W9-DFC-425

# Information, Organization and Management

Arnold Picot · Ralf Reichwald · Rolf Wigand

# Information, Organization and Management

Springer

Prof. Dr. Dres. h.c. Arnold Picot
Ludwig-Maximilians-Universität Munich
Munich School of Management
Institute for Information, Organization
and Management
Ludwigstr. 28 VG II
80539 Munich
Germany
picot@lmu.de

Prof. Dr. Prof. h.c. Dr. h.c. Ralf Reichwald
Technical University of Munich
TUM - Business School
Chair for Information, Organization
and Management
Leopoldstr. 139
80804 Munich
Germany
reichwald@wi.tum.de

Prof. Rolf Wigand Ph.D.
University of Arkansas at Little Rock
CyberCollege
258A ETAS Building
2801 South University Avenue
Little Rock, AR 72204-1099
USA
rtwigand@ualr.edu

ISBN 978-3-540-71394-4        e-ISBN 978-3-540-71395-1

Library of Congress Control Number: 2008925000

© 2008 Springer-Verlag Berlin Heidelberg

Cover design: WMXDesign GmbH, Heidelberg

Printed on acid-free paper

9 8 7 6 5 4 3 2 1

springer.com

# Preface and Acknowledgements

This book has a long history. The three authors' research foci are in related areas and they have worked together on numerous projects in organization research, organization design, information systems and the use and application of information and communication technologies. In addition they exchanged ideas for over 25 years. This occurred in the form of publications, at conferences in joint sessions and on joint panels in Europe and North America, by guest lectures and through visiting professorships at their respective universities. Toward the end of the 1980s the idea to write a book jointly and publish it simultaneously in English and German emerged from this cooperation. After numerous meetings, the authors were fascinated at the time by the idea to utilize new communication media in this project enabling *virtual teamwork* and, in a sense, practice what they preach.

Transatlantic telecooperation, however, proved itself at times more difficult than anticipated: The complexity of this book project, the rapid development of the new technologies and their deployment resulted in substantial changes of the subject matter addressed and demanded an intensive dialogue among the authors. The subsequent development of the concept and content of the book had to be clarified and discussed. The boundaries and limits of telecommunication and telecooperation, as well as the book project reached a crisis stage.

During a most productive, week-long meeting in April 1994 in the Brewster Inn at Casenovia Lake in New York the project was revitalized and a new conceptualization together with a new work plan materialized.

Throughout these efforts we gained an experience that may also be a subject topic for this book: The authors encountered the boundaries and limits, but also the support potential of information and communication technology, especially the Internet and its e-mail and file transfer services. This technology enabled the formation of a *virtual team*, as well as the accomplishment of a complex project. All of this was only possible of course on the basis of commonly shared values and trust which were developed initially through face-to-face interactions. The general recognition that complex projects have to pass through a serious crisis before they find a suitable and goal-directed conclusion can certainly be confirmed in our case.

The realization of our project may in part be attributed to the engaged cooperation of our respective research teams. The innovative concept of the "boundaryless firm" and the opportunity to help shape the new "management leadership in the Information Age" excited and motivated them to contribute to this book in some fashion. These teams too were virtually connected and thus contributed essentially to efficient geography- and time-expanding coordination of the final product. In this fashion we were enabled to bundle knowledge and this cooperation approached the limits of co-authorship. The individual authors worked on the development of various chapters in numerous locations throughout the world and while on various sabbatical and research leave projects as well as on numerous long transatlantic and transpacific flights.

A surprisingly difficult aspect turned out to be our desire to publish this book in English and German simultaneously. The creation of both language versions really was not all that difficult. Some portions of the book were written right from the beginning in German while others started in English. Consequently a "two-language" manuscript was available that in each case was further developed by the other authors and their teams and was translated and adapted. The English and German versions are therefore not literal translations of each other. They differ also content-wise as appropriate for the country-specific audience and their respective "textbook culture".

For conceptual and content contributions we thank in particular Robert Benjamin, Wolfgang Burr, Juan-Ignacio Conrat, Burkhard Hermens, Gerhard Hesch, Claudia Höfer-Weichselbaumer, Wolf-Guido Lutz, Donald A. Marchand, Kathrin Möslein, Johann Niggl, Hans Sachenbacher and Dianne Lux Wigand. For their valuable editorial support we thank, Rudolf Bauer, Nico Grove, Hans Koller, Johann Kranz, Barbara Kreis, Rahild Neuburger, Heiner Röhrl, Sven Scheuble and Birgitta Wolff. Carsten von Glahn, Tanja Ripperger and Angela Shelley contributed in various translation efforts expertly and with much enthusiasm. Markus Böhme, Christine Bortenlänger, Martin Braig, Jorun Cramer, Hermann Englberger, Christine Graap-Lippert, Florian Haase, Beth Mahoney, Florian Pfingsten, Ulla Raithel, Dieter Riedel, Peter Rohrbach, Andrea Schwartz, Eckhard Wagner, Axel Wiemers and Stefan Zeilner contributed and assisted in the creation and design of figures, as well as other editorial tasks. We thank Ilse Evertse, the editor and proofreader of this book. The authors thank Mary L. Good, Dean, College of Engineering and Information Technology, as well as Dan Berleant, Chair, Department of Information Science and Robert B. Mitchell, Chair, Department of Management, all with the University of Arkansas at Little Rock for their continued support. Last, but by no means least, we would like to thank Mr. Jerry L. Maulden and the Jerry L. Maulden-Entergy Endowment for continued support as well as Nico Grove and Johann Kranz for the coordination and the finishing of the book. We would like to thank them all sincerely for their excellent and much committed work and cooperation with the authors. The responsibility for content and potential errors remains of course with the authors exclusively.

It was surprising for us that in spite of all sorts of globalization and digitalization efforts in the publishing and media fields apparently no model for tandem-solutions in the management literature exists within English and German language regions. Numerous discussions and meetings were necessary until two equally respected and expert publishing houses agreed to become cooperative partners for this project. John Wiley & Sons, Ltd. as the publisher of the 1997 volume for the English-language region and Gabler Verlag is the publisher of the book for the German-language region. This German edition is now in its 5$^{th}$ edition and has enjoyed great success in the German speaking regions of the world. We would like to thank Dr. Reinhold Roski and Mrs. Roscher (Gabler) for their and their colleagues' always constructive and cooperative work. We appreciate especially the support and cooperation by Dr. Werner Müller and his team with Springer Verlag for the present book. The earlier mentioned first version of the book has been substantially changed and revised and, for all intents and purposes, the current version more than ten years later is indeed a very different book.

We welcome of course any sort of feedback on this book and would like to thank our readers in advance. They can reach us at the addresses specified on preceding pages and, of course, via e-mail.

Munich and Little Rock, March 2008                                Arnold Picot
*(picot@lmu.de)*

Ralf Reichwald
*(ralf.reichwald@wi.tum.de)*

Rolf T. Wigand
*(rtwigand@ualr.edu)*

# Table of Contents

# Table of Figures

# Abbreviations

| | |
|---|---|
| ACD | Automatic Call Distributor |
| ACS | Automatic Call Sequencer |
| ANSI / SPARC | American National Standards Institute / Systems Planning and Requirements Committee |
| API | Application Programming Interface |
| ARIS | Architecture of Integrated Information Systems |
| ATM | Asynchronous Transfer Mode |
| | |
| CATeam | Computer Aided Team |
| CBT | Computer-Based Telelearning |
| CD-ROM | Compact Disc – Read Only Memory |
| CIM | Computer Integrated Manufacturing |
| CORBA | Common Object Request Broker Architecture |
| CPU | Central Processing Unit |
| CRS | Computer Reservation System |
| CSCW | Computer Supported Cooperative Work |
| CSF | Critical Success Factors |
| CTI | Computer Telephone Integration |
| | |
| DCF | Discounted Cash Flow |
| DGB | German Federation of Trade Unions (Deutscher Gewerkschaftsbund) |
| DIN | German Industrial Standard (Deutsche Industrienorm) |
| DQDB | Distributed Queue Dual Bus |
| DSS | Decision Support System |
| DTB | German Futures Exchange (Deutsche Terminbörse) |
| | |
| E-Mail | Electronic Mail |
| ECR | Efficient Consumer Response |
| EDI | Electronic Data Interchange |
| EDIFACT | Electronic Data Interchange for Administration, Commerce and Transport |
| EVA | Economic Value Added |
| | |
| FDDI | Fibre Distributed Data Interface |
| FTP | File Transfer Protocol |
| | |
| GDSS | Group Decision Support System |
| GII | Global Information Infrastructure |

| | |
|---|---|
| GPRS | General Packet Radio Service |
| GSM | Global System for Mobile Communication |
| HSCSD | High Speed Circuit Switched Data |
| HTTP | Hyper Text Transfer Protocol |
| IEEE | Institute of Electrical and Electronic Engineers |
| INMARSAT | International Maritime Satellite Organisation |
| IPX / SPX | Internetwork Packet Exchange / Sequenced Packet Exchange |
| ISDN | Integrated Services Digital Network |
| ISO / OSI | International Standard Organisation / Open Systems Interconnection |
| JIT | Just in Time |
| LAN | Local Area Network |
| MVA | Market Value Added |
| NC | Numerically Controlled |
| NII | National Information Infrastructure |
| ODA / ODIF | Office Document Architecture / Office Document Interchange Format |
| OMG | Object Management Group |
| OMT | Object Modeling Technique |
| OOA | Object Oriented Analysis |
| PaCT | PBX and Computer Teaming |
| PBX | Private Branch Exchange |
| PC | Personal Computer |
| PCMCIA | Personal Computer Memory Card International Association |
| PCN | Personal Communication Network |
| POSDCORB | Planning, Organizing, Staffing, Directing, Coordinating, Reporting, Budgeting |
| PPS | Production Planning System |
| RDA | Remote Database Access |
| RISC | Reduced Instruction Set Computer |
| ROE | Return on Equity |
| ROI | Return on Investment |
| RONA | Return on Net Asstes |
| SA | Structured Analysis |
| SDW | Simultaneous Distributed Work |
| SOM | Semantic Object Model |
| SONET | Synchronous Optical Network |
| SQL | Structured Query Language |
| STEP | Standard for the Exchange of Product Definition Data |

| | |
|---|---|
| T/TTS | Task/Team Support System |
| TCP/IP | Transport Control Protocol/Internet Protocol |
| TQM | Total Quality Management |
| UCD | Uniform Call Distributor |
| US-GAAP | Generally Accepted Accounting Principles |
| VRU | Voice Response Unit |
| W-LAN | Wireless Local Area Network |
| WAN | Wide Area Network |
| WWW | World Wide Web |
| XML | Extensible Markup Language |

# Chapter 1

# Information, Organization, and Management: The Corporation Without Boundaries

## 1.1 Changes in Competitive Environments and Corporate Structures

We think of corporations as self-contained, integrated structures. They are physically located in office buildings and production plants where the corporation's employees usually work and where the required machines, equipment, materials, and information can be found. From the perspective of most observers – from both theory and practice – these physical structures and the contractual relations between corporations define a corporation's boundaries. Naturally, a corporation constantly crosses its own boundaries when transferring goods to and from markets, procuring input goods, selling finished products, and borrowing or investing capital. Nevertheless, this type of boundary crossing between the corporation and its market denotes a clear perception of inside and outside, of membership and non-membership, and of interfaces between the corporation and its markets.

In today's economy, many areas no longer match this textbook model of corporate boundaries. Network organizations, telework, cooperative networks, virtual organizational structures, and telecooperation are no longer simply buzzwords, but are often found in the real world. They are reactions to new market and competitive environments that are influenced by modern information and communication

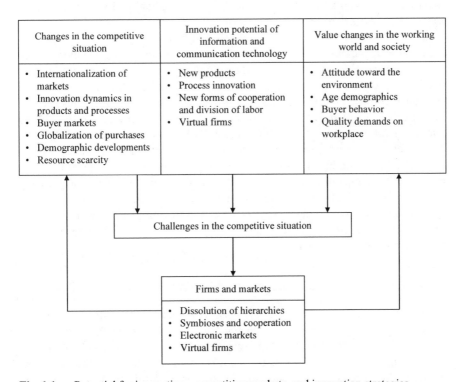

**Fig. 1.1.** Potential for innovation, competitive markets, and innovation strategies

technologies. Traditional corporate boundaries are beginning to blur, to change internally as well as externally, and, in some cases, to dissolve. Multi-layer corporate hierarchies that primarily function by means of orders and obedience are increasingly replaced with decentralized, modular structures characterized by autonomy, cooperation, and indirect leadership. This development is associated with changes in competition and technology. Figure 1.1 illustrates this new situation with regard to corporations and markets.

## 1.1.1   Changes in Competitive Markets

There have been drastic changes in a variety of corporations' competitive conditions. Goods, labor, and information markets are increasingly globalized. The use of new communication networks provides worldwide access to previously difficult to reach markets. Competition is intensified through new competitors' entrance into formerly local or proprietary markets. East Asian suppliers' success, especially in the field of industrial mass products, is impressive. Since the opening of the borders to East European markets, suppliers have emerged whose national economies allow the production of industrial goods at substantially lower costs and – while simultaneously improving the quality of their goods and services – are increasingly gaining access to world markets. Today, qualified service providers offer their services worldwide by means of data networks.

In addition, we observe a shift from seller to buyer markets. Buyers have become more demanding and are no longer willing to accept organization-related coordination problems such as long product delivery times or interface problems. With the current demand for greater product quality, this new buyer behavior has a substantial influence on new goods and service development. This holds true for the consumer goods industry, investment goods, and all types of services. Many competing products are of very high quality, which is taken for granted today. Real product differentiation often occurs only in the service offered after a product's sale. Above all, buyer markets require corporations to be customer orientated and flexible. Competitive strategies must fundamentally reevaluate the business and management goals of 'flexibility', 'time' (development and delivery times), 'quality' and 'costs'. Turbulent markets, time, and flexibility are often the decisive criteria for competition: Consequently, corporations have to adapt to changing demands quickly and efficiently.

## 1.1.2   Changing Value Systems of the Working World and Society

The development described above has been superimposed by radical changes in the working world and society. This change has taken place since the 1960s and is, at least in highly developed industrial societies, similar throughout the world. Changes in the working world reveal themselves most noticeably through an increasing reluctance to accept a subordinate position, to fulfill an obligation or execute tasks without some degree of autonomy. In the 1970s, this led to the implementation of new forms of labor organization in industrial corporations that aimed at improving labor conditions in the sense of increased worker autonomy. However, these new forms did not have a lasting effect: Numerous models for the humanization of the work place failed due to a superficial and narrow understanding of efficiency. Today, values such as personal responsibility, autonomy, self-realization, and individuality are becoming more important; simultaneously, their potential with regard to quality, flexibility, increased work efficiency, and overall organizational performance is being (re-)discovered.

On a much broader scale, these changes in the value system manifest themselves in society in a change of attitude towards resources, the environment, and in the utilization of technological potential. One important reason for the working world's changed attitude is the increase in traffic, and the decrease in available space in densely populated cities. Every day, millions of people make use of mass transport for work with the associated risks, time loss, and stress. In densely populated cities, rental costs are constantly increasing, and are, in turn, reducing disposable income. Ecological damage, stress, and the loss of valuable time are negative social costs for which there is no compensation. On the other hand, changes in working conditions raise serious questions about industrial production, services, the optimal location of work places, as well as about products and services' potential market success.

## 1.1.3 Innovation Potential of Information and Communication Technology

Information and communication technologies play a special role in change and reorganization processes. These technologies' dramatic performance increase, miniaturization, and integration, as well as their capability to transform work, enhance productivity, and liberate workers often lead to a completely new application potential for business and society at the product and process levels. In conjunction with production, energy, material, and transport technologies, drastic changes have occurred. These changes are characterized by capacity, mobility, cooperative work, integration, openness, distribution, and globalization. With the help of these and other technologies, numerous new service markets have developed in related fields.

These new technologies have, however, also greatly contributed to the innovation dynamic in the product and process innovation area. Microelectronics alters products and production processes and turns many machines into quickly aging ones as new technologies with increased capacities and capabilities come on the market more rapidly.

Owing to these technologies' growing number of applications, as well as their related structural potential for change, there is an increased awareness of the well-known fact that corporations, markets, industries, politics, and society are essentially constituted by information and communication. It follows that new performance qualities and new forms of economic process design evolve that continually alter business, management, and science's abilities and methods. Furthermore, new information and communication technologies offer many new opportunities for structuring new production forms based on the division of labor in order to meet new demands, changes in consumer behavior, the changed value system, and the resulting challenges for the working world. New forms of cooperation within and between corporations – team concepts and group work, telework, work in mobile offices or in decentralized work places, and modular organizations all the way to virtual corporations – are examples of new ways of working that have been enabled by information and communication technologies.

The information society, which primarily manifests itself in the link between and diffusion of individual and mass communication media, together with the intensification of competition due to the growing number of suppliers, strengthens the buyer's position and turns customer value into a corporation's market success. Many services can be globally obtained today, which is exemplified by software production and particularly by procurement markets for immaterial goods that distribute their goods worldwide.

### 1.1.4  New Organizational Concepts: Overcoming Boundaries

A variety of factors often limit corporate activities, especially factors such as physical distance and a lack of space and time, knowledge deficiencies, production bottlenecks, and a lack of flexibility. These barriers and boundaries can be overcome through the use of newer information and communication technologies in competitive processes. Moreover, these technologies offer new solutions in respect of various business innovations.

- Regional or national borders are of lesser importance in the definition and organization of economic activity as communication and transport are facilitated.

- The implementation of entrepreneurial concepts facilitates the integration of communication with a third party, which contributes to eradicating corporate boundaries in the sense that there is no longer a clear differentiation between inside and outside.

- Knowledge boundaries can be extended and overcome more quickly through the worldwide access to knowledge carriers and knowledge bases.

- Capacity restrictions are eliminated due to the flexible integration of required resources.

- Employees' limited specialization and qualifications become less important because processes and people's novel bundling and integration capabilities are enabled, amongst others, by information and communication technologies.

The trends described above serve as examples, which will be analyzed in more detail in subsequent parts of this book. These trends demonstrate that traditional concepts of organization construction and function need to be rethought. Today, organizations are very seldom regarded as self-contained, permanent, integrated, and clearly defined structures that are easily distinguishable from their environment. Fundamental organizational innovations are on the agenda, namely the transition to completely new entrepreneurial concepts and new forms of an economic division of labor within and between organizations.

These new organizational forms can be observed in modularized, partly virtual, enterprises. They are problem-specific and flexible within an open, symbiotic network and enable value-added processes. In addition, they utilize the innovative technical and organizational potential of, for example, telecooperation, electronic markets, and interorganizational system integration.

### 1.1.5   Barriers to Organizational Innovations

It is well known that especially organizational innovations diffuse slowly due to various persistent counteractive tendencies. Examples of such barriers are: a lack of understanding of new challenges and the forces driving this change, a lack of adaptability and readiness to change, as well as fear of the consequences of new structures. These barriers prevent the organization from developing swiftly. Changes may therefore occur too late. An in-depth examination of the potentials for change and the forces that drive them may contribute to the dismantling of such barriers.

## 1.2   Transition to New Organization and Management Models

### 1.2.1   Tayloristic Industrial Organization: Productivity Under Stable Conditions

Insights into the new competitive environments are well known. Numerous publications on new competitive strategies indicate future courses of action. These insights are, however, difficult to translate into action. Traditional industrial organizations' experiences still dominate everyday corporate activities, given that the Tayloristic factory organizations' success story forms the 'guidelines for successful management.' This type of organization is largely based on Frederick W. Taylor's work (*Principles of Scientific Management*) (Kanigel 1997), which influenced firms' structures, productivity, and value chain conceptualizations, as well as classic management tools – leadership, incentives, and control systems.

Hierarchies, the functional division of labor in the organizational structure, as well as the one-best-way concept (Kanigel 1997) were fundamental characteristics of the classic industrial organization. The Tayloristic labor organization's dominating formal principles were:

- Focus on work methods, on maximum work specialization, and job breakdown;
- Separation of managerial and operational work; and
- The physical exclusion of all planning, governing, and controlling tasks from the manufacturing area.

Industrial production's complex coordination problem could therefore be 'optimally' solved by providing and coordinating production factors. The individual was, however, integrated into the production process as a functional production factor, responsible for receiving and implementing directions. Communication relationships followed that of the hierarchical structures, i.e. formalized, hierarchical communication along official channels with fixed and strict rules. Communication between a superior and subordinate was prescribed by their roles, with the superior giving the orders that the subordinate followed.

Strategies to increase the efficiency of the industrial production of goods essentially result from traditional management and organization concepts. These strategies were developed at the beginning of this century through the principles of scientific management. Industrial production strategies focused mainly on mass production in large corporations, achieving considerable success through the systematic development, perfection, and application of methods to optimize manufacturing processes. This success was, however, only achieved through the satisfactory utilization of economic activity in long-term, stable basic conditions and through the latter's apt application in clear guidelines for entrepreneurial action. The following are the basic premises of the success of traditional efficiency strategies:

- Products' relatively long life cycles;
- Stable sales markets;
- Limited number of competitors with known strengths and weaknesses;
- Low-cost natural resources and low environmental burdens for firms; and
- The general availability of highly motivated, well qualified or easily qualifiable workers.

As long as these economic and social conditions were applicable, the classic principles – Burkhart Lutz calls them industrial innovation strategy's "principles of common wisdom" – assured corporate success. Today, the basic conditions have changed and new principles are required. Moving away from these traditional principles is, however, not an easy task. These principles have been reinforced over decades and are currently "hard-wired" into the definitions of tasks and management responsibilities, into educational programs' design, qualification and employee competencies, into business information systems' selection and implementation, as well as into the format of a firm's external relations.

Stable market conditions, product longevity, and high productivity rates justified this type of industrial organization until the late 1970s. The industrial sociologist Konrad Thomas comments on this development: "The division of labor, assembly line production, and performance incentives have given industry a productivity boost which, together with the methods of rational corporate design, is correctly labeled as the second industrial revolution by G. Friedmann. Nothing makes more sense than to judge the legitimacy of the applied methods by their efficiency."

## 1.2.2    New Models: Flexibility and Capacity for Innovation

These changing competitive environments require corporate flexibility and a capacity for innovation instead of fixed productivity increases based on the division of labor. The flattening or even eradication of hierarchical structures is necessary. Traditional departmentalization and hierarchical levels are no longer important. Precisely prescribed communication structures are being replaced by direct group communication that cannot be channeled directly and specifically. Managerial and operational tasks' integration, as well as the merging of services and production into self-contained value chains raise additional questions regarding the organizational boundaries, also in geographical terms: The more the principle of autonomous organizational units permeates the value chain, and the more autonomous units can be coordinated through information and communication technologies, the more the site location debate becomes the focal point.

When economic advantage can be realized through a change in location, for example, through closer market proximity, through the exploitation of cost advantages, through an increase in employees' quality of life, and through transport and supply advantages, the trend towards geographic decentralization – meaning organizational units' change of location – follows organizational decentralization. This concerns the location of entire corporations, of modular organizational units, groups, and individual workplaces. It is therefore no longer surprising that new forms of labor and the division of labor, such as telecooperation and telework, are intensely discussed in the course of corporate organization's modularization and restructuring. Moreover, this makes the pursuit of new competitive strategies possible. For many years, Porter's hypothesis dominated strategy deliberations: You either pursue a cost leadership strategy or a differentiation strategy. This popular perspective was much criticized. There are many empirical examples of firms with hybrid competitive strategies – understood as a synthesis between cost and differentiation strategies – that achieved impressive success. Examples are Dell's manufacturing of individually configured PCs, or a growing number of companies' mass customized manufacturing of clothing. The trend toward such hybrid strategies is nurtured by the mass customization movement. This movement substitutes the old contrast between flexibility and productivity with a flexible, as well as highly productive, market supply in some industries.

Figure 1.2 provides an overview of the way in which new models shape efforts to adapt to entrepreneurial structures. These new models emphasize the necessity

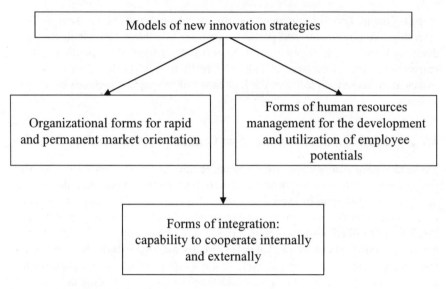

**Fig. 1.2.**    New models for innovation strategies

to redesign the entrepreneurial organization and corporate management. The guiding idea is to strengthen innovation capability through the development of new organizational strategies to replace traditional productivity-oriented models.

### Decentralization and Modularization (Chapters 5 and 8)

Changes in the basic conditions and the importance of structural change in respect of maintaining and securing competitiveness mainly require distinct capabilities to adapt to market changes by:

- Reintegration of manufacturing and service functions into self-contained and holistic processes that focus on customer value in respect of in the creation of business value;

- Direct communication in new forms of work organization among all participants in a value-creating process;

- Increasing employees' capability to process market information, to interpret such information correctly, and to act in a customer-oriented way;

- Nurturing employees' capacity to recognize their organizational unit's contribution to the total corporate value creation and market success, and to adjust their daily decisions accordingly; and

- New roles for managers and employees in less hierarchic organizations.

Through the extensive reintegration of managerial tasks into industrial production processes, future industrial work will be primarily organized in autonomous groups.

The reengineering concept also propagates the integration (beginning with market orientation) of industrial performance processes into teamwork, ideally starting with the supply of material and ending with the delivery at the buyer's location.

**Technical and Non-technical Forms of Integration (Chapters 4, 6, 7 and 8)**

Future forms of global collaboration within the corporation have been necessitated by decentralized and geographically dispersed organizations in a business world that is increasingly based on the international division of labor. These developments demand that the future employee has the capability to act within technical and non-technical networks.

Network membership implies highly valuable social connections inside and outside the organization, whose success and stability depend on compliance with certain rules. These rules are concerned with interaction with other team members from different societies and cultures. All network participants are responsible for communication with customers and market partners who live by different norms and rules, for managers in global teams' handling of various expectations, and also for the evaluation of alternatives actions (as well as their usefulness and costs). A case can be made for cooperation in the areas of development, sales, marketing, logistics, assembly, etc. whenever service chains, alliances with competitors or other forms of vertical or horizontal cooperation are established.

It follows that employees have to develop qualifications with respect to the difficult field of communication. The increased deployment of networks has given rise to important questions regarding the creation of trust and the maintenance of interpersonal relations in a global working world. Cooperations also require new evaluation methods and tasks. They must, for example, deal with questions concerning the usefulness and costs of cooperation, and, in a cooperative process, the joint effects' measurement and contribution with regard to budgeting and profit utilization.

**New Forms of Human Resources Management for the Development and Use of Employee Potentials (Chapters 9 and 10)**

Holistic organization structures are innovative corporate concepts that redefine the division of labor, coordination forms, and effectiveness context. The development and exploitation of employee capabilities and potentials are decisive for the realization of these corporate concepts. New organization forms of management and labor offer important premises. As long as autonomous groups and flexible, problem-dependent networks are sensibly integrated into the value creation process, they have the required prerequisites to unfold employees' creativity and performance potentials, to foster motivation, and create economic benefit. The insights gained from the debate on the structure of work confirm that meaningful job content, a manageable work environment, the quick feedback of work results, as well as adequate qualification, autonomy, and responsibility provide individuals with the possibility of self-realization and, thus, increase their willingness to perform.

These considerations may resolve much of the previous friction and may bring the employee's goals in line with those of the firm. These process frameworks form new strategy development and controlling concepts.

## 1.3    Structure and Special Features of This Book

### 1.3.1    A New Management Theory

This book deals with the above-mentioned changes' causes, trends and forms at the corporate level and at the level of economic competition. In addition, these developments are regarded in the light of the opportunities and perspectives that result from these changes, the difficulties encountered in handling them, and the challenges that they present for management. The fundamental importance of changes in information and communication's price-performance relationship for economic organizational forms is demonstrated. More specifically, the effects that the actual and expected outcomes of further reductions in information and communication costs (and the simultaneous increase in information and communication performance) will have on the division of labor structures within and between corporations and markets. Figure 1.3 depicts various arrangements of coordination forms in relation to their dependence on underlying tasks.

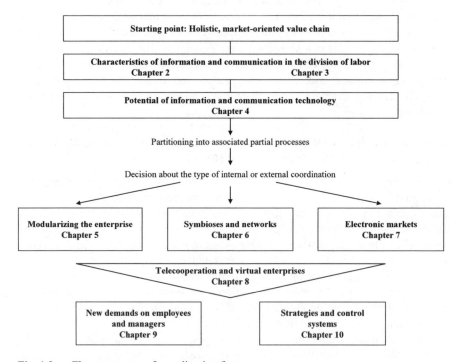

**Fig. 1.3.**    The emergence of coordination forms

In the past, the focal discussion in business management and design was concentrated on highly-specific and largely unvarying tasks, as carried out in traditional hierarchies. Today, however, this discussion has shifted: The focal point is the entire market perspective. In order to address this perspective, we need to determine the relevant competitive, technological and institutional basic conditions, and the appropriate and corresponding coordination structures while considering suitable value-adding steps. Information and communication technology's performance potential is enjoying increasing attention, with products, processes, structures, as well as entire value chains' information dimension playing an increasingly important role. We are aware that the vast majority of all value-adding activities are information and communication focused. Entrepreneurial value adding is increasingly shifting towards the information domain. Organization and management structures have to adapt to cope with these developments. Consequently, completely new design options, opportunities, and requirements are created for corporate management. In this respect, this book can be regarded as a new management theory for the information society.

## 1.3.2 The Boundaries of "Boundarylessness"

The ideas and concepts presented in this book offer recommendations in respect of a multitude of challenges. The authors do not, however, offer a panacea and "magic bullets." Considering the situation-specific approach to organizations upon which this book is based, organizational solutions are only efficient under certain basic conditions. When these basic conditions change, new organizational recommendations are warranted. For example, currently, questions addressing the new design or redesign of value chains dominate many discussions and we believe that this book contributes to this realm. However, as soon as these reconstruction efforts have made progress, other complex themes requiring different solutions will evolve. At the end of each chapter, we offer a few detailed suggestions regarding the boundaries and limits of the ideas and concepts.

## 1.3.3 An Overview of the Structure of the Book

The following sections offer a brief overview of each chapter. Chapters 2 and 3 provide the theoretical foundations for all subsequent chapters, dealing with the fundamentals of and the explanations for changes in the competitive environment. Chapter 4 explicates key concepts and describes the potential of newer information and communication technologies. Chapters 5 to 8 examine typical corporation structures and directions, as well as market development and trends. Chapter 9 discusses the human factor's special role in the organization without boundaries. Chapter 10 is devoted to the changed demands required of business management and controlling.

**Chapter 2** is dedicated to the theoretical foundations of various exchange relationships in markets and in the corporation. Furthermore, this chapter focuses specifically on information and communication's crucial role in market dynamics and competition. It shows the way in which information and communication influence dynamic corporate competition, the division of labor and, thus, the organization. Organizational forms, understood as institutional structures of processes based on the division of labor, contribute as far as possible to a frictionless and motivated task completion and, thus, to efficiency improvements in the division of labor, information and communication. Market process theory and new institutional economics are important reference theories in this area.

**Chapter 3:** An in-depth discussion of processes based on the division of labor within and between corporations requires a more detailed analysis of the relevant information and communication processes. Chapter 3 prepares the basis for this discussion by describing fundamental information and communication models that, in turn, provide insights into information behavior. With the help of these basic theories, and together with the economic theoretical foundation established in chapter 2, new communication and information forms' possibilities and limits, as well as new organizational solutions are derived. The reader is presented with fundamental social-scientific concepts of interpersonal communication, as well as empirical evidence of human information and communication behavior in organizations.

**Chapter 4** deals with information and communication technologies' potential for organization development within the marketplace. The focus is on these technologies' development trends at the levels of information or information systems (hardware, software) and communication's (networks, services) technical infrastructure. Both areas are increasingly integrated, offer new performance potential and provide support for different corporate structures and processes. We also highlight information and communication system levels and information deployment levels.

**Chapter 5** deals with internal hierarchies' dissolution due to competition and technology. When the modularization of firms is addressed, traditional, multi-layered hierarchical structures are replaced by relatively independent, process-oriented units that are only loosely coordinated. Two examples of prerequisite are: The appropriate optimization of performance strength and depth, and information and communication systems' appropriate and purposive design. This trend can be observed at different organization levels, at the macro level (e.g., the holding company), at the intermediate or meso level (e.g., business segments) and at the micro level (e.g., the island principle, group work). In all cases, self-steering mechanisms (automatic control) are strengthened, hierarchies are flattened, and integral processes are supported by information and communication technology. All of this occurs in a unified way under one responsible person or group.

**Chapter 6:** The dissolution of corporate boundaries within extended relationships (external relationships) that, in turn, lead to symbioses and networks is the focal point in chapter 6. Intensified competitive dynamics and new communication possibilities lead to a more intense, problem-specific collaboration with third parties, sometimes even in the areas of the own core competencies. Consequently, organizations' traditional entrepreneurial boundaries blur in favor of strategic networks or alliances, whether these are vertical or horizontal. Besides discussing the causes and forms of this development, this chapter also discusses the information and communication-technical implications, as well as the special challenges for management.

**Chapter 7:** Not only is the coordination form 'corporation' and/or 'hierarchy' impacted by the new information and communication possibilities, but 'market' as a coordination form is also impacted. Electronic markets enable new forms of market coordination and may offer firms new options for the marketing of products and services. This chapter presents electronic markets' forms and developments and describes the conditions for and patterns of their emergence and functioning, as well as their requirements regarding management and technology.

**Chapter 8:** The degree of freedom in the design and application of the new information and communication technology not only relates to organizational aspects, meaning the choice of new coordination forms, but generally also to the physical dimension of completing division of labor processes, i.e. forms of geographical decentralization. Thus, these new technologies help to overcome physical boundaries at the levels of the individual workplace, the department and the entire corporation. This leads to the formation of telecooperation as a work form. Telework, telecooperation, location-independent work at local, regional and global levels, their technical and organizational prerequisites, as well as the resulting requirements for management are thus discussed in this chapter. These developments show the emergence of telecooperation work forms, which may therefore be regarded as prerequisites for the virtual enterprise concept.

**Chapter 9:** The expansion of human performance boundaries is an important concept for the organization without boundaries. This chapter is dedicated to managers and employees' new roles in the boundaryless organization. To some extent, the above-mentioned change processes, enabled by information and communication technology's performance increases in the intensified competition, make new demands on participating individuals. They are therefore based on the premise that all actors acknowledge these new demands and are able to fulfill them. Therefore, a new role, that of the human factor, is associated with these organization changes. This refocusing of organization and management design on the role of the working individual is the result of the value system changes in the working world and society, of the need for new, interdisciplinary qualifications, and of managers and employees' changed roles in organizations with few hierarchical levels. These developments demand a new and holistic conceptualization of value-added processes.

**Chapter 10:** In an economic world, characterized by the dissolution of legal, organizational, spatial and temporal boundaries, we ask the inevitable question: What actually holds companies together? In this context, a central role is played by joint strategies and control systems through which performance processes can be oriented towards a supraordinate goal. We demonstrate that in the organization without boundaries, controlling is not superfluous. Quite the contrary: Controlling has become a central integration function whose scope ranges from the support of indirect management concepts to the coordination of interfaces, the design of incentive systems, and the development of trust relationships, which includes information and knowledge management.

### 1.3.4  Special Features of This Book

In view of this book's structure, a few special features need to be highlighted:

**Theoretical Foundation**

The book is not limited to a descriptive inventory of certain phenomena. Without a solid theoretical foundation, many statements concerning the discussed developments have an ad-hoc character and are merely eye-catching or just plain fads. Therefore, in a deliberate and relatively detailed manner, this book begins with a number of relevant basic theories that highlight the role of information and communication in the competitive process and in managing the division of labor. A foundation is therefore offered for the management, organization, and implementation of new information and communication technologies. These foundations are complemented with theories addressing the relationship between technology and organization development, theories on organization and motivation, as well as with theories on organization change.

**Linking Organization, Information, and Communication Technology and Management**

The book offers a useful insight into important information and communication technology developments whose application potential enables the realization of new organizational and managerial forms. The link is made between the fields of management, information, and organization (which are usually analyzed without reference to technology) by considering relevant technological developments. Many technology-centric descriptions offer far too few discussions of an organizational or human resource nature. In this book, the authors take on the difficult challenge of viewing and examining information and communication's technical and non-technical aspects and the link between them.

**Modular Scheme**

The book deals with a large number of subjects from various disciplines. It starts with the organization's basic theoretical foundations, information and communication, then discusses information and communication technology's development trends, different forms of restructuring and managing corporations, as well as human resource development. It can be assumed that the reader is somewhat aware of some of the problem areas discussed in this book, yet wants to study others in more detail. The text is therefore structured into ten, relatively independent, modules related to each other through a cross-referencing system. Based on the level of knowledge and interests, the reader may prefer to read the individual modules. We recommend that a reader who is less familiar with the underlying theories start with the chapters that provide the theoretical foundation (chapters 2, 3 and 4).

**Applied Orientation**

Besides the theoretical foundation provided, the book focuses on the development of practical perspectives to provide managers with orientation support. Management faces the special challenge of identifying and exploiting opportunities in the currently occurring change processes. Consequently, all chapters provide managers with implementation-oriented summarizing statements and recommendations.

**New Models of Competitive Organization and Leadership Strategies**

Corporate management is currently in a process of reorientation and rethinking. The traditional patterns of successful entrepreneurship are no longer necessarily valid, necessitating a quest for new models. Chapters 5 to 10 are dedicated to this task. In each of these chapters, conclusions are derived in respect of management. This means that guidelines have been developed for innovation strategies that are suitable for the changed conditions in the markets, in the working world, and in society.

*Chapter 2*

# Market Dynamics and Competition: The Fundamental Role of Information

# Case Study Chapter 2: The Rise and Fall of Netscape

The Internet's astounding history is closely linked to the similar astounding story of Netscape Communications. Exemplary elements and developments of the Internet economy are mirrored in this firm's development, for example, the entrepreneurial dynamics and the partially changed economic rules of the game, which among other related topics are addressed in this chapter.

Although computers had already been non-centrally connected via ARPANet in the 1960s and have utilized the TCP/IP protocol – the platform-independent communication standard (see chapter 4) – since the early 1980s, it took until the mid-1990s before the Internet became a true mass medium (Sen-newald 1998). One of the reasons for this rather slow diffusion rate was that for a long time there was no software that enabled suitable visual and user-friendly access to Internet data (Quittner / Slatalla 1998).

The National Center for Supercomputer Applications introduced such inno-vative software in 1993 with the browser "Mosaic." One of the leading pro-grammers at the time was the then 20-year-old Marc Andreessen, a computer science student at the University of Illinois (Hamm 1998b).

Mosaic was distributed free of charge and diffused rapidly via the Internet. In 1994 Jim Clark, a former Stanford University professor who had already achieved success with Silicon Graphics Inc., took note of Marc Andreessen's browser. He recognized the Internet's potential and, with Andreessen, founded Mosaic Communications, which soon became known as Netscape Communica-tions, in Mountain View, California. Clark and Andreessen suspected that the sale of browser software alone would not generate long-term revenues (Quitt-ner / Slatalla 1998). Right from the start, it was the firm's intended strategy to generate demand for Internet software with which to operate web servers through the free distribution of the browser software (Bamford / Burgelman 1997). The attractiveness of this relationship was to be enhanced for business customers through the integration of an encryption system with which to exe-cute transactions securely (Quittner / Slatalla 1998). Netscape programmers, most of whom had been recruited from the former Mosaic team, developed the new browser "Netscape Navigator" unusually quickly by dividing the work into many modules and working in parallel. There was continuous coordination within a flat organization (Quittner / Slatalla 1998). The employees were highly motivated, as stock options would allow them to participate in the firm's suc-cess when the firm went public. Netscape Navigator was first distributed via the Internet towards the end of 1994, gained more than 75% of the browser market within just four months (Quittner / Slatella 1998), and became a de facto industry standard. On August 9, 1995, Netscape was listed on the stock ex-change. By the end of the first day of trading, the initial purchase offer of $28 had more than doubled to $58 (Bamford / Burgelman 1997). Netscape's success was also a signal for competing software firms that Clark's vision of the Internet as a mass medium was slowly becoming a reality. Microsoft had already presented its first version of "Internet Explorer" in August 1995 and, in December 1995, announced that it regarded the Internet as a crucial business domain, after Bill Gates in his first edition of *The Road Ahead* had negated the importance of the Internet. In order to close the gap between its program and Netscape, Internet Explorer was distributed free of charge to all customers (private individuals and firms) (Quittner / Slatalla 1998). In addition, Microsoft exploited its existing relationships with hardware producers to ensure that both Internet Explorer and the Windows operating system were installed on new computers. In spite of legal challenges in the ensuing months and years, Netscape lost its share of the browser market to Internet Explorer (Cusumano / Yoffie 1998). Despite numerous reconceptualizations of its strategy, Netscape Communications could not sustain its early successes. Finally, Netscape Communications was bought by America Online in 1998 and was thereafter closely associated with the hardware manufacturer Sun Microsystems (Sager et al. 1998). Jim Clark had already withdrawn from the Netscape Communications management and formed a new venture with Healtheon (Hamm 1998a).

## 2.1    Why Corporations and Markets?

The basic intention of economic activity is to satisfy human needs. Although human needs are infinite, the goods with which to fulfill them are scarce. This scarcity has led to the formation of economic institutions that, while they cannot eliminate scarcity, at least minimize it. This scarcity sets the stage for various economic phenomena such as the exchange of goods, the division of labor, competition, markets, and corporations. In keeping with 'modern' standards, few natural commodities can be directly consumed, requiring a combined process to largely transform them into consumables. This process is divided into a variety of individual steps resulting in a complex nexus of economic activities.

The fundamental premises to address the scarcity problem are (Picot 1998c):

- Production detours;
- Innovation;
- Division of labor and specialization.

The term "production detour" is attributed to the Austrian economist Böhm-Bawerk (1909), and is derived from Menger (Menger 1871). He classifies economic goods according to their proximity to final consumption. Consumer goods are therefore first order goods. They are produced from preliminary products through specific means of production, which are second order goods, which in turn stem from pre-products and higher order means of production.

Production detour describes a product's position in a higher order, i.e. its productive use beyond final consumption (e.g., the use of grain as seed instead of food, the use of materials and labor to produce tools). In this sense, a production detour is commensurate to an investment: Production detour implies sacrificing present consumption for the sake of productivity increases and, in turn, an increase in future consumption options. Based on given resources, production detours lead to an increase in the need satisfaction potential. Scarcity can be further reduced if consumption or production becomes more efficient or effective through the utilization of innovations. The available resources are then deployed more economically, or more cost effectively so that, for example, a better yield is achieved with the same amount of seeds. Innovations may therefore also be interpreted as a special form of production detour: Labor is not utilized as a direct product-generating factor, but for the creation of new ideas that improve products and processes.

The division of labor and specialization contribute most to reducing scarcity. Division of labor and specialization are mutually dependent. They are related to humans' limited temporal and cognitive ability to master substantial assignments alone. Complex assignments therefore need to be systematically broken down into single tasks until such a task completion lies within the scope of an individual's capacities. In most societies, this process has led to the extensive division of labor. Concentration on single tasks enables the development of specific knowledge, abilities, and processes with which these tasks can be efficiently completed. The principle of creating and using specialized skills, which Aristotle as well as, more recently, Adam Smith (see Smith 1999 [1776]) proposed, leads to considerable productivity increases in the completion of partial tasks. A more productive use of given resources implies the possibility of satisfying a larger number of needs. This mechanism can be observed at all levels of economic activity, beginning with personal, intra-firm or interfirm specialization, and the division of labor all the way to sectoral, regional, national or international specialization and division of labor.

In order to combine partial tasks with specific production methods or consumer goods, services must be exchanged. Partial tasks that are carried out through the division of labor must be reunited in a coordinated way in order to complete the entire task, for example, the production of a car. This process results in a nexus of various exchange relationships. This coordination of partial tasks does not occur automatically, but is a task in itself, also requiring resources. Exchanges between economic actors have to be initiated, negotiated, and completed, for which the exchange partners require information.

In neoclassical microeconomic models, this fundamental basis for the coordination of economic activities was mainly ignored. It was assumed that prices reflect all the information required and that determining prices did not cost time or money. In turn, it was assumed that the search for information was problem-free as well as cost-free, thus providing everyone with identical levels of information. However, the main stumbling block in coordinating economic activities is in the unequal distribution of information and the considerable efforts involved in obtaining it (see Hayek 1945).

Everybody has different and constantly evolving experiences, knowledge, and abilities. The human capacity to process information is limited, which accounts for the continually changing information asymmetries in all fields of the economy. These asymmetries are the basis of all labor-divided activities and entrepreneurial initiatives. Simultaneously, the search for and evaluation of information with regard to, for example, potential exchange partners' abilities and intentions, require resources.

The various forms of scarcity reduction – production detours, innovation, division of labor / specialization, as well as the resultant exchange and coordination activities – view information as purposeful knowledge (Wittmann 1959) of essential importance (Picot 1998c):

- Production detours are often complex and require time, thus necessitating professional competence, as well as information on their future needs and demand.

- Innovations are based on previous knowledge and are at first nothing but an idea, i.e. information, which can then be realized.

- In the end, the division of labor / specialization, as well as exchange and coordination requires information when decomposing tasks as a whole, assigning partial tasks to individuals, controlling task completion activities, as well as when consolidating individual tasks and / or the exchange of services.

This latter point deserves particular attention due to the importance of the division of labor and specialization, and has also been indicated as an organization problem (among others by Picot 1982; Milgrom / Roberts 1992). This organization problem has arisen because information itself is a scarce good. If the required information is not available, deficiencies – caused by faulty organization – may be created in the business process (Picot / Dietl / Franck 2002): The insufficient division of labor leads to constantly changing activity steps, making the development of specialized knowledge and know-how almost impossible. The flip side of this coin is, however, an exaggerated form of specialization resulting in monotony, which is just as unproductive. Deficiencies in the area of exchange and coordination may arise when people do not execute the tasks assigned to them, or when the delivered components do not mesh or fit. These deficiencies – and thus the problems of organization – can be divided into two parts (Milgrom / Roberts 1992; Wolff 1995):

- Coordination problems occur when actors in business processes lack information, for example, do not know which task steps they have to follow and execute. Coordination problems are thus problems of nescience.

- Motivation problems result from actors' conflicts of interest: Contractors may know which tasks need to be carried out, but do not carry them out as their aims differ from that of the principal or contracting authority. Motivation problems are thus problems of unwillingness to perform.

Coordination and motivation problems with regard to the division of labor / specialization, as well as exchange and coordination may trigger the potential loss of productivity gains. The chief concern of the organization problem is eliminating these deficiencies in the process of organizing through coordination and motivation. One should not forget, however, that this also requires resources. Accordingly, the organization problem is an optimization task through which an organizational form is sought that will exploit productivity increase through the division of labor and specialization. Furthermore, this organizational form will consider the use of resources with regard to exchange and coordination, so that a maximum number of needs are met (see figure 2.1). The decisive question here is: Which instruments will support coordination and motivation best?

The costs arising from the usage of resources for coordination and motivation are referred to as transaction costs (see, e.g., Picot 1982). Transaction costs are the "production" costs of an organizational activity. In other words, the costs of the information and communication that is required for the preparation, execution, and control of the division of labor and specialization, as well as of exchange and coordination. The scale of transaction costs is primarily influenced by the characteristics of the relevant transactions (see section 2.3.3).

An empirical study by John J. Wallis and Douglass C. North (Wallis / North 1986) shows the considerable importance that transaction costs possess with regard to the coordination of economic activities. These two researchers examined the scale of the US economy's transaction costs between 1870 and 1970. In their study, they differentiated between transformation services and transaction services. In

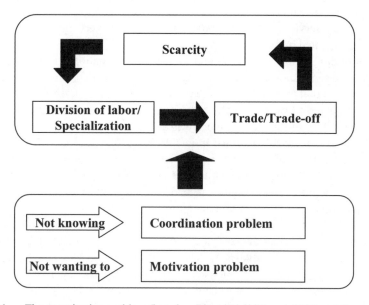

**Fig. 2.1.** The organization problem (based on Picot / Dietl / Franck 2002, p. 10)

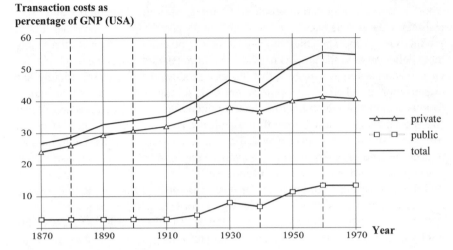

**Transaction costs as percentage of GNP (USA)**

**Fig. 2.2.**     Proportion of transaction costs of the US gross national product (based on Wallis / North 1986, p. 121)

order to identify transaction services, they analyzed those economic activities taking place in the context of market transactions. They consequently grouped diverse economic activities together as transaction industries, such as financial, insurance, as well as wholesale and retail activities. In addition, they evaluated transaction services within companies in non-transaction industries (e.g., manufacturing, raw materials, and agriculture). Wallis and North also studied the contribution of public transaction services. On the whole, they provided very impressive results, which are presented in figure 2.2.

These findings show the substantial increase in the national income realized through the provision of transaction services. Whereas in 1870 only one-fourth of all economic activity was related to the provision of transaction services, this percentage amounted to over one-half (55%) of the total realized income in the US economy in 1970. In this period, there was also a notable growth in government activities. This percentage increased from 13% in 1870 to 25% in 1970. This indicates that most of the national income was spent on information and communication, thus on coordination purposes. Furthermore, Wallis and North's study illustrates the growing strategic significance of the emergence of information and communication technologies during that time.

This study clearly reveals the structural changes in the US national economy, such as the transition from an agricultural to an industrial economy, the growth in services and government activities, the change in corporation size, and the resultant importance of economic coordination activities. The study also emphasizes an additional consequence of the fundamental economic purpose – overcoming the scarcity problem. Although the division of labor and specialization have enabled or still enable increases in productivity through improved efficiency in transformation processes, these gains can only be realized through exchange activities, which, however, require economic resources too. Consequently, transaction costs, like the costs of transformation processes, are a limiting factor with regard to economic growth. "Until economic organizations developed to lower the costs of exchange, we could not reap the advantage of ever greater specialization." (Wallis / North 1986, p. 121).

This implies nothing more than the need to weigh the advantages of further specialization against the related increase in those coordination costs. It is even possible that the advantages of a certain degree of specialization could be exhausted by the coordination costs. The increase in transformation process productivity would inherently set its own economic limits through an increase in coordination costs. Organizational or technological institutions and innovations that support the reduction of exchange costs are thus of great importance for economic development as a whole. Parallels can be drawn to intra-organizational exchange of services.

The long-term analysis of the production costs of varying firm sizes is based on the exploitation of economies of scale. This means that production costs decrease when firm size increases and there is a simultaneous increase in the degree of specialization. This empirical insight, valid in the past, was applied to the production of services and markets under stable circumstances. Coordination costs decrease relative to firm output, as mirrored by the traditional learning curve model. However, under volatile circumstances – when change factors influence the production process as much as market demand – decreasing production costs are quickly overcompensated by ever-increasing coordination costs, i.e. the costs of adaptation and modification. Production firms therefore no longer achieve economically attractive low unit costs.

Inevitably, these facts shift the focus towards the central importance of various coordination mechanisms with respect to economic activities. Coordination mechanisms are therefore evaluated and designed according to their potential to coordinate economic activities yielding the lowest degree of friction. Moreover, to solve these challenges, information is required that is made available through the use of information and communication technologies. These technologies, however, trigger their own effects on the organization of enterprises and markets. An analysis of these changes is presented in sections 2.2 and 2.3, which present a discussion of the fundamental importance of information in markets and enterprises. The focus of section 2.4 is the economy of information production, distribution, and utilization. Based on these deliberations, section 2.5 addresses market and enterprise changes brought about by improved information and communication technologies. Corporations and markets are the two poles on a continuum of possible coordination mechanisms, presenting dichotomous organizational forms of economic activities. Based on their different properties, a variety of options arise for the design of minimal coordination forms. To recognize these options, the fundamental functions and effects of markets and corporations must first be understood.

## 2.2      Markets and Entrepreneurship

A market is an economic place in which the supply of and demand for goods meet, thus enabling exchange processes between sellers and buyers that have become necessary due to the division of labor and specialization (see section 2.1). For the analysis of real market developments, we can draw upon two quite different theoretical approaches: Neoclassical market equilibrium theory and Austrian market process theory. While market equilibrium theory examines conditions determined by fundamental market data such as technologies and preferences, the central focus of market process theory is on the changes brought about by unequal information distribution. In order to understand markets better, we will first describe fundamental ideas of market equilibrium theory (section 2.2.1) and then market process theory (section 2.2.2) (for a detailed comparison see, e.g., von Lingen 1993).

### 2.2.1   Market Behavior and Market Equilibrium

The crux of the predominant market equilibrium theory (e.g., Kreps 1990) is the interaction between actors and markets. Here, coordination occurs through the price mechanism: Based on comparative pricing, the actors (households and enterprises) choose from and / or offer available goods, so that their utility and profit are maximized. The market is in equilibrium when all voluntary exchange processes are completed, i.e. when the quantities offered are equal to those demanded. The main interest in neoclassical market equilibrium theory is centered on these equilibrium conditions: Whether or not they exist, how they are characterized and by which price-quantity combinations, and which properties they exhibit with regard to efficiency, unambiguity, stability, etc. The characteristics of equilibria are not only comprised of fundamental market data (available technologies, individuals' preferences, the quantity and type of initially available resources), but are also dependent on the market form (monopoly, a quantity oligopoly, price oligopoly, full competition, etc.). In contrast, the market equilibrium theory abstracts quite extensively from institutional general frameworks. In this sense, a neoclassical organization, for example, can be fully described by means of a production function that is a system-indifferent fact (Gutenberg 1965). Consequently, the contractual relations between the actors within the organization are not considered (see section 2.3).

Market equilibrium theory is primarily suited to analyze the effects of fundamental market data on the price system in the equilibrium state. One should nevertheless note that these results are primarily valid for mature and transparent markets due to strict neoclassical theory assumptions with regard to the distribution and processing of information in markets:

- Consumers possess complete information about each good's characteristics and utility generation.
- Producers have access to all production technologies.
- All actors know the prices of all goods and have unlimited capabilities to process information.

Through these assumptions, which are based on the underlying model, the problems as a consequence of unequal distribution of market-relevant information are avoided at the outset. Since buyers are fully informed, it is not necessary to search for products or to control their quality. Since all prices are known, similar goods are always traded at uniform prices. Moreover, in the general equilibrium model, as well as with high-volume purchases, the assumption is made that the pricing process occurs via a hypothetical auctioneer. This auctioneer continuously "calls out" new prices until that point in time when the market achieves equilibrium. No actual transactions take place until this point is achieved. It follows that no transactions are allowed at the prices reflected by a market in disequilibrium (Kreps 1990). Market events are very orderly at any point in time when complete information is available. "'Complete information' and 'equilibrium condition' (general allocation equilibrium) [are therefore] characteristics of the *'information death of an economic society'*, i.e. a situation in which all economic activities draw to a close." (Kunz 1985, p. 32 f., italics in the original). Through its fundamental assumptions, the neoclassical market equilibrium theory primarily has a normative character (Güth 1996). It is furthermore helpful in understanding factors that determine equilibrium. One should nevertheless note that the market equilibrium theory abstracts from problems resulting from incomplete and unequally distributed information. The theory thus disregards the importance of the market and competition as institutions for the distribution of information and knowledge (von Hayek 1945). In section 2.1, we already pointed out that in reality, more than half of all economic events are transaction activities, i.e. information and communication processes. Information activities may therefore not be disregarded when accurately examining division of labor-based systems. They play a central role in the understanding of any economy.

## 2.2.2 Market Process and Entrepreneurship

Market process theory differs from the neoclassical equilibrium theory in that the recognition, deployment, and importance of information gaps and incomplete information constitute the starting point for an analysis of market processes. Consequently, information and time are the key building blocks of this theory. Market process theory was particularly important in influencing the Austrian economists Carl Menger (1923 [1871]), Ludwig von Mises (1949), Friedrich A. von Hayek (1945, 1994), as well as Joseph A. Schumpeter (1993 [1934]). One therefore also speaks of the "Austrian School" and / or Austrianism. Austrianism is not, however, a consistent and integrative theory, but rather a structure of varying approaches whose commonality lies in understanding the market as process-like events. We furthermore follow Kirzner's (1978) explication that will later be complemented with Schumpeter's evolutionary approach (1993 [1934]).

### Kirzner's Theory of Market Processes

The starting point for the market process theory is the (uneven) distribution of knowledge in society. It is not just technical subject matter knowledge that is economically relevant here, but especially knowledge regarding the special circumstances of location and time, in which differing amounts and levels of information are expressed regarding markets or technology applications (von Hayek 1945). Contrary to the exponents of the neoclassical market equilibrium theory, von Hayek (1945) does not view the economic problem as having to calculate an equilibrium's existence and characteristics on the basis of given preferences and technologies, since no one person may ever posses the entire prerequisite knowledge required to do this. The actual question is rather how information about preferences and technologies is obtained and how this may be dispersed among the market participants. It is precisely this goal that the pricing system achieves.

The market process theory therefore starts – as does the neoclassical equilibrium theory – with producers and consumers who interact according to the technologies and preferences within a given market (Kirzner 1978). In an effort to improve their original situation, these actors enter a market to buy or to sell goods and services. In doing so, they have certain prior expectations regarding performances and services that they believe they will have to deliver, and reciprocal services that they expect to receive from their exchange partners. Consequently, they construct prior plans, i.e. buying or selling intentions. These plans may be realized better or less well during a market period. Accordingly, the underlying expectations regarding market participants' plans are fulfilled retrospectively, or they are not. Assuming that for illustrative purposes each actor would only want to buy or sell a part of the respective product, the following typical cases are distinguished (see figure 2.3):

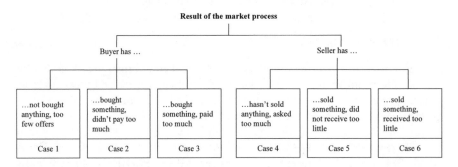

**Fig. 2.3.** Possible results within a market period (according to Plinke 1999, p. 60, based on Kirzner 1978, p. 11)

Cases 2 and 5 denote a situation of fulfilled expectations as encountered in a market equilibrium: The relevant actors' purchases and/or sales were retrospectively optimal, since their prior expectations were realized. The remaining four cases explicitly take into account the possibility of unfulfilled expectations and/or unfulfilled plans. These plans are neglected by the market equilibrium theory, and/or excluded from the outset, through the auctioneer construct.

If people were not adaptive, they would reenter the market with the same expectations and plans in the next period. If, however, they realize that in the previous period they had made decisions – unsatisfactory in hindsight – that were based on wrong information, they will revise their expectations and plans. These changes are modified in respect of rational actors so that they follow the laws of supply and demand systematically: If, for example, the offer to buy was too low (case 1), the next price will be higher. If the offer for sale was too high (case 4), then the offer will be lower in the next period, etc. "This series of systematic changes in the interconnected network of market decisions constitutes the market process" (Kirzner 1973, p. 10). The underlying understanding of the market is therefore a priori dynamic.

The closing of information gaps and the deployment of disequilibrium situations within this market process occur spontaneously, i.e. without interference from a central planning office. In the neoclassical equilibrium model, the fictitious auctioneer mentioned above (see section 2.2.1) is thus replaced by decentralized transactions between individual actors. The driver of the market process is the market participants' learning aptitude in conjunction with the desire to design and configure, and to improve their own lot. The latter notion is expressed in the concept of human beings as "homo agens" of the market process theory (von Mises 1949).

In addition, entrepreneurs develop the market process further. Kirzner (1978) illustrates this by means of a thought experiment in which he uses the extreme example of buyers and / or sellers incapable of 'learning' from their experience on the market. He then introduces new, clever actors – whom he calls entrepreneurs – into this hypothetical market. The entrepreneurs are neither interested in buying nor in selling. They discover, however, that in a market disequilibrium the price differences can be utilized as arbitrage, i.e. it is possible to achieve gains without risks. For example, an entrepreneur buys from a seller, who is asking a price that is far too low (case 6), and sells these goods at a higher price. However, these opportunities for gain and profit are always temporary, since the exploitation of a knowledge and / or information advantage through arbitrage is, as it were, a signal to the other entrepreneurs to exploit the situation in a similar way. These other entrepreneurs are likely to offer the sellers, who are incapable of 'learning', a slightly better offer.

As this example demonstrates, competition in the market process is inevitable: Entrepreneurs must always ensure that they offer their market partners more attractive conditions than their competitors. This process of competition continues until the opportunity for gain and profit has been completely eroded, i.e. a situation in which supply and demand are in complete harmony. In the process, entrepreneurs communicate knowledge and information about the market – including the value and the relative scarcity of goods – to passive market participants who (in this thought experiment) could not acquire it on their own (Kirzner 1978). Accordingly, based on their superior information, which the price system was unable to handle adequately during the disequilibrium situation, entrepreneurs take on a coordination function (Casson 1982). The entrepreneurs did not seek this specific market knowledge of location and time of gain and profit opportunities. It was rather their alertness that allowed them to take advantage of existing but undiscovered opportunities. It is this latter characteristic that distinguishes entrepreneurs (Kirzner 1979).

In reality, however, market participants are not incapable of learning. In fact, (see the Austrian market process theory) all actors have an entrepreneurial element when they perceive a risk-free opportunity for gain and profit, which is then exploited, or they seek the favor of potential exchange partners by making increasingly better offers. The market process is further developed in both cases, since the actors gradually approach their limits while participating successfully in market developments (Kirzner 1978). On the one hand, the speed and the course of market processes depend on the market participants' resourcefulness. On the other hand, the diffusion of information depends on technical capabilities, since actors can only be resourceful if the right information is available. This leads to special information markets in which market-relevant knowledge itself becomes the product. Consequently, reciprocal transactions occur between information markets and material goods markets. When, for example, it is cheaper to obtain information on information markets, the informational differences on goods markets even out since arbitrage is alleviated. Information markets therefore have considerable influence on the competitive environment within markets for goods (see section 2.5.2).

In the course of the above-described market process, coordination occurs in two forms (von Hayek 1994):

- The individual plans of individual actors are aligned reciprocally so that they are compatible, i.e. mutually realizable.

- The supply of goods and services is shifted to those actors who can operate at the lowest cost.

During the course of the market process, disequilibrium and inefficiency are therefore abolished gradually. In both cases, knowledge that was previously unavailable in a concentrated form is acquired and distributed. Von Hayek (1994) thus speaks of "competition as a discovery method." At the same time though, we need to realize that this process is never concluded: Not only do market data such as the available resources change, but the actors themselves may be interested in changing the existing market data by introducing innovations into the market, which Schumpeter (1993 [1934]) specifically emphasizes.

### Schumpeter's Theory of Economic Development

According to Schumpeter, the entrepreneur's innovation function consists of the "implementation of new combinations" (Schumpeter 1993 [1934], p. 111). These innovations may correspond to the following aspects (Schumpeter 1993 [1934]):

- Introduction of a new product;

- Introduction of a new production method;

- Development of a new market;

- Development of a new procurement market; as well as the

- Implementation of a new organization structure.

With the introduction of an innovation, entrepreneurs interfere with the regular course of production as well as with the exchange on the market. Entrepreneurs' goal is to make a profit through their knowledge advantage, which is expressed by these new combinations. The profit arises in that entrepreneurs (in line with Schumpeter's theory) take advantage of the gap between the price of resource deployment and the price of the products that they produce (Schumpeter 1993 [1934]). For a certain period of time, entrepreneurs may in fact be more successful than their competitors. Others will, however, try to participate in this money-making opportunity by imitating their competitors. Realizing such gains will therefore only be possible as long as the competing imitators have not eroded the profit margin. Schumpeter's entrepreneur is characterized as a "creative destroyer" of existing structures. The introduction of new products or processes alters the equilibrium (Schumpeter 1993 [1934]): An innovation can replace existing goods (e.g., the replacement of typewriters by computers), as well as ultimately enabling new products and services (e.g., computer software). Innovations, it follows, change the fundamental scarcity of goods within the economy: Some resources become more valuable, while others lose their importance.

It is therefore clear that Kirzner's and Schumpeter's perspectives of entrepreneurship complement each other to a certain degree: While Schumpeter views the entrepreneur as the cause of changes, moving away from the previous equilibrium ("creative destruction"), Kirzner emphasizes the role of the entrepreneur in the convergence towards the (new) equilibrium ("arbitrage") (Casson 1987). Consequently, a continuous market process evolves in the form of a convergence towards equilibrium and a turning away from this, due to its creative destruction. Both entrepreneurship concepts have the special importance of information in common: Ultimately, opportunities arise for entrepreneurs because competence and knowledge are distributed unevenly in the economy. This uneven distribution enables information advantages and permits an entrepreneurial exploitation of information divergences, albeit through arbitrage (Kirchner's entrepreneur), or through innovation (Schumpeter's entrepreneur). Entrepreneurship is therefore composed of the recognition of economically relevant information or knowledge advantages and the practical exploitation of such divergences. Entrepreneurial achievement is the creative bridging of thus far completely unconnected and / or incompletely connected information spheres through the use of entrepreneurial ideas. This entrepreneurial activity may be taken for granted as far as trade is concerned. Goods are bought from sellers and are then offered on the market on terms that meet the time, place, as well

**Fig. 2.4.** The fundamental entrepreneurial idea as creative bridging between information spheres (based on Picot 1989a, p. 4)

as quantity. The basic context applies equally well, but in a more complex way, to firms that do not trade. Between purchasing and sales, the creation of goods and services is an especially intensive transformation step. In both cases, information advantage and knowledge differences between two information spheres are recognized and are capitalized on economically (see figure 2.4).

The above-mentioned examples illustrate that an entrepreneurial idea's realization is usually more complex than Kirzner's arbitrage model. The market process theory (like neoclassical pricing theory) abstracts from all questions regarding the performance slump of the transformation process, the organization of the supply relationships, and contracts' design and implementation. For a more complete analysis of economic events, additional theoretical approaches are required that examine the above-mentioned organization problems.

## 2.3    Theories of Organization

The core of the organization problem lies in the scarcity of economic goods and the resultant economic problems, as well as the possibility of these problems being reduced through the division of labor (see section 2.1). Consequently, the determination of tasks based on the division of labor and the selection of appropriate forms of coordination and motivation are central issues related to organization in and between corporations, as well as in the economy as a whole. Economics offers many theoretical instruments and models with which these organization problems could be solved. Section 2.2 examined market theory solutions that specifically address the question of how actions can be coordinated in a decentralized way. As a field of research, new institutional economics has recently received much attention in scientific literature and in practice. Similar to the Austrian market process theory, new institutional economics also emphasizes the importance of information and communication for the coordination of economic activity. Institutions that facilitate the rationalization of information and communication processes are its core research field. They function as mechanisms to stabilize expectations, which in turn facilitate the coordination of production based on the division of labor. In the following, we offer a brief survey of those parts of institutional economics that are of special relevance for the theory of organization: Property rights theory (section 2.3.2), transaction cost theory (section 2.3.3), as well as principal-agent theory (section 2.3.4). In section 2.3.1, we first offer a short overview of the common elements and assumptions of all theoretical approaches to institutional economics.

## 2.3.1   Institutions and Contracts

Institutions are "… socially sanctionable expectations related to the actions and behaviors of one or more individuals" (Dietl 1993, p. 37; translation by authors). They function as mechanisms to stabilize expectations, which in turn facilitate the coordination of production based on the division of labor.

New institutional economics deals with the effects of institutions (i.e. contracts, organization structures, language, and money) on human behavior, as well as with possibilities of efficient formation and / or evolutionary development, and with the rational design of institutions. The new institutional economics is therefore based upon two fundamental assumptions: "(i) [I]nstitutions do matter, (ii) the determinants of institutions are susceptible to analysis by the tools of economic theory." (Mathews 1986, p. 903). The creation of institutions can also be explained with the help of game-theoretical reflections: Ullmann-Margalit (1977) and Kunz (1985) differentiate between self-maintaining institutions and those requiring supervision. Self-maintaining norms are formed wherever participants benefit more from the creation and observation of institutions than from behavior not authorized by institutions. Compliance with a norm that benefits the participants does not have to be controlled, since a deviation would itself cause disadvantages for the actors. Examples of self-maintaining norms are the language rules of interpersonal communication (sentence structure, grammar), money, or basic traffic rules such as driving on the right side in the Americas and continental Europe. Conversely, conflicts of interest can arise between participants through the creation of and expected compliance with institutions requiring supervision. Norms that must be monitored are characterized by individuals behaving as rational actors (from their own perspective) by not contributing to such norm creation and / or by not respecting those that have been created. The creation of standards is a prime example of norms requiring supervision (see Besen / Saloner 1988).

The emergence of self-maintaining norms and norms requiring supervision can be explained with the help of game-theoretic models. For example, the creation of self-maintaining games can be modeled as cooperative games, in which all participants can improve their position through group-conforming behavior (see figure 2.5).

In this example, the actors each have a choice between two ways of behaving: They can either drive on the right or on the left side of the street. If the actors choose different sides of the street as their driving norm, they risk a collision, and

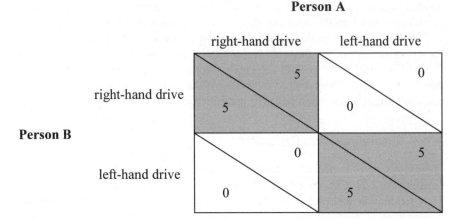

**Fig. 2.5.**   (Pure) coordination problem: choice between two norms (based on Picot / Dietl / Franck 2002, p. 16)

they have to drive with considerable care (utility value of each equals 0). If, however, both drivers agree on which side to drive as a norm, the traffic becomes more efficient and safer (utility value of each equals 5). There does not seem to be a conflict of interest between the actors. However, in order to have the advantages of a common norm, they must agree on which one of the two possible norms to choose, through, for example, an appropriate agreement.

Thus, information and communication are required to solve the coordination problem. If, to begin with, there is a norm, it sustains itself since the actors have no interest in deviating from this norm. Conversely, partially conflicting participant interests could arise with norms requiring supervision. Norms requiring supervision are characterized by individual actors finding it individually rational to contravene the originated norm.

Norms requiring supervision, their creation, and compliance can be described with the help of what is known as the prisoner's dilemma (e.g., Ullmann-Margalit 1977). Prisoners' dilemma situations are characterized by the actors being allowed to choose freely between alternative plans of action and by the constellation of expected action results designed in such a way that the optimal solution will be systematically missed. This happens because all actors ultimately try to maximize their individual results at the other actors' cost. Cooperation cannot take place because all the partners anticipate these behaviors. The prisoner's dilemma belongs to the category of non-cooperative games. Consequently, the final situation presents all the participants with worse results than would have been possible with cooperative behavior. A typical example of the prisoner's dilemma is illustrated by the following situation (Luce / Reiffa 1957): Two thieves are arrested by the police and are separately interrogated. Each thief has the option to either refuse to give evidence, or to confess to the crime, thus betraying his fellow thief. If both of

**Thief 1**

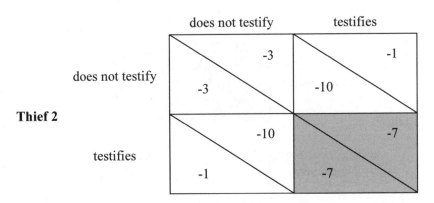

**Fig. 2.6.**    Motivation problem: the prisoner's dilemma situation (based on Picot / Dietl / Franck 2002, p. 17)

them should refuse to give evidence, they can each expect a maximum of three years' imprisonment. If both confess, they will each receive a seven-year sentence. If only one of the thieves confesses, he can expect a sentence of one year (chief witness regulation), whereas the other thief will receive ten years' imprisonment. Since each thief assumes that his fellow thief will betray him in order to free himself, they will not take the strategy that would be optimal for both of them – not to give evidence and to each receive a three-year sentence. Instead, each thief will give evidence in an attempt to prevent the other from improving his situation at his cost. In turn, a less than optimal situation will be realized (see figure 2.6).

The prisoner's dilemma is evidently a motivation problem: Even if the actors know that remaining silent is the better solution for both, and even if they were to agree to such a strategy, they – based on the constellation of utility values – always have an incentive to deviate from this collective optimal solution and to contravene any other deals if these cannot be enforced. An institution must therefore be able to overcome the actors' unwillingness. This means both controlling actors' behavior and punishing norm deviations so that after punishment fewer benefits are provided than with conforming behavior. Consequently, with regard to motivational problems, the sanctionability of expectations is of particular importance. Within the framework of our example, this may be done, for example, by a mafia organization that punishes confessions appropriately (Holler 1983). Through this threat, the game result is transformed to such an extent that not confessing constitutes the optimal strategy for each of the prisoners (see figure 2.7): Cooperative behavior thus becomes *incentive compatible*. From an economic perspective, an analogous function takes over the constitutional state jurisdiction that oversees compliance with laws and prosecutes legal infractions.

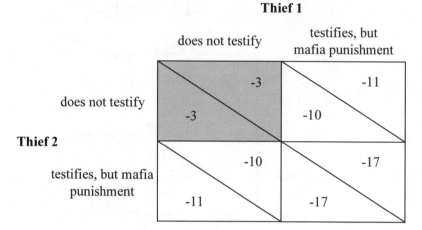

**Fig. 2.7.**    Solution of the motivation problem by means of norms requiring supervision (based on Picot / Dietl / Franck 2002, p. 18)

Contracts that specify contractual partners' behavior (coordination aspect) and the sanctions to be expected if they do not behave in accordance with these (motivation aspect) are important for the solution of coordination and motivation problems. In an economic sense, a contract is viewed as "each binding explicit or implicit agreement about the exchange of goods or services between people who concur with this agreement, since they expect a betterment from it" (Wolff 1995, p. 38). A distinction is often made between classical, neoclassical and relational contract types (MacNeil 1978; Williamson 1990).

Within the new institutional economics framework, organization structure design is analyzed by means of contracts. Currently, the new institutional economics does not constitute a consistent and integrated theoretical structure. It is rather comprised of several approaches – methodologically mostly related – that overlap, complement one another, and are partially related to one another. The following three points of departure have all these approaches in common:

- Methodological individualism;
- Individual utility maximization;
- Bounded rationality.

Methodological individualism is a linking element of nearly all economic theories. Within the framework of this research concept, social structures such as enterprises, but also the state, are analyzed by focusing on the aims and decisions of individuals who operate within these structures (Schumpeter 1908).

The assumption of individual utility maximization is also a common element of economic approaches. This axiom asserts that all actors pursue their own self-interests: In accordance with individuals' perceived limits of actions and preferences, they choose an alternative that promises them maximum value. The concept of opportunism, which is understood as "self-interest seeking with guile" is related to individual utility maximization (Williamson 1975, p. 26). The acceptance of opportunistic behavior stresses that actors will put up with and approve occasional negative consequences for other people solely for individual utility maximization, as illustrated by the prisoner's dilemma.

New institutional economics emphasizes actors' bounded rationality. According to Simon (1959, p. xxiv), human behavior is "*intendedly* rational, but only *limitedly* so" (emphases in the original). The boundaries of rationality are a result of incomplete knowledge and our limited information-processing capability. In this sense, people can only be rational with regard to their subjective, incomplete information. This is why Simon (1959) also speaks of subjective rationality. As already elaborated on in section 2.1, it is this incomplete information, with its partial aspects of coordination and motivation, which allows the organization problem to evolve in the first place. As already mentioned, part of the theoretical approaches of the new institutional economics are the property rights theory (see section 2.3.2), transaction cost theory (see section 2.3.3) and principal-agent theory (section 2.3.4). These theories are addressed briefly. Their relevance will be demonstrated in respect of determining enterprise boundaries, explaining the dissolution of enterprise boundaries, as well as in respect of the emergence of new organizational forms for internal task fulfillment.

## 2.3.2   Property Rights Theory

At the heart of the property rights theory (Coase 1960; Alchian / Demsetz 1972; Picot / Dietl / Franck 2002) lies the right to take action and the right of disposal (property rights), as well as their effects on the behavior of economic actors. The point of departure here is the observation that the value of goods and people's actions depend on the rights assigned to them. For example, firm motivation largely results from its right to acquire profits and gains. Firm motivation and its value will diminish if the right to acquire such profits and gains is limited, for example, by taxes and deductions. Besides the general assumptions of the new institutional economics (methodological individualism, individual utility maximization, limited rationality (see section 2.3.1)), property rights theory is essentially based on property rights, external effects, and transaction costs.

Property rights are the focal point of the property rights theory. Property rights are understood as those rights to action and disposal that are related to a good and to economic entities, and are based on legal regulations and contracts. Property rights have object-related, as well as person-related aspects. They determine the rights of an individual pertaining to the use of a good. By allocating property rights, transaction rights are created, but also obligations for those benefiting from such rights, as well as transaction restrictions for those who do not have property rights to the specific good. Consequently, from the distribution of property rights, certain incentive effects may emanate from individuals' behavior.

Property rights associated with a good may be divided into four single rights (Furubotn / Pejovich 1974; Alchian / Demsetz 1972):

- The right to use a good (usus);

- The right to alter a good's form and substance (abusus);

- The right to acquire gains arising from a good and the responsibility to assume any losses that may result (usus fructus);

- The right to sell a good to third parties (capitalization and / or liquidation rights).

With regard to the actors, it is necessary to differentiate whether or not they possess all these partial rights (total allocation) and whether or not these rights are only partially allocated (partial allocation). On the other hand, the same partial right may be allocated to a single individual or may be distributed between several individuals. One speaks of attenuated property rights when rights to action and disposal are partially assigned and / or are allocated to multiple individuals.

Attenuated property rights carry the risk of external effects. External effects refer to all those (positive and negative) side effects of individuals' actions that are not recompensed via the market, or those for which individuals have to pay themselves. Since rights to action and disposal are not fully specified in attenuated property rights, or are allocated to several actors, individuals' actions do affect the utility of the remaining actors. If, however, property rights are strongly diluted, excessive negotiation costs inhibit a contractual agreement, in which case the external effects that lead to a loss of welfare remain.

Communication products, such as telephones, networked computer systems, etc., are a good example of the above. They are differentiated in that a single user's utility specifically depends on the number of individuals who can be reached via these products on a common network (Blankart / Knieps 1995). Each new participant brings positive external effects for the existing actors within a network, as their communication possibilities increase. In this case, the right to use this product (usus) is obviously attenuated, since communication products are by definition always used by at least two people – a sender and a receiver (see chapter 3). The same is true for any gains arising from the use of the product (usus fructus).

If a buyer of components invests in a data processing infrastructure and connects to the electronic warehousing system of the firm's suppliers, both the buyer and the supplier can save costs. The buyer does not therefore have the full right to appropriate all gains (usus fructus) resulting from the data processing investment. Thus the supplier is likely to be willing to contribute to the expenditure on the system implementation. In doing so, the positive external effect of the buyer's decision with regard to the supplier's gain is internalized.

Network effects also occur with telecommunication networks. Each e-mail account becomes more valuable with each new Internet user, since the number of communication relationships that is theoretically possible increases (see section 2.4.2). Contrary to the above example, it is actually not possible to internalize external effects – in order to balance the utility – through payments, as the negotiations required by the vast number of affected participants would lead to enormous costs.

This example clarifies the importance of the third central element of the property rights theory – transaction costs. In a world without transaction costs, all allocation of property rights would be equally efficient: If information and communication were free and if there were an infinite amount of free time available for negotiations, even individuals affected by attenuated property rights would negotiate just as long as it would take for all external effects to be internalized. This is what the Coase theorem (Coase 1960) maintains. In the real world, however, quite considerable transaction costs do arise (see section 2.1) and not only through negotiations, but above all during the development, allocation, transfer, and enforcement of property rights (Tietzel 1981). This addresses the costs of information and communication, including the opportunity costs of the time required for the initiation and execution of a service exchange.

Generally, property rights should be allocated in such a way that as many nearly complete rights bundles as possible are linked to the utilization of economic resources and assigned to actors so that they are stimulated to use resources responsibly and efficiently. This increasing complete allocation is, however, only economically meaningful as long as the reduction of welfare losses as a result of external effects is larger than the transaction costs. Figure 2.8 illustrates this trade-off.

The property rights theory contributes to a differentiated picture of the firm. According to the methodological individualism perspective, it is regarded as a multi-person structure and dynamic meshwork of contractual relations (Kaulmann 1987). Property rights theory is therefore applicable to the analysis of all decisions that lead to a change in the rights to action and disposal within the firm. Property rights theory may therefore offer valuable recommendations for in-depth questions concerning the organization's internal design (Picot 1981).

Consequently, property rights should be dissected in some detail. This will subsequently lead to a new allocation of property rights in the form of changed competency and resource allocations (see chapter 5). The goal of organization design must be the most efficient allocation by means of organizational rules that address internal lines of action through expertise and function bundling, as well as the delegation of responsibility. The safeguarding and enforcement of property rights play an important role in economic activities.

Actors' willingness to act increases with the degree to which they can personally acquire the benefits of their activities. This phenomenon is of special importance for research and development activities. There are various institutional regulations, such as copyright and patents, to protect knowledge. Without institutions that describe the rights to the disposal of information and that simplify their enforcement of these rights, innovative knowledge production would be considerably inhibited.

**Total effect**
**Transaction costs**
**Welfare losses**

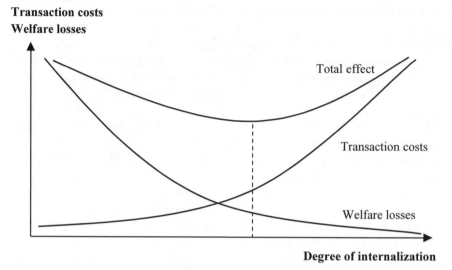

**Degree of internalization**

**Fig. 2.8.**    Trade-off between welfare losses through external effects and transaction costs (based on Picot / Dietl / Franck 2002)

## 2.3.3  Transaction Cost Theory

The transaction cost theory's fundamental unit of analysis (Coase 1947; Williamson 1990; Picot / Dietl / Franck 2002) is the individual transaction. The latter is defined as the transfer of property rights. The costs occurring in this process are referred to as transaction costs (Picot 1991b) and they cover:

- Initiation (e.g., research, travel, consultation);
- Agreement (e.g., negotiation, legal department);
- Execution (e.g., process control);
- Control (e.g., quality and due date monitoring); and
- Adaptation (e.g., additional costs due to subsequently submitted qualitative, cost or target date changes).

The magnitude of these transaction costs depends on the characteristics of the activities to be performed, as well as the chosen integration and / or organizational forms. It is the goal of transaction cost analysis to find an organizational form that minimizes the transaction costs of given production costs within a given production capacity. Transaction costs are therefore the efficiency measure for the appraisal and choice of various institutional arrangements. These are organizational forms such as market and enterprise (hierarchy), but also intermediate forms such as longer-term cooperative arrangements. Enterprises in the form of integrated,

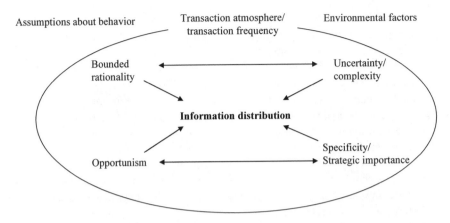

**Fig. 2.9.**   Factors influencing transaction costs (Picot / Dietl / Franck 2002; based on Williamson 1975, p. 40)

division-of-labor-based entities only have the right to exist if they can handle the coordination and motivation problems associated with the delivery of goods and services better – i.e., at lower transaction costs – than this would be possible by dealing with an external partner from the marketplace.

Factors influencing transaction costs can be systematically represented through Williamson's (1975) organizational failure frameworks (see figure 2.9).

Central components of the organizational failure framework are, on the one hand, the environment's specificity, strategic importance, and uncertainty and, on the other hand, the behavioral assumptions opportunism and bounded rationality. The greater the obsolescence that arises when the required resources for a task accomplishment are not deployed as intended, the higher a transaction's degree of specificity, as these resources are being used for the next best utilization (Klein / Crawford / Alchian 1978). For example, during the conclusion of a business relationship, non-specific resources such as standard software can be utilized as before without any limitations. On the other hand, specific investments, such as special machines, require a refitting to prevent them losing their value entirely (e.g., customer data).

In general, we identify the following types of specificity (Williamson 1990):

- Site specificity: Investments in localized assets;
- Physical asset specificity: Investments in specific machines and technology;
- Human asset specificity: Investments in specific employee skills;
- Dedicated assets: Specific investments in non-specific assets that would, however, constitute excess capacity if the transaction is discontinued.

The specificity of a performance relationship may change frequently during the course of a contractual relationship. A buyer, for example, has a choice beforehand of different suppliers that all offer just-in-time delivery. However, once a certain supplier has been chosen, replacement barriers arise, as the link to the logistics concept requires certain specific investments in information technology, etc.: The performance relationship has become specific retrospectively. Such a conversion is called a fundamental transformation (Williamson 1990).

This dependency through specificity can be exploited opportunistically, for example, by increasing delivery prices. Specificity becomes problematic when the behavioral assumption of opportunism has been fulfilled, i.e. when the actors, where applicable, maximize their own benefits at the contractual partner's cost (see section 2.3.1). Transaction cost theory therefore recommends that, generally, specific transactions should not to be carried out by means of short-term relationships but that these should rather be strongly and hierarchically integrated by means of a long-term contractual relationship.

For such a decision, one also needs to consider the activity's strategic importance, i.e. its contribution to the final product's competitive position. If the production of goods and services is specifically and strategically important, the fundamental capabilities can be interpreted as core competencies according to Prahalad and Hamel (1990). Core competencies should in any case always be organized within and not external to the firm. There is a need for transactions that are indeed specific, but only of little strategic importance. The specificity of such transactions should be reduced so that long-term outsourcing becomes possible. An example of such a development is the general trend toward business standard software (see chapter 4). On the other hand, proprietary software solutions are preferable when specific, difficult to describe non-standard processes are strategically important, as often happens in the production area (see chapter 5). Uncertainty as an environmental factor is expressed in the number and extent of unpredictable task modifications. In an uncertain world, the fulfillment of a contract is complicated by frequent changes in due dates, prices, conditions, and quantities. All of these imply changes and modifications of contracts and thus the acceptance of higher transaction costs. The environmental conditions' uncertainty is not, however, a problem until it is encountered in conjunction with the behavioral assumptions of bounded rationality, as cognitive skills and capabilities could then be overtaxed. Williamson describes this situation, when information is distributed asymmetrically and there is the risk of an information advantage being opportunistically exploited by a transaction partner, as an information wedge (Williamson 1975). These constellations of asymmetric information are also of central interest in the principal-agent approach (see section 2.3.4).

Besides the four influencing factors and the possibility of an information wedge, two additional factors need to be considered: Transaction frequency and the spirit in which transactions occur. These two elements of the organizational failure framework are of subordinate, but not insignificant, importance when choosing efficient forms of integration. Transaction frequency determines the payback period and the economic profitability of hierarchical entrepreneurial structures or long-term cooperative relationships. Frequently recurring transactions make the creation of a firm's own in-house capacities, or the finalizing of long-term cooperative contracts

Internal development or production

Capital investments in suppliers/customers
Local and regional supplier aggregation

Development cooperation
- with subsequent internal production
- with subsequent external production

Long-term agreements
- about specific, internally developed parts
- about specific, externally developed parts

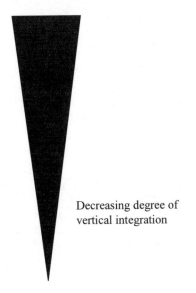

Decreasing degree of
vertical integration

Annual contracts
- with open dates of delivery and quantities
- with fixed dates of delivery and quantities

Spontaneous purchase on the market

**Fig. 2.10.** Examples of alternative decisions for optimizing the delivery of goods and services (based on Picot 1991, p. 340)

seem cost efficient rather than merely sporadically occurring exchange relationships that may be conducted on the open market.

The spirit in which transactions occur also influences the transaction costs of varying forms of integration considerably. This spirit encompasses all of the organization's relevant social, legal, and technological general conditions. They include the transaction partner values, as well as the fundamental technical infrastructures that facilitate the interaction between the transaction partners that could decrease the transaction costs. Information and communication systems may expand the possibilities of rational behavior, the specificity of a transaction, and reduce transaction costs. They thus influence design of the optimal organizational form (see section 2.5.1).

The above discussion suggests that there is a multifaceted spectrum of in-between forms, i.e. forms ranging between the two extreme forms of market and hierarchy. They bridge elements of the market, as well as of the hierarchical organization, which includes, for example, long-term entrepreneurial cooperatives, strategic alliances, joint ventures, franchise systems, licensing, dynamic networks, as well as long-term purchasing and supply contracts. These hybrid organizational forms have been examined in line with transaction cost theory for several years. By taking this into consideration, it is possible to unfold a continuum of organizational forms between the extreme forms of the pure market-based organization, with its short-term, spot-market contracts, and the pure hierarchical organization based on unlimited work contracts. The seemingly simple choice between firm-internal and firm-external creation of goods and services emerges as a complex optimization task within a broad continuum of possibilities (see figure 2.10).

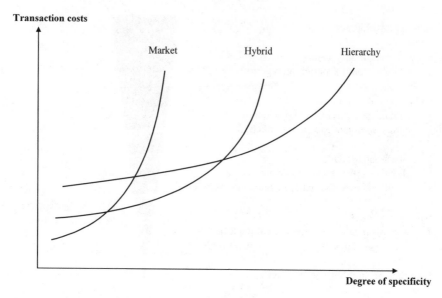

**Fig. 2.11.**   Integrated forms and specificity (based on Williamson 1991, p. 284)

The advantage of each of these organizational forms depends on the combination of the above-mentioned influencing factors and their respective impact on the transaction costs. Figure 2.11 illustrates how the transaction costs of three organizational forms may vary depending on the specificity of the goods and services to be rendered, assuming that all other factors of the organizational failure framework, as well as the production costs and services are fixed.

Regardless of their degree of specificity, hierarchies (firms) have the highest fixed transaction costs, which include bureaucracy costs (Williamson 1990). The hierarchical organizational form makes a multitude of incentives and control mechanisms available that facilitate the execution of specific transactions. Consequently, transaction costs increase relatively evenly with an increasing degree of specificity. Conversely, market transactions incur the lowest fixed costs, since they have no longer-term contractual relationships. The variable transaction costs of increasing specificity are therefore very high, since the risk of opportunistic exploitation requires precautionary measures to ensure a proper choice of contractual partner, agreement regarding the contractual content, control measures for the delivery of goods and services, etc. Generally, hybrid organizational forms face a lesser threat of opportunistic exploitation (although larger within hierarchies), since longer-term relationships ensure that the interests of contractual partners are at least partially equal and also increase the potential for sanctioning opportunistic behavior. Hybrid organizational forms, however, trigger higher fixed transaction costs that increase slightly with increasing specificity as when executing a transaction via the market (although the increase is greater with hierarchies). If the specificity of the delivery of goods and services is low, the expensive incentive and control mechanisms of hierarchical integration forms are not efficient. Consequently, such transactions ought to occur via the market.

On the other hand, vertical integration is sensible at a high degree of specificity, since hierarchies are better suited for coping with the consequences of an information wedge. Finally, hybrid organizational forms are advantageous for the broad class of tasks of middle-range specificity. The emergence of firms can be validated by means of the transaction cost theory framework (Coase 1937), as well as by the observation that firms' boundaries are becoming increasingly blurred and that firms are, as it were, disintegrating (see section 2.5.1, as well as chapter 6). Valuable design recommendations may be deduced from transaction cost theory. Likewise, recommendations may be generated with regard to internal organization design (see chapter 5), or with regard to the spatially decentralized, firm-spanning task accomplishment that would not be realizable without information and communication systems that can decrease transaction costs (see chapter 8).

## 2.3.4 Principal-Agent Theory

The principal-agent theory (see, e.g., Ross 1973; Jensen/Meckling 1976; Picot/ Dietl/Franck 2002) is concerned with the principal-agent relationship that is based on the division of labor, is characterized by asymmetrically distributed information and uncertainty about the occurrence of certain environmental situations, as well as the contract partner's behavior. Principal-agent relations are entered into when one party (principal) delegates decisions and implementation competencies to another party (agent). In a principal-agent relation, agents make decisions that not only have an impact on their own welfare, but also influence their principals' level of utility. The agent is the informed partner. The principal-agent theory examines the contract underlying the principal-agent relationship and/or the metaphor of the underlying contract between parties, if this is not explicitly described. Hence, the contract between the principal and agent is the central unit of analysis. The principal-agent approach focuses on determining the optimal contractual design required to steer and control the principal-agent relationship.

The principal-agent theory's important elements include the principal-agent relationship, agency costs, the typology of information asymmetries, and the determination of appropriate institutional integration forms as the organizational design of potential principal-agent relations. Moreover, the principal-agent theory may also be regarded as the study of internal relationships within an institution. From the principals' perspective, it explains (positive analysis) the principal-agent relationship and its design (normative analysis).

Agency costs are the efficiency criterion. According to Jensen and Meckling (1976), these costs are comprised of three components:

- The principal's monitoring and control costs;
- The agent's signaling and guarantee costs;
- The remaining loss of welfare (residual loss).

The first two cost types arise from measures for the reduction of uncertainty. Residual loss is an indication of information incompleteness, so that transactions that would inherently increase welfare will not be – or will be only partially – executed. Accordingly, parents may, for example, do without a babysitter whom they would use if they actually knew about him or her. Between the mentioned cost types, partial trade-off relationships are found: Increasing residual loss may be minimized, for example, through increased monitoring and control expenditures. These expenditures may, in turn, be reduced by the agent's credible signaling and specified guaranteed services. The institutional arrangement that minimizes agency costs should be chosen for the actual execution of the delivery of goods and services.

Based on the underlying information asymmetry between the principal and agents, the classification of the focal principal-agent relationship plays an important role. Three problem types can be differentiated on the grounds of their causes (Spremann 1990; Picot / Dietl / Franck 2002):

- Hidden characteristics;
- Hidden action;
- Hidden intention.

**Hidden Characteristics**

The problem of hidden characteristics arises before a contractual agreement is reached, i.e. if principals are not familiar with agents' characteristics or with the services that they offer. The resultant risk lies in the potential selection of undesirable contractual partners due to adverse selection. The traditional example of this phenomenon is the used car market with Akerlof's famous article on 'Market of Lemons' (Akerlof 1970), as potential buyers (principals) of used cars whose value are unknown, will start by assuming that they are of an average quality. Assuming that these cars' value on the total market is equally distributed and ranges between $10,000 and $30,000, the average value would be around $20,000. This would be the maximum price that buyers would be willing to pay. If sellers (agents) were, however, to know the true value of these cars, they would only be willing to sell cars at this price if their true value were below $20,000. This consequently leads to a systematic negative selection of contractual partners: At any arbitrary price, only those agents whose goods and services are exactly as good as or worse than (due to a lack of information about the average price) the principals' offer will be willing to engage in a transaction. Since the interested party is not going to agree to any disadvantageous transaction, this market will subsequently collapse. Such problems may also arise, for example, when hiring new employees or in the relationship between lenders and borrowers. To solve this problem, the principal-agent theory offers two solutions: On the one hand, signaling, screening, as well as self-selection contracts are mechanisms that reduce the information asymmetry between principals and agents. On the other hand, instruments that enhance the alignment of interests prevent the exploitation of existing information asymmetries.

Signaling means that agents signal their characteristics and / or performance characteristics to principals so that an understanding of a principal-agent relationship can be achieved. Such a signaling function may assume the form of, for example, potential agents' work or education certificates. Conversely, with screening, the initiative starts with principals seeking additional information about agents' characteristics and / or their past performance. Examples of such screening activities are the administration of various tests during the application process or creditors obtaining information from credit agencies. In self-selection situations, principals offer agents a menu of contracts that are structured in such a way that agents' choice of contract reveals their hidden characteristics. Accordingly, cost sharing is common in insurance contracts. A high degree of cost sharing is only meaningful for agents when liability obligations are unlikely. By choosing a high degree of cost sharing, agents thus reveal their low risk assessment. A high degree of cost sharing may be interpreted as an instrument for the equalization of interests if agents can influence their overall risk assessment: As agents have to share the damage, it is in their interest, as well as that of the insurance to ensure that no damage occurs.

**Hidden Action**

In contrast to the problems of hidden characteristics, hidden action only becomes relevant after the closing of the contract, i.e. after having chosen a contractual partner. Hidden action denotes that principals are only aware of the results of agents' actions, but not familiar with these actions. This occurs when agents' behavior cannot be observed or principals lack the knowledge required to judge agents' behavior. Therefore, a supervisory board (principal), for example, cannot judge whether or not the board of directors' (agent) chosen strategy was in the interests of the owners. It follows that principals cannot tell whether or not a negative result is due to agents' actions or due to unfavorable environmental conditions. The resultant moral hazard, which is triggered by hidden action, is that agents might take advantage of the scope of options open to them and act contrary to principals' interests. This may occur if, for example, agents fulfill their tasks carelessly, or do not exert themselves.

In order to limit the potential impact of moral hazard, the principal-agent theory recommends monitoring to reduce information asymmetry (e.g., reporting systems and control mechanisms). In doing so, principals can acquire a better understanding of agents' behavior and apply immediate sanctions if necessary. Another alternative is the implementation of incentive systems, especially through some form of revenue sharing such as a sales commission, through which the two parties' interests are aligned. Agents may, for example, be offered a contract that partly bases their salary on their results. However, if principals are risk neutral and agents are risk averse, it is efficient – as far as welfare aspects are concerned – if the principals take on all risks emanating from environmental influences and offer agents a fixed salary contract. Nevertheless, as

already mentioned above, agents may then have little incentive to exert themselves as their remuneration does not depend on their efforts. Although a fixed
salary contract is efficient, it provides few incentives. Consequently, for motivational reasons, principals should leave a portion of the risk with agents. There
will, admittedly, be a residual loss due to this inefficient partitioning of risk.

## Hidden Intention

Hidden intention refers to principals' irreversible intermediate inputs or sunk costs.
After signing a contract, and based on this specific investment in the transaction,
principals end up being dependent on agents, as they now have to rely on their services. This risk of opportunistic exploitation is called a hold up. It also demonstrates
the logical relationship between the principal-agent theory and the transaction costs
approach: In both cases, the investments' specificity is the risk trigger.

Interest alignment through ownership of unique and retractable resources is recommended to control the hold-up problem. This can be accomplished, for example, through vertical integration, by closing long-term delivery and service contracts, and / or through the creation of mutual dependencies by requiring security
in the form of collateral or "hostage taking" (see, e.g., Spremann 1990).

The three cases of information asymmetry are again presented in figure 2.12. A
clear-cut, definitive attribution of institutional integration to specific information
asymmetries is not possible (Spremann 1990). Since the information asymmetries
referred to above often surface simultaneously in business practice, in many cases,
only a combination of various institutional forms of organization will provide an
efficient solution. The principal-agent theory's important business application areas
are found in the design of incentive and information systems. Spatially decentralized task accomplishment (telecooperation) is a main contributor to information

| Information asymmetry / Differentiation criteria | Hidden characteristics | | | Hidden action | | Hidden intention |
|---|---|---|---|---|---|---|
| Information problem of the principal | Qualitative characteristics of the performance of the contractual partner are not known | | | Efforts of contractual partner not known, not observable, no basis for judgment | | Intentions of contractual partner are unknown |
| Cause of problem or essential influencing factors | Concealment of characteristics | | | Monitoring possibilities and costs | | Resource dependency |
| Behavioral leeway of agent | Prior to the signing of contract | | | After the signing of contract | | After the signing of contract |
| Problem | Adverse selection | | | Moral hazard | | Hold up |
| Type of problem-solving | Removal of information asymmetry by: | | Interest assimi-lation | Interest assimi-lation | Reduction of information asymmetry (monitoring) | Interest assimilation |
| | Signaling/ screening | Self-selection | | | | |

**Fig. 2.12.** Overview of principal-agent theory (based on Picot / Dietl / Franck 2002)

asymmetries, mainly to the hidden action problem, thus increasing the latter drastically (see chapter 8). There are similar concerns regarding the hidden characteristics problems in electronic markets (see chapter 7). The principal-agent theory can contribute to making these new organizational forms more efficient.

## 2.4    Information and Network Economy

Starting with the organization problem, the preceding sections in this chapter have shown what enormous importance information has with regard to economic events. It has become clear that many aspects of markets' and enterprises' observable reality are directly ascribable to the scarcity of information as a resource. Section 2.2 therefore illustrated that successful entrepreneurship is based on information advantages. In the course of time, this information is dispersed throughout a market in the form of competition and information gaps are thus closed. The focal point of section 2.3 was the choice of organizational form. It was shown that the optimal structure greatly depends on the costs of information and communication.

Accordingly, systematic planning in respect of information as an entrepreneurial resource is just as significant as planning for human, financial, and material resources. On closer examination, information has various characteristic attributes that distinguish it from other goods (see, e.g., Picot / Franck 1988; Shapiro / Varian 1998; Reichwald 1999; Wigand 1989):

- Information is an immaterial good that is not consumed after multiple uses.
- Information is consumed and transported via media – if required – at the speed of light.
- Information is transmitted in an encoded format and requires common standards to be understood.
- Information reduces uncertainty, yet its own production and utilization are tainted by uncertainty.
- Information is compressible and yet expands during utilization.

In the following, we examine the effects of these peculiarities on the value-added process of information products. We will analyze the value-added steps of the production (section 2.4.1), distribution (section 2.4.2), and utilization (section 2.4.3) of information.

### 2.4.1    Production of Information

The production of information may be subdivided into two processes: The new production of information and the re-production of already existing information (Hass 2002). New production concerns, for example, the creation of a book manuscript or a program code. Re-production occurs when a manuscript or program code ("master") is duplicated, which may in turn be distributed as a copy. There-fore, the consumer of information does not receive an original, but always a copy (with identical content). In other words: Contrary to material products, it is possi-ble to simultaneously distribute information as a copy while retaining the original.

Original information is the basis of the new production of information. Original information is comprised of raw data such as goal-oriented news about markets, already existing software objects, etc. Derivative information is extracted from this original information through processing. Information processing is differenti-ated according to the extent to which the signal content (e.g., the market volume in dollars), signal system (numbers or graphics), and signal medium (monitor screen or paper) are changed (see, e.g., Kosiol 1968; Bode 1993).

Translation of information merely affects the form, not the content. Existing in-formation is simply coded into another signal system, somewhat analogous to numbers being visualized in the form of graphs, or entering written information into an electronic application system. The actual production of new information occurs through the original information's transformation, which produces new signal con-tent through information input. This information production may occur either ana-lytically or synthetically. In analytical information acquisition, more derivative in-formation is created from the original information (e.g., dividing an order into in-formation about price, quantity, quality, etc.). In synthetic information acquisition, however, new, derivative information is created from diverse original information (e.g., the calculation of the mean and variance from a data series). Thus, the in-formation is, as it were, compressed.

When original or newly generated derivative information is placed on and taken over by another signal medium, this is called transmission. In such a re-production, the signal content and signal system remain unchanged, but the signal medium is changed (e.g., when a software program is recorded on a CD-ROM). There is a further classification, as we refer to transport when not only the signal content and system remain unchanged, but also the signal medium, and the information is just sent to another location (Bode 1993).

The two phases of information production – original production through trans-lation and transformation and re-production through transmission and transport – are distinguished by very different characteristics. Creating information for the first time is generally a very elaborate and a costly process. In the long run, this is a consequence of the embedded uncertainty in the production of information. When, for example, a new computer operating system is developed, there is rela-tively little prior knowledge of the extent to which research efforts will be re-quired, as numerous problems could arise or other ideas for improvement be iden-tified during the development process. The development usually manifests itself as an iterative process during which the software – an information product – is im-proved until reaching a level considered ready for market introduction. Compara-ble examples are the creation of a book manuscript, music, movies, etc.

On the other hand, the re-production of information has become very affordable through the use of hard drives, CD-ROMs, books, etc. With the utilization of the

Internet as a medium, information distribution's marginal costs approach zero. A decisive factor in this is that the mass-produced copies of an information product are always copies of the original: Information therefore only needs to be produced once before its use by an unlimited number of people. Consequently, considerable economies of scale result from this form of information production: Most of the costs lie in the transformation of original information into derivative information.

Conversely, the costs of the duplication and distribution of information are low. With the increasing diffusion of information, the first production costs are disseminated over an increasing number of copies, decreasing the average cost per copy. The degression of fixed costs is the result of the concentration tendencies in information-intensive industries, such as the media and software industries, because producing information only once and then duplicating it, is more efficient.

This concentration is further reinforced by the strong price competition that is driven by the prevailing low marginal costs (Shapiro / Varian 1999; Hass 2002). Within a given firm, this cost characteristic allows enormous cost savings by making existing information available to many employees through effective knowledge transfer (see chapter 3).

## 2.4.2  Distribution of Information

The transfer of information content (communication) always occurs in a coded format: The content is coded by means of symbols from a symbol system and is stored and / or transferred via a medium (the symbol carrier). For communication to occur, the recipient must be able to decode the message received. It is therefore essential that the symbol system be mutually understood at a syntactic, semantic, and pragmatic level so that the intended content can be inferred from the read symbols (see chapter 3). Based on the medium utilized, an additional, compatible technology may be required to utilize the medium. Media theory distinguishes between primary, secondary, and tertiary media (Faulstich 1988, pp. 21, 31 ff.).

Primary media (people media) are those media that require no additional technology when communication occurs (e.g., a lecture). Secondary media (print media) are characterized by the sender's utilization of technology (e.g., printing of a text book). Tertiary media (electronic media) mainly require the recipient to utilize additional technology. Here we distinguish between decoding on the hardware level (e.g., the reading of a CD-ROM) and on the software level (e.g., the presentation of Hypertext Markup Language via a web browser). This use of technology requires tertiary media to have additional standards so that the information can be decoded. The body of rules on which the interaction between actors is based, is called a communication standard (Buxmann / Weitzel / Koenig 1999). Such standards, for example, English grammar or the rules of Hypertext Markup Language (HTML), are the basis of any type of communication between people and machines.

All actors who use the same standard form a network. Such networks are characterized by their value – despite potential capacity bottlenecks – increasing with the number of connected users due to positive external effects, called network effects, between the actors: Each new participant increases the value for the actors already participating in the network. Network effects are subdivided into direct and indirect effects (Katz/Shapiro 1985). Direct network effects realize a utility increase through the immediate physical connection between the network participants (e.g., data exchange via the Internet).

Each new participant thus creates an additional communication possibility for all previous users and consequently increases the network's value. Indirect network effects are present when the utility of the participants increases with the network size, but when this increase in utility is not triggered via the immediate communication relationships between the actors. In this case, the actors are connected with a virtual network (Shapiro/Varian 1998). Indirect network effects are, for example, characteristic of operating systems: A widely distributed operating system increases the availability of complementary application software, thus making the system more attractive. Besides the availability of complementary products, learning effects may also cause indirect network effects (Thum 1999). Many products are therefore complex and demand a certain degree of know-how.

These difficulties are decreased if the use of such products is based on known standards, for example, in the form of an integrated user platform. Moreover, the more these products are utilized, the easier it is to find service providers and other users who may be of help when problems arise. While many products have indirect network effects, direct network effects are characteristic of communication goods, which is why standards play a special role. They decrease information and communication costs (transaction costs) and increase the availability of information. Consequently, they increase the quality of decisions (Buxmann 1996). Standardization, however, also increases costs in the form of change and conversion, as well as expenditure on learning, etc. The introduction of standards thus always implies a loss of utility through reduced product differentiation (Farrell/Saloner 1986). Standards are therefore specifically problematic as far as product characteristics are concerned due to the differing preferences of the users of these products. Moreover, transaction costs arise from the negotiation and coordination processes of choosing a standard (Wigand/Steinfield/Markus 2005).

On the whole, there is a trade-off between information costs and standardization costs (Buxmann/Weitzel/Koenig 1999). If, for example, employees in a virtual organization cooperate on a project, they need to communicate. An exchange of information is best handled technically if all the participants use the same data format for all documents. Some employees may therefore have to install and learn new software. In addition, an agreement needs to be reached on the communication standard that should be chosen, with all the employees likely to prefer their specific software or software with which they are already familiar. If no consensus can be reached, these employees cannot exchange data electronically, and the work results will suffer. A compromise might be the use of conversion programs, such as with EDI (Electronic Data Interchange). A conversion is, however, required for each individual information exchange, but this is often imperfect and expensive.

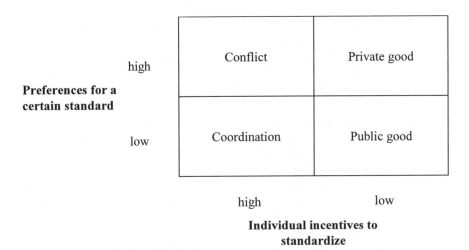

Fig. 2.13. Typology of standardization processes (based on Besen / Saloner 1989, p. 194)

The various types of standardization processes can be generalized via Besen and Saloner's (1989) scheme (see figure 2.13). The essential influencing factors are first of all the actors' interest in a standard becoming mandatory and, secondly, their preference for a specific standard. The desire to participate in the standardization process increases with the potential to reduce information costs by reducing the transaction costs that arise during the standardization process. Preferences for a particular standard are especially pronounced when its specification impacts the use of the good to be standardized, or when not all available standards permit the continued utilization of existing complementary products or accumulated know-how. Four different types of standardization processes are consequently identified:

### Coordination

A true coordination problem occurs if the interest in a generally valid standard is high (without there being a specific preference for a certain standard). An example of this is the already mentioned preference for driving on the left vs. the right (see section 2.3.1).

### Conflict

Admittedly, the above example only worked when this road traffic standard was introduced for the first time. One has to anticipate conflict as far as achieving a common standard for formerly differing networks is concerned. Although creating a common standard appears attractive, simultaneously, there are strong preferences for (differing) standards: All actors would like to implement their standard in order to avoid the standardization costs due to the subsequent conversions that would be required. This adherence to a chosen standard is also referred to as lock-in (see, e.g.,

Shapiro / Varian 1998). This effect is comparable to fundamental transformation in transaction cost theory (see section 2.3.3).

Lock-in effects are of strategic interest to the providers of standards, as they force customers to use a particular standard and consequently reduce price competition. The resulting power to control a market can be exploited by means of higher prices for subsequent and complementary products. These conflictual situations often lead to tough competition between vendors of differing standards, which is aimed at achieving the swiftest diffusion of their specific standard: The greater the number of actors who use a particular standard, the more attractive this network becomes, and the greater the number of new participants who are likely to choose this standard.

Market penetration can be rapidly achieved by giving away products and product samples. This strategy is especially promising in respect of information goods, since the actual costs of the non-physical reproduction and distribution are not only minimal, but – due to the lock-in effect – an opportunity also arises to gain from establishing a specific standard (Zerdick / Picot / Schrape et al. 2001). Such a gain is advantageous when the producer or vendor has property rights to such a standard and is able to control its use. This is called a closed or proprietary standard (Grindley 1995). Since no one is able to offer goods with this standard without permission, considerable profits can be achieved with these exclusive products or via their licenses. The specifications of open standards are generally freely available and may be used by anyone (e.g., HTML).

Accordingly, it is likely that, after an open standard has been successful established, there will be many vendors of this standard, while the lock-in makes the user independent of the producer or vendor, and the competitive pressure increases for the latter. Open standards are therefore the most difficult to exploit. In general, though, it is easier to establish open rather than closed standards: Through the larger number of vendors, the distribution within the market (and also the availability of complementary products) increases, also resulting in the network's value increasing. On the other hand, the system's life cycle costs decrease for the user, while the competition within the standard increases. For the parties within such a conflict, there is a trade-off between absolute market penetration and relative market power: Open standards permit the standard to penetrate quickly and comprehensively, which is, however, associated with loss of control. Closed standards on the other hand, are more difficult to establish, although they permit a more precise controlling of further development, as well as a better skimming of profits (Grindley 1995; Shapiro / Varian 1998).

**Private Good**

A conflict such as the above between various vendors is unlikely when there is little incentive to establish a common standard. If there is a strong preference for specific specifications, a market-wide standard is unlikely. Within a closed user group (firm, network, etc.) there may nevertheless be a movement towards standardization (private good). Since such a specification is user-specific, this is called a type (Kleinaltenkamp 1993). Such a type may in time become a standard, as happened with the IBM personal computer.

**Public Good**

If there are few incentives for universal distribution and the interest in a certain standard is weak, this refers to a public good (e.g., daylight saving time). This does not mean, however, that standardization would not be advantageous. In such situations, prohibitive transactions costs often prevent a decentralized negotiation solution (see section 2.3.2). Public institutions may help producers and users to jointly determine a specification. Such a set of rules may initially merely serve as a (de jure) norm (Kleinaltenkamp 1993), but through appropriate adoption by market participants, it may in time become a (de facto) standard.

## 2.4.3 Utilization of Information

In the economic context, information exchanged through communication ultimately serves to prepare for actions. In the words of Martin J. Beckmann, it is the "raw material … from which decisions are made." (Albach 1969, p. 720). Since information is a scarce good, its utilization should occur in an economically rational manner.

Information's economic value is determined by the juxtaposition of the utility of information with regard to problem solution and decision processes and the costs with regard to the relevant information acquisition and production activities. An optimal information level is achieved when the additional costs of information activities are commensurate with the net utility increase gained through acquired information. Unfortunately, the utility of information is not known in advance, but only manifests itself when it is actually acquired and utilized. Information is therefore an experience good (see chapter 7), but since it is also an immaterial good, Arrow's information paradox becomes apparent (Arrow 1962): The value of information only becomes truly known to the buyer when he knows it. At that point, however, he has already absorbed the information and there is no longer a need to acquire it.

This does not mean that an appraisal of information – and thus a rational information acquisition – is impossible. It is, however, associated with uncertainty, which is why information value is a stochastic magnitude. Decision theory defines the yield obtained from specific information as the difference between the expected revenue when making a decision with this information and the revenue realized when making a decision without this information (Marschak 1954; Laux 1998). It is thus equivalent to the decision's expected improvement as a result of this information. An example is the value of principals' screening procedures in the selection of suitable contractual partners (see section 2.3.4). We assume that initially principals (e.g., entrepreneurs) do not have any information about the agents (applicants). They do, however, have the possibility to carry our various screening procedures, such as the use of references.

The more precisely principals are enabled to differentiate between good and bad candidates, and the greater the value of a correct decision is (i.e., the higher the costs of a wrong decision), the greater the value of such a screening becomes. In practice, however, it is almost impossible to determine the value of information exactly. However, based on previous experience, it is often possible to at least compare the effectiveness of different screening instruments. In this process, the source of information serves as a surrogate benchmark. Consequently, brands have a special role in respect of information goods, as their reputation vouches for the quality of the information.

Nevertheless, rational information acquisition is limited by people's bounded rationality (see section 2.3.1). This normative perspective of human information behavior should therefore be complemented with a positive analysis (see chapter 3).

## 2.5 Changes in Firms and Markets Through Improvement in Information and Communication Technology

The above observations include several important consequences for further contemplation of the organizational forms of economic activities. From a theoretical perspective, the fundamental importance of information and communication for economic activity has become clear (see sections 2.1 – 2.3). This perspective was complemented by an economic analysis of information (see section 2.4). Although the mentioned principle characteristics of information have not changed with regard to its production, distribution, and utilization, the technology that enables the production of information, distribution and utilization was indeed revolutionized in the past (see chapter 4). The economic importance of the improvement of information and communication technology does not so much lie in the absolute increase in information, but rather in the available information being ubiquitously and inexpensively accessible and electronically processable (Shapiro / Varian 1998). The integration of data streams and data inventories is no longer limited to the enterprise-internal domain, but increasingly comprises suppliers and customers as well. Thus, traditional boundaries fade, blur, and blend. Since organizational forms ultimately emerge as a result of the scarcity of the resource information and the resultant transaction costs, this scarcity (impacted by information and communication technology) manifests itself within firms as it does within markets (Picot / Hass 2002; Bieberbach 2001).

Fundamentally, we identify the following changes:

- The decline in transaction costs differs with regard to various organizational forms. Hence, the boundaries of existing organizational forms change.

- Transaction costs decline absolutely, realizing additional welfare-providing transactions.

These two aspects are discussed in greater detail in sections 2.5.1 and 2.5.2. Additional consequences for firms' strategy and leadership are discussed in chapter 10.

## 2.5.1  Boundary Changes in Organizational Forms

Transaction costs theory deals with the comparative superiority of the various organizational forms (market, firm, hierarchy). Given a transaction's specific characteristics (especially specificity and strategic importance; see section 2.3.3), an analysis compares the resulting transaction costs of each organizational form. An improvement in information and communication technology reduces transaction costs. The assumption that decreasing transaction costs lead to an increasing effort in marketing and delivery of economic goods and services has, since the 1980s, been described as the move to the market hypothesis (Malone / Yates / Benjamin 1987). These developments are also observable in the relatively recent worldwide trend towards outsourcing information technology skills and services.

The following arguments explain these developments (Picot et al. 1998c):

- The use of information and communication technology increases market transparency. Information about offers can be distributed electronically and is immediately available worldwide. This in turn enhances regional competition and leads to a more efficient international division of labor. Transaction processes' individual tasks can also be automated (e.g., price comparisons). At the same time, these electronic markets (see chapter 7) ensure an accelerated diffusion of information, resulting in increased entrepreneurial competition (see section 2.2.2). On the whole, the advantages of vertically integrated organizational forms are acknowledged with regard to the exchange of information.

- Simultaneously, market entry barriers decrease because information and communication technology offers customers direct worldwide access (disintermediation, see Benjamin / Wigand 1995). Consequently, it becomes easier for specialized suppliers to achieve a minimally optimal organization size, resulting in increasing market efficiency.

- Many process steps can be standardized and automated through the deployment of information and communication technology. Consequently, these work processes become less specific and may be outsourced to external suppliers specializing in these processes and exploiting the (often worldwide) economies of scale (outsourcing). Simultaneously, new markets emerge for services that were previously only available within a firm.

Figure 2.14 again illustrates that services with high degrees of specificity (from $S_2$) are fundamentally more efficient for organizations within firms (hierarchy) and, correspondingly, for services with low specificity (0 to $S_1$), market organizational forms apply, and for mid-range specific services ($S_1$ to $S_2$), hybrid forms apply (see section 2.3.3). The introduction of new information and communication technologies may be interpreted as suggesting a decrease in fixed and variable (i.e., an increase in the specificity of) transaction costs. Transition zones continuously move towards hierarchical organizational forms on the right ($S_1$ to $S_1$', $S_2$ to $S_2$') through the corresponding shifting of the curves. In other words: The change

**Transaction costs**

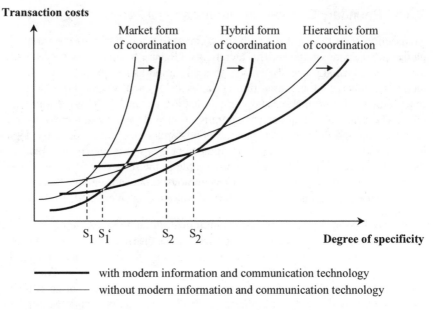

Fig. 2.14. Move to the market due to decreasing transaction costs (based on Picot / Ripperger / Wolff 1996, p. 71)

from market to hybrid organizational forms only becomes worthwhile when a
higher degree of specificity is achieved. There are, however, also countermove-
ments that somewhat qualify the move to the market hypothesis (Picot 1998c):

- With the improvement of information and communication technology, the
  information element of many products also increases generally, for example,
  in the form of increased research and development efforts, or by being connected to networks with common standards. Therefore, the economies of
  scale of the information production and distribution of these goods gain increasing importance and favor concentration of such efforts (cf., chapter 7).

- The advantages of improved information and communication technology
  ultimately only favor the distribution of knowledge that can be represented
  by signals. A hierarchical organizational form remains dominant in respect
  of implicit knowledge (chapter 3), which is difficult to articulate and therefore not part of electronic processing, as vertical integration economizes on
  information costs (Demsetz 1988).

- Firm-spanning information and communication technology systems evolve
  from networking, which allows the entire value chain to be better controlled (e.g., within the context of an efficient consumer response). The result is an expansion of hierarchical mechanisms towards once market-like
  organized inter-firm domains.

Which of the aforementioned trends – market-like or hierarchical design – dominates ultimately depends on the relevant transaction's characteristics. The example of firm-spanning information technology integration specifically demonstrates that the traditional, sharply differentiated attribution of hierarchical mechanisms to firms and market-like mechanisms to markets is no longer valid. This is due to the new information and communication technologies blurring the formerly clear boundaries between the market and firm. This is especially true in respect of a number of new organizational forms that only became feasible as a result of the improvement of information and communication technologies (e.g., telecooperation and virtual organization; see chapter 8).

## 2.5.2   Expansion of Organizational Forms

This chapter has so far analyzed a given transaction's most efficient organizational forms and how these are changed by the improvement of information and communication technologies. This examination contributes to the understanding of the observable changes to organizational structures.

New transactions and the resultant increase in economic activities are other, but equally important, consequences of decreasing transaction costs. As was demonstrated in section 2.1, transaction costs limit the reduction of scarcity through the division of labor / specialization, as the achieved productivity gains are partially diminished due to the required exchange and coordination processes. New information and communication technology leads to a decisive decrease in the costs per transaction, thus making transactions possible that were previously not feasible due to the transaction costs being more than the possible exchange profit. The market's expansion manifests itself specifically in the form of electronic commerce (see chapter 7), which enables consumers and businesses alike to trade nearly any goods on new platforms such as worldwide auctions. Similar developments are also observable in banking, insurance, manufacturing, and retail / wholesale markets (Beck / Wigand / Koenig 2005), as well as in mortgage markets (Steinfield / Wigand / Markus / Minton 2005): Decreasing transaction costs, smaller minimum order sizes, increases in transparency, much speedier decision-making, the extension of trading hours, and many other features enable previously inconceivable transactions and deeper worldwide market penetration. Additional exchange gains can be realized through the enhancement of the value creation of transactions. This especially applies to the observable transition from mass production to personalized (customer-specific) production. Consequently, each transaction becomes more valuable, since products can be customized to buyers' specific needs, resulting in their willingness to pay for this added value.

This individualization of the mass markets is especially easy to achieve with information products, as access to already produced information is available at almost no incremental costs. Furthermore, this information can be shaped to suit the customer's specific needs and requirements: An Internet-based newspaper that is customized to its readers' unique reading preferences generally costs no more than making the original newspaper available to all customers. The individualization of industrial products is generally more expensive, but is often also possible through modularized product design and configuration and the worldwide bundling of similar customer orders (Piller 2001).

Decreasing transaction costs not only make new market-like transactions possible, but also increasingly hierarchical ones, since improved information and communication technology makes higher specificity and larger organizations manageable. Coase (1937) already presumed that technical innovations that reduce the costs of organizing spatial distribution and increase management's capacity to process information could make the emergence of larger firms possible. Organizations' growth therefore becomes possible in those areas where the transaction costs of intra-firm organization had previously limited the utilization of economies of scale on the production and procurement side. Consequently, we frequently observe a partial introduction of market-like organizational mechanisms within the firm, for example, in the form of cost and profit centers that exchange services with each other at market-oriented price levels. In this context, it is possible to put the trend towards modularization into perspective (see chapter 5): Decreasing transaction costs permit property rights to be more precisely allocated (see section 2.3.2); at the same time, the integration of individual modules into a firm through scale advantages enables favorable access to sales and procurement markets. Consequently, market-like and hierarchical organization mechanisms intermingle.

## 2.6    Implications for Management

This chapter demonstrated the importance of information and communication for the firm's management processes and the effects and benefits of improved information and communication technology.

We started with the problem of scarcity. Scarcity is mainly dealt with through the division of labor and specialization. Consequently, coordination and motivation are necessary for the efficient design of the resulting exchange and coordination processes. Coordination and motivation problems only arise because information itself is a scarce good. Information's imperfection and unequal distribution also mold the dynamics of markets. Entrepreneurship is ultimately based on information leads that tend to erode during the course of evolving competition.

The exploitation of information leads always requires a form of organization. The choice of an organizational form may be interpreted as an attempt to manage the scarce resource information as efficiently as possible. The management of information therefore has to deal with the special characteristics of information as a good. These characteristics gain added importance as the networked economy increases.

Against the backdrop of a networked economy, markets and firms transform themselves by means of better information and communication technology. It is therefore becoming increasingly difficult to view firms as relatively closed, integrated structures (Picot/Reichwald 1994; Wigand 1997). The interface between firms and markets, i.e. the clear delineation between the firm's inside and outside fades, or is at least blurred. Instead, we increasingly encounter organizational forms that lie between firms and markets, such as network organizations, cooperative network configurations, virtual organization structures, and telecooperative structures. These are the results of reactions to new market and competitive conditions and the possibilities enabled by new information and communication technologies.

These factors often lead to the structures of what used to be considered typical economic activity being discontinued. Robust manufacturing technologies, as well as long-lasting organizational forms and leadership structures are changed in favor of flexible forms that can be quickly adjusted and enabled to meet the new realities and conditions. Instead of clear and manageable regional business activities, we encounter a global orientation. Consequently, there are also changes in the institutional frameworks with which firms are confronted and that have to date largely delivered stable and manageable foundations for entrepreneurial activities.

A multitude of new institutional circumstances, that firms have to increasingly face, arises from their strong interconnectedness, as well as from the internationalization of business activities. On the whole, changed market and competitive conditions, as well as the innovation potential of the new information and communication technology have led to entrepreneurial boundaries being fundamentally reformulated.

# Chapter 3

# Fundamental Information and Communication Models: Insights into Communication and Information Behavior

## 3.1   The Importance of Information and Communication in Organizations

Information and communication are essential for human interaction and are the cornerstones of its very existence. The ever-increasing variety of information and communication forms, as well as the various forms of media in both the business and private world demonstrates their escalating significance. In order to fully grasp the advancements in this field, it is necessary to explain the various principles of information and communication in conjunction with their theoretical models. While the previous chapter served as an introduction to this topic, this chapter aims to explain the concept in more detail.

Information and communication models and theories are valuable tools that can be used for the interpretation of entrepreneurial behaviors, as well as for the design of new entrepreneurial structures (Wahren 1987; Picot/Wolff 1997; Kieser/Hegele/Klimmer 1998; Reichwald 1999). Interestingly, information and communication behavior models and theories were not developed until long after other areas in economic phenomena had already received considerable attention. One reason for this is the relatively late acknowledgement of information as a production factor in economics. When one considers that other production factors such as land, labor, and capital have been studied in great detail and that their influence on economic activity has been demonstrated, the construction of models that describe information and communication phenomena is a relatively new concept. Although information was recognized in most situations addressed by economists, it was considered a given and thus did not receive proper attention.

Information and communication may be examined in various contexts. Both promote interpersonal understanding (section 3.2) and are associated with various behavioral options, restrictions, and problems (see section 3.3). Information should furthermore be regarded as a type of commodity similar to other types of commodities that must be produced and maintained. Many different theories and models have been developed while focusing on these particular aspects. These theories and models are used to identify certain key factors that influence the quality of the actions and institutions associated with information and communication. In turn, these are decisive in overcoming information and communication barriers. This chapter discusses the intricacy of communication barriers and the necessity of using not only one but several approaches to solve practical information and communication problems.

Advancements in information and communication technologies have led to increased flexibility with regard to arranging and establishing information and communication relationships. In addition, they have been particularly useful in creating unique alternatives for cross-corporate communications.

At the same time, there are certain types of communication problems that may become more serious over time and new ones that may arise. Models that are designed to explain different types of communication processes can be a useful aid in the process of identifying and reducing obstacles that prevent an organization from overcoming internal communication barriers, as well as its organizational boundaries. The same holds true for models of information behavior, coordination, and information production.

Towards the end of this chapter, the various approaches of the communication process models are reexamined. Their differing traditions – which exist in the theoretical as well as in the practical world – have helped to create diverse perspectives. Consequently, there is no standard communication model. Aspects of specific models that are significant with respect to specific explanation and design problems can therefore be singled out and combined with other models' aspects. The combined theory can then be applied to overcome communication barriers.

## 3.2    Selected Models of Information Behavior

Information is essential for any task that needs to be completed within any organization. In order to ensure that the person responsible for a particular task receives the necessary information, a certain level of reciprocal communication is required. This is especially true for organizations whose various labor levels differ greatly. The different aspects of the reciprocal communication of information will be discussed in greater detail later in this chapter. This section will primarily focus on actors' actual information and communication behavior and / or the behavior of those responsible for task completion when dealing with information.

It seems logical for actors to adjust their information demand according to the information need. They should furthermore first use existing information before asking for more. Finally, they should search for and analyze any information that is relevant to the decision to be made, and use this information to make an educated choice. Nevertheless, various research and empirical studies have shown that decision makers do not necessarily follow this systematic and analytical procedure.

All too often, the relevant information is available, but is not used in the decision-making process. Surprisingly, the search for relevant information actually takes place after a decision has already been made, and the information is no longer required. The subsequent acquisition of information thus only serves as justification for the decisions already made.

In the search for information, non-relevant or unimportant information is often requested, which is not particularly helpful and often just hinders the decision-making process. This is exactly why the management of information within an organization is very important (Reichwald 1999; Wigand 1988).

### 3.2.1   Information Need and Supply

Information need is defined according to the type, quantity, and quality of the information that persons require in order to complete tasks within a certain timeframe. Due to its unique nature, information need is hard to define and largely depends on the decision makers' objectives and personality. An information-oriented analysis of a particular task is called an objective information need. This is used to define the type and quantity of the information required to complete this task.

In contrast, a subjective information need considers the decision makers' personal views and specifies the information that they feel is relevant for the completion of a specific task. Usually, the subjective and objective information differs. Within an organization, it should be the information management's responsibility to match the subjective information need with the objective one. This objective becomes more complicated with tasks that are unstructured, complex or unpredictable. In the end, only a fraction of the originally requested information is actually required.

Only that area where information demand and information supply overlap, leads to an actual transmission of information, which is called information supply (Picot/Reichwald 1991; Picot/Wolff 1995; Reichwald 1999). The part of the information supply that is objectively required for the completion of tasks represents the status of the information. Figure 3.1 illustrates this situation. However, the definition of the task itself depends on the given level of information and on the status of the information.

When attempting to match an objective information need with a subjective one, it is sensible to utilize a system that allows the person responsible for the task to provide input. The system should simultaneously allow the task's original content to be taken into account. A particularly useful system in this regard is the critical success factors (CSF) method (Rockart 1986).

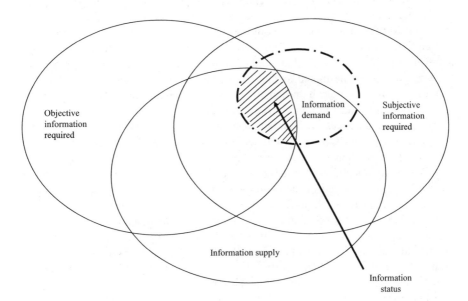

**Fig. 3.1.**   Information need and information supply

CSF takes into account those factors and parameters of the task that are of particular relevance. The utilization of this method requires a meeting between CSF specialists and decision makers, which allows the decision makers to be made aware of those factors that require the most attention. Additionally, the information need of specific tasks is identified and analyzed through interviews with the decision makers. We need to be aware that the definition and implementation of the task depend on the information status. In this sense, information needs research and task analysis complement and support each other.

## 3.2.2  Newness Confirmation Model

Ernst and Christine von Weizsäcker developed the newness confirmation model (von Weizsäcker 1974) and used it for the analyses of the action-promoting effect of information. According to this model, the pragmatic effect of information is closely related to previous experiences in that it requires information not to involve too many new experiences or too many past ones. Total originality, as well as full affirmation is considered the extremes of a continuum within which the pragmatic effect of information becomes apparent. Figure 3.2 illustrates this continuum and the pragmatic content of information.

Totally original information does not have any pragmatic effects. If the receiver is unable to link new information to previous experiences, i.e. to an existing contextual framework, this information cannot be used in an action-oriented way. The information then becomes useless.

The information "the Yen is dropping" will, for example, have a different pragmatic effect on investment fund managers than on laypersons not involved in the stock market. Such information would be an action-oriented message for managers and would possibly drive them to buy or sell stocks and bonds in response. Conversely, laypersons would most likely have no response whatsoever, since this information cannot be linked to their framework and cannot be processed. Information can only develop its pragmatic effect if it contains added confirming elements that can be linked to previous experiences.

If there are an excessive number of confirming elements, there will be a decrease in the information's pragmatic effect at the other end of the continuum. The more confirming elements information contains, the less action-promoting effect it has. The pragmatic effect of information that only includes confirming elements is basically nil. At this end of the continuum, it can longer be regarded as information, just as a message. A professor who, for example, visits a high school classroom will (we hope) not gain much relevant new information and knowledge.

Communication is only productive when there is a healthy mixture of new elements balanced with confirming elements. This means that a high degree of newness between two people from very different contextual backgrounds could cause significant communication problems. This problem is often observed in multinational organizations and is much more likely to happen there than at their regional counterparts.

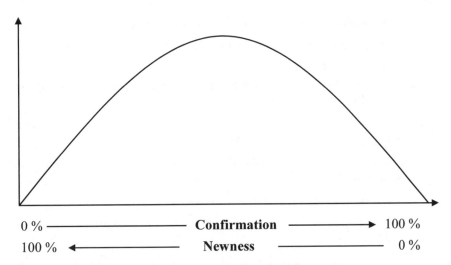

0 % ———————————— **Confirmation** ————→ 100 %

100 % ←———————————— **Newness** ———————— 0 %

**Fig. 3.2.**   Confirmation, newness and pragmatic information (based on Schneider 1988, p. 220; Weizsäcker 1974, p. 99)

### 3.2.3  Information and Communication Behavior According to O'Reilly

O'Reilly observed the institutional conditions of human information processing by relating information and communication behavior to organizational context variables (O'Reilly 1983). He developed an integrated perspective of the connection between organizational context variables, information and communication behavior, the level of information, and actors' decisions based on all of these. Ultimately, decisions are a function derived from the use of information. Relevant context variables include: The organization structure, the existing incentive and control systems, the norms and value systems, as well as the characteristics of the tasks to be completed. Information and communication behavior is furthermore influenced by the predominant context of the formal and informal power relations. O'Reilly formulated different statements that refer to the relationship between context variables and information behavior. Accordingly, the probability that information will be considered is greater:

- If the decision maker regards it as central to the task at hand (this can lead to a difference between the subjective and objective task definition);

- If the information is better linked to the decision maker's relevant planning, control, and assessment systems since reward and punishment are deduced from these;

- If it has a strong influence on activities that are positively sanctioned by a control system (conformity);

- If it benefits the personal goals of the decision maker;

- If it does not lead to conflict within the relevant organization departments or their affiliated partners;

- The easier it is to access the information (organizationally, regionally, and intellectually);

- The more compact and the easier it is to comprehend the information (e.g., a diagram with a short summary);

- The more personal or relatable the information is (the advantage of verbal communication);

- The more trustworthy the information source is; and

- The more powerful the information provider is in comparison with the decision maker.

All of these factors are ultimately influenced by the cost-benefit calculations of the decision maker. Information is far more likely to be used the less its acquisition costs are and the greater the expected utility is, or the higher the eventual penalty for its non-consideration is.

### 3.2.4   Information as a Signal and Symbol

O'Reilly (1983) implicitly states that the quality of decisions improves with an increase in the decision maker's information and knowledge. However, since the quality of the actual information or the decisions based on it is hard to judge, it raises considerable assessment issues. According to Feldman and March (1981), in such situations, it is not unusual for a decision maker's visible information behavior to be used as an evaluation substitute with which to assess the quality of information and / or the decisions based on it. They emphasize that information behavior can have important signaling effects on observers. This means that decision makers can create support for their decisions and confidence in their quality by signaling information-seeking activities to their external environment. This results in the original content of the information being substituted by visible information behavior signals. The decision's evaluation is therefore influenced by the transmission of meta-information (information about other information). However, this means that changes need to be made to the overall assessment and incentive criteria and, consequently, to individual controlling possibilities.

This implies that decision-related information behavior can be substituted by signaling information activities. Even if the actual quality of the decision suffers, its implementation can be positively influenced by means of the signaling of a suitable information behavior. This increases a decision's credibility while preventing it from being criticized. In this case, information is not a tool for the objective evaluation of decisions, but is used to refute existing or expected criticism.

Decision makers are far more likely to be reprimanded for making a bad decision due to a lack of information than for requesting too much information for a good decision. This encourages the tendency to request too much information and increases the costs of information acquisition unnecessarily. Moreover, this is especially likely to occur where decision makers are held accountable for their decisions, but not for the costs of their information-seeking activities.

People who relate an increase in prestige or power to the possession of information will seek and provide information, even if it is not required for their task completion. This can also lead to an added activity in the information search due to their cost-benefit calculations.

Subjectively based decisions, as well as the signaling effects of information behavior, play an important role in the solution of objective problems when compared to that of factual professional information. This type of communication effect influences the way information is transmitted, the choice of communication media, the communication behavior of decision makers, etc.

## 3.2.5 Information Pathologies

In addition to the correct choice of communication media, potential malfunctions in organizational knowledge processing have to be anticipated to ensure a well-functioning supply of information functions and successful communication processes. Malfunctions can influence the level of success for the production, transmission, and application of information. They are also described as information pathologies (Wilensky 1967; Scholl 1992). They include "avoidable mistakes, in other words, producible information that is not produced, acquirable information that is not acquired, available information that is not or incorrectly transmitted and... transmitted information which is misunderstood or not put to use" (Scholl 1992, p. 901, translation by the authors).

Based on Wilensky's model, Scholl describes three dimensions in which information pathologies could arise: Actor-related, interaction-related, and knowledge-based information pathologies. His theory is based on the assumption that actors do not knowingly misuse or distort information.

Actor-related information pathologies are the result of deficiencies in the basic human make-up. Knowledge acquisition occurs through the gradual assimilation of new information and experiences with existing knowledge, as well as through the modification of existing knowledge that could previously not be assimilated due to a lack of understanding. Consequently, new information can only be assimilated if a link can be established to existing knowledge. If these links are missing, potential new information cannot be processed. In order to reduce these kinds of information pathologies, the new information's level of confirmation needs to be increased. Systematic continuous education can achieve this. This theory is very similar to von Weizsäcker's newness confirmation model (see section 3.2.2).

Insufficient information demand often has similar results, which is often caused by a lack of general knowledge or the capacity to look beyond the task at hand, i.e.

the ability to see the whole picture. The longer a person is engaged in the same tasks that always require the same information, the stronger this effect becomes. The ability to acquire new information becomes severely inhibited.

Individuals who are naïve or biased and lack a broad general knowledge are prone to information overload. Conversely, individuals who have a comprehensive knowledge base are far more likely to identify patterns within large volumes of information. This should enable them to sort through the information and add the relevant aspects to their knowledge.

Another source of actor-related information pathologies is people's inclination to perceive only that which they wish to and which they think will suit their personal framework. This constructivist view (see section 3.3.6) can lead to a distortion of people's perceptual abilities. Examples of this are the *not-invented-here syndrome*, meaning the total rejection of uncommon ideas (especially in business) or persistent clinging to a visibly weak viewpoint in order to protect one's self-esteem.

Interaction-related information pathologies occur when there are faulty communication processes. While an exchange of information and opinions generally leads to an increase in knowledge, these exchanges seem to be preferred with like-minded individuals. This is primarily due to the high degree of affirmation between people with similar opinions. However, since very little new information is presented in such interactions, there is also a limited degree of information exchange. In many cases it is more rewarding for both sides of a conversation if the topic is controversial, or if both sides have different knowledge and different views.

On the other hand, due to the human pursuit of consistency, affirmation of one's opinion has greater value than contradiction. There is a tendency for communication barriers to develop when experts from different areas interact. This is usually caused by differences in fundamental knowledge and the use of different and specialized terminology.

In addition to the classic semantic "traps" within interactions, which specifically cause many misunderstandings, there is also the conscious and structural distortion of communication content. In hierarchy-based distortions, negative information that is sent to higher levels tends to be camouflaged or hidden in order to avoid sanctions, or to ensure promotions and advancement. However, information distortion also occurs within the same hierarchy level when there is a personal interest or competitive advantage in doing so. There may be invisible structures in bureaucratic organizations that tend to distort information as it travels along long communication channels, thus hindering adaptation and innovation. In economic theory, the conscious distortion of information is described as influence activities (Milgrom / Roberts 1992, p. 271).

Knowledge-based information pathologies are based on people's assumptions regarding the characteristics that valid knowledge should generally possess. For example, many people harbor the rather simplistic view that knowledge should be clear and verifiable. Such a factual view tends to lead to black-and-white thinking and the dismissal of contradicting opinions. This naïve approach also includes exaggerated facts and a preference for quantitative "hard facts" over quantitative information ("soft facts"). Within many organizations, perceptions (declarative knowledge) are favored above experience and vice versa. While knowledge-based information pathologies do depend on each individual's attitude, when imprinted on the organizational environment, they can turn into an essential and vital element of the corporate culture (see Habermas's concept of the living world and Luhmann's concept of autopoietic social systems (see section 3.3)). The breaking down of such culture-based information pathologies is difficult and normally takes a long time.

## 3.3 Selected Models of Communication Behavior

In order to gain a clear understanding of the communication process, it is necessary to define what the object of the communication process is and how the process works. The following example serves as illustration: If a person is told to "go jump in a lake" by another person and the first person actually does so, a communication process has occurred between the two actors. However, if the first person is pushed into a lake by the other, it can be argued that there had been no communication between them. It is important to understand the difference between an induced action (being pushed) and a spoken message (being told to do something).

In the first situation, the message receiver can determine the consequences of various reactions to being told to go jump into a lake, such as refusing to jump. Conversely, in the second situation, there is a definite cause and effect relationship. The person being pushed into the lake is given no choice of an alternative action or to react to the situation. Communication depends on the receiver of the message being able to choose from various actions and having the possibility to react. There is a difference between signals and other causes of actions. A signal can cause various reactions, which may then also serve as signals. Since a signal does not only cause a single reaction signal but an unlimited variety of reaction signals (Gallie 1952), there is an endless chain of feedback with signals bringing about other signals. Following this logic, a simple push cannot be perceived as a process of communication, since a fall into a lake is not a reaction signal. It is simply the physical result of the push.

### 3.3.1 Three-Level Model of Semiotics

Scientific research involving the objects and functions of different communication processes is known as semiotics (see, e.g., Eco 1977). Semiotics pertains to three different levels of communication: The syntactic, semantic and pragmatic levels. Syntactics refers to the analysis of signals and the relationship between multiple signals, while semantics is the analysis of the relationship between signals and their respective meanings. Finally, pragmatics refers to the analysis of the effect that signals have on their users and receivers.

The following is an example of semiotics in a common situation. A professor says to a student, "If your upcoming presentation isn't significantly better than your last one, I have my doubts regarding your grade." At the syntactic level, there is the question of an accurate transmission of the message. Can the student clearly discern what the professor has said? Or could this process be influenced by other factors such as the professor's indistinct speech, or the distracting background noise?

At the semantic level, the student must interpret the words correctly to accurately process the professor's message. Does this student, for example, realize that the phrase "have my doubts" implies a bad grade?

The pragmatic level is more ambiguous, dealing with the intentions of the phrase, as well as the receiver's reaction to it. The professor's intentions are to motivate the student to work harder. However, depending on the student's interpretation of the statement, as well as the professor's intentions, the student may either try harder or give up altogether.

The three semiotic levels should not be examined independently, since they tend to overlap and build upon one another. All the levels deal with signals, their relationships with one another, and the rules of application. The pragmatic level is the most comprehensive of the three. This level takes all the personal, psychological, and contextual factors into consideration that distinguish one communication event from another. In addition, the intentions and practical consequences related to the communication process are analyzed. This level should be regarded as the conceptual foundation for various communication models. Figure 3.3 illustrates the use of semiotics in a potential communication process.

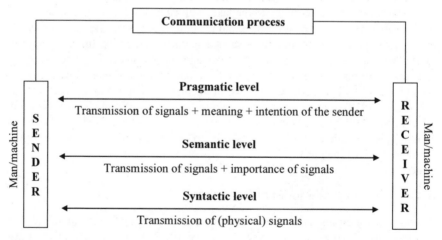

**Fig. 3.3.**     Levels of information transmission analysis (based on Reichwald 1999, p. 231)

Terms such as signal, sign, message, and information are often associated with communication procedures. When using semiotics as an outline, these terms can be separated and defined in order to further show their importance in a variety of procedures. At the syntactic level, signals and signs are regarded as observable objects. There is a focus on the relationships between signs and signals, and the formal rules of these relationships. These terms do not, however, emphasize meaning or interpretation. They are used to describe the problems associated with correct and complete transmission and/or to analyze the array of sign combinations (grammar).

The semantic level deals with the relationships between signs and their designata, i.e. their designated meanings. Since signs always refer to some type of object, event or situation, the user determines each sign's meaning. When both the sender and receiver attribute an identical meaning to the transmitted sign, i.e. if there is a semantic agreement, this is a message. It should be pointed out that this level does not deal with the actual effects of messages.

The effects of messages are discussed at the pragmatic level, which concerns the clarification of the intended and/or actual message and its effect on the receiver. When a sign's meaning is linked to its intended purpose or action, a message becomes information. If this approach is followed, information can be interpreted as purpose-oriented knowledge. This clearly demonstrates that information generates action.

Information can be distinguished from data by means of this three-level method. One essential criterion for this distinction is the difference in their context and purpose. Data represent meanings that are not immediately purpose oriented. Information can, however, be considered purpose-oriented in certain instances and contexts. Thus, while data are more closely related to messages, the definition of data is far more restricted. It is generally used in situations where messages are generated, processed and transmitted by electronic means. In comparison, the term message is only used in written or verbal communication.

Communication models are based on different action levels. Their main focus is on information and its various effects. Messages and signs should, nevertheless, also be considered, since they are a fundamental part of information. Focusing on them, however, poses other problems that soon become apparent in respect of the technical communication model.

## 3.3.2 Technical Communication Model

Shannon and Weaver's technical communication model is the basis for dealing with a variety of technical questions related to information and communication (see Shannon/Weaver 1949). This model's focus is on the communication process's syntactic level. It emphasizes the categories signs, sender, receiver, capacities, redundancies, and encoding and/or decoding, which are comparatively easy to measure by means of mathematical-statistical procedures. Shannon and Weaver's model illustrates the transmission channel that a message travels from a sender to a receiver (see figure 3.4).

Certain sign combinations (messages) are selected and/or created from an information source, with the latter only occurring in certain cases and according to specific rules. The transmitter modifies these signals (encoding), which are then routed over a transmission channel to the receiver. At this point, there is a reverse modification (decoding) and the signals are transmitted to their intended destination.

The technical communication model is especially suitable for the analysis of noise that might occur during a transmission. When noise is present, the received signals no longer resemble the original signals. Nevertheless, a prerequisite for a successful communication process, especially one intended to encourage particular actions, is the syntactic accuracy of a transferred message.

The technical modeling of a communication process is crucial for successful message transfers. This is especially true for the telecommunications field. One remedy for the problem of noise is the transmission of redundant signals to neutralize noise. Noise can also be identified through inconsistencies in the redundant signals (e.g., test digits for electronic data transfer).

Although this model deals with distinct circumstances and problems, it can only be used as a starting point for the analysis of the communication process, as the sender and receiver are only analyzed technically and are regarded as static objects. In order to describe the communication phenomenon fully, models dealing with the semantic and pragmatic level of communication need to be utilized.

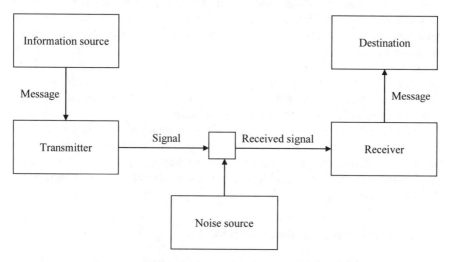

**Fig. 3.4.**   Technical communication model by Shannon / Weaver 1949

## 3.3.3   Axioms of Communication, Communication Interference and the TALK Model

### 3.3.3.1   *Axioms of Communication According to Watzlawick, Beavin and Jackson*

In contrast to the newness confirmation model (see section 3.2.2), which depends on the degree of newness of information, Watzlawick, Beavin and Jackson take a different approach when describing the pragmatic effect of communication. They developed a comprehensive, socio-psychological-oriented model of human communication that focuses on behavioral effects. Their model describes the general characteristics of human communication and offers five axioms of communication that are illustrated in figure 3.5 (see Watzlawick/Beavin/Jackson 1976). Noise in human communication processes can be identified by means of these axioms and possible remedies determined.

One of this model's fundamental assumptions is that some communication noise is actually caused by pragmatic communication conditions, which thus help to create paradoxical communication situations. The contradictory request, "Be spontaneous!" is a perfect example. These situations can only be explained at a meta-level by means of meta-communication. While technical sender-receiver models usually have a linear character, Watzlawick et al. stress a circular communication process instead; this process allows each of the communication partners to influence the other through its alternating feedback effects.

| | |
|---|---|
| Axiom # 1: | One cannot not communicate. |
| Axiom # 2: | Every communication has a content and relationship aspect. |
| Axiom # 3: | The relationship of the communication partners is established by the use of punctuation during encounters. |
| Axiom # 4: | Human communication makes use of digital and analog modes of communication. |
| Axiom # 5: | Communication is based on symmetrical and complementary relationships. |

**Fig. 3.5.**    Axioms of communication according to Watzlawick, Beavin and Jackson 1990

The first axiom asserts that any form of behavior is a form of communication and that all behavior conveys a message. Therefore, one cannot not communicate. Even when an employee walks past a manager without saying a word, this behavior sends a message. Thus, it is a form of communication. This is an important insight, since it allows communication-theoretical analysis of interpersonal interaction problems without requiring explicit communication in the traditional sense. Consequently, all human behavior is open to interpretation.

The second axiom maintains that all communication contains a content aspect and a relational aspect. The content aspect is only concerned with the transmission of facts, for example, the head of the department presenting the department's monthly financial report to subordinate employees. Conversely, the relational aspect refers to the interpersonal relationship between communication partners that, under certain circumstances, lays the foundation for the interpretation of content. An example is praising or criticizing the boss for the monthly report's positive or negative results. Communication therefore not only conveys facts, but also influences the social bonds between communication partners. The less complex these social relations are, the easier facts can be exchanged, since less communicative effort is required to clarify the relational aspect.

The third axiom addresses how the communication partners' relationship is established by examining the use of punctuation during encounters. Watzlawick et al. describe punctuation as a combination of the interpretation and causal perception of the communication partner's statements and behaviors. There is, for example, a punctuation problem when a manager continually criticizes his subordinates. While the manager is criticizing these persons' lack of initiative, the subordinates regard the constant criticism as the reason for their poor performance. Different uses of punctuation can also lead to context-dependent communication interferences. Often, these can only be solved by means of a discussion of the communication's original meaning (meta-communication). Such divergences in punctuation can occur easily, particularly in intercultural communication, which often lead to considerable misunderstandings and even the failure of the communication process as a whole (Keller 1992).

The fourth axiom distinguishes between digital and analog communication. Digital communication mostly occurs in written or spoken language. Due to its clear syntax, it is especially suitable for the transmission of the content aspects of communication. Analog communication mostly occurs outside the actual language's scope, for example, through mimicking, gestures, and intonation. Although it does not have a clear syntax, it has various semantic possibilities and mainly serves to convey relational aspects. Returning to the second axiom's example, the data and financial report's presentation (digital communication) can occur in either a critical, concerned tone or in a positive one (analog communication). However, the intended message can be conveyed without explicit praise or criticism by employing analog communication.

The fifth axiom focuses on the distinction between symmetric and complementary communication relationships. Symmetric relations exist when all communication partners perceive themselves as being on the same level. An example of this would be co-workers with similar job titles and responsibilities, and all the partners have the same communicative possibilities. On the other hand, complementary relationships exist when communication partners can compensate for their differences – as between a boss and his subordinates.

Despite their five axioms of communication, Watzlawick et al. still do not offer a complete or self-contained communication model. Their theories do, however, shed light on some important aspects of communication, which, in turn, have considerable influence on interpersonal communication. They are thus able to offer useful recommendations for the design of intra-firm and inter-firm communication, as well as the implementation of types of communication media. An important point is that different media have different ways of conveying the content and relational aspects of communication. Each situation requires an appropriately targeted media form in order to communicate the message in a suitable manner. A fax machine is, for example, well suited for the fast and clear transmission of printed data (content aspect, digital communication), but not for interpersonal exchanges. On the other hand, when reprimanding an employee – a situation in which the relational aspect plays a major role – face-to-face contact is more appropriate, since the required analog communication is difficult to convey by means of technical media.

### 3.3.3.2   Communication Interference According to Schulz von Thun

Based on the work of Watzlawick, Beavin and Jackson (1967), Schulz von Thun (1993) developed an expanded socio-psychological perspective on interpersonal communication. According to Schulz von Thun, every message contains four different components. Much like the Watzlawick et al. model, he believes that every message contains content and a relational aspect. In his expanded model, he introduces two more aspects to the communication process: Appeal and self-revelation. Appeal is used to have a certain effect on the communication partner. The other aspect, self-revelation, maintains that any form of communication can include an intended improvement of one's public image, as well as unintended self-disclosure. These four aspects are analyzed with respect to their intentions and / or effects on the sender and the receiver. Rather than being a separate communication model, Schulz von Thun's work is just a further development of the Watzlawick et al. model.

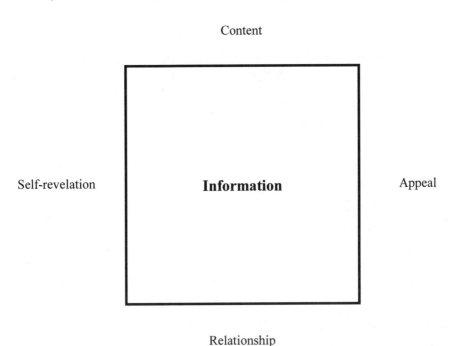

**Fig. 3.6.**    Four sides of a message (based on Schulz von Thun 1993, p. 14)

According to this perspective, communication interferences are inevitable, since both the sender and receiver interpret the sent and received messages differently. For example, a supervisor's message to a subordinate, "Mr. Smith, you work too much," can be applied to all four aspects. In reality, the supervisor is trying to stress the content and is simply alluding to the fact that Mr. Smith works ten hours a day instead of eight, but Mr. Smith may interpret these words as a criticism and conclude that the boss is unhappy with him and his performance.

One reason for such a message misinterpretation may lie in the interpretative key (much like punctuations in the Watzlawick et al. model) that receivers use and that is derived from their self-image. This type of misunderstanding can lead receivers to respond in a manner that seems inappropriate to senders in the light of their original message. These conflicts can only be solved when both communication partners use some kind of meta-communication. They have to mutually communicate how a message is to be interpreted in order to agree on its underlying meaning. This process requires both partners to be willing and able to reach such an agreement at the meta-level, which, however, is not always a realistic prospect. Another important point in avoiding such misunderstandings at the relational and self-revelation level is the issue of standardization and the individuality of communication processes (Koller 1994).

### 3.3.3.3    The TALK Model According to Neuberger

The TALK model was developed by Neuberger (1985) as a continuation of Watzlawick's communication theory. It was developed as the theoretical foundation of communication instruction in organizations and is especially useful for the analysis of interpersonal communication. This model focuses on four aspects of communication processes: Fact presentation, expression, direction, and contact (see figure 3.7).

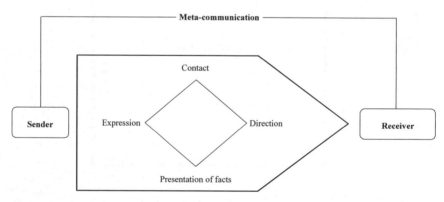

**Fig. 3.7.**    The TALK model (based on Neuberger 1985, p. 13)

The fact presentation aspect ("It is") is closely related to the content aspect of Watzlawick, Beavin and Jackson's second axiom. The central aim is to use communication as a tool for solving real problems. In the problem-solving process, Neuberger makes a distinction between five distinct phases: Problem formulation, requirement and goal explanation, development of alternative solutions, assessment of alternative solutions and the relevant decision and, finally, implementation and management of the solution.

The expression ("I am") deals with the information that one, willingly or unwillingly, provides about oneself during communication. There is a focus on non-verbal communication, but this type of communication is easily misunderstood. Neuberger makes a clear distinction between expression (the reflection of internal emotions) and impression (effect on the partner). These are not necessarily the same.

The directional aspect ("You should") emphasizes that the sender of a message is trying to affect the receiver in a certain way. This can be done directly ("Work harder!") or by means of manipulation techniques ("The President will be here tomorrow and that will give you a good chance to show how meticulously your team works together.").

Contact is primarily concerned with the parts of communication that focus on the relationship between communication partners. This is where, once again, similarities can be found to the second axiom by Watzlawick et al. Most communication processes deal mainly with the development and nurturing of relationships. The actual content of the communication is not as important. Sometimes this is hard to understand. If a colleague asks, "How are you today?" it would be wrong to address the content of the question, as the question is rhetorical, expressing emotion and not a real question. One should relate the message to the relationship level and answer in a similar, friendly fashion.

Meta-communication plays a crucial role in solving communication problems. When communicating about communication, the use of the above-mentioned four aspects could be extremely helpful.

### 3.3.4  Speech Act Theory According to Austin and Searle

Speech act theory is based on Austin's lectures and the work of Searle, his student (Austin 1989; Searle 1994). Central to this theory is the question of the pragmatic aspect of a communicative statement, i.e. the search for the function of communication. Is the function of a communicative statement just a message, i.e. a transmission of information? The speech act theory argues against and demonstrates other possibilities for the use of statements.

Austin provides the following example. During a wedding ceremony, the statement "I do" is not a message. It is actually the execution of an agreement. Saying "I do" in front of a justice of the peace or a church official does not mean that a marriage has been entered into as a result of the statement. Only a bride and groom can enter into a marriage (Austin 1989, p. 29). A greeting, thanks, a threat, and a court sentence are similar statements; they all depend on the specific reaction to them and the action taken.

Language and statements can be used to make people act. Statements become speech actions or "speech acts." A message is just one type of statement. While statements with message characteristics are examined for their level of truth, this method is not recommended for speech acts. Speech acts are used to substantiate commitments. With these types of statements, the real question is the relevant conditions required for success or failure.

Statements that are also used for negotiations, such as the "I do" during a wedding ceremony, are also referred to as performative expressions (Austin 1989). Negotiations that are executed with statements are referred to as illocutionary speech acts. This theory has focused specific attention on a wide spectrum of negotiations and actions, leading to multi-faceted communication. Searle (1993) combined these different facets into five categories that he calls the "taxonomy of illocutionary speech acts." These are presented by means of examples (see Searle 1993; Winograd / Flores 1992; examples taken from Talib 2002):

- A directive act: The speaker wants the listener to do something.

- A commissive act: The speaker indicates that he or she will do something in the future.

- An expressive act: The speaker expresses feelings or an emotional response.

- An assertive act: The speaker expresses a particular belief in certain facts or circumstances.

- A declarative act: The speaker's utterance results in a change in the external non-linguistic situation.

All of these speech acts are interdependent. On the one hand, performative statements can only be attributed to illocutionary speech acts in context. On the other hand, the conditions of their success cannot be isolated for analysis. A simple metaphor describes the way specific speech acts combine to provide new insight into organizations and computer systems, supporting this new perspective: Speech acts are like "dance steps" that combine to make a conversation and, which in turn creates "a pattern of mutual responsibilities" (Winograd / Flores 1992).

Based on this approach, organizations can be interpreted as networks of conversations. Computer systems thus take on the role of conversation support systems (Winograd / Flores 1992). This new concept of information and communication technology's role in organizations that are based on the speech act theory has helped to create a whole new class of conversation-oriented systems. These influence today's news and group support systems, as well as the extensions of workflow design and business process re-engineering (see chapter 4). Speech act theory not only influenced the work of Winograd and Flores, but also built the foundation of the mechanisms for coordinating actions as presented by Habermas.

### 3.3.5 Mechanisms for Coordinating Actions According to Habermas

The theory of communicative action focuses on the conditions of communication (Habermas 1981). It clarifies the conditions and fundamental patterns of human interaction and uses these to develop a comprehensive social theory. Although it is not Habermas's intention to create a communication model, his work provides important factors for the understanding of human communication.

His primary interest is the description of social action. He furthermore analyzes mechanisms for coordinating activities that facilitate the regular and stable interconnectivity of operational actions (Habermas 1984). Since the coordination of actions is closely related to communication processes, important theoretical conclusions relating to communication can be drawn from Habermas's research. Within the framework of semiotics, these factors can be assigned to the pragmatic level of communication.

There are two fundamental coordination methods for the management of function-oriented single actions (negotiations): Coordination is primarily achieved through the actors' reciprocal participation or through the creation of a rational agreement between them. The methods differ in that they are dependent on the actors' personal attitudes and expectations. In reciprocal participation, the attitude and expectation are success-oriented. Conversely, a compromise-oriented attitude leads to a rational agreement. According to Habermas, an actor cannot simultaneously take on both attitudes, since they negate each other.

In his research, Habermas tested these two attitudes in different situations and circumstances. He also drew a distinction between social and non-social situations. Non-social negotiation situations refer to an objective world with all its qualities and conditions. Social negotiation situations refer to a societal world in which certain rules are essential for the society. From this, Habermas developed three different negotiation methods (see figure 3.8).

| Action orientation / Action situation | Success-oriented | Compromise-oriented |
|---|---|---|
| Non-social | Instrumental action | -- |
| Social | Strategic action | Communicative action |

**Fig. 3.8.** Action types according to Habermas

Social negotiation situations and their differences need to be clarified for a better understanding of negotiation-based communication. In success-oriented negotiation, actors regard their opponents as an object. They will achieve their goals, even if this involves manipulation, deception or fraud (e.g., in an aggressive marketing strategy). Conversely, compromise-oriented actors treat their partners as "co-subjects" (Kirsch, 1992). Through reciprocal communication, the actors are able to clarify their intentions. The goal is to develop a mutually agreed upon negotiation procedure. The actors do not manipulate each other, but instead try to find consensus and common solutions to a problem (e.g., a family searching for a vacation destination).

Habermas refers to compromise-oriented negotiation as communicative action. This term serves to illustrate the importance of communication as a guiding mechanism for the coordination of negotiation. Other methods that do not require communicative agreement, such as money or power, can of course be used to influence negotiation. Habermas argues that these (non-communicative) methods are being increasingly applied in areas in which a communicative action orientation should be used, as in families, friendships, and other groups. Compromise-oriented negotiation (communicative) is based on agreement and can be compared to the previously mentioned example of telling someone to go jump into a lake. In contrast, success-oriented negotiation is comparable to pushing someone into the water.

Communicative action leaves room for alternative courses of action that can be assessed by means of communication processes until mutually beneficial consensus is achieved. An agreement that is achieved through communication is dependent on three assessable validity claims and an actor can lay claim to any of them. First, when presenting facts from the objective world, the actor lays claims to the validity of truth. Second, when creating and renewing interpersonal (social) relationships the actor lays claim to the validity of (normative) correctness. Finally, for expressive statements such as personal experiences or emotional impression, the actor lays claim to the validity of sincerity. An actor will always lay claim to all three validity claims, but one claim will usually dominate. If the listener does not accept these claims, an agreement (and thus communication) cannot take place.

Both parties need to use a strategy geared towards agreement if communication interferences are to be resolved. The use of manipulation or deception would make achieving an agreement impossible under the observed communication conditions. One of the actors would simply fake the meta-communication, using it to pursue his or her own goals.

In Habermas's theory, another important aspect for the understanding of communication processes is the concept lifeworld(s) (Lebenswelt(en). The term lifeworlds is used to describe a certain life and language form that determines an actor's possibilities and limits with regard to thinking and speaking. A lifeworld encompasses the entire background knowledge that makes communicative action possible. This means that statements or messages do not have a context-independent or denotative meaning, but are always based upon certain experiences and thought patterns. This can lead to considerable communication problems between actors who come from different lifeworlds.

Wittgenstein (1953) refers to language games and their rules, which humans have to follow within a certain lifeworld so that they can communicate with other members within that lifeworld. These rules and background knowledge are learned through socialization processes during which a belief system is developed. The cultural rules of the society in which the actor is raised are an example. It follows that the meaning of a sentence is based on the context of the individual's background knowledge.

Considerable communication interferences and misunderstandings can occur when communication partners do not have shared lifeworlds. This is especially true of corporations from different regions whose employees come from different cultures. Contemporary business literature provides extensive examples of intercultural communication problems between American and / or European corporations and corporations from Asia (see, e.g., Keller 1992).

However, intercultural communication problems are not only limited to dissimilar cultures, but can also arise in the same culture, for example, between the employees and management within a single corporation. This might occur when the people working together do not share the same private lifeworld that can be regarded as the original lifeworld. The better co-workers adapt to the organizational and, therefore, derivative lifeworld of their corporation besides their private living and language forms, the more this shared lifeworld becomes a suitable foundation for functioning communication.

## 3.3.6   Communication from a Radical Constructivist Perspective

A different perspective on information and communication processes, and thus on the principles of communication, can be gained from radical constructivism. Radical constructivism describes a certain viewpoint on the functioning of human cognition. According to this view, no form of comprehension depicts a true reflection of reality, but merely represents an internal construction of (external) reality. The nervous system's cognitive processes generate this perception. This perspective on human cognition was strongly influenced by the work of neurobiologists Maturana and Varela (see, e.g., Maturana / Varela 1987) and may be understood as operating at different levels.

Operational self-containment refers to the informational level, but not to the material level (energetic openness). Informational self-containment therefore means that a cognitive system receives no direct information from its environment. The cognitive system itself generates the information that it processes. For example, the same event can cause different mental reactions in different persons, which depend on their respective mental states up to that moment.

Since a cognitive system does not possess direct access to an external reality, it cannot reproduce it. All it can do is to create a construct of this reality and hope that this construct is appropriate for its own survival. This means that there are no right or wrong constructs of reality, but only more suitable and less suitable ones. Nobody can judge the degree to which a construct of reality really represents "true" reality. All cognitive systems are equally closed.

This viewpoint has important consequences for the evaluation of communication. When cognitive systems are self-contained in the above-mentioned sense, information cannot be transferred from one system to the other during communication processes. Consequently, successful communication has to be explicable by means of other approaches.

In language psychology, we find a differentiation between the denotative and connotative meaning of language symbols. The denotative meaning expresses the relationship between a symbol and a real object. The word "dog," for example, describes a certain species of mammal that has been domesticated by humans. Comparatively, the connotative meaning comprises all emotional and evaluative links and therefore determines the interpretations that are related to a particular symbol. The connotative interpretation is specific to each individual. A person who has been bitten by a dog assigns different connotative meaning to this word than a successful dog breeder.

From a radical constructivist viewpoint, words – strictly speaking – have no denotative meaning. This view argues that communication occurs entirely through the connotative attribution of meanings to symbols. Consequently, no instructive interactions can take place in a communication process; a sender cannot influence a receiver in a convincing manner. Communication can, however, occur when the receiver's construction of a message is similar to the sender's intended meaning.

Based on common, identical or similar experiences and events, i.e. through similar processes of socialization, identical or similar cognitive states develop, resulting in identical or similar constructions of reality (consensual fields). Communication functions best when the interpretation of communication takes place within such a consensual field.

Consensual fields are closely related to Habermas's theory of a lifeworld (Lebenswelt). When two communication partners interact within consensual fields, they interpret symbols (e.g., certain terms, gestures) in a relatively similar manner. Communication only becomes possible because similar cognitive states cause symbols to trigger similar reactions.

When two Americans talk about a dog, they will usually regard it as a pet, whereas in China it might be considered a meal. The anecdote about the American couple in a restaurant in China illustrates the fatal misunderstanding that can arise when two people from different consensual fields communicate. The woman pointed to her poodle sitting at the table and then to its tail to express that the dog needed something to eat. The waiter took the poodle into the kitchen, returning later with the dog prepared as an "appetizing" meal.

### 3.3.7  Interpretation of Communication According to Luhmann

Luhmann's (1994) perspective with regard to radical constructivism is that modern society's most important communication areas are operationally self-contained systems. Based on Maturana and Varela's work, he developed a terminology to help describe social systems in a more detailed manner (autopoietic system). These systems create their own interpretation patterns, which are independent of other systems, and refer exclusively to these (self-reference).

Sociologist Luhmann maintains that autopoietic social systems are formed through the use of communication. Accordingly, it is not the living elements (humans or groups of humans) that make up the system aspects but the communicative ones. Communication is therefore a necessary element for the emergence of social systems such as organizations (e.g., corporations and markets). In autopoiesis, these elements are created by the social system itself and communications are also construed as decisions in these organized social systems. Corporations and markets do not only consist of decisions, but also produce the decisions that form them (Luhmann 1986).

Luhmann's major contribution to the understanding of communication is his argument that the results of communication processes cannot merely be attributed to a single actor or to a pair of communication partners. Generally, communication processes have a far-reaching effect, especially at the pragmatic level. Single communication processes, which are first and foremost attributed to a single communication pair, make a contribution to the constitution of the social system to which they belong. In his work, Luhmann stresses the independence of social processes from a methodological individualism in the context of the communication process.

The models of communication presented in this section demonstrate how much the construction of models, and hence their explanatory content, depend on the viewpoints of specific theorists. It furthermore shows how aspects that are irrelevant for such viewpoints are intentionally neglected.

The contributions to the description and explanation of communication processes by the authors Watzlawick, Beavin and Jackson, who were all influenced by psychology, are principally based on the study of individual communication processes. Conversely, the authors Habermas and Luhmann, who were influenced by sociology, focus more on the effects of communication than on the social construct as a whole. In contrast, Shannon and Weaver's technical communication model deals mainly with the technical explanation of communication interferences. Furthermore, the TALK model, as well as the Austin and Searle model, is built on the foundation of these models.

All these models present partial approaches to the description and explanation of economically relevant communication processes. Although there is no self-contained, comprehensive theory of human communication, these different approaches offer various perspectives that can be used in a situational approach to describe, analyze, and finally design communication phenomena.

## 3.4    Task-Medium-Communication

Task, medium and communication are all interdependent. The type and the extent of the required information are dependent on the specific task for which it is needed. The quality of decisions (within the specific task's framework) and the actions that are based on them are generally influenced by the cross-communication between the relevant decision makers. For example, the type of task, as well as the required communication influences the choice of appropriate medium (communication tool). In turn, this choice influences the task fulfillment and the quality of the communication process.

This chapter will examine different perspectives that are used in deciding on appropriate media choices. It will explain how these choices can be used to promote action.

## 3.4.1   Perspectives in Media Selection: Results of Media Choice Research

Different tasks pose different challenges for communication. The question of which media are better suited for the various challenges depends on each particular task. The question of which technology is best suited to support communication tasks, especially tasks in management communication, is the main focus of many media-choice research projects that are currently being conducted.

Time and again, this research shows a correlation between communication task criteria and the communication method's characteristics. However, this same research also shows that as far as adequate media support is concerned, there is an essential difference in the content and relationship aspect of human communication (see, e.g., Goecke 1997; Reichwald 1999; Moeslein 1999; Reichwald / Moeslein 1999). Which factors should therefore be considered when choosing an appropriate medium?

Media support is required whenever it is impossible to communicate directly (face-to-face). This can be done through a letter, fax, e-mail, SMS or even the telephone or a videoconference. The variety of media choices that are used to support human communication is abundant and new, alternative forms of communication are regularly introduced. However, the success of the communication process depends greatly on the medium chosen.

This relationship between successful communication and media choice has become a major focus of communication research. Research is examining the extent of different media types' influence and the reasons for specific types being chosen. Furthermore, research is exploring the question of how the choice of medium influences the success and failure of communication. Based on different media theories, the perceived influencing factors of certain media types are forwarded as the reasons why they are chosen for specific applications (Moeslein 1999; Reichwald / Moeslein 1999a).

- Subjective media acceptance theory states that individual work-style and communication preferences influence media choice. (Does the medium support the desire for speed and user-friendliness?)

- The social influence approach claims that the choice of medium is based on how well it will be accepted by the communication partner. (What does the other side prefer?)

- The task-oriented approach to media choice is based on the basic requirements of the communication task that the medium needs to fulfill. (How well does the medium fulfill the task requirements?)

- Media richness theory claims that in respect of analog and digital communication, the medium's objective characteristics are dominant. (Is the medium "rich" or "poor"?)

None of these theories can individually explain why different forms of media are chosen over others and there are still many open questions in this area of research. However, the current research does point to the following: New technology cannot be judged solely on its potential to surmount space and time boundaries. Only when other influencing factors are considered and their functioning methods explained, can one understand why – in today's world of telephone, videoconferencing and multi-media – organizations still spend considerable time and money in order to have "personal" communication (e.g., Pribilla / Reichwald / Goecke 1996; Goecke 1997; Reichwald et al. 2000; Reichwald / Moeslein 2001).

**Media Choice According to Media Acceptance Theory**

According to the subjective media acceptance theory, the use of a particular type of media depends on the relevant task. Consequently, media choice depends on more than a medium's objective performance standards. It is far more likely that the subjectively perceived usefulness of the medium will determine whether it is accepted or rejected. According to this theory, "perceived usefulness" and "perceived ease of use" are the central yardstick for media acceptance (Davis 1989).

The perceived usefulness or perceived ease of use with regard to media utilization cannot be influenced. While the subjective estimation may be based on personal characteristics, there is a greater emphasis on experience and personal history with the medium, which create a positive association. Certain qualifications are required to utilize a media type fully (and to gain a feeling of proficiency), which necessitate instruction, education, and / or training. These qualifications are required in respect of preparation for media acceptance, as well as for profitable media utilization.

**Media Choice According to the Social Influence Approach**

The social influence approach, also known as the collective media acceptance theory, maintains that besides individual preferences, the social setting is especially influential in the acceptance or rejection of media types. This means that an individual's media choice will depend on the media that colleagues, business partners, and management use, as well as the symbolic meaning associated with the utilization of the medium and on how well it is distributed and utilized (Goecke 1997).

How much attitude, experience, and patterns of use in the work environment influence media choice was already apparent in Smith's early empirical research (1987). His work showed that 20% of the variances that occurred during e-mailing in a work environment were based on superiors' pattern of use.

The role that the symbolic meaning of the media utilization plays, becomes evident in, for example, some organizations where the media use of upper-management is viewed as a sign of innovative ability. In other organizations, however, management's personal preference regarding media utilization is not considered pertinent.

A communication medium's significance and diffusion need to take the "critical mass" phenomenon into account. Communication media normally only achieve their usefulness potential when an individual has enough communication partners (see chapter 2). The more users a medium has, the more attractive it becomes. When the number of users reaches a "critical" limit, the decision to use that medium becomes obvious. Social factors and norms, as well as symbolic associations and collective use patterns all influence personal media choice.

## Media Choice According to the Task-Oriented Approach

In the early 1980s, German researchers first pointed out the relationship between the communication task and the communication medium with their model of task-oriented media choice (Klingenberg / Kränzle 1983; Picot / Reichwald 1987). Research on the introduction of new media forms has led to the discovery of a fundamental correlation between task and utility in communication. Different tasks present communication with different challenges. Alternative media forms are able to meet these challenges in different ways.

The task-oriented suitability of a medium determines whether or not it is acceptable. The model shows that every business communication has four basic prerequisites. In keeping with the task content and the decision maker's assessment, these prerequisites are of differing importance for the task solution (see figure 3.9).

| Task related prerequisites for communication channels | | | |
|---|---|---|---|
| Accuracy | Speed/user-friendliness | Trustworthiness | Complexity |
| • Transmission of the exact wording<br>• Documentability of the information<br>• Simple processing<br>• Verifiability of the information | • Short transmission time<br>• Short preparation time<br>• Quick response<br>• Simplicity of the communication event<br>• Transmission of short messages | • Transmission of confidential content<br>• Protection against tampering<br>• Authentication of the sender<br>• Interpersonal creation of trust | • Need for unequivocal understanding of the content<br>• Transmission of difficult subject matter context<br>• Execution of controversies<br>• Solution of complex problems |

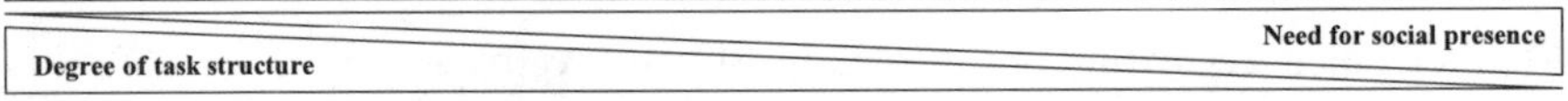

Degree of task structure                                                    Need for social presence

**Fig. 3.9.** The task-oriented communication model (based on Reichwald 1999)

Accuracy in communication is an essential requirement in organizational leadership, as well as coordination processes that involve technical tasks. These types of communication processes require administrative exactness, especially with regard to documentation and the conveying of shared information. Formal administrative decision-making with regard to investment ventures is a good example of top-management's cooperation processes. These decisions require special accuracy with regard to the contextual aspects of communication.

The speed and user-friendliness of communication are important when information needs to be shared quickly and efficiently. If communication processes require rapid arrangement or reaction (especially in unexpected situations), speed and user-friendliness are essential.

Trustworthiness is demanded in communication processes that involve the realization of value-oriented agreements in which interpersonal trust development is important as a social aspect of communication. The trait "trustworthiness" also includes communication partners' requests to be protected against unauthorized access to and tampering with messages, as well as the identification of a message's sender.

Complexity is a characteristic of communication tasks, especially those concerned with clarifying difficult content. It also applies to questions related to complicated subjects or personal matters that both parties need to understand. It can also strain the directness of dialogue, requires immediate feedback, as well as the interplay between verbal and non-verbal communication.

These four basic prerequisites are the requirements for all business communication relationships. In the foreground are effective task fulfillment and uninterrupted understanding between the communication partners. The choice of media will depend on the task and the decision maker's subjective assessment (Reichwald 1999). The highest priority for optimal task support is that a choice of media should be available and that the work environment should be configured to support and provide them. This applies to both the successful conclusion of business affairs, as well as to management's everyday work.

### Media Choice According to Media Richness Theory

Media richness theory, which differentiates between "poor" and "rich" communication forms, provides an especially interesting explanation for media choice. According to this theory, technical and non-technical communication forms have different capacities regarding the transmission of analog and digital information. Face-to-face communication during an interpersonal encounter is, for instance, considered a "rich" communication form. It offers a variety of parallel channels (speech, intonation, gestures, mimic, etc.), enables immediate feedback, provides a rich spectrum of possible expressions, and allows the immediate perception of personal temperament and emotions. In contrast, the exchange of documents (letters, fax, e-mail, etc.) denotes a "poor" communication form with a low degree of media richness.

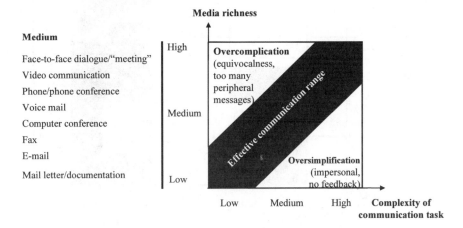

**Fig. 3.10.**   The media richness model based on Daft and Lengel (following Rice 1992)

The above illustration depicts the model of "poor" and "rich" media forms developed by Daft and Langel (1984, 1986) on the basis of empirical research. This model classifies different communication forms according to their "richness" and covers the spectrum from personal dialogue to a letter.

The model goes one step further by taking the "lean and mean" approach that rich media are automatically better than poor media. However, the opposite is true. The range of effective communication lies somewhere between over-complication (unnecessary complications) and over-simplification (improper simplification). Which medium "fits" depends on the complexity of the task at hand (Rice, 1992).

- Communication through "rich" media forms becomes more effective the more complex the task is.

- Communication through "poor" media forms becomes more effective the more structured the task is.

The Daft, Lengel and Trevino (1987) research is interesting, because their discovery that successful leaders distinguish themselves by utilizing a media approach was in line with the theory. "Media-sensitive" managers, whose media choices were based on theoretical media-choice rules, were twice as likely to be considered "high performers" than managers who, contrary to the model's recommendation, use their media choice for various tasks. The latter are therefore substantiated as "media insensitive" (see figure 3.11).

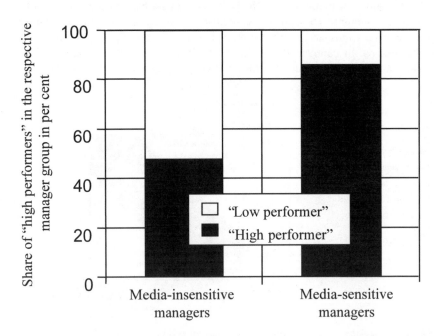

**Fig. 3.11.**   Media sensitivity and management success (based on Daft / Lengel / Trevino 1987)

If the Daft and Lengel model is correct, management's media support faces significant consequences. Which communication system should management use to fall within the effective communication range? This is where the question of media choice meets the question of media impact. These questions are addressed in the following section.

## 3.4.2 Perspectives of Media Effects: Results of Media Impact Research

The relationship between the utilization of various types of communication media in management and their impact on management behavior is clearly demonstrated by Grote's (1994) research. This research describes a manager's leadership behavior by means of two completely separate dimensions: Locomotion (also referred to as achievement or goal oriented) and cohesion (also referred to as colleague or group oriented). The appropriate combination of these leadership dimensions is regarded as significant for the specific success of different leadership styles.

If management is solely focused on the attainment of contextual work goals, it runs the risk of neglecting the equally relevant success factors within the work climate. This can lead to poor performance due to dissatisfaction in the work place. However, if management is wholly employee oriented, it is likely to have a high level of job satisfaction, but low performance levels.

Grote's questionnaire-based research showed that there is a difference of opinion regarding the media types that support performance and / or group orientation in management. Consequently, the utilization of technology-based communication media is primarily suitable for supporting locomotion within teams of co-workers, while cohesion is encouraged by face-to-face communication. This raises the question whether the variety of new "media rich" technologies will continue to have the same substitution effects on communication forms and social presence that are presently observed and whether they will also influence management structures and the development of organization culture.

### The Impact of Media Utilization on Work and Management Cooperation

While few doubt that the spread and use of new media are changing work, cooperation, and management procedures, there is still very little knowledge on this subject in media-impact research. With the exception of a few projects (e.g., Beckurts / Reichwald 1984; Grote 1994; Goecke 1997), most of the assumptions about media influence are based on studies that were not specifically focused on management procedures. Insights from other work-related procedures cannot, however, be easily applied to these types of management procedures. This complicates pure analytical assumptions and predictions about the expected effects of media utilization and development tendencies in the management domain. Current research in this area continues to present surprising and unexpected results.

Optimistic expectations regarding media utilization effects were previously focused on reducing "personal" communications, time saving techniques, especially
concerning face-to-face interaction, or on reducing meeting time and business
travel. On the whole, the focus was to reduce managers' demanding daily communication duties through the use of supportive media systems. A closer inspection
of current top management time and activity profiles, especially in relation to
management studies from the 1970s (when most of the current media were not yet
developed), presents an altogether different picture.

A comparison of time and activity level research from the 1990s (Pribilla / Reichwald / Goecke 1996) with studies conducted in the 1970s (Mintzberg 1973) is
problematic. It can, however, be attempted because the research methods in the
two studies are comparable.

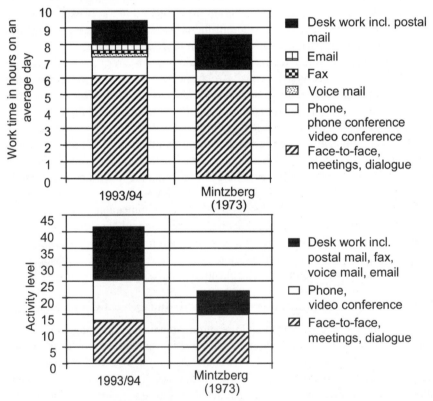

Results from a total of 28 observation days 1993/1994 and
25 observation days 1969/70

**Fig. 3.12.**   Comparison of time and activity profiles of upper level managers (Pribilla / Reichwald / Goecke 1996)

Figure 3.12 shows the comparison between the Pribilla, Reichwald and Goecke (1996) study and that of Mintzberg (1973). The average use of e-mail, fax, and voicemail was obviously not a valid question at the time of the Mintzberg study. The increase in telephone communication in the latest study is surprising, as there are more options for communication available today than there were at the time of the Mintzberg study. The biggest surprise, however, is the almost unchanged degree of face-to-face communication. It seems that a manager in the 1990s, just like a manager in the 1970s, spent an average of six hours or more on personal interaction or meetings per day.

Contrary to all assumptions about the substitution of face-to-face communication – especially as far as surmounting long distances is concerned – this comparison shows that the degree of face-to-face time in upper management has in no way been substituted by the increased use of modern communication tools. Whether this result is transferable to specific multimedia amenities in managers' work environments cannot be fully supported at this time. However, one thing is certain: Face-to-face communication remains a constant in managers' communication behavior. As in the past, it continues to play a dominating role in all areas of business (Kieser / Hegele / Klimmer 1998).

Similar to previous studies (Beckurts / Reichwald 1984), this result therefore demonstrates that face-to-face communication's issues do not change. The problem of absenteeism and unavailability that affect face-to-face communication in management continues. How can the information stream be maintained during times of absence from the workplace? The assumption is that various technical media innovations can be utilized.

The difference in the work hours (an apparent increase) of the participating managers in the more recent study (see figure 3.12) raises questions as to the cause of this difference. There is a substantial increase in the degree of communication by means of electronic media and a decrease in the amount of "desk time" during the workday. However, most managers reported that there was not enough time to complete normal activities that require time behind the desk (reading reports, working on new concepts, and / or preparing presentations) and that these tasks were usually done during non-working hours (nights or weekends).

Management is caught in a time-trap. Deadlines, high volumes of tasks, quick responses in critical situations, customer care, relationship management, leadership within the organization, and networking are all matters that take up valuable time. The managers in the 1996 study had a workload that was almost twice as high as those in the 1973 study. In the light of current reorganization trends, the situation at the upper management level threatens to expand even further into other areas of management and to continue to deteriorate (Reichwald et al. 2000).

The utilization of media, especially those designed for synchronization (voice mail, fax, e-mail etc.), can help reduce this current work overload. If the current standard for face-to-face communication remains the same and the number of face-to-face contacts continues to increase, there needs to be a stronger focus on telecommunication. In addition, traditional mail communication can be substituted by the use of modern media.

The conclusion of this time and activity comparison (in relation to the media impact) indicates that upper management perceives the advantages of media utilization – especially with regard to asynchronized forms of telecommunication – as the quickest and most comfortable way to remain in contact with both close and long-distance communication partners. It should be noted that these new media forms have also contributed to an increase in the workload and have strengthened expectations regarding immediate feedback, reactions, and quick decisions. In the telecommunication field, new media offer a way to control work and management processes by circumventing traditional demands for physical presence in face-to-face communications. They also allow tasks to be completed (regardless of time and regional differences), contacts and relationships to be maintained, and reduce reaction and negotiation time.

Simultaneously, currently available communication tools are also helping to increase the degree of communication activity. This is leading to an increase in managers' normal workload, while fragmenting the average workday, and (especially with heavy users) causing an increase in travel activity (see Pribilla / Reichwald / Goecke 1996). This telecommunication paradox will be explained further in chapter 8. The application of new technologies has shown that they serve as problem solvers for managers' time and activity dilemmas, but are also creating new ones. Communication and management research now face many open questions.

## 3.5    Knowledge Models

### 3.5.1    The Meaning of Knowledge

In contrast to information, which is defined as a signal with symbolic meaning, knowledge is defined as an action-oriented combination of information that takes experiences from a corresponding past content into account. This means that knowledge strongly depends on people and / or organizations, while information can be independently interpreted or processed.

Knowledge encompasses all the perceptions and judgments that individuals have collected about their environment and are all built on past experiences, observations, and conclusions based on them. Personal history is responsible for creating personal belief systems.

Knowledge also encompasses all of an individual's cognitive and neurological abilities that have shown useful when individuals deal with the world around them. In addition, it covers the skills of the collective, which create their own standards of knowledge elements and are based on the combined efforts and abilities of individuals (see Scheuble 1998). The content of this definition of knowledge can be systematized by means of three categories: The object, the context, and the transferability (see figure 3.13).

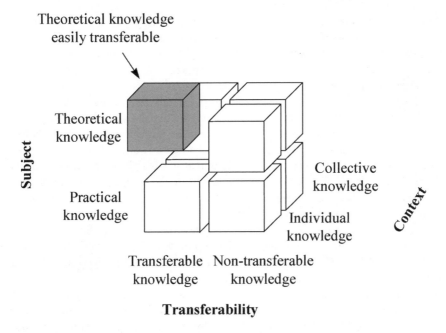

**Fig. 3.13.** Systematization of knowledge (based on Scheuble 1998, p. 10)

The issue with regard to the object is the distinction between theoretical and practical knowledge. When it is related to the context – within which each of the knowledge elements unfolds its impact – the difference between individual and collective knowledge can be distinguished. Individual knowledge categories can be differentiated further, according to the degree to which barriers hinder the transfer of knowledge between actors. This leads to the distinction between transferable and non-transferable knowledge that, much like a value, is placed at either end of a continuum. The types of knowledge that can be found in the literature can be interpreted as alternative definitions of the cubes in figure 3.13, or as partial aspects of these elements.

The concept knowledge has been a primary focus of epistemology research for more than two thousand years (for further explanation, see Moser/Nat 1995). The different rudiments of this philosophical tradition are usually oriented towards the Plato-based concept of knowledge as the true explanation of perception. The philosophical definition of knowledge is therefore linked to the perception of reality. According to this way of thinking, knowledge encompasses all of the awareness that individuals have about themselves and the world around them.

One could also regard this as an individual's view. This view has to be a trusted image of the world (worldview). Interestingly though, it does not have to be correct. However, the relationship of this worldview with the "real" world has to have a certain level of verification. In keeping with the philosophical definition of knowledge, this does not mean that the view has to be correct in order to qualify as knowledge. It merely means that it is considered a truthful worldview as it has been authorized in some way. There are many ways of verification. One extreme way is through science, which subjects perception to a systematic and objective authorization process.

Another extreme are myths and traditions, which are considered accurate due to their social legitimacy. The difference between the two extremes is not the result, but their approach. While many scientific theories have been found to be false, most traditions contain some aspect of the truth (e.g., Sowell 1980).

Knowledge is not a given, but something that needs to be learned. Individuals do this by taking their interactions with the world around them and interpreting them so that they can then analyze and organize them. They therefore create a world-view on the basis of their experiences. This view is then used for decision-making, recognizing consistency, making assumptions, and drawing conclusions. Sometimes new experiences also lead to the realization that a previously held world-view is incorrect. These "revisions" of one's knowledge base can happen in every day life, as well as in science. Consequently, knowledge is always provisional.

Up to this point, theoretical or abstract knowledge of something has been described. Theoretical knowledge is described by Ryle (1949) as "knowledge that" and by James (1962) as "knowledge about." However, reducing the knowledge concept to an abstract or theoretical level is inappropriate, since it does not take into account all the practical skills and abilities that are important for economic dealings. Practical knowledge encompasses all the practical skills and abilities that enable theoretical knowledge to be more than a purely intellectual phenomenon.

Although knowledge is always individual, it is formed by exposure to the individual's surroundings (Nelson/Winter 1982; Simon 1991). Collective knowledge is therefore like a mosaic: It is composed of individual elements in order to create a common function. Individual knowledge is the substance of collective knowledge, but is nevertheless more than just the sum of its parts.

Without going into the details of the reciprocal adaptation process between individuals and their surroundings, it can be argued that there is such a thing as collective knowledge (see, e.g., Berger/Luckmann 1967). This is because individual knowledge is developed by means of an interaction process with this individual's physical and social environment, which is influenced by individual exchanges that in turn impact individual knowledge.

Collective knowledge is that knowledge that can only be controlled by a collective as a whole. This does not mean that this type of knowledge is synonymous with a routine or a culture as many authors maintain. Knowledge is always held by an individual. Just as a mosaic is composed of various stones, collective knowledge is composed of various knowledge "building blocks."

Collective knowledge can also be differentiated into practical and theoretical knowledge. A collective's theoretical knowledge is shared knowledge. The attribute "shared" emphasizes that this is knowledge that belongs to all of the collective's individual members. Typical examples are an organization's myths and traditions and the jargon that project team members use.

When discussing collective knowledge, the literature more often than not refers to its practical aspects. These practices (March/Simon 1958; Nelson/Winter 1982) are the well-rehearsed result of a group of people's action and decision-making and represent their own knowledge standard in respect of quality. The self-contained character of collective knowledge makes it possible to analyze collective business actors, such as an organization or company, by means of the same procedures that apply to individuals.

An especially interesting question is the degree to which knowledge is transferred from one actor to another. This applies to both the encouragement of knowledge transfer, as well as the prevention of unintended knowledge transfer.

A transfer implies the effective transmission of knowledge from one actor to another. The purchase of a physics book, researching a patent at the patent office or attending a lecture do not qualify as a knowledge transfer. A knowledge transfer is only successful when the receiver is able to reiterate the information as the original knowledge "owner" conveyed it. In this context, the implicit character of knowledge is important (Polanyi 1962, 1985) as it can negatively affect transfers.

The degree to which knowledge can be articulated is not the only determinant of the transferability of knowledge. Knowledge that cannot be put into words can often be transferred visually (Moeslein 2000). When, for instance, interns are learning a new trade, they do this by largely observing, imitating, and practicing that which their instructors demonstrate (Nonaka/Takeuchi 1985). Frequently, it is not even necessary to observe knowledge owners doing their task, as just looking at the end product is often sufficient to gain the fundamental knowledge required to create it. This is often referred to as reverse engineering. On the other hand, there are many examples of extensively articulated knowledge that is very difficult to transfer.

## 3.5.2 Knowledge Between Coordination and Motivation

As a central production factor, knowledge is manageable. The task of knowledge management is to optimize the knowledge flow within and between organizations (see chapter 10). Since knowledge management is firmly rooted in an organizational context, it is caught between coordination and motivation (Milgrom/Roberts 1992). Coordination and motivation measures largely determine the ability and drive of the employees in an organization who, as carriers of knowledge, are responsible for managing it. In this sense, it is important that the organization's leadership finds appropriate coordination and motivation measures. Only then can knowledge management succeed.

Within the coordination aspect context, there is the question of which actions employees need to carry out to help achieve organizational goals. To begin with, the "do not know what to do" should be addressed. There are two relevant factors when examining an organization's knowledge management: The coordination between people and the coordination between people and machines.

The first factor is relevant in all areas that require the coordination of knowledge flows by means of hierarchies, group constellations, and / or formal information pathways. The coordination between people and machines is especially important with regard to the use of databanks that are responsible for transmitting targeted information. This can be as simple as an office memo or a newsletter, but can also apply to the creation of an office intranet designed to influence and control information flow.

Within the motivation aspect context, there is the question of the types of conditions that have to be developed to enable all employees to contribute to knowledge management. The motivation of the actors to generate, transfer, and use knowledge depends greatly on the material and immaterial incentives that are in place.

In order to introduce knowledge management successfully (see chapter 10), organization rules, motivation, and incentive systems need to be developed that not only enable employees to contribute (coordination aspect), but drive them to contribute (motivation aspect).

## 3.6    Information, Communication, and Trust

Trust is an elementary principle in organizations, especially with regard to interpersonal exchanges and relationships. Not only is the development of trust based on information and communication processes, but information and communication behaviors also depend on the degree of trust that has already been established. This interaction between trust, information, and communication will be discussed in this section.

Trust can be examined from various viewpoints (see, e.g., Schottländer 1957; Barber 1983; Zündorf 1987; Gambetta 1988; Schmidtchen 1994; Ripperger 1998; Luhmann 2000). First the meaning of trust within and between organizations is examined, i.e. the meaning of trust in the intra- and interorganizational context. Next, the relationship between the trust mechanism and actors' individual information behavior is examined (information behavior and trust), while focusing on the problems associated with reciprocal information behavior (trust and reciprocal [information] behavior). Finally, the interaction between trust and communication is explained, including how this affects intercultural aspects (trust development and communication and trust development in the international and intercultural context).

### 3.6.1   The Meaning of Trust in the Intra- and Interorganizational Context

As an elementary organization principle, especially with regard to interpersonal exchanges and relationships, trust plays a central role when it comes to business performance relationships (Albach 1980; Fukuyama 1995; Ripperger 1998). Trust is not just essential in micro-economic transformation and reorganization processes, but also in more flexible business structures (Bleicher 1995). Trust is an essential prerequisite for business structures' existence, since it is the primary characteristic of network organizations, as well as virtual and distributed business structures (e.g., Powell 1996; Sydow 1996; Handy 1995; Loose / Sydow 1994; Wurche 1994; Reichwald et al. 2000).

These types of organizations are distinguished by an accelerating degree of geographical and organizational decentralization. Based on modern information and communication technology, these decentralization processes vary greatly. Starting with intra-organization structures, such as modularization and internal networks, these processes can continue beyond the organizational borders and can even assume a virtual organizational form.

Currently, geographic and organizational decentralization measures are expanding the business capacity of employees and partners. At the same time, it is impossible to restrain this newfound capacity with traditional control and monitoring systems, as this would require additional costs that would have to be partially recouped through decentralizing efforts to increase efficiency levels. Here, trust can be a valuable mechanism by filling the "control vacuum." The maxim that "trust is good, but control is better," is thus transformed into the goal to replace control with trust in those areas where control is too costly or absent.

The establishment of trust within and between organizations can be encouraged by means of social norms and institutional ground rules (Zucker 1986; Creed & Miles 1996; Kramer & Tyler 1996; Ripperger 1998, 1999). Organizations that have a high level of trust generally have a higher level of social capital than more opportunistic ones and can use this to realize higher profits. Consequently, trust – especially in newly formed organizations – can become a business advantage.

## 3.6.2 Information Behavior and Trust

The problem with trust can be described as a problem of risk-filled preparatory effort (Luhmann, 2000). The trust "giver" hands over control of events and resources to the trust "taker" and in doing so gives the taker the opportunity to do harm (breaking trust) as well as to assist (honoring trust). By giving trust, the giver has to take the unsecured risk that harm may potentially be done.

Understanding problems associated with trust deals with two assumptions about human information behavior: Limited rationality and optimism. Trust only becomes an issue when there is uncertainty about another person's motivational disposition (intentions). This means that trust givers cannot be fully informed about trust takers' true motives and intentions and can make a mistake in their assessment of the other (limited rationality). It also means that the trust taker does not always convey accurate information and in certain instances can knowingly hide or distort information in order to make a profit at the giver's expense (opportunistic behavior). This leads to a principal-agent relationship between the trust giver and the trust taker (see chapter 2). The trust giver, who takes on the role of the principal, is generally less informed about the intentions of the trust taker (agent) than vice versa. With this in mind, trust can be defined as in Figure 3.14.

| Trust is ... | |
|---|---|
| **Trust actions** | ... the voluntary delivery of a risk-filled preparatory effort while ignoring explicit contractual safeguards and controls against opportunistic behavior ... |
| **Trust expectations** | ... in the expectation that the trust taker is motivated to voluntarily forego opportunistic behavior. |

**Fig. 3.14.**    Trust – trust expectations and actions (based on Ripperger 1998, p. 45)

The trust behavior of the trust giver is based on the subjective assessment of the trust taker's trustworthiness (see also Deutsch 1960a, 1960b, 1976). The trust giver is generally not well enough informed to be sure of success when acting. The only option that the trust giver has to overcome this information deficit is to take information available from the past and transfer it to the present. Consequently, trust givers protect themselves through their personal experiences and those of third parties.

Depending on the underlying information, there are three different categories of trust (see figure 3.15). General trust describes a person's general willingness to trust, regardless of the specifics of a particular situation (see Rotter 1971, 1980; Petermann 1996). Such trust is usually regarded as a personality trait. Based on personal past experiences, people are more or less willing to trust other people.

In comparison, specific trust is based on the subjective assessment of a particular person's trustworthiness in a specific situation (Petermann, 1996). For example, a doctor who is needed for a very complicated medical procedure will make a professional and trustworthy impression.

The trust giver does not, however, solely rely on personal experiences, but also relies on the experiences of others. When dealing with third parties' experience with the trust taker, this is referred to as reputation. Reputation is basically public information about the past trustworthiness of an actor. When there is no way to draw a conclusion about the quality or reliability of a product, trust plays an important role in organizations that do not have any verifiable information about a potential business partner and in business conducted on the Internet (see Koch / Moeslein / Wagner 2000).

When the experiences of a third party have no direct bearing on the trust taker, but are based on interactions with third parties within a shared social context, they constitute a social system's atmosphere of trust (see Ripperger 1998). A culture or organization's basic conditions greatly influence the likelihood of opportunistic

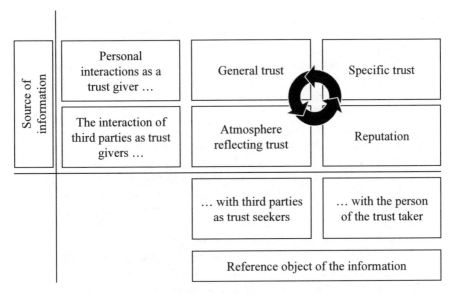

**Fig. 3.15.** Typical trust categories (based on Ripperger 1998, p. 99)

behavior within a particular system, i.e. the number of actors behaving opportunistically differs from culture to culture. The more positive experiences gained from relationships in a particular social environment, the better the quality of the trust atmosphere usually is.

There are interdependencies between these categories. It is generally true that in a particular situation, the degree of general trust is influenced by the degree of trust expectation. It can also be assumed that in a social system with a good trust atmosphere, an actor's general trust (with regard to other members within the system) is usually higher than in a system with a poor trust atmosphere. Within a social system, the nature of reputation influences the subjective perception of the quality of the trust atmosphere. This means that the reputation of a potential trust taker will influence the trust giver's trust, although it is no substitute for personal experience.

A situation's degree of familiarity will determine which trust category is the most important (e.g., Ripperger 1998). If a situation involves a high level of familiarity, trust expectations are likely to be based on general trust, the reputation of the potential trust taker, and the trust atmosphere of the social environment. Conversely, when a situation is less familiar, there is a likelihood of situation-specific trust.

### 3.6.3 Trust and Reciprocal Information Behavior Reciprocal Altruistic Behavior and Social Capital

The norm of reciprocal behavior (reciprocity norm) is considered a universally applicable norm in all cultures (Gouldner 1960). It is constructed from the following two behavior rules: People should not harm those who have helped them and people should help those who have helped them. This form of reciprocity can also be described as reciprocal altruistic behavior.

Reciprocal altruistic behavior within a group is based on the same principle as the above, as it is also based on reciprocal assurance. The benefits of this type of behavior tend to be higher for the receivers than the costs associated with using it. If one member trusts that another will reciprocate this behavior at a later point, this can lead to long-term benefits for both sides (Trivers 1971).

Reciprocal altruistic behavior can be a key incentive for the recognition of trust and investment in trust relationships. However, reciprocal altruistic behavior also depends on a minimum level of trust, especially with regard to the user's appreciation of and willingness to reciprocate. Examples of this behavior can be found in both humans and animals, i.e. warning cries regarding approaching danger, saving the life of a drowning person or donating blood.

Trust becomes possible and even grows through reciprocal altruistic behavior. Both foster the development of social capital, which is generated when the relationships between actors are altered to a point that allows cooperative conduct (Coleman 1990). Actors who maintain social capital can count on the cooperative conduct of a third party and can, for example, use that person's resources to expand their own.

Social capital is primarily developed in interpersonal exchanges and social settings resulting from the moral entitlement to and expectations of reciprocal altruistic behavior. However, trust is still the main focus in the production of social capital. Organizations with an unchanging trust atmosphere will have a higher level of social capital and, thus, more cooperation opportunities than their counterparts with more opportunistic cultures (see, e.g., Cohen / Prusak 2001). The development of trust should therefore be encouraged through an appropriate institutional framework.

The exchange and sharing of information is a fundamental manifestation of reciprocal altruistic behavior in every day life. In many cases, the transmission of information does not as such cost the messenger much, but makes the receiver very useful. Nevertheless, the information often loses some of its value as soon as it is shared. In many instances, the exchange of information is only valuable if the informant receives valuable information in return. The reciprocal transfer of valuable information generally leads to a high level of trust. The following section discusses the problems associated with interorganizational information transfer.

### The Information Transfer Dilemma: Problems with Interorganizational Information Transfer

This theory is based on game strategies: Two players have the option to either cooperate with each other or not. Both players' dominant strategy is to be uncooperative. Regardless of how they behave, one player's uncooperative behavior will always seem more advantageous than the other's cooperative behavior. If they are both uncooperative, they will, however, both benefit less than if they were cooperative. In a single game, both players will generally remain uncooperative, but in multiple games, cooperative behavior may develop.

In computer simulations, this tit-for-tat strategy (Axelrod 1997) has been shown to be the most effective. Tit-for-tat is a heuristic approach requiring cooperation in the first round and copying of the partner's behavior in all subsequent rounds. The cooperation between the players is maintained until one player decides to be uncooperative. In the following round, the partner will copy this uncooperative behavior until the cooperation is terminated.

The prisoner's dilemma type of situation can be applied to interorganizational information transfers (see, e.g., Hippel 1988; Schrader 1990). Two organizations, A and B, each have information that the other does not. The value of A's information is equal to that of B. Each value is based on two components: The basic value of r and the added value of $\Delta r$. The added value is based on the information advantage that the one organization has over the other. This advantage is lost during an information transfer, leaving only the basic value. The model of the information transfer dilemma is depicted in figure 3.16.

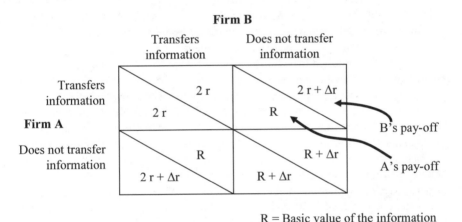

Fig. 3.16. Structure of the information transfer dilemma (based on Schrader 1990, p. 27)

If the assumption of a one-round game is abandoned, then, as previously mentioned, cooperative behavior between two organizations is possible. While the non-transfer of information may be profitable in the short term, one organization's cooperative behavior can lead to a long-term, mutually beneficial relationship between the two organizations. The model demonstrates that interorganizational information transfer is only economically viable when the information's basic value is high and the added value is low. On the other hand, competitive behavior occurs when information's basic value is low and the added value is high.

It has been demonstrated that this type of information exchange is only possible when there is a reasonable level of trust and a prospect of a long-term partnership. In an empirical study, Schrader (1990) came to the conclusion that informal interorganizational information transfer can positively contribute to the success of both organizations. He also discovered that the decline in efforts and reciprocal efforts over time, as well as a certain blindness concerning successful cooperation relationships, which is associated with competitive thinking, is often the reason for rejecting such information transfer. This contradiction between cooperation and competition is not, however, unsolvable.

### 3.6.4   Trust Development and Communication

Trust development and communication are strongly interconnected (Bittl 1997). The development of trust depends just as much on communication as some forms of communication depend on trust. Consequently, communication has an impact on the degree of trust between communication partners. Trust is only viewed as a problem when the trust giver is uncertain of the trust taker's morality and true motives.

The trust problem is a result of the trust giver's information asymmetry (inconsistencies) and the possible risk of being taken advantage of by the trust taker. Communication can overcome or strengthen information asymmetries. Someone is trustworthy when, "… he understands the intentions that he conveyed to another through words or implied behavior, is aware of what has or has not been communicated by his behavior and by what he knows to be true or will soon be true through future behavior" (Ripperger 1998, p. 139; translated by the authors).

In comparison, people are untrustworthy when, through their communication behavior, they create the illusion of benevolent intentions in order to gain trust, but actually intend to inflict harm on others for their own benefit. It is especially the intent to deceive that is transferred with the conveyed message that separates honest communication behavior from dishonest behavior (Baier 1986). The trust of trust givers is supported by the assumption that they, through what they communicate, do not intend to deceive anyone. The development of a trust relationship therefore depends on trust takers' clear communication that they recognize the concerns of the trust givers and will adjust their behavior appropriately. This can be done through verbal communication, for example, a promise, but can also simply be accomplished by convincing behavior.

The building of trust is often based on easily interpretable situations and presumes the ability to correctly understand third parties' communicative utterances and signals. This requires a minimum level of agreement and understanding on the syntactic, semantic, and pragmatic level (see section 3.3.1), as well as with regard to specific behavioral norms and customs. People also have different ways of subjectively filtering other people's facial expressions, gestures, and utterances. They are therefore not always able to correctly interpret other senders' messages and their meaning.

To truly understand the meaning of certain communicative utterances, people need to learn these in the context of multiple interactions. This develops a basis of repeated experiences and a minimum level of trustworthiness (Luhmann 1988, 2000). "Trustworthiness increases the certainty of expectation by simplifying the correct interpretation of trust situations, thus reducing the immanent subjective uncertainty of trust and the possibility of misinterpreting information and communication and, therefore, the risk of making an error" (Ripperger 1998, p. 107; translated by the authors).

### 3.6.5  Trust Development in the International and Intercultural Context

In the global economy in which organizations operate, cooperate or even merge across cultural and geographic boundaries, trust development plays a critical role. The significance of trust in international or intercultural transactions is, in contrast to domestic business transactions, the fact that it generally involves a greater number of national and international laws and governances.

In an international context, a contract's explicitness (a functional equivalent of trust) loses its effectiveness (Ripperger 1999). On an international level, contract negotiation is generally more complex and therefore not as comprehensive as on a domestic level. The implementation of a contract across international borders is more cost-intensive, time-consuming, and less enforceable than in a domestic setting. Additionally, most international contracts do not take the increased need for flexibility into account. Consequently, there is a greater demand for trust in an international context. At the same time, trust building between different cultures has its own fundamental problems.

When one is familiar with a culture and its institutions, as well as with the norms of social interactions, one is better able to evaluate the behavior of others and the consequences of transactions. Trust is built through the belief that the message being sent (consciously or subconsciously) is the truth. The legitimacy of a communicative utterance is easier to assess in a culturally familiar environment, because people from different cultural backgrounds emphasize clarity in communication less than people from the same culture. Consequently, a verbal agreement may mean a great deal in one culture while it is meaningless in another, or a lie may be regarded relatively harmless in one culture while yet another may regard it as a malicious act.

Facial expressions, gestures and other communicative utterances are often associated with different meanings in different cultures. Last but not least, communication can be even more difficult if there are problems with the ability to speak the other's language. These communicative complications therefore make trust development across cultures problematic. Consequently, the trust required for information transfer on an international level is less likely to be available than on a domestic level.

In many cases, there is a lack of personal experience with people from other cultures or subcultures, which could help to build a foundation for general trust. Moreover, it is difficult to obtain accurate information on the reputation of a potential transaction partner, or on the current state of a specific social system's trust atmosphere. Even the acquisition of situation-specific information, which is required for specific trust settings, becomes problematic in an international context. In addition to cultural differences, geographic distance and / or time differences also need to be dealt with.

The general level of trust in foreigners can vary across different cultures (Fukuyama 1995). Fukuyama, for example, describes China as a culture in which trust is given freely to family members but rarely to foreigners. This makes building the trust required for cooperative relationships with Chinese organizations difficult. Much like with virtual organizations (see chapters 8 and 10), trust development in an international and / or intercultural context presents a trust dilemma. Not only do these types of transactions increase the demand for trust but for all the reasons just mentioned, trust development across cultures is indeed problematic.

Nevertheless, trust development can be fostered under certain circumstances. Ripperger (1999) describes different methods for the development of trust in bilateral and multilateral transaction relations within an international context. The following recommendations take into account that the development of trust is often a cost-intensive and relationship-specific investment. This investment is only amortized over time through repeated transactions and the gain of equivalent cooperative profits.

(1) Transaction relations can be developed within long-term relationships. This generally leads to an increase in the number of transactions, as well as in attainable cooperative profits, thereby increasing the willingness to do business in a trustworthy manner. Willingness to enter into longer-term cooperative relationships can be signaled through specific investments such as a purchaser's investment in the production facilities of a supplier, which in turn increases credibility.

(2) Increasing the exclusiveness of a transaction relationship can have a similar effect. By decreasing its number of international transaction partners, an organization increases its future cooperation profits where there is trustworthy behavior on both sides (loyalty premium). However, this situation involves a higher risk (e.g., loss of production if parts do not arrive or are defective), thus requiring a higher level of trust.

(3) At first, cooperation gains can be kept low and be increased incrementally. This allows an organization to influence the loyalty premium of its partners, thus providing incentives for trustworthy behavior.

(4) Furthermore, the possible risks of the trust-giving organization should be low at first. By testing potential trust takers' trustworthiness in a low-risk situation, organizations are better able to judge their motives and intentions (especially their loyalty and opportunistic premiums), thus decreasing the risk of misjudgment in situations where more might be at stake.

(5) Another useful tool for trust development in international transactions is the use of brokers (e.g., import / export companies and banks). International transac-

tion partners do therefore not deal directly with each other, but use brokers in their respective countries. Using brokers can increase the number of transactions (and reduce their time-frame), as well as efficiency and trust as they negotiate the various transactions on a local level.

(6) Brokers are a special form of trust intermediaries. The cost of trust development between two actors can be reduced if they have a common, already established trust relationship with a third party (a trust intermediary) who is then used to establish a chain of trust between the two actors. In the international context, any organization can generally fill the role of a trust intermediary, whether it is a bank or any other institution (i.e. a business organization or the local chamber of commerce).

(7) Conversely, the trust takers can also induce and encourage trust through the use of certain signaling measures such as collateral or specific investments. The application of these measures leads to a reduction of the opportunistic premium for the trust giver.

(8) Finally, trust can be developed through the creation of a trade coalition or a business network, thus encouraging the formalized embedding of transactions into a multilateral context within a definable system. A required part of trust development is revealing the identity of the transaction partners, which is defined by the group or system to which they belong. However, certain institutional regulations have to be developed to encourage trustworthy behavior within this group or system. This type of encouragement can be achieved by means of regulations (such as lower transaction costs, more resources, and/or access to interesting potential partners), if the group's attainable corporation profits are higher than those of another group, and if opportunistic behavior is not tolerated (i.e. immediate dismissal from the group may follow). This principle has been applied since the Middle Ages, starting with the trade coalition of the Maghribi dealers (Greiff 1989), is also the basis of the New York diamond exchange (Bernstein 1990), and is currently used by eBay Inc. for its online auction system.

## 3.7   Implications for Management

This chapter has explored the problems of information behavior, communication behavior and understanding, media choice and its effects, knowledge and knowledge transfer, as well as trust development. The different information and communication theory models have demonstrated that these problems can become debilitating factors for organizations and partnerships.

It has become clear that there are various reasons for actors' information behavior being less than optimal:

- Deviation between the subjective and objective information need;
- The inadequate practical impact of information due to it being too new or largely just confirming existing information;
- Inefficient use of information due to an insufficient institutional framework;
- Visible information behavior as a measure of information's quality or as the basis on which decisions are made;
- Information pathologies based on actors, interaction, and knowledge.

It has also become apparent that disruptions between two actors' comprehension can occur on many levels:

- Semiotics levels: Syntactic, semantic, and pragmatic disruptions in the communication between actors;
- Technical disturbances during the transfer of information;
- Psychological and socially based disruptions in human communication exchanges;
- Disruptions at the level of speech: Speech acts;
- Disturbances at the level of strategic and communicative behavior through manipulation or different lifeworlds (Lebenswelten);
- Disruptions based on false or missing overlapping consensual spheres due to different constructions of reality.

As the basis of an organization, communication also provides options for structuring an organization. New possibilities in media-supported communication have also led to more possibilities to provide structure and design suggestions. The entire spectrum of communication options is available to today's organizations. The interplay between task, medium, and communication was therefore also discussed in this chapter. We examined:

- Fundamental questions about appropriate task-related media choice; and
- Fundamental questions about task-dependent media effects in communication processes.

A summary was provided of the answers to these questions and the open questions that remain were explained.

There is also an increasing emphasis on the knowledge factor in organizations. It is therefore becoming more important to design measures and motivation / incentive systems that not only encourage employees to contribute to the generation, transfer, and use of knowledge (coordination aspect), but that also make them want to do this (motivation aspect).

When examining the different aspects of information, communication, and trust, certain points need to be reiterated:

- The meaning of trust in the intra- and interorganizational context will continue to receive more attention in the new decentralization trends that are currently discernible and in the resultant expansion of employees and partners' behavioral scope.

- Trust is based on information. Depending on the information on which it is based, it is possible to differentiate general trust, specialized trust, reputation, and trust atmosphere.

- The advantages of reciprocal altruistic behavior and the social capital that it generates create an important incentive for trustworthy behavior. Trust development should be encouraged in organizations through appropriate frameworks and measures. Trust is a basic requirement for interorganizational information transfer, which in turn benefits all parties involved.

- Trust and communication are intertwined. Trust development depends on communication and the quality of a communication process depends on a certain level of trust. Trust development is generally easier when others' communicative utterances are relatively easy to decipher. However, this requires a minimum level of agreement on the syntactic, semantic, and pragmatic communication level (i.e. a certain amount of trust).

- The trust dilemma becomes apparent in an international or intercultural context. Differing international laws and regulations are the cause of low efficiency in explicit contracts, while the demand for trust is increasing. However, different cultural backgrounds, a low level of trust, and the basic rules of communication that are required hinder trust development. Trust can nevertheless be developed through the application of certain measures.

Actors' successful communication within and between organizations depends strongly on the types of "typical" behavior observed with regard to dealing with information, communication channels, and media, as well as the development of information and communication systems. Whatever the root of problems with communication, they have to be dealt with through the management of information and communication and be reduced by taking appropriate measures.

This is especially relevant for cross-organizational information and communication relationships. The underlying process, however, gives rise to a twofold problem. The first is that there are certain communication problems that emerge as a result of geographic distance and time differences and/or technical incompatibility. Furthermore, there are the problems associated with the management of information across organizational boundaries. This means that systems need to be developed that not only cater to a targeted enterprise-oriented management, but that require the coordination of multiple managerial interests. Accordingly, there has to be a general reduction in cross-organizational responsibilities regarding system development, fewer complex agreement mechanisms should be developed, and there should be less tolerance of single-minded and opportunistic behavior.

It is impossible to know to what extent, compared to traditional organizations, the organizational use of modularization concepts, virtual organization structures, and symbiotic arrangements increase problems. The implementation of modern information and communication technology (i.e. electronic archiving systems and document management, databanks, and artificial intelligence systems; see also chapter 4) cannot fully penetrate the human barriers of rationality and information processing capacity, but can come close.

Many problems involving the information behavior of employees can be addressed through the implementation of information and communication technology (ICT), for example, shared databanks or new possibilities to access information that was previously difficult to obtain due to the distances to the information source. Besides and together with ICT, problems with information processing can, in many cases, be overcome through the creation of an organizational environment that is conducive to human communication. For instance, even the best ICT cannot solve the lack of information sharing in the prisoner's dilemma situation, but by adding information-sharing requirements to long-term contracts and by means of cooperation based on mutual trust, it can be overcome. Additionally, organizational regulations can create positive incentive structures for sufficient information gathering and the efficient use of information (i.e. budget regulations regarding information gathering).

In contrast to traditional, highly integrated organizations, the above problems regarding communication behavior and understanding can intensify or even increase in symbiotic organizational forms or telecooperative structures (see chapters 6 and 8), since larger distances have to be overcome. Distances between organizations continue to increase. Consequently, the amount of transmission errors on the syntactic, semantic, and particularly the pragmatic level of communication, as well as obstructions in human communication exchanges due to the difficulty in determining relational aspects will increase. Greater distances increase dependency on the reliable transfer of electronic information. Consequently, the transfer of knowledge and the development of trust also become more difficult.

This leads to the conclusion that the efficiency advantages of organizational frameworks have to compensate for these looming communicative disadvantages or, where possible, have to deal with them by purposively implementing modern information and communication technology and appropriate incentive systems. Conversely, the modularization of an organization (see chapter 5) helps to reduce communication problems when tasks that have previously been carried out in separate and spatially dispersed organizations are combined into organizational sub-units that can act independently.

The ideas discussed in this chapter will be expanded on in the following chapters and combined with other theoretical approaches. This will help to create an overview of what the driving factors of decentralization are, how organizational boundaries are restructured or dissolved, what role information and communication technology plays in this process, and how the newly formed organizational framework created by this change can be managed. It is essential that organizations and their information and communication technologies complement one another; organizations can then practice new forms of coordination that will not threaten the internal harmony of newly developed structures.

*Chapter 4*

# The Potential of Information and Communication Technology for Corporate Development

## 4.1 Benefits and Adoption Levels of Technology

New information and communication technologies (ICT) harbor novel potentials for our way of life, the development of society, for the future of the industrial democracy, and for new and innovative organization structures. Nevertheless, assessments of such technical potentials and predictions of technology utilization are rarely confirmed by subsequent development, and often they are just plain wrong.

When Johann Philipp Reis presented his telephone prototype in 1861 or Alexander Graham Bell transmitted his famous line, "Watson, come here; I want you." to his assistant Thomas Watson in 1876, the exact utility of this medium was not at all clear. At best, modest success was expected. At the turn of the 19th century, the telephone was therefore used, for example, to transmit operas and concert events. Not until 1919 did the number of telephone connections exceed a million subscribers. In 1994 there were more than 600 million landline connections worldwide and the way the phone was utilized had changed as radically as the perception of time and space had (Becker 1995; Sterling 1995; Flichey 1994). Meanwhile, cell phone connections far exceed landline connections. In 2006, there were more than 2.7 billion mobile phones in use ("2.5 billion …," 2006). China Telecom alone is adding more than four million subscribers a month or close to two every second (Cyran/Hutchinson 2007). The historical development of the phone is by no means an isolated case as far as the failure to predict potential and realization is concerned: "I think there is a world market for maybe five computers," predicted Thomas Watson, the president and founder of IBM in 1943. Likewise, the graphic user interface, without which no operating system can function today, was regarded as an interesting gimmick and its potential underestimated.

In the more recent past, misjudgments with regard to the information and communication technology domain have been quite common. These incorrect forecasts are mainly due to people's tendency to make predictions based on linear and monotone extrapolation of actual development trends. In doing so, they often underestimate future developments and misjudge these developments' potential direction and rate of change (e.g., Dörner 1989). Keeping these restrictions in mind, the following overview presents a few basic potentials of information and communication technology.

Due to the number and variety of technical possibilities, it seems to make little sense to deduce universally concrete recommendations for the efficient deployment of information and communication technology. Strategic considerations make it far more imperative to formulate information and communication technology requirements. This top-down philosophy is well illustrated by the three-level model of information management. This model is presented below and used in the following sections.

## The Three-Level Model of Information Management

The task of information management is the effective (goal-oriented) and efficient (economic) deployment of information in the firm. This can be accomplished on three differing but connected levels (Wollnik 1988; Picot/Reichwald 1991; Wigand/Picot/Reichwald 1997).

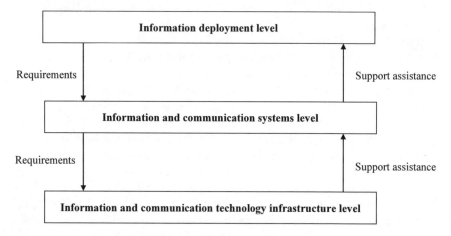

**Fig. 4.1.**    The three-level model of information management (based on Wollnik 1988)

**The information deployment level:** On this level, all information demand and supply is planned, organized, and controlled in respect of all essential organizational purposes (internal and external). The management of information deployment is the firm leadership's specific task. Ultimately, this task concerns the setting of priorities regarding the planning and controlling of information as well as the documentation required, all of which need to be systematically made accessible. This level defines the requirements of and involves the support services from the information and communication systems level.

**The information and communication systems level:** Information and communication systems are the synchronized arrangements of resource-based, organizational, and technical elements that meet the need for information. This includes, for example, standardized accounting systems, production planning and controlling systems, as well as enterprise-specific product, and customer information systems. It is the role of the information and communication systems management to determine the structure of these systems by combining their elements appropriately. These efforts need to take the demands and requirements established in the first level into consideration. Simultaneously, this second level defines the requirements of and involves support services from the third level.

**The information and communication technology infrastructure level:** At first, the technology infrastructure's components may be regarded as benefit-neutral or benefit-free service providers (Wollnik 1988), i.e. their benefit for the organization only lies in the goal-directed combination of single infrastructure components and their deployment in a task accomplishment context. Infrastructure-related decisions include decisions pertaining to computer configurations, system architecture, and network solutions.

## 4.2 Information and Communication Technology Development Trends

The levels of the information deployment of information and communication technology systems and infrastructures are influenced by fundamental development trends that we will address next. We present a rough differentiation between overlapping and application-related trends.

### 4.2.1 Overlapping Trends

#### 4.2.1.1 Increase in Capacity and Performance

Technology's most notable potential for enterprise development is based on the increased performance capacity of computers and networks. This is especially evident with regard to the processing and transmission speeds and storage capacity of

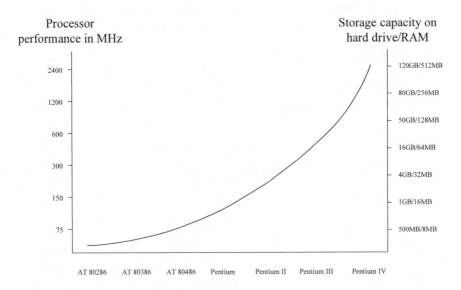

**Fig. 4.2.**    The development of microcomputer processor speed and storage capacity

the various storage media. Closely linked to these developments is the increased performance of the software running on these platforms, which is conveyed as functionality, robustness or user friendliness. The continuing explosive increase in information and communication technology's capacity is the catalyst for an entire range of additional potential developments, some of which will be addressed in the subsequent chapters. Figure 4.2 reveals the exponential development of technical aspects as exemplified by PC processor speeds and storage capacity expansion.

**Increase in Computer Architecture Performance**

The shortcomings of the traditional "von Neumann architecture" within computer architecture disappeared long ago (Hennessy/Patterson 1994). This architecture comprised a program-controlled computer whose instructions and data were stored in a single memory. At that time, these were revolutionary ideas that meant that the construction was program-independent because the program instructions were stored in its memory. This revolutionary development offered great flexibility compared to the hard-wired architecture. Bus architecture – an expansion and conversion of the von Neumann concept – connected the main memory to other specialized components such as the central processing unit (CPU), as well as to input and output components by means of a negotiation component (the bus) for the first time. The bus plays a very important role in this concept, as it is an open-ended transmission line that connects all competing components on an equal footing. This architecture can be compared to a normal comb whose teeth represent connections to bus participants – the bus structure therefore differs from a star or ring-like architectural concept. In the course of technological development, the capacity limitations of the pure von Neumann architecture were quickly recognized due to its inherent and technical barriers to miniaturization. As the only connection between the computer components, the bus proved to be a bottleneck with regard to processing speed. Consequently, this led to new, innovative computer architectures (Hwang/Briggs 1985; Bode 1990). Superscalar, vector, and massive parallel computers, which exceed conventional processor performance multiple times, fall into this category.

Aside from performance increase through fundamental architectural changes, the computing performance of the traditional components of the "von Neumann computers" also increased rapidly due to newly developed technologies in their design and manufacture. These included RISC technologies, increased clock rates, intelligent pipelining, and increased bus width. In 1965 Gordon Moore, an Intel co-founder, ascertained that the capacity of integrated circuits doubles every 18 months (Moore's Law). Experts estimate that this rule of thumb will be valid for the next decade.

**Increase in Computer Network Performance**

When considering downsizing strategies, it is no longer sufficient to merely examine individual computer hardware to assess their system performance. With the migration from centralized data processing on mainframe computers to distributed processing on networked workstations, the need for network performance matching that of mainframes became essential. Fiber optic cable and new transmission methods have increased throughput and capacity while decreasing error rate. In the area of local networks, the industry utilizes current state-of-the-art technology such as Fiber Distributed Data Interface (FDDI) and Fast Ethernet (IEEE 802.3u) at 100 Mbit/s, or Gigabit Ethernet (IEEE 802.2ae, 2002) at up to 10 Gbit/s. In comparison, traditional Ethernet functions in the range of 10 Mbit/s. At present, network technology performance doubles in bandwidth every six to eight months. This is much faster than computing system performance increases.

Besides transmission capacity, the type of switching is also important for the performance capacity of a network. Here, two basic types of communication connections can be distinguished. Circuit switching allows the synchronization of the sender and receiver through a line that is exclusively available for the duration of the connection (e.g., the phone). Another type of connection is packet switching. This is the partitioning of the data into small blocks, called packets, which are then transmitted from the sender to the receiver. The connections for each individual packet's transmission are configured step by step from one node to the next. The next network node has to be determined at each point of the transmission path, which means that the entire transmission is usually subject to a degree of uncertainty. The advantage of circuit switching lies in its higher transmission success rate, whereas the packet switching versions' strong points are their robustness and better utilization of the available bandwidth. If a network node fails or drops out in a packet-switched network, the data packets can immediately be diverted via available nodes to an alternative transmission route.

There are several types of networks. A local area network (LAN) is characterized by its limited extent of only a few miles and its high transmission rate. The number of connections is limited, usually no more than a few hundred stations (e.g., within a firm). By connecting several LANs via network interconnections, a larger number of network connections become possible. LAN or W-LAN operators have many choices regarding their network's premise and they alone are responsible for the network. Different types of cable and radio links can be used as transmission media. Depending on the transmission medium, the transmission rate ranges from 1 Mbit/s up to several Gbit/s. A metropolitan area network (MAN) is the evolution of local networks and supports increased communication needs within a high-density area. This network's transmission rate lies between 100Mbit/s and 1 Gbit/s and fiber optic cable is generally utilized. These networks may be administered publicly or privately. A wide area network (WAN) connects different geographic regions, sometimes spanning countries. Network operators are usually private or public telecommunication companies. The term global area network (GAN) is also used for globe-spanning networks with high transmission rates such as the satellite business system (SBS). There is no precise WAN demarcation; therefore, the largest interconnection of networks in the world, the Internet, is formally described as a WAN.

The demand for increased bandwidth has become increasingly important, especially with regard to WANs. The large number of simultaneous users worldwide has led to a large volume of data transmissions that need to be transmitted quickly.

The underlying architecture that connects cities and countries resembles that of traditional road traffic: Via a dedicated main traffic route – the data highway – important nodes are connected worldwide. Similar to highway on and off ramps, entry and access to this information highway are only possible at certain locations. At present, the only methods employed for the realization of long-distance transmission networks are frame relay, DQDB, and ATM, each of which offers different levels of technological development:

**Frame relay** is a widely used technology but due to its narrow bandwidth, it is nevertheless not optimally suitable for a fast information highway. It is an optimized, packet-switching technology with transmission speeds of up to 44 Mbit/s.

**Distributed queue dual bus** (DQDB) technology has two buses, each of which works only in one direction, thus offering much better performance. Just like on a conveyer belt, empty and / or filled cells are transmitted via these buses, reaching their destinations with speeds of up to 140 Mbit/s.

**Asynchronous transfer mode** (ATM) offers speeds ranging between 25 and 622 Mbit/s, with future technological advancements promising speeds up to 2.5 Gbit/s. This technology is based on broadband-based ISDN networks and utilizes a fixed packet size. Through the configuration of a virtual channel, which is a virtual

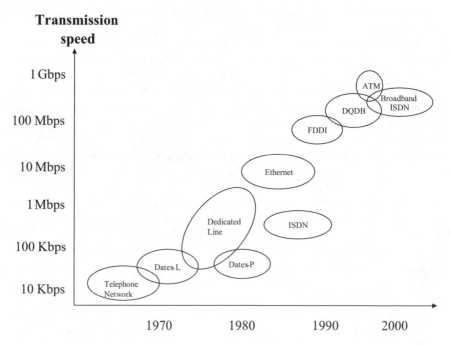

**Fig. 4.3.**    Development of communication technologies (updated and based on Geihs 1995, p. 4)

connection between the sender and receiver, a fixed path is created by means of which user information can be sent in very small, subdivided packets. Given that decisions regarding the packets' route are made beforehand, this reduces the efforts required to check and correctly distribute the individual packets considerably as well as simplifying the allocation of costs. ATM switches – network access components that no longer require network participants to execute access algorithms – are responsible for ATM technology's high speed. The sender merely submits the individual data packets at the ATM switch and not, as many local networks require, together with other network participants, which would require the transmission to be coordinated.

Figure 4.3 offers an overview of some key communication technologies' transmission speeds and dates of origin. One should note that the ordinate is based on logarithmic scaling, which emphasizes the specific increase in the transmission speeds of the corresponding technologies.

**Miniaturization**

Miniaturization has brought a remarkable reduction in the size and weight of hardware components with a simultaneous performance improvement. The manufacture of ever-smaller integrated circuits due to increased integration density – i.e. the quantity of switching elements per surface area on a chip – is increasingly approaching the limits of natural boundaries through, for example, heat development, physical size limits, and other factors. The size of a printer is, for example, limited to the size of the paper and a notebook keyboard's size to the size of human fingers. A phone has to cover the distance between the ear and the mouth and must offer sufficient space for a keypad. The current super-thin notebooks achieve their minimal size and weight not only through component miniaturization, but also by economizing on the configuration. Consequently, many peripheral devices and interfaces are no longer an internal component of these devices, but are external accessories.

While serviceability and other external constraint factors have become manageable through, for example, folding keyboards and extensible print head control, considerable heat development due to highly integrated circuits poses a yet greater challenge. Given the current state of knowledge, the problem of overheating microprocessors is best addressed by a reduction in integration density. By utilizing a reduced processor instruction set, the number of required integrated circuits is reduced. By linking this hardware technology with an optimizing compiler, it is thus possible to achieve an increase in performance while keeping the size of hardware components the same. This concept is used in RISC (reduced instruction set computers) architectures.

Parallel to processor-level miniaturization efforts, entire component group miniaturization offers another potential. Accordingly, it has become possible to manufacture a Bluetooth interface and a hard drive PMCIA card (or PC card) as small as a matchbox. This technology, used in laptops and notebooks, is based on the standardization of insertion cards that comply with the Personal Computer

Memory Card International Association's (PCMCIA) specifications. The interface logic recognizes each card's function individually, making it possible to exchange these cards.

### 4.2.1.2   Cost Development

On the whole, the costs of electronic information processing have decreased by a factor of more than 100,000 during the last 25 years. In 1975, for example, the cost of information processing was $100 per instruction and processing second, which was reduced to less than $0.001 in 1999. Similarly, the $300 that a three-minute telephone conversation between New York and London cost in 1930 shrank to less than a dollar in 1999. These cost reductions continue: It is expected that within the next few years, for example, the telecommunications industry's bandwidth will increase four-fold every two years, decreasing costs simultaneously. These developments influence scarcity ratios negatively, leading to a massive utilization of communication and information technology in nearly all application fields. They also specifically enable automation and support via communication and information technologies in application areas that were previously inconceivable. This leads to massive productivity increases, higher innovation rates, and shorter product life cycles. Consequently, firms face completely new demands: Through matching pricing strategies, they are forced to either take advantage of early adopters before new, more powerful successor products appear, or to arrange the rapid distribution of products and services as quickly as possible to exploit network effects (see chapter 2). In this context, apart from traditional absorption and penetration strategies, typical pricing strategies are the follow-the-free strategy (see chapter 2), as well as the shareware price model.

### 4.2.1.3   Internet and Globalization

An additional aspect of the development of information and communication technology infrastructures addresses their distribution beyond national boundaries, i.e. their globalization. The goal is to provide information and technology developments, as well as to develop international standards worldwide. This becomes very clear in the light of Internet developments.

#### Globalization of Voice Transmission

GSM (global system for mobile communications) was developed in 1982 as a digital cell phone network. In the meantime, GSM has become the effective standard in Europe and Asia and covers about 130 countries. The GSM-based personal communication network (PCN), which was created in 1991 under the digital cellular system 1800 (DCS 1800) label, is a worldwide communication concept. The technology faces very challenging demands regarding the best possible reduction in waiting times and delays in telephony transmissions worldwide. The use of satellites as a transmission path is therefore essential.

**Globalization of Data Transmissions: Internet**

The Internet has increasingly become the focus of a global information infrastructure vision of the worldwide transmission of data. Its role as a common, worldwide data network is increasingly being consolidated. Since its commercialization, the "network of networks" has been growing exorbitantly. In November 2007, there were about 1,244 billion Internet users worldwide in over 100 countries (Internet Usage Statistics, 2007). Figure 4.4 provides a breakdown of this number per world region.

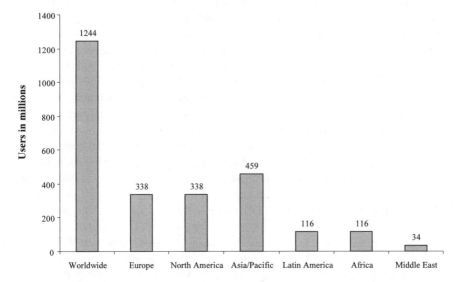

**Fig. 4.4.**    Worldwide Internet users in November 2007 (Internet Usage Statistics 2007)

Due to its original military objectives, the Internet was first conceived as a network within which a fully decentralized administration is possible. It has no central coordinating authority, nor a place that controls the various services. However, organizations have surfaced that give trend-setting advice and are generally viewed as standard-setting organizations. Among these are the Internet Engineering Task Force (IETF) for the Internet in general and the World Wide Web Consortium (W3C) for the World Wide Web and related technologies.

The basis of communication on the Internet is the transmission control protocol / Internet protocol (TCP/IP). As with the ISO / OSI standard, a layered structure is provided; there is, however, nothing with which the individual layers can be directly compared. The Internet's increasing popularity is essentially based on TCP/IP features and services. In the meantime, a multitude of services and applications have become available. Due to the Internet's open character, new services can be implemented in a decentralized way at any time. Figure 4.5 offers an overview of the most important services on the Internet.

| Basic systems | Bulletin board systems | Directory systems | Data systems | Information search systems |
|---|---|---|---|---|
| • Telnet<br>• Ftp<br>• Email<br>• Http | • Listserv<br>• Mailing lists<br>• News | • Finger<br>• Whois<br>• X.500<br>• Netfind | • Alex<br>• Prospero | • Hytelnet<br>• Archie<br>• Gopher<br>• Wais<br>• World wide web |

**Fig. 4.5.**    Classification of Internet services (based on Scheller et al. 1994, p. 2)

Telnet permits interactive access to remote computers. FTP is the file transfer protocol service for the transmission of data between two computer systems. The transmission of text (including inserted files) occurs by means of e-mail. The World Wide Web (WWW), originally developed at CERN (the European Organization for Nuclear Research), is based on a client / server architecture. A distant server keeps information ready in its data pool and a local client prepares this information for presentation on the monitor by means of browsers. Information and documents on the Web are obtained by means of a unique address called the uniform resource locator (URL). The transmission of multimedia data is based on the hypertext transfer protocol (HTTP). An important and much discussed aspect of the Internet is the protection of transmitted data against unauthorized access and manipulation. On the Internet, the relevant methods are primarily based on the encryption of information. At the protocol level, these methods include, for example, the secure socket layer (SSL) and the secure HTTP (S-HTTP), while at the data level, we find procedures such as a digital signature (electronic signature) and RSA (encryption), as well as self-made solutions such as those used by many banks to safeguard authenticity and / or access. At present, however, consumers make little use of digital signatures. They are mainly used by firms to certify the authenticity of program parts embedded on their websites (e.g., Java applets or ActiveX controls). The increasing importance of the safety of electronic data transmissions on public networks, especially the Internet, has also been recognized by the legislature in order to create a uniform legal basis for electronic transactions.

There are few trust centers, i.e. institutions that issue digital keys and chip cards and guarantee their authenticity. Many problems still need to be addressed, mainly of a technical nature, for example, questions regarding the enormous security requirements that trust centers have to fulfill, before uniform and full-fledged legal authorization will be possible. Individual physical characteristics such as fingerprints or the retina, which offer many more variables, present user-friendly and highly secure procedures to instantaneously identifying someone.

Internet philosophy and technology are being increasingly used within firms. These intranets, as they are called, serve as a type of corporate network for internal information flow. This information is only available within the firm. Once the information network transcends the firm, an extranet has been established. An extranet is characterized by its enterprise-spanning technical network of closely cooperating value-adding partners. Furthermore, extranets, together with network structures (see chapter 6) and a transmission medium for EDI, play an important role. The technical foundation of both concepts is – as is the Internet's – the TCP/IP protocol pair as well as Internet services. In contrast to the Internet, access to intranets and extranets is only available to a limited set of users. Firewalls screen intranets and extranets from the Internet, thus providing protection from unauthorized use. It is consequently possible to take advantage of the Internet benefits without having to deal with its disadvantages (mainly regarding security). The various areas of a wide-range extranet generally utilize the Internet as a link. This utilization of a public network as a means to transport data makes a considerable reduction in costs possible compared to traditional proprietary networks, because only the connection costs (provider fees) have to be covered, while the construction and maintenance costs of an own network do not apply.

### 4.2.1.4   *"Natural" User Guidance*

The user-friendliness of information technology is still improving. Forms of use that delay implementation or that make implementation unnecessarily complicated inhibit multifaceted technological systems from achieving their full user potential. The ease, with which complex software can be used, can be regarded from different viewpoints.

One viewpoint is intuitive use: The user should be able to use a system as efficiently as possible without having to expend much effort on learning (by studying handbooks, manuals, training sessions or experimenting). Here, the graphical user interface (GUI) is important, as the recognition of the standardization of recurring control elements and the use of understandable icons lead to effortless use and, thus, higher productivity (Möslein 2000). The least number of movements (mouse movement, activation of icons, dragging and dropping of objects) should therefore be used to perform the most frequent actions. Contextual help functions that answer the user's targeted questions regarding the user interface elements, help functions that allow natural language queries, as well as quick help features (e.g., "tool tips"), etc. allow user questions to be answered quickly and directly without major search efforts. Object orientation, which will be described in more detail later, is another user interface that allows intuitive and productive use. The user manipulates objects (e.g., documents) with the system, which offers suitable actions for context-sensitive processing. This enables uniform, integrated user interfaces in which a complex of applications functionalities that had in the past been separate – often as individual and separate programs – fuse with one another so that only objects (office documents such as text, databases, presentations, tables, but also instructions, invoices or orders) are manipulated in a context-dependent way. The "how" and perhaps the "where" are no longer the focus. The "what" is.

Another view is the "natural" user input. Traditional input devices, such as the keyboard to input numbers and / or text and the mouse to manipulate graphical user interfaces, will remain important. Appropriate software is becoming increasingly available for newer input forms, such as voice recognition to input text and instructions verbally, which will be an integral component of many operating systems in the future. There is also an increase in touch screens use. By allowing the use of words and gestures, these devices allow people to use their natural forms of expression and communication. Consequently, information systems are seamlessly integrated into the user's daily environment and productivity is increased through the acceleration of work processes in comparison with traditional input methods. Although dictated text still needs to be entered via a keyboard at present, voice recognition systems may make this step redundant in the future. Another example of voice recognition input is that by merely mentioning the names of business partners, they can be automatically dialed as the telecommunication system is linked to a database of names. The user therefore no longer needs to search for a number in a telephone database or needs to enter it.

Other forms of "natural" interaction between man and machine will increasingly allow people to move naturally within an information and communication systems environment. A stylus can already be used as an input device on a touch-sensitive surface and complements input via mouse and keyboard. Systems that recognize people's line of sight are already utilized to control special military systems, while various research and development projects are addressing this application's use in civilian offices. It should therefore be broadly utilized within the next few years. Three-dimensional, interactive work areas are likewise being researched. Nevertheless, current computing systems are not as yet powerful enough for such applications.

In this context, the "roomware" concept is also interesting: Parts of office and building furniture such as desks, shelves, doors, and walls become interactive, computer-augmented and networked objects; real environments and the virtual information space merge. Research into demonstrations, display, input, and communication systems is in various stages of development, especially with regard to supporting cooperative work by means of, for example, project and conference rooms' furnishings. Examples of these developments are various "cooperative landscapes": "DynaWall," a touch-sensitive display wall ("electronic wallpaper") is several feet high and wide, while "InteracTable" is a networked projection table with a touch-sensitive surface that allows the displayed objects to be manipulated with a finger or pen and information to be input via voice and / or pen. Large automobile manufacturers and advertising agencies' research and development units are very interested in these developments. Some of this information technology is already used by the Metro Group, Europe's largest retailer, in its Future Store, a futuristic grocery store in Rheinberg, Germany that is open to the public (see: http://www.metrogroup. de/servlet/PB/menu/1009740_l2/index.html).

The new forms of user interactions by means of "roomware" are closely associated with the intelligent workplace. On entering the room, employees are identified by means of, for example, an active badge or sensors on the door-handle, the specific work context is loaded, and the heating and air flow adjusted to the specific person's preferences. The future work place is sometimes envisaged as location-independent, i.e. the employee becomes a nomadic worker: Personal work data can be transparently transferred between the home and different offices, conference rooms, etc. Office equipment and fittings such as lights and heaters are also networked and report their status, making preventative maintenance possible. The goal of the intelligent workplace is not only to enable new forms of cooperation, but also to improve employees' quality of life and to reduce the use of energy. Besides individualizing the environment by recognizing the user, a building management system that attempts to adjust environmental variables such as airflow, lighting, humidity and heating according to the prevailing weather conditions is also part of this development.

### 4.2.1.5   Object Orientation

Object orientation has been investigated for many years. This approach does not portray a problem world – which could be, for example, schedule management or an enterprise – according to traditional functional procedures, but is based on the components (objects) from which this world is constructed. The object orientation concept was created by the inventors of the programming language SIMULA (Dahl / Myrhaug / Nygaard 1970) and was later integrated into the programming language Smalltalk (Goldberg / Robson 1989). From this perspective, the separation between data and function has disappeared and has been replaced by structuring, which occurs by means of module boundaries. The fundamental building blocks are no longer procedures and data, but conditions, activities, and communication. Typical objects that can be modeled within an enterprise are, for example, human resources administration, individual workers, and departments. Detailed information on the concepts of object orientation and the object modeling of problem areas can be found in Meyer (1990), Graham (2000) and Coad / Yourdan (1991).

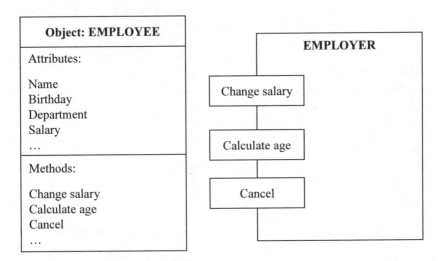

**Fig. 4.6.**   Object structure (Graham 2000)

Within an object orientation framework, the entire modeled world is totally comprised of equal objects that fundamentally follow the same set of rules (although individual objects may behave differently). These objects are comprised of attributes and behaviors (routines, methods); collectively they are called features or members. They communicate with one another via messages when the sender requests the receiver to process a certain task. The receiving object carries out the requested activity after it has been received. After the activity's execution, the receiving object reports the success or result of its efforts, for example, a calculation, to the sending object. The interfaces of the individual objects are precisely defined, i.e. which messages an object is allowed and by whom these may be sent are determined exactly. This concept is called encapsulation (see figure 4.5 for the design and visible interface of an example object of a class called "employee"). Furthermore, all objects are self-dependent, i.e. only they determine how they handle a request via a message, as long as the result corresponds to the specification. No other object, except they themselves, may change their status. Moreover, during the program's actual run-time, objects meet their assignments dynamically (e.g., concretely allocating values to characteristics).

All similar objects (e.g., employees) are combined into one class scheme, which describes the full configuration of all the dependents of that class's essential characteristics and behavior. Classes may therefore inherit from other classes, i.e. a class (subclasses) can take other classes' (upper classes) features (and possibly rename or redefine these features) and may add their own, additional features. These inheritance relationships are labeled specializations. A class 'employee' could, for example, inherit from a class 'person.' During the programming, only the classes are described and not the objects used during the program's actual run-time. During the running of the program, concrete objects are instantiated from the class descriptions; these objects communicate with one another, react to messages and then process and solve the posed problem during this interaction.

The advantages of the object-oriented approach are the structuredness of object-oriented modeling of the problem world. This results in software that is highly flexible and comprehensible and that can be easily expanded, scaled, and changed as a result of its modular approach – qualities that are indispensable for ever more complex modern systems. Through the modular approach, individual components (classes) can be reused in a multitude of different scenarios and applications, leading to time and cost savings in new software development. One perspective of critical importance is the demand for reliable, as well as correct and robust software. Here, the design by contract theory (Mandrioli / Meyer 1992) is applicable. According to this theory, software creation is based on the result of precisely documented contractual agreements between clients (requests) and suppliers (routines) that rely on mutual commitments and explicit assurances. The software thus utilizes messages, encapsulation, inheritance, and additional characteristics to implement object orientation. When these ideas are consistently followed and applied, the created software has a high degree of reliability.

To date there have been few programming languages capable of translating the concepts of object orientation. Eiffel is an example of such a language (Mayer 1992).

Currently, many widely used programming languages such as C++ or Java incorporate object oriented characteristics, although their procedural origins are still apparent. In the light of their advantages, programming languages that are strongly object oriented may enjoy increased acceptance in the future. Their current disadvantages, such as higher resource needs, memory, and computing power, should be of lesser importance over time. The ideas of object orientation, originally developed at the programming language level, are increasingly used in the analysis of software project problems (see sections 4.4.5 and 4.4.6). They are also increasingly used in the analysis of enterprise and organization structures (e.g., the concept of business / objects, see also chapter 10).

### 4.2.1.6 Convergence

Over the past few years, a development has taken place that is a prerequisite for the formation of new economic structures within the "Internet" marketplace and which is best described as convergence. "Convergence describes ... the evolutionary process of the coalescence of the originally largely independent media, telecommunication and information technology industries. It denotes the convergence of the technologies, as well as the linking of their value-added chains and the coalescence of the markets as a whole" (Zerdick / Picot / Schrape et al. 2001, p. 140). The term convergence largely means coalescence at a specific point, merging, agreement, and uniting for a common goal. Digitalization technology, which enables the transmission of multifaceted contents via the same medium, makes this possible. The rapid growth in computer performance, the drastic decrease in computing and storage capacity costs, the considerable progress made in transmission technologies, the deregulation of the telecommunication markets, as well as the market participants' creativity and imagination have allowed digitalization technology to develop quickly (Yoffie 1997). One of the first companies to propagate digital convergence was NEC Corporation, which had already had a banner with the slogan "C&C" (Computers and Communications) in 1977 (Yoffie 1997).

Greenstein and Klemma (1997, pp. 203 ff.) distinguish two ways in which the boundaries between the markets for information and telecommunication technology blur. On the one hand there is convergence into substitutes, which indicates the functional coalescence of once different products leading to their exchangeability and, on the other hand, the convergence into complements, which describes the functional extension of several products and / or their increasing interplay, with their combined use offering new possibilities not found in their separate use.

Earlier, the three media, telecommunications and information technology industries, had already had common interests and mutual complements. More recently, they have increasingly merged and their formerly separated vertical value chains have merged into a new multimedia market with several horizontal sections (Collis / Bane / Bradley 1997; Zerdick / Picot / Schrape et al. 2001). The multimedia market includes the integrated convergence of media, telecommunications and in

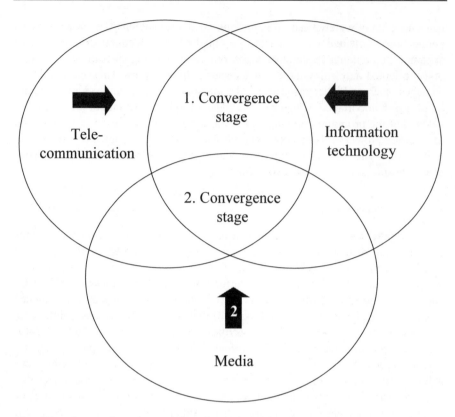

**Fig. 4.7.**    Stages of convergence (based on Adstead / McGarvey 1997, p. 10)

formation, and communication technology tasks and benefits. This process is comprised of two stages (Zerdick / Picot / Schrape et al. 2003) that are schematically depicted in figure 4.7.

In the first stage, the added value between the telecommunication and information technology industries fuses. Electronic information processing systems utilize the telecommunication sector's features and technologies to exchange data. The Internet expansion since 1993, which has seen the annexation of many formerly separate networks, has drastically accelerated this process. The currently occurring second convergence stage is characterized by the media, telecommunication, and information technology sectors' increasing convergence, resulting in growing and more important overlapping areas.

Convergence has led to new competitive relationships arising between enterprises that were formerly active in separate markets. Media contents are no longer exclusively disseminated via broadcast networks, such as radio, cable or satellite, but increasingly via telephone and computer networks. Conversely, new technologies enable communication services to be affected via broadcast networks. Information that was previously only available to the consumer at certain transmission times and reception areas is now available without temporal or geographic constraints. Terminals such as televisions sets, phones, and computers, which were previously limited to only one sector (i.e. media, telecommunication, and information technology), increasingly have functionalities that cover several of the three sectors. Consequently, television sets may, for example, be used as a display device for Internet content, computers for telephony or for the display of radio content. Transmissions may occur either via traditional channels or via computer networks. Likewise, it is possible to receive and depict Internet information on a mobile phone.

Newer content distribution forms such as blogs and specialized services like Brightcove Inc., Roo Group Inc., and Blinkx make the widespread distribution of content possible. The underlying technology makes it easy for any producer, including home-movie aficionados and television networks, to distribute their videos to many websites. All three parties – the video producer, the site that displays the video, and Brightcove, the middleman – can share revenue from the resulting advertisements or sales. At the time of writing, Brightcove has a sales staff of two who sell 15 and 30-second commercials that are shown prior to many videos wherever they are played. The video producer usually receives the largest portion of any advertising revenue, but Brightcove shares a portion with the hosting site and keeps a portion for itself. Consequently, blog operators can become a small multimedia or cable company. This media model undoubtedly poses a considerable challenge to the media industry, while simultaneously offering innovators and entrepreneurs an opportunity. Previously, film, TV, and video material producers were dependent on other big companies such as the broadcast networks, cable systems, etc. to deliver their product to an audience. Today, these new forms of distribution allow anyone to be a producer with literally an endless number of potential outlets.

These changes require new strategies adapted to the multimedia market's conditions (e.g., based on the CHESS principle, see Yoffie 1997). It is therefore understandable that certain traditional firms have problems staying afloat in this changing market, whereas small, young firms often achieve surprising results. The emerging uniform communication infrastructures and services, as well as the increasing availability of information also lead to economic change potentials in other sectors of the economy such as financial services and trade. Examples of such potentials are virtual marketplaces and other e-commerce applications (see chapter 7, as well as Zerdick / Picot / Schrape et al. 2001).

### 4.2.1.7 Virtualization

Within the technology development framework, a trend can be observed in all market and organization changes – virtualization (see also section 4.4.1, as well as chapters 8 and 10).

Virtual does not mean actual, apparent or real (Scholz 1994; 1997). Virtuality does not exist as such: Virtuality always refers to an object. Although it is non-existent, a virtual object has full functionality and may be treated from the outside as if it were real. The term was originally used in a technical context in expressions such as virtual memory or virtual machine. Today, we link virtuality with reference objects such as products, enterprises, and markets. In the meantime, there are many definitions and systematizations that are differentiated with regard to their choice of reference object and type of differentiation (Picot/Neuburger 1997a; Wigand/Imamura 1997).

From a customer's point of view, it is possible to envision a "virtual service network": Via, for example, the Internet, customers compile services that meet their requirements and promise the best solutions, thus creating a "virtual" total product.

From the enterprise's point of view, one can differentiate between a virtual product and a virtual division of labor. Product virtualization is a result of the information sphere's (e.g., the Internet) increasing shift in customer contact, distribution, and sales. Physical processes are increasingly being partially or fully substituted by virtual processes and this development is epitomized in the expression "from marketplace to market space" (Haeckel/Nolan 1993). Consequently, market structures are virtualized in developments such as electronic markets, teleshopping, and electronic commerce (see chapter 7). The potential of a virtual division of labor can be realized in the organization of economic value generation by utilizing alternating partners flexibly and regardless of existing limitations (Picot/Neuburger 1997a; Reichwald/Möslein 1996b). The virtual division of labor is comprised of several stages. Virtual co-workers are separated spatially and temporally and are integrated via telecommunication into business events (see chapter 8). Virtual teams bring internal and external team members together for a project's duration. Virtual enterprises are created from the problem and task-related integration of geographically dispersed organization units that participate in a specialized value-adding process (see chapter 8). This may involve both external and internal modules or organization units.

As a result of all of these developments – regardless of the specific underlying organization model (see section 4.4.1) – there is an increasing virtualization of market and enterprise structures. Organizational forms change and make different demands on the supporting information and communication systems than traditional markets and hierarchies do. System design and configuration (see section 4.4.4) have to incorporate these discernable organizational developments. System development has to address the challenge of suggesting ways in which these structural demands can be translated into suitable system architectures.

## 4.2.2  Applied Trends

### 4.2.2.1  Mobility

The development trend towards information and communication technology infrastructures is especially important with regard to the dissolution of organizational boundaries. This dissolution of boundaries refers to increasing mobility, i.e. the possibility to simply and conveniently change location (see Reichwald 2002). Currently, data can be transmitted via worldwide networks from nearly any location. Integrated solutions such as a briefcase equipped with a PC, printer, fax, and phone utilize this communication capability, which is in a sense a combination of mobile computing and mobile radio. Notebooks and PDAs are increasingly able to connect to data transmission networks such as Bluetooth, W-LAN, and GPRS. Developments in the mobile telephone sector are also characterized by increased miniaturization and the consequent price reductions.

In the US, the mobile phone service industry is concentrated in four large national carriers (AT&T, Verizon, Sprint/Nextel, and T-Mobile) that have dominated the industry since September 2005. This high degree of concentration is a relatively recent development. When the industry initially evolved, the US government issued two licenses to operate phone service per geographic market, which were issued to a large number of companies. The current consolidation occurred after a lengthy history of voluntary mergers and acquisitions. The US mobile telephone industry has therefore transitioned from the Federal Communications Commission's (FCC) dispersed industry to a concentrated industry as a result of voluntary acquisition and merging actions by wireless phone carriers.

The major US carriers use one of two network technologies, GSM (Groupe Spécial Mobile or Global System for Mobile Communications) or CDMA (Code Division Multiple Access). Most phones are designed for either one or the other, and each technology has its characteristic strengths. In general, GSM phones – used by AT&T and T-Mobile – provide more talk time on a battery charge, usually five hours and more. They also exchange photos and other data better with computers and other mobile devices without having to go through the wireless network. Many GSM phones with Bluetooth capability can wirelessly swap their address book with other phones, or beam photos directly to a printer or photo kiosk. Since GSM is more widely used across the world than CDMA, many phones sold in the US will also work in Europe and Asia. However, GSM phones do not have the analog backup required when the digital network is inaccessible, as in some rural areas.

CDMA phones, used by Alltel, Sprint, and Verizon, use higher-speed data networks and most provide analog backup. They are also more likely than GSM phones to have historically useful features, such as a standard 2.5 mm headset connector. Nextel, which merged with Sprint in 2005, uses a proprietary network technology that is incompatible with CDMA and GSM.

Cell phones have become a permanent part of the landscape. In 2006, there were more than 145 million subscribers, who spent an average of $47 a month on a local service. A small but steadily growing number of people use a cell phone as their only phone. Most major phone manufacturers and cellular service providers are promoting a new generation of equipment that allows users to do much more than merely make phone calls. An excellent example of these developments is Apple's iPhone.

Despite its popularity, cellular service has a reputation for problems: Dead zones where service is unavailable, calls that inexplicably end mid-conversation, inadequate capacity so that calls aren't connected, hard-to-fathom calling plans, and frequent errors in bills. Problems of this kind explain why as many as one third of all cell phone users maintain that they are ready to switch carriers.

### 4.2.2.2  Cooperation

Cooperation as an information and communication technology potential is particularly important in cooperative support and group work applications. The development of computer-supported, specialized task accomplishment started with the use of mainframe computers at the organization level. In the following years, desktop computers mostly provided the support that individuals required to carry out their tasks (Grudin 1991). According to Grudin, the first approaches to support cooperation by means of suitable hardware and software date back to 1984. Earlier, related efforts were called office automation, although information technology was not their main focus.

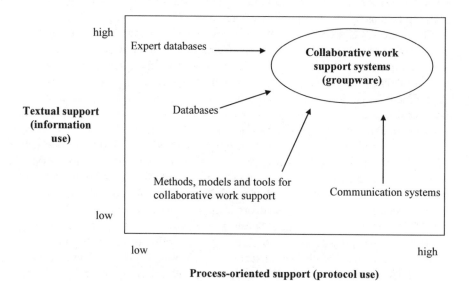

**Fig. 4.8.**    Contextual and process-oriented forms of support of cooperative task accomplishment (Picot / Reichwald 1991, p. 299)

A first differentiation can be made in the area of computer-supported group work by asking whether the information and communication technology support of group work influences the content of the cooperation or its operation (see figure 4.8), i.e. a differentiation is made between information support and process support (Picot / Reichwald 1991). Databases that are used in group work, for example, mainly serve as information support, while a telephone and most communication technologies usually support the process to which they are connected. Regardless of the type of support, computer supported cooperative work (CSCW), the generic term, denotes all partial aspects of computer-supported cooperative work (Borg-hoff / Schlicher 2000). Within the spectrum between pure information support and pure process support, we describe database and expert systems, group cooperative work systems, group decision support systems, as well as process control systems in the following sections.

### Database Systems

A database system, consisting of a database and the database management system (the software that manages it) is the basis for making relevant data available for individual as well as group work. To fit the multitude of available database systems into a common classification scheme, the American committee for standardization issues (ANSI / SPARC) developed a three-level architecture for the design of database system in 1975 (see ANSI / SPARC 1975, as well as figure 4.9). For the first time it was possible to distinguish between physical aspects – such as data storage, optimization and security, the user's requirements, and application systems – and the actual logical configuration of the database system. Moreover, these aspects could be independently designed, so that the database's conceptual (logical) model remained unchanged by modifications made in the layers above and below it.

The effects of this level-oriented architecture, as depicted in figure 4.9, can be illustrated by the following example: Two users, one in the Financial Planning Department, the other in Production call up stored company data via the database system. Both users only receive data for processing that are necessary for the execution of their respective tasks. The actual interaction with the users occurs at the database system's external level, the sub-schemata level, where the two users each

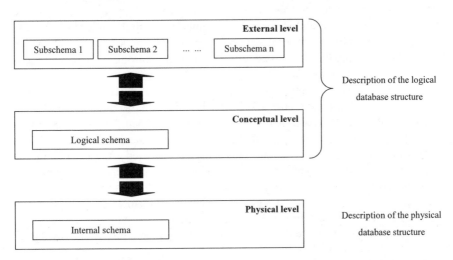

**Fig. 4.9.**    Three-level architecture of a database system (Picot / Reichwald 1991, p. 347)

see their specific view of the data. If a third user needs access to a subset of relevant data, this becomes possible without the levels below being modified. An increase in data volume may require additional database management features, such as the optimization of the data's physical storage by means of an index, which may be added at any time. This intervention on the internal (physical) level is possible without any adjustments to the other levels and occurs without the user noticing anything.

## Expert Systems

A stored knowledge base allows conclusions and inferences, thus generating new knowledge. An even higher level of information support can be achieved through an expert system. Similar to a database system, such an expert system allows information retrieval through access to a data quantity that the user can direct by means of queries. This knowledge base differs from a database in that it has rules that permit an intentional definition of the subject matter context. By representing knowledge as a number of rules in this special way, an expert system makes it possible to generate new information by extracting consequences and inferences.

In an expert system, interaction with the user not only includes the knowledge base but also the components inference mechanism and dialog control (Liebowitz 1988). The inference mechanism mainly serves to *prove* the user's query in respect of the knowledge base. The statement expressed in the query is then checked and verified for compatibility with knowledge stored in the knowledge base. Based on this line of thinking, it is thus possible to reveal a number of facts from the knowledge base. This occurs through the specification of free variables in the query, i.e. variables that are assigned values during the course of the inference processes and that are displayed on the computer screen via the dialog component. The dialog control is the interface with the user and is mostly interactive. In addition, an explanation component is available through which the user may retrace the expert system's decision and reasoning process and thus examine these processes critically.

The following is an example of an expert system: The knowledge base contains two facts, Jones is Miller's boss and Miller is Baker's boss. Simultaneously, the rule that if A is the boss of B and if B is the boss of C, then A is the boss of C is also stored in the knowledge base. At first glance, this may appear obvious, but in electronic processing these relationships must be specified. A user submits the query whether the employee Jim Jones is Mark Miller's superior. The submitted query reads: Jones is boss of Miller. Through the available information, facts, and rules in the knowledge base, the expert system then attempts to prove that this query is correct. By substituting the variables A, B and C with the names Jones, Miller, and Baker into the only available rule, the true condition can be deduced. The system's answer is: Yes.

The following query is submitted as a second question: Jones is the boss of A. During the course of *proving* this relationship, the free variable A is substituted with the value Miller, because the fact that Jones is Miller's boss is stored in the knowledge base. By applying the rule, the system will therefore find the value Baker. The computer screen will in fact display: Miller, Baker.

The above-described form of deriving specific statements from a general set of facts is known as deductive inference. An interesting expansion of this concept is statistical inference, which attributes probability values to the knowledge base, from which conclusions can then be derived by means of fuzzy knowledge. It is therefore possible, for example, to describe the fact that Jones is Miller's boss with an 80% probability. This possibility offers interesting perspectives with regard to the human ability to express (approximating) presumptions.

A total of three different expert system user modes can be distinguished, all of which are used interactively via the dialog control: The deduction of answers from questions (the user as client), the expansion of the system's knowledge base (the user as tutor), and the output of knowledge base facts as the basis of further human utilization (the user as student) (Michie 1980).

**Workgroup Systems**

As part of cooperation in process support and due to individual group members' temporal and geographical dispersal, we differentiate four different communication types (see figure 4.10, as well as figure 8.1) supported by groupware (DeSanctis / Gallupe 1985; Borghoff / Schlichter 2000; Krcmar 2002). In the following, we examine groupware systems and highlight the group decision support system (GDSS), joint editing and e-mail.

Group decision support systems (Maass 1991; Krcmar 2002) are an example of synchronous communication support in the same location. As a subclass of decision support systems (DSS), the focus of research by Keen and Scott Morton (1978), this system is able to support a group of decision makers in finding a solution to poorly structured problems through computer-supported methods such as brain-writing,

| Presence of participant | At the same time (synchronous) | At different times (asynchronous) |
|---|---|---|
| **In the same location** | • Comprehensive computer-supported session<br>• Computer-supported meeting moderation<br>• Group decision support system<br>• Presentation software | • Calendar management for groups<br>• Project management software<br>• Text filtering software |
| **In different locations** | • Audio and video conferences<br>• Screen sharing<br>• Spontaneous interaction through instant messaging within the computer network | • Electronic conferencing and bulletin boards, e-mail<br>• Tools with which to structure conversations<br>• Joint editing |

**Fig. 4.10.** Synchronous / asynchronous and distributed / not distributed communication (based on Krcmar 1992, p. 7)

determination of preferences or techniques for idea structuring. In order to create the best possible atmosphere for meetings and discussions, the conceptualization of such systems often also utilizes group dynamics aspects and ergonomic general conditions.

A distributed, asynchronous or synchronous work situation can be supported by joint editing during which various users revise the same document, possibly even simultaneously. When, however, only one person revises documents, which are thereafter shared with other individuals asynchronously, we speak of electronic mail or e-mail.

Video conferencing is a specific kind of computer-supported group work. This is a form of communication enabled by audio and video technology through synchronous telecommunication. This form of communication is the closest to having the advantages of classical face-to-face communication. The minimum bandwidth requirements are 64 Kbit/s, which is approximately equivalent to narrow-band ISDN. On the other hand, a multimedia conference via high-performance workstations has much higher demands with regard to bandwidth: Required transmission speeds of about 100 Mbit/s are not unusual.

## Workflow Systems

Workflow systems offer the highest form of process support for a group (see also chapter 5.4.3.3). In contrast to the above-mentioned workgroup systems that have cooperation (i.e. the commonality of the work to find a solution) as the main focus, workflow systems focus on the sequence of supported procedures. By using a process control system, various co-workers' activities can be coordinated temporally by integrating application programs and tools. The system automates the course of the process, i.e. the user is sequentially given the individual steps for execution. Since the execution of the individual tasks does not necessarily have to be carried out on the same computer, the separate processing of client/server environments lends itself well to this type of application.

Administrative demands on a workflow system are, for example, integrating text processing systems to generate documents, the possibility of determining the routing of documents, the simple regulation of proxy situations, etc. Functions that are also part of business processes are the relaying of data from one application program to the next so that the system is able to address application programming interfaces (APIs), i.e. program interfaces.

"Workflow" order processing includes, for example, the capture of order data, as well as the activation of a credit-rating module that compares data stored in a database with newly submitted data. Once the financial solvency of the customer has been determined, the next step is the transmission of the order data to the warehouse management. The information that addresses the step to be carried out next can be compared to a traditional floating file's register. The electronic floating file of the workflow system automatically sends a file's relevant contents to the relevant persons and also makes the tools available that are required to complete this task. In each of these tool or module activations, the system automatically provides the module with input data. In our example (the credit rating), it is first the customer data and then the order data. These requirements have to be explicitly programmed for each module activation within workflow systems while taking the programming interface (API) of each appropriate module into consideration.

The comparison of the process control system to the traditional floating file fails in one specific regard: While the electronic version can be sent simultaneously to two different persons for parallel processing, this is nearly impossible with regard to the conventional, paper-based form. A considerable advantage of the electronic process support of many enterprise processes is therefore the ability to handle process elements in parallel. Furthermore, when compared to manual process execution, it is this flexibility advantage, which leads to quicker and better adaptability. There is, moreover, the possibility to automate several sequential steps, such as an automated credit check when an order has been entered or the automated re-ordering of goods when warehouse stock reaches a certain minimal threshold.

### 4.2.2.3   Distribution

The distribution aspect describes the trend toward decentralization at the level of information and communication technology infrastructures. A progressive dissolving of central structures has occurred over the last decade with regard to data management, as well as the functionality of application programs. The explanation for this increased effectiveness and capacity of computer networks is that the problem of information processing transmission bottlenecks has become unimportant, thus making data distribution to and functioning on other computers possible. An important prerequisite for this distribution to other computers within a heterogeneous system landscape is standardization, an aspect that will be addressed later. However, in some areas, there has recently been a trend in the opposite direction, i.e. back toward centralized data processing on application and terminal servers. This development may be due to the more costly maintenance and the high hardware costs of the actual implementation of distributed systems. Furthermore, the high performance capability of modern work stations can meet several simultaneously connected users' computing needs – an activity that was previously the domain of mainframe computers.

**Distribution of Data**

The aspect of data management that transcends the boundaries of firm-internal computers deserves separate examination. C. J. Date (1999) encapsulated the demands and requirements for a distributed database as: "To the user, a distributed system should look just like a non-distributed system." From this basic rule – called the transparency requirement – twelve rules are derived that have not as yet been wholly implemented by any commercially available software. Nevertheless, these rules serve as an excellent guide for the assessment of distributed databases. The most essential aspects are addressed below.

The local autonomy rule refers to the necessity for separate locations to be self-reliant. There should be no function-determining dependencies between individual locations nor should this be imposed by a central entity, as a partial system failure will affect other locations. Conversely, one of the rules is that users should perceive all the data as being stored in a central location – theirs. Date refers to this as the demand for location independence. The demand for data to be unfragmented is derived from concepts regarding data's physical storage. For reasons of efficiency, data should be stored in the location with the largest demand for such data, even if they logically belong together. Human resources data that are of interest for a London subsidiary should, accordingly, be stored in London, just as the Los Angeles human resources data should be stored in Los Angeles. Nevertheless, the user, regardless of location, has all human resources data available.

Likewise, there is a rule to be allowed to implement controlled redundancy across the separate locations, i.e. the requirement for replication independence. Data copies may thus be kept at various locations to facilitate the user and system administrator's speedy access, with the system ensuring the consistency of the various copies.

Similarly, there is a need for distributed query processing for efficiency reasons. This rule refers to the simultaneous processing of a query on the databases at all locations where fragments of the relevant data files are kept. This possibility likewise requires distributed transaction management through which, for example, consistency damage due to a node's failure can be avoided within a database.

Transcending static distribution, newer approaches attempt to utilize the possibilities of a more dynamic, location-independent distribution of data files. Object migration, a key term, means approaches that permit data objects to migrate within a worldwide distributed system (e.g., flight record systems) and allow them to dynamically move to locations where there is a greater need for them.

## Distribution of Functionality

In a distributed system, the transparent distribution of internal functionality is the foundation of the integration of externally available functionality. Consequently, the integration of different users at different locations can only occur through the externally invisible duplication of single location systems by means of connected, equally invisible coordination. In a closed information and communication system, distribution and integration concepts are thus always connected in one form or another. As a method of internal functionality distribution, the client/server concept, which will be addressed in the next section, enables the optimal placing of tasks at the best suitable entity and, thus, the integration of all computers in the network's computing power.

The term client/server should first be examined with regard to its abstract meaning (Borkoff/Schlichter 2000). This simply implies that a requester, the client, has a task that is processed by a service provider, the server (see figure 4.11). As far as information technology is concerned, the participating actors may take on different guises, their roles as client and server may even be fully interchangeable.

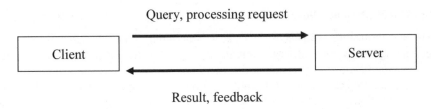

Fig. 4.11.   The client/server concept

Figure 4.12 shows a possible depiction of the fundamental application system architecture from a client/server perspective. Each component can change its functionality. The actual application, comprising a modeling, presentation, and control part, utilizes a hierarchy of abstraction levels within the storage medium. A production planning and control system, for example, utilizes certain algorithms to calculate completion dates and throughput times that can be assigned to the modeling component. Routines from the presentation component can be displayed on the screen, and the output screens that display the calculated values can be linked by means of routines from the control component.

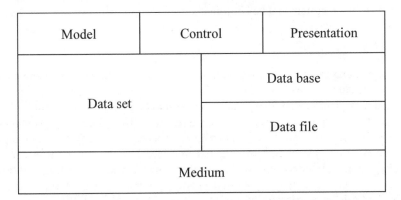

Fig. 4.12.   Application system architecture from the client/server perspective

The lower levels refer to the storage of data and individual data sets can be accessed from here, or data can be processed directly. On the medium, data file, database, and presentation levels, it is already possible to use the client/server concept in a network; however, this concept's transfer to other modules is also conceivable. Consequently, the distributed query processing described above is an example of a client/server relation on a database level; the relevant database servers are the nodes that are busy with the execution of the posed query. In traditional local networks, however, file servers have to coordinate connected clients' access to all data files. A disk server may be utilized, for example, in configurations in which a narrow medium such as a CD-ROM drive is made available to several clients.

**Standardization of Client / Server Databases**

The standardization of database interfaces is required to include database servers in heterogeneous application environments. The ISO (International Organization for Standardization) is one standardization body. In addition, there are manufacturer alliances such as the SQL Access Group or X / Open, but also individual standardizations such as those of Microsoft and IBM.

The ISO's international norm for database access is the remote database access (RDA) standard. This provides clues for the conversion of, for example, SQL-formulated, manufacturer-specific database queries into a neutral format. In turn, this neutral database may then be converted by means of the ISO's seven-layer model between the client and server. We also find guidelines for the conversion of response – a message back to the client. A distributed configuration with several database servers has, however, not as yet been addressed.

An important consortium of manufacturers with regard to object-oriented client / server systems is the object management group (OMG), which, with more than 700 members, is the largest consortium worldwide for the coordination of function calls over a network. The latter is defined by the OMG-specified common object request broker architecture (CORBA) (OMG 1992). Consequently, objects from different manufacturers and in different programming languages can be integrated into a distributed system and be coordinated through mutually utilized services.

*4.2.2.4    Integration*

There are strong trends toward integration with regard to hardware, as well as relevant system and application software. Different computer architecture and system techniques are coordinated or aligned with regard to their relative compatibility with other system components. Based on their interoperability with other system components, they are also integrated into heterogeneous network and system landscapes. Diverse systems' interoperability has become increasingly important, especially in conjunction with the trend towards globalization. The enormous success of products such as Java, a largely system-independent programming language, and concepts like CORBA is primarily due to this transformation.

An additional level of integration is the consolidation of application programs within a uniform user interface. In the context of the Internet and intranet, the browser plays an important role as the universal client for various application and user interfaces, as well as providing access to various servers. Even office software packages that formerly came with self-contained applications such as word processing, presentation programs, and / or databases are increasingly being presented with a uniform user interface. Various functions can be transparently and modularly activated via a control center. In addition, document creation applications now include Internet functionality so that created documents can be published directly on the World Wide Web.

Another aspect of integration is the consolidation of formerly separate task and functional areas into a large software product with coordinated components. This has allowed corporate management systems (such as SAP) to be introduced that comprise and support all the stages of an organization's value-adding processes and depict the organization structure of the company.

In the following, we address integration trends at various levels. The discussion focuses on computer networks, data, as well as forms of data.

## Integration of Networks

The integration of existing local networks usually only occurs through their connection to what is called a backbone network. Such a network, which has the same role as the human spinal column, is capable of integrating several existing local networks by means of special links that require no major reconfiguration efforts. The network component at the interface between the local and backbone network is called a gateway. It takes care of the translation between the connected networks' different protocols, transmission bandwidths, and standards. The asynchronous transfer mode (ATM) high-speed transmission method (see section 4.2.1) was designed, for example, for its suitability as a backbone technology. An ATM gateway can thus efficiently handle the required translation and transmission of user data.

## Data Integration

At another level of integration, data summaries required within a company are a prerequisite for the integration of information. The summary of data from different functional areas, which is also a vertical summary within and external to the enterprise is labeled data integration. Data integration enjoys all the advantages that the central administration of enterprise-relevant data offers while, simultaneously, being the prerequisite for a corresponding configuration of enterprise-wide processes. A major advantage is that the multiple capture of identical data can be avoided. Order information that is, for example, needed in the finance department, as well as in production only needs to be captured once to be available to both departments. An integrated database is largely free of redundancy, which simultaneously ensures consistency, since the possibility of conflicting information in redundant databases is avoided.

## Media Integration

Integration also occurs within the media. The term multimedia includes communication media such as language, graphics, and video. Five media are currently considered for merging in a user interface: Text, vector and bit-mapped graphics, audio, and video. The audio and video media differ considerably with regard to technical demands as real time execution is demanded. For moving pictures or sound sequences to be reproduced, they have to be recorded and / or sampled continuously. On the other hand, media text and graphics only require a single, temporally non-critical digitalization. Figure 4.14 shows a comparison of the different media's storage needs.

| Storage needs of digitalized information | |
| --- | --- |
| 1 page of typewritten text (black and white) | 2 KB |
| 1 page of graphics (24 bit/picture element) | 50 KB |
| 1 video (stationary picture) | 200-700 KB |
| 1 minute audio in stereo | 5.3 MB |
| ... compressed | 1.3 MB |
| 1 minute video moving pictures | >1 GB |
| 1 page color print | 20 MB |
| 1 movie (color, 90 min. uncompressed) | 1 TB |

**Fig. 4.13.**   Storage needs of digitalized information (based on Wolff 1993, p. 12)

An improvement of audio and video data quality is possible by increasing the sampling frequency. This, however, increases the capacity required from the underlying transmission medium, despite sophisticated compression algorithms. An example is video data's real-time or live transmission, which requires a bandwidth of 140 MB/s. This transmission speed is presently only possible by using high-speed networks such as the DQDB or ATM technology (see section 4.2.1). This capacity problem is not limited to transmission, but also surfaces with regard to the storing of media data. For the dissemination of multimedia data, high capacity media such as CD-ROM or DVD are preferred, whereas fast hard drives with high storage capacities are chosen for the processing of high performance data. In spite of all the technical difficulties that the integration of media faces, its economic importance, especially in the office work domain, is becoming a focal point (Koller 1994; Picot / Neuburger 1997b).

*4.2.2.5   Standardization*

Standardization (for the economic basis of standardization, see section 2.4.2) is aimed at establishing generally accepted and publicly available rules that enable different systems to be used (compatibility). Systems that follow such rules are called open systems. The official definition of open systems as provided by IEEE's (Institute for Electrical and Electronics Engineers) Technical Committee on Open Systems relates to the complete and consistent number of international technology and functional standards for the specification of interfaces, services, and formats regarding the guaranteeing of the interoperability and portability of applications, data and persons (Bues 1994, p. 22).

In this regard, openness is a prerequisite for integration, specifically with regard to integration-determining factors such as interoperability and portability. Interoperability (the cooperation among different components) and portability (the transferability to other systems) can only be guaranteed when suitable manufacturer-transcending standards are adhered to when information and communication technology infrastructures are designed.

The term standard denotes a specification that users have broadly accepted. Basically, we differentiate between de facto and de jure standards. De facto standards are created in an evolutionary way in practice so that a specification is sufficiently supported within the market. They are the result of market-based selection processes, associations, and federations' activities or cooperation (Zerdick / Picot / Schrape et al. 2001). Moreover, they emerge in an expanding market when a certain change in procedures offers a relative advantage in comparison to alternative procedures (Gates / Myhrvold / Rinearson 1997, p. 83). Examples of this are the network protocols TCP/IP and IPX / SPX, but also the database standard OBCD. De jure standards, however, are mandatory standards that have been developed by industry consortia or official institutions. In a more narrow sense, these standards enjoy immediate force of law and are viewed as coercive.

In the US, the American National Standards Institute (ANSI) addresses a variety of standards. It is a private, non-profit organization that administers and coordinates America's voluntary standardization and conformity assessment system. The Institute's mission is to enhance the global competitiveness of the country's business and quality of life by promoting and facilitating voluntary consensus standards and conformity assessment systems, and safeguarding their integrity.

At the European level, there are essentially three authoritative organizations in the information and communication technology domain: The Comité Européen de Normalisation (CEN, European Committee for Standardization) for the standardization of information technology in general, the Comité Européen de Normalisation Electrotechnique (CENELEC) for electrotechnical concerns, and the European Telecommunications Institute (ETSI) for the telecommunication sector. The Information and Communication Technology Standards Board (ICTSB) coordinates the overlapping areas of these organizations. CEN-issued European standards are obligatory for nations within the European Union (EU) and the European Free Trade Area (EFTA), and are also adopted as national standards by the organization members. These standards are not, however, legally binding.

At the international level, the International Organization for Standardization (ISO), the International Electrotechnical Commission (IEC), and the International Telecommunications Union-Telecommunication Standardization Sector (ITU-TS) – formerly called the Comité Consultatif Internationale de Télégraphique et Téléphonique (CCITT) – are analogous to the European and American standards institutes. In the information technology standards area, the ISO and IEC's fields of activity overlap to some extent. In order to address this overlap, the Joint Technical Committee 1 Information Technology (JTC1) was founded in 1987. The ISO's main members are the national standards-setting institutions of its member states, although the latter are not obliged to accept these standards. The World Trade Organization (WTO) is, however, striving towards a stronger obligation for its member states to adopt ISO standards. In this regard, the US and Japan specifically have some catching up to do.

Official norms and standards, such as the ISO/OSI reference model depicted below, compete with industry standards such as the TCP/IP, IPX/SPX. The standards that evolved in an evolutionary way in practice are often considerably more assertive than their counterparts developed through negotiations. In some areas, governments and commissions address norms and standards to improve standards. These are de jure standards that have the force of law. Many of the most successful standards are, however, de facto standards that the market has identified (Gates/Myhrvold/Rinearson 1997). In both cases, efforts towards standardization reflect a desire for openness, compatibility, and integration. There is, in other words, a perceived need that manifests itself in non-profit manufacturer alliances. Examples of such alliances are the X/Open Consortium, which focuses on the standardization of the operating system UNIX; the World Wide Web Consortium (W3C), which recommends specifications for WWW data formats; and the Open Applications Group, which address document type definitions (DTD) for XML, as well as describing business objects.

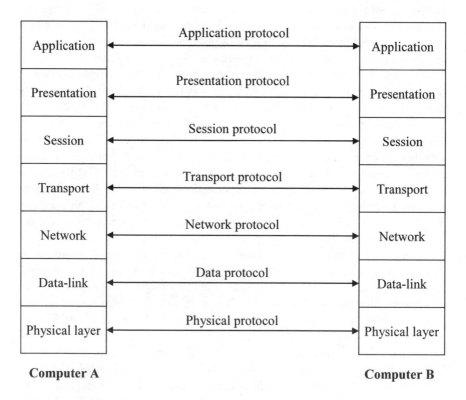

**Computer A**                                                                 **Computer B**

**Fig. 4.14.** The ISO/OSI 7-layer reference model

## Network Standardization

A first step toward openness is standardization at the network level. The OSI 7-layer reference model (see figure 4.14) for the structuring of OSI computer networks is conceptually the foundation of the interoperability of network architectures. This model's individual layers are assigned certain tasks (Tanenbaum 1989). A layer's functionality is based on the services provided by each of the layers below it. These services' elementary functions are the error-free transmission of individual bits through a given technical medium at the lowest layer, the physical layer. Communication between corresponding layers on different participating computer systems depends on a standardized language, the protocol. The two most important protocols on the Internet, TCP, and IP (transport control protocol and Internet protocol) are assigned to levels 4 (transport layer) and 3 (network layer) respectively. Via TCP, a virtual connection is established between the source and the destination computer, while the IP is responsible for the transmission of data on the route between the sender and receiver.

## Standardization of Data Exchange

On the ISO / OSI reference model's presentation and / or application layers, standards have to be integrated for electronic data interchange between firms. This is referred to as electronic data interchange (EDI) (see chapter 6) and enables efficient inter-firm communication. This is why EDI is considered the core basis of the efficient consumer response (ECR) concept. The uniform standards utilized on

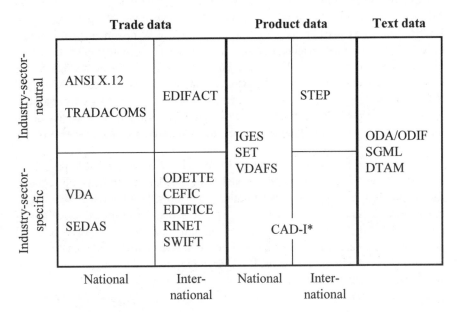

**Fig. 4.15.** Standards for trade, products, and text data exchange (Neuburger 1994, p. 22)

the transport layer are prerequisites for the uninterrupted transmission and processing of data. A great number of standards have also been developed for commercial data, as well as for product and text data (see figure 4.15).

In respect of commercial data interchange, there are, besides a few national or industry sector-specific standards, the ISO standard EDI for administration, commerce and transport (EDIFACT) that is used across industries and internationally. This comprehensive body of rules and regulations with a total of more than 600 different data elements is coordinated through the creation of what is called subsets to address the concrete needs of individual communication partners and industry sectors. Consequently there are, for example, ODETTE for the automotive industry, CEFIC for the chemical industry, and EDIFICE in the electronics sector. An example of the standards developed for product data is the ISO standard STEP (the standard for the exchange of product definition data). It is especially well suited for the exchange of CAD data. For the exchange of text data, there is the office document architecture / office document interchange format (ODA / ODIF) developed by ISO. The goal is not only to capture text, but also to describe formatting information, layouts, footnotes, etc.

The introduction of EDI within a firm is usually very costly. Consequently, smaller and medium-sized firms, especially suppliers, will only introduce EDI if larger firms pressure them to do so. This also explains why, despite its potential, EDI has not enjoyed widespread diffusion. This may be changing, however, due to the Internet data format XML (extensible markup language). XML (see W3C 1999) is a simplified subset of SGML (structured generalized markup language) that was developed to fulfill the need for a more powerful language than the previously used HTML (hypertext markup language) to describe WWW documents. In contrast to HTML, it allows the meaning of a structured document's content to be described. Similar to SGML, XML is also a meta-language, i.e. it allows newer descriptive languages to be described. These characteristics are the basis of the use of XML and XML-derived languages as a universal data format. Moreover, this universal data format could eventually allow data to be exchanged effortlessly between and at the interfaces of web servers, databases, enterprise planning systems, office software, and any other programs.

By combining EDI and XML, the entry costs for firms interested in participating in EDI can be considerably decreased since smaller investments are required for the previously complicated development and tools. In addition, EDI / XML is much more flexible, as information can be processed and transmitted regardless of the underlying business processes and communication standards. Even bilateral agreements and / or locally / firm-internal developed standards can be incorporated into this concept without problems. It is therefore quite possible that economies of scale and strategic advantages – anticipated since the 1970s – will be realized (Neuburger 1999).

### 4.2.2.6   Dematerialization

Besides virtualization, which describes the conceptual existence of objects that do not really exist, there is a purely physical trend towards the dissolution of tangible objects into sheer electronic information – dematerialization.

This denotes the disintegration of the medium and the information, i.e. separating information from its usual carriers, then storing and transmitting it electronically. This "change from physical atoms to digital bits" (Zerdick / Picot / Schrape et al. 2001, p. 16) by means of digitalization has become possible through performance increases gained from computer systems and networks (section 4.2.1). Information that is stored in a digital format can be captured and managed by microprocessors, be duplicated as often as needed, be stored at very low costs, be transported via networks, and can reach global markets regardless of borders (Zerdick / Picot / Schrape et al. 2001).

The trend toward dematerialization is revealed in various areas: Traditional mass media (Sennevald 1998) utilize the possibilities of the Internet by making content simultaneously available in traditional distribution channels. Moreover, they make exclusive online content available to a broad audience by means of low-cost "transport" and regardless of geographical reach. Some print media even offer immediate electronic "duplicates" of their print products in Adobe's portable document format (PDF). Usually, however, electronically presented content requires additional editing and redesign for presentation on the Internet and for suitable viewing on a computer screen. This procedure is different from the one required for traditional media products, thus starting a new value chain (Sennevald 1998). Even information that has been electronically available on physically distributed data carriers such as music CDs or data CD-ROMs is increasingly being distributed electronically via data networks. This requires the efficient use of compression procedures such as MP3 for audio data to minimize the amount of data to be transmitted as much as possible. Through simple copying and cross-border data traffic, the generation and distribution of illegal copies (pirated copies) are easily done. In order to control such illegal behavior, suitable technical security procedures, such as electronic certificates of authenticity (e.g., "water marks" for the identification of sound data), will need to be created. Especially in the music business, music firms resist new distribution methods via electronic networks (e.g., peer-to-peer), as they fear that their dominant market position is being threatened (Zerdick / Picot / Schrape et al. 2001; Wigand 2003).

Within the area of financial services, forms of electronic banking are also increasingly replacing paper receipts, checks, and written orders. Around the clock electronic transmission and automatic processing of processes such as account management or stock trading allow considerable savings with regard to staff and bank branches. In turn, this leads to the emergence of online banks that interact with their customers only by phone, in writing or, preferably, via the Internet. The resultant cost savings can be passed on to the customer. Often such Internet-based banks whose services are exclusively electronic, offer more attractive terms than conventional banks do. The explosive increase in Internet connections (see section 4.2.1) has led to an increase in the number of customers who wish to take advantage of electronic banking via data networks, as it is independent of location and time-of-day. Accordingly, more and more conventional banks offer online banking in addition to their traditional services in the hope of reducing the previous costly branch-based customer services.

In comparison to numerous other countries, the term 'electronic banking' is somewhat of a misnomer in the US. It should rather be called electronic bill paying, as full-fledged electronic banking is still not possible on a regular basis. Furthermore, account holders can only electronically pay the bills of those companies that the bank lists and approves. To date, it is impossible to transfer an amount from an account at bank A to another account at bank B and often even impossible within the same bank without paying exorbitant fees such as $25 per transaction. True electronic banking at modest fees has been possible in Western European countries for several decades.

The company-internal information flow has replaced traditional paper-based information with electronically stored and distributed information. Increasingly, the flow of letters, memos, and other correspondence is generated and stored electronically. They can therefore be quickly retrieved from a central storage point by those authorized to do so and easily changed. This information may be readily stored on hard drives or CD-ROMs. Similarly, the distribution of digital information internally and externally is increasingly occurring via a data network in the form of e-mail instead of traditional postal mail. For security purposes, these documents may have digital signatures affixed to them. However, the paperless office will continue to be wishful thinking for the foreseeable future.

## 4.3     Information Deployment Within the Firm

### 4.3.1     Identification of Information-Intensive Business Areas

Given the numerous possibilities to influence entrepreneurial success by means of information and communication technologies, some kind of a grid or matrix to assist in the search for promising application areas seems desirable. Porter and Millar (1985) presented such a matrix in the form of an information-intensity portfolio.

The portfolio concept is based on the following fundamental idea: Just as there are capital-intensive and / or material-intensive business areas, a business area may also be information intensive. It is exactly those information-intensive business areas of a firm that have to be identified, as it is there where competitors, as well as the enterprise itself may discover great opportunities. Targeted information management activities may contribute to business success. Porter and Millar suggest two dimensions for the operationalization of information intensity (see figure 4.16). The in-

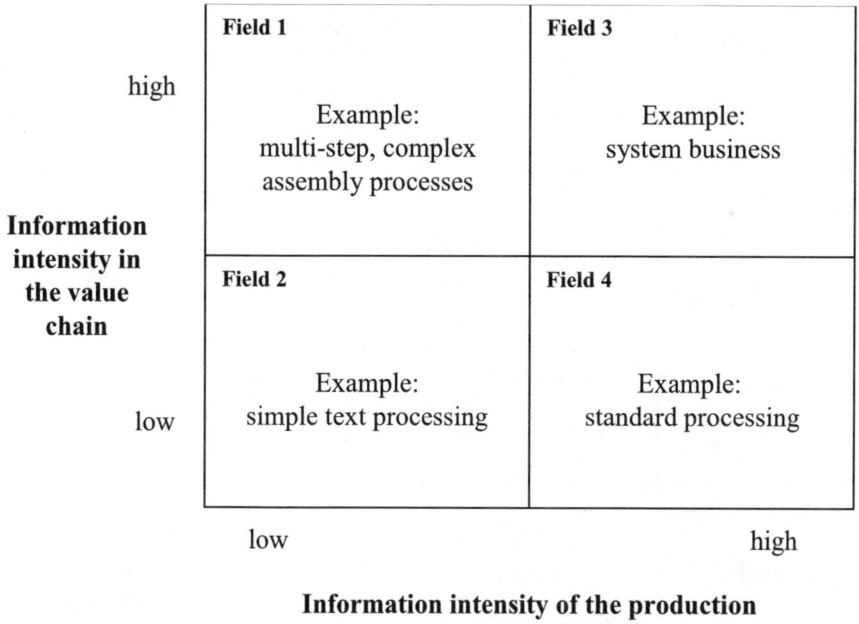

| | Field 1 | Field 3 |
|---|---|---|
| high | Example:<br>multi-step, complex<br>assembly processes | Example:<br>system business |
| **Information<br>intensity in<br>the value<br>chain** | **Field 2** | **Field 4** |
| low | Example:<br>simple text processing | Example:<br>standard processing |

low                                                           high

**Information intensity of the production**

**Fig. 4.16.**   Information intensity portfolio (Porter / Millar 1985; based on Picot / Reichwald 1991, p. 273)

formation intensity in the value chain not only describes the role of information in procurement, logistics, production and sales, but the information intensity of production also relates to the need to explain products and services. This is reflected, for example, in the need for consulting and training, documentation and / or product information. Based on these criteria, individual business areas and / or partial functions are positioned in the portfolio matrix.

Complementary to the information intensity is the current competitive position and the business area's attractiveness. The strategic competitive position influences the urgency with which information technology and communication systems are deployed. If a firm enjoys a strong competitive position in successful and future-oriented markets, the deployment of information and communication systems is of great importance.

It is possible to deduce strategic directions and priorities for information management by means of a joint examination of business areas' information intensity and competitive position (Krüger / Pfeiffer 1988, also see figure 4.17). Business areas' very successful position and high information intensity demand aggressive development strategies and the subsequent deployment of information and communication systems. When there is a downward shift in the overall business area, information and communication systems play a less important role, requiring the

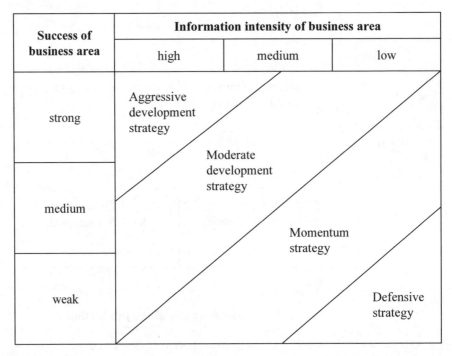

**Fig. 4.17.** Strategy-oriented development and deployment of information and communication systems (Krüger / Pfeiffer 1988; in accordance with Picot / Reichwald 1991, p. 275)

pursuit of moderate development strategies, momentum strategies or even defensive strategies.

With regard to achieving a strategic competitive advantage, the presented model still has a weak point (Ciborra 1994). If one expects a strategic information system to actually be capable of creating a strategic competitive advantage for the firm, it has to at least meet the following three requirements: Generate an added value for the firm, have a largely proprietary character, and should not be immediately imitable by competitors.

The approach by Krüger and Pfeiffer (see figure 4.17) presented above mainly generates non-proprietary solutions, i.e. solutions that are in principle available to all market participants. Only a new understanding of information system planning processes seems to promise a solution to this dilemma (Ciborra 1994). Just as innovation strategies form the foundation to achieve sustainable competitive advantage in the production and process area, an innovation-oriented approach may also result in sustainable advantages in information management. Section 4.5 will again address this aspect in a discussion of management perspectives for the deployment of information and communication technology in the firm.

### 4.3.2   Information and Communication-Oriented Design of Business Processes

Once the business areas that appear to be meaningful for the targeted and improved deployment of production factor information have been defined, the next step is to examine the affected processes to establish their real information needs. If needed, processes may have to be adapted to make technical support easier. Taking an abstract look at business processes, one realizes that a number of activities transform a certain input into a certain output.

This perspective is not just inadvertently congruent with those of automatons (see section 4.4.2), because an automaton may actually be understood as the formalization of processes. The difference between the two terms can be found in the properties of their activities. These activities, which constitute the basis of an automaton, have to be described exactly; an effort that is generally unfeasible in respect of business processes. Within an organization's context, a process also has other important parameters such as the time required or the technology platform utilized. These processes may be manual (e.g., the manual sorting of postal mail) or automated (e.g., the sorting of account statements with a specifically designed machine). The above-mentioned elementary activities are arranged within a flow-oriented diagram to describe a process. From a formal point of view, the notations of function and process modeling, which are described in section 4.4.5, are also available to describe this process. Without further addressing the resultant technical details, the following discussion will take a broad view of this process. In line with Davenport's (1993) observation that process innovation is the fusion of information technology with the human factor, we too regard the term process as a mere stringing together of elementary transformations. Although the process innovation concept relies on new information technologies, a process's success nevertheless basically depends on employees' motivation and upper management's degree of engagement with regard to the strategic vision. Information technology is the cornerstone of this paradigm and manifests itself as either an enabler or disabler.

The process orientation propagated by Davenport and others (e.g., Picot / Franck 1995) increasingly incorporates a customer orientation. An improved costing orientation may, for example, be achieved by introducing process cost accounting. In all these general frameworks, it is important to design processes that do not eventually solidify, thus forming barriers against the rest of the organization's dynamics. An example of this is the introduction of workflow systems that hinder the "cementing" of organization structures by means of workflow structures that are adaptable to changing conditions.

### 4.3.3   The Life Cycle Model for the Production of Information

Based on the determined information needs, the information supply has to be planned, organized, and controlled. One method that could be applied is the critical success factor method. The life cycle model for the production of information lends itself to the analysis of demand fulfillment (Levitan 1982) (see figure 4.18).

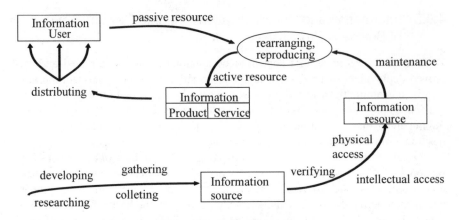

**Fig. 4.18.** Life cycle model for the production of information (based on Levitan 1982)

The life cycle of information production starts with potential information being recognized within a quantity of data. After the relevant data have been collected and acquired, this forms the information source. Several steps are required to transform an information source into an information resource. The information source needs to be verified, mechanisms have to be established to access it physically and intellectually, storage capabilities have to be made available, and various legal, organizational, and economic stipulations need to be considered. The information resource fulfills the information user's information needs, adopting either a passive or active condition. If the resource is only utilized through the information user's initiative, it is labeled passive, i.e. it is a user-active information resource. In its active condition, the resource is transformed into information products and services that are transmitted to the information users, for example, in the form of regular reports or mailing lists, or messages based on the surpassing of or failing to meet thresholds levels (Szyperski 1980). This situation also lends itself to demonstrating the difference between the push and pull principle. While the push principle makes information available (active information resource), the pull principle requires a user-active search for information (passive information resource).

The advantage of a life cycle model is that various "production steps" of information can be identified and configured. These may then be utilized as the starting point for answering questions regarding the planning of the resource 'information.' Simultaneously, the various steps within the life cycle model offer important starting points for potential support services through information and communication systems. These starting points must also be recognized and converted by means of information management.

### 4.3.4 Value Added Through Information and Communication

The design and coordination of organization structures and business processes with suitable information technology are ultimately aimed at the generation of and / or increase in value. If value added cannot be achieved, one should seriously question the entire effort.

In the past, many managers somewhat naively assumed that the introduction and / or application of information technology generated the desired value added almost automatically. Today, however, we look back on several projects that amount to nothing more than the simple automation of existing bureaucratic processes. The anticipated strong increase in efficiency did not materialize. This discrepancy essentially resulted from the assumption that information technology automatically results in financial value added. This perspective is analogous to the hypodermic needle model suggesting that when we are ill, we only need a shot in the arm to be cured. The view that the relationship between the deployment of information technology and value added was of such a trivial nature was unsubstantiated. Nevertheless, value added effects can materialize in the form of efficiency (e.g., return on investment (ROI)) or effectiveness (e.g., quality of management information) (Kuhlen 1995; Wigand 1995a; Reichwald 1999).

The following case is an example of where the introduction of information and communication technology did not lead to value being added and might even have resulted in value depreciation. In the 1960s, the publisher of the **Scientific American** wanted to implement an information system (Boehm 1988) to automate certain manual steps in the subscription process to increase their efficiency. The subscription processes mainly comprised the scrutiny and sorting of the received mail with regard to new orders, subscription renewals, and / or gift subscriptions. The data were then transferred to punch cards and manually archived. In a very work-intensive session, labels, invoices and other forms were monthly generated from the archived data. Due to the increase in demand, the publisher was soon no longer able to handle this work and sought the assistance of a software company. The solution proposed and ultimately adopted, was essentially to replace the manually managed punch card archive. As before, the mail was visually inspected, sorted, and the information transferred to punch cards. In a next step, the latter was transferred to tape and processed on a minicomputer for administrative purposes. Now, the required forms could be generated from the electronically archived data at the end of each month.

Interestingly, the subscription administration costs increased. The quality of the services decreased and the workers' morale was abysmal. The main reason for these developments was the technology-centric perspective of the information system planning and realization. According to the programmers and systems developers, the extremely complex and admirable program had a slight shortcoming: Due to a single, very trivial data entry error in the data stored on the punch cards, the entire system's read operation was halted and the entire punch card set rejected. The card containing that error had to be found manually, corrected, and the run started anew. Consequently, additional control loops were built into the manual capturing on punch cards. Additional validity checks (e.g., checking the renewal of non-existing orders) had to be introduced as well. Additional staff had to be employed and new forms had to be developed for the inclusion of newly created exceptions.

This example clearly demonstrates that the mere introduction of information technology rarely generates value added. In addition, organizational and human resource aspects, such as ascertaining the underlying work processes in detail and correctly and / or involving co-workers in planning this information system from the beginning, need to be considered. This could have made a success of the *Scientific American*'s project. If one wishes to achieve a value enhancement, one should rethink the entire process from an organizational, technical, and human resources perspective. What effect would it have had on the project's success if, for example, the need to capture the data on punch cards had been questioned?

### 4.3.5   The Productivity Paradox

The impossibility of determining a direct, rule-based relationship between information technology and value added is not only evident in individual cases such as in the example above, but also in the broader perspective beyond the service industry as a whole. The catch phrase "productivity paradox" (e.g., Brynjolfsson 1993; Gründler 1997; Picot / Gründler 1995; Piller 1998c; Thurow 1992; Strassmann 1990; Wigand 1995a) denotes the well-known phenomenon of the missing correlation between investments in information and communication technology on the one hand and productivity on the other. Roach (1991) calls this overinvestment in computer technology. This is particularly appropriate with regard to the services sector that comprises approximately 85 percent of all installed information technology in the US.

According to various reports, the US economic output increased by 30 percent between 1980 and 1990, while the number of workers increased by two percent, the number of salaried staffers rose by a total of 33 percent. Simultaneously, worker productivity rose by 28 percent, but the productivity of salaried staffers decreased by three percent. New technology, hardware, and software found their way into the office, but the net effect was nevertheless negative productivity development. Brynjolsson (1993) offers similar results and also calls attention to the much discussed but difficult to explain relationship between information and communication technology and productivity. In other studies, however, Brynjolfsson and Hitt (1993, 1995a, 1998) draw attention to clear productivity improvements due to information and communication technology at the entrepreneurial and industry levels.

---

1. Reinvesting of the employee-related savings
2. Redistribution of the gains among the businesses within an industry
3. Delay with the realization of profits
4. Inability to measure inputs and outputs
5. Political resistance
6. Mismanagement of information and communication technology
7. Inadequate reorganization of business processes

---

**Fig. 4.19.**   Explanations for the information technology productivity paradox

Various explanatory approaches have been offered in this regard. Picot and Gründler (1995; Gründler 1997) divide their explanation into seven categories (see figure 4.19).

The gains do not become obvious outside the business if employee-related savings are reinvested. Savings in the form of lower labor costs are specifically not obvious in the administrative area; rather, there is an improvement in the work quality. A second aspect is the redistribution of gains among businesses within an industry. The assessment of industry-spanning productivity should therefore be undertaken from the perspective that a possible increase in productivity in individual firms within a competitive market is distributed across the entire industry. Such an increase in productivity is therefore not, in an economic sense, reflected in a directly measurable way. The delay in the realization of profits is due to two aspects. First, the specific industry that makes the new information and communication technologies available to the market has to develop these products' quality and service structure. From the user's point of view, this leads to delays due to potential errors in the products, especially if the manufacturer does not provide support. Second, learning and adaptation difficulties lead to delayed payback from this information technology.

The inability to measure inputs and outputs correctly is the most frequent and plausible explanation for the productivity paradox. Advantages in the form of improved quality, speed, variability, customer service, and / or flexibility are not usually taken into consideration in prevalent evaluation and assessment methods. Owing to the time between inputs and outputs, there is the additional problem of accounting for inflation. Political resistance is another explanation offered for the productivity paradox. Given certain circumstances, employees may cling to the traditional system and way of doing, resist reorganization, and the deployment of information and communication technology. The mismanaging of information and technology refers to the responsible decision makers' inadequate assessment of the resulting benefit. The introduction of information technology is often not executed with the company's interest in mind, but is based on widely varying personal motivations. The inadequate reorganization of business processes is due to the wrong deployment of information technology, which is often no more than the "electrification" of the existing processes without the organization and staff structure being adapted as well. The consequences are inefficiencies and the potential "cementation" of the organization structure.

## 4.3.6  Appraisal of the Economic Efficiency of Information Deployment

With the increasing importance of information as a production factor, the problems associated with the appraisal of the economic efficiency of information deployment have intensified. Increased information and communication technology networking in the business has made traditional calculations of economic efficiency largely obsolete. Why are networked information and communication systems in organizations so difficult to appraise? The traditional investment appraisal model for a controlled investment object has been invalidated because – besides investment expenditures on technology – intense parallel efforts to address the change to and adaptation of the organization and human resource should be taken into consideration. Consequently, the object of appraisal cannot be an isolated, single effort but should be entire groupings (bundles) of measures with partially delayed and spatially displaced economic efficiency effects.

The appraisal of the economic efficiency of newer information and communication technology thus faces problems in theory and in practice. These problems can essentially be grouped into six problem categories (see chapter 10.5.4, as well as Picot 1979a; Picot / Reichwald 1987; Reichwald 1999; Wigand et al. 1997, and figure 4.20):

- Measurement problem: Which measurements and / or indicators reflect the effort and utility effects most accurately?

- Situational problem: To what extent do prevailing and specific situational conditions influence economic efficiency effects?

- Integration problem: In which segments of labor-divided activities in firms do the effects of economic efficiencies arise?

- Attribution problem: How can temporally delayed or spatially dispersed economic efficiency effects be attributed?

- Innovation problem: How can the innovative applications of new technology that transcend mere substitution of traditional work processes be appraised?

- Holistic problem: How can the complex, interdependency in the organizational, technical, and human resource system as a whole be taken into consideration during an appraisal of economic efficiency?

These identified problem areas define the effective appraisal of economic efficiency prerequisites. When these are translated into the performance characteristics of an ideal appraisal process, this means:

- Relevant economic efficiency criteria need to be defined in monetary and non-monetary terms (measurement aspect).

- There should be no restrictions as far as taking temporally and spatially dispersed cause-effects relationships into consideration (attribution aspect).

- Those economic efficiency criteria that address shortcomings within the deployment area in need of change should be emphasized (situational aspect).

- The transparency of the dependency relationships between the implicated partial systems and integration effects, as well as economies of scope need to be guaranteed (integration aspect).

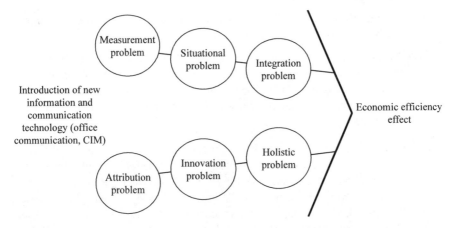

**Fig. 4.20.** Appraisal problems of networked information and communication technology
(based on Reichwald / Höfer / Weichselbaumer 1993, p. 16)

- Innovation effects have to be incorporated into the economic efficiency
  approach, for example, with regard to market supply considerations (innovation aspect).

- Besides purely technology-related cost and performance measures, more
  comprehensive effects (organizational effects, qualification effects, humane
  effects, and external effects) need to be considered. However, this means
  that an information and communication technology appraisal can only be
  meaningful in an information and communication systems context and with
  regard to the goal-oriented deployment of information and communication
  in the business (holistic aspect).

Traditional investment calculation methods do not meet these demands. They are,
however, still widely used in practice, as they are simple to manage. Many newer
suggestions for the appraisal of the economic efficiency of information and communication technology deployment attempt to confront the shortcomings of traditional methods.

If one wishes to evaluate the effectiveness of a new appraisal approach, it
makes sense to first ask questions concerning (Schumann 1993):

- The type of method: Does this involve a purely quantitative, purely qualitative or a combined ("expanded") appraisal approach?

- The type and quantity of the targeted measure to be evaluated: Do these involve one-dimensional or multidimensional evaluation methods?

- The method's application area: Is this a decision aid to generate a new information and communication technology solution, a supporting tool to
  use during the introduction, or a control tool to use after implementation
  of the solution?

- The extent of the procedure: Is this an isolated support tool or a comprehensive appraisal methodology?

- The perspective: Are the characteristics of individual technical solutions isolated effects of singular solutions, the integration effects of appraised integrated information and communication systems, or is a holistic concept being offered for strategic information and communication technology planning?

An overview of newer procedures for the appraisal of the economic efficiency of information and communication technology is offered, for example, by Kredel (1988), Nagel (1919), Schumann (1992; 1993), as well as by Reichwald, Höfer and Weichselbaumer (1996). In the following, we briefly present the approach towards a networked economic efficiency concept (Reichwald / Höfer / Weichselbaumer 1996) as an example of an expanded economic efficiency approach (see also section 10.5.4).

Extended economic efficiency approaches offer an interesting vantage point to demonstrate the advantages of networked appraisal projects. The appraisal basis is ultimately the extent of the effectiveness, i.e. the suitability of measures to achieve a goal. From this perspective, an organizational and technical change in the business should be classified as economic if it is possible to achieve pursued interests more successfully. Changes thus need to be viewed and compared from different viewpoints (multi-level perspective). The appraisal of economic efficiency should capture all direct and indirect cost and performance results from the employees' perspective, from the entrepreneurial level, as well as from a societal perspective. Figure 4.21 provides an overview of the fundamental concept of the evaluation approach.

Central to the appraisal approach to networked economic efficiency are the participation of different company interests groups in the appraisal process, as well as the equal consideration of people-related, economic (costs, time, quality, and flexibility), and societal criteria in the context of the extended appraisal of economic efficiency. Different interests groups' participation is important, as investments in information and communication technology are usually very complex and uncertain. Only when employees from the company's affected areas are included, can their experiences and know-how be utilized. At the same time, however, each economic efficiency result is essentially manipulable. All appraisal methods are based on subjective assumptions and estimations. Even in traditional, purely monetary, investment calculation methods – which are often postulated as objective – estimations have to be made about future cash inflow and outflow, interest rates, etc. Marginal changes in these assumptions can lead to a situation in which the relative advantages of the appraised alternatives shift considerably, making the original appraisal results useless.

A relatively balanced perspective may be generated in that all affected interest groups participate in the appraisal, present their objectives, and bring about a joint

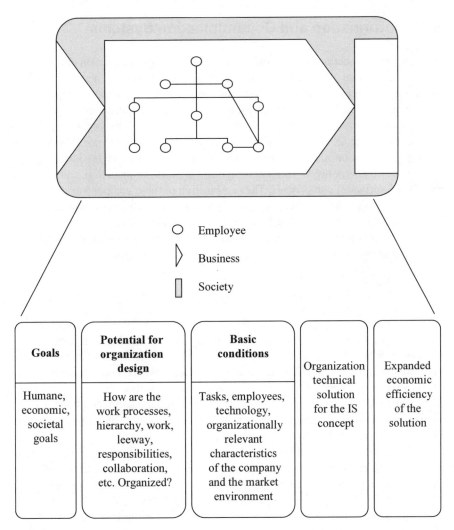

**Fig. 4.21.** Fundamental concept of the evaluation approach of networked economic efficiency (based on Reichwald / Höfer / Weichselbaumer 1996, p. 120)

exchange of interests or consensus. This will ensure that the various aspects of
company events are highlighted so that individual, as well as entrepreneurial and
societal goals are considered, and a holistic perspective can be formed of the consequences of an appraisal of economic efficiency. These deliberations are especially important, as decisions or developments can be assessed, but their actual
consequences cannot be fully anticipated. This is particularly true with regard to
newer information and communication technologies.

## 4.4     Information and Communication Systems

In the preceding section, we addressed the deployment of information and communication technology in companies after ascertaining information needs and taking the productivity paradox into consideration. However, for a company and its development in the market, a meaningful integration of the company information and communication system is required for the planned support to be implemented (see, e.g., Mertens et al. 2000). Technology should serve the company, not the other way around. Information and communication systems unify human resources (qualification, motivation), organizational (design and process organization), and technical (hardware, software) components. The combination of these components determines information and communication systems' structure and influences their efficiency with regard to organizational task accomplishment. Different tasks make specific demands on organization structures; different organization structures require specific support by means of information and communication systems.

### 4.4.1     Information and Communication Systems and Forms of Coordination

Transaction cost theory demonstrates that the suitability of organizational and co-ordination forms depend on the characteristics of the specific tasks and exchange relationships (see chapter 2.3.3). During specialized task accomplishment, these characteristics influence the information and communication problems that need to be dealt with. From this perspective, alternative organization structures may be viewed as alternative paths to solve these problems as economically as possible (Picot / Reichwald 1991; Picot / Freudenberg 1997).

If the specificity and variability of task characteristics (both described as low and high) are regarded as a criterion for the magnitude of information and communication costs, four organizational forms can be distinguished through which the classified tasks can be accomplished (see figure 4.22). Each of these organizational forms (hierarchy, market, strategic network, and modular firms) makes different demands on the support of information and communication systems. Due to information and communication technology's increasing penetration, new opportunities suggest themselves in respect of task accomplishment design that may ultimately lead to the virtualization of business and market structures (see chapter 8). In turn, new and changed demands on the support of information and communication systems arise from this.

**Hierarchical coordination forms** (in field 1) occur with highly specific, stable tasks. Here, information and communication systems fulfill the function of internal regulation and control structures. Consequently, there is a need for horizontal regulation and control structures within and between the individual functions (along the value chain processes), as well as vertical regulation and control structures between the top management layer and the operative units (along the hierarchy).

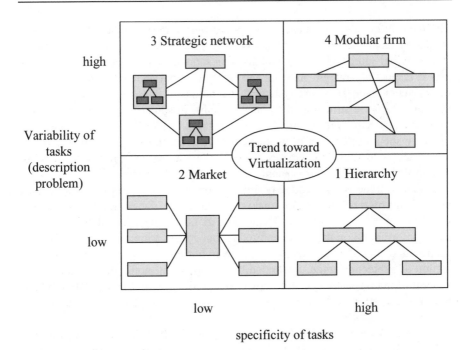

**Fig. 4.22.** Organizational forms and macrostructures of information and communication systems (based on Picot / Reichwald 1991, p. 292; Wigand / Picot / Reichwald 1997, p. 132)

By systematizing and following the criterion of their respective operating reach (in consideration of their vertical regulatory and control range between operative units and entrepreneurial direction) the following classification suggests itself (Mertens 2001; Mertens / Griese 2000; Scheer 1990):

Quantity-oriented operative systems process information about the status and course of quantity-oriented, primary value-adding processes. They are, for example, utilized in industrial manufacturing, in the various partial phases of construction with regard to work scheduling, the control of manufacturing processes, and even with regard to the quality assurance of computer systems. Together with computer-supported PPS systems, they form the foundation of computer integrated manufacturing (CIM). A prerequisite is a logically uniform database (which may be physically dispersed) that all partial systems can access. Quantity-oriented operative systems deliver data input for value-oriented accounting systems, which partially consist of, for example, stock accounting, asset accounting, as well as debit and credit accounting. They make the financial consequences of quantity-oriented processes visible.

Analysis, reporting and control systems mainly operate by means of cost and results accounting methods. These systems should make information available to support the management (controlling) mid-range planning and control processes.

The input information for the systems is derived by means of selection and consolidation from the operative, quantity, and value-oriented systems, as well as from external sources. Planning and decision support systems should provide support in respect of strategic planning and entrepreneurial policy decisions at the top management level. These are systems that should contribute to the improved management of poorly structured decision situations. In spite of rigorous research efforts, such system concepts are still very abstract. There is, however, consensus that they should offer a set of methods and / or decision models, as well as direct online access to suitable databases. Internal and external information (e.g., about market share and competitors) should flow into these databases.

A data warehouse is frequently utilized for the information technology support of an enterprise's decision-making. Contrary to the operational databases that store only current data on a fragment of the enterprise, a data warehouse stores information on the entire enterprise that covers a longer period (mostly as snapshots of the operative data). A data warehouse is defined as a logical "collection of subject-oriented, integrated, time-dependent, non-volatile data for the support of management decisions" (Mertens et al. 2000, p. 61; translation by authors) and comprises the components data management, data organization, and evaluation / processing.

The **market coordination form** (field 2) lends itself to the exchange of unspecific, stable services, i.e. standard products. Since the characteristics, qualities, conditions, etc. of standard products can easily be illustrated, markets are increasingly becoming "mediatized" by means of information and communication systems and transformed into electronic markets (see chapter 7). Traditional trade levels are losing their importance due to these developments, since electronic media can inform buyers comprehensively about deals on the market and they are thus less dependent on local suppliers. Electronic media are very well suited to integrate many supply and demand relationships. Consequently, they offer more and quicker possibilities for business transactions. In addition, this improved market transparency by means of communication and technology systems also enables the automated processing of order, billing, and payment transactions. Aside from this brokering effect, the "mediatization" of transactions may also lead to integration and interlinking effects between the value chains of companies in the electronic market. These expanded integration effects, however, presuppose that the market, as well as company-internal communication is based on uniform and standardized data formats and transmission protocols.

**Strategic networks** (field 3) are organizational forms that are developed for the coordination of unspecific but highly variable services. They consist of relatively independent, specialized small and medium-sized companies that manage joint tasks in close, strongly specialized exchange relationships. Initially, a lead or broker firm takes on the firm-spanning coordination function (Jarillo 1988; Ochsenbauer 1989).

Firm-spanning information and communication systems are deployed for the fine-tuning of the network partners' performance contributions. EDI or the extranet (see section 4.2.1) are very important in this regard. They can support secondary administrative tasks (e.g., the exchange of invoice data or computer-supported transmission of payment notices), as well as primary value-adding processes (e.g., electronic order systems for just-in-time production; distribution systems between manufacturers, shipping agents, and traders; and/or remote diagnostic systems for technical installations).

Highly specific and strongly variable tasks give rise to particular appraisal and dependency problems that cannot be satisfactorily solved by means of formal, bureaucratic systems. It makes sense to develop **modular firms** (field 4) by forming closed, process-oriented units that may arise at differing levels (see chapter 5). Information and communication systems take on a rather subsidiary function by supporting information exchange within and between modules. Beyond individual information processing, systems can provide computer-supported teamwork and collaborative work support, as well as support group work by providing appropriate content and processes (see section 4.2.2).

### 4.4.2 Formalization as a Prerequisite for Information and Communication Technology Design

Human information processing capability is limited. Information and communication technology offers an opportunity to expand the human boundaries of information entry, storing, and processing and thus contribute to the expansion of human performance limits with regard to space, time, and speed. Herein lies the fundamental potential of the technical media, a potential that is nonetheless also limited by fundamental boundaries. It is not so much the possible technical boundaries, such as restrictions regarding processing speed, storage capacities, and/or transmission speed that manifest themselves directly in the user's everyday usage of information technology and communication media that concern us. These slowly lose their relative importance due to processors, storage media, and transmission channels' continuous performance improvements and capacity increases. The computer-aided theoretical limitations of data processing, which are also valid for hypothetical computing models with unlimited processing performance and storage capacity, are of far greater importance. These are the boundaries of formalization and computability – central research topics of theoretical computer science.

We briefly address a few aspects of formalizability in as far as this is important to understand the limits of fundamental information and communication technology performance. For more on this topic, the reader is referred to the following authors: Sipser (1997), Cohen (1991), Engeler and Läuchli (1988), Hopcroft and Ullman (1979, 2000), Sander, Stucky and Herschel (1995), Schöning (2001), and Stetter (1988).

Computer systems are developed with the demand that they support people in the management of information processing problems. Ultimately, however, computer-aided data processing always means the execution of specific calculation instructions on the available information. Problem solving with the aid of a computer (i.e. a formal description of the problem to be solved) always precedes the formulation of the problem-solving instructions, as well as the determining of the required information. This implies that without formalization there is no implementation, without implementation there is no information and communication technology system.

The most important question is therefore for which problems it is actually possible to find formalizations and what such formalizations should or could look like. Closely related to this is a multitude of additional questions: What description techniques are available for the specification of problems and/or problem-solving instructions? Which forms of expression are suited to certain description techniques? When certain problems are difficult or nearly impossible to formalize, is this due to the selected description technique (e.g., the programming language)? Which properties characterize general description techniques, i.e. techniques that are in principle suitable to formally describe problems (and their solutions)?

In the context of information processing, a precise and finite number of written processing rules are denoted as algorithms. Despite its ancient roots, the algorithm concept still plays a fundamental role in data processing. It dates back 1200 years to the mathematician Al Chwarismi, who lived at the Caliph of Bagdad's court and was the first to exclusively refer to mechanical rules for calculation with written numbers. Leibniz generalized the term algorithm to include fixed rules for the processing of general symbols (characters) and character strings that may have an arbitrary meaning (Bauer/Wössner 1981; Bauer/Brauer/Jessen 1992). Good examples of algorithms are computer programs in which the actual programming language used for the formulation is completely irrelevant. Only the unambiguous and finite specified sequence of elementary processing steps, which determines how input data are step-wise converted into output data, is essential. An algorithm thus describes the mapping of a set of valid input data to a set of output data. However, not all such mappings can be implemented by means of an algorithm. Currently, we also increasingly view formal problem specifications in descriptive languages as algorithms. Although they do not exactly specify the processing sequence, they nevertheless enable a machine-based (mechanical or electronic) interpretation and problem solution. In general, informal references and instructions, recipes or handicraft instructions do not meet the requirements for machine-based interpretability and feasibility. Consequently, they do not fall under the term algorithm.

However, not all problems are solvable through algorithms. One of the most interesting aspects of theoretical computer science is the existence of proof that the set of problems is larger than the set of solutions. Consequently, there are no algorithmic solutions for certain problem formulations such as the "busy beaver function" (from the colloquial expression for an "industrious person"), which is a non-computable Turing-machine-based problem. There are indeed many examples of extensive research and development project failures when, in the search for algorithms for demonstrably unsolvable problems, this fundamental theoretical knowledge was not taken into consideration.

Through its characteristic as a processing instruction for a specific input parameter, each mathematical formula represents an algorithm. Basic algorithms that are applied in miscellaneous application areas are: Search and sorting algorithms, algorithms for the processing of character strings, and / or algorithms for solving graph and network problems (see, e.g., Knuth 1997; Knuth 1998; Ottmann / Widmayer 1996). The field of business administration works with a multitude of useful algorithms for special application areas, such as calculation rules for order quantity optimization, throughput and capacity scheduling, machine scheduling planning, and path minimization in the area of production management.

Computer programs written in common programming languages merely represent a special case of algorithm formulation. In general, an algorithmic description can be developed with the help of mathematical constructs based on what is called formal languages, or by using abstract computer models such as pushdown automata or Turing machines. The latter are abstractly notated, symbol-processing machines that are theoretically capable of executing the specifically described algorithm. Next, we briefly present a few basic formal description models.

Real world problems can be dealt with autonomously by an individual task bearer, by persons in division of labor arrangements, as well as by additionally including technical support media. As long as individuals act autonomously, it may suffice if they have an implicit image of the intended aim or solution method in mind. However, to transfer tasks and subtasks to other actors, the solution method or the objective needs to be formulated in a language (see figure 4.23).

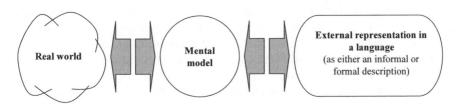

**Fig. 4.23.** Modeling

Informal or semi-formal description in the form of natural language usually suffices for communication between human information bearers. However, to transfer tasks to a computer in the sense of the above-described algorithm concept requires a highly formal task description governed by strict and precise formation rules. Such formal descriptions are formulated in formal languages, such as programming languages, which are artificial. Just like their less formal counterparts, they are determined by a certain basic vocabulary, an alphabet, and a set of rules – the grammar. The latter indicates how words and sentences of the language are to be constructed from the elements of the alphabet, i.e. which character strings, composed of the alphabet's elements, belong to the language vocabulary. The syntax of a formal language is thus clearly established, its semantic is well defined, i.e.

the correctness and meaning of a sentence in this language are always unambiguously determinable. For example, in the case of programming languages, the rules for building the language – whether or not a given program text is formally correct within that language – and the semantic meaning of a syntactically correct program have all been established (for semantics levels see chapter 3.3.1).

The syntax (spelling rules) of a formal language may be affected in various ways, for example, by specifying formal grammars – sets of rules that determine the language – or by means of what is known as automata models – abstract machines capable of exactly understanding the specific formal language's sentences (and no others).

How do these language-theoretical considerations fit into the business context? In their most powerful form – the Turing machine – automata models can all calculate computatable and, consequently, computer-supported solvable functions (Church's thesis). It is therefore important that automata models represent sequences of operations. Such an operational sequence describes the transformation of inputs into outputs, a fact that is of great importance for the formalization of business processes. Approaches to workflow modeling (i.e. the description of operational events with regard to information technology support) often utilize automata as a means to describe these events.

Finite automata (state-transition diagrams) represent the simplest and, due to the ease with which they can be implemented for practical descriptive purposes, the most important automata class. Figure 4.24 depicts a conversation network based on speech act theory that is modeled as a finite automaton (see chapter 3.3.4). The network describes a possible conversation course for the conversation type "order" as it is represented in the coordinator system, the first and probably best known computer system for explicit conversation support. The nodes of the diagram specify the possible states during the course of the conversation process; the edges represent the occurring speech acts. From the entry point, node 1 leads person A's request to node 2. From this point on, the further path depends on person B's speech act: A refusal leads to node 8, a promise to node 3. This type of modeling forms the foundation for an entire class of newer systems for communication and decision support in organizations (for the basic principles of the action workflow theory see Winograd 1986; Winograd/Flores 1986; Medina-Mora et al. 1992).

The traditional view of information processing and communication processes makes use of a central entity, as well as a sequential order of processing steps. However, just as we today know that the traditional, largely centralist view of organization structures only reflects a special case within the spectrum of centralization and decentralization in the field of management, the central control of technical information and communication systems can be classified into a continuum of varying degrees of dispersion. Analogous to this, organizational events, as well as the traditional, largely sequential perspective of technical processes are only a special case within the spectrum of sequentialization and parallelization.

There is a recognized need for a thorough study on the degrees of freedom of dispersion (i.e. within the centralization and decentralization spectrum) and concur-

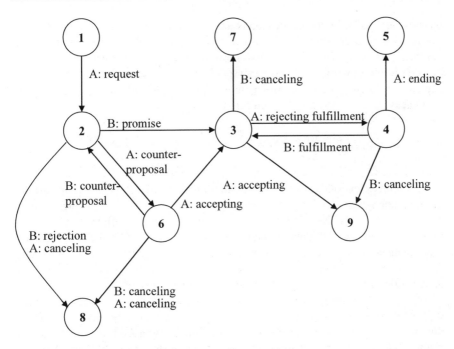

**Fig. 4.24.** Example of a conversation network modeled as an automaton (Borghoff/
Schlichter 1998, p. 187)

rency (i.e. within the sequentialization and parallelization spectrum). Although research has for several decades been devoted to bringing about a better understanding of cooperating processes, our existing knowledge of the organization of distributed systems and concurrent processes is still rather limited compared to our
knowledge of sequential events.

An important approach for the description of distributed, concurrent systems is
the Petri net model (e.g., Baumgarten 1996; Reisig 1990; Starke 1990). In 1962,
Carl Adam Petri's dissertation created the basis of this descriptive approach with
which it is also possible to depict temporal relationships. Today, Petri nets are
used in many application areas, for example, in the description of human interaction processes, technical communication events, and also in business transactions.
This will be discussed in more detail in section 4.4.6.

In the context of technical applications, an important Petri nets application area
is the modeling of communication protocols. Such protocols are necessary to safeguard a regulated information exchange, exclude undesired network behavior, and
ensure a minimum level of fault tolerance in computer networks (see section 4.2).
Nationally and internationally, standardized communication protocols (e.g., the
ISO/OSI reference model, see section 4.2) are currently mostly too complex to be
tested comprehensively in practice. Network models therefore facilitate a clear description of formal analysis and/or the simulation of extensive test runs. In the

business application context, Petri nets are becoming increasingly important with regard to the description, analysis, and simulation of office events and general business processes. They allow the description of structured events, based on the division of labor, within and between organizations, while not being limited to the depiction of purely sequential processing steps, but also allowing the description of processing alternatives and concurrent processing steps.

## 4.4.3   Limits of Formalization

Data processing requires communication and communication requires language. While communication between people can utilize informal linguistic tools, the use of computer systems and the technical communication between computer systems always require formalized communication. The possibilities of formalized communication are, however, limited by the powers of expression of formal languages and their characterizing models (mathematical constructs, logical calculus, grammars, and / or automata). Computability theory deals with questions regarding which problems are describable by means of which language classes and the limits of describability. These questions are, however, of little interest in the case of computer-supported data processing, because real computers are, strictly speaking, only finite automata. The reason for this lies in the finite memory. More comprehensive problem classes require a theoretically infinite memory for the implementation of specific formal automata models. No matter how large the available memory, no matter how fast the processor, or how long the available computing time may be, time and memory are always finite under real application conditions. The modeling assumptions of unlimited memory or unlimited time are unreal.

But what can computers actually achieve given these real constraints? Complexity theory deals with this question. This theory also established the need for resources requirements to process problems that are solvable in principle and attempts to classify problems according to the extent of their resource requirements. Consequently, it is possible to provide the prerequisites for basic time and effort estimates in the computer-supported data processing area. It is also easy to demonstrate that even for many problems for which there are formal language and / or algorithmic solutions, there can be no exact computer-supported solution. Numerous business problems fall into this complexity class, including the "traveling salesman problem," in which the most economic transport route needs to be determined for an arbitrary number of travel destinations, and an analogous problem, the "optimal machine scheduling planning" problem. Such problems can generally only be meaningfully handled by means of heuristics, i.e. procedures that are not based on scientifically proven knowledge, but on hypotheses, assumptions, and experience.

Even within a static problem world in which problems can actually be described well, there are limits to practical computability. Furthermore, reality "complicates" the situation: The business problem world is subject to constant changes that vary in intensity. Formal descriptions are, however, static. Moreover, real problems change with the sheer effort of describing them. Nevertheless, intensive work is currently being undertaken with regard to new and further development of system specifications. An "ideal" system description's main characteristics are, among others, correctness, unambiguity, completeness, verifiability, and consistency. Researchers within the field of information systems do not doubt that in time it will be possible to provide a comprehensive model of the social system "enterprise." In the light of economic theory, however, this objective seems doubtful. In 1987 Ciborra had (alluding to the development of comprehensive enterprise data models) already highlighted the fundamental problem of the realizability of formal enterprise models: "Now, if this were possible, the enterprise would not have any reason to exist according to the transaction cost view: its dissolution would be warranted on efficiency grounds (reduction of overhead costs)" (Ciborra 1987). In accordance with transaction cost theory (see chapter 2.3.3), an enterprise that can be holistically modeled cannot be efficient. Based on its evident describability, it would no longer be possible to hierarchically coordinate it. Transaction cost theory therefore contradicts the possibility of a comprehensive description and depiction of the enterprise (Ciborra 1987; Picot 1989b).

In other words, a comprehensive description of an institution's information architecture would immediately deprive this institution's coordination mechanisms of their authority. The moment that an enterprise's information structures are formalized, it is possible to utilize this formalization to decrease the transaction costs associated with the enterprise's information and communication activities. As already indicated in section 4.3.2, such formalization may, for example, be regarded as a basis for the deployment of information and communication technology. Another opportunity arises during enterprise reorganization efforts, i.e. when its hitherto (e.g., hierarchical) organizational form is altered.

The ever-increasing diffusion of information and communication technology infrastructures has led to the predicted reorganization effect already manifesting itself in practice. Monolithic organization structures disband in favor of decentralized, dispersed and network-like organization architectures. Current information models cannot, however, support organizations' mutability towards modular or virtual structures; they inhibit the change process. Modular, network-like or virtual organizations do not arise out of thin air but arise from existing organization structures through organization change. To date, current description techniques can scarcely support this change process.

## 4.4.4  System Development

The engineering-based development of software by means of scientific methods and tools (i.e. software engineering) is usually viewed as a life cycle – the software development life cycle. Within this framework, two fundamental approaches are initially distinguished (McDermid / Rook 1991): On the one hand there is the project management perspective that carries out software development according to chronologically linked phases, while, on the other hand, there is a rather more technical approach in which distinct software design stages are differentiated. A classic example of the former approach is the waterfall model originally developed by W. W. Royce (1970). This name comes from the step-wise depiction of individual project phases, which is associated with a waterfall (see figure 4.25).

In this model, there is a strict division between problem-area-specific and implementation-specific activities, which is conveyed by the explicit separation between the analysis and design phases. The output of the concept analysis phase has no implementation instructions, which means that the specific department is largely responsible for this. In contrast, the drafting of the technical concept is mostly done by the responsible information technology department in the design phase, as concrete implementation-specific decisions are made here. To date, the waterfall model has undergone many enhancements, such as the introduction of validation steps and feedback loops between the phases, to guarantee improved quality assurance in the development process.

Prototyping is one example of the technology-oriented approach. It is the development of an executable pre-version (prototype) of the final software version. This method permits the early linking of users and thus counteracts the consequences of possible imprecise specifications. Prototyping can be classified into three forms

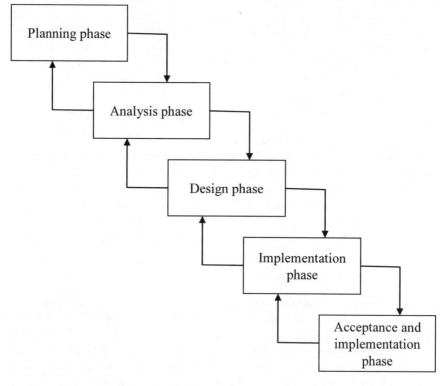

**Fig. 4.25.** The waterfall model of software development (based on Royce (1970))

(explorative, experimental, and evolutionary) and assumes an important role, especially with regard to object-oriented system development. The differences between the various prototyping types are determined by their specific goals (Pomberger/Blaschek 1993). As an illustrative object, the explorative prototype is a way of ensuring a maximum of complete system specifications. The experimental prototype reflects an approach that allows the software's usefulness to be tested while relying on partial specifications, i.e. it is an attempt to test the feasibility of specific goals. Evolutionary prototyping, in which the prototype is developed stepwise until the end product is achieved, is of greatest interest for software development.

Barry Boehm (1988) achieved the linking of two differing development methodologies (the phase-oriented and technique-oriented approaches) via his spiral model (see figure 4.26, as well as Hesse/Merbeth/Frölich 1992). Here, the analysis, design, implementation, and testing project phases are embedded within an iterative framework, making an improved prototype available after each phase. A planning phase, risk analysis, as well as the mentioned project phases for the generation of the actual software, together with an evaluation by customers is planned for each of these prototypes.

Owing to the high level of complexity of modern software systems, such methodologies are becoming increasingly important for software development, especially since classic, phase-oriented procedures have failed as an exclusive structuring concept. In view of this shortcoming, various extensions of the phase model were undertaken. Among these efforts, two models contribute specifically to object-oriented software development: The cluster model by Meyer (1989) and the fountain model by Henderson-Sellers and Edwards (1990).

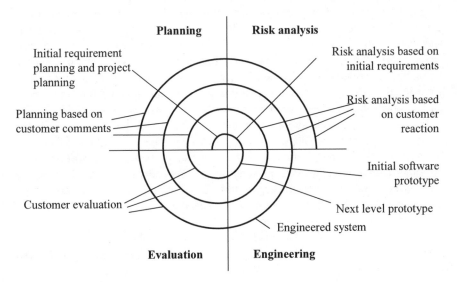

**Fig. 4.26.** The spiral model

## 4.4.5  Modeling of Information Systems

As an abstraction of reality, the model is the focal point of both project phases, i.e. analysis and design. In this regard, software is mostly specified beforehand by means of graphical notations that, in turn, provide a basis for the comprehensive planning of the peripheral conditions such as project duration or occurred costs. The modeling of software is usually related to two aspects: the system's dynamic functionality and static structures. In accordance with this dichotomous partitioning, one primarily differentiates between functional modeling and data modeling. Object-oriented modeling of software is another approach that is being increasingly used. In object-oriented modeling, the problem world has been classified into objects, i.e. independent but interacting components, each with its own characteristics and behavior.

One well-known functional modeling method is the data flow diagram developed by Tom DeMarco (1978) within the structured analysis (SA) framework. The data flow diagram provides the system specification process with tools and methods that provide order and precision by guiding and developing a structured specification. The essence of this notation method is limited to three key elements: The activities, data flows indicated by arrows, as well as data sources indicated by two parallel lines. The analyst's challenge is to link tasks with the aid of the data flow arrows in order to capture the functional aspects of the software to be specified. Included in the capturing of the function aspects is a hierarchical concept, the structured analysis, which enables a relatively simple way of learning and is a comprehensive method for specifying top-down dynamic relationships.

The second aspect of a system description refers to the static relationships within it. Six years after the first publication of the relational database model by E. Codd (1970), Peter Pin-Shan Chen (1976) presented his method of modeling data and their mutual relationships. This entity/relationship approach has meanwhile become the standard method for data modeling and is viewed as a mature concept. It combines three different elements and is therefore structurally relatively simple. By using the essential elements (i.e. entity, property, and relationship), it is possible to depict objects, object properties and the relationships between objects. The following example should simplify the understanding and use of these terms: In the entity/relationship terminology, the term entity may refer to a customer, a product or an order. The characteristics of entities – called properties – are, for example, customer names and addresses, product prices, and order numbers. The possible relation between the three entities would, for example, be the connection "has placed an order," the link between the customer, the product that was ordered, and the specifics pertaining to the order.

This entity/relationship approach has been considerably improved (see, e.g., Date 1999). Among the most important improvements are the specification of relational complexities, i.e. the specification of the maximum number of possible relational partners and the further detailing of the relationship terminology into specializing and decompositional relationships. An example of the first variant, also known as the "is-a relation," would be the relationship between the entities BMW, Mercedes, Audi, etc. and the entity automobile ("BMW is-an automobile"). The listed automobile models are forms of the entity automobile, whereas a decompositional relation (i.e. the relation "has-a") has automobiles components as members. An example of the latter is the relation between the automobile entity and the entities body, engine, gearbox, frame, etc. ("automobile has-a body").

Software systems always combine static, as well as dynamic elements. Consequently, there is a general need for the deployment of a model that combines data and functions (methods). Nevertheless, one should be aware of the difficulty of combining both perspectives. The parallel development of the two models demands intensive coordination between the relevant employees, especially since the interdependencies between the static and dynamic perspectives are usually very strong. The separation of data and functions therefore seems somewhat hindering, but this is due to the software development history and the database systems.

The object orientation approach offers a possibility for improvement (see section 4.2.1). In this concept, the delineation between data and function is dissolved and partitioning occurs along modular boundaries. The term aggregation is used here to denote the summary of an object's components, which includes executable operations. Aggregation thus forms the basis of modern system development, which considers such concepts as reusability, dynamic data exchange, compatibility, client / server, etc. Within this context, one should also note the programming by contract concept, the basis of modern system development, which considers concepts such as correctness, robustness, expandability, reusability, and compatibility (Meyer 1990). This modular view of the software system enables better planning and coordination of software developers, as well as more flexible and clearer customization and maintenance.

Rumbaugh et al. (1991), as well as Coad and Yourdon (1991) are proponents of the object-oriented modeling approach. It makes sense to consider the classification of this and other procedures in conjunction with the context in which they originated. Rumbaugh's method, object modeling technique (OMT), essentially utilizes already known concepts that can be categorized as evolutionary procedures, while the procedures used by Coad and Yourdon are better described as revolutionary. The constituent concepts of Rumbaugh's object modeling technique are an expanded entity / relationship diagram, a data flow diagram, as well as a state transition diagram that depicts events occurring within the system. In contrast, Coad and Yourdon use an integrated notation, object-oriented analysis (OOA), which utilizes one of the three different views of the software to be developed via integrating notations. It already offers the advantage of an integrated examination of data (properties) and functions (behavior) during the analysis phase, making a subsequent consolidation less likely to require changes.

In 1997, the Object Management Group (OMG, www.omg.org) looked for a standard for the exchange of object models and chose the unified modeling language (UML, http://www.uml.org/). Since the most important players in object technology area are either OMG participants or those who align themselves with the OMG standard, UML has emerged as the standard notation for business process and object modeling.

## 4.4.6  Enterprise Modeling

When modeling is applied to real objects, such as enterprises, it is necessary to incorporate the capturing and integration of actors into the model. The aspect "who" must therefore be added to the software system aspects "how" and "with what" and, eventually, "when" to enable a realistic depiction of reality. This leads one to the organization and events model. With regard to enterprises, the organization model essentially includes the organizational units, i.e. the enterprise structure. In the event model, the chronological relationships are modeled, i.e. which event triggered which action and which further events are caused as a result of this are taken into

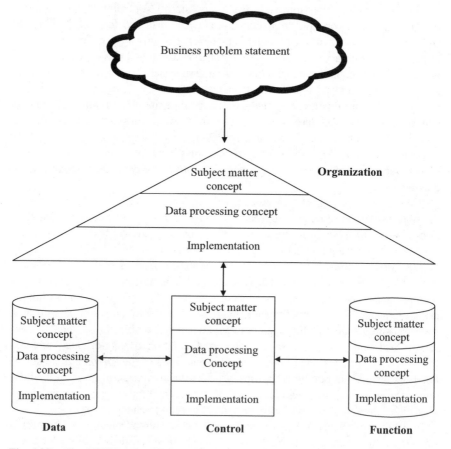

**Fig. 4.27.**  The ARIS concept (Scheer 1997)

account. Planning software for workflow systems such as Scheer's ARIS Toolset and / or the product Bonapart (see, e.g., Krallmann / Klotz 1994) offers modeling tools that enable certain activities to be assigned to specific actors.

Even though the four levels of modeling (data, functions, objects, and events) are not always explicitly considered in all known methods and models, all four dimensions are always included. Important approaches to enterprise modeling are Scheer's architecture of integrated information systems (ARIS) and the semantic object model (SOM) by Ferstl and Sinz.

Scheer's ARIS concept (1994) approximates the above-mentioned four-dimensional perspective best (see figure 4.27).

Within the overall enterprise modeling framework, this concept describes four perspectives of the information system: The data, function, organization, and control perspectives. Events are introduced into the model from a control perspective and serve as the basis for linking the function and data perspectives. The result of such a linkage is the event-driven process chain (EDPC). The assignment of individual functions to organization units provides a link to the organizational perspective. Figure 4.28 provides a simple example to illustrate this.

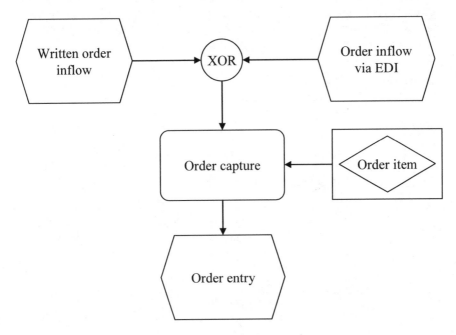

**Fig. 4.28.**   The event-controlled process chain "order entry"

The two events "new order" and "new order via EDI" occur exclusively in respect of a given order and trigger the function "order capture." This function uses the data object "order item" and results in the event "order entry."

The semantic object model (Ferstl / Sinz 1990, 1991) is an attempt to minimize the structural breaks between the various perspectives on the enterprise. Embedded within a comprehensive procedural model, a top-down approach is used to interactively develop data, functions, organization units, and events. At each level of refinement, a comprehensive model becomes available that reflects all dimensions, ensuring a structurally continuous collaboration. The final specified result, the conceptual object scheme, could be used as the basis for the actual software development. The model's consideration of organizational aspects gives the design process a holistic perspective.

The basis for the modeling of the event-driven dynamic system enterprise is found in both ARIS and the SOM Petri net, although in a deviating form. This modeling method, discussed in section 4.3.2, allows chronological relationships to be described by means of two different types of network nodes.

On the one hand, a Petri net describes local states, which are often called conditions or objects, and are usually depicted as circles. These states or conditions may contain symbols called markers. The second type of network nodes refers to events, which are depicted as rectangles. Events and local conditions are reciprocally interconnected, i.e. an event leads to a condition, and from a condition an event may occur, etc. Events, indicated by rectangular symbols, may potentially bring about changes in their local conditions by rearranging the markers contained within "local

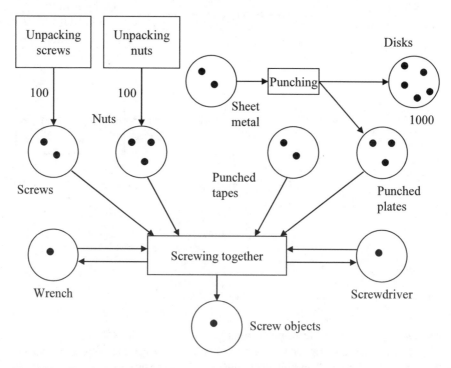

**Fig. 4.29.**  Simple Petri net model: sheet metal and screws (Baumgarten 1996)

conditions." These changes can be described mathematically, making a control and analysis of the number of relative temporal intervals and sequences of events possible with the net.

In the example (see figure 4.29) of the event "screwing together," one requires a screw, a nut, a punched tape, and a punched plate. One will also need a wrench, a screwdriver, and a container with sufficient space for new objects. All of the resources required for this event are symbolized by abstract markers. The "screwing together" activity may be simulated within a Petri net by removing relevant markers from already stored containers and the storing of certain markers in object containers.

Thanks to its instinctive naturalness and closeness to reality, the object-oriented approach as utilized in SOM and also in ARIS (Bungert / Hess 1995) for the modeling of enterprises is enjoying ever-increasing popularity. For a theoretical discussion of object-oriented enterprise modeling, see Lutz (1997) and for an applied approach see, e.g., Taylor (1995).

## 4.5   Implications for Management

In the often-exaggerated pursuit of ever newer and better management concepts, companies are confronted with a multitude of different recommendations. Approaches such as lean management, total quality management, empowerment, quality circles, and / or reengineering were often regarded as a cure-all for a firm's problems. Decision-makers who did not embrace the management concept *de jour* had to justify their decision and had to face general incomprehension. Within these developments, which are often strongly influenced by various trends, it has become increasingly difficult to discern truly seminal ideas from the multitude of quick fixes (see Wigand 1995d).

Over the last 50 years, change has mainly been applied to the functional hierarchy, which has been the dominant organization model. For a reconfiguration, one has to identify core processes that not only cover the entire enterprise, but also include the suppliers and customers. The process is the focal point, i.e. it is not what an enterprise produces that is of central concern, but how this is produced with the support of partners, suppliers and, possibly, customers. However, even when firms have identified the correct processes, it is still a difficult, not to be underestimated, task to design these processes and develop them continuously. Information and communication technology plays a decisive role in this procedure. Nevertheless, its potential can only be fully exploited if it is appropriately deployed. The optimal alignment of processes with the superimposed information and communication technology is the fundamental presupposition for a successful transformation to an adaptable and flexible organization.

The explanations in section 4.3.4 emphasize that there is no direct correlation between information and communication technology deployment and derived value. We should therefore pay more attention to the business strategy and / or the organization's goals. The requirements derived from them in respect of information technology should be taken into consideration in conjunction with the requirements arising from the actual organization of business processes. We also need to recognize the reciprocal relationship: On the one hand, business strategy and processes define their requirements with regard to information and communication technology implementation while, on the other hand, information and communication technology enables the implementation of newer strategies and processes. The skill lies in finding the optimal degree of information and communication technology deployment, i.e. the optimal organizational fit.

In order to achieve this, several iterations may be required during the implementation, which are always followed by improvements, adjustments, fine-tuning, and calibration that are quite similar to the self-regulatory mechanisms in a cybernetic system. Not until a suitable linkage has been established between the information and communication technology, the business strategies, goals and processes, and the organization has adapted itself to these changes can improvement with regard to efficiency and effectiveness be expected (Wigand 1995a).

Beside minimal sufficiency, we may also strive to achieve an innovative deployment of information and communication technology. The deployment of the production factor information should be as novel and unique as possible to ensure survival in the light of international competition. In this regard, Ciborra (1994), for example, offers an approach with his seemingly contradictory guidelines. He argues that these seven paradoxes describe a new "systematic" organizational approach to controlling innovative information system development. They are suited for fostering learning processes and creativity, and also move the need for control to the background.

Striving toward innovative information and communication technology solutions, as well as the right organizational fit is the key to surmounting the performance limits of organizations. This not only refers to the firm's traditional boundaries with regard to geographic limitations, distance, speed, and working hours, but also to employee awareness and perceptual limitations. The vision of an adaptable and flexible enterprise can be realized by continually aligning information technology, business goals, strategies, and organizational processes, as well as by expanding the organization boundaries. This is supported and fostered by the continuously increasing potential of information and communication technology.

# The Dissolving of Hierarchies – Modularizing the Enterprise

# Case Study Chapter 5: The "Spaghetti Organization" of Oticon

After a period of intensive rationalization and economization, a major change took place at Oticon, the traditional Danish hearing-aid producer. A radical decision was made to almost overnight remove and reorganize the hierarchical structure of the 120 staff members at the headquarters in Copenhagen. All individual workplaces, spaces, and supplies were abolished. Oticon employees no longer had an office, a desk, or even a personal computer. In their place, a new architectural concept, a new innovative technical infrastructure, new ways of using supplies, and new rules for task completion and collaboration were introduced (e.g., Hagström 1995a, 1995b; Kao 1996).

Today, entire customer-oriented projects that start at the product development level and end at the market level are the focal point of teamwork. A responsible manager and promoter from the ten-person top management team oversee these projects by providing contacts and opening doors within the organization. There are no longer set working rules and employees are not obligated to be present at fixed working hours. Each employee is responsible to the rest of the team for input to help achieve the team goal. Individuals are assigned to a resource pool, and they can apply for projects on the basis of their personal interests.

As a rule, employees simultaneously work on several interdisciplinary projects. The principle is that specialists from one area should take on roles from other areas to gain skills and insight into the workings of the organization's different areas. Consequently, for example, an engineer, who is usually responsible for the programming of microchips, can participate in the development of market strategies and also be responsible for the correspondence with Spanish business partners.

A crucial Oticon principle concerns the spatial proximity of the project members: Whenever possible, face-to-face communication is preferred.

At first, the employees met the reorganization with great enthusiasm. A wave of project initiatives led to the innovation of new projects, which are the main source of the company's income today. Production cycles were also cut in half. After some time, however, the original "spaghetti organization" met with resistance. After the initial euphoria had died down, many employees were not satisfied with the reorganization. Even though the increase in decision-making input and independence was generally motivational, many Oticon employees wanted monetary incentives. Many projects on which the employees worked were also suddenly discontinued or never completed.

Today, Oticon has extended the original organization with competence centers that mediate between different projects. The organization's individual parts have also been modified to provide a clear hierarchical framework. The Oticon example shows that there is no "one best way" for organizations, but that individual organization and employee situations need to be considered to create a dynamic organization (Foss 2001).

## 5.1     Fundamentals of Modularization

In the last few years, research and experience from business practice have provided increasing evidence that changed competitive conditions require companies to reorganize. The crux of this criticism concerns large-scale companies with strong hierarchical and dysfunctional organization structures. Much has been said about the end of the "dinosaurs" and that they will be replaced by modularly built, highly flexible, "flotilla" organizations (Drucker 1990). Many authors are of the opinion that company reorganization should be undertaken by flattening hierarchical structures (Bennis 1993; Davidow / Malone 1993; Picot / Reichwald 1994; Wigand 1985). These theories will be discussed in detail in this chapter.

Modularization as an independent organizational principle needs to be defined before the causes and economic explanatory approaches of the above developments are discussed. An analysis of the proposals suggested in the literature for the reorganization of the value chain by means of "fractals," "segments" or "modules" (Warnecke 1992; Zenger / Hesterly 1997; Wildemann 1998) indicates considerable similarity between these concepts. By combining their fundamentals, one arrives at the following:

Modularization means a reconstruction of the company organization on the basis of integrated, customer-oriented processes with relatively small, observable elements (modules). These are revealed through decentralized decision competency and results-based responsibility, which leads to stronger coordination between the modules through non-hierarchical coordination forms. The common fundamentals of modularization concepts are applicable on different organizational levels (Gerpott / Boehm 2000): From modularization on different working levels to the development of autonomous groups up to breaking up the entire organization into largely independent profit centers.

### 5.1.1   Characteristics of Modular Organization Forms

The main goal of dividing companies into modules is to reduce the complexity of performance development and to gain a closer proximity to the market. The modularized company should be able to react quicker and more flexibly to market changes, customer demands, and competition. The specific characteristics of the above definition will be examined in more detail in the following section.

**Restructuring of the Company Organization**

Modularization is an intra-organizational reorganization form (Schwarzer / Krcmar 1994). This form differs from the new organizational forms (network and / or virtual organizations) – discussed in chapters 6 and 8 – that involve relatively long-term or case-specific co-operational relationships between different organizations and / or organizational units (interorganizational perspective).

It is assumed that the value-added process occurring in modules is highly specific and cannot, in certain instances, be applied to the market (see transaction cost theory discussions in chapter 2). The object of reorganization, in the sense of modularization concepts, is thus the "classic" organization, which is characterized by long-term contracts and property rights. However, this does not mean that property rights of complete modules such as those created through further development of the organization cannot be transferred to third parties.

**Process Orientation**

Besides promoting modularization concepts, the reorientation of organization units towards processes (i.e. the chains of connected activities for the production of products or rendered services) (e.g., Picot/Franck 1995) encourages many contributions to the company's general organization (e.g., Striening 1988; Harrington 1991; Davenport 1993; Österle 1995a, 1995b; Picot/Franck 1995; Gaitanides 1996). This emphasizes the contrast with previous, primarily functional and/or work-oriented organizational concepts that concentrate on optimal productivity through specialization.

The main goal of this process orientation is the reduction of organizational obstacles in the performance process. In the last few years, obstacles such as communication barriers, goal conflicts or waiting time between the different functional departments have all been identified as some of the main causes of companies' deteriorating competitive capability (e.g., Gaiser 1993). They can trigger long production cycles (Reichwald/Sachenbacher 1996b) and high costs when customer contracts are involved. The latter often arise when problems such as poor quality or a lack of flexibility to react to market changes are noticed too late (Sanchez/Mahoney 1996; Baldwin/Clark 1998).

From a modularization and organization theoretical point of view, orientation toward processes rather than functionality becomes an object-oriented modeling and structural approach (see chapter 4). In principle, modularization concepts are similar to the well-known functional organization. However, a recent development is the transformation of object-oriented structures at all organizational levels. In addition, the organization structure not only targets finished products during modularization, but also interim products (monetary and other services).

**Customer Orientation**

Although module orientation generally emphasizes organizational activities (internal and external products) as its goal, the importance of customer orientation should not be ignored. This is developed through the customer who has a key role in defining the requirements of the services to be rendered and, consequently, also in the process. Through an object-oriented perspective of internal products and processes, the internal purchaser of services also develops an expanded awareness of the customers. This means that modularization efforts have to complement the current requirements of total quality management (TQM), which demand continuous attention to service quality along the entire value chain (e.g., Mizuno 1988; Weaver 1991; Oess 1994).

The emphasis on customer orientation by market-oriented and trade-based processes has an interesting side effect. According to customer-oriented fundamental principles, the reorganization of market-distant organizational areas, such as research and development, finance departments, and / or human resources, can lead to a restructuring of the value chain's market level. For this restructuring to occur, an exact definition has to be developed of internal customers and their specific needs.

## Integration of Tasks

The demand for a widespread integration and / or completion of tasks merged within a complete module is directly linked to process and customer orientation. This demand is created by applying process orientation in order to integrate as many activities as possible for the development of (interim) products. According to organization theory, this is possible as organizational obstacles should be avoided by means of strongly interdependent tasks. The minimum size of a module arises from the process steps for a clearly definable interim product. However, this is problematic, since – depending on the task – the process viewpoint can be too highly dependent on the task integration along the value chain. This can cause the borders of control to be crossed by a small margin (in the sense of the above definition of modularization). This will be discussed in more detail later in the chapter.

## Developing Smaller Organization Units

A process orientation trait that all modularization approaches have in common with most current reorganization approaches is the building of small units, which may be considered the fundamental concept of modularization (Weber 1995). Its goal is to adapt the organization structure to the problem capacity of people and / or a small, manageable group of people. This is aimed at specifically preventing complex errors, additional costs, and delays.

Depending on the task and due to human factors, the boundaries of control are different and can cause visible fluctuations when determining an appropriate size for "small units." Frese correctly points out that this is a "relatively small number of people" (1993, p. 1004). However, empirical research results suggest that there is a ceiling. Peters and Waterman (1984) determined that when an organization level reaches about 500 employees, work conflicts, fluctuations, and dissatisfaction increase at a disproportional rate. A maximum size of approximately 15 people is suggested for partially autonomous groups, which is the fundamental form of modular organization units.

Besides the previously discussed demand for the completion of tasks within modules, this leads to module building facing a second fundamental demand. The scale and complexity of a task assigned to a module have to consider the capacity of the people and / or group as a determining factor. A conflict that is difficult to solve can arise when, from a process-oriented point of view, the most meaningful minimum size for task integration exceeds the boundaries within which a module can be overviewed and controlled by even a small margin. Through the implementation of new information and communication technology (ICT) (see chapter 4), which help to expand these boundaries, these conflicts can be greatly reduced. These new technologies, much like the re-engineering movement (e.g., Davenport 1993; Hammer / Champy 1993), play an important role as "enablers" of modularization.

Furthermore, increasing emphasis is placed on reducing technological and procedural dependencies to a minimum, even during the creation of products and services. Through the partitioning of services into mostly independent and functional subsystems with defined interfaces, certain fields and tasks can be targeted and isolated from others. Likewise, the modularization principle has for years been utilized in the software field in an effort to reduce production time. However, even in other areas, such as the automotive industry, emphasis is increasingly being placed on product modularization to structure and synergize different areas. Finally, it is easier to outsource closed function modules to external partners (see chapter 6).

As a general rule, the advantages of product modularization outweigh the disadvantages, although there is always the danger that a module will become completely independent. This means that it is possible to lose track of the production as whole due to the continuous optimization of different areas. The utility of products and services should therefore be regularly checked for its overall appropriateness and competitiveness in the field with regard to close-to-market competitors, as well the company's goals.

### Decentralized Decision-Making Competency and Responsibility for Results and Performance

A further shared characteristic of the modularization concepts is the relocation of decision-making competency, as well as responsibility for results and performance to the modules. The concrete levels of this reintegration of task planning and administration are based on their approach and assignment. Fundamentally, the subsidiary principle (see Picot 1991c) is followed as a guideline for the decentralization of management functions. This means that decision-making competency and responsibility for results and performance should be kept at the lowest possible level within a hierarchy (as close as possible to the value-added process). This means that decision-making competency that is close to the process will increase the company's flexibility greatly through many decentralized and customer-oriented groups (see Beuermann 1992), and through the elimination of long decision-making processes that are vulnerable to mistakes. At the same time, the added task responsibility should increase employee motivation and strengthen the incentive for fair trade. Consequently, the management role changes from that of the traditional boss to "coach" (see chapter 9).

### Non-hierarchical Coordination Forms Between Modules

As previously explained in chapter 2, the proponents of traditional economics assume that markets are coordinated by what is called an "invisible hand." The crux of this concept is that the price mechanism, which coordinates the activities of the individual market participants, focuses market information, and signals trade possibilities, thus creating an optimal resource allocation.

Alfred Chandler, the late well-known Harvard business historian, conversely argues for the "visible hand" of management. He refers to the hierarchical coordination of business activities through an organization's management. "Self-regulation" through market mechanisms is superseded by the "external regulation" of the organization participants by the management within the hierarchy.

Recently, it has become clear that besides the "visible hand" of management concept, large organizations in particular are trying to apply market-similar coordination mechanisms to the coordinate largely autonomous organization units (e.g., Picot / Ripperger / Wolff 1996; Frese 2000; Bieberbach 2001). These mechanisms such as the internal market-oriented transfer price, should allow the "invisible hand" of the market to become more useful.

As an alternative to hierarchical coordination, the use of "softer" measures, such as the development of a particular organizational culture, are also discussed (e.g., Wilkens / Ouchi 1983). With its emphasis on the organization's goals, the problem of the coordination of modular organization units gives rise to many questions that need to be addressed (see section 5.2). However, the application of new information and communication technologies (ICT) creates new possibilities to control coordination tasks and improve them through human influence (see section 5.2). First, the dysfunctions of traditional organizational forms need to be discussed before implementation forms of modularization can be presented.

**Hierarchy and Modularization**

The term hierarchy generally describes the structure of senior and subordinate positions within an organization (e.g., Welge 1987; Kappler / Rehkugler 1991). Within this structure, positions are the smallest organization units to which specific tasks are assigned in a relatively "people-neutral" manner. Generally, the building potential and the formation of relationships between positions will be established first (position-based hierarchy). An indication of a hierarchical relationship between positions is the one-sided allocation of services and decision-making capabilities in favor of the higher-level, authoritative positions over the lower-level positions.

While one person usually holds the authoritative position, it can also be held by a group of people (for instance a commission or committee). In practice, a position-based hierarchy is also a concrete people-based hierarchy linked to a corresponding power and status-based hierarchy. Organization theory research into hierarchy and / or its alternatives cannot be done without considering the sociological factors associated with it, such as the acceptance of power structures within companies and organizations.

In respect of the topic vertical integration, the term hierarchy has an even wider definition within the organization theory literature (e.g., Picot 1991b). Here, "hierarchy" is regarded as the extreme form of the organizational linking of parts of the value-added chain, which is in contrast with the case-by-case completion of transactions in the market, as well as with hybrid organizational forms (see chapter 2).

In this context, long-term work contracts are used as the basis for service exchanges and are therefore the most important indication of a hierarchy. The direct connection to the above fundamental concepts of hierarchy is based on the fact that these long-term contracts are the very reason that, in comparison to service exchanges, extended directive and control authorization is possible (see chapter 2).

Today, the typical dysfunctions of hierarchical organizational forms are known (e.g., Bennis 1993; Peters 1993):

- Long decision processes on the "authoritative path." This causes inflexibility in the face of market changes, as well as high coordination costs during turbulent market conditions;

- Market- and process-distant decision makers;

- Information filtering and distortion problems;

- Concentration on regional goals, since only the top hierarchical levels have the ability to see the entire process;

- Inadequate acceptance of the hierarchical coordination by means of directives, especially in connection with an authoritarian leadership style.

From this short observation of the different definitions of hierarchy and the very different dysfunctions related to them, it is obvious that many different factors have to be considered in order to assess the relationship between hierarchy and modularization. In respect of the previously discussed conclusions, the theory of the "de-hierarchization of companies" can, for example, be interpreted in many different ways when regarded from a modularization viewpoint:

- as the reversal or flattening of position-based hierarchy;

- as the transformation of a person-based hierarchy to a commission-based hierarchy;

- as the reduction of the degree of vertical integration in the value-added chain.

While this theory can be accepted in many respects, a complete de-hierarchization, as the theory title suggests, cannot be expected (Kühl 1995).

It is therefore obvious that a comparison between hierarchy and modularization requires different viewpoints. Selected aspects of modularization theories will be discussed in greater detail below.

### Bureaucracy and Modularization

The work of Max Weber is often used as a reference for the general characterization of bureaucracies (Weber 1922). He describes a few of the characteristic features of bureaucratic organization (summarized by Derlien 1992; Kieser 1999):

- Full-time employees;

- Separation of (private) budget and operation;

- Hierarchy of senior and subordinate positions;
- Scaling of directive and control authorization;
- Compliance and reporting;
- Formal divisions based on spatial and professional competency;
- Strict observation of rules, which leads to an impersonal process;
- Supervision and regulation of the paper flow to ensure security and control.

While the details of Weber's bureaucracy model are based on public administration, most of this model's definitive features can also be applied to organizations in the private sector. There is often a reference to "bureaucratization" when an organization shows signs of the above-mentioned features. In the same sense, an organization that is moving away from this structure is referred to as being in the process of "de-bureaucratization." With this in mind, Frese (1993) refers to the modularization concepts of large organizations as the "de-bureaucratization effect."

At first, Weber's model was merely regarded as the ideal concept of bureaucracy, but it has provided a wide spectrum of approaches to bureaucracy criticism (Derlien 1992). These primarily address the different dysfunctions of bureaucracies from the risk of individual bureaucratic structures developing a life of their own to the loss of the "human" aspect, and viewpoints regarding their efficiency. Within the new organizational concepts (e.g., modularization) discussion, new concepts have been developed that are especially useful within institutional economics, such as the property rights theory, transaction cost theory, and principal-agent theory (see chapter 2). The modularization principle will be discussed in greater detail later in this chapter.

The focus of bureaucratic criticism is concentrated on hierarchical characteristics (e.g., Bennis 1993). The most frequently mentioned bureaucratic organization dysfunctions are the examples discussed above in connection with hierarchy. In this light, it is clear why the terms hierarchy and bureaucracy are used relatively undifferentiated in the literature.

However, when examining the connection between bureaucracy and modularization, it should not be forgotten that the characteristics of a bureaucracy (in Weber's sense) clearly contain more aspects than those of a hierarchy. This is especially true with regard to rule-observation within the procedures of a bureaucracy. It is within this context that Kieser and Kubicek (1992) emphasize that the widely believed assumption of de-bureaucratization – especially relating to the building of small organization units – is generally untested. They assume that general rules will become more important for the coordination of teams (also see Reichwald/Koller 1996b). However, this does not apply to the strict and fixed rules that lie at the heart of bureaucracy, but more to the application and use of behavioral maxims, norms, and values as suggested in many of the new organizational concepts (see chapter 9).

The comparison between bureaucracy and modularization in respect of limited competency-based assignments can be likewise explained. There seems to be a preference within modularization concepts for the expansion of competency-based but autonomous organization units that are oriented towards a stronger process, thus leading to a stronger customer focus. At the same time, the necessity of task assignments will result in limited competency with regard to functionality. It is therefore also impossible to address the proposition of the diametrical contrast between a "bureaucratic" and "modular" organization from this perspective.

**Taylorism and Modularization**

The dominating design principles of the Tayloristic production concept are (Taylor 1913):

- The personal separation of anticipated and executable work;
- The concentration of the work methodology on an extensive job segmentation according to the performance principle;
- The separation of all planned, leading, and controlling tasks in the area of production.

The industrial organization model of the continuous production flow is based on this principle. In management studies, these models are linked to Taylor and Fayol. To this day, the methods and principles of their organizational philosophies still have influence on large industrial organizations (see chapter 9).

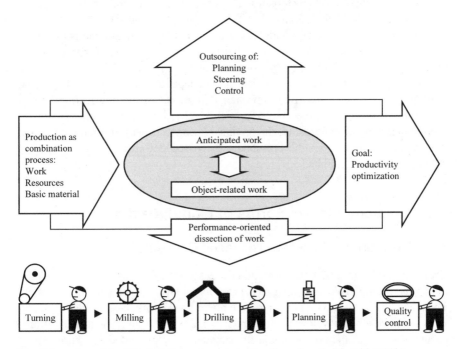

**Fig. 5.1.**  A model of Tayloristic work organization (based on Reichwald 1993b)

A two-tier workforce system was developed from the principle of the separation of all planned, steering, and controlling tasks in the area of production. This is found in management and production sectors, thus creating the "blue-collar" and "white collar" work environments and the "wage receiver" and "salary receiver." The strongly work-dependent performance factors of production areas required a strict hierarchical management structure that implemented highly bureaucratic rules. This did not just influence the production area, but was carried over to the organization as a whole.

Tayloristic organization principles were developed against the background of the never-ending demand for mass-produced products, traditional production technologies, as well as the lack of innovation with regard to industrial products. Based on this competitive situation, organizations' main goal was usually the highest possible level of productivity, known as output level per time unit. Through the development of organizational procedures, especially in the production sector, this method led to a permanent increase in production volume (Reichwald 1992a).

The decomposition and schematization of procedures were also meant to lead to a reduction in the demands made on the individual. The individual would then become a "functional production factor" and could therefore be made responsible for his / her actions. This became the production-based and cost-based theoretical premise for determining the optimal degree of task assignment (e.g., Reichwald 1977).

The task-based organization principles of hierarchy, bureaucracy, and Taylorism reveal reciprocal characteristics. This often leads to an unwarranted equating of the principles, especially in the literature (see chapter 9). It should also be noted that in many cases, especially with regard to extensively standardized goods (e.g., mass-produced goods), other efficient alternatives are presented if market conditions are stable. In addition, to date observations and research have demonstrated that a comparison between modularization concepts and those of organizational principles is an over-simplified approach. The effect of modularization cannot simply be deduced from the converse of hierarchy, bureaucracy, and Taylorism shortcomings. More importantly, the predictable consequences of a modularization need to be deduced from the previously discussed definitive characteristics of modular organization units.

## 5.2   Implementation Forms of Modularization

### 5.2.1   The Spectrum of Modularization Concepts

Reorganization concepts, which were initially described as the fundamental principles of modularization, have been suggested as apt for all levels of company organization: The macro level (overall organization), the micro level (workplace development and work organization), as well as the intermediate meso level (departments and / or procedures). Although they share similar fundamental principles, modularization efforts take on different orientations on the various organizational levels.

On the overall organization level, module building is oriented towards competition-based top-level goals such as market proximity and / or leading-edge technology. On the process-based level, it is focused on task chains. On the work and organization level, the primary focus is on the employees and the ICT to support them.

Modularization concepts often reveal different focal points within a specific level, which compete with one another directly. Conversely, within the different modularization endeavors, potential conflict points can occur between the different levels. It should be noted that a chosen modularization form could become less beneficial if changes are made to its general conditions. It would then be necessary to return to a stronger orientation towards functionality. The following sections will provide an overview of the currently available modularization efforts, thus providing an overview of the limitations of modularization in general.

## 5.2.2   Modularization Concepts at the Organizational Level

### 5.2.2.1   Profit Center Structures with Centralized and Decentralized Modules

A characteristic of many organizations with modularized structures is their formation into many, relatively independent profit centers (Frese 1995). On higher modular levels and / or segments, these are then categorized according to different criteria, such as business areas and products, core competencies, and / or regions or markets (Wittlage 1996). The Swiss-Swedish ABB is a classic example of a profit center organization with a relatively small, coordinated central managerial unit (e.g., Koerber 1993). The top of this company is comprised of about 100 employees located at the headquarters in Zurich, Switzerland.

On examining the profit center organization, the classic conflict between the centralization and decentralization of task-assignment is again center stage and needs to be dealt with in an appropriate manner. A complete centralization is likely to fail, due to its overwhelming effect on the central managerial unit. At the same time, a decentralized solution will not work if there are no centralized procedures and / or adequate infrastructures. This means that even decentralized organizations require a certain degree of cross-sectional tasks, such as strategy development, accounting, controlling, finance, human resources, technology development, etc. (Koller 1997; Scholz 1997).

An increasingly popular solution for this conflict is a management holding firm form of organization (Buehner 1987, 1993). Management holding firms are a decentralized form of business area organization. It represents an organizational affiliation in which the business activity of several entrepreneurial and legally independent partial organizations is accountable for a profit center. The leadership of the affiliation, which often represents only a small number of the total employees, is responsible for supervising the subsidiaries. This is especially relevant with regard to global strategy, personnel management, accounting, as well as the coordination of cross-sectional tasks (see figure 5.2).

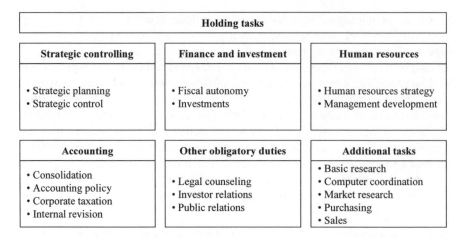

**Fig. 5.2.**    Tasks of a management holding company (based on Bühner 1993)

A holding company is therefore responsible for finance, technology, and management synergy. Operative synergy (e.g., the shared use of distribution systems) is realizable through business segments. The business segments' greater accountability helps to increase employee motivation and makes different segments more agile. Another advantage is the structural and strategic flexibility, such as in the joining or removing of business divisions, and / or certain divisions entering a partnership with an external partner.

### 5.2.2.2    Modularization Through Business Divisions and Products

The traditional form of dividing the organization structure according to market-oriented segments is generally known as a divisional organization. Alfred Sloan first applied this at General Motors during the 1920s. As a general rule, this means that in the sense of object-oriented centralization, the organization is divided into different product groups on a second hierarchical level.

   Modern modularization concepts fine-tune the object-oriented divisional organization by building market-oriented modules (often legally independent), which comprise everything from the smaller business segments to individual products. In addition to the strongly product-oriented differentiation during module building, coordination facilities are developed on higher levels. This can be done through groups within the top management who are held responsible for specific business segments. The goal is to encourage the exchange of know-how between related profit centers and, consequently, the use of technological synergy potential in the organizational affiliation.

### 5.2.2.3    Modularization Through Core Competencies

Another form of module building on the overall organizational level is the implementation of long-term organization units for the continued development of core competencies (Prahalad/Hamel 1990) and/or capabilities (Stalk/Evans/Shulman 1992). According to Prahalad and Hamel, the core competency concept specifically emphasizes the meaning of the development and control of key technologies that can be applied to different products. Canon, whose wide spectrum of products arose from three core competencies, is an excellent example of the targeted development and combining of core competencies.

Stalk, Evans and Shulman (1992) argue that, in addition to core competencies in the sense of key technologies, there needs to be proficiency in the fundamental

| Canon core competencies | | | |
|---|---|---|---|
| | Precision engineering | Precision optics | Micro-Electronics |
| Basic camera | ■ | ■ | |
| Compact fashion camera | ■ | ■ | |
| Electronic camera | ■ | ■ | |
| EOS autofocus camera | ■ | ■ | ■ |
| Video still camera | ■ | ■ | ■ |
| Laser beam printer | ■ | ■ | ■ |
| Color video printer | ■ | | ■ |
| Bubble jet printer | ■ | | ■ |
| Basic fax | ■ | | ■ |
| Laser fax | ■ | | ■ |
| Calculator | | | ■ |
| Plain paper copier | ■ | ■ | ■ |
| Battery PPC | ■ | ■ | ■ |
| Color copier | ■ | ■ | ■ |
| Laser copier | ■ | ■ | ■ |
| Color laser copier | ■ | ■ | ■ |
| Navi | ■ | ■ | ■ |
| Still video system | ■ | ■ | ■ |
| Laser imager | ■ | ■ | ■ |
| Cell analyzer | ■ | ■ | ■ |
| Mask aligners | ■ | ■ | ■ |
| Stepper aligners | ■ | | ■ |
| Excimer laser aligners | ■ | ■ | ■ |

**Fig. 5.3.** Core competencies exemplified by Canon (based on Prahalad/Hamel 1990, p. 90)

value-added processes that are essential for competitiveness. They use Honda, which is also mentioned by Prahalad and Hamel (1990), as an example to point out that this company's core competencies were most certainly a reason for its gradual expansion into the motorcycle, lawnmower, generator, and car markets. However, another reason is Honda's less visible and unusual (core) capabilities in the vendor management and product development areas.

In comparison to the classic portfolio made up of entrepreneurial fields, business areas, and market segments, these examples show that the care and development of organizational portfolios also depend on core competencies and / or core capabilities. In a modularized organization, therefore, superordinate, coordinated modules have to be developed for this task (Prahalad / Hamel 1990). In this area, a certain centralized tendency becomes recognizable (for example, the founding of a competence center). However, if core competencies are to become useful for customers, decentralized units with a certain market proximity have to nurture an efficient exchange of information between customers and the organization.

### 5.2.2.4  Modularization Through Regions and Local Single Markets

The increasing need for organizations to act as a regional market participant on international markets leads to another form of modularization: The development of regionally specific organization units (e.g., Koerber 1993) as close as possible to particular markets. This is especially relevant for highly developed markets whose customers are attracted to innovative products, since these markets often lead the way to global mass-market. Simultaneously, this tactic also targets customers with a preference for local vendors and products.

Similar to modularization that is based on business areas and products, the division of today's regional modules also demands that their markets activities be coordinated so that synergy effects can be utilized. This can once again be done by establishing superordinate modules for regional areas on the highest level of the organization structure.

### 5.2.2.5  Conflict Potential at the Organizational Level

The creation of modular organization units for a particular organization's different business areas, core competencies, and regional markets cannot be accomplished without a certain degree of overlap. Modularly organized organizations are therefore often structured in a (sometimes multiple) matrix from their top level downward. Conflicts of interest are unavoidable in this organization structure, even if, as a rule, the direct line of employee allocation follows a certain matrix path. Generally, organizations accept these conflicts, although it is important to recognize and try to resolve them. In this process, individual profit center managers play an important role. Basically, they have to serve many masters to achieve equilibrium between the different interests that develop within the matrix structure (e.g., Koerber 1993).

Within modularly structured organizations, the demands made on the management in these interface positions are extremely high.

A too extreme modularization can be dysfunctional, even at the organizational level and can lead to the need for reorganization. In the previously mentioned example of the Swiss-Swedish ABB, as a module, each corporate affiliate belonged to a matrix organization, but also to a national subsidiary and a business area. Since the company operates in 140 countries, this proved to be too complex. Consequently, this led to a reorganization during which the business segments were strengthened to reduce the influence of the national affiliates.

Another area of conflict at the organizational level is the task assignment between the centralized and decentralized modules. It is important to recognize and exploit the correct specialization advantages here. These specialized advantages can either be in the process and customer specialization area, or in the overall organization infrastructure and cross-divisional specialization areas. Tasks that involve high process and customer specialization and therefore require knowledge about specific customer-oriented procedures to resolve problems (Picot 1999; Picot / Dietl / Franck 2002) should be undertaken within the decentralized, market-related and process-oriented modules, and / or specific departments.

However, problem-solving tasks that involve a high function and infrastructure specialization, in the sense of a high level of overlapping methodical and technological aspects, should generally be managed comprehensively, i.e. centralized. Activities from both sides are very often regarded as important, which leads to the development of hybrid coordination forms that are a compromise between infrastructure and functionality specialization advantages and process requirements.

As long as the cause of conflict is a communication problem and not a problem of the reconciliation of spheres of authority, information and communication technologies (ICT) can serve as an "enabler" of flexible problem solving within the organization. This allows customer-oriented processes to be regarded as function-specific information pools. Traditional organizational problem-solving techniques, such as a matrix structure, working groups, project management or information exchange can all be realized with the help of ICT.

Further supportive elements, such as a competence center, replace traditional functional sectors and as such assist the decentralized organization units as advisors for and coordinators of all the organizational activities in this particular area (see Koller 1997). This creates a flexible combination of infrastructure and / or function-oriented modules ("centralization") with process and customer-oriented modules ("decentralization"). Examples from the banking industry illustrate this. A credit institution specializing in certain process transactions (specifically in monetary transactions) can be combined with a credit institution that specializes in the consumer industry, despite its different ways of presenting customer services, such as face-to-face contact, telephone banking or on-line banking (Picot 1997a; Picot / Neuburger 2000; see figure 5.4).

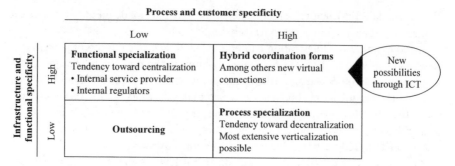

**Fig. 5.4.**     Strategic norms for (de)centralization of functions (based on Picot 1997b)

## 5.2.3   Modularization Concepts on the Process-Chain Level

### 5.2.3.1   *Institutionalization of Business Processes*

In conjunction with task expansion and object orientation, functional and cross-divisional process orientation is becoming more important. Continuous transaction and process-chain orientation can achieve a significant reduction in information transfer and waiting time and, therefore, a reduction of the entire production time and working processes (as exemplified by the case studies on reengineering by Hammer / Champy 1993 and Reichwald / Sachenbacher 1996b).

Concepts regarding process-oriented restructuring have been discussed for quite some time (e.g., Gaitanides 1983). The ideal goal is to completely replace the previously used functional organization structure with process-oriented organization units and the persons in charge of these units (the "process owners"). Typical examples of such business processes include order processing, purchasing, and / or product development (Fromm 1992). Generally, business processes encompass important parts of the value-added chain.

### 5.2.3.2   *Segmentation and Island Concepts*

Concepts for the creation of process-oriented organization units were first developed for the production sector (e.g., the "focused factory" model by Skinner 1974). There are already several established applications in this area that have been demonstrated as successful in practice. Examples include the product island concept by Wagner and Schumann (1991) and the production segment concept by Wildemann (1998) (see figure 5.5).

The fundamental characteristics of segmentation and island concepts are very similar to the previously mentioned principles of modularization: The development of small process and customer-oriented units, largely autonomous task areas, decentralized decision-making competency, and results-based responsibility.

| Product island | Production segment |
|---|---|
| (Based on Wagner / Schumann 1991) | (Based on Wildemann 1994) |

Consolidated completion of a product group
• Spatial
• Organizational

Holistic work content:
• Planning tasks
• Executing tasks
• Controlling tasks

Extensive self-control of the product island within the organizational framework

Market and goal alignment
• Formation of differentiated product/ market/production combinations
• Strategic success factors

Product orientation
• Coordination efforts
• Performance complexity
• Vertical range of manufacturing

Several steps in the logistic chain Integration of several company-internal value chains

Transmission of indirect functions
• Controlling
• Material supply, transport
• Assembling
• Quality control, maintenance

Costs and result responsibility

**Fig. 5.5.** Fundamental characteristics of the product island and product segments (based on Wagner / Schumann 1991; Wildemann 1998)

On the one hand, these organizational concepts have been transferred and applied to non-related sectors. A well-known example is a distribution island in which order processing and modifications are combined for specific products (Bullinger 1991; Weissner et al. 1997). On the other hand, expansion right up to the organizational level – in the form of organizational segments – has also been suggested (Bullinger / Seidel 1992; also see figure 5.6).

This demonstrates that "bottom-up" modularization approaches start at the process level and develop to an ever-expanding integration of value-creating steps. These then converge with the "top-down" approaches that are derived from the organization's original division.

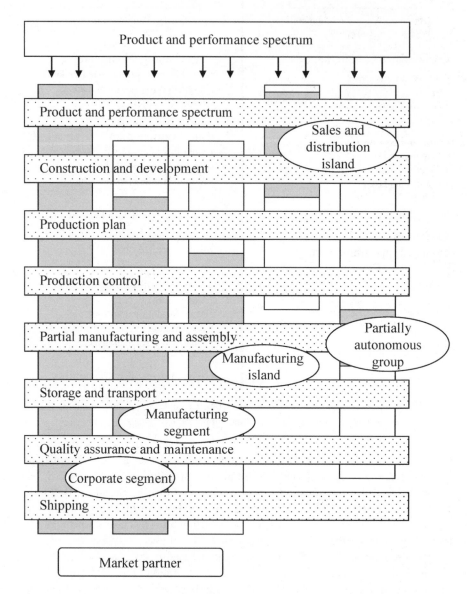

**Fig. 5.6.**    Modularization concepts along the value chain (based on Bullinger / Seidel 1992)

### 5.2.3.3  Conflict Potential on the Process Level

When modular organization units are instituted on the process level, conflicts can arise in different ways. For example, the extent of a task on the process chain may be too great, so that even the use of ICT cannot help. Temporary hierarchical structures are necessary for these types of process chains.

Conflicts may arise at the interface between modular units, for example, between the production islands and production segments (see figure 5.6). It is therefore important to avoid goal divergences between cooperative modules (Weissner 1997). Likewise, conflicts of interest may occur between similar modules, for example, between the manufacturing segments of related product lines, especially when indivisible resources, such as expensive production machinery, have to be shared. At the process level, the tension between the centralized and decentralized allocation of resources is therefore a serious problem for which only tailored solutions are appropriate.

General conflict potentials can specifically arise at the process level if corporate management and their advisors plan and implement the reorganization of corporate processes in a top-down manner. Such an approach can, nevertheless, lead to a swift implementation of reorganization plans, although it can also provoke considerable resistance from affected employees. These types of acceptance problems can be reduced and possibly overcome through the adoption of participative elements in the planning and implementation phases of reorganizational measures (Picot/Franck 1995).

Personnel resistance to change, such as employees clinging to old habits and thought patterns, can eventually lead to the failure of process organization and modularization. The resulting dilemmas can be avoided if the management makes its intentions, goals, and the consequences of the upcoming organization changes known well beforehand. Management also needs to integrate skills concepts into the reorganization plans, which will prepare the employees for more complex and demanding tasks (Nippa 1995).

## 5.2.4  Modularization Concepts at the Labor Organization Level

### 5.2.4.1  Autarky Model Versus Cooperation Model

As far as the application of new information and communication technologies are concerned, there are primarily two design possibilities for creating autonomous units at the labor organization level (Picot/Reichwald 1987, p.125): First, an attempt can be made to integrate tasks in such a way that an entire process can effectively be completed by one employee. In this case, emphasis is placed on the self-sufficient processing of the associated technical managerial tasks (autarky model). Second, it might prove necessary or sensible to assign the entire task and/or process to a team from the very beginning. Since the focus of this organization design is on the coordination and cooperation between and among group members, this form is known as the cooperation model.

A particular development that arises from these two characteristics is their effect on top-level management. In the autarky model, management uses electronic media independently and regardless of their location (in the office, on vacation, at home). In the cooperation model, management uses media through cooperative partners who are there to assist them (secretaries, coworkers, staff).

Empirical research on the use of new communication technology indicates a tendency towards the autarky model (Pribilla / Reichwald / Goecke 1996). Nevertheless, top management's use of new telemedia forms depends on their specific work situations and tasks.

Realizing forms of the autarky and / or cooperation models at the labor organization level requires both fully integrated single workplaces and semi-autonomous groups. Hammer and Champy make an analogous differentiation by referring to a "case worker" and a "case team" (1993). Both forms of modularization at the lowest organization level have their own strengths and weaknesses and impressive examples are available of both. These forms will be separately discussed in the following sections (e.g., Hammer / Champy 1993; Davenport 1993).

### 5.2.4.2 Fully Integrated Single Workplaces

Organizational concepts at the labor organization level that correspond to the autarky model are also referred to as "all-round processing" or "integrated single workplaces." Although they both describe the smallest form of modular organization units, they can be exceptionally productive. There are numerous examples of the successful implementation of this concept, particularly in service areas with the closest proximity to customers. Hammer and Champy (1993), for example, report noteworthy breakthroughs in respect of credit institutes and insurance companies' cycle times and service quality, which have been achieved through one-stop (one and the same single person), computer-supported full processing of customer applications (as opposed to multiple specialized persons for various steps of the application). These authors cite the more personal contact with customers as a further advantage of integrated task processing. Aside from the latter, personal contact also prevents a problem that often occurs in practice: The status of an activated order cannot be determined (e.g., in respect of customer inquiries or required changes), as nobody is directly responsible.

Recommendations have also been made for the extensive self-sufficient task processing of the industrial R&D area (e.g., Ehrlenspiel / Ambrosy / Assmann 1995). It has, for example, been recommended that construction and production planning workplaces should be integrated, allowing one employee to directly complete related partial tasks from both areas. This would allow more rapid iteration loops in the product development process.

However, in the R&D area, the deficiencies of the autarky model are already clearly visible: Whereas the relatively standardized construction and planning tasks in the area of the detailing and finishing of product designs can be handled independently, innovative development tasks often require the creative potential of teams.

The autarky model reveals interesting results in top management work situations when new telecommunication media are applied. On the one hand, empirical research shows that telemedia sharply increase the pressure experienced in the work situation through an increase in temporal constraints (Mueller-Boehling/Ramme 1990). On the other hand, the new media provide new solutions for problem solving. The autarkic application of telemedia enables an increase in information flow, as well as increased flexibility and greater cooperation with remote partners. Furthermore, consistent with the autarkic model, the personal use of synchronized media (e-mail, fax and voicemail) reduces the use of assistants by 30% (Pribilla/Reichwald/Goecke 1996). The autarkic use of media also provides top management with temporal advantages and with internal and external partners for global cooperation.

The cooperation model, however, offers the best approach to the cooperative accomplishing of ad hoc tasks by using the best time management and least capacity. It offers a useful approach to reduce the fragmentation of managerial work. The assistance provided by e-mail communication helps top management to realize face-to-face communication with many on-site participants. This also applies to the coaching of small teams (see chapter 9). Furthermore, the possibility for direct communication with many people, regardless of hierarchical status, is conducive to the transmission of company goals and helps to create a company atmosphere (Pribilla/Reichwald/Goecke 1996).

## 5.2.4.3 Semi-autonomous Groups

The semi-autonomous group is the normal organizational form for the implementation of the cooperation model at the labor organization level (see chapter 9). Through the extensive reverse integration of managerial tasks into the primary functional area, groups made up of eight to ten diversely qualified people can complete the entire value-creating process of less comprehensive tasks areas, or at least a large section of the value chain. In an ideal case, this process ranges from procurement to the final assembly of a distinct customer order (e.g., Frieling 1992; Martin 1992).

The development towards the greater use of semi-autonomous groups is focused on the human being (Heinen 1986). The autonomous group as an organization model was propagated in the 1970s as the labor model that corresponds best to basic human needs. This model has all the requirements that support the development of human creativity and productivity potential, as well as promoting motivation and economic utility if it is meaningfully integrated into the value-creating process. Insights from the labor structure debate substantiate (see chapter 9) that humans are given a better opportunity for self-development through sensible job responsibilities, a healthy work environment, timely feedback of results, as well as through sufficient qualifications, scope for action, and responsibility. Simultaneously, there is a greater personal willingness to perform and increased respect from others, which means that individual goals can be better aligned with corporate goals (Womack / Jones / Roos 1990; Reichwald / Hesch 1993).

## 5.2.5   Conflict Potential at the Labor Organization Level

As mentioned at the beginning of this chapter, modularization approaches at the direct labor organization level are based on the resources available for task completion, the employee potential, as well as on new possibilities to support these by means of ICT. At this level, the most important conflict potential therefore lies in the acceptance of new organizational forms and new ICT. Some examples of possible causes of conflicts at this level are:

- insufficient technical qualifications to complete the expanded tasks (especially with regard to the relevant information and communication technology application);

- the lack of social competencies for self-organization and conflict management within the group;

- internal tension within the group stemming from disproportionate abilities and skills, as well as the differing levels of willingness to perform (especially in evaluations based on group performance), etc.

### Potential for Conflict Between Modularization Concepts at Different Corporate Levels

The debate on the centralization versus decentralization of direct or indirect functions at different levels of the corporation has a long-standing tradition, and is often at the center of controversial discussions. The current spectrum of decentralization approaches is certainly wider than ever before. Then there is the extent to which decentralized organization structures at the labor organization level are compatible with decentralized organization structures at the intermediate and macro levels. Although numerous questions are still unanswered, there are already a few promising approaches for important partial aspects.

One of the main inter-level problems is the coordination and synchronization of the modules at the various levels. As discussed previously, an inherent risk of autonomous organization units is that individual interests will be pursued at the cost of corporate interests. Hierarchic coordination structures are therefore generally maintained to coordinate the operative modular units at the labor organization level, as well as at the process and corporate levels (Reichwald / Koller 1995, p. 21). In these hierarchies, the manager's role undergoes a distinct change – from supervisor to moderator and / or to coach (see chapter 9).

Corporations are increasingly applying such "hybrid" organizational forms and realizing that traditional hierarchic coordination – goal setting through a central authority and the reporting of results through operative levels – contradicts self-organization and self-control within modules. These corporations therefore often make the transition to setting goals together with the employees of the modular units to reduce such interference. They thus attain a more effective coordination, as well as a motivational effect (Reichwald / Koller 1995, p. 23).

Likert's (1961) system of overlapping groups, which seems to have been rediscovered in the search to find modularization applications, goes one step further. This approach suggests coordinating corporations' activities through a system of hierarchic but overlapping groups (see figure 5.7). One employee from each of the subordinate groups functions as the "linking pin" between the levels and the next higher group.

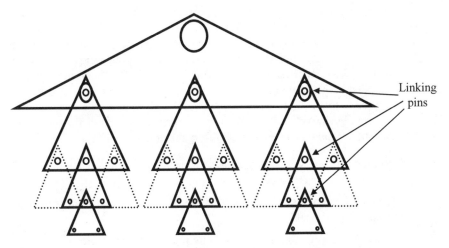

Linking
pins

**Fig. 5.7.**    The system of overlapping groups (based on Likert 1961)

This overlapping group approach provides an outstanding possibility to link modular units at different corporate levels. Simultaneously, it enables group-specific advantages to be realized in respect of mutual loyalty and cooperation. This increases the acceptance of the commonly agreed upon goals and guarantees their implementation.

This coordination approach (in a slightly modified form) was also used by the "sociocratic" model (Pfefferkorn 1991; Endenburg 1994), which has been put into practice in the Dutch corporation Endenburg Elektrotechniek. It can be deduced that in order to have an effective coordination between the modules in the sense of a corporation's goals, participation in organizational goal setting needs to be regarded as rewarding.

Further conflict potential between modules at different levels arises from the centralization and / or decentralization of functions in corporations. The tenet formulated by Bühner (1993, p. 12) for the management holding company can be applied in this case. He states that nothing that is essential for modules' success should be centralized. In this respect, module interests often contradict supraordinate interests. In turn, the decision concerning the decentralization of functions (mainly in large corporations) is a complex, multiple-step process that also needs to be mutually agreed upon and implemented with employees' participation.

## 5.3    The Competitive Advantage of Modularization from the Theoretical Model Perspective

### 5.3.1    Explanatory Approaches to Competitive Strategy

As a result of their contribution to business process reengineering and modularization concepts, the advantages of new competition requirements are frequently used as an argument to justify these efforts In the process, depictions that are based on single case studies tend to dominate as their universally applied arguments make them plausible (Hammer / Champy 1993; von Kober 1993). Theoretical models are rarely applied in the literature.

An exception to this is Frese's (1993, p. 999) reflections on the "model function of medium-sized business structures for large corporations." He distinguishes the following as the essential efficiency goals of organizations:

- Resource efficiency: avoiding unused capacities and the uneconomical allocating of scarce resources;

- Market efficiency: utilizing synergies by coordinating appearances on sales and supplier markets;

- Process efficiency: optimizing the entire process, for example, in respect of cycle time, quality, service or flexibility.

The functional organization of large corporations is therefore regarded as an expression of the primary quest for resource and market efficiency. However, in the face of the increasing dynamics and uncertainty of markets, the growing importance of process efficiency is stressed.

Consequently, the competitive strategy of a corporation has a distinct influence on its coordination requirements and, thus, on the organization structure (see also Chandler 1962). Starting from this assumption, Frese developed a competitive strategic model to consider the advantages of 'small units.' This model is analogous to Porter's (1995) systematic classification of competitive strategies, which have been modified by taking the different production types into consideration (see figure 5.8).

The result of Frese's model is that the importance of process efficiency increases from strategy type A to strategy type C. The competitive advantages offered by forming small organization units depend on the specific corporate strategy and the related importance of process efficiency. Nevertheless, the general development of markets has forced more and more corporations to adapt the strategy types B and C.

| | Differentiation (Delivery service or quality orientation ) | Type B Differentiation according to marketing products | Type C Differentiation according to customer products |
|---|---|---|---|
| | Cost- Orientation | Type A Cost leadership | (Inefficient strategies) |
| | | Market Production (Standardized products) | Customer Production (Alternative products, individual products) |

(left vertical label: Internal strategy dimension)

External strategy dimension

**Fig. 5.8.**   The systematization of strategies (based on Frese 1993 and Porter 1995)

## 5.3.2   Institutional Economics as an Explanatory Approach

### 5.3.2.1   *Modularization as Adaptation of Property Rights*

From the property rights theory (see chapter 2), modularization can be interpreted as a redistribution of property rights within an organization. The rights to action and / or implementation competencies, which are horizontally distributed in functionally and hierarchically organized corporations, are combined in these modules in a process-based way. Simultaneously, the rights of disposal and / or decision competencies are transferred vertically from the management to the lower levels that are closer to the process (Picot / Schneider 1988).

This aspect of the modularization concepts is similar to the basic recommendation of property rights theory with regard to organization: Assign property rights to actors whenever possible. This generates an incentive to act in a responsible and efficient manner. In addition, high transaction costs related to property rights transfer (in some cases from instruction-oriented, hierarchical coordination forms) can be avoided.

The transfer of property rights to individual modules generally refers to the right to use the available resources in the sense of the prescribed task (*usus*). Conversely, there are considerable differences between the modularization concepts of the different corporate levels regarding the extent to which further property rights are transferred. This is due to the concepts not having been fully developed in respect of property rights distribution.

The right to retain profits from business activities, as well as the responsibility to carry one's own losses (*usus fructus*) is increasingly transferred to higher levels of modularization (modules such as cost centers or profit centers). However, it is unusual for corporate management to completely abandon these property rights. This applies to rights such as the right to carry out strategically relevant capital resource shifts between modular units. Even in modularization, the far-reaching property rights of alienated use and / or the alteration of goods (*abusus*), as well as disposal to a third party, essentially remain in the hands of the owners or their directly authorized representatives.

The incomplete attribution of property rights to the direct actors can mainly lead to the risk of external effects. The only way to limit these effects would be through measures allowing employees to hold a share of the corporate capital. This is, however, a topic that is rarely discussed in the context of modularization concepts.

### 5.3.2.2    Modularization from the Transaction Cost Theory Perspective

Transaction cost theory was originally developed to explain the emergence of corporations as centralized, hierarchically coordinated forms of production (Coase 1937; Williamson 1975). It also proved to be a valuable instrument for analyzing the efficiency of organization structures (e.g., Picot 1982). In this generalized application form, it is very helpful to explore and explain observable centralization and decentralization tendencies such as modularization efforts. Transaction costs are a central element within the organization structure and, in this context, can be interpreted as information and communication costs to coordinate organizational tasks based on the division of labor (see chapter 2).

According to transaction cost theory presumptions, efficient organizational forms are characterized by low transaction costs in comparison to alternative forms of organization. Hence, we need to know to which degree and under which conditions a corporation's modularization is linked to transaction cost reduction and if it presents an advantageous organizational approach to a transaction cost perspective.

As previously discussed when analyzing the essential features of current modularization concepts, modularization describes the creation of object-oriented organization units around processes. These organization units, which are rather autonomous and responsible for their own profit, are therefore quasi-enterprises within the corporation. Consequently, transaction cost theoretical viewpoints serve as an explanatory model for the degree of vertical integration that is economically useful (Picot 1991) and that can be analogously transferred from the corporate level to the modular organization unit level.

The integration of production processes into a modular organization unit would therefore be recommended if high specificity and strategic importance were major performance features (Picot 1991). Greater transaction frequency and high environmental uncertainty would support this tendency.

On examining the current competitive situation, one observes that process qualities such as order processing time or flexibility in respect of customer needs have become as important from the customer's point of view as physical product features. Consequently, processes are regarded as a strategic factor.

Furthermore, processes are less prone to imitation. This is in direct contrast to products on the market that can be analyzed and eventually copied by others. This means that a strategic differentiation by means of processes comes to mind and is also successfully practiced by many corporations (e.g., Stalk / Evans / Shulman 1992). Process-oriented modularization can also be justified on the basis of transaction cost theoretical viewpoints of the degree of vertical integration. The above-described environmental uncertainty due to market turbulence and the pace of innovation supports this fundamental argumentation.

The trend towards process-oriented modularization can also be justified when taking the coordination requirements of current value-creating processes into consideration. The frequency of cross-functional and cross-departmental transactions often increases when the competitive importance of processes increases. Consequently, transaction costs (the costs of initiating) arising from having to agree to, process, adapt, and control single transactions are especially high for traditional, functionally structured organizations.

The reasons lie in the often-deplored interface problems between functional fields. These are due to different departmental goals, organizational cultures, and different terminologies. Only when additional market opportunity costs (e.g., through late market entry) are compared with the actual coordination costs, does the extent of the economic importance of these transaction barriers become fully obvious.

Interface problems can be successfully reduced through organizational integration of partial processes with the most frequent transactions, which will drastically decrease transaction costs. In this process, communicating in a common language and an atmosphere of trust, which evolves through close collaboration, play an important role in decreasing transaction costs (Ouchi 1980). In this context, the view of modules as small, manageable units has a trust-building effect. Another positive factor is due to the social control in small groups, which helps to decrease the risk of opportunistic behavior that normally causes high transaction costs (e.g., through costly control measures).

Small, process-oriented units imply an increased demarcation – i.e., in a functional sense, decentralization. From a transaction cost theoretical perspective, it is therefore necessary to examine whether improved coordination at the process level, which occurs in some cases, is related to coordination problems and, therefore, to a significant loss of synergy potential in a functional sense. Consequently, an analysis has to be done with regard to which type of specificity is more important in an individual case: Technical specificity (here, along the process) or infrastructural specificity (see Picot 1990; Picot / Reichwald 1991). This differentiation is examined further when discussing modularization concepts at different corporate levels and their conflict potentials.

### 5.3.2.3   Modularization and Principal-Agent Problems

The principal-agent theory (see chapter 2) provides valuable hints for the theoretical justification of current modularization concepts. The crux of this theory is the risk inherent in the buyer-contractor relationships that the contractor (agent) may deviate from the agreement with the buyer (principal), which introduces latitude for different behaviors. The theory mentions the principal's incomplete information on asymmetric information distribution, as well as deviations between the principal and the agent's goals as decisive factors that give rise to principal-agent problems, thus causing the latter to behave in an opportunistic manner.

These economically relevant (negative) consequences of principal-agent problems are a loss of prosperity caused by the agent's behavioral deviations. In addition, there are the consequences of the principal's non-value-creating expenditure on control and the agent's trust-building costs (guarantee costs). These agency costs are the efficiency criteria when evaluating modularization concepts from the principal-agent theory perspective.

Principal-agent relationships occur in almost any kind of corporate structure. This is due to the emergence of organizations regularly being related to the allocation of the decision and disposal rights of owners. However, in a corporation, these buyer-contractor relationships only become problematic if there are substantial information asymmetries, as well as goal deviations between the principal and agent. In two respects, this is especially relevant with regard to hierarchical, functionally structured organizations: Between corporate management and functional areas in particular and between central authorities and executive positions in general. In the following, we take a closer look at the extent to which modularization concepts counteract these principal-agent problems.

The first problematic principal-agent constellation in functionally structured hierarchies concerns the buyer-contractor relationship between general management and managers in functional areas. The focus is on observable deviations between the market requirements as a whole, i.e. the objectives to which general management has to pay attention, and the actual behavior of managers in functional areas. In real-life situations, there is a tendency towards departmental optimization, which generally leads to sub-optimal results in respect of overlapping goals such as total cycle time, total costs, and / or total quality (the quality of the value-added process as a whole).

Special attention has to be paid to those objectives that are actually relevant to managers in functional areas, as well as to their leeway. Managers' goals are primarily derived from the result indicators that are used to measure their performance. In practice, departmental performance indicators still tend to dominate, and focusing exclusively on them could eventually lead to suboptimal overall results. Area managers' other personal goals, such as striving for as many employees as possible in order to increase their status, could even lead to increased divergence from the corporate goals.

An analysis of an area manager's scope for action reveals a paradoxical situation. Although managers do theoretically have significant latitude with regard to action, this is often substantially limited by area-oriented controlling parameters, which contradicts the process orientation that the market requires.

As the principal, corporate management can change agents' objectives in a way that is suitable for the market by modularizing and appropriately aligning the management structure's process orientation. Nevertheless, a simultaneous alignment of the controlling system is also required, for which only few conceptual reflections are available (for controlling systems see, e.g., Küpper 2005; Hahn 2001; Horváth 2002).

Another interesting manifestation of principal-agent problems in hierarchical organizations is the general buyer-contractor relationship between authorities and executive positions. The principal-agent problem manifests itself in employees at all levels in the form of business-damaging and opportunistic exploitation of their latitude. Typical manifestations of this 'moral hazard' (see chapter 2) are, for example, high absenteeism, inattentiveness at work, and a lack of commitment to productivity improvement.

Although such statements have not been empirically substantiated, theoretical reflections based on principle-agent theory suggest that currently there is an increase in moral hazard in hierarchical organizational forms. On the one hand, the tendency towards employees having better qualifications and increased knowledge of their rights has enabled them to better identify their latitude. On the other hand, observable changes in social values (see chapter 1) have led to an increased discrepancy between corporate objectives and personal goals, as well as to an inadequate acceptance of hierarchical management and control systems. It is therefore possible that qualified employees in executive positions in strictly hierarchical organizations will increasingly take advantage of their identified latitude, also in respect of their personal interests.

If one examines the measures suggested by modularization concepts with the above in mind, one realizes that those suggestions are largely similar to the principle-agent theory's general recommendations that moral hazard should be restricted (see chapter 2). A further aspect is certainly that small, surveyable units allow better information and control possibilities. Their transparency allows information asymmetries to be reduced. The "blind spots" of the controlling authority are thus substantially reduced. The social control found in team structures helps to reduce individual employees' latitude and, thus, the pursuit of "private" goals. However, these improved control possibilities cannot be regarded as the main advantage of modularization in respect of principle-agent problems. Ultimately, one has to assume that resourceful (de-)motivated employees will always discover and exploit other latitudes regarding behavior.

The decrease in the discrepancy between employee objectives and their organization unit's economic goals has a far greater impact on the avoidance of principal-agent problems through modularization. The suggestions embedded in modularization concepts that decision competencies should be delegated to modules and that teams should be organized agree with the recommendations of the principal-agent theory in this respect. However, new principal-agent problems can arise during modularization if a goal discrepancy between the module's interests and those of the corporation as a whole is not prevented through appropriate coordination measures.

One solution to reduce principle-agent problems has scarcely been considered in modularization concepts: Profit sharing for employees to increase their incentives on behalf of the corporation as suggested by the theory (see chapters 2 and 9). This aspect is certain to become more important in the future, if one takes into consideration the often-stated prognosis that business organizations will increasingly develop into 'open systems of shareholders' (e.g., Laske / Weiskopf 1992).

### 5.3.3  Communication Theory Perspectives

The results of communication research (see chapter 3) reveal that a manageable number of agents' intensive interactions can have a positive effect on the efficiency of information and communication processes. Much of the work done in this area emphasizes close proximity, as well as common value and subject contexts to cope efficiently with complex tasks (e.g., media richness theory, as well as chapter 3). This is based on the fact that in the context of communication, actors' mutual relationship is always available (Watzlawick/Beavin/Jackson 1990). A limited number of communication partners, as well as frequent interaction help to ease the interpretation and transmission of the relationship content. Common tasks of organization modules also help to transmit issue-related information (e.g., O'Reilly 1983).

A modular organization structure can be beneficial for individual decision-makers, since the complexity of the information can be limited to certain areas and new information can be classified in a targeted manner. Individual information reception and processing pathologies (i.e. perception distortions based on self-concept and hierarchy) can become more transparent and can be regulated by the group.

However, membership in organization modules can also lead to the development of a partial community of values, especially if the environment is regarded as unsafe or hostile. Distortions in the information and communication process, which can be observed at the individual level, can in theory also appear at the level of interaction between the group and the rest of the organization. The "groupthink" phenomenon can lead to wrong decisions being made if the group norms lead to distorted perceptions (Janis 1982). Consequently, there is increased emphasis on management to create a higher-ranking community of values (Reichwald/Bastian 1999).

### 5.3.4  Modularization and Motivation

Insights from industrial science substantiate that human motivation is generated by comprehensive tasks, adequate leeway, a transparent environment, as well as speedy feedback of work results. The results of studies conducted by Hackman support the predicted advantages of modular organization structures in respect of employee motivation (Hackman 1969, 1977). The possibilities to integrate tasks, together with a higher level of individual responsibility and greater latitude for action (see figure 5.9), offer opportunities for work enrichment and self-realization.

The results of the work done by Herzberg (Herzberg et al. 1959 and chapter 9) point towards the same general direction. In his two-factor approach, Herzberg distinguishes between what he calls hygiene factors and motivators. Hygiene factors are those conditions whose insufficiency creates employee dissatisfaction and

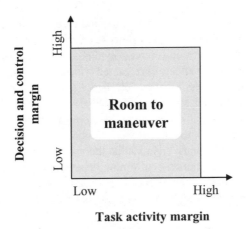

**Fig. 5.9.** Model of room to maneuver (based on von Rosenstiel 2002)

whose existence does not lead to performance motivation (according to Herzberg, e.g., salary, external working conditions or relations with colleagues). Motivation to perform is triggered by the same motivators that are also responsible for employees being content at work. It is noteworthy that, according to Herzberg, the four most important motivational factors (performance, recognition, work content, and responsibility) can be positively influenced by the creation of small, self-contained, and mostly self-organized units in the sense of modularization concepts. An impression of one's own performance and, therefore, the basis of personal recognition and recognition from others can only develop through integrated work. The formation of modules based on relatively self-contained process chains can deliver the necessary organizational prerequisites.

Within modular units, the principles of self-organization and self-responsibility tend to be more interesting and more versatile and, as such, they are responsible activities and thus have positive effects on motivation. Nevertheless, the principle of (horizontal and vertical) task integration on which these measures are based, presumes that employees should have significantly higher qualifications. Therefore, a lack of relevant qualification measures can hinder the acceptance of new organization concepts by a substantial part of the staff, as indicated, for example, in Frieling's (1992) case studies.

These insights into the advantages of small units and team structures are not new. They had already been mentioned in the discussion on the humanization of the labor environment in the 1970s (e.g., Picot/Reichwald/Berbohm 1985; Reichwald 1990), but could not, however, be applied in practice. From today's perspective, one realizes that these concepts were introduced too early. Only the radical change in competitive conditions, as described in chapter 1, have resulted in the economic benefits of these modularization concepts being fully realized.

These benefits are mostly based on motivated and therefore more flexible and more creative employees thinking in a more process-oriented manner.

Meanwhile, this competition-oriented evaluation of new organizational concepts and their motivational effects have gained widespread acceptance. Today, even leading advocates of business organization theory stress the motivational effects of modular and/or segmented structures (e.g., Frese 1993, p. 1003). Consequently, there has been a shift in the interpretation of the term 'motivation': Whereas motivation was interpreted as an expression of work satisfaction by the 1970s' ergonomics-based discussion, contemporary organization theory publications primarily consider motivation as an effect of market-conforming behavior. In this sense, Frese (1993, p. 1017) stresses the motivating effect of creating market pressure within the corporation through, for example, the introduction of profit centers.

The following statement by Bennis (1992, p. 10) can be considered as characteristic of the new, economics-based perspective of the rediscovered modularization concepts: "While various proponents of 'good human relations' have been fighting bureaucracy on humanistic grounds and for Christian values, bureaucracy seems most likely to founder on its inability to adapt to rapid change in the environment."

## 5.3.5 Task-Oriented Approaches

Work distribution requires coordination and coherence, which generally require a certain amount of effort. The use of alternative organization structures can help to minimize coordination costs. One of the most important insights of situational organizational research is the view that there is no optimal way (optimal organization structure). A realistic approach is that the most appropriate structure to minimize coordination and communication costs depends on the specific characteristics of the organizational task. If the task requirements change, new solutions need to be considered for the organizational problems (e.g., Picot 1999).

Attempts to develop a task typology have been useful to examine the relationship between a task and a suitable organizational form (e.g., Picot/Reichwald 1987; Nippa/Reichwald 1990). On this basis, the current need for reorganization by means of modular organizational units can be justified. Furthermore, industrial manufacturing was always emphasized in the past.

The characteristics of a task are responsible for determining the concrete definition of organization's processes and structures (Perrow 1970; Picot 1999). This general insight is successfully applied for decisions with regard to production management. Characteristics that describe tasks and their underlying situation are the basis of decisions with regard to production management (e.g., Schomburg 1980; Picot/Reichwald/Nippa 1988; Frese 1989; Zäpfel 1989; Frese/Noetel 1990). The characteristics of tasks concerning production management are also based on the specific features of the services offered and on the type of market.

The dominating characteristics used to designate a production task are its complexity (the number of elements that have to be considered and their connection) and its variability (the degree and the predictability of the changes) (Reichwald/

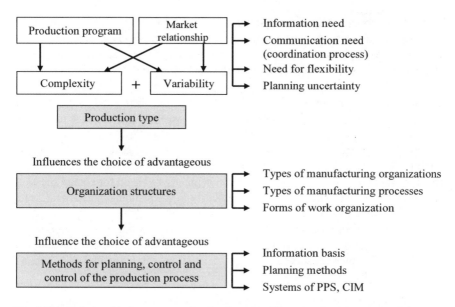

**Fig. 5.10.** Relationship between production-based problem, production type, and decision field (based on Reichwald / Dietl 1991, p. 406)

Dietl 1991). These specifications demand requirements with regard to production management's situation-appropriate design. The complexity of the production task is greatly influenced by the production program and variability as a result of an industrial firm's relation to the market. Figure 5.10 demonstrates this situational perspective (see also Reichwald 1984; Picot 1990; Reichwald / Schmelzer 1990).

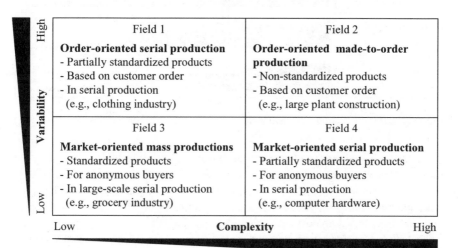

**Fig. 5.11.** Production-based task fields (based on Reichwald / Dietl 1991)

If the characteristics of complexity and variability were to be combined for a pro-
ductivity-based economic situation description, the four fields with different parameter values depicted in figure 5.11 would develop. Field 2 shows a production
situation that is normally encountered in plant engineering and construction investments (high complexity and highly variable performance programs). Field 3 is
representative of a production situation within the consumer goods industry with
mass-produced goods (low complexity and barely variable performance program).
Fields one and four depict mixed forms.

Depending on the task field, different requirements arise in respect of the information and communication structures, as well as the production planning methods.
This is triggered by the different information demands and need for communication
and coordination, and, therefore, the dissimilarity in the planning situations (Zäpfel
1989; Reichwald 1990). The four basic situations as illustrated in figure 5.11, as
well as the viewpoints expressed in figure 5.10 help to build three production
types whose requirements with regard to the planning situation and organizational
solutions are further illustrated in figure 5.12 (Picot / Reichwald 1987; Nippa /
Reichwald 1990).

| Characteristics \ Production type | Type I Order-oriented made-to-order production | Type II Mixed serial production | Type III Market-oriented mass production |
|---|---|---|---|
| Information need | Very high | Medium | Low |
| Need for flexibility | Very high | Medium | Low |
| Coordination process | Very high | Medium | Low |
| Planning uncertainty | Very high | Medium | Low |

**Fig. 5.12.** The production types and their characteristics (based on Reichwald / Dietl 1991)

The order-oriented unit production (type I) is highly relevant because it allows for
individual products to be produced. The customer determines the characteristics of
the product. Industrial firms with order-oriented unit production are faced with a
risky planning situation. Their competitiveness lies in their ability to swiftly produce products based on customer specifications.

The market-oriented mass-production type (type III) is characterized by its stable
planning situation. The production program and process have little need for flexibility and coordination between production and the market. This enables standardized

services and reduced costs, while differentiation aspects tend to play a less important role. The determination of the product characteristics is based on the planning uncertainty in any anonymous market.

The mixed serial-production type (type II) is a mixed form of the two previously mentioned production types, and is therefore characterized by average planning safety.

These three production types can be described as ideal types. However, in real-life situations, their diversity does not live up to expectations. Simultaneously, the perspective offered by these production types leads to a task-oriented approach to solutions and structure-based decisions in production planning and controlling (process decisions). The task-oriented production types offer a certain level of ideal freedom in respect of an organization's design (see figure 5.13).

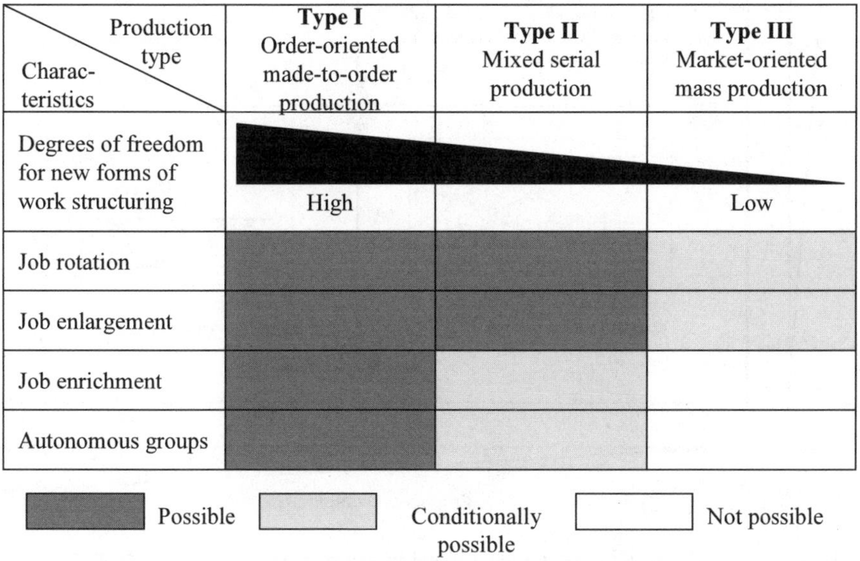

| Characteristics \ Production type | Type I Order-oriented made-to-order production | Type II Mixed serial production | Type III Market-oriented mass production |
|---|---|---|---|
| Degrees of freedom for new forms of work structuring | High | | Low |
| Job rotation | | | |
| Job enlargement | | | |
| Job enrichment | | | |
| Autonomous groups | | | |

Possible ☐ Conditionally possible ☐ Not possible

**Fig. 5.13.** Production type and degree of freedom with regard to organization design (based on Reichwald/Dietl 1991)

As long as industrial performance was largely dominated by products of low or, at best, average complexity and specificity with regard to long-term, constant needs (i.e., markets were stabile and customer wishes were uniform (sellers' markets)), organization models characterized by the division of labor and hierarchy were considered as efficient as any others.

In current industrial practice, however, there is a growing tendency towards a customer-oriented, individual production, such as in the automotive or industrial sector. This intensive interaction between industry and market requires a high level of flexibility in all areas of industrial services. The above-mentioned competitive conditions are the reason for the visible tendency towards type I and, partially, type II production types. Consequently, this opens the possibilities to apply concepts such as job rotation, job enlargement, job enrichment, and autonomous groups (see chapter 9). At the same time, there is a need for reorganization towards modular structures. These developments will continue in the future. Figure 5.14 shows this trend from an organization-internal viewpoint.

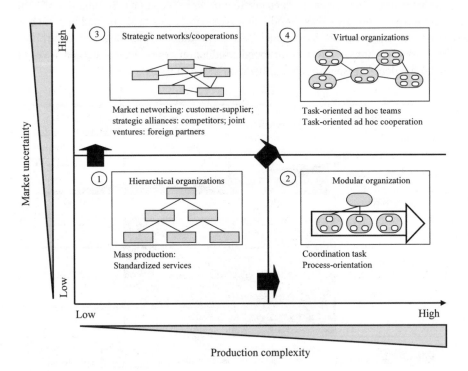

**Fig. 5.14.** Change in the market situation and need for reorganization (based on Pribilla / Reichwald / Goecke 1996)

Changing service characteristics, task characteristics and market demands, in addition to higher levels of complexity and variability require autonomous team structures in production and other organization areas so that these forms can adapt faster and more efficiently. The trend towards modularization has therefore been verified from the task-oriented approaches of organization theory.

## 5.4     The Role of ICT in Modularization

### 5.4.1   ICT Requirements in Modular Organizational Forms

The holistic integration of tasks along the value chains of modularized corporations requires corporate-wide coordinated information and communication systems (Pribilla et al. 1996). The most important task is to supply the decentralized modules with the necessary high-quality information in a timely manner. In order to guarantee access to the required data and information and their specific decentralized processing, all business information systems must be integrated and linked through networks. This is the only way that, for example, production-related customer inquiries could be reliably managed and controlled in order processing.

Modern information and communication technologies (ICT) reveal high potential, especially with regard to the coordination of modules. Although the integration of process and function-oriented units is problematic, these technologies make this possible. Based on the corresponding information and technology infrastructure, the completion and / or processing of specific tasks can at any time be integrated into modules required for coping with a task. Figure 5.15 illustrates this principle by means of an insurance company's customer service.

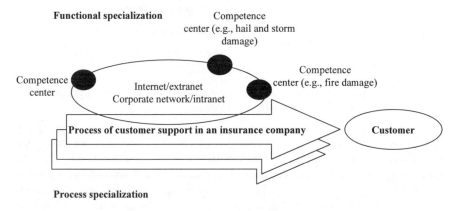

**Fig. 5.15.**  Virtual linkage between process and functional specialists

In the customer service process, the necessary know-how can be integrated through access to a competency center (e.g., through the use of an extranet or a corporate network). The more independent a module becomes, the more important ICT becomes: It is used for the coordination and virtual connection between modules. In order to access the necessary data and information, all organization information systems have to be fully integrated and networked. This is the only way to allow production-based tasks (such as customer questions in the order processing) to e reliably completed and controlled.

In order to meet these requirements, the entire diversity of objects, resources, and functions in a corporation, as well as their interaction would have to be mapped by information and communication systems. Such highly complex information and communication systems (e.g., integrated PPS systems) are still difficult to control in corporate practice and require considerable capital and know-how input.

Instead of attempting to map the corporation in its complexity, modularization leads to an opposite development. The observable trend is towards self-organization, which is supported by the often tailor-made application possibilities of modern information and communication systems (see Figure 5.16). "Self-organization comprises all processes that evolve from a system by themselves and create, improve, or maintain order in this 'self'" (see Probst 1992, col. 2255 – 2269, translation by authors).

| Process-related prerequisites | ICT technical support |
|---|---|
| Decentralized access and exchange of information, timely and need-driven use of information by various co-workers | Communication technology networking of computing capacities, integrated and/or distributed applications architecture with distributed database, intranet, extranet |
| Support of decision-making | Decision-making support systems |
| Support of autarkic generalists instead of various specialists | Workplace systems, expert systems |
|  | Workgroup systems, intranet |
| Tools to support group work |  |
|  | Workflow systems, intranet |
| Process-oriented support of structured workflow |  |
|  | Utilization of the telecommunication infrastructure, |
| Firm-spanning exchange of data | EDI, intranet, extranet |

**Fig. 5.16.**   The requirements of modular, process-oriented organizations in respect of ICT and potentials for solutions

Self-organizing complete entities (modules) form at all levels of the enterprise. They have the following general characteristics: They are autonomous, meaning they are self-regulating. Design, control, and development competencies are distributed throughout the system. They have redundancy at their disposal, meaning that each self-organizing unit has a capacity for autonomous actions. In addition, self-organizing systems are self-referencing, meaning they delineate themselves vis-à-vis their respective environment. Nevertheless, self-organizing systems maintain links with their environment through a few open interfaces.

Such self-organizing whole entities (modules) are created at all levels of the corporation by means of the modular organization's process-oriented arrangement. When totally integrated into the corporate value chain, all modules at each of these levels will autonomously complete their own tasks. This results in simple, clearly defined structures. The simplification of the process goes hand in hand with the simplification and reduced complexity of information and communication systems. This insight leads to a basic understanding of the use of information and communication technologies.

Modern information and communication systems need no longer cover all eventualities of complex-structured processes. However, they must be tailored to a lean core process and its specific task and information requirements. It is obvious that such individualization of information and communication systems is incompatible with centralized information-processing solutions. Thus, modern information and communication systems that are tailored to lean core processes can be primarily realized and supported by means of distributed, decentralized information-processing solutions. Consequently, the functional task support within modules has to be ensured first and, second, the links between the modules have to be mapped by the information and communication system.

This leads to the fundamental question regarding the degree to which standard software can fulfill business requirements by means of modern ICT. The prerequisites for a corporation's sustained competitiveness are core competencies and highly specific tasks. They distinguish a corporation from its competition and are necessary for long-term survival on the market. This is particularly true in respect of the information technology support of relatively unique core processes, which is therefore of special value for the corporation.

However, standard commercial software mostly supports standardized processes. Whereas traditional complex process structures always contained a high degree of standardized processes, this only presented a minor problem before, but modularization and concentration on core processes require specific functionalities. Therefore, modern software tools must meet new requirements, such as the ability to provide corporate-specific and, thus, individual solutions quickly and easily while simultaneously taking the integrity of the common data into consideration.

ICT's adaptation to corporate-specific circumstances is known as customizing. With the help of a special program, called the customizer, functional building blocks of modular standard software, which optimally support customer and corporate-specific processes, are combined into a (new) program.

A more decisive factor than the information technology support of core processes is their corporate-wide coordination and integration. The reasons for this are first, (passive) provision of an information and communication infrastructure in the form of networks and integrated databases and, second, (active) process coordination, for example, through workflow systems.

The swift development in the area of ICT offers solutions to many of the challenges being faced. These are summarized in figure 5.16 (column two) and will be discussed further in the following chapter.

## 5.4.2  Potential of ICT Support of Modular Organizational Forms

As already explained in detail in chapter 4, the modern information and communication technology potential is an essential prerequisite for the further development of new organizational concepts. The possibilities offered by communication technology networks in respect of computer capacities and the potential of integrated, distributed application architecture with distributed databanks play an especially important role in the modular organizational form.

Networks of differing physical size ensure the timely supply of current data and information to local workplaces. The application of telecommunication infrastructures and electronic data interchange (EDI) is necessary for the networking of physically separated corporate or business units (see chapter 6), as well as for cross-corporate linkage (Neuburger 1994).

Through the high transmission capacities of modern communication networks, interactive and multimedia applications can be increasingly realized, even over long distances. This enables the use of groupware systems to be extended to cross-corporate processes through, for example, the use of an extranet (see chapter 4). A closely linked, cross-site development with a supplier would then, for example, become possible in the sense of simultaneous engineering (Kuhlmann et al. 1993; Gerpott / Winzer 2000).

The efficiency of modern information and communication networks facilitates system configurations that are in accordance with self-organizing units' typical mix of centralization and decentralization. Systems of this type are known as client-server architectures (Geihs 1995 and chapter 4), which means that server programs offering certain services (e.g., special databases) are installed on designated computers within a network. The programs on the remaining workstations act as clients, using these services through the network when they are required. For a database inquiry within a centralized configuration, a workstation either simply acts as a terminal of the central computer (host) or copies all the data through the network lines and processes the inquiry locally.

In contrast, client-server architecture only requires one command to be sent from the client to the database server, which then processes the inquiry and only returns the "results" to the client. Further processing of the data, such as formatting and graphics, takes place locally, on the client. Only truly relevant data are therefore transmitted through the network, reducing the network's load and supporting local task integration and delegation of decisions. Decentralized modules also have access to electronic decision-supporting systems, expert systems, and individually programmable workplace systems for further functional support of designated tasks.

A client-server architecture also facilitates the coordination of single modules through common information and knowledge bases in the form of integrated distributed databases (see chapter 4). In the past, databases were centrally stored on mainframes to allow integrated data processing. The current trend is away from centralized database solutions and towards distributed database systems. Consequently, only task and process-relevant data are stored locally and decentrally, whereas the data that are less often used, are stored centrally or in other areas. The various databases maintain contact with one another, although to the user they appear to be a centralized database (Jablonski 1991). The organization's modularization therefore goes hand in hand with ICT's modularization of the required databases.

In addition, process-oriented information and communication systems are necessary for the coordination of modular units. Currently, however, the workflow systems described in section 5.4.3.2 are the only type of process-oriented software on the market, whereas all other software types (e.g., PPS systems) only partly deserve this description. The frequent attempt to support process structures by combining existing functional software modules only increases information and communication system complexity, and contradicts the goal of complexity reduction through modularization. New developments with regard to process-oriented software can therefore be expected in future.

In this context, the increasing distribution of cross-organizational standard software packets (Enterprise Resource Planning or ERP) needs to be pointed out. These complete software products encompass diverse functional solutions, such as materials management, production planning and controlling, accounting and human resource management, and combine these into process-oriented units.

Owing to the interchangeability and interoperability of modularly built systems, customers and suppliers can easily be integrated into the internal data exchange. A few providers already offer standards (e. g., R/3 from SAP), especially in branches in which there is an intensive exchange of data. However, the decision to implement such a system is often criticized as it only offers a limited possibility for strategic differentiation. As a rule, the implementation of such an ERP system is associated with a higher degree of organization-wide integration and formalization than that of its common standard package counterparts. The software is also often based on generic task solutions and can limit organizations, since integrating the software requires a great deal of effort.

In many cases, the organization has to fundamentally adjust itself to the software, which means that the implementation of an ERP requires a great deal of re-organizational effort. Consequently, the highest management level first needs to establish the degree to which the benefits of greater information and operations transparency between the different areas of the organization offset the drawback of uniformity (Davenport 1998).

### 5.4.3 Task-Oriented ICT as a Prerequisite for the Efficiency of Modular Organizational Forms

#### 5.4.3.1  Basic Considerations Regarding ICT Task-Efficiency

The increased information technology penetration within corporations has led to an important change within the business information-processing infrastructure. The multi-functionality of new information and communication technologies and the resultant wide array of application possibilities are creating new conditions for business performance. They are both production and organization technologies, thus impacting the physical production process in manufacturing, as well as information processing in the office.

Information technology is becoming an increasingly versatile resource due to the performance spectrum of the new technology being available decentrally and the open design possibilities of hardware and software systems. Technology is increasingly assuming a tool-like character: It can be applied for both standardization and individualization. This change in infrastructure affects all business design options in respect of working conditions, organization structures, and employee qualifications (e.g., Scott / Michael 1991; Davenport 1993; Iacono / Wigand 2005).

The emergence of new business information and communication infrastructure specifically facilitates new forms of division of labor. Partial processes, which have until now been assigned to functionally specialized workplaces and work groups, can be completed in an integrated and object-related manner with the help of multifunctional information and communication systems. This task integration can occur horizontally (integration of different types of activities at the operative level), as well as vertically (integration of planning, decision, and control tasks).

The underlying organization model is crucial as far as the organizational consequences of the use of technology for the division of labor are concerned. With the autarky concept (see Picot / Reichwald 1987), the deployment of technology in management and in work processing is supposed to make those responsible for a task independent of assistants and individuals in other positions.

The goal is to provide those responsible for a task (managers, developers, designers, office workers) with multifunctional technology at the workplace, so that they can, for example, independently undertake text generation, graphics and image processing, as well as communication processes, information filing, and information retrieval.

In contrast, the cooperation model is based on the retention of the division of labor processes. Team-related processes are encouraged for task completion. All participants within a cooperation should be able to complete their tasks more efficiently through the use of information and communication technology. To summarize, the autarky model expedites productivity increase by reducing the division of labor, whereas the cooperation model concentrates on increasing efficiency in teamwork by improving communication relationships.

Keeping this in mind when examining the literature on business process reengineering approaches and case studies, one realizes that they present a more or less innovative implementation of the autarky and / or the cooperation model (Picot / Reichwald 1987; Nippa 1995). With such a task-oriented approach, the following recommendations are made: The greater the degree of structuring of tasks and the lower the degree of variability and complexity, the more beneficial the autarky model is (e.g., case management for insurance companies). On the other hand, the cooperation model is more practical in task areas that are not as structured and have a higher degree of change and complexity (as in research, development or project management). Both models are based on extreme cases with interesting mutual combinations.

### 5.4.3.2   ICT in Support of Autarkic Full Processing of Well-Structured Tasks

Numerous information and communication tools have been developed to support autarkical and / or independent processing of interwoven, well-structured task combinations. The various terms are summarized by the generic term "workplace technologies."

Workplace technologies are aimed at the optimal technical support of single workplaces. The specific requirements can be identified through a job analysis on the workplace level. Possible analysis objects are, for example, the problem structure, activity structure, activity content, as well as the characteristics of an individual workplace's activities.

The development of individual systems based on single workplace requirements has been a central issue for information system development since about 1975 (Grudin 1991). The appropriate design of the database, as well as the corresponding mechanisms for the generation, processing, preparation, and evaluation of information is of great importance. Integrated word processing, spreadsheet, presentation, and database programs are therefore implemented. Traditionally, the focal point is information processing's content aspect and not its interpersonal relationship aspect (Picot/Reichwald 1991, p. 255). Even when common information resources are used, the single autonomous person responsible for the task will usually be technically isolated, enabling an "undisturbed" work environment (e.g., the transaction mechanisms and blocking protocol of present database systems).

The support philosophy in the outlined workplace systems is especially appropriate when the task structure is actually tailored to autonomous, individual work. In principle, each task has elements of individual work. However, when task complexity increases, team-like cooperation becomes more important. The specific requirements of this cooperation aspect are the focus of the following outlined workflow and work group technologies.

### 5.4.3.3  ICT Support of the Cooperative Processing of Well-Structured Process Chains

An adequate information and communication technical support of corporate process chains (e.g., order processing and procurement) requires the targeted examination of overlapping task correlations besides the examination of single workplaces. This is primarily the field in which workflow systems are applied (Hilpert 1993; Hasenkamp/Kirn/Syring 1994; Götzer 1997; Rosemann/Uthmann 1997).

Workflow systems, which mostly operate by means of document management systems, permanently support the handling of business processes according to set rules. They offer support services in respect of process generation, organization, and control, as well as process tracing, process information, and process termination. As a rule, workflows are modeled with the help of state transition diagrams. This means that workflows undergo a step-by-step examination, with each step bringing about a change in the state of the technical system. Alternative subsequent steps, which are determined by the new system status, are then available. The information technology representation of the processes not only guarantees the correct processing sequence, but can also provide for timely processing by means of scheduled intervals or linking to certain results.

Workflow systems can be classified into transaction-oriented and ad-hoc-oriented systems (Palermo/McCready 1992; Jablonski et al. 1997). In transaction-oriented workflow systems, the process sequence with all its variations is extensively determined, with no user intervention envisioned. In contrast, ad-hoc-oriented workflow systems enable the user to intervene in the process steps, as well as redefine the workflow. Consequently, transaction-oriented workflow systems are mainly based on well-structured, long-term stable processes that, from the beginning, can be clearly described by means of rules and procedures, whereas ad-hoc-oriented workflow systems can also support transitory processes.

The key advantage of workflow systems lies in the possibility to further process an event's objects without disruptions in the media flow. Paper-based objects (letters, invoices, policies, drawings, expert opinions, file notes, reports, forms, etc.) are scanned and electronically stored. All of the objects belonging to a series of events can then be combined in an electronic circular that, besides the original paper-based documents, also includes all the created objects. Consequently, the advantages of electronic data processing (transport, access, actuality, etc.) can be realized in each of the processes' steps. Recorded objects can be exclusively used by one user, but can also be duplicated as often as necessary. In contrast to difficult to control physical duplication, the workflow system assumes responsibility for version update and control. Consequently, processes can be dynamically split up and run in parallel, leading to drastic reductions in running and transport times.

Negative effects from workflow systems lie in reduced informal contacts (Wohlenberg 1994; Jablonski et al. 1997). The associated danger of isolation from coworkers can be confronted and overcome through regular meetings or the introduction of group rooms, etc. There is no doubt that workflow systems also have a considerably larger control potential compared to traditional, paper-based work methods. These potential dangers can be deterred from the beginning through appropriate data protection laws and business agreements.

An additional problem area is that many workflow system implementations still occur without taking the organization's circumstances into consideration (e.g., Bornschein-Grass 1995, p. 110; Weiss/Krcmar 1996). Therefore, besides the further development of business process support through workflow systems, the prevalent research focus is on a stronger consideration of organizational requirements in their application.

### 5.4.3.4    ICT Support of Cooperative Processing of Poorly Structured Task Combinations

Work group technologies should support the collaborative efforts of groups through the utilization of information and communication technologies. The focal point should not only be on pure functional aspects, but on events and business processes. There is therefore a search for cooperative applications that, on the one hand, allow flexible data processing and, on the other, enable process-oriented communication between team members (Wohlenberg 1994).

The identification of work group system requirements should start at the organization level and should take the following into consideration: The technical relationships and dependencies, the cooperation and communication relationships between the participants, as well as the specifics of the socio-technical environment. The technical progress in the areas of telecommunication, distributed systems, as well as multimedia applications has contributed greatly to the development of support systems for work-related team structures.

Group support systems are currently available under the following labels: Groupware, computer-aided team (CATeam), task/team support system (T/TSS), and computer-supported cooperative work (CSCW) (Nastansky 1993). The most frequently used classification of computer support for groups is based on two characteristics of group work – the differences in time and location. Four support forms arise from the comparison of group work's synchronous and asynchronous progress, as well as its physical proximity and/or distance (see chapter 4).

In contrast to the targeted isolation of the workplace technologies of the individual user, work group concepts concentrate on users' deliberate cooperation: Cooperative relationships and, under certain circumstances, collision relationships between team members will be made explicit in the context of the application. One of the central design strategies of work group systems is not isolation, but "awareness"; i.e., the conscious perception and experience gained from cooperative work processes engaging with one another (Borghoff/Schlichter 2000).

There are several empirical studies available on the use of group support systems (e.g., Wohlenberg 1994, p. 52 and the indicated empirical studies). Computer conferences are presently used for the coordination of and agreement on group processes and/or for idea generation. However, group support systems used in respect of complex decisions, negotiations, and differences of opinions, or when the communication partners have never met are more problematic (e.g., Kilian-Momm 1989). With appropriate preparation, the use of decision support systems for groups, as well as electronic meeting rooms has also demonstrated to have positive effects on the procedures and results in group decision processes (Krcmar/Lewe 1992; Grueninger 1996).

In contrast, empirical insights into groupware tools appear more refined. Groupware tools are aimed at supporting asynchronous group communication (e.g., group appointment calendar, multiple author systems, and group knowledge bases and/or agent systems). These systems generally have a high support potential when several group members process several information objects in the application field.

Unfortunately, negative effects have also been identified, such as group members having to be very willing to work together, because the system's use is associated with individual information leads being reduced and, consequently, power positions weakening. Forced changes to the group members' personal work styles, personal contacts being replaced by information technology, and increased control can further reduce the chances of realizing the potential utility of groupware systems. It is therefore important that affected employees should already participate and be offered training early in the introductory phases.

Today, the possibility for the integration of the outlined groupware developments with each other as well as into existing systems is still considered technically problematic. The associated disruptions in the flow of media, i.e., changing from one medium (e.g., paper) to another (e.g., e-mail, SMS, telephone) is the main point of criticism of work group technologies (Bornschein-Grass 1995, p. 108; Teufel 1996).

## 5.5   Implications for Management

Current organization theory and practice have led again to the close scrutiny of the modularization of the organization. At the heart of all modularization concepts lies the holistic, market-oriented goods and services process. This process should be partitioned into its associated partial processes, for which particular efficiency criteria need to be established (e.g., the magnitude of the transaction costs). Moreover, it should be determined if they should be carried out within the organization, or by specially chosen external partners (see chapter 6), or be procured externally from the market (see chapter 7). There are appropriate modular concepts for highly specific organizational processes that have to be carried out within the organization, which will be discussed next.

The guiding principle is to form small, easily manageable, and mostly self-organizing organization units (modules) in order to establish holistic customer-oriented processes and, thus, to take advantage of the synergy and motivation effects resulting from the integration. This allows the demands for competitiveness – discussed earlier – to be better met. Through the organization of the company's emphatic focus on customer-oriented processes, market orientation clearly becomes the central focal point, while considering modularization and the greater delegation of decision-making authority to these modules.

The organization's operative flexibility (e.g., in the case of new customer demands) is increased by avoiding interfaces in customer-relevant processes, reducing communication paths, and having relatively flat hierarchies. The modular organization structure simultaneously offers the possibility to build and remove relatively easily individual modules, which also offers highly structural adaptation capabilities in respect of dynamic market conditions. Today's demands for high innovation expertise throughout the organization are addressed by the modules' immediate access to the market, the motivational holistic task structure, as well as the direct and informal communication possibilities.

Modularization as an organizational approach can be used on all levels of an organization. On the level of the organization as a whole (macro level), modules can be implemented for entire divisions in the organization or regional markets, as well as for core competencies or even strategic planning and coordination. On the level of organizational processes (meso level), modules can be implemented for process classification from a simple production segment to complete organization segments (e.g., a total product production process). On the work organization level (micro level), similar fundamental modularization principles lead to the development of partially autonomous groups and fully integrated individual workplaces.

In a modularized organization, this can be compared to Warnecke's (1992) propagandized "fractal factory," i.e., similar, compact structures on all levels.

In modularization, new information and communication technologies play a central role. They are often – quite correctly – referred to as the actual "enablers" of process-oriented reorganization (e.g., Davenport 1993), since they transcend the former borders of interrelated processes and have created new paths for today's modularization concepts. As a rule, the benefits of small organization units or teams (flat hierarchies, self-organization, stronger motivation, social control, etc.) are only realized through the implementation of new information and communication technologies, which also enables the integration of interrelated processes.

Modularization is a holistic approach, which must also consider the people working within the organization. Employees and management have to develop a new role relationship within modularized organization units (see chapter 9). The role of the employee as the trigger for and key factor of radical organization changes is being reexamined. A general demand for higher qualifications and increasing demands for improved work quality are regarded as possibilities (with the appropriate information technology support) to close the divide between executable and anticipated work. The transition to team-oriented work forms that are associated with the realization of modularization concepts also make new demands on employees' social and expert competencies.

# Dissolution of the Company – Symbiosis and Networks

# Case Study Chapter 6: Colliers International Property Inc. – An Example of a Worldwide Entrepreneurial Network

How can one organize a service with a worldwide demand, which is, however, based on regional needs and demands and therefore requires a local supplier presence with regard to service delivery and know-how? What looks like a quadrature of the circle, Colliers International Property Inc. (www.colliers.com) offers customers of its commercial real estate business through its worldwide network of offices. Colliers' offices are not branches of a worldwide company, but legally independent real estate brokers and enterprises that view themselves as independent members of a worldwide network. Colliers offers "full service" regarding all commercial real estate aspects: The spectrum ranges from services such as buying and selling, to the renting and managing of commercial real estate, the management of financial services, market research, and communication services. With its worldwide networks, Colliers can offer global firms a complete one-stop service package.

Colliers was founded in 1974 after a merger of several real estate firms in Australia. It first expanded to Southeast Asia, then to Canada. In 1985, Colliers joined a leading group of US commercial real estate firms and thus gained access to the US market. Colliers' headquarters, which are responsible for coordination worldwide, were relocated to Boston. In 1989 all Colliers offices were electronically connected, greatly enhancing communication possibilities and allowing the company to truly offer worldwide business. All of Colliers' members have used the groupware Lotus Notes since 1995, which has made worldwide access to common databases possible. On the whole, the communication flow was made much more efficient (Knoop / Applegate 1997). The firm grew rapidly, with 50 new partners joining the network between 1995 and mid-1999. Today, this global real estate services firm has 10,092 employees in 267 offices in 57 countries (see, http://www.colliers.com/Corporate/About/). There are several regional centers around the globe.

Colliers' organization is a typical example of a hybrid organization form: The members are legally independent enterprises and no capital fund integration is required between members, nor a capital investment in Colliers. Members pay an annual service fee, based on a formula, for the services offered by the Colliers headquarters, which include communication, coordination, and the organization of conferences. Members have to use the Colliers logo and designate one employee as their "Colliers manager." This individual is then the formal contact person for the headquarters and other members, and has to ensure that the firm follows Colliers' global quality standards.

Colliers also centralizes other functions: The worldwide use of Lotus Notes as the communication standard was initiated by the headquarters. Furthermore, a central key account manager is deployed to handle long-term full service contracts with global firms and will be the responsible person in respect of the customer. This key account manager coordinates and controls the participating members' activities, while they utilize their regional know-how of the specific real estate market. This hybrid organizational form with its mixture of centralized and decentralized activities enables Colliers to take advantage of the economies of scale enabled by a globally operating conglomerate, but without losing its marketability. The latter is of decisive importance given that all real estate business is ultimately local.

## 6.1    The Basic Idea of Hybrid Organization Structures

There is an increasing trend in business practice for traditional entrepreneurial structures and firm boundaries to be dissolved into hybrid alliances with external partners. The fundamental idea behind such alliances is based on the notion of global cooperation, which can be described as follows: An enterprise enters into an intensive relationship with other – legally and economically independent – firms by incorporating these firms into the execution and completion process of its tasks. Consequently, alliances are formed that may have negative (dependencies), as well as positive (synergies) effects (Gemünden / Ritter 1998).

In order to prevent partners from opportunistically limiting or exploiting dependencies, these hybrid arrangements are usually of a long-term nature. They aspire towards a tightly networked relationship between the partners that is based on mutual trust. The various manifestations of such arrangements, such as networks and / or joint ventures, change the legal and economic boundaries of the enterprise: Company boundaries become pliable as the intersection between enterprise and market can no longer be described appropriately. While the company has to date merely dealt with standardized partial market tasks, external market partners are now being increasingly involved in the company's original tasks. This blurs the traditional market-near company boundary (specific vs. standardized services) ever more and, at the same time, almost leads to the company dissolving. These hybrid forms of organization are also increasingly shifting legal boundaries. In fact, a new, legally independent business unit is created for joint ventures that cannot be clearly associated with any partner. Internationally oriented, dynamic networks traverse national legal boundaries, which may lead to a clash between differing national laws.

In the following three cases, the traditional economic boundaries have been changed or dissolved: Dissolving occurs when, in an effort to optimize its real net output ratio, a company is increasingly disintegrated vertically and thereafter procures standardized services from the market. On the other hand, dissolving of a company also occurs when business location boundaries and limits can be overcome through the use of information and communication technology and when office workplaces can be moved to employees' homes (see chapter 8). Thirdly, a company undergoes a dissolving process when external third party involvement in the original (i.e. specific and/or precarious) entrepreneurial tasks becomes compulsory through company-internal (e.g., a lack of know-how or capital) or company-external factors (e.g., EDI, see chapter 4), or when this involvement occurs voluntarily. This outsourcing of tasks and competencies to third parties leads to a cutback of the company's field of activity, as well as its boundaries becoming increasingly diffuse; they can no longer be exactly demarcated. The company task to bridge supplier and buyer markets in a well-conceived way and to offer customer-oriented services (see section 2.2) are now seldom achieved in traditional markets, but are increasingly achieved within a shifting symbiosis with third parties. This chapter will focus on these forms of dissolving entrepreneurial boundaries.

## 6.2   Explaining the Development of Hybrid Organizations

In the following, we will address the core competency theory, transaction cost theory, and contractual theory as approaches that may describe or explain the dissolving of entrepreneurial boundaries and the commitment to hybrid arrangements with third parties.

### 6.2.1   Core Competency Theory as an Explanation for Hybrid Organizations

Increasing competitive pressure forces a firm's management to optimize the coordination between entrepreneurial tasks, the range of services and products, and the competitive environment even more consistently than before. A too wide range of services and products requires far more management capacities, know-how, and capital. These resources are then no longer available for the company, which limits the company's flexibility within its competitive environment. This is why there was a call to recapitulate the core competency concept (Prahalad/Hamel 1990; Strautmann 1993, see also section 5.2.2.3), which has actually been realized.

Core competencies are primarily a company's technical, technological, sales and marketing, as well as its organizational capabilities. There are three possibilities to identify core competencies: "First a core competence provides potential access to a wide variety of markets. ... Second, a core competence should make a significant contribution to the perceived customer benefits of the end product. ... Finally, a core competence should be difficult for competitors to imitate" (Prahalad/Hamel 1990, pp. 83ff.). Consequently, core competencies are concerned with company-specific capabilities, and have to be accompanied and supported by complementary competencies, which are distinguished by specialization, volume, and integration advantages. They are, however, not as crucial as core competencies to achieve strategic success; hence, other market participants and not the company itself often control them. The following example illustrates this point: In automotive engineering, the manufacturers' core competence lies in the construction of engines, but the electronic anti-block system is a joint development with large suppliers (such as Bosch and / or Nippon Denso).

Companies often need to forge cooperative agreements and strategic alliances with other companies to develop core and complementary competencies so that they can realize their competitive strategy (e.g., Bleicher 1992; Gerybadze 1995). Consequently, a company can acquire supportive complementary competencies (Reve 1990) without having to build them itself. Peripheral competencies, on the other hand, are of so little importance for the company's competitive position that they do not have to be built internally nor in cooperation with other companies. They may simply be acquired externally on the market by means of short-term purchase or service delivery contracts.

Only internal awareness and the nurturing of core competencies are therefore essential from the core competency theory perspective. The enterprise should limit itself to its strategic core, its actual business concept. Goods and services that lie beyond these own competencies may often be acquired far cheaper from third parties – either directly from the market or through the creation of cooperative and strategic alliances with external partners (Jarillo 1998).

It therefore seems possible to determine efficient company boundaries from the core competency theory perspective. In business practice, it is becoming increasingly clear that for various reasons companies are involving other companies in the building and expansion of their core competencies. The required competencies can then be acquired quickly and cost-effectively. Philips, for example, cooperated with Sony to develop the compact disk and the associated optical storage technologies, as two large companies could better manage the development costs and standardization efforts than one. Optical storage technology is one of Philips' core competencies (Prahalad / Hamel 1990).

It is difficult to develop a clear-cut delineation between core competencies and complementary competencies. Accordingly, we sometimes find criticism of the core competencies concept's high level of abstraction with regard to analysis, and there have been calls for the pivotal theoretical terms and research results to be clearly substantiated (Reve 1990).

Reve (1990), for example, reveals that the theory's pivotal terms – core competencies and complementary competencies – can be formulated more rigorously. He proposes a theoretical transaction cost interpretation of these terms (see also Strautmann 1993). According to Reve, core competencies manifest themselves in specific local investments or justify themselves through highly specific fixed assets and human capital. However, core competencies can also be generated through transaction-specific investments, i.e. through investments in a specific service relationship with a certain customer. Complementary competencies are conversely distinguished by the average specificity of fixed assets, human capital, transaction-related investments, as well as by average local investments. By using theoretical transaction cost considerations, it is easier to determine the optimal integration form and, thus, the most efficient company boundaries for core and complementary competencies. The traditional theoretical transaction cost approach is discussed in the next section to explain the hybrid organizational forms that developed from it.

## 6.2.2   Choosing Company Boundaries from Transaction Cost Theory Perspective

First, a demarcation is required between the dissolving of company boundaries by means of hybrid arrangements and the problem of vertical integration and / or disintegration. Section 2.3.3 discusses the market-hierarchy paradigm and alternative coordination mechanisms for the completion of tasks based on the division of labor, i.e. the market, hierarchy, and cooperative organizational forms.

With the help of transaction cost theory, company boundaries can be determined in the sense of their specific internal field of responsibility for the delivery of goods and services, as well as their exploitation. These company boundaries have to be determined anew if key factors (specificity and uncertainty), behavioral assumptions (opportunistic behavior and bounded rationality), information distribution, the atmosphere in which transactions occur, and the entry barriers to know-how and capital are changed (see section 2.3.3). This re-determining of the company boundaries leads to an integration of those tasks whose specificity has increased significantly and to the outsourcing of those tasks whose degree of specificity has decreased significantly. Consequently, there is a new delineation of the intersection between the enterprise and market, with the market especially having to manage the production of standardized goods and services. This is a permanent optimization process that is unavoidable in a dynamic economy with shifting performance and tasks characteristics.

Besides company boundaries having to be newly determined because the most important influencing factors have changed, the justification of hybrid arrangements is an especially important aspect of organization change within an enterprise's life cycle. In contrast to the adaptation of company boundaries, external partners cooperate in the production of original (i.e. specific and highly uncertain), goods and services when cross-border arrangements are justified. Hybrid arrangements are usually developed after the company has identified its boundaries and limits within the market, which occurs in the context of the make or buy decision. It is then that the company seeks to develop close, long-term cooperation with external third parties, which is also pursued for the fulfillment of core tasks that have been identified within the context of the make or buy decision. If third parties are incorporated for the creation of these specific core tasks, it is no longer possible to clearly determine where one company begins and the other company (with a hybrid arrangement) ends, due to the combination of the resources and the common task accomplishment. The strong connection between the dissolution of the enterprise as a result of symbiotic arrangements and the problem of vertical integration thus becomes clear.

There is a multitude of varying forms of partnerships that blur entrepreneurial boundaries: Cooperation, strategic alliances, joint ventures, networks, franchising and licensing agreements, keiretsu, inter-company clans, and others (see section 6.3). We need to ask ourselves under which conditions, to what degree, and in which form a company dissolves itself by justifying hybrid arrangements, and what the economic advantages and disadvantages of this process are.

The following four influencing factors have been identified as reasons for the dissolving of entrepreneurial boundaries (Picot 1993c):

- Average specificity of tasks;

- High degree of uncertainty in the environment;

- Changes in the transaction conditions and atmosphere (technical advancement, especially within the information and communication technology, trust, and the transaction partners' common value systems);

- Market entry barriers based on a lack of capital or know-how.

### 6.2.2.1    Classical Transaction Cost Theory Explanation: Average Specificity of Tasks

Transaction cost theory recommends a hybrid integration form (e.g., a long-term cooperative agreement) as a suitable coordination model in respect of partial tasks of average specificity (i.e. with complementary competencies) and average uncertainty. Specific, average-range goods and services cannot be procured from the market like standard goods and services, as they will have to be adapted to the highly specific core of entrepreneurial activities. On the other hand, it makes little sense to create or deliver such goods and services of average specificity oneself, since the characteristics of the goods and services to be coordinated do not require costly hierarchical incentive and sanctioning systems.

Transaction cost theory (see section 2.3.3) suggests the delivery of goods and services through third parties for the efficient integration of tasks of average specificity. This third-party relationship can be safeguarded against opportunistic exploitation through long-term basic agreements and cooperation treaties. The first reason for justifying hybrid arrangements has therefore been established: The average specificity of the partial delivery of goods and services leads to high transaction costs in both market and hierarchical task execution. Many single-source agreements and inter-company, simultaneous engineering approaches can be regarded as cooperative symbiotic arrangements.

### 6.2.2.2    High Task Uncertainty as Justification for Hybrid Arrangements

In the previous considerations, the role of the degree of environmental uncertainty in respect of the execution of a specific transaction was not considered in detail. In reality though, an increasing environmental uncertainty had been evident for some time. High uncertainty is reflected in non-predictable, frequent changes in the delivery of goods and services, characterized within a set of qualitative, quantitative, due-date-related, political and technical parameters. When environmental uncertainty increases strongly, even highly specific partial delivery of goods and services (i.e. core products) should be carried out with external partners if possible. Moreover, external partners should be given access to core competencies, since specific investments in a dynamic environment are strongly exposed to the danger of devaluation. In a highly uncertain environment, such investments are far riskier than in an environment with low uncertainty. Accordingly, companies will more than ever be on the lookout for partners who are willing to share this risk in such uncertain environmental conditions, as well as with regard to highly specific investments. Through this symbiotic partnership, additional economies of scale and relative advantages can be realized during the relatively short life span of these types of investments, which a single company could not realize.

In the case of highly specific investments that are afflicted with high uncertainty, the argument for a hybrid arrangement is even stronger for tasks of average specificity. Under such conditions, the inclusion of external partners – even in the enterprise's quintessential core areas – is the most efficient solution to stay competitive. Research and development cooperation, and distribution and production alliances are examples of cooperative and networked arrangements with legally and economically independent external partners.

### 6.2.2.3   Encouraging Symbiotic Arrangements Through Changes in the Transaction Conditions and Atmosphere

Changes in the transaction conditions may stimulate hybrid arrangements. In the following, we examine the influence of information and communication technology (ICT) and trust on the justification and development of hybrid arrangements.

**Information and Communication Technology**

Transaction costs can be considerably influenced by the appropriate use of ICT, so that hybrid arrangements with external partners or even market-based coordination instead of hierarchical solutions become economically meaningful. From the transaction cost theory perspective, the deployment of appropriate information and communication technology may lead to a reduction in transaction costs. The original efficiency issues in the changeover from one coordination form to another are shifted in the direction of market-based coordination (see section 2.5). This implies that market and hybrid coordination forms are now capable of efficiently generating the delivery of goods and services that have hitherto been transaction cost intensive, i.e. they can generate more specific core tasks characterized by a greater degree of uncertainty. The importance of hierarchy decreases, but that of market-based and symbiotic solutions increases. Consequently, ICT fosters an organization's market and symbiotic orientation (Picot / Ripperger / Wolf 1996).

Existing trends towards the organization's dissolution through hybrid arrangements such as networks and joint ventures can be reinforced and favored. However, when embarking on such forms of cooperation, enterprises should pay attention to the technical compatibility of systems to prevent the costs of adapting the technical infrastructure from eliminating any efficiency gains achieved by the overall cooperative effort.

Inter-company ICT can support cross-company cooperative work and coordination in many functional areas (see figure 6.1). When appropriate ICT – especially modern telecommunication infrastructures – is available, contacts between potential transaction partners can be established much easier. Furthermore, coordination is also possible over long distances (e.g., Reichwald / Koller 1995). With ICT's appropriate integration into company processes, the coalescing of value-adding chains may also be realized. Inter-company processes and transactions may be sped up and simplified (see chapter 4) by means of videoconferencing services, data transmission services, value-adding services or electronic data interchange (EDI). EDI (Picot / Neuburger / Niggl 1994) has a specific potential in this regard (see section 6.4). EDI that is based on accepted standards (e.g., XML) can support task accomplishment in existing cooperative networks and strategic alliances, as well as making hybrid arrangements possible in the first place (Neuburger 1994).

| Business area | ICT-supported cooperative form | Effects |
|---|---|---|
| R&D | • Exchange of information<br>• Coordinated or collaborative R&D<br>• Design and utilization of collaborative infrastructures | • Economizing on resources<br>• Time advantages<br>• Increase in market power<br>• Nurturing of creativity<br>• Better capacity utilization<br>• Better access to resources |
| Purchasing | • Collective procurement, transport<br>• (Partially) automated warehousing | • Utilization of large customer advantages (e.g., discounts)<br>• Cost, time, and quality advantages |
| Production | • Exchange of components<br>• Exchange of free capacities<br>• Building and utilization of collaborative production sites | • Cost, time, and quality advantages<br>• Utilization of scaling effects<br>• Risk sharing<br>• Better capacity utilization |
| Marketing/sales | • Exchange of information (e.g., customer database)<br>• Reciprocal takeover of distribution and/or customer services<br>• Joint advertising, PR or marketing promotion activities<br>• Design of joint service offers (e.g., hotline) | • Access to new resources<br>• Risk reduction<br>• Saving of funds for competitive purposes<br>• Increased customer utilization through the integration of value-added services |
| Market research | • Exchange of information and results<br>• Joint market research<br>• Building and use of joint market research establishments<br>• Joint development of support systems<br>• Joint market monitoring | • Access to new resources<br>• Avoidance of parallel research<br>• Specialization advantages<br>• Innovation potential through possibilities to combine products and/or services |

**Fig. 6.1.** ICT support potential in cross-company cooperation (based on Reichwald / Rupprecht 1992)

The Internet (see chapter 4) makes a worldwide computer network available, which also offers small and symbiotically networked firms highly affordable communication capabilities and enables a multitude of new communication forms between companies. Many hybrid arrangements, such as networks, are hardly conceivable without state-of-the-art information and communication technology support. However ICT may not only be utilized for the execution of standard processes, but also for simplifying cooperation with third parties in specific, complex, and dynamic task areas.

At times, the deployment of technology to support market or cooperative symbiotic processes faces intrinsic boundaries, which particularly surface when, for example, personal presence and interpersonal face-to-face communication are required to solve ICT problems. The building of trust between cooperative partners, joint strategic decisions, and creative solutions to unstructured problems cannot be realized without personal contact. Telecommunication can therefore only play a supporting role in the preparation and post processing efforts.

**Trust and Shared Values**

Trust and shared values (Handy 1995; Mathews 1994 and see section 3.6) are also important components of the transaction conditions. Similar to ICT, they facilitate and speed up agreement on and execution of transactions, thus decreasing costs and also facilitating hybrid arrangements in the form of a symbiosis in respect of cross-company fulfillment. The risk of prevailing dependencies being opportunistically exploited is lower than with anonymous market transactions. Trust and a shared value system stimulate and reinforce existing tendencies in respect of the justification of hybrid organizations. Trust between transaction partners reduces the need for highly specific, contractual prior specifications of future events or for explicit arrangements regarding the dividing of the cooperation's financial rewards. Mutual trust makes the need for expensive and elaborate protective mechanisms to prevent opportunistic behavior unnecessary. Long-term transactional relationships are expedient for the development of a trusting atmosphere. Such relationships make it easier to overcome prisoner's dilemma situations that may arise through a lack of trust (see section 2.3.1). In long-term transaction relationships, it is counter-productive to engage in opportunistic behavior for the attainment of short-term advantages at the cost of the cooperative partners.

### 6.2.2.4    Entry Barriers to New Know-how and Capital Markets as Justifications for Symbiotic Arrangements

Entry barriers to new know-how and capital markets (Picot 1991b; Picot/Reichwald 1994) also contribute to the softening of company borders by means of symbiotic arrangements. In an uncertain, competition-intensive environment, those core competencies with which an enterprise initially built its competitive position can devalue quickly. It is therefore crucial for the enterprise to continually build new core competencies that may lead to entrepreneurial success. Thereafter the company has to address the question of the degree to which a cooperative solution is needed to develop the knowledge and capability that are required for task accomplishment, or whether fostering know-how internally, for example, through education and advanced training is more advantageous. Neither solution option may, however, be available to the company. In a number of cases, building new core capabilities internally also triggers high transaction costs and the capabilities are only realized very slowly. A market-based know-how acquisition usually has cost and time advantages.

However, external procurement of the needed know-how is not always possible. In this context, the information paradox describes the phenomenon (see section 2.4.3) that maintains that a buyer is unable to judge the information to be acquired because it is unknown. As soon as the buyer has acquired the information, it is no longer required, as this knowledge is now known.

Transfer problems in respect of tacit knowledge may also make the purely market-based external procurement of know-how more difficult. It is often application-specific knowledge – acquired through experience – that is of importance for the building and development of a core competence. Owing to its implicit and difficult to comprehend nature, the transfer of such knowledge is limited or impossible through the use of words, figures, and maps. The information paradox and the tacit knowledge phenomenon are inhibiting factors when externally procuring new knowledge from the market. Even if these difficulties were controllable, external procurement would still face the general problem of a potentially strong dependence on external specialists.

These three know-how entry barriers can be overcome easier and quicker with a long-term, close cooperation with external knowledge suppliers that is based on mutual trust (which is also true in the context of joint venture contracts). In a long-term cooperation, the information supplier does not have to fear that there will be no reciprocal gesture from the information buyer after the information has been supplied. If there is a symbiotic relationship between the information supplier and information buyer, it is also possible to transfer tacit knowledge "on the job" (as in joint project work) through joint problem solution. The possibility of opportunistic exploitation of dependencies that have developed is a lesser problem in long-term exchange relationships than in short-term, market-based contracts. It is possible to build internal core competencies and areas of business through long-term partnerships, while sharing risks with partners.

The limited availability of capital – and the simultaneously required high and risky capital expenditure – for the development of core competencies increases the need for hybrid arrangements. They make realizing future capital-intensive strategies, which should actually be implemented within the company, much easier. The limited availability of capital often forces even very large companies to cooperate with external third parties with regard to their core business areas.

In summary, it is apparent that a lack of know-how and capital can make life more difficult for companies to go it alone and they may be forced into hybrid arrangements with external partners. It is also often necessary to soften company boundaries somewhat when building new core competencies so that cooperative partners can bring in new knowledge and capital into the company.

## 6.2.3 Modeling the Enterprise as a Network of Internal, External, and Hybrid Contracts

From the core competency theory perspective, the company's boundaries become blurred when it is forced to embrace external partners in order to build core competencies (see section 6.2.1). From a transaction cost theory perspective, company boundaries become blurred when external partners are involved in the fulfillment of highly specific or uncertain tasks that were – originally – enterprise tasks. Finally, we have to examine the contract theory contribution in respect of an explanation of hybrid arrangements (see section 2.3.1).

The dissolution of the enterprise through hybrid organizational forms can be explained from a contract theory perspective when the enterprise is modeled as a network of internal and external contracts (Aoki/Gustafson/Williamson 1990). The company's hierarchical structure is constituted of internal contracts with the company member (e.g., work contracts). They are usually incomplete and relational in nature. Highly specified tasks are especially well suited for internal fulfillment. Arrangements such as joint ventures, franchising, and licensing agreements, which are used to fulfill tasks of average specificity, are controlled by external contracts (cooperation contracts and franchising agreements). Bilateral relationships with external partners, which are used to fulfill tasks of low specificity (i.e. standardized tasks) are also managed by external contracts (spot market contracts) in which the delivery of goods and services is fully specified. Internal contracts and the previously mentioned traditional external contracts for short-term external procurement from the market determine traditional enterprise boundaries. These entrepreneurial boundaries are, however, becoming blurred through the first-mentioned category of external contracts (cooperation contracts and franchising agreements), which justify hybrid arrangements.

Hybrid arrangements are also entered into when, for highly specific tasks, external contracts are concluded with independent third parties, instead of the requisite internal work contracts that one would expect in this situation. The advantage of hybrid arrangements is that the enterprise can transcend its organizational and therefore also its resource and performance boundaries. Consequently, the enterprise can secure support and resources from the market and unlock new expansion possibilities. Efficiency gains are not only realized through an appropriate differentiation between the enterprise and market in the context of make or buy decisions, but also through hybrid arrangements. There is, however, a risk that external partners will be more involved in the fulfillment of company tasks than previously and could, for example, acquire more knowledge about the company's internal affairs than is desirable. Stronger dependencies than originally planned could then occur.

The traversing of entrepreneurial boundaries through hybrid arrangements can therefore create extraordinary opportunities, but may also generate serious contractual and management problems (Reve 1990). The realization of opportunities, as well as the prevention of opportunistic behavior by transaction partners must be guaranteed through efficient contracts. This task gains significance in that cross-company, long-term networks are often based on incomplete, relational contracts. These networks require special contractual (hard) and extra-contractual (soft) protective mechanisms and therefore often resemble symbiotic contracts (Schanze 1991).

## 6.3    Implementation Forms of Hybrid Organizations

### 6.3.1  Overview

No one has to date succeeded in systematizing hybrid organizational forms consistently and placing them on a continuum between market and hierarchy. All systematization approaches describe an organizational form's degree of vertical integration and base the differentiation between market-near and hierarchy-near organizational forms on this. Imai and Itami (1984), for example, utilize the art of decision-making, as well as the duration of a relationship to describe hybrid-processing mechanisms (Baur 1990). The vertical degree of integration increases with an alliance's duration over time and with the possibility to coordinate assignments. Kappich (1989) mentions the extent and type of protection against opportunistic behavior as criteria. The vertical degree of integration should therefore increase with an increase in the scope for opportunistic behavior. Benjamin, Malone and Yates (1986) use the degree with which business partners are selected ad hoc as a criterion for the degree of integration. Vertical integration depends on the degree to which, for example, suppliers are selected in advance for future procurement tasks and no longer compete with one another. Schneider (1988) aims at the shape that the influencing of business partners takes. With market-near organizational forms, the results of actions are increasingly influenced by the price mechanism, while with hierarchy-near forms, actions are directly influenced by direction-giving possibilities. Figure 6.2 presents an overview of these criteria.

| Imai/Itami (1984) | • Art of decision-making<br>• Duration of the relationship |
|---|---|
| Kappich (1989) | • Type and extent of the need for protection against opportunistic behavior |
| Benjamin/Malone/Yates (1986) | • The degree of the ad hoc selection of business partners |
| Schneider (1988) | • The form of the influencing of business partners |

**Fig. 6.2.**    Criteria for the evaluation of the degree of integration

The dependency relationship between exchange partners is closely linked to the degree of specificity of a performance delivery. Most descriptive efforts aim to identify the degree of integration by means of the degree of dependency on business partners. Hierarchy-near organization forms are identified as market-near forms by means of a larger and / or a mutual dependency relationship between business partners.

One-sided dependencies make the use of potential power possible. In such cases, a vertical dominance prevails (Baur 1990). Such dominant forms define middle and long-range relationships between legally independent, but unilateral economically dependent partners. These dominant forms reveal a relatively high degree of vertical integration and thus entail a hierarchy-near organizational form. Examples of this are tasks with a comparatively high degree of specificity but of rather little strategic importance and / or rare occurrence.

In contrast, the term cooperation denotes an amount of collaboration that equals that between legally and economically independent enterprises. Cooperative agreements are usually entered into for tasks with average specificity and of average strategic importance and distinguish themselves by a certain, but not very high, degree of vertical or horizontal integration. In this sense, cooperative arrangements have a symbiotic character with a mutual dependency.

We will next describe varying forms of dominance and cooperation, illustrating their characteristics and manifestations. Within the literature and business world, there is a range of terms that describes certain forms of organization mechanisms between a market and hierarchy. These are terms such as strategic alliances, strategic (value-adding) partnerships, strategic cooperative efforts, joint ventures, etc. They can all be summarized by the term cooperation. However, they all refer to different forms of cooperation. Similarly, one speaks of vertical, horizontal, and / or diagonal forms of cooperation (e.g., Sydow 1992a). The varying forms are the topic of section 6.3.2. Forms of dominance also have a wide range of terminology. The range stretches from semi-vertical integration or vertical semi-integration to licenses and / or equity stakes. These forms of dominance are examined in section 6.3.3. The question of which of the highlighted symbiotic or dominant organizational forms should to be chosen under specific conditions is addressed in section 6.3.4.

Different manifestations and peculiarities of multilateral organizational forms will also be described. Such inter-company networks consist of a variety of legally independent enterprises that are more or less loosely coupled. The term network has never been linked with a certain market or hierarchy-nearness. Networks are therefore best described as hybrid organizational forms that, depending on their relational forms, may be designed with either market or hierarchy-nearness. Networks also have a wide variety of terminology. We find terms such as strategic networks, dynamic networks, and value-adding networks that are partly used synonymously, but may at times also indicate different network types. These are described in section 6.3.5.

## 6.3.2 Cooperative Forms

As a term, cooperative forms denote a mid to long-term contractually regulated cooperation between legally independent companies for the collaborative completion of tasks (Rotering 1990; Schrader 1993; Balling 1997). Such cross-company cooperation occurs via mutually beneficial efforts and is thus symbiotic in nature. Cooperation is considered when it offers advantages that cannot be delivered by any other organizational forms. Frequently mentioned advantages of cooperation are time, cost, know-how, scale, profit and benefit advantages, as well as the reduction of risks such as market entry (e.g., Poert/Fuller 1989; Vizjak 1990; Rupprecht-Däullary 1994; Bronder 1995). This does not, however, reveal what this common task fulfillment should comprise and what concrete forms the relationship should take.

Tröndle (1987) describes the character of cooperation by, for example, using degree of autonomy and independency as criteria (Rotering 1993). Companies participating in a cooperative effort are autonomous to the degree that they themselves can decide to accept or terminate cooperation without having to seek permission from a higher-ranking entity. They are therefore equal partners within the cooperative effort. This perspective can be expanded. Companies are also autonomous when, within their relationship with another partner, no direct pressure or potential power is applied to initiate or terminate a long-term cooperation. At this point, it is apparent that there are differences between cooperation and controlling contracts.

As soon as cooperation commences, interdependencies start developing between cooperation partners. These interdependencies are based on all the facts considered in collective decision-making. Within a cooperation, a large number of decisions are made jointly, which may have to be negotiated within decision-making bodies and are binding on both cooperation partners (Brockhoff 1989). Cooperations are therefore a form of resource consolidation (Vanberg 1982). In this consolidation, both the nature and quality of the resources to be contributed to the cooperation, as well as the sharing of the output are generally addressed by coordination and/or negotiation processes. In an unbalanced negotiation situation, the weaker partner would never agree to cooperation.

Additional characterizing features that are frequently mentioned are that cooperation is formed voluntarily and its contractual agreement is always explicit. The first characteristic allows cooperation to be well delineated from the dominant forms addressed in the following section. The voluntary nature of cooperation implies that it is only agreed upon when both partners expect an increase in profits through cooperation. This is not necessarily true of dominant models. Moreover, cooperation always occurs through explicit contractual agreement. As we will demonstrate, dominant forms may also arise from explicit contracts. The explicit agreement to cooperate is often viewed as the definitive characteristic of cooperation. Rotering (1993) defines cooperation, for example, as a long-term, explicitly agreed upon and unilaterally rescindable collaboration between companies.

Cooperation is often linked with a strategic component. In this context, we speak of strategic alliances, strategic partnerships or, in the context of networks, we refer to strategic networks. This should clarify the goal of cooperation: To create competitive advantage for the cooperation partners.

**Systematizing Cooperation**

Cooperation may be systematized according to various points of view. With regard to the direction of the cooperation, vertical, horizontal, and diagonal forms of cooperation can be distinguished (Büchs 1991; Bronder 1995). Vertical cooperation refers to a company's consecutive steps within the value chain such as cooperation with the customer and supplier. Such cooperative forms are often described as value chain partnerships and they belong to the same business area (e.g., the close cooperation between a manufacturer and supplier in the automobile industry). In a horizontal cooperation, companies in the same business area, as well as the same value chain (e.g., R&D cooperation within microelectronics firms) cooperate. Diagonal cooperation is agreed upon between firms in differing business areas and in various value chain steps (e.g., banks and IT companies).

Cooperation may relate to the entire enterprise or to a few functional areas only. If the collaboration pertains to a few functional areas, functional cooperation can be further differentiated. Logistic cooperation, for example, is one form of collaboration in which companies agree upon a close and long-term contractual coordination with regard to logistics. Marketing cooperation refers to companies collaborating with regard to sales, marketing, and customer service. Technology cooperation occurs when companies, especially within the R&D area, collaborate to jointly develop new technologies and / or to undertake technological development.

Additional systematization possibilities are, for example, the range of cooperative efforts (national / international), the duration of the cooperation (temporary / permanent), the degree of the mutual economic dependency, as well as the degree of telecommunication support.

**Examples of Cooperation**

There are numerous examples of cooperation between enterprises in various areas of business and industries. The microelectronics industry has an especially high level of cooperative efforts (e.g., Wigand 1988). These symbiotic partnerships are motivated by two reasons. First, the development and production of a new microchip generation require very high investment costs that one company alone can no longer carry, since competing developments may lead to considerable market risks. Second, in this industry, successful market activities require a very high degree of technical standards that constitute a quintessential value factor for the buyers. To develop actual standards, a considerable market share is required that can often no longer be achieved or maintained by just a single company.

The companies Apple, IBM, and Motorola therefore formed a strategic alliance for the development of standards for an RISC processor that was developed in a joint research and development center. In a further strategic alliance, these companies combined to found the company Kaleida with which to create a future multimedia standard. Apple brought its considerable technology know-how to this cooperation, while IBM contributed its considerable experience in the implementation of de facto standards and its excellent market access. An example of a marketing partnership is that between Siemens and SAP. The computer manufacturer has access to medium-size enterprises, while the software company SAP can offer suitable, new software. These providers offer various components for a new systems technology (hard and software as complementary goods). Through a close working relationship, compatibility problems can be very effectively solved (Picot / Hass 2002).

An example of cooperation at specifically the regional level is the development of regional networks (clusters). These networks concern companies and institutions that are geographically close to one another and that are integrated into a cluster of activities (Knyphausen 1999). Technology-oriented networks specifically show promise of a high added-value level and innovation potential. Among the best-known examples of regional entrepreneurial concentrations are Silicon Valley near San Francisco and similar centers such as Silicon Glen near Glasgow. Porter (1990; 2001b) explains the success of such regional cooperative structures as resulting from national and regional location factors. Important competitive factors such as capabilities, knowledge, and innovation are often more similar within regions than internationally. They can be developed in a concentrated way and thus improve the competitive advantage of companies internationally.

Regional cooperation may pursue two strategies. Regional networks within a country aim at attracting direct investment funds from abroad. Cooperation abroad is, on the other hand, the reason for the acquisition of know-how in various value chains. Cooperation of this type may be found, for example, in the biotechnology sector: With the laboratory facilities that Bayer AG acquired from Miles Corporation (whose headquarters are in Elkhart, Indiana) in 1978, it started a corporate-wide pharmacological research center in West Haven (the Yale cluster), which is also supported by the Cutter Laboratories in Berkeley in the production technology area.

## Organizing Cooperation

There are many ways of organizing cooperation (Fonatanari 1966; Fleischer 1997; Olesch 1998). There are formal organization structures or the cooperation can be a loose, informal structure. If, for example, the cooperation refers to only a single contract, there seem to be no immediate need to embed the cooperation within a formal organization. If the participating parties decide on a formal organization structure, there are two longer-term cooperative efforts from which to choose: A joint venture and a consortium.

In a joint venture, participating companies cooperate via a specifically created and legally independent company, the cooperative venture. Each participating company contributes a differing amount of resources. Cooperating companies usually participate in equal degrees and amounts (Liessmann 1990). Joint ventures are especially found when a single company can no longer handle highly complex tasks by itself, as in the aerospace industry or in microelectronics. In order to share the high R&D risks, as well as the financial burden, and to increase its market (often protected by national governments), appropriate super projects in the form of international joint ventures are put into place. Such projects include the development, production and, some times, the sales and distribution of such goods.

A second possibility for the organization of cooperation in a symbiotic form is project collaboration. In a consortium, as this organizational form is called, the participating companies agree to carry out one or more carefully delineated projects jointly. Consortia are usually formed for a limited duration, as there is no intention that this should be a long-term cooperation. In super projects, a consortium can reduce the risk that the individual cooperation partners run. The consortium members' economic and legal independence are also maintained. Typical examples of consortia are large construction project. Banks may also get together in consortia so that they can offer more credit or issue more stocks and shares.

Various standardization efforts within the information and communication sector are an additional example of cooperation between companies within the context of consortia. Such collaborative activities are, however, rarely described as a consortium, but nevertheless do have typical consortium characteristics. X/Open, for example, is a project group that operates in this way and whose purpose is to standardize the different variants of the UNIX operating system. Various companies are therefore working together to develop a uniform operating system standard, although they basically compete against one another with their proprietary UNIX designs. At the same time, though, they realize that they can only gain competitive advantage in respect of other operating systems if they can offer their customers a uniform and standardized UNIX operating system. This joint standardization activity has all the characteristics of a strategically important cooperation between the participating companies.

## 6.3.3   Forms of Dominance

In contrast to cooperative forms of collaboration between companies, forms of dominance indicate unilateral economic and financial dependencies (e.g., Baur 1990). Forms of dominance have a hierarchy-like character – especially when compared to cooperative forms – due to the limited economic dependence of the two related companies.

This vertical integration is only efficient when tasks have to be organized that – although they have a relatively high degree of specificity – do not necessarily require company-internal processing because they are of little or mid-level strategic importance or they occur infrequently. The way the contract is designed permits the dominant company to have a strong or less strong influence on the partner's business activities (e.g., Gerpott 1993). This can lead to decisions being made by a decision committee not comprised of equal voting rights that alter the profit levels of all the participants. The dominant company has instruments of power with which decisions can be enforced, even if this means that it will suffer economic disadvantages. There may also be various contractual regulations between the parties that can shift the power in favor of one of the partners. Figure 6.3 offers an overview of possible forms of vertical dominance, as well as the reasons for an unequal distribution of power (Baur 1990).

| Vertical dominance forms | Reason for the power position |
|---|---|
| Quasi-vertical integration | Ownership of specific production factors |
| Vertical quasi-integration | Importance of the customer for sales as a whole |
| Implicit contracts | Threat to discontinue tacitly assumed contract renewal |
| De facto vertical integration | Geographic location of the supplier |
| Partial integration | (Credible) Threat to completely integrate a production step |
| Licenses | Possibility of withdrawal of know-how |
| Equity stake | Establishment of proprietorship |

**Fig. 6.3.**    Important vertical forms of dominance (based on Baur 1990, p. 101)

These varying forms of dominance are distinguished according to their underlying working relationships. If, for example, the buyer of certain goods has rights to the supplier's production means, this is a quasi-vertical integration. Although the suppliers in such a situation run less risk by not having to invest in specific equipment or facilities, they have almost no negotiation power to implement anything to their own advantage. When, for example, delivery conditions need to be renegotiated, suppliers have almost no possibility to negotiate a price range despite the high specificity of the services that they offer. Buyers may threaten to withdraw the production means and fulfill the order themselves or to ask for a completely new bid. The suppliers, which are merely the owners of these production means, therefore have fewer possibilities for opportunistic behavior. Consequently, the quasi-vertical integration may be an appropriate alternative to a fully integrated (hierarchical) production of specific goods and services. Suppliers may be offered technical know-how without having to fear the costs associated with opportunistic behavior (Männel 1996). Examples of a quasi-vertical integration of goods and services are found in the automobile industry where an automobile manufacturer constructs a metal pressing plant – to which it has rights – with a supplier company.

Suppliers within vertical quasi-integration cooperation may generate a vast amount of turnover from a single very large customer. This customer may, however, threaten the weaker company with the termination of its business relationship. If this were to threaten the company's existence, the weaker company could agree to certain concessions. The dominating buyer could then exert greater control over the supplier's business and influence the production process considerably. The buyer may, for example, demand that the production process and goods logistics be precisely tailored to meet the stronger company's needs so that, for example, just-in-time delivery conditions are optimized. Despite all these advantages, which are similar to those that a hierarchical organization offers, the buyer does not have to carry all the risks for the production of goods and services. These risks remain with the legally independent supplier. The supplier's only countermeasure is the opportunity to develop a mutual working relationship. One such possibility may be the development of specific know-how. Through innovation such as an anti-blocking system, a supplier within the automobile industry may, for example, try to build a specific negotiation position with regard to buyers. Aside from typical examples within the automobile industry, tendencies towards vertical quasi-integration may be found where there are considerable size differences between business partners and, therefore, considerable concentrations of market power.

Implicit contracts are closely related to vertical quasi-integration. They are based on the threat to discontinue contract renewal that has always occurred quietly and tacitly. In contrast to explicit contracts, the weaker company has no possibility to insist that contracts should be adhered to in their entirety and to have this legally enforced if required. Consequently, it may become compliant with regard to the dominating business partner's wishes. An important advantage of a fully integrated hierarchical organization thus becomes available through an implicit contract between business partners whose power is distributed unequally, without having to deal with its disadvantages. The weaker party is almost totally dependent and there is a possibility that it may be influenced without having to incur any costs, while the stronger partner is independent of the weaker one.

Another vertical dominance form is de facto vertical integration. This may manifest itself in the form of location-specific investments of the supplier. A supplier may, for example, locate close to a buyer in order to optimize just-in-time delivery. The more this supplier limits its possibilities of supplying other buyers, the more it develops a location-specific dependency on this single customer. Consequently, the same potential for power arises as with the other dominant forms. An example of a de facto vertical integration is Recaro, a manufacturer of car seats, which located to the automobile manufacturer Daimler-Chrysler's immediate neighborhood in Bremen, Germany. Although this supplier is still legally independent, it is – at least in the vicinity – strongly dependent on the dominating automobile manufacturer.

A partial integration occurs when a buyer seriously threatens to integrate a supplier's production stage. The buyer should obviously either have the appropriate technical facilities and capacity to do so or should be able to acquire them swiftly. In addition, the buyer should not suffer any major production cost disadvantages due to a lack of degression effects. It should be kept in mind that realizing a partial integration – irrespective of available capacities – requires time, which then offers the supplier an opportunity to consider countermeasures. A partial integration therefore constitutes the weakest form of vertical dominance.

Besides the above-discussed forms, vertical dominant forms may also be realized by means of licenses, as well as through equity stakes. In respect of licensing, we assume that the license issuer owns a patent or has specific experience with a certain technology (von der Osten 1989). The patent owner has the possibility to utilize this technology in its in-house production or to extend others the right to manufacture this technology under a license agreement. There are some advantages to issuing a license that in-house production does not have. Within the context of the license contract, the license issuer can specify how a technology should be applied. Only certain types of utilization are usually permitted, for example, those preventing the licensee from passing the technology to third parties. Consequently, the license issuer controls the diffusion of know-how despite its utilization outside the company. Additional control can be exerted by specifying regional usage and thus avoiding conflict with the license issuer's own production and regional plans or competition with other licensees in other regions. License issuers frequently specify compliance with certain quality standards, limit production quantities, and / or maintain some influence on the pricing structure. License issuers can thus influence the licensee's business policy considerably.

This licensee's economic dependency on the license issuer depends on the degree to which it has relinquished the right to develop its own know-how base. The license issuer may threaten to cancel the license contract, be unwilling to renew an existing license agreement or refuse to offer new know-how in the form of licenses in future. The risk of opportunistic behavior in such a unilaterally dependent relationship may be reduced by granting counter-licenses. Frequently, the granting of licenses offers quick access to markets. This is especially true with regard to foreign markets with unfamiliar conditions, customer needs or trade barriers; granting a license is therefore a suitable way for one's own know-how to gain market access.

Another way to limit opportunistic behavior is through equity stakes. Whether the equity stakes are unilateral or mutual depends on the dependency relationship. If, for example, the supplier requires specific investments to enable production improvements, this could lead to a potentially dangerous unilateral dependency relationship, as the buyer may refuse to pay the agreed upon price for the products as soon as the investments have been made (hold-up problems, see section 2.3.4). If the supplier anticipates this risk, these investments will not be made, which would also be to the buyer's disadvantage. In order to avoid this, the buyer may want to offer the supplier an equity stake. This serves as a safeguard against buyer exploitation. If both sides require investments, monitoring, and controlling possibilities, a reciprocal cross-ownership relationship helps to decrease the incentives for opportunistic behavior.

## 6.3.4  The Selection of a Symbiotic Coordination Form

We have not yet addressed which concrete organizational characteristics should be and / or must be present in a symbiotic coordination form. An analysis of the prevailing resource interdependency between participating companies may contribute to finding the most suitable organizational form for a symbiotic arrangement. Teece (1986) and Dietl (1995) gained important insights into the relationship between resource interdependency and organizational form (see also Picot 1993c; Picot / Dietl / Franck 2002), which will be highlighted in the following section.

An economically advantageous symbiotic relation between companies requires at least one company to deploy resources through which greater benefits may be achieved than through a single company. The resources that are relevant for a symbiotic relationship are called interdependent resources. Such resource interdependencies allow important conclusions to be drawn with regard to the design of symbiotic relationships. Three different types of resource characteristics need to be considered in this respect: Dependency, potency, and plasticity. The dependency of a resource is conveyed when it, together with other companies' resources, generates greater benefit than the resources would if used individually. An example is the available knowledge within a group compared to the knowledge available to the individuals within a group. A resource has great potency when other resources depend on it; for example, when a business's continuation depends on the extension of a bank credit line. When a resource is dependent but not potent, this is called unilateral dependence; if a resource is dependent and potent, this is called reciprocal or mutual dependence. The plasticity of a resource refers to the fact that the way in which this resource is likely to be utilized may not be predictable or only limitedly predictable. The more difficult it is to predict a resource utilization, the more plastic the resource is, for example, employees with a large knowledge base may be viewed as a plastic resource.

If two companies plan to start a symbiotic relationship, an assessment of these resource characteristics allows various typical structuring situations to be distinguished. Each situation requires a specific type of organization structure for an efficient symbiotic relationship (Dietl 1995). Consequently, the type of resource dependency is largely determined by the three above-mentioned resource characteristics (plasticity, dependence, potency). There are varying organization structure recommendations that depend on the combination of the three resource characteristics and on the distribution of the resources by means of the cooperating partners (see figure 6.4).

If the resources of company A are dependent on company B's potent and very plastic resources, this unilateral dependence always carries the risk of a hold-up and moral hazard (see section 2.3.4). This occurs when, for example, company A owns production facilities whose economic benefit is strongly dependent on company B's technical know-how. Simultaneously, company A has considerable difficulties in monitoring the application of B's know-how and in assessing it. The only efficient solution is for A to achieve uniform resource management through a

|  |  | Resources from company A | | |
|---|---|---|---|---|
|  |  | Dependent | Potent and of little plasticity | Potent and of high plasticity |
| Resources from company B | Potent and of high plasticity | Case 1: Majority interests, acquisition or merger | Case 3: Stake in equity from B to A | Case 5: Joint venture |
|  | Potent and of low plasticity | Case 2: Issuance of license | Case 4: Consortium | Case 6: Stake in equity from A to B |

**Fig. 6.4.**   Selection matrix (based on Dietl 1995, p. 580)

high degree of integration, for example, through a buyout of B or by acquiring a majority interest in B (case 1).

If company A's resources are dependent and company B's potent resources have little plasticity, a different structure is recommended (case 2). In this case, the resources required from B can be adequately described and can be transferred within the context of a more or less complex contract (e.g., a licensing agreement). Such a contract cannot, however, be formulated by taking all the details and possible future developments into account. It should be primarily supported by confidence and trust-building measures. The advantage is that in this form of symbiotic relationship it is possible to specify the essential aspects of the contract. Adherence to the contract can be controlled and one may check, for example, if certain goods or information were delivered or not. Licensing agreements with companies in the Third World for the manufacture of steel, chemical products or trucks are examples of such specification.

When both sides have potent resources, there is a mutual or reciprocal dependency (cases 3 and 6). The company whose resources are the most plastic has an advantage over the other company, since its contribution to the joint task fulfillment is more difficult to control. The resultant risk of moral hazard behavior has to be limited through appropriate actions such as a (minority) stake in the company with the greater resource plasticity. This equity stake serves as security for the side with less resource plasticity, as the company with greater resource plasticity is now unlikely to exert its opportunistic possibilities against its partner. An example of this type of symbiotic relationship is the cooperation between airlines, hotel chains, and / or car rental companies. Airlines often own a minority interest in such cooperating companies.

If two companies are mutually dependent and have equally low resource plasticity, a consortium is the most efficient organizational form (case 4). The parties agree to carry out a joint, relatively well-defined project through which both will gain benefits as a result of synergy effects and the sharing of the risk. Examples of this are consortia of construction companies or cooperation between banks in respect of the issuance of stocks and bonds.

When both parties bring potent and very plastic resources into cooperation, both sides face the possibility of morally hazardous behavior (case 5). Since one partner cannot sufficiently control the other's contribution to the common enterprise, each party has the possibility to deliver less than it promised. If one party behaves in this way, it may realize certain cost advantages for itself, while both parties share the loss in benefits. This problem can be efficiently addressed by each party contributing its resources to a joint venture. A common body alleviates the mutual control, reduces the possibilities for opportunistic behavior, encourages the development of a common culture and, through trust building, tries to contribute to achieving the common goals. Examples of joint ventures are joint research and development projects to which both parties contribute qualified human and technological resources.

## 6.3.5  Enterprise Networks

Our discussion has so far been focused on bilateral cooperation and / or dominance forms. Forms of cross-company cooperation do not have to be limited to bilateral relationships. It is possible to carry out a cross-company task fulfillment through contractual relations with a variety of legally independent companies. This leads to a network of cross-company cooperation in which many companies may participate (Gomez / Zimmermann 1999). For this form of cooperation, no particular descriptive label has yet emerged. In the literature, we find terms such as dynamic networks (Jarillo 1998; 1998), strategic networks (Sydow 1992a; Wigand 1997, p. 3), value-adding networks (Pfeiffer / Weiss 1992), cooperative networks (Thorelli 1986), business webs (Hagel 1996), and value webs (Wigand 2004).

In general, such networks may have a more hierarchical or more market-based character. Accordingly, they may be allocated to either the cooperative or the dominant forms of cross-company cooperation. When cooperative relationships form the basis of cooperation, these are called cooperative networks (Thorelli 1986). Examples are research and development alliances, merchandise management systems (with a majority of the companies participating), and rationalization communities between suppliers, buyers, and shipping agents for efficient transport processing (Wolff / Neuburger 1995). Other networks are differentiated in that one or more companies have a leadership role. These focal companies coordinate the process of cross-company task fulfillment (Sydow 1992a). There are long-term contractual relationships with conditions similar to a hierarchy between focal companies and the other participating companies.

An example of a network enterprise (see Sydow, e.g., 1992b and others) is the Italian clothing company Benetton, which offers high-quality fashion collections. It acquires its textiles from about 350 legally independent, but economically dependent suppliers. The suppliers are partially located near the few production sites. The own manufacturing is essentially limited to very demanding operations, while labor-intensive standardized tasks are usually outsourced to relatively small supply firms. Benetton controls the production process that is mostly based on the division of labor, while the competition-centric tasks such as designs and quality control are carried out internally. Benetton also centrally coordinates the suppliers' tasks. The suppliers are economically dependent, since they themselves do not deliver a complete product that could be sold to consumers. In return, Benetton guarantees the supply firms a stipulated share of the earned profits. The sale of the textiles is handled by approximately 4,200 businesses with which Benetton has franchise contracts. In addition, there are 75 independent commission-based sales agencies between Benetton and these businesses. These agencies look after the individual businesses and coordinate regional advertising activities. Benetton itself exerts considerable influence on the sales channel. It also derives several benefits and advantages from this network arrangement. There is a relatively low need to invest and Benetton is flexible to react to fluctuations in demand, which consequently greatly reduces its business risks. The risks do not disappear of course, but they are passed on to the dominated business partners. Consequently, a cross-company cooperation concept is realized that often serves as a role model for other reorganization efforts. This form of the intensive division of labor is only possible through the appropriate use of IT.

Another example of a multilateral network is a keiretsu. A keiretsu is a typical Japanese form of cross-industry company cooperation (Sydow 1991). The core of a keiretsu group usually consists of a bank, a retailer, and an industrial manufacturing company. These companies, together with about 20 to 30 other business partners from various business areas, form the inner circle of the group. Especially the inner-circle companies meet regularly to exchange information and to coordinate their business strategy. In addition, the wider keiretsu circle also includes suppliers of companies from the inner circle so that the total network is comprised of up to 100 companies.

Besides personal relationships, a keiretsu group also has various forms of economic integration such as mutual equity stakes in one another's companies, as well as mutual supplier relationships. The participating firms nevertheless maintain their decision-making autonomy, i.e. there is no institutionalized management. Competition is therefore largely maintained. Even though a company within a keiretsu chooses other keiretsu members as transaction partners, there is no obligation to do so. Consequently, business relations between companies from different keiretsu networks are also possible.

The keiretsu bank has a central position within the keiretsu as a whole. It provides the members with the required financial means and services to implement necessary adaptation and restructuring measures. If one of the companies were to be threatened with insolvency, the keiretsu bank would accept security for the required credit. If the troubled company's management is unsuccessful in solving its financial problems, the keiretsu bank could exert pressure to have the management replaced by a designated crisis management team. The general retailer also has a crucial position in most keiretsu. Through its sales and distribution activities, it has direct contact with customers and thus gains important market information. With this information, the general retailer can influence product development very specifically. It therefore often coordinates the keiretsu-internal know-how transfer, the execution of very large projects, and / or the founding of new companies.

These achievements show that within a keiretsu, economies of scale can be used, for example, in the financial area or in strategic planning, without the risk of slowing down important market and competitive powers, which might happen with a full integration.

The virtual company is a form of temporary coordination (see chapter 8). This form of cooperation manifests itself in companies concentrating on single areas of the value chain to bundle their competencies. The trend toward enterprise and competence-focused segmentation does not necessarily lead toward an optimization of the entire value chain. The virtual organization concept offers a potential solution (Picot / Neuburger 1997a; Mertens / Faisst 1997; Ettinghofer 1992; Reichwald / Möslein 1996b; 1997; 1997a). Virtual enterprises are artificially created companies that address the solution of customer problems and integrate different companies' core competencies along the value chain (Picot / Neuburger 1997a; Rayport / Sviokla 1996).

After the underlying task has been executed, virtual organizations usually dissolve themselves. In the virtual organization configuration, the focus is not so much on the available resources, but on the necessary competencies. Their integration into the virtual organization is possible regardless of where they are physically located. Consequently, virtual organizations support the market orientation of acquisition and sales areas.

## 6.4   The Role of ICT

### 6.4.1   Demands on ICT

The development of symbiotic organizational forms makes special demands on the design of information and communication technology (ICT) relationships between the participating companies. We need to consider organizational and human resources configuration problems to implement suitable information and communication systems, but will also need to consider various technical requirements. The technical prerequisites for symbiotic coordination forms do not at first seem to differ principally from those of the company-internal execution of tasks. In cross-company communication relationships, various additional considerations may make the successful use of ICT more complex. This includes the bridging of considerably larger geographical distances and differing time zones.

Different forms of information may be exchanged between the companies within a symbiotic organization relationship. These include information exchange that is simple verbal communication, face-to-face communication, the exchange of documents (e.g. with the assistance of EDI), and electronic communication via Internet and Extranet.

Verbal communication dominates, especially when initiating symbiotic relationships, as well as when solving poorly structured problems, which requires the generation of interactive and creative information. Communicating by telephone over a distance is a fast and convenient form of telecommunication that enables interactive coordination and problem solving (without the communication partners having to engage in face-to-face contact) even in respect of difficult task problems.

On the other hand, face-to-face communication has a holistic character. It cannot be achieved by means of technical communication. In situations in which personal contact between communication partners is absolutely necessary, ICT can merely fulfill a lower level function. For example, when preparing for a personal meeting, written documents can be quickly exchanged or important information may be requested during ongoing negotiations on an ad hoc basis and even over long distances. The holistic character of personal communication can, however, be approximately achieved by means of multi media videoconferencing. A videoconference attempts to replicate meetings' typical communication situation without the participants having to be in the same location. For this application, ICT must be capable of integrating moving pictures, language, and data. This may be required, for example, to intensively exchange knowledge and to coordinate complex problems in cooperative research and development efforts.

In the organization of administrative tasks, especially routine standardized tasks, we mainly find the exchange of text documents such as letters, contracts, minutes, and memoranda. Documents in paper form have the important advantage of being recognized as documentary evidence within a court of law. The signature below a text testifies to the correctness of its content and is thus of importance in judging a sender's declaration of intent. Aside from this evidence-providing function, written documents also have a representative function, for example, by means of a letterhead or its design. These requirements limit the possibilities of substituting the transmission of texts by means of telecommunication media such as e-mail. The demand for legal validity and authenticity could be achieved by introducing digital signatures, which somewhat simplify electronically supported business relationships. This substitution is desirable for two reasons: Transmission times are greatly reduced compared to postal cycle times and a paper-based communication requires the content to be entered into the recipient's electronic application system too, which is cost and time-intensive, as well as prone to error. The use of a fax does reduce transmission time, but it does not substitute the potential need for data to be entered again. The overall goal is smooth text processing across the recipient's application systems. To increase the availability, traceability, and speed of the operation of documents techniques like document management systems (DMS) are utilized. The same is required with regard to the transmission of technical drawings and graphics. For example, in cross-company research and development projects, the quick and cost-effective transmission of construction drawings is especially very important. Under certain circumstances, this might even be the prerequisite for meaningful company cooperation.

Electronic Data Interchange (EDI) may support symbiotically integrated companies' execution of similar and repetitive information and communication processes. EDI is a form of inter-company communication in which business and technical data, as well as common business documents such as texts, figures, and graphics are structured according to standardized formats and are exchanged between different companies' computers by means of open electronic communication processes (see chapter 4 as well as Picot/Neuburger/Niggl 1991; 1995). A prerequisite for application systems compatibility is appropriate standards on the transmission and information/data levels. Internet technology and especially extranets (see chapter 4) are of increasing importance as a suitable infrastructure for the transmission of EDI data. On the information and data level, a long-term goal is to develop a comprehensive (i.e. international and cross-industry) standard: EDI for administration, commerce, and transport (EDIFACT). Since it is almost impossible to cover all relevant information and data types, EDIFACT subgroups have been formed. In contrast to the evidently bilateral EDI agreements, these subgroups focus on business-area-specific EDIFACT solutions (see chapter 4). We may assume that companies that communicate with multiple partners from differing business areas prefer the complete EDIFACT. Companies with business-area-specific communication relationships are likely to prefer the EDIFACT subsets. In conjunction with the Internet standard XML (extensible markup language), efforts are underway to integrate the EDIFACT concept with XML's flexibility to make the deployment of EDI attractive for all companies (see chapter 4). In principle, all business and communication partners should be considered in respect of the deployment of EDI (see figure 6.5).

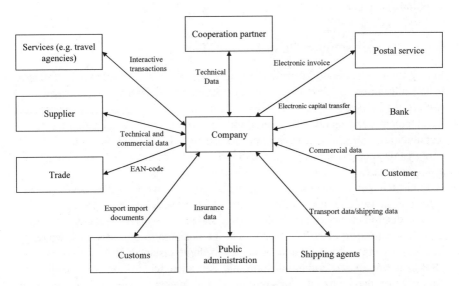

**Fig. 6.5.** Electronic communication relationships (based on Kilian/Picot/Neuburger 1994, p. 44)

Typical examples are logistic partnerships or vertical dominant forms in which large numbers of documents that accompany transactions have to be exchanged between the participating businesses (e.g., JIT relations in the automobiles industry). The use of EDI (based on the Internet and XML) essentially lies in avoiding transmission problems between media and in processing documents without interruption. Consequently, delivery documents and invoices, for example, no longer need to be printed or sent to the purchaser on paper. Instead, the electronic data are sent to the information systems departments of both companies, as well as to the participating banks.

EDI could therefore leverage the assimilation of the organization structures and processes of communication partners. Linking application systems by means of EDI supports tendencies that lead to the integration of organization structures and processes and lastly, to the cross-company integration of planning and control systems. This is especially important in symbiotic company relationships, as it encourages the coordination of the participating companies' organization structures and processes, as well as their planning and control systems. Kleinaltenkamp (1993) refers to this as business integration. It is necessary to coordinate and finetune the various companies' structures and processes exactly in order to, for example, optimize just-in-time delivery relationships or to lead rationalization communities to success. If this were to be possible by means of EDI, we should not be surprised if a trend were to emerge toward cross-company network structures between customers, suppliers, banks, shipping agents, public administration, as well as service organizations in an empirical research project analyzing the organizational effects of EDI (Kilian / Picot / Neuburger 1994). EDI can therefore stimulate symbiotic arrangements with other companies.

## 6.4.2   Implementation Potential of ICT

In chapter 4, we already identified the basic potentials and development trends of ICT. Building on the described symbiotic arrangements and their requirements in respect of ICT (see section 6.4.1), we will now emphasize important technological development trends and their meaning for symbiotic arrangements. Communication technologies, especially telecommunication networks and services that form the core of this section, are of particular importance within the context of symbiotic arrangements.

Public telecommunication networks are undergoing two important developments. First, considerable improvement in transmission capacity is expected (see section 4.2.1.1) due to new transmission technology and protocols. This will create the technical foundation for electronic business in the business-to-business area, which requires considerable transmission capacities for large distances (e.g., Frazier / Herbst 1994). Internet-based communication and data channels are of considerable importance for the realization of communication-intensive enterprise relations. In addition, many countries are expanding and modernizing their telecommunication infrastructure through the increased use of fiber optic cable. The overall goal is to build a global information infrastructure (GII), i.e. a globally available high performance telecommunication network with, as far as possible, uniform transmission technology offering a multitude of telecommunication applications. This will enable and support cross-border symbiotic arrangements such as cooperative international research and development efforts. The design and utilization of Intranets and extranets based on the Internet standard protocol TCP/IP play a special role in the development of company networks by supporting location-independent collaboration and minimizing media flow discontinuity.

We observe a trend towards telecommunication services being increasingly integrated within a single transmission network. In the future, we may expect a single high performance telecommunication network that offers an entire range of services such as phone, data exchange, messaging systems, radio, and television transmissions.

Close communication technology connections and the associated network integration trends may lead to the development of cross-company electronic groups or hierarchies. Cross-company electronic groups are formed when a variety of companies have close communication links with common standards as a result of their cooperative relationships. Open communication possibilities are therefore available within such groups and between its members, thus requiring only minimal expenditure on coordination when communication relationships change. Such cross-company electronic groups come quite close to being an electronic market as a coordination form (see chapter 7). They do, of course, differ in that their membership is rather small and in that they have common objectives. Examples of such electronic groups are merchandise management systems, rationalization communities, and research and development alliances between various companies.

A cross-company electronic hierarchy is concerned with the longer-term electronic integration of the information systems of two or more legally independent companies. The dominant company may exert its influence with regard to the assimilation of organization and business processes. Other companies cannot, however, readily participate in such electronic hierarchies, as the deployment of proprietary application systems and standards strengthens the hierarchical character by reducing the outside options of the companies integrated within the electronic hierarchy.

In respect of dominant forms, it may actually be the dominant company's strategy to permanently bind the dominated companies in a dependency relationship by deploying specific ICT. Ford Europe's communication strategy may be an example of this. Ford uses a proprietary communication system (Fordnet), as well as its own EDI standard that is especially well suited to meet its needs (Hartzheim 1990) to communicate with its suppliers. This strategy could lead to a situation in which potential new business partners refuse to apply this proprietary system, thus making a business relationship impossible. In fact, although dominant forms cannot be created by such electronic integration, it does reinforce the dominant character of existing hybrid arrangements.

## 6.4.3  Problems and Risks

Besides the described potentials, ICT deployment also creates various problems and risks. These factors may lead to circumstances in which ICT's potential to develop symbiotic organization forms may or may not fully evolve.

Even where there is a telecommunication infrastructure, it does not as such guarantee the success of symbiotic arrangements. In addition, cross-company collaboration demands a high level of technical performance capacity. Various tasks, such as in research and development, are based on the transmission of pictures and large amounts of data over great distances. Considerable transmission speeds and capacities are also required for multimedia applications and videoconferences. An intensive exchange of pictures, multimedia applications, and technical data increases the risk of a capacity bottleneck in transmission networks.

High transmission capacities, as well as low tariffs are required for transmission services. Deregulation and increased competition on all levels of the telecommunication sector, especially on the network level, allow a competitive and varied selection of transmission and telecommunication services (Burr 1995).

The deployment of ICT is often associated with security and legal risks and, in as far as anticipated, these risks may limit the formation of symbiotic coordination forms (e.g., Borghoff / Schlichter 2000; Krcmar 2002). During the transmission of data, security aspects make important demands on cross-company communication relationships and on the infrastructure that supports it. During transmission, technical errors may occur that may not be recognized by security controls or by validity checks at the receiving end. There is, moreover, a risk of deliberate data manipulation on the transmission route from the sender to the receiver, as at least one other actor, such as the transmission network provider, is involved in the transmission of data besides the two communication partners.

Consequently, the legal question arises of who is responsible for loss or damage due to faulty or manipulated data transmission. A good example is a faulty transmission of a certain order, which then leads to the delivered quantity being far too low. This may lead to a production bottleneck or perhaps even to a loss of production for the buyer, who thus suffers financial losses. To date there is no clarity regarding the question of who is responsible when, for example, an automobile manufacturer experiences production shutdown when too few or the wrong goods are supplied due to faulty data transmission. Considerable legal problems may therefore arise from trying to clarify who is responsible for the damage. Many of these problems can be solved through the increased use of digital signatures, electronic certificates, and data encryption. Furthermore, various safety devices have been suggested that should make potential damage and loss calculable. The legal system no doubt needs to adapt itself to these new communication conditions.

The possibilities to realize and expand symbiotic coordination relationships flexibly, increase with the diffusion of uniform transmission and data standards. Standards such as TCP/IP and an expanded EDI and XML basically create open communication conditions in which the initiation and development of new symbiotic business relationships may occur without elaborate agreements regarding transmission and format rules.

## 6.5    Implications for Management

When partners make their resources available to others within a collaboration, opportunities for symbiotic arrangements lie primarily in the expansion of these resources (especially capital and know-how). Since symbiotic arrangements between companies are not limited to the national level, but are increasingly also utilized across countries, an opportunity arises to exploit the regional and global potential flexibly and to take advantage of the international division of labor. In the long run, international symbiotic arrangements aim at utilizing differences in wages, differing levels of know-how, and differences in national laws (e.g., internationally differing regulatory standards with regard to the environment and social security laws). At the international level, symbiotic arrangements not only blur company boundaries, but also make national boundaries less important for companies' international activities.

Symbiotic arrangements with other companies have to be planned and organized just like any other economic activity. The management of symbiotic arrangements demands that conditions be created for close collaboration with other companies, that the risks associated with this blurring of company borders be controlled, and that business opportunities associated with symbiotic arrangements be utilized. Following suggestions are derived for the management of symbiotic enterprise alliances based on various theories.

### Infrastructures as a Prerequisite for Cooperation

A key requirement for an enterprise to enter a cooperative arrangement is the presence of stable, viable, and affordable infrastructures. They contribute significantly to the transaction conditions by reducing the transaction costs of inter-company collaboration. Part of these infrastructures is of a:

- Technical nature (telecommunication networks, including broadband, traffic routes, maintenance, and recovery);

- Institutional nature (e.g., corporate law, competition law, labor law, and property rights);

- Personal nature (e.g., public schools, universities, and very large project organizations).

Part of the infrastructure is also the private infrastructure available within companies such as jointly utilized corporate networks, computing facilities, and extranets. These public and private infrastructures are an essential prerequisite for symbiotic arrangements such as networks, franchising systems, and strategic alliances. Generally, we know that symbiotic arrangements make different demands on the available infrastructures and ICT systems than traditional markets and hierarchies do. Symbiotic arrangements are often supported, intensified or even enabled by ICT. Conversely, the deployment of new ICT changes the possibilities for collaboration substantially. Through innovative ICT, it is possible to realize completely new

and hitherto unknown forms of symbiotic arrangement in an economically efficient way. The spectrum of known and new symbiotic organizational forms that
may have evolved and / or will still evolve in the course of time is currently still in
a rudimentary form. Their development leans toward cross-enterprise and cross-
location networked structures as a model of future-oriented innovation strategies
(see chapter 1), which makes increasing demands on the existing infrastructures.

Technical infrastructures can only support symbiotic arrangements effectively
and efficiently if these infrastructures are relatively stable and capable of development. If there are no such infrastructures (as in developing nations or in the suc-
cessor nations of the former Soviet Union) or if they are barely developed at all,
the company cannot dissolve on the ground of its symbiotic arrangements, but
must actually find ways to integrate better. Difficulties with other companies also
arise after entering into symbiotic arrangements in an unstable legal infrastructure.
This can be observed in Russia where there is a widespread lack of legal framework and where the formation of strategic alliances with domestic and foreign
partners is difficult to achieve, if not impossible. Companies are therefore forced
to seek a higher-level of vertical integration.

It is management's primary task to design and build the required company-
internal infrastructure so that symbiotic arrangements become possible. Moreover,
management is expected to guarantee access to the required infrastructures, as well
as to explore new, possibly more favorable organizational forms for symbiotic task
accomplishment in cooperation with other companies. The company will thus be
strategically positioned to pursue future innovative organization development.

**Trust, Common Norms and Values: Ten Rules of Trust Formation**

Common norms and values, as well as mutual trust are further cooperative elements
in the transaction conditions that enhance arrangements and decrease transaction
costs (see chapter 3). This implies that the company has the capacity to design and
build cross-company collaboration as a strategic, competitive-advantage-enabling
and potentially secure organization. Within the context of symbiotic arrangements,
the building of trust and common values is encouraged by long-term collaboration,
but not guaranteed. It is therefore important that both partners keep to the written
and unwritten rules of cooperation, which, as it were, serve as the constitution of the
symbiotic arrangement (a type of network or cooperation constitution).

An example of this is TCG (Technical and Computer Graphics), a group of 24
mid-sized Australian firms in the computer services sector (Matthews 1994). Each
of the companies in this group has specialized in a certain area of information
technology. Economically and legally, the firms are largely independent. TCG is
therefore organized as a network. The individual companies acquire orders from
outside the network and execute these orders by subcontracting their partner companies. TCG appears to be a homogeneous entrepreneurial unit to external groups,
i.e. the subcontracting relationships are not apparent to the business world. In the
past, the enterprise group was very successful, as it was able to develop efficient
governance structures for the management of the inter-company network relation-

ships. Essential elements of this "interorganizational governance structure" (Matthew 1994, p. 16) are:

1. Independence of the coordinated network firms through bilateral contracts: This does not exclude the possibility of crossover capital investments between individual firms within the network.

2. The firms' preference for one another when closing contracts: This behavioral rule gives the enterprise group its identity. The signing of contracts with firms not belonging to the TCG groups is, however, still possible.

3. Exclusion of competition between the network firms: This rule is the foundation for the mutual trust between the network firms.

4. Mutual non-exploitation: Network firms forego any financial gains from transactions with member firms. Joint jobs are billed to the member firm on the basis of cost-plus contracts. This rule also enhances trust development between the network participants and avoids the formation of a hierarchy between economically strong and weak network firms.

5. Flexibility and ensuring the group firms' autonomy: Group firms do not have to seek the other partners' approval to sign contracts with external partners or to build new business areas.

6. The network's democratic constitution: There are no proprietors in the entire enterprise group, no holding company, and no central planning committee. The network keeps together due to the established business relationships between the firms.

7. Non-observance of the rules leads to expulsion from the network: The possibility to implement sanctions ensures that the member firms adhere to the rules.

8. Entry of new firms into the network: New firms' entry into the network is generally welcomed and desirable. This rule allows the network to continue expanding and to permanently renew itself.

9. Withdrawal of firms from the network: No member firm is kept in the network against its will; it can withdraw at any time.

10. Relationships of individual network firms with external third parties: Each firm has the possibility to enter the market with its own goods and services so that it is not entirely dependent on subcontracting within the network. This consequently prevents the emergence of a buyer-subcontractor hierarchy between the network firms.

These ten rules form the TCG constitution. They provide the network's coherence and its developmental dynamic. According to Matthews, these rules were never explicitly written down, but emerged in an evolutionary way in practice. Matthews (1994, p. 19) remarks: "Above all, the study of the governance structure of networks brings the issue of trust back to the center of attention. Trust is not a natural but a social construct. It is produced from the norms that govern people's behavior and their commercial interactions."

This example clearly illustrates that a common company constitution may stimulate the capability for cross-company collaboration if it favors fairness and openness and enables the formation of trust, as well as common values and norms. Management's primary task is to develop and enforce rules for performance relationships between symbiotically integrated companies, as well as to nourish a cross-company culture in the firms within the symbiosis. In conclusion, the transaction conditions (i.e. basically, the infrastructure of the transactions and the mutual trust of the transaction partners) have a special meaning within symbiotic arrangements. This may be an essential determinant of the success of a symbiotic arrangement.

Aside from creating technical prerequisites for symbiotic integration, management's role is still to control the risks associated with symbiotic arrangements. These risks may result in companies losing their identity and/or their competitive advantage. The risk of losing identity is especially high when companies with very different cultures and traditions enter a symbiotic integration. The risk then arises that the integrated company components either have not developed their own entrepreneurial culture and identity, or that the culture of the dominant symbiosis partner will displace the culture of other symbiosis partners. In both cases, the symbiosis may sooner or later be revoked because, for example, the coordination between the partners turns out to be unexpectedly difficult and too transaction cost intensive due to differing value expectations.

Under such circumstances, the integrated company components are often dissolved or entirely taken over by one of the partners. Depending on the circumstances, this may mean the loss of critical core competencies. This also addresses the second issue in respect of symbiotic arrangements – the loss of market advantages and the emergence of unilateral dependencies.

## Theoretical Design Recommendations

The core competency theory, as well as transaction cost theory provides valuable design recommendations with regard to controlling the above-mentioned two risks. Both theories point out that core competencies and/or specific performances should be realized internally by the company itself and only as an exception in cooperation with external partners. In addition, transaction cost theory recommends that this cooperative integration should also be ensured through trust and common values or through long-term contracts between the partner companies. If companies disregard these recommendations, they may face the loss of core competencies that can only be rebuilt with considerable effort. They may also risk unilateral dependencies that would need considerable resource expenditures to overcome.

A case in point is IBM, which in 1983 decided to acquire Microsoft's operating system (DOS) and Intel's processor for its first personal computer, instead of developing these core products itself. Consequently, IBM lost many of its core competencies in these areas, while its unilateral dependency on Microsoft and Intel increased. Its renewed building of core competencies – to minimize this dependency – (the development of the OS/2 operating system and the PC microprocessor) required considerable effort. Its Power PC project was only partially successful as a result of a new symbiotic relationship with Apple and Motorola. OS/2 failed completely in the private PC user market.

Such strategic aspects are the focal point of both the core competencies and transaction costs theories. The possible boundaries of symbiotic network application in respect of the organization of task accomplishment on the basis of the division of labor may be derived from both theories.

In summary, the management of symbiotic arrangements between various companies has mainly rendered the following services:

- Examination of the technical, legal, and human resources prerequisites for a symbiotic arrangement with other companies (cooperation capability);

- Appraisal of the opportunities that may result from a symbiosis with another company;

- Consideration of the risks.

The above discussion makes it clear that the management of future-related and innovative company development has to place particular emphasis on the management of information and communication technology infrastructures, on the management of inter-company contractual integration, and on developing a cross-company management culture.

# New Forms of Market Coordination – Electronic Markets

# Case Study Chapter 7: Covisint – An Electronic Marketplace for the Automobile Industry

Many automobile manufacturers concentrated their efforts on optimizing the entire value chain through to the building of the "3-Day Car" (Howard, 2005). Setting up electronic marketplaces and places of cooperation is supposed to make a crucial contribution to improving the efficiency of value creation despite the increasing complexity caused by ever decreasing development periods and the growing diversity of vehicle models. Even though it turned out to be a complete failure, the best-known example of such a marketplace was Covisint, an artificial name that combined the words collaboration, vision, and integration. In February 2000, DaimlerChrysler, Ford, and General Motors announced their campaign to set-up a standardized global e-marketplace for the automobile industry. Renault and Nissan joined this campaign in April 2000. From April 2001, Covisint provided a broad array of products and services for its international clientele. In May 2001, Covisint held the world's then largest Internet auction with a total turnover of approximately $4 billion within just four days. In a further expansion stage, Ford implemented the first pilot version of a Covisint sub-supplier portal in February 2002. In the final stage of expansion, it was envisaged that up to 5,000 sub-suppliers would have access to over 80 applications via this portal.

As an application and service platform, Covisint had positioned itself between all companies involved in automobile manufacturing, i.e. not only between the Original Equipment Manufacturer (OEM) and the largest sub-suppliers (Tier 1). The goal was to drastically reduce the complexity of the communication connections between the market players. If, for instance, a sub-supplier created a connection to a manufacturer using one of the supply chain applications provided by Covisint, it could expand this application to include other car manufacturers without any additional effort. The applications and services were bundled in Covisint and were specially tailored to meet the automobile industry's requirements. Some products were, however, also used in other industries: The Internet-based collaborative product development in the area of aircraft construction and the Internet-based transmission of inventory data in real time in the field of the chemical industry.

The automotive B2B landscape suffered a setback in 2004 when the Big Three automakers abandoned Covisint with its highly touted cooperative effort to source parts, share documents, and solve supply chain problems. Covisint insiders reported that the envisaged electronic supply chain never quite materialized: Only three to five percent of all transactions were in fact conducted electronically as envisaged; 97–95% of all transactions were carried out through traditional communication means (i.e. fax and phone). It never took off – countless new CEOs, corporate rebirths, and profitability predictions could not change the fact that many suppliers felt they were being squeezed and preferred using established firms such as Freemarkets and their own systems. Covisint's exchange was sold to Freemarkets (itself bought by Ariba) and the more promising data messaging business was sold to Compuware for $7 million. Despite Covisint's failure, there were, however, a few successes: The Big Three's OEConnection replacement part venture has been successful, although growth has slowed.

## 7.1 Basic Concept of Electronic Markets

The concept of electronic markets has been discussed in-depth in the literature ever since Malone, Yates and Benjamin (1986; 1987) published "Electronic Markets and Electronic Hierarchies." Many authors have continued to develop this concept in numerous ways since then (Picot/Reichwald 1991; Ciborra 1993; Schmid 1993; Krähenmann 1994; Picot/Reichwald 1994; Benjamin/Wigand 1995; Picot/Bortenlänger/Röhrl 1995, 1996; Schmid 1995; Choi/Stahl/Whinston 1997; Wigand 1997; Shapiro/Varian 1998; Koch/Möslein/Wagner 2000; Bieberbach 2001; Schütt 2006). The Internet's rapid worldwide growth has increased interest in electronic markets from a scientific, economic, and political perspective. The development of electronic markets has led visionary authors to assume that the world is on the threshold of a new business age in which previous economic rules will no longer be in force (Rayport/Sviokla 1994; Kelly 1997) and small companies will compete with multi-nationals through their access to global markets (Applegate et al. 1996). Nevertheless, skeptics point out that the actual development of electronic markets is still a far cry from these assumptions (Bichler/Segev 1998). Despite this criticism, the constant growth in revenues attained from trading an increasing number of physical goods and services over the Internet can be observed.

To date, the literature has not provided a uniform definition of the term electronic market. "E-terms" are overzealously used for all economic activities taking place by electronic means (e.g., "electronic commerce," "electronic business," "electronic markets," "electronic marketplaces," "electronic marketspaces," etc.). These terms are usually applied vaguely and inconsistently. This is not surprising, since the field of electronically aided market and corporate processes is subject to strong dynamic forces due to the rapid development of the supporting technology.

In the current context, the collective term electronic commerce denotes any type of economic activity conducted via electronic connections. The range covered by electronic commerce extends from electronic markets to electronic hierarchies, and also includes types of electronically supported corporate networks and alliances (electronic networks). Electronic markets therefore form a single selected institutional and technical platform for electronic commerce. Their common feature is the market coordination mechanism.

It is important to first examine the way in which these markets function more closely before providing a definition of electronic markets. Markets within our

**Market transaction phases**

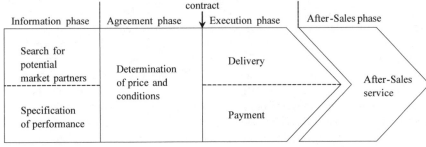

**Support via the Internet**

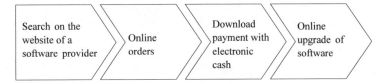

**Fig. 7.1.**    Internet support of market transaction phases

economic system are places of exchange. It is here where supply and demand meet (Wigand 1997; 2003). The basic characteristics, tasks, and forms of markets when regarded as processes were discussed in detail in chapter 2: After the hierarchy, the market is the second basic form of economic coordination (Coase 1937; Williamson 1975, 1985). The market exchange process includes the information, agreement, and execution of transaction phases (Schmid 1993). These phases are followed by the after-sales service phase. The latter phase is the one in which the relevant services are provided to the buyer after the actual transaction has been executed.

Electronic markets arise through the mediatization of market transactions, i.e. the electronic depiction of the communication relations between market players. One form of mediatization of market transactions is to support a transaction's individual phases by using information and communication technology (ICT), which is a constitutive characteristic of an electronic market (Schmid 1993). Figure 7.1 indicates the individual transaction phases and, through the "Purchase of Software" example, how these phases can be supported by the Internet information and communication system.

The degree to which technical information and communication (I&C) systems support a transaction's phases depends on the intensity of their information. These phases also have different infrastructural requirements. It is possible to support an information phase well if, for example, the I&C system can easily locate information on suppliers, prices, and products, and prepare it for the information seeker in a suitable way. In the agreement and execution phase, however, attention is focused on the safety requirements of the I&C system. The after-sales phase needs communication channels that can be individualized as far as possible. The ability to support market transactions by means of technical I&C systems largely depends on the characteristics of the traded goods (Korb 2000). Delivery in the execution phase can, for instance, only be supported if the traded item is information-based, otherwise other technical systems must be used (Steyer 1998). In section 7.3.1, the connection between the characteristics of goods and their support by means of I&C systems is considered in greater depth. Technical I&C systems' support of market transactions is in itself insufficient to characterize an electronic market.

The growing importance of open I&C structures (notably the Internet), which everybody can basically access, and which permit a wide range of goods and services to be traded, requires a definition of electronic markets that takes the type of goods into account. It is useful to delineate the boundaries of markets based on industrial economics, which is the basis of the substitutive and/or complementary relationships of goods traded on a market. According to this delineation, a market comprises "either a homogeneous good or a group of various products that are close substitutes (or complements) of at least one good of the respective group. It is assumed that the interaction with 'the rest' of the economy stays within limits" (Tirole 1995, translation by authors). In the following sections, the examination of electronic markets is based on a definition that takes this aspect into account (Bieberbach/Hermann 1999). According to this definition, an electronic market is a sub-market of a specific commodity market distinguished by technical information systems supporting the contract conclusion and individual phases of the market transaction.

This definition also leaves leeway for the specific delineation of an electronic market, but compared to other definitions, its advantage lies in the economic relationships of the traded goods being regarded as a defining criterion and not the underlying technical I&C infrastructure. One can, for example, speak of the electronic market for books or the electronic market for air travel. Information and communication systems that permit buyers and sellers to exchange information on prices and products (e.g., via the Internet) are called electronic marketplaces (Bakos 1991). Similar to physical marketplaces, they provide the infrastructure for the activities of the market players. The following section considers the functions of electronic marketplaces and their significance for electronic markets in greater detail.

## 7.2    Types of Electronic Markets

### 7.2.1    Closed Electronic Markets

In the science sector and in practice, the first approaches to electronic markets date from a time when no one could have foreseen the current importance of the Internet or other open communication platforms. Closed electronic markets were therefore the initial focal point (Malone/Yates/Benjamin 1987). The reservation systems Apollo and SABRE, which had already been developed in the early 1970s by

United Airlines and American Airlines, are early examples of such systems. This sector is characterized by well-structured mass transactions and trades in non-storable goods (e.g., seats on a particular flight). This is conducive to the use of information technology. A large number of travel agencies and airlines were connected to the two systems, which were then able to offer and provide air travel in open competition (Malone / Yates / Benjamin 1989).

These systems have undergone further development over the years. Today, there are competing booking systems (e.g., AMADEUS, GALILEO, and SABRE) developed and operated by several airlines all over the world. It is also possible to gain access to the systems of suppliers in related industries (e.g., hotel chains, car rental companies, and shipping companies). An essential feature of these systems is that it is possible to jointly book services with all the suppliers involved. In addition, it is possible to integrate automatic payment services (e.g., via credit cards, electronic cash systems).

Reservation systems were originally designed for the business-to-business area: The buyers of tourist industry services were unable to gain direct access to the booking system. The travel agency therefore acted as an intermediary. This enabled one to choose the best offer in a booking system, although the full potential of possible market relationships was not covered because the system could only mediate between connected partners. This meant that the customer's selection was restricted to the range provided by the reservation system used by a travel agency (Hanker 1990). This restriction is losing importance due to the possibilities provided by the Internet. Today, end customers are able to gain direct access to almost all reservation systems via various online travel agencies and make travel bookings (see section 7.2.2).

The development of electronic markets in the financial sector started almost as early as the first flights bookings. Like the travel industry, financial markets also have many characteristics that are conducive to the use of information and communication technology and thus foster the development of electronic market trading (see section 7.3.1.2). The first steps toward developing electronic stock market information systems were already taken at the end of the 1960s. The first electronic stock exchange trading system (CATS: Computer-Assisted Trading System) was used in 1977 in Toronto. Today, it would be hard to find a dealer who works without access to real-time online services, computer-aided analysis tools, and the possibility to route orders to linked stock exchanges.

However, when information and communication technology is introduced to stock exchanges, the existing organizational form is frequently retained: The number of those entitled to access remains restricted to prevent investors from directly trading stocks and shares. Banks and brokers also often endeavor to retain their exclusive access and their intermediary position (Hanker 1990; Schmid 1993). Safety has also been increased during transactions due to the restricted group of participants (see section 7.3.2.3). The German securities trading system XETRA, which is operated by the Deutsche Börse AG, is a good example in this regard, as only official dealers may be linked to this system. In addition to financial markets, numerous commodity exchanges and commodity future exchanges are further examples of closed electronic markets.

The feature that these closed electronic markets have in common is that they are centrally managed by one operator (market maker), who creates the electronic market with the aid of an I&C system as a service provider for buyers and suppliers. Users interested in this system can be connected to it, thus becoming part of a group of buyers and suppliers, which is managed and restricted by the market maker. The market maker can also act as a buyer or supplier, as in the above-mentioned example of a flight-booking system. Obviously, the market maker then endeavors to gain an advantage for his or her own benefit. With the Apollo reservation system that commenced operations in 1976, United Airlines attempted to do the same by initially only accepting bookings for its own flights. SABRE, the competing system run by American Airlines that was launched on the market only a short while later, also included the flights of other companies and was thus preferred by many travel agencies. To avoid being crowded out of the (reservation systems) market, Apollo was also opened to other airlines. The competition between the systems therefore ensured that the competition distortion between the systems was reduced. Both airlines did, however, try to gain an advantage by ensuring that their own flights always appeared first on the list of possible connections. This practice was prohibited after a lawsuit filed by the US antitrust enforcement agency, the Federal Trade Commission (Malone / Yates / Benjamin 1987). Although the systems no longer discriminate in favor of a particular market player, they are still a lucrative source of income for the operating companies. The role of the market maker is also becoming less important in new electronic markets. Currently, the Internet provides an open platform on which basically anyone can act as a supplier, buyer or intermediary. There is no centralized control or restriction of access on this platform.

## 7.2.2   Open Electronic Markets

It is possible to differentiate between functions in electronic markets based on open platforms such as the Internet. The central market maker is replaced by a number of actors with various functions who can be systematized in a three-level model (see figure 7.2). Electronic marketplaces, trading and market support systems generally have to bring supply and demand together and enable or support market transactions. Buyers, suppliers or third parties (intermediaries) can operate these systems.

### 7.2.2.1   Electronic Marketplaces

The electronic market place is the lowest level of the electronic market as an organizational form. An electronic marketplace is an information and communication infrastructure that can appropriately serve as the basis of a market-like coordination of services (Wigand 1997; Bieberbach/Hermann 1999; Bieberbach 2001). Consequently, an electronic marketplace is a necessary but inadequate requirement for an electronic market. Based on this marketplace, however, the electronic market can emerge through exchange processes between suppliers and buyers. This distinction between the market and the marketplace is in line with the Anglo-Saxon literature's traditional differentiation between the market and the marketplace, therefore "the market as an abstract organization and the one in a geographical sense" (translation by authors, Nieschlag/Dichtl/Hörschgen 2002, p. 92; also see Wigand 1997). Electronic markets assume the function of geographically defined places (Beam/Segev 1997).

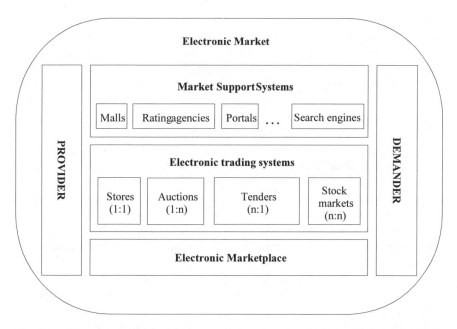

**Fig. 7.2.**    Three-level model of electronic markets (based on Bieberbach/Hermann 1999)

In the flight-booking example, the electronic marketplace is the main computer on which the database with the available seats and booked reservations is stored, as well as the terminals at travel agencies and airlines connected to the main computer. In the case of Internet trade, the electronic marketplace is the Internet infrastructure with the related standards (TCP/IP, etc.) and services (WWW, etc.). A further example is a television channel that is linked to a return channel (e.g., home order television and telephone). In the following, the focus will be on the Internet, as it has emerged as the most important trading platform of all.

## 7.2.2.2   Electronic Trading Systems

Electronic trading systems are based on electronic marketplaces to which suppliers and buyers are connected. These systems are specifically focused on coordinating and executing the exchange of products and services in an electronic marketplace. Individual suppliers, buyers or third parties (intermediaries) can operate these trading systems, which, depending on the number of suppliers and buyers, can be divided into four categories: Stores (1:1), auctions (1:n), tenders (n:1), and stock exchanges (n:n).

### Electronic Stores (1:1)

Like normal business transactions, electronic stores are usually operated by one supplier (dealer or producer). The supplier enters into a relationship with an individual buyer via this type of store. A contract and an exchange of goods and / or services materialize, if appropriate, after negotiations have been conducted (Choi / Stahl / Whinston 1997). On the World Wide Web, this kind of store is a website where one can compare, select, and order products. An electronic market is created when various electronic stores compete for customers.

Companies often start their Web presence by merely supplying information on the company and its products as a support for other sales channels. An electronic store is created if order and payment methods are added to this information. Among such a store's objectives are an increase in revenue through the new sales channel and a reduction in advertising and sales costs (Timmers 1998). However, if the company already has other sales channels, cannibalization might occur. The automobile industry, for example, met with fierce resistance from powerful car dealers when it first attempted to sell vehicles over the Internet, which led to the basis of this business disappearing. If, however, the Internet's potential is not tapped due to concern for traditional sales channels, there is a risk that competitors will exploit the cost advantage that the Internet offers and will make cheaper offerings.

The most important advantages that Internet shopping offers customers are improved convenience by avoiding shopping trips, the 24-hour availability of these stores, and the ease with which a comparison can be made of various supplier offerings. The time saved should specifically not be underestimated. The average US consumer, for instance, spends 1.5 hours per week buying food, visiting a shop 2.5 times per week to do so (Burke 1998). Shopping online could therefore save much time. In countries with strict closing-time laws, or if high additional labor costs have to be paid for night shifts, 24-hour availability is of special importance. The system allows an electronic store to receive orders at any hour, which the employees then process during normal working hours. Customers do not as yet classify being able to compare offers as an important advantage; however, this is expected to gain in importance as online shopping increases and as customers who are more sensitive to prices enter the market (Wigand / Chen / Nilan 2000).

**Auction Systems (1:n)**

In auction systems, several buyers compete with one another for a supplier's service and / or product. In traditional markets, auctions have to date had an outsider role, although they are increasingly appearing in electronic markets. The reason is not only that auctions can be automatically and cheaply executed by means of online software, but also specifically that an Internet auction allows more customers to participate. The critical mass of participants required for a meaningful auction is thus achieved more easily. In the light of the growing significance of online auctions, a brief description of the four most important auction mechanisms follows.

The best-known and also most widespread auction method on the Internet is the English auction. This method is particularly suitable when the price of goods such as antiques and collectables is difficult to determine in advance. It is, however, also used for almost all other kinds of goods found in electronic markets (Beam / Segev 1998; Schmidt / Weinhardt / Horstmann 1998). In this type of auction, having started with a minimum bid in open competition, buyers must outbid one another again and again.

There are two ways of ending the auction. One is for the online auction to run for a given period of time, usually a week (Beam / Segev 1998), and then to close. The alternative is for the auction to close when no new bids have been made for a certain time. The person with the highest bid when the auction closes receives the goods at that price. The advantage for buyers is that they might get the goods at a price lower than the maximum amount that they would have been willing to pay. They then pay only slightly more than the person who bid the longest was willing to pay. The price is thus determined at a slightly higher level than the second-highest amount that all the buyers would have paid.

The Dutch auction is particularly suitable for goods needing to be sold swiftly due to their rapid loss in value. The flower auctions in the Netherlands are the best-known example of such an auction, which is thus also named after them (van Heck / Ribbers 1998). At this type of auction, the auctioneer starts with a high price and gradually decreases it until signaled by a buyer willing to buy at this price. The bid is accepted and the auction ended or continued with another, identical product. If the buyer fails to act strategically, his / her willingness to buy is signaled when the price announced is lower or the same as the intended buying price. The buyer acts strategically by indicating willingness to buy at the price announced shortly before the time when other buyers are expected to signal their willingness to buy. The price that is arrived at therefore strongly depends on the buyer's expectations concerning other buyers' willingness to purchase and their strategic behavior. This type of auction has not as yet been established on the Internet.

With a first price sealed bid auction every buyer submits a single secret bid and the person with the highest bid wins. This was advantageous prior to the establishment of electronic auctions, as English and Dutch auctions required all the bidders to be present in the same room. Compared to those procedures, the first price sealed bid auction saved transaction costs. However, this advantage is no longer important in electronic marketplaces, which is why this type of auction is seldom used on these marketplaces. With regard to pricing and related strategic behavior, this type of auction is equivalent to the Dutch auction.

Finally, the second price sealed bid auction, also called the Vickrey auction, functions in the same way as the first price sealed bid auction, the only difference being that the highest bidder does not pay the price offered but the price of the second-highest bid instead. It has been shown that the price that is arrived at is fractionally lower than that at an English auction, namely exactly the second-highest that all the buyers are willing to pay (Vickrey 1961). Compared to the English auction, the Vickrey auction has the advantage that lower transaction costs are incurred, as everyone is only required to submit one bid.

This means that, in theory, it is superior to the English auction. It is, however, rarely used by Internet stock exchanges. Some suppliers initially held Vickrey auctions on the Internet, but discarded this practice due to a lack of interest. This may be explained by customers being unfamiliar with this method and by the element of entertainment that the English auction offers, which more than compensates for the greater effort involved (Beam / Segev 1998). Vickrey auctions are of greater significance in business-to-business auctions.

**Electronic Tenders (n:1)**

Electronic tenders (reverse auctions) are a mirror image of the auction systems: A buyer specifies a commodity or service, and several suppliers then compete to provide this. It would be equally possible to use the four methods described above in this regard. In practice, there is a difference in quality because the competing suppliers are usually companies, which is why the entertainment and play aspect is of less importance. A well-known example is the provider Priceline (www.priceline.com) through which customers can openly invite tenders for a trip by providing travel data and a price. Airlines, hotels, etc. can then compete and undercut this price. If a cheaper price materializes within a specified timeframe, this trip is automatically booked on behalf of the customer.

**Electronic Stock Exchanges (n:n)**

As far as electronic stock exchanges are concerned, the market largely consists of a single I&C system. The way that the electronic markets that emerge in this system function most closely approximates the perfect market. In this kind of market, there are many suppliers and many buyers, and a common, generally revenue-maximizing price is established with the aid of defined mechanisms. There are several methods that can be implemented to establish such an auction. Two basic methods are briefly described:

In the classic double auction, suppliers and buyers first make bids. The buying bids are then sorted in descending order and the selling bids in ascending order. The example in figure 7.3 shows buying and selling bids sorted for a unit of an imaginary commodity. Once the bids have been made, the auction is closed and the auctioneer determines the price at which the maximum revenue is possible. This is done by going through the list with the selling bids, starting at the lowest price, and the list with the buying bids, starting at the highest price, matching as many offers as possible. In the example, this results in a price of $134 for which three units of the commodity are tradable (see figure 7.3 printed in bold type). Any change in price would reduce the possible revenue. Once the price has been determined, the possible revenues are generated. Following this, the auction is opened again and the process starts anew.

| *Sell* | *Buy* |
|:---:|:---:|
| **$120** | **$140** |
| **$134** | **$135** |
| **$134** | **$134** |
| **$140** | **$134** |

**Fig. 7.3.**   Matching in the double auction

In a continuous double auction, buying and selling bids can be submitted continuously. If a new buying bid is received, a test is carried out to determine whether it matches an existing selling bid. If so, the revenue is generated, otherwise the new buying offer is sorted into the existing list. The same method is applied to new selling bids. Securities exchanges are usually based on this method.

Electronic stock exchanges are of special importance for standardized goods in business-to-business markets. Examples of such goods are electricity exchanges such as the European Energy Exchange in Leipzig (www.eex.de), which offers a spot or forward market for electricity.

### 7.2.2.3   Market Support Systems

Finally, there are market support systems on the third level of the reference model. In contrast to trading systems, they do not only process the actual exchange of goods and / or services, but also support suppliers and buyers during the various transaction phases (see figure 7.1). In traditional markets, trade primarily assumes these functions such as information, advice, bundling, logistics, and insurance. However, very sophisticated differentiation and specialization have arisen on the Internet.

Examples of support for the information phase are electronic malls, portals, search engines, rating agencies, price agencies, etc. Malls combine various stores under one common "virtual roof," thus making a preliminary selection for buyers and / or creating a joint marketing platform for suppliers (www.qualitymall.com).

Portals are general points of entry into the World Wide Web through which the person searching can find a desired market partner or buying recommendations (e.g., www.yahoo.com) within a specific classification scheme. Their most important function is to attract as much attention as possible and to sell this as a service to their advertisers and customers (see section 7.3.2.1). Search engines permit the user to carry out a specific search based on certain keywords and categories throughout the entire World Wide Web (e.g., www.google.com).

Rating agencies evaluate suppliers and goods and / or services on the network and thus help their customers find a suitable trading partner (e.g., www.consumer-reports.org). Other consumers can also contribute to these evaluations by publishing their experience with certain products or services on an opinion platform on the Internet (e.g., reviews.cnet.com, mypicklist.com, usuggest.com, dooyoo.co.uk). In contrast, price agencies have the task of finding the cheapest offer for a precisely specified service and / or product (e.g., www.priceline.com, www.pricescan.com). At present, many of these support functions are free of charge and are financed by advertising or cross subsidization.

Market support systems for the agreement phase are less widely available. Online auctions have, however, adopted initial approaches by offering their customers bidding agents. At English auctions, these agents make bids on behalf of the customer until the bid is won or until a given, maximum price is reached (e.g., proxy bidding at ebay.com). From the customers' point of view, the English auction thus almost becomes a Vickrey auction, as transaction costs are reduced. It is more difficult to implement systems for automated negotiations between two partners, as the complexity of the negotiations is a major problem if the goods are not fully standardized. The negotiation system must be able to indicate small changes in the price, performance or conditions in the customer's order of preference to make comparisons. However, only a few software programs are capable of offering this feature (Beam / Segev 1997; Piller / Stotko 2002).

To support the contract conclusion, trust centers offer the possibility of signing with legally binding effect by means of computer networks. A reliable, neutral center (trust center) confirms that an electronic signature is genuine, which saves the trading partners from having to send paper documents to and fro.

In the execution phase, e-cash and credit card companies offer to process payment transactions that are directly related to a purchase. In the case of e-cash (electronic money), this involves encrypted codes sent by the sender to the recipient, who either passes these on or credits them to a bank account. Contrary to normal electronic payment services, this money, like (real) cash, ensures anonymity, i.e. it is impossible to determine through whose hands electronic money has passed.

A distinction must be made between digital and physical products in respect of the delivery of the goods (see section 7.3.1.1). Digital products can be directly sent over the network or even downloaded by the customer and thus do not pose a logistical challenge – if the required bandwidth is available. In electronic markets, physical goods are usually dispatched through parcels services, which, as the external service provider, assume the sales logistics. Consequently, an increase in parcel services is expected as electronic markets' revenue increases. Supply chains are usually shorter in electronic markets since the goods are no longer required to be transported to intermediate dealers. The manufacturer (or wholesale warehouse) sends goods directly to the final customer after the contract has been concluded (van Heck / Ribbers 1998; see section 7.3.2.3).

The WWW emerged as particularly suitable for the after-sales phase very early on. The Internet can be a valuable complement to a telephone customer hotline, particularly if problems occur with the purchased products. Customers can search for answers to frequently asked questions and to their specific problems, and are only required to contact customer advisors in very difficult cases. Users also support one another via forums and mailing lists and in virtual communities (Reichwald / Fremuth / Ney 2002).

Furthermore, it is possible to download updates for digital products that become rapidly outdated (e.g., virus protection software) from the Internet. In the business-to-business area, extranets play a special role in the after-sales phase. By means of a password, customers and business associates are given the opportunity to gain access to a company's intranet from the outside and to view service information, online manuals, lists of contacts, etc. In addition, further repeat orders or orders for services can often be placed over an extranet.

## 7.3  Approaches for the Explanation of Electronic Markets

This section attempts to explain electronic markets and the special economic characteristics of such markets. In section 7.3.1, the products and services traded in electronic markets are examined. The special role that information plays in the flow of market processes, as well as the role of information as a traded commodity in electronic markets is considered. Section 7.3.2 analyzes the economics of electronic markets, starting with the special requirements of trading in digital products. Following this, the effects that electronic markets have on competitive conditions are examined. In a final section, light is shed on the new challenges that trade intermediaries face from electronic markets.

### 7.3.1  Products and Services in Electronic Markets

The breakneck speed at which the Internet is spreading confronts almost every company with the question whether, and especially how, it can use this network. As accurate as the statement may be that generally any good – irrespective of whether it is a physical good or a service – can be sold over the Internet (Choi / Stahl / Whinston 1997), it is also true that there are greater advantages to the electronic transactions of some goods than to others. Realizing these advantages is decisive for whether the suppliers and / or buyers of the good gain an additional benefit. This additional benefit is, in turn, the basic requirement required to trade successfully in electronic markets (Wigand 1997; Albers 1999; Koch / Möslein / Wagner 2000). Below, the characteristics of goods and / or services are examined on the basis of a taxonomy of goods and information economics. These are of key importance for this issue.

### 7.3.1.1   Information as Marketable Goods in Electronic Markets

The suitability of goods for trading in electronic markets depends, among other things, on the transaction phases (see figure 7.1) that can and should be supported by I&C systems. The more phases this involves for a given good, the more it is likely to be suitable for trading in electronic markets. According to this assumption, goods are particularly suitable if all phases, from the information phase to the delivery and the after-sales phase, can be supported. Differences between various types of goods specifically occur in the execution phase, as only information can be transported over the electronic market's underlying I&C infrastructure (usually the Internet) as an economic good, whereas all other goods must be sent by the supplier to the buyer via a physical infrastructure (see section 7.3.2.3). Consequently, one should distinguish between information goods and physical goods when attempting an analysis based on a taxonomy of goods.

Information can be traded as an economic good if it is "appropriate, existent, available, transferable, and scarce, and meets an effective market demand" (translation by the authors, Bode 1997, p. 461). The transfer of information always requires carrier media such as paper, cables, celluloid or air in the case of the spoken word (see section 2.4.2). Information goods can be divided into information products and information services (Bode 1997). Information services differ from information products because they require an external production factor (i.e. provided by the buyer). These services are created in interaction with the buyer, for example, business consulting services or auditing. Conversely, there is no such interaction when information products are produced: The information is produced autonomously by the producer and stored on a physical carrier medium. Texts in paper books or newspapers, or pieces of music recorded on CD are examples of information products. The distinction between information products and information services is made in the same way as the distinction between physical goods and traditional services (see figure 7.4).

Information goods can be digitized in electronic markets, sent over computer networks, and processed by computer processors (Zerdick / Picot / Schrape et al. 2001). Information products thus become digital products in electronic markets (Choi / Stahl / Whinston 1997; Albers et al. 2001). These characteristics make digital products ideal merchandise for electronic markets. Software, online magazines, digitized music or films are examples of digital products. As a result of their digitization, all transaction phases of information goods can be supported. Owing to

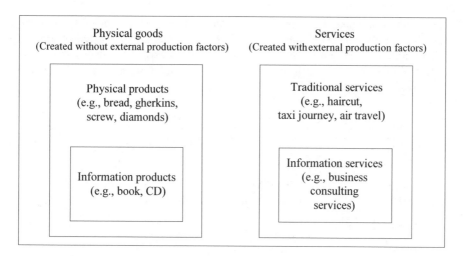

**Fig. 7.4.**    Information in a taxonomy of goods

their increasing economic importance and because requirements to produce and distribute them differ from those of traditional goods, digital products are also the focus of attention in many analyses of electronic markets and / or e-commerce (see section 7.3.2.1).

However, information services can also be digitized and transported through I&C systems. Examples of this are investment advice or training via a videoconferencing system. Nevertheless, the economic potentials of electronic markets cannot be developed to the same extent for information services as they can for digital products, as the I&C system also requires direct interaction between the supplier and buyer. One way for suppliers of information services to better develop the potentials of electronic markets is to substitute the services with information products, particularly computer software (Hermann / Bieberbach 1999). Figure 7.5 presents examples of information services whose substitution with digitizable information products is favored in electronic markets.

These are usually standardized services that can be provided in an automated way by I&C systems such as a simple bank transfer transaction. However, the technical progress made in the development of computer hardware and computer software is pushing the limits of automation further and further so that increasingly complex services can be mapped in computer systems. The substitution of information services with information products took place and is, of course, also still taking place outside electronic markets. Figure 7.5 provides further examples of this substitution process.

The substitution effect has far-reaching economic consequences for the creation of the relevant information goods. The automated creation of information products leads to cost reduction potentials resulting in a decline in the prices of these goods if competition functions properly. The extent to which these advantages actually lead to an improvement for the buyer also depends on how complete the substitution is from this buyer's point of view. If, for example, a bank customer attaches greater importance to information received during a personal advisory session than to the same information retrieved from the Internet, the information product is not a complete substitute.

| Information service | Information product | |
|---|---|---|
| • Telling stories<br>• Opera<br>• Performance by a court jester | • Book<br>• Gramophone record<br>• Late night TV show | |
| • Banking advice<br>• Book trade<br>• Tuition<br>• Consulting a doctor<br>• Advice obtained from a travel agent<br>• Transport timetable<br>• Translation service | • Online banking and analysis tools<br>• Communities and online ordering<br>• Learning software and online support<br>• Expert system<br>• Photos, videos, hotel descriptions, support with choice and online booking<br>• Online timetable database<br>• Translation service | Substitution through electronic markets |

**Fig. 7.5.**    Examples of the substitution of information services with information products (Hermann / Bieberbach 1999, p. 71)

In addition to the possibility of substituting information services with digitized goods, electronic markets provide an opportunity to bundle information services and products anew. Based on the banking advice example, this can mean that simple information can be retrieved from the bank as an information product and that the customer can obtain additional advice from a person via a videoconference if required. Suppliers of digitized information products can use the characteristics of electronic markets to their advantage to adopt various price and product strategies, which are examined in depth in section 7.3.2.1.

In about 1995, long before the Internet investment bubble even began and Amazon.com was just beginning to sell online, few, if any, retailers could predict whether business-to-consumer (B2C) e-commerce would catch on with customers, or whether the Internet would ever rival stores and catalogs as a serious additional sales channel. Although digital products are ideal for trading in electronic markets from a theoretical perspective, selling physical products such as clothing or books dominated the initial phase of e-commerce. Currently, much travel and insurance are specifically found in e-commerce, i.e. traditional services are sold and not digital goods. Books, computer software, music, and information products are among the most widely sold goods. In fact, suppliers still sell computer software, which is most suitable for digitalization, to buyers on physical carrier media and not over the Internet. With Forrester Research Inc. predicting that by 2009 almost 40% of all US households will be making at least one online purchase each year, Internet retailing has clearly come of age and remains the US retailing industry's fastest-growing sales channel.

US Internet retailing is a $135-billion industry according to the trade publication **Internet Retailer**. By all accounts e-retailing is exploding and has shown a steady growth of roughly $15 billion or better each year. Some refer to this growth as analogous to the way stores and catalogs grew in the last half of the last century. In the beginning, i.e. the 1990s, web retailing grew from nothing to $109 billion in 2005. 2006 reported online retail sales of $135 billion and predictions are that this volume will grow to $900 billion by 2016, accounting for 15 percent of total retail sales (*Internet Retailer* 2007).

Retailers worldwide have been struggling with the issue of strategic multichannel retailing, i.e. the use of traditional stores (*brick*) and online sales channels (*click*). The underlying difficulty is to assess the expected role that sales channels should play in the eyes of the consumer, i.e. the buyer. Should there be more or fewer traditional stores or do buyers appreciate more online purchasing options? Should the product mix in both channels be the same or should there be variations? What adjustments need to be made as the buying population changes and ages? Many companies such as Wal-Mart have adopted a hybrid strategy between the two channel choices and are poised to roll out or reduce either channel according to consumers' long-run preference. Companies have recognized the importance of presenting customers with one uniform face, no matter which shopping channel is used to connect the store, catalog, call center, and online operations. The electronics retailer Circuit City, for example, has designed a business strategy that places the Web at the very center of its operations. The company guarantees that in-stock items ordered online will be available for pick-up at a store within 24 minutes of the customer placing the order. Circuit City even offers preferred parking spaces right at the store entrance for Web customers picking up their orders.

The top ten US retail businesses and their respective 2006 web sales volumes are depicted in figure 7.6.

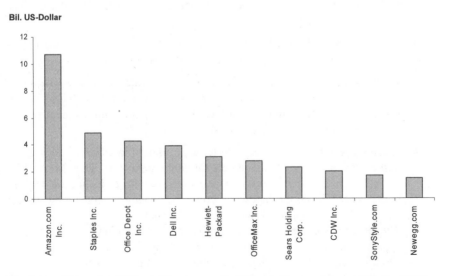

**Bil. US-Dollar**

**Fig. 7.6.**   US top ten 2006 retail businesses (in billions) (Source: Internet Retailer 2007)

The following are some specifics characterizing this steadily growing industry:

- **Sales Power:** While there are easily tens of thousands of retail web sites operating in the US, the top 500 e-retailers in 2006 accounted for 61% of all online sales.

- **Growth Engine:** As a group, the top 500 grew their online sales by 21% in 2006 and accounted for a total of $83.6 billion of the nation's $136.2 billion retail web sales.

- **Online Sales by Industry:** A total of 145 (or 29%) of the top 500 e-retail businesses in the US are owned by store-based retail chains, 89 (or 18%) by catalog and direct-marketing firms, 42 (or 8%) by consumer branded manufacturers, and 224 (or 45%) by pure plays or web-only retailers. Since they control an even larger share of the biggest sites, retail chains accounted for 41% of online sales reported by the top 500 in 2006, catalogers 14%, manufacturers 14%, and pure plays 31%.

- **Online Growth by Industry:** Of the 500 e-retailers, retail chains and web-only merchants grew their online sales faster than anyone else, achieving growth rates of 23.4% and 23.6%, respectively. By comparison, catalogers in the top 500 grew their e-retail sales by 21.2%% and consumer-branded manufacturers by only 9.1%.

- **The Big vs. the Small:** In 2006, the fastest growing retail web sites in the US were found in the second tier of the top 500 e-retailers. Thirty-three of the 50 fastest growing e-retail sites consisted of e-retailers that were ranked between 251 and 500 overall. As a result, the top 100 e-retail sites – though still dominant as a group – saw their share of total top 500 sales decline from 87% in 2005 to 86% in 2006.

- **The $1 Billion Group:** In 2006, 17 companies recorded online retail sales of $1 billion or more compared to just 14 the previous year.

- **Everything Sells Online:** Twelve of the 14 merchandising categories tracked in the top 500 registered double-digit growth rate in 2006, with the fastest growth rate coming from the hardware / home improvement sector, which expanded its online sales by 42%.

- **Winners & Losers:** In percentage terms, Lumber Liquidators achieved the best e-retail sales growth among the top 500 with a 400% gain. Meanwhile eCOST.com turned in the worst performance with a decline of 41% in online sales. While the hardware / home improvement sector grew fastest online with a 42% growth rate in 2006, the runner-up was not far behind. The merchants in the largest category (in terms of numbers of merchants) – apparel / accessories – continued to show that shoppers have no qualms about buying fashions online. The combined 2006 web sales for this group rose by 41% to almost $10 billion. Conversely, only one category – sporting goods – experienced a decline in online sales in 2006, reporting an 8% drop from 2005. This decline was, however, the result of certain sporting goods retailers being reassigned to other categories as a result of acquisitions.

**Concomitant Changes in Advertising**

Considerable changes can be observed in the world of online sales and associated advertising, with the most significant changes occurring in favor of various forms of online advertising. A major shift is occurring away from traditional broadcast as well as print media advertising to online forms of advertising in which fine-tuning and precision measures are applied much more effectively and precisely to reach a specifically targeted audience. In past television advertising, media buyers worldwide placed an advertisement on a television show that attracted the highest concentration of target customers. The available audience measures are, however, at best rough approximations based on past surveys of samples of viewers. Advertising has always faced the difficulty of having to judge whether expensive advertisements succeed in driving sales. In the early days of advertising, John Wannemaker quipped, "I know exactly that one half of my advertising is wasted; the problem is I don't know which half." Online advertisers, however, can be much more scientific and precise in where they place their advertisements. Specialized behavioral targeting firms have developed techniques to track the online habits of potential customers. Accordingly, when searching for products, web users may, for example, be fed highly targeted advertisements based on their preferences and past searches. Advertisements can therefore be far more streamlined and will be targeted at the user most likely to respond, enabling advertisers to generate measures to track the effectiveness of their advertising and marketing efforts. At times, success may be determined within minutes and adjustments can be made almost on-the-fly, depending, for example, on how many people clicked on an advertisement, the length of time a consumer spends with an advertisement, what a user does after viewing the advertisement, etc. These evolving changes in online advertising spending are reflected in figure 7.7.

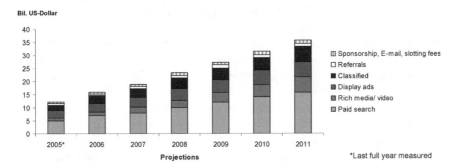

**Fig. 7.7.**   US online advertising spending by format (Source: Steel, Emily. Advertising's brave new world. The Wall Street Journal, May 25, 2007, p. B3)

In addition to the digitizability of products, there are evidently other characteristics of goods that are important when trading online and in electronic markets. These are dealt with in greater depth in the following section.

### 7.3.1.2   Information Economic Approach

As shown in the approach based on a taxonomy of goods, the suitability of digital products for trading in electronic markets arises from the fact that the execution phase can also be fully supported by electronic means. The reduction in transaction costs in electronic markets is, however, not primarily dependent on how many transaction phases can be supported but on how high the overall reduction in transaction costs for all phases is as a result of mediatization. In electronic markets, it is possible to reduce the transaction costs of every phase (Picot / Bortenlänger / Röhrl 1997). The greatest savings potential can be realized in the information phase when the search for information on potential market partners is carried out and the information in their offerings is compared. I&C technology is very good at specifically supporting these activities (Schmid 1993).

From the information economic perspective, goods are systematized according to their search, credence and experience characteristics (Nelson 1970; Darby / Karny 1973; Weiber / Adler 1995a) as follows: Goods or services with mainly search characteristics can be fully evaluated by the buyer searching for appropriate information prior to a purchase. As far as goods or services with mainly experience characteristics are concerned, the buyer evaluates these after the purchase because the quality can only be determined after their use or consumption. The buyer cannot evaluate goods with mainly credence characteristics either before or after the purchase, as this requires time and expertise.

In addition to these three categories, it is possible to introduce a fourth category, namely intensive consulting services (Korb 2000). This involves packages of services for which the supplier provides very intensive consulting services prior to the conclusion of the contract. Owing to the special features of the consulting service that precedes the actual purchase, and which plays an important role in electronic commerce, it appears necessary to examine this fourth dimension too. It is rather difficult to determine the moment when the characteristics of the service and / or product can be evaluated for purchases involving intensive consulting. In addition to the actual purchase, the consulting service is an important factor that contributes to the realization of the transaction and / or should actually be regarded as a part of the transaction.

The consulting service comprises aspects of all three of the known types of characteristics – the search, experience, and credence aspects. Strictly speaking, however, it is possible to evaluate the service or product characteristics only after the conclusion of the contract because, although the consulting service is provided prior to the conclusion of the contract, the consumer cannot actually evaluate the service or product until afterwards. In reality, there are only few goods that can be clearly allocated to one of these categories, as all three types of characteristics are to greater or lesser degree present in every good. The allocation of characteristics to certain goods depends on the specific buyer's subjective perception of the service or product. Categorizing goods according to their information economic characteristics is therefore not generally valid. Rather, these characteristics are specific at a certain time for specific buyers, although they can be ascertained in buyers through empirical surveys (Weiber / Adler 1995b).

In the context of this systematization, it is possible to provide an explanation for computer hardware, books, and travel having a leading position as goods traded in electronic markets on the Internet. The information required by buyers for their evaluation, such as price, technical features, and specifications, can be communicated efficiently and effectively through electronic markets. In addition, multimedia depictions can clearly illustrate the goods' basic and additional benefits for customers. Primarily, these goods have search characteristics whose specifications can be communicated to the buyer by the I&C system underlying the electronic market (Korb 2000).

Products are less suitable for electronic trade if, however, their quality and functionality can only be evaluated by sampling (smelling, feeling, tasting) since the buyer must then employ different methods to obtain this information. Even though there are already prototypical applications for the transmission of smells via the Internet, interactive media primarily target human hearing and vision. The media can only reduce buying uncertainties regarding perfume or wine to a limited extent (Rohrbach 1997). Selling these kinds of goods in electronic markets requires activities by the supplier that, through the restricted possibilities of the communication medium, will compensate the buyer for the sensual experience of the buying process.

If goods are sold through the various sales channels on electronic commerce, the traditional classification of goods into search, experience, and credence goods shifts. Especially goods with properties that can be defined as search characteristics in traditional trade can be transformed into primarily experience goods. For example, goods sold electronically can only be examined visually, since checking these with the aid of human sensory organs is no longer possible. In addition, only one good is displayed as an example and not the good that is actually sold. Nothing about the goods themselves has changed, but the possibilities of evaluating their actual characteristics are now restricted in the light of the large number of goods. To solve this information-related problem, tools must be applied that will compensate for these disadvantages. However, it must also be taken into account that certain experience characteristics of a good in traditional trade can become partial search characteristics due to the increased information potential in e-commerce (Korb 2000).

Information goods – and thus also digital products (see section 7.3.1.1) – always have experience and credence characteristics (Shapiro / Varian 1998; Choi / Stahl / Whinston 1997). This is caused by an information paradox (see sections 2.4.2 and 6.2.2.3): To evaluate information, one needs to know it; but once one knows the information, one no longer needs to buy it. Suppliers of information goods therefore have to develop strategies to resolve the information paradox in order to tap electronic market potentials.

One strategy for overcoming the information paradox is to provide individual parts of an information good free of charge to buyers so that they can form an opinion of its quality without knowing all its parts (Shapiro / Varian 1998). Typical examples of this are newspaper headlines and movie trailers. Other possibilities include initially providing an information product free of charge for buyers to test for a certain period and then requiring compensation after the expiry of this test phase. Suppliers of computer software often use this method when buyers use their software on a permanent basis (e.g., word processing programs). Similar to computer software, another characteristic of digital products is frequently used to overcome the information paradox: Its easy modification. The buyer is supplied with a slightly different version free of charge although the functions of this software are restricted (see section 7.3.2.1). The buyer can then test the quality of the product, acquiring the full, unrestricted version if satisfied. Patent protection is a legal instrument for bypassing the information paradox: A buyer can obtain information on an invention's characteristics in the patent specification. However, this information can only be used for economic purposes in return for appropriate license fees.

Another strategy for successfully selling goods with experience and credence characteristics through electronic markets is to use information substitutes to reduce the buyer's uncertainty prior to the purchase (see chapter 2; Weiber / Adler 1995a). The transfer of these substitutes is supported by their multimedia representation possibilities in electronic markets, since service or product-spanning information substitutes (such as reputation and degree of awareness) and service or product-related information substitutes (such as guarantee and price) can be transferred through this media. In addition, virtual communities can contribute to a reduction in uncertainties (Armstrong / Hagel 1996, 1997). Furthermore, standards are increasingly being established that reduce uncertainty about quality during purchase and increase the share of search characteristics in goods with experience and credence characteristics. Reviews of books that evaluate the quality of publications are an example of quality seals. Since the buyer must trust information substitutes in order to accept them as a replacement for the personal evaluation of goods' characteristics, their effectiveness specifically comes into effect in repeated or longer-term transaction relationships.

Overcoming quality uncertainty is a function that intermediaries, as independent third parties, can assume in markets (Choi / Stahl / Whinston 1997). The intermediary guarantees the quality of a good for a buyer, which means that the buyer is not required to personally procure information on goods' characteristics. There are major differences between intermediaries' role in electronic markets and their role in traditional markets. Overcoming quality uncertainty is one of the most important tasks – and therefore also one of the most interesting business areas – that intermediaries carry out in electronic markets. Section 7.3.2.3 deals with the new role of intermediaries in greater depth.

In summary, it can be stated that goods' suitability to be traded in electronic markets is largely determined by their information economic characteristics. These determine how well the information phase can be supported by an I&C system. However, the characteristics of a good based on a taxonomy of goods are decisive for whether transaction phases can be supported at all. Only information services and information products can be fully supported in the execution phase. The decisive issue is, however, the total reduction in transaction costs that can be realized in electronic markets throughout all of a good's phases. A significant reduction in the information costs in respect of goods with a predominance of search characteristics can carry more weight than, for example, a reduction in the execution costs of digital products.

Certain goods' information economic characteristics depend on a great many factors and can also be influenced by electronic market suppliers. The suitability of products and services therefore varies. Figure 7.8 summarizes the goods-related factors that are important in respect of goods' suitability for electronic trading.

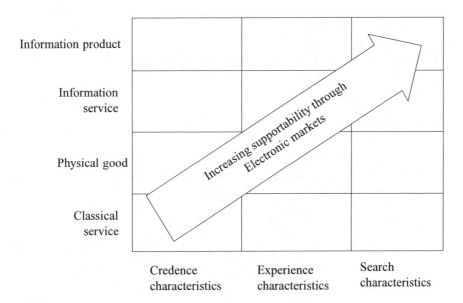

**Fig. 7.8.**    Ability of electronic markets to support transactions

## 7.3.2   Economics of Electronic Markets

### 7.3.2.1   *Economics of Digital Products*

Although the digitizability of products is only one of the characteristics that enables them to be traded in electronic markets (see section 7.3.1.1), analyzing the unique economic characteristics of digital products' production and distribution helps to explain how electronic markets function. Trading in electronic markets means major changes for all affected commodity markets. However, the most fundamental change will take place in markets for digitizable information products, since the basic principles underlying their production and distribution are changed by networked I&C technology (Reichwald 2002). Doing business with digital products is the crux of electronic commerce (Choi / Stahl / Whinston 1997). The economics of digital products is characteristic of the economic rules of the Internet.

Moreover, digital products, driven by technological innovations, are becoming increasingly important in modern economies. For example, the media, software, consulting, databases, and financial services markets that are relevant for digital information products are among the strongly growing markets (Zerdick / Picot / Schrape et al. 2001). It is a fact that "… the Internet economics' application area no longer only relates to the … media and communication sectors, but is increasingly becoming an economic theory that provides fundamental basic knowledge for all economic sectors" (Zerdick / Picot / Schrape et al. 2001, p. 157; translation by the authors).

The economic examination of digital products is carried out in two stages. First of all, a description is given of how the characteristics of the production and the widespread distribution of information products lead to economies of scale and network effects, and what the implications for suppliers are. The second stage discusses the strategies that can be implemented to realize the revenue potentials of digital products.

### Economies of Scale and Network Effects with Digital Products

It is often emphasized that the Internet also offers small companies – even the smallest ones – the opportunity to join global electronic markets (e.g., Schwartz 1997. Wigand 1997). Creating an initial presence on he Internet incurs relatively little costs, as a website set up on rented servers suffices initially. Investments that have to be made in technical infrastructure are just a fraction of the costs that would be required to enter a traditional market. In addition, a technical range to approach customers all over the world is available from the outset. One should note, though, that large-scale electronic commerce applications, including such necessary features as load-balancing, mirror sites, as well as intrusion and security measures could very quickly become rather expensive. Although the Internet certainly also contributes to the spread of new forms of work, for example, small offices and home offices (SOHOs) (Reichwald et al. 1999), it is also obvious that just a few companies dominate many electronic markets on the Internet. Despite the large differences in their services and forms of revenue, the best-known Internet companies, for example, Amazon, Yahoo!, and Google share the common experience that as they grew, they achieved competitive advantages in their markets. Scale benefits in electronic markets are based on economies of scale on the supply side and network effects on the demand side.

In traditional markets, economies of scale play an important role in respect of industrial goods. As the production quantity of, for example, automobiles increases, the average costs incurred with the production of another vehicle decrease. The reasons for this are, for example, the use of larger plants, more efficient manufacturing methods with a higher degree of specialization and division of labor, favorable purchase terms for larger quantities, and the realization of learning effects over time. In traditional markets, economies of scale are nevertheless limited. They are restricted by various factors, for example, an increase in coordination costs as the company grows (see chapter 2). In contrast to industrial goods' economies of scale, there are no limiting factors in respect of digital products. On the contrary, the economies of scale increase as the number of sold products increases (Zerdick / Picot / Schrape et al. 2001).

Economies of scale play an important role in the (re-)production of information in electronic markets (see chapter 2). The production of the first unit of an information product entails relatively high costs, additional units (copies) mean low costs, while electronic markets on the Internet entail hardly any costs at all. The larger the quantity of information products that a supplier can sell, the cheaper they become. In turn, the quantity of sold product increases. Competitors find it very difficult to catch up with a supplier that has succeeded in creating a lead with successful sales of a specific digital product.

The network effects induced on the demand side are just as important for the economies of scale in electronic markets. Section 2.4.2 describes the differences between direct and indirect network effects, and the significance of network effects and standardization for information and communication markets. Direct network externalities mainly occur in the I&C infrastructure area in electronic markets, for example, on the WWW as an electronic marketplace, and with communication services and products such as an e-mail service. Indirect network effects occur in a large number of digital products, for example, compression standards for digital music and software to create texts and pictures. With regard to these network effects, various products' compatibility, the learning effects of users of programs that are already on the market, and the certainty that the product will also be compatible with future products are all decisive factors for the decision to purchase. Potential buyers' expectations about the future distribution of a product have great significance for the decision to purchase (Tirole 1995). Many users will only decide in favor of a product if they expect that it will be successful in the future as well. In turn, the building of such expectations depends partially on other market players' choice.

Network externalities lead to a supplier also gaining competitive advantages over other suppliers as the distribution of its product increases. While the utility of its own product increases, those of competitors become less attractive to buyers due to their lack of these advantages. In an extreme case, a winner-takes-all market emerges as a result of network externalities. This enables a supplier to increase its advantage until it has a monopoly once a certain market share has been exceeded (Shapiro / Varian 1998).

Figure 7.9 provides an example of the development of market shares in a winner-takes-all market: Two competitors start off with almost the same market share in a new market for a digital product with network effects, for example, new soft-

ware for playing music on the Internet. While the market shares are almost the
same, within a "battle zone" there is still competition between the two suppliers.
As soon as one supplier succeeds in significantly increasing its market share, the
advantage is reinforced by network effects, and the disadvantages for the competitor increase. The competitor then leaves the "battle zone." The result is a winner
that can dominate the market as a monopolist and a loser that leaves the market.
Whether a specific market is a winner-takes-all market depends positively on the
strength of the network effects and negatively on the customer's need for different
product versions (Shapiro / Varian 1999). Due to digital products' very short innovation cycles, these monopolies are constantly under threat from new products –
or announcements about new products – and cannot be maintained for a long period
of time (Zerdick / Picot / Schrape et al. 2001).

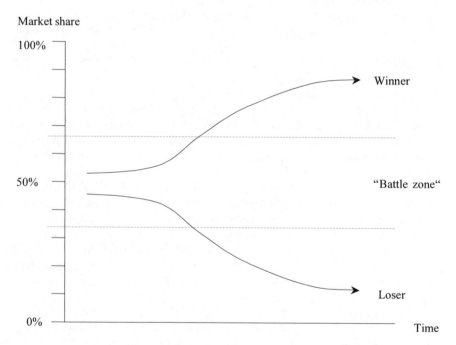

**Fig. 7.9.**   Winner-takes-all market (based on Shapiro / Varian 1998, p. 177)

Suppliers of digital products face the strategic challenge of achieving the necessary distribution with their products as long as the market is in the "battle zone,"
and thus exploiting positive network effects to their own ends. To achieve this
goal, the number of users of their products must exceed a critical mass, after
which the positive network effects will be strong enough for the product to continue to proliferate and reach all potential buyers (see section 7.3.2.3). The strategies that enable suppliers to reach these goals are presented below.

## Strategies for the Realization of Economies of Scale

To exploit network effects, suppliers must distribute their products as rapidly and as extensively as possible. As far as price strategy is concerned, a penetration strategy is the traditional instrument with which to achieve this goal (Simon 1992). This price strategy entails new products being placed on the market at a very low price, in some cases below production costs, in order to rapidly achieve high sales figures and market share. In traditional markets, this strategy aims at achieving economies of scale in production in order to establish competitive advantages that cannot be overtaken. The company makes a profit by exploiting its dominating market position to increase prices and / or by not passing on the cost advantages involved in mass production to buyers. The low prices in the product's launch phase constitute an investment in the yields that are eventually expected from the market share and quantities.

The penetration strategy appears in its most extreme form in electronic markets: Companies give their products away to achieve favorable network effects. This strategy is particularly suitable for digital products because hardly any costs are incurred in the production of additional units once the first unit has been produced (see Chapter 2). The rapid spread of the Internet browser Netscape Navigator at the end of the 1990s was a spectacular example of the initially successful implementation of this strategy. On superficial examination, Netscape and other suppliers' temporary Internet success with giving away products appears to invalidate the economic rules of traditional markets (Kelly 1997). However, these companies too were pursuing a longer-term strategy by giving away information products: Distributing their products was an investment in eventual profits.

As a second step, a supplier attains revenues in various ways after distributing a free product (Zerdick / Picot / Schrape et al. 2001). It can, for example, sell enhancements or updates of the free basic version, charge fees for the use of the product after a free test phase, sell complementary products or use its product as an advertising medium and sell its users' interest to other companies. A systematic overview of the forms of revenue, as well as the price and product strategies for digital products that have been outlined here is provided in the following sections.

Potential users' subjective perception of the product advantages is crucial if a critical mass is to be reached (Rogers 1995). Consequently, it is important for the supplier to convincingly communicate these advantages to buyers and to reduce possible uncertainties about the product's future distribution – and thus its future utility. An important strategy in pursuit of this goal is the establishment of standards (Tirole 1995). The strategic advantages and disadvantages of standardization for suppliers of information goods are discussed in section 2.4.2. A supplier can also reduce buyer uncertainty by investing in advertising and PR measures to increase awareness of itself and its product.

To ensure the distribution of large quantities of a product, interested buyers must not only be aware of it, but it must also be available to them. The Internet provides ideal technical conditions for the rapid, inexpensive, and mass distribution of digital products. The supplier must, however, ensure that interested parties can download the product onto their computers smoothly and quickly. The advantage of this strategy for the supplier is that products can be copied and passed on by the buyers themselves without a loss of quality (Shapiro / Varian 1998). At the same time, the supplier must safeguard its potential revenues by not permitting a product to be passed on free of charge. Managing the intellectual property rights of information products is key in this regard (Shapiro / Varian 1998).

The supplier can also exert an influence on potential customers' expectations by announcing future products. If a supplier announces a new product version that enjoys a high degree of awareness, some buyers delay their buying decision until the announced product has appeared on the market. This enables a larger number of users to be reached as soon as the product appears.

### Forms of Revenue

Determining price and product strategies for digital goods can be analytically divided into two sub-areas (Zerdick / Picot / Schrape et al. 2001): The form of revenue decision and the price policy decision. When choosing a form of revenue, the supplier determines whether it will finance its services through, for example, user fees or advertising income. This decision is then followed by the selection of a specific price and product strategy, i.e. what, for example, the fees or advertising prices should actually be and on what basis they should be calculated. Figure 7.10 provides an overview of the forms of revenue systems used by information suppliers.

In direct forms of revenue, suppliers receive their income directly from information buyers, whereas in indirect forms of revenue, suppliers provide information free of charge and receive compensation for their services from other companies or from the state, which in turn refinances this through consumers by means of taxes or higher product prices.

Direct forms of revenue are divided into use-related and use-unrelated revenue forms. The use-related forms are based on the quantity of information acquired by a buyer (e.g., the number of newspaper articles retrieved from an archive) or on the time granted to access the information offered (e.g., time-based user fees for online services such as AOL). With the direct use-unrelated forms of revenue, the price payable is not related to the duration and volume of the information use. For one, the buyer pays non-recurrent fees to acquire the right of unrestricted use. These fees include flat-rate license fees (e.g., for the use of software), connecting charges, and payment for a special receiver (e.g., a pay TV decoder) with which to retrieve the information. Use-unrelated payments can also be levied intermittently. This category includes subscriber fees that are, for example, paid on a monthly basis for the use of an online service or, for instance, Germany's mandatory monthly radio license fee for public broadcasting.

A distinction is made between indirect forms of revenue based on information suppliers' source of finance. Financing through other companies is more important: Based on users' demand for information, information suppliers can offer these

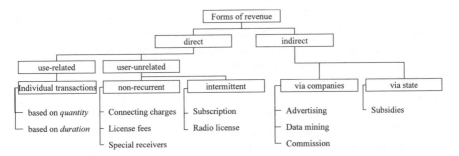

**Fig. 7.10.**   System of revenue forms (based on Zerdick / Picot / Schrape et al. 2001)

companies various services. Financing through advertising is an indirect form of revenue that is of paramount importance. Advertising companies gain buyers' attention and pay the supplier of the information that has attracted this interest. Closely related to this form of revenue is indirect financing by means of commissions. The third company pays the information supplier an appropriate share for successfully brokered transactions that were initiated by the buyer's attention being drawn to the product or service. The third form of indirect financing that is especially suitable for the Internet is based on the use of data mining and the subsequent reselling of customer information gained through this method. The information supplier therefore collects data that buyers leave about themselves when retrieving information. This might be personal data that the user has to provide to gain access to the information or data about user behavior gathered automatically when the information is retrieved. This data can then be sold to interested companies. Data protection laws do, however, strictly limit this source of income – at least in Europe. State subsidies finance information offerings that are eligible for subsidization if sufficient private financing sources cannot be found. An example is Internet teaching provided by a state-financed university.

Suppliers of information products can combine these forms of revenue at their discretion: An online service may, for example, be financed by a combination of non-recurrent connecting charges, basic monthly rentals, time-dependent user fees, and advertising on its start page.

**Price and Product Differentiation**

When determining a specific price policy in electronic markets, the possibilities of price differentiation play a key role (Skiera / Spann 2002). Reference is generally made to price differentiation if a supplier demands different prices from different buyers for identical units of its good. However, this definition is inadequate for the analysis of real markets, since there are hardly any goods with identical attributes (Tirole 1995). Price differentiation therefore also applies when a supplier asks different prices for goods that are not completely identical but are generally similar (Skiera 1998). If, for example, depending on the booking period, different prices are demanded for a flight, this can be referred to as a price differentiation.

According to Pigou (1920), a distinction is made between three types of price differentiation (Tirole 1995): A first-degree price differentiation occurs if the supplier can obtain an individual price from each individual buyer, and this price is exactly equivalent to the maximum amount that each individual is willing to pay. With second-degree price differentiation, the supplier provides a range of different versions of its product at different prices. Buyers can now choose between the different versions themselves and are required to pay different prices for them. With this method, the buyers disclose what they are willing to pay through their decision in favor of a certain version. Shapiro and Varian (1999) accurately refer to second-degree price differentiation between digital products as "versioning" (Shapiro/Varian 1998; see also Skiera/Spann 2002), as the supplier must be able to offer different versions of its product to realize this strategy. Third-degree price differentiation occurs if a supplier offers its product to different groups of buyers at different prices. These groups may be formed, for example, by various affiliations to social groups (e.g., students) or by regional differences (e.g., home country and abroad).

By adopting a price differentiation strategy, suppliers endeavor to determine, as far as possible, what buyers are willing to pay and thus to maximize their profits. This is fully successful if a supplier can apply a first-degree price differentiation. In reality, however, this goal can only be achieved if buyers are prepared to disclose the maximum amount they are willing to pay.

Characteristics of digital products also affect the determination of a pricing policy. Digital products are especially suitable for price differentiation strategies as they can be simply and inexpensively bundled, differentiated, and tailored to cater to buyers' needs (Choi/Stahl/Whinston 1997; Shapiro/Varian 1998; Skiera 1998; Piller 2001; Hermann 2002). Moreover, personalized digital products reduce buyers' incentive to enter arbitrage transactions, i.e. trading the product between buyers who have to pay different prices (see section 2.2.2).

The Internet especially favors the possibility of price differentiation, as it is possible to gain information on individual buyers through data mining (Bakos 1998; Shapiro/Varian 1998). The supplier can use information about, for example, preferred information offerings or previously purchased products to submit offers specially tailored to the needs of individual buyers. The electronic exchanges and auctions described in section 7.2.2.2 can also be used as price differentiation tools since, in these types of markets, prices materialize through the prices offered by individual buyers and not by buyers simply accepting or rejecting fixed price quotes.

A price differentiation can also be based on certain groups of users. First of all, it is important that such groups are as homogeneous as possible in terms of their price sensitivity. Secondly, the groups with higher prices must accept that there are group-related features that lead to lower prices (e.g., lower prices for students). In this respect, there is no fundamental difference between electronic and traditional markets. However, greater market transparency can lead to the erosion of group-related price maintenance strategies (Shapiro/Varian 1998) because the different groups become aware of the differences in prices and then refuse to accept this practice.

Versioning offers digital product suppliers in electronic markets ideal prerequisites to pursue second-degree price differentiation strategies. The aim is to create as high a value as possible for the buyer by tailoring the product as far as possible to the buyer's needs and by skimming off the largest possible part of this value through the price (Shapiro / Varian 1998; Hermann 2002; Skiera / Spann 2002; Piller / Stotko 2002). For versioning, the supplier must therefore identify product characteristics whose different attributes will significantly influence the customers' use of this product. Figure 7.11 provides an example of digital product characteristics that could be the subject of versioning, as well as the characteristics of (potential) users, all of which could lead to differences in users' willingness to pay for the products.

| Product dimension | Characteristic | Opposites of the utility continuum | Example |
|---|---|---|---|
| Time | Topicality | Immediate or later access | PAWWS financial networks (real time and delayed share prices) |
| | Duration of availability | Long-term or short-term use | Lexis/Nexis database (on-screen use or download) |
| Quantity | Scope of performance | Business or private use | Scope of database |
| Quality | Picture resolution | Pictures with high or low resolution | 10MB for gloss picture or 600KB for matt picture |
| | Legibility | Monitor or hard copy | Printed or online version of a technical book |

**Fig. 7.11.**   Examples of the versioning of digital products (based on Zerdick / Picot / Schrape et al. 2001)

Versioning's success depends on whether the supplier manages to clearly differentiate between the different versions of a product line (Zerdick / Picot / Schrape et al. 2001). Cheap versions should therefore not be of a very high quality, as no one would otherwise be prepared to spend more on the high-end versions. A slight difference in price between a high-end and low-end version might, however, contribute to users moving from the low-end version to the high-end one (Shapiro / Varian 1998). The digital product's characteristics and buyers' requirements determine the number of eventual versions, as well as the exact differentiation of the differences in the various versions' price and quality. Correctly defining these parameters is therefore a strategic success factor for suppliers of differentiated information products.

Another strategy adopted by suppliers to generate revenues from network effects is to exploit complementarities (Shapiro/Varian 1998; Zerdick/Picot/Schrape et al. 2001). As a first step, the supplier distributes an information product free of charge, which rapidly achieves a critical mass of users and related positive network effects. A second step is selling the complementary information products that are required to use the free product. This strategy is particularly promising with product systems that require individual products to function interdependently as complements so that total utility is achieved. The supplier therefore exploits the fact that if the customer changes to an alternative system consisting of complementary goods, additional costs are incurred, which effectively binds the customer to the supplier's own system (lock-in effect). A classic Internet example is Netscape, which distributed its Internet browser free of charge, generating revenues by means of the complementary software for Internet servers (see chapter 2). This strategy is older than electronic markets and was already used by Rockefeller, who gave away oil lamps to sell oil at the beginning of the 20th century. Today, this strategy is adopted, for example, by suppliers of mobile phone networks that subsidize mobile devices in order to make money by means of user fees.

Another way of differentiating between digital products is by combining individual information components to form a customized information package, which is called "bundling" (Shapiro/Varian 1998; Choi/Stahl/Whinston 1997). In other words, suppliers bundle components and sell them to the customer at a fixed price. A typical example of the bundling of information products is a daily newspaper. The supplier gathers news from various fields and then sells it to the buyer 'bundled' in a newspaper issue. Generally, information can be bundled and billed according to its quantity and duration of use. Direct, use-unrelated forms of revenue (see figure 7.9) with non-recurrent or periodic payments are also part of bundling strategies.

The newspaper example also serves to illustrate that digital products' advantage over that of information products on traditional media (e.g., paper) lies in the possibility of un-bundling it. Information products can therefore be individualized: Customers can combine news for online newspapers, for example, dowjones.com, as they please without having to refer to superfluous information as in daily print newspapers. Many authors have therefore predicted that bundling will remain a niche in electronic markets (e.g., Choi/Stahl/Whinston 1997). However, analyses have proved that suppliers of information products can boost their profits through bundling strategies under specific conditions (Bakos/Brynjolfsson 1998). Bundling can even out deviations in various customer groups' willingness to pay for separate, unbundled information products, thus increasing the supplier's revenue.

Moreover, bundling can be used to introduce new information products to a market (Shapiro/Varian 1998): For example, a software supplier may integrate a demo version of a new program into its old software to draw its customers' attention to it. Bundling can also be used as a strategy to resolve the information paradox. Readers of a newspaper might, for instance, be completely unable to assess beforehand what news they wish to receive. This means that the information bundled by a newspaper's editorial office might also contain articles whose utility is only recognized once they have been read. In this case, the bundling of such articles is a valuable service for which the buyer is also willing to pay.

At present, bundling is frequently a price strategy on the Internet, as putting a price on individual information components would entail excessive transaction costs. For the above-mentioned reasons, the bundling of information products will make sense even if improved payment methods (micro-payment) make it possible to charge separately for the smallest information components.

### 7.3.2.2 Competition in Electronic Markets

In answering the question of how market electronization impacts competition and strategy, two effects, which were described at the beginning of this chapter, are especially important: The electronic communication effect and the electronic brokerage effect (Malone / Yates / Benjamin 1987). The former implies that information can be transmitted ever more rapidly and cheaply, also over long distances. The latter signifies that modern information and communication systems act as brokers, i.e. they bring suppliers and buyers together (see section 7.2.2.2). They also have advantages over their human counterparts as they can process a larger number of bids within a shorter time, and thus tend to provide suppliers and buyers with a wider selection. In addition, they are usually cheaper. The Frankfurt securities exchange is a good example of this: Its electronic system Xetra (Exchange Electronic Trading) can process more than ten times as many orders per day at about one fifth of the costs per order than a traditional floor trade can. One consequence of these effects is the merging of markets that were previously geographically, temporally or sociodemographically separate. Individual suppliers and buyers can clearly expand their operating range through information and communication networks and overcome geographical market boundaries. In principle, it is thus possible to globalize these markets, although high transport costs (compared to the purchase price), the perishability of goods, legal regulations or cultural barriers (e.g., language) are limiting factors in some classes of goods. However, temporal and sociodemographic market boundaries are also becoming less important as shop closing time is irrelevant in electronic markets, and people have fewer social inhibitions in certain of these shops because they are not being watched by other customers. As a result of these developments, more extensive markets are emerging with a greater number of market players (Sviokla 1998).

A second development very closely connected to this, is the increasing transparency within markets. Information and communication technology allows information on suppliers, buyers and the traded products to be far easier collected and compared than in traditional markets. Above all, a comparison between different manufacturers' products is simplified through the decrease in search costs, and decreasing switching costs ("Your competitor is just one mouse click away").

A third development is the change in communication between market players. It is no coincidence that the Internet has only been significantly used as a marketplace since the introduction of the WWW. Its multimedia possibilities far surpass any previous standard of media richness on the Internet (see Chapter 3; and Möslein 1999 for details). However, even today communication in electronic markets still occurs through standardized, technical interfaces with relatively low media richness. Direct face-to-face communication is usually not (yet) possible, and the customer is generally not served by a human but by software. This is detrimental to personal customer contact, trust, and customer retention.

There is fiercer competition between market players as a result of the increased transparency, which led to the expansion of these markets, and the resultant decrease in customer retention. Since most of the markets in Western industrial countries are buyer markets, the fiercer competition leads to suppliers suffering an erosion of profits (Sviokla 1998; Hagel / Armstrong 1997). In seller markets, the greater transparency can lead to price increases, although this will probably be an exception (Gebauer 1996).

To date, however, no significant price reductions resulting from electronization have been observed in electronic markets on the Internet; the level of prices has remained largely the same as the customary level in the catalog mail order business. This may be a temporary phenomenon though, since many companies have only relatively recently set up the Internet as a sales channel and are still operating at a high cost level. On the other hand, there is a tendency towards better off customers, who find shopping convenience more important than a lower price, being reached through the Internet. As the Internet continues to spread to yet wider segments of the population, the price war on the Web might intensify significantly (OECD 1998).

Suppliers are naturally not interested in their profits being eroded and attempt to counteract the above-mentioned developments by adopting various strategies. To prevent cut-throat price competition, suppliers endeavor to create artificial intransparency on the markets to prevent a comparison between prices. Particularly obscure pricing is one way of doing this. Online securities, whose complicated tariff systems are based on those of airline and telephone companies, are exemplary in this regard. In addition, suppliers attempt to prevent software agencies from making automated price comparisons. An example is the failure of the software BargainFinder, which was supposed to search the Internet for the cheapest audio CD on a customer's request. Suppliers responded swiftly and blocked their sites to BargainFinder (Bailey / Bakos 1997).

A second method of preventing excessive market transparency is to ensure as great a differentiation of the products as possible, extending as far as customized mass production (Pine 1993; Piller 1998a, 2001). Mass customization is not only a way of personalizing marketing inexpensively, but also of creating products and services in line with individual customers' needs. In keeping with certain basic requirements, related personalized prices are adjusted individually to what customers are willing to pay (see section 7.3.2.1). The individualization demanded of mass customization also requires personalized communication, which can be achieved through interactive media (Korb 2000; Piller 2001; Reichwald / Piller 2002). Finally, there is a wide range of possibilities to increase customer retention, many of which are adopted from traditional marketing. This includes, for example, targeting customers individually, loyalty bonuses, unique additional benefits, and the systematic prior announcement of new products. The establishment of strong brands on the Internet or the transfer of brands from other markets is particularly important, as the lack of trust in suppliers as human counterparts can be substituted by trust in well-known brands (see section 7.3.1.2 and Reichwald / Bullinger 2000). The cause of the lack of trust in the electronic trade, which may be perceived more or less strongly, lies in the uncertainty of buyers, which may have various causes. Incomplete information about the transaction partner's behavior, about external influences, any new general conditions that influence market behavior, and one's own contribution to the transaction are probably the most frequently given reasons for uncertainty (Korb 2000; Piller / Stotko 2002).

In addition to the customer retention strategies mentioned, there are new strategies in electronic trade that utilize the new technical possibilities of the WWW. Virtual communities in line with Hagel and Armstrong (1997) are the best-known examples in this regard. With this strategy, a supplier attempts to set up a discussion forum for its customers and potential customers on its website. This forum enables them to discuss the company's products and exchange experience and advice.

There is a distinction between commercial and non-commercial use of electronic communities. The first electronic communities, initially known as news groups, are currently often commercialized by advertising, product and service offerings, sponsoring, as well as by offers for cheaper products or services for their members (Seeger 1998). In contrast to non-profit communities, whose initiator is mostly a wholly private individual, commercial communities are established by companies. In their own way, both types of communities are important in respect of shedding light on their role in the reduction of information asymmetries. The advantage for customers is that they receive valuable information and assistance, can make suggestions, and even voice complaints. The advantage for suppliers is that they receive customer feedback very cheaply and may obtain valuable suggestions for new and further developments by observing or participating in the community. On the one hand, suppliers gain information on their customers that can be used to specifically target them, thus strengthening customer relations. On the other hand, it reinforces customer relations, as the customers themselves are able to trigger "their" supplier to make modifications as a result of their involvement. It has, however, been noted that customer retention strategies and customized offers should not only be established in the after-sales phase. More than ever before, transactions should focus on customers and their needs during each phase of the buying process.

Apart from all the strategies employed as a response to the increase in competition, there is still one important trend in electronic markets, especially on the Internet, that also counteracts the development of perfect competition: It is called the economy of attention (Goldhaber 1997; Franck 1998). This concept is based on the notion that there is a wealth of freely available information on the Internet and that it is therefore no longer a scarce resource. Conversely, potential customer attention is scarce, which gives rise to competition between suppliers for this attention. Advertising is an important instrument in this competition. Creating awareness is a key success factor for companies on electronic markets. A high level of awareness also affects potential buyers' expectations when new products with network effects are introduced (see section 7.3.2.1): If the company has already established a high degree of awareness, it is regarded as more likely to sell a sufficient number of new products (Shapiro / Varian 1998).

### 7.3.2.3    The New Role of Intermediaries

The changes arising from the electronization of markets for producers and consumers have also had an impact on intermediaries. The term intermediary is generally used to denote any actor on a market who is neither a supplier nor a buyer, but either facilitates the overall functioning of the market or first enables the market to function, receiving a commission or similar compensation for this (see Benjamin / Wigand 1995; Wigand 1997; Reichwald 2002). Wholesalers and retailers, brokers and auction houses are examples of such actors. Typical intermediary functions are as follows (Malone / Yates / Benjamin 1987; Buxmann / Gebauer 1997, Bailey / Bakos 1997; Wigand 1997):

- Supplying market players with information about goods and other market players to save transaction costs: The basic idea is that not all of m suppliers are required to contact all of n buyers to find the most suitable market partner (m*n contacts). Instead, the information is collected at a central point and passed on to the market players (n+m contacts). The information function can also incorporate the intermediary that provides support to fix prices (e.g., a stock exchange) or acts as a broker or intermediary.

- Organizing the bundling and distribution of goods and providing the infrastructure required for this (e.g., market hall): For example, the primary function of a supermarket chain is to provide the most important daily requirements (bundling) close to home so that shoppers can buy them (distribution).

- Gaining the trust of market participants and, on this basis, acting as a quality assurer or assisting customers in their buying or selling decisions: Intermediaries have little incentive to behave opportunistically, as they generally carry out transactions frequently and therefore have to take their reputation into account.

- Taking over additional services such as processing payments, financing or safeguarding against risks.

Initially, the discussion about the effects of the electronization of markets on intermediaries was largely restricted to the information function. It was often argued that intermediaries would probably become superfluous due to the lower costs of information procurement, as customers could directly interact with the producers (disintermediation) (Wigand / Crowston 1999; Benjamin / Wigand 1995; Wigand

1997). A typical example of this development's potential is taken from the field of the clothing industry (Benjamin / Wigand 1995). Figure 7.12 presents aggregated depictions of an industrial value chain for a shirt that extends from the manufacturer, via the wholesaler and retailer, to the final consumer. Value chain 1 presents the traditional form of sales. When each added value is aggregated, the customer pays $52.72 per shirt. The second row presents the same value chain when the wholesaler is bypassed (disintermediation of the retailer, although the wholesaler may be retained). This results in a price of $41.34 for the consumer, which is a 28% saving compared to the traditional case. If modern information and communication media were to enable every intermediate stage to be bypassed and the customer could hence be directly contacted, this would have even greater effects. The price payable for the shirt decreases to $20.45 for the final consumer, a 62% drop compared to the traditional sales channel. Naturally, the manufacturer will endeavor not to pass the entire difference on to the final consumer. The competition in the specific electronic market will ultimately determine who will profit most from cost reductions (see section 7.3.2.2).

It therefore appears that despite economic incentives, disintermediation on the Internet is not occurring as extensively as expected (Bailey / Bakos 1997; Buxmann / Gebauer 1997). The following reasons are regarded as primarily causing the as yet low degree of disintermediation (Picot / Bortenländer / Röhrl 1997):

The insurance function of the intermediaries: Banks are a good example of this function. Their specific knowledge of the special circumstances relating to time and place and their general know-how permit them to conduct more efficient screening and monitoring than private individuals. Hence, they can largely overcome adverse selection and moral hazard problems. This means that taking on non-payment risks can be analytically understood as an insurance service (Böhme 1997). Similar security services are assumed by the trade. Such services include the quality assurance of products, advisory and exchange services, as well as other measures that reduce the risk entailed in a purchase. This example demonstrates that intermediaries do not only have specific know-how of the primary transactions involved in the transfer and announcement of products and services, but also of indirect, supporting secondary transactions, such as financial transactions, insurance, and logistics (Himberger 1994). Intermediaries furthermore realize economies of scale when providing these services. Disintermediation thus requires a reorganization of the functions carried out by conventional intermediaries and new institutions, but often such reorganization is carried out by entirely new actors within the underlying industry (Wigand 2003).

The market power of intermediaries: Another reason for the low degree of disintermediation is the market power of conventional intermediaries. S.W.I.F.T., an international banking network for the electronic exchange of money, serves as an example in this regard. Only banks can access this network, as they are reluctant

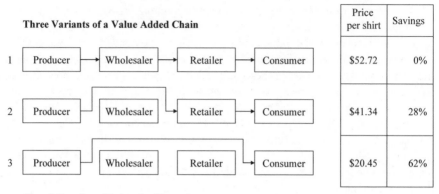

Fig. 7.12.   Value chain in the shirt industry (based on Benjamin / Wigand 1995)

to lose their monopolistic position as the coordinator of cashless payments (Picot / Bortenlänger / Röhrl 1997). To dispense with the services provided by intermediaries, non-banks must invest in setting up a new infrastructure. The establishment of this kind of infrastructure might, however, be a lengthy process, as uniform standards have to be created in order to exploit network advantages. The creation of such a system can therefore fail due to a lack of critical mass (see Niggl 1994 on problems when establishing standards).

The critical mass problem: The producers of goods and services who approach buyers without employing the services of intermediaries are faced with this problem. This is due to a market's attractiveness increasing with the probability of other market players being attracted to it and, therefore, the number of participants increasing. In other words, every additional participant increases the advantage for the existing participants (Economides 1994). Intermediaries agglomerate suppliers and products and thus increase a market's attractiveness for buyers. It can therefore be more difficult to attain a critical mass of participants and exploit positive network externalities without intermediaries. Essentially, intermediaries' function is to attract the attention of as many market participants as possible (see section 7.3.2.2).

In summary, it can be concluded that the broad base of intermediaries is not expected to disappear, but that their role in electronic markets is changing (e.g., Bailey / Bakos 1997):

- Two opposite trends can be observed in respect of the information function: On the one hand, suppliers and buyers can meet more easily on the Internet due to the simplification of information procurement. This tends to make intermediation superfluous. On the other hand, however, the number of potential trading partners is increasing sharply due to worldwide networking, which makes an overview of the market more difficult and intermediaries more important. Depending on the market, this will lead to either a greater or lesser need to provide information. In markets characterized by a large number of buyers who purchase on an irregular basis, for example, consumer goods or books, intermediaries' significance is likely to increase. However, in markets characterized by a manageable number of market players with regular exchange relationships, for example, the supplier markets of large industrial companies, electronization will probably lead to the substitution of intermediaries.

- This also applies to the bundling of services. While the need for bundling might remain high for sporadic purchases in markets with little transparency, buyers will bundle desired services themselves, particularly in the business-to-business area. However, one reason for bundling might also be because selling packages of services is one way for suppliers to determine whether customers are willing to pay higher prices (see section 7.3.2.1). Generally, bundling in electronic markets occurs logically, while physical bundling and distribution (of physical goods) are mostly taken on by traditional parcel services (see section 7.2.2.3).

- Since there is no longer direct personal contact between suppliers and buyers and it is therefore very difficult to build human trust, the trust function is gaining increasing importance in electronic markets (see section 7.3.1.2). Well-known brands that customers trust and which represent a certain quality and reliability thus become an important asset on the Web (Evans / Wurster 1998). However, the development of trust institutions is also gaining significance in respect of executing processes, because exchanges Burgterrasse of services and / or goods and payments over the network must be safeguarded (trusted third parties; see section 7.2.2.3).

Nevertheless, we must recognize the demise of, for example, travel agents and the steady onslaught on the traditional role of stockbrokers. Specialization in respect of the intermediation function can also be observed on the WWW. While a conventional intermediary often provides a broad spectrum of services ranging from information and advice to distribution and financing, Internet intermediaries usually specialize in supporting individual phases of the exchange of goods and / or services on markets. For example, they operate electronic trading systems, assist market players in searching for partners, bundle the services of other suppliers, and carry out quality assurance (see section 7.2.2). The possibilities that the Internet provide for bundling products and / or services can be simultaneously exploited with the bundling of specialized services by forming telecooperative corporate networks and virtual enterprises (see chapter 8).

The conclusions can be summarized as follows: Three types of changes are occurring with regard to the marketing stages of commerce's traditional value creation. The substitution and / or the extinction of intermediaries are referred to as disintermediation. This applies primarily to digitizable goods, such as software and information, but increasingly also to other sectors in which suppliers target customers directly. Transintermediation is the term used when the intermediate trade is replaced by new intermediaries. These kinds of changes are especially visible in the brokerage business, such as in real estate and job and partner brokerages. Moreover, new intermediaries are pushing their way into the electronic market. This development is referred to as reintermediation or hypermediation. New types of intermediate trade, such as content providing, search engines, portals, and community suppliers are emerging. Their tasks lie in the area of information, security, and brokerage. It is particularly in this new area of intermediation that profits are expected (Wigand 1997; Schneider / Gerbert 1999; Albers / Peters 2000; Wigand 2003).

## 7.4 The Role of Information and Communication Technology

In recent years, technological developments have had a revolutionary impact in electronic markets. There is every indication that this turbulent development will continue. For a long time, electronic markets were merely a niche and were only of relevance in respect of highly standardized goods in the business-to-business area (e.g., securities, flight tickets). The breakthrough in the business-to-business area was not achieved until the introduction of the World Wide Web. It provided the first convenient and multimedia user interface and allowed the Internet to expand to private households. For the first time, it was possible to also advertise and sell goods on electronic markets that require multimedia presentation.

Besides modern information and communication technology's constitutive role in respect of electronic markets in their current form, new technical possibilities also play a decisive role with regard to their development potential. The worldwide availability of the Internet has, for example, enabled the emergence of highly specialized markets that would have failed in local or regional markets due to a lack of critical mass (Picot 1998a). The Internet is, moreover, already showing signs of departing from the traditional pricing model in which suppliers offer goods at a fixed price and buyers can decide whether they want to buy or sell at this price (e.g., supermarkets). More flexible mechanisms such as exchanges and auctions are gaining in importance on the WWW. This is made possible by suitable software that inexpensively performs pricing procedures that are to some extent very complicated. Furthermore, market players are now able to participate in auctions, exchanges, etc. through information and communication networks without their physical presence being required. From an economic point of view, this signifies these markets' enhanced efficiency.

Technological developments that will have a major impact on the possibilities offered by electronic markets are already anticipated for the coming years. The continued spread of the Internet, which the introduction of easy-to-use end devices seems to indicate, is of key importance in this regard. It will be interesting to see whether a convergence (i.e. a merging) of end devices will occur. Similar to the convergence phenomenon observed in telecommunication and data networks, the functionality of end devices is no longer necessarily determined by only one service. The limits of traditional equipment functions have been eliminated by the integration of telephony, the retrieval of texts, the sending and receiving of faxes, and radio broadcast through multimedia PC.

Similar trends can also be observed in the TV domain. In this regard, there is a specific development towards Web TV or Web Video as part of the overall Web 2.0 developments (e.g., Wigand 2007): An integration of Internet and TV/ Video, the contents of which, depending on the concept, can be interactively retrieved via a PC or a TV set with a set-top box. It is expected that this will lead to an expansion of particularly business-to-consumer markets. In the future, Web EDI will play a greater role, especially in the business-to-business area. Order forms filled in on the WWW are automatically converted into EDI or EDI/XML messages (see chapter 4) and processed as such by the supplier. The continued expansion of the bandwidths of transmission media will clearly improve the ability to depict products on the WWW and thus enable more goods and services to be offered through networks (see section 7.3.1). Above all, a breakthrough will be experienced in sending information products directly through the Internet and in providing information services through the area-wide introduction of video communication. Several researchers estimated that in 2007 60% of all Internet traffic is the transmission of video materials (Wigand 2007).

In the shorter term, the enforcement of standards for electronic payments on the Internet is especially of crucial importance. Chip cards and e-cash systems that use encryption procedures could allow goods and/or services to be paid for directly and safely without any additional expense.

## 7.5    Implications for Management

Electronic markets have gained importance through the progress made in information and communication technology. To meet the challenges and seize the opportunities arising from this, managers must understand the new rules of the Internet economy and modify their strategies to suit the changed setting. Electronic markets' potential cannot be realized to the same extent in respect of all products and services. Whether an additional advantage is created for suppliers and/or buyers above those of traditional markets is crucial in this respect. The starting point for examining the performance spectrum is the transaction process as a whole, from the search for information to the execution of the business transaction. In this regard, the innovation potential in the information phase is of key importance.

To be successful in electronic markets, the supplier must succeed in effectively communicating information on its goods / services that is relevant for its customers by means of the underlying I&C infrastructure. The supplier must check whether its own spectrum of services / goods is suitable and how the information can be prepared to meet this medium's requirements. Spatial, temporal, and socio-demographic market limits are losing their significance as a result of the new global communication networks. Companies thus have the possibility of penetrating new markets, but also regard themselves threatened by new competitors in their long-standing markets. Innovative services in electronic markets also enable new business areas. Markets that previously failed due to a lack of critical mass can now develop through worldwide networking. The redefinition of a company's markets and competition is therefore a necessary prerequisite for success on electronic markets. Online marketing creates new potential for companies, for example, in respect of cost reductions, customer convenience, through-put times, and capital tie-up or the bypassing of marketing levels.

Many companies that currently conduct their sales and marketing through traditional channels are hesitant about doing business online because they fear a cannibalization of their previous sales channels, which are, in some cases, very profitable or powerful. However, they then run the risk of being crowded out by new competitors that exploit the potential offered by online sales. A proactive strategy that actively seizes new opportunities is required to achieve success on electronic markets. Dealers and other intermediaries should therefore become aware of the transformation of their role. Competition has increased through the greater market transparency, the lower costs incurred in switching suppliers ("Our competitor is just one mouse click away"), and the loss of personal customer contact.

Successful actors in this environment use the economies of scale and network effects of electronic markets. These can be primarily observed in respect of information products but are also spreading to other electronic markets. Companies that manage to attract as much attention as possible and reach a critical mass of customers quickly achieve success on electronic markets. These goals are pursued by making high investments in publicity for the own company and by adopting an aggressive pricing policy – which may mean giving away products. Profits can, however, only be made from the company's ultimate strong market position.

Awareness is an important instrument for building trust to reduce customer uncertainty. Reputation must therefore replace the personal relationship between the seller and buyer as far as possible. Customer expectations are also important for new products' distribution and success, and only a well-known supplier can influence these expectations. Once a supplier has achieved a good position on the market, its aim must be to retain customers and, simultaneously, to optimize revenues. Electronic markets also require creativity in the form of revenue and price strategies: Prices and products are differentiated and individualized; the key to this is customer information.

Attention has become a scarce commodity that can be traded. Electronic exchanges and auctions are replacing the traditional "take-it-or-leave-it" fixed price model. Many of the emerging electronic markets are also characterized by particularly fierce competition and very short market life cycles. Furthermore, competitors' head start in winner-takes-all markets is very difficult to catch up with. It is thus becoming more and more important for companies to identify emerging markets at an early stage, enter them at the right time, and achieve a strong market position. The fierce competition within existing value chains might even erode profits at some stages. Consequently, it will often be necessary to continue one's presence and to face competition even in unprofitable business areas in order to retain customers (and not become cannibalized) and win new ones. Innovative managers identify future profitable stages and penetrate new business areas.

*Chapter 8*

# Overcoming Location Boundaries:
# Telecooperation and Virtual Enterprises

# Case Study Chapter 8: "The Worldwide Group" – A Future Work Scenario?

In order to understand how location boundaries can be overcome in the scenario presented below, we have to envision employee Tara Rodgers's ordinary working day by moving a number of years into the future. Rodgers works for the "Worldwide Group" (management consultants) and is jointly responsible for a marketing campaign that has to be planned in less than eighteen hours. This scenario, developed by Jarvenpaa and Ives (1994), illustrates certain aspects of the future world of employment, giving us an idea of how to use information within a different technical, organizational, legal, and social setting. In the future, unlike the physical transport of goods and people, information activity will expand rapidly: A transatlantic flight will still take at least five hours; on board, food and drinks will be served in the usual way, but communication systems will support and partially replace transport systems. This setting is further elaborated upon in this case example below.

"As the pilot retracted the 787's landing gear, passenger Tara Rodgers linked her personal assistant to the onboard computer built into the armrest. Although this plane's systems were no longer state of the art, the display screen was larger and of higher resolution than that available on her assistant system. It also provided access to the airline's electronic amenities. She chose to tune into the airline's audio system, which provided capabilities similar to those engineered into her personal assistant – connection to the in-flight entertainment, the ability to listen to ground control, as well as the special circuitry required to eliminate the plane's background noise. She touched an icon on the screen in front of her and called up the in-flight service menu. She cancelled dinner, and eliminated such nonessential messages from the flight personnel as the pilot's sightseeing instructions. She requested a glass of port for two hours later. She did not expect her electronic documents to attract the attention of the European Community's customs and immigration systems, but she authorized the system to wake her if an onboard interview with immigration officials was requested. By speaking softly into a microphone plugged into the arm rest, she completed her custom's declaration electronic forms. The flight number, date, and trip duration had already been completed by the airline's computers. She wondered if the customs people knew, or even cared, about the massive knowledge base and expert systems that were contained in her personal assistant system or the wealth of information and tools that were immediately accessible using the worldwide data network to which her firm subscribed.

Rodgers barely noticed the selection of soft classical music that served as background to her audio system. Her personal profile, stored in her assistant – or was it the airline's frequent flier database –, had chosen the type of music and preset the volume based on her personal preferences. The personal profile would also suggest that her morning coffee be served with cream but not sugar.

With the touch of another icon, Rodgers began to make arrangements for her brief stay in Oxford. This was a spur of the moment transatlantic crossing, so she had left with no hotel reservation. The electronic reservation agent her firm subscribed to had meanwhile booked her into the charming guest house she had been so delighted with during her last visit to Oxford. Using her travel agent's virtual reality simulator, she wandered into the rooms with open doors (available to be rented this evening) and selected one with lovely pink wallpaper, a canopied bed, and a view of one of the colleges. She then booked a car to pick up at Heathrow and transport her to Oxford. She could have looked at a short video segment showing where to meet the cab. Closer to the time of arrival, she could even look at a prerecorded introduction to her driver or talk to him or her directly. Assuming on-time-arrival, which the onboard computer informed her, was 95 percent likely, and normal early morning traffic, she would arrive in Oxford five hours before her meeting with Professor Fearl and the prospective customer. For the first two hours of the flight there was a great deal of work that needed to be completed. But first she called home to talk to her husband and proudly watched her littlest one take a few more faltering steps around the living room. (...)

With a touch she activated her electronic messaging system and listened again to the message from a senior partner of her consulting firm that had prompted this sudden trip to London. 'Tara, this morning I was forwarded from our London office a message that had come in from Professor Frank Fearl at Templeton College at Oxford. Fearl is a well known B-School academician with the ear of many of Europe's CEOs. Apparently over the years Fearl has worked closely with our U.K. and European offices on a number of projects that have proven mutually beneficial to us, Fearl, and clients. London believes that Fearl may have the inside track on a most promising opportunity, but we need to move quickly and decisively.'

'The prospective customer is Empire Software, a U.K.-headquartered firm that specializes in the production of integrated software systems for the international freight business. Sir Thomas Baker-Knight, CEO of Empire, is in residence at Templeton College for three days attending a Managing Directors forum. Over coffee, Baker-Knight expressed a concern to Professor Fearl that his firm is not embracing the tumultuous advances in software engineering and that his management team is poorly prepared to respond to competitive threats from a variety of unexpected quarters. In an informal discussion, Baker-Knight expressed considerable interest in a tailor-made educational offering for the firm's top 100 employees. Fearl has set up a follow-up meeting with Baker-Knight for tomorrow afternoon at Templeton to explore this further. He thinks that with quick action, we might be able to land this without an arms-length call-for-proposal process. Fearl suggests a joint effort between Templeton and Worldwide, where we would use our contracts to supply expertise not available to Templeton. (...) I've checked your availability over the next two days and it appears that we can reassign most of your responsibilities to other associates. Hopefully, you can pick up the remainder from your airplane seat or hotel room. Your contact person in the U.K. is Jeremy Wainright, a partner in our London office. (...)'

Rodgers then listened to the forwarded messages from Professor Fearl and from Jeremy Wainwright in the London office. (...) While she waited, Rodgers prompted the assistant to identify an initial list of individuals who might add value to the program. Using just her firm's database, she checked on availability over the next six month and watched video clips of several professors working with an executive audience. She called one in Oregon who had worked with her and Baker-Knight years before. His enthusiasm for the planned program and obvious respect and fondness for Baker-Knight were so great that she asked him if she could use his automatically recorded remarks, and contagious smile, during her presentation tomorrow. Rodgers then contacted Cinko Kolors, a multimedia services company to which her firm often outsourced graphics work. Cinko Kolors front-ended for a variety of small, often one-person, graphics consultants that tended to work out of small towns, artists colonies, resort locations. These graphic artists provided multimedia artistic talent while Cinko Kolors marketed services, kept the artists' technology up to date, took care of the bookkeeping, and provided technical expertise and training. Inducements from the Singapore government, coupled with that island nation's superior information technology infrastructure, had led Cinko Kolors to establish their legal headquarters there.

Cinko Kolors ensured that the customers received worldwide presentation consistency, copyright clearances, a standard of quality, and onsite presentations equipment for the end user. Because of the lateness of the hour and short time horizon, Cinko Kolors first offered Rodgers an artist on Kuai. Rodgers viewed several short segments of the artist's work and then, using Cinko Kolor's database, gained assurance of his ability to deliver in a timely fashion. From her own firm's files Rodgers retrieved and reviewed a previous project for which this same artist had received high marks. Satisfied, Rodgers forwarded logos from her own firm, as well as that of Empire along with names, titles, pictures of Templeton, pictures of Empire's corporate headquarters, and the information that would permit the artist to access the previous multimedia presentation. Cinko Kolors would collect, and share with the original multimedia design consultant, a standard fee if that presentation were modified for reuse. Through the next hour Rodgers and the multimedia artist discussed the initial story board for the ten-minute marketing presentation. Site venues, talent presentation clips, and segments from her would be forwarded to a companion multimedia artist in London who would complete the work. The final rough cut of the promotional piece would be available for Rodger's review upon arrival in Oxford. Cinko Kolors would ensure that presentation equipment was available both at her guest house and at Templeton. That would still leave several hours for final edits and perhaps even inputs from Fearl, Wainwright, the firm's European managing director, or Japanese partner who had supervised the Tokyo project and was now cruising the Caribbean.

Rodgers wrote up a summary of her activities thus far and forwarded it and the various working documents and contact people to Wainright and The Worldwide Group's database. She also took the liberty of recording a 5:30 a.m. wake up call for him. If the human resource profile on him was accurate, she could trust him to pick up the ball and move it forward while she caught a little sleep. She set a relative wake up call for herself for 45 minutes before the plane touched down in London. Her personal profiler would ensure that a gentle voice would awake her with some sweet words of encouragement.

As the flight attendant arrived with the port wine, Rodgers reviewed the personal assistant's profile of Tom Baker-Knight. When she came to work for The Worldwide Group, the information in her old portable had been transferred to the assistant and, for all she knew, to the Group's central data banks. Although she had been far less experienced in those days, she had the sense to record the wine Baker-Knight had ordered and so much enjoyed five years before. She forwarded the name and year to Wainwright, who with his alleged penchant for detail, perhaps might be motivated to get an Oxford wine merchant to embellish the Templeton College wine cellar before tomorrow's meeting. Sipping her port with some satisfaction, she downloaded a short story into the audio system and reclined the seat. (Jarvenpaa / Ives 1994, pp. 30 – 34)"

Tara Rodgers airplane 'office', and the other nodes she interacts with illustrate the essence of a dynamic network: a globally dispersed and dynamic web of knowledge nodes drawn together on a one-time basis to address a unique problem. A knowledge node can be an individual knowledge worker, a team of knowledge workers, and / or an independent organization. Among the knowledge nodes making up the web in our scenario are Tara Rodgers, Jeremy Wainright, Cinko Kolors, their graphic artists, a graduate student at Irvine, and the Japanese partner aboard the cruise ship in the Caribbean. Knowledge nodes have their own distinctive competency. For instance, the Cinko Kolors' knowledge node adds value that cannot easily be provided by the various artists the firm represents.

This scenario gives us a first impression of what new forms of problem solving and task accomplishments may arise from new and future technology. Perhaps some of them will be achieved more quickly (e.g., technological), some of them more slowly (e.g., organizational), while others will be achieved in ways that differ vastly from those depicted here. Nevertheless, the "Worldwide Group" example gives us some indications of what the future may entail (e.g., a "global Web") (Reich 1991) and virtual organizations (Davidow / Malone 1992).

Actually, this organizational form demolishes the firm's traditional boundaries, particularly with regard to space, time, and in a legal sense. The coordination of tasks no longer occurs in static or predefined structures. There is a problem-specific and dynamic linking of resources to accomplish specific tasks. This is an organizational form that in part, but also in its entirety, may be short-lived and transitory, in other words, it may entirely dissolve after the problem has been solved, or may be capable of adapting itself through a dynamic reconfiguration to meet highly variable task demands.

In the following sections, we will first address the fundamental aspects of the various forms of the dispersed organization. Thereafter we offer various theoretical approaches to dispersed organizations and examine the role of information and communication technology in this setting. The virtual organization as a specific resultant of telecooperative work forms is presented in section 8.2.2.

## 8.1    The Fundamental Idea of Dispersed Organizations

Large areas of business applications are increasingly contradicting the traditional picture of the enterprise as an integrated, methodically organized, and relatively stable product of the production of tangible assets and services: Strict hierarchies dissolve themselves into flat, modular structures (chapter 5). Traditional organizational boundaries blur in symbiotic, network-like entrepreneurial relationships (chapter 6). Technical infrastructures revolutionize markets (chapter 7) through the step-wise dissolution of spatial and temporal restriction. The increasing dissolution of locations, as well as the conditions for and implications of this for actual and future organizational forms, is the focal point of this chapter.

Virtual organizations are an outgrowth of these developments. They therefore function more like spider-webs than networks. They are opposites of organizations that, with regard to ownership and contracts, have relatively well-defined boundaries, have a steady location, relatively permanent resource assignments, and controlled process structures. According to Aristotelian philosophy, virtuality may be regarded as an idealized goal of a boundless organization (Legrand 1972, p. 269). It may also be regarded as an organizational form that considers virtuality in the same sense as information systems researchers might, i.e. as a concept of performance improvement. This perspective also regards concrete locations where the actual work is carried out as systematic and dynamic (Mowshowitz 1991; Szyperski / Klein 1993).

We will next address fundamental aspects of the dissolution of the work location, as well as questions pertaining to the drivers and organizational manifestations of dispersed work locations. The virtual organization as a specific result of telecooperative work forms is presented later.

### 8.1.1   "Anytime / Anyplace": A Vision of the Dissolution of Space and Time

The "Worldwide Group" scenario describes only a few examples of potential future work models. In part, this future scenario has already been embraced: We not only work on airplanes, but also at desks, in shops, on building sites and while traveling. Human beings rather than databases will continue to be the carrier of relevant, personal, and confidential information. This organizational form of task accomplishment will not necessarily always be the most suitable one for human beings, the most suitable environment, and the economically most efficient organization model. The choice of the most efficient organization models always depends on an assignment's characteristics and context. We therefore need a systematic conceptualization of spatial and temporal options as a basis for such a model's organizational use. A particularly simple and graphically pleasing conceptualization is the "anytime / anyplace matrix" (see chapter 4 and figure 8.1).

This foursquare map illustrates a two-dimensional differentiation between time and space, depending on whether the interaction takes place at the same location or at different locations, at the same time (synchronous) or at a different time (asynchronous). These settings can be grouped into four basic situation types.

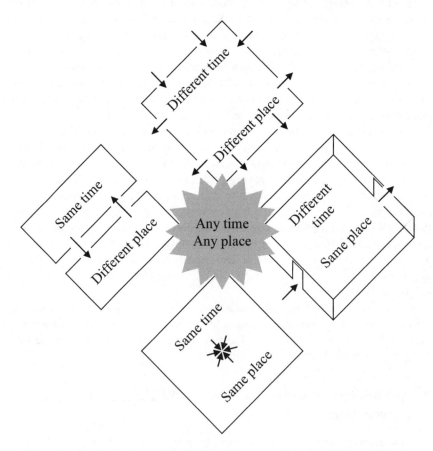

**Fig. 8.1.**     Anytime / anyplace matrix (O'Hara-Devereaux / Johansen 1994, p. 199)

Accordingly, current technologies that support cooperation (e.g., groupware) can be assigned to each square in figure 8.1 (also see chapter 4). With today's developments, this model needs to be expanded with the dimension "mobility." A number of information technologies have evolved that support and enable location-independent mobile work forms by going beyond dispersed work locations and stationary cooperation.

But what is the meaning of "anytime/anyplace" for the organization of production processes based on the division of labor? It definitely does not mean that it does not matter under which spatial/temporal constellations task accomplishment occurs. Although organizational rules will not be supplanted by new technological developments, organizational scope will be expanded. Organization theory also needs to confront these expanded degrees of freedom (e.g., Remer 1994) with new questions. Specifically, these are questions pertaining to the division of tasks and coordination when the work location is dispersed and independent.

As discussed before, organization is always necessary whenever a task has to be accomplished that cannot be accomplished by only one person within one step. In this context, organization has three aspects: (1) to divide tasks appropriately, (2) to bring together the resulting individual activities, i.e. to coordinate the execution of individual activities, and (3) to ensure motivation during task accomplishment. It follows that organization is therefore the reciprocal interplay between task division, coordination, and motivation. The accomplishment of an assigned task requires the accomplishment of coordination and motivation tasks. New information technologies change the possibilities for accomplishing assigned tasks (IT as production technology, see Malone 1988), for accomplishing coordination tasks (IT as coordination technology, see Malone 1988), as well as for accomplishing the design of motivation systems (Picot/Ripperger/Wolff 1996). New information technologies therefore increasingly emerge as a platform for the accomplishment of tasks based on the division of labor (IT as mediating technology, see Ciborra 1993).

## 8.1.2 The Problem of Location in Business Management Theory

Spatial proximity is the characteristic feature of "same time/same place" organizations in respect of people involved in various task accomplishments. This is contrary to organizations with dispersed work locations and/or those that are location independent. Currently we know very little about the actual meaning of spatial proximity and/or its non-existence, as well as about the possibilities of replacing it in the context of organizational task accomplishment. Obviously, spatial distance is primarily a communication problem when accomplishing tasks.

Chapter 3 already described the spatial setting of communication partners with task-related needs and the choice of appropriate means of communication. Task-specific demands on communication channels need to be considered and they need to be specified from a user's perspective. The problem of organizations with dispersed work locations becomes obvious at this point: Certain – especially non-specific and complex – problems demand mostly synchronous, verbal communication means and spatial proximity between the communication partners. The better information and social presence are effectively exchanged and conveyed – despite the use of media during communication processes – the less of an issue the problem of spatial distance is for task accomplishment in work-dispersed locations.

A survey of 500 academics and engineers in industrial research and development (R&D) indicates that even with employees concentrated in one location, social presence and face-to-face communication occur only on a relatively small scale (Kraut/ Egido 1988). Only one-fifth of the personal communication processes that occurred between colleagues on the same floor were observed between employees whose offices were on the same floor but in different corridors. Communication between co-workers on different floors was even less. Consequently, the spatial grouping of people, who are responsible for achieving various tasks, at central locations does not necessarily guarantee the required social presence (Kraut/Egido 1988).

New solutions need to be specifically found for a large number of or frequently changing cooperation partners. Currently, problem-related face-to-face meetings of cooperation partners, which require all the participants to be more mobile, compete with media-supported cooperation processes. A prerequisite for better fulfilling task-related communication needs is to extend the performance spectrum of technical channels in terms of information richness (see section 3.3.8, as well as the overview of information richness theory by Markus 1994, p. 503 ff.). Consequently, media-supported task accomplishment (telecooperative work forms) can gradually expand into task areas that were previously reserved for direct forms of interaction.

Currently, multi-media communication enables us to express ourselves by means of virtual realities. Multimedia communication makes virtual conferencing possible and product development is supported by virtual prototypes before the physical product is manufactured. Establishing virtual environments in which to complete mutual tasks, allows information-related activities to be a partial substitute for true spatial proximity. Within the near future, media-supported connections between real but dispersed work locations, in the sense of a joint reality and/or collaborative augmented reality, is more likely than true virtual reality (e.g., Grenier/Metes 1992; Harasim 1993; Barnatt 1995).

## 8.1.3  Driving Forces of the Dissolution of Work Locations

In order to understand organizations with dispersed work locations, we must first address the driving forces behind the dissolution of work locations. The role of information and communication technologies as the engine of these developments has been mentioned often. The creation of new technology alone is, however, by no means a guarantee that this technology will actually be used. Examples abound of technology application failing due to a lack of market or societal acceptance, or not being deployed due to their utilization benefits being inadequately quantifiable (see section 8.3.3 and Englberger 2000). Even though we may not yet be able to explain these developments in their entirety, it is meaningful to point out the three essential levels that influence these developments:

- The market and business environment level;
- The value added and business model;
- The level of people and their work.

**Drivers of Workplace Dissolution on the Market and Business Environment Level**

New technological possibilities are usually considered the trigger of dispersed and location-independent work models and organizational forms (e.g., Grenier/Metes 1992; Allen/Scott Morton 1994; O'Hara-Devereaux/Johansen 1994; Reichwald et al. 2000).

Four major trends are of central importance as driving forces:

- The miniaturizing of information technology through the continuing integration of microprocessor components;
- The reduced cost of computing power;
- The reduced cost of storage;
- The increase in electronic connectivity, as well as the increased transmission capacity and reduced cost of telecommunication networks.

New information and communication technologies make the dissolution of workplaces possible. In fact, current developments with regard to the environment, society, and politics demand this. Workplace dissolution can be realized, for example, through ecological, transportation, and traffic-related policies. Besides other developments, considerable benefits resulting in sustainability are expected from telecommunication applications: "It is difficult to think of tools that have intrinsically a lower *material* (including energy) *intensity per unit service – MIPS –* than telecommunication equipment" (Schmidt-Bleek 1994). Electronic data transmissions instead of sending paper documents, the creation of virtual instead of real prototypes, telecommuting instead of real commuter traffic are just some of the many possibilities. Telecommunication applications may, moreover, realize benefits (including sustainability) within regional and structural economics politics. Further examples are the creation of additional, non-agricultural employment possibilities, especially for younger people. In addition, such developments may increase the income and the economic power of citizens living in rural and remote areas. Finally, this can lead to a decrease in labor migration and brain drain, as well as rural areas being preserved as an equal and self-contained living space.

## Drivers of Workplaces Dissolution on the Value Added and Business Success Level

The economic drivers of workplace dissolution are expectations of improved resource productivity and, consequently, a better competitive position, as well as the development of new markets.

Currently, firms' greater resource dependence, especially with regard to know-how and capital, favors the growing tendency towards the dissolution of work locations. Consequently, completing ever-increasing complex tasks within a global competitive setting requires, for example, an optimal combination of knowledge and service providers. Knowledge, capabilities, and skills are, nevertheless, not distributed homogeneously throughout the world, but developed under prevailing historical, cultural, and structural conditions. It is, for example, unlikely that the best aerodynamic scientist, the most innovative airbag developer, and the smartest chassis designer will be found in one central location (like Detroit or Chicago) and that they all have optimal management support for their work. Although global sourcing has already become a fully accepted strategy, employee selection still occurs mainly locally. Human resources will generally follow the maxim: The workplace is where the firm is located. Only in a location-dispersed and/or location-independent organization can heterogeneous performance profiles – targeted at a supra-regional or international level – be combined and utilized (e.g., Simon/Bauer/Jägeler 1993).

As mentioned previously, companies have to develop a far-reaching customer orientation. This increased creation of customer-specific problem solutions demands that customers are closely integrated into the service delivery process. The customer moves from being a pure consumer to a user with an after-sale orientation and thereafter to a "prosumer" integrated within the delivery of goods and services (Toffler 1980; Reichwald/Piller 2002; Piller/Stotko 2002). Consequently, isolated, side-by-side value added processes need to be linked. New information and communication technologies offer a number of capabilities through which this can be achieved (see chapter 7). Telecooperation and distributed value-adding structures can support customer integration if they are aimed at achieving closer proximity to the customer.

To a large extent, a firm's competitiveness depends on the economic processes of the production of goods and services. Four targeted dimensions that can influence profitability through organizational and technical measures are (see Reichwald/Hoefer/Weichselbaumer 1993): Cost, time, quality, and flexibility. New organization designs and technical concepts that promise positive effects on these dimensions have a realistic chance of being implemented and transformed. If these concepts also have a positive influence on human work situations and take external company effects into consideration, the prospects are promising.

There are numerous arguments in favor of a positive economic assessment of organizational and technical concepts pertaining to workplace dissolution. They are the drivers of the introduction and transformation of telecooperative work forms. Just a few are presented here for illustrative purposes:

- **Cost Factors**: Regional and national differences in salaries and wages (and / or in employee costs) are often the key drivers of the relocation of organizational activities. The high cost of real estate in metropolitan areas also triggers spatial decentralization of organization units.

- **Time Factors**: The exploitation of differing time zones and / or internationally differing work patterns and holiday regulations through work location dispersion allow organizational processes to be streamlined.

- **Quality Factors**: The targeted use of national strengths and skills makes improved fulfillment of quality goals possible (e.g., software development location and adaptation in terms of language and regional or national skills).

- **Flexibility Factors**: There is an increasing need to respond flexibly to changing demands. This necessitates permanently adapting a firm's capacity and performance limits to problem-specific demands. The virtual organization as an outcome of telecooperative work (presented in section 8.2.2) largely meets the demand for flexibility.

### Drivers of Workplace Dissolution on the Level of People and Their Work

Everything seems to indicate that Western industrial nations have undergone a far-reaching change in values since the early 1960s (see Klages 1984; von Rosenstiel / Djarrahzadeh / Einsiedler / Streich 1993; for an overview see von Rosenstiel 2002). This change in society's fundamental values and preferences has also led to the world of work making new demands and having new expectations. Jobs and working conditions that enable employees to harmonize their profession and private lives, and also include a high degree of self-sufficiency and flexibility are in demand. Acknowledgment, recognition, and personal development are the most salient motivating factors, especially for younger employees with high qualifications and high job expectations.

In the future, firms will have to carefully consider these continuing changes and new requirements. New organization models and economic goals cannot be realized without embracing employees' personal goals. Finally, enterprises will only survive and maintain their competitiveness as long as they can consistently use and develop human potential. In addition, management has to provide practical organizational and technical conditions to take advantage of employees' creative potential. In the final analysis, each individual firm will only survive if it pursues and utilizes these developments deliberately.

In many ways, telecooperative work models and organizational forms suit the new value system well. They enable individual ambitions in respect of self-determination, mobility, and independence, regarding this as a basic element of organizational concepts. Resistance at the management level is considered the main barrier to implementing telework, and demonstrates how far firms are from fully integrating their business aspirations and the aspirations of their employees (Reichwald et al. 1997).

## 8.2     Implementation Models of Dispersed Organizations

### 8.2.1     Telecooperation as Media-Supported Production of Goods and Services Based on the Division of Labor

Figure 8.2 provides an overview of the dimensions of media-supported work, the definitions used, and the aspects examined in this chapter. In the following section, telecooperation is viewed as a generic term for the media-supported production of goods and services based on the division of labor from three perspectives.

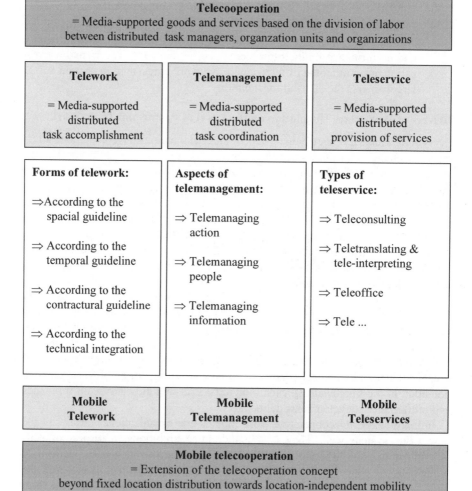

**Fig. 8.2.**     Telecooperation dimensions (based on Reichwald et al. 2000)

Each of them provides answers to one of three central problems:

- The telework perspective pursues the question of how human work is shaped by spatial distribution and mobility requirements.

- The telemanagement perspective examines how such a distributed task fulfillment can be coordinated.

- The teleservices perspective asks questions regarding the resulting products and services.

### 8.2.1.1 Telecooperation: Development from the Fixed Work Location to the Dispersed Work Location

There is much speculation on what future telecooperation will look like. Different models offer outlines of tomorrow's world of employment during a time of change in structures and values. They furthermore include new opportunities for enterprise action and individual goals, for supplying markets, for cooperation, and inventive ideas in respect of services and product marketing. Additionally, these models contain outlines of a novel image of man and tomorrow's world of employment. A workplace in familiar surroundings, such as a telecenter close to home, or a mobile workplace close to a customer, in a hotel, or in a vacation home provides employees with new forms of creativity and organizational leeway. An employee will not only be able to take advantage of flexible working hours and bear the responsibility of self-organization and motivation, but may (unfortunately) risk exclusion and isolation from other employees.

Information technologies enable the rearrangement of traditional business value chains. Furthermore, they make the restructuring of the organization's location, decentralization, as well as an increase in autonomy and the transfer of workplaces to residential areas possible. These trends towards organization restructuring can currently be observed. The predicted final stage will be the location-dispersed organization, i.e. the entreprise délocalisée (distributed enterprise) (Benchimol 1994), the global workspace (O'Hara-Devereaux/Johansen 1994) or the distributed organization (Grenier/Metes 1992). By means of the any time/any place vision, we have already gained a first impression of the consequences for the future world of employment. Although we have discussed some of the driving forces that may trigger and improve these trends, we cannot predict what kind of structures these organizations will have in the future. Moreover, we still do not know how to systematize and draw a clear dividing line between various successful types, many of which are discussed in the recent literature and have been partly experimented with in practice. The basic framework of these developments as depicted in figure 8.2 may be useful in this context.

Entrepreneurial organizations can be differentiated with regard to their location as follows:

- Location-bound organizations;
- Location-dispersed organizations;
- Location-independent organizations.

While participants in location-bound organizations mainly cooperate directly in the production of goods and services based on the division of labor, location-dispersed and location-independent (mobile) task accomplishment occurs through media support. The term telecooperation therefore denotes the entire spectrum of media-supported production of goods and services based on the division of labor.

In section 8.1, we already indicated that accomplishing tasks always means the coordination of tasks. This reflects the difference between telework as a media-supported, distributed achievement of tasks and telemanagement as a media-supported, distributed coordination of tasks. Since telecooperation pertains only to information-related tasks, the resulting product is always information. The product of telecooperation is a service and is labeled teleservice.

The differentiation into telework, telemanagement, and teleservice suggests three perspectives of telecooperation:

- The design, work performance and conditions (telework);
- The management of distributed task accomplishment (telemanagement);
- The delivery of results, their markets and customers (teleservice).

We examine each of these perspectives in the following sections.

### 8.2.1.2    Telework: Teamwork and Autonomous Individual Work

Telework is a recent, but not an entirely new phenomenon. The British FI Group, founded in 1962, is attributed with being the first to explicitly implement the concept of telework by having female programmers do their work at home. Today, this project is regarded as a precursor of the current practice of telework (e.g., Godehardt 1994). The academic discussion is based on Jack Nilles's research (1976) during the 1973 oil crisis in the US. He analyzed the possibilities of substituting commuting with data transmission and coined the term "telecommuting." This expression is still prevalent in the US and is largely synonymous with the English term "telework." The first steps towards telework were taken in the 1970s, followed by intensive academic examination and numerous euphoric predictions during the 1980s. Surprisingly few practical advances were, however, made in the eighties. Telework's current popularity is due to recent innovative concepts in economy, research, and politics. These developments were supported by numerous national and international initiatives and congresses (e.g., the conferences Telearbeit (1994), Telework (1994), Telecommute (1994)). The term "telework" is preferred as it implies work being done at a distance rather than on commuting, especially since much telework is done that has little to do with commuting aspects as such. The term also includes notions of independent, alternating, mobile and, generally, tele-cooperative forms of work. It further implies media-supported, dispersed task accomplishment utilizing a multitude of forms and types of workplaces. In the meantime, four basic forms of distributed work have emerged that, as basic forms of spatial decentralization for companies, offer new potential for flexibility (see figure 8.3 as well as Reichwald et al. 2000):

**Home-based telework** comprises all forms of telecooperation that is based on work from the home.

**Center-based telework** includes all forms of the bundling of teleworkplaces in telecenters (telework centers, teleservice centers) created for this purpose. The primary goals of telework centers, is to bundle companies' outsourced workplaces locally. Teleservice centers are mainly intended to provide customer-oriented tele-services by utilizing a suitable organizational form.

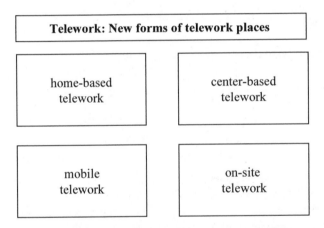

**Fig. 8.3.**     Four fundamental forms of the spatial flexibility of workplace design (Reichwald et al. 2000)

**On-site telework** denotes telework at the customer or supplier's location or, generally, at the value-adding partner's location. In many career tracks it is currently an everyday occurrence to work "on site" while staying in close contact with the organization via telecommunication media (customer-based work).

**Mobile telework,** i.e. location-independent work at a "mobile workplace" is also rather common these days, but this tends to be a form of dispersed work that is not often taken into consideration. Through the implementation of information and communication technologies (mobile radio, mobile computing), considerable reorganization and support potentials have arisen for management, as well as field service work in industry and services, but also for the craft, trade, and construction professions. These technologies' potential benefits have not as yet been fully exploited.

Up to this point, the discussion of the basic forms of telework has mainly addressed the differing approaches to the spatial flexibility of workplaces. When exploring the possibilities for telecooperative task accomplishment, the working hours and schedule, type of contract, and type of technical infrastructure should also be considered in addition to exploring the workplace (see figure 8.4 and Reichwald et al. 2000).

| Forms of telework | |
|---|---|
| **Workplace**<br>• Home-based telework<br>• Center-based telework<br>• On-site telework<br>• Mobile telework | **Working hours and schedule**<br>• Permanent – part time<br>• Fixed – variable<br>• Synchronous – asynchronous |
| **Contractual Regulation**<br>• Teleworker<br>• Telemanager | **Technical infrastructure**<br>• Offline telework<br>• Online telework |

**Fig. 8.4.** Forms of telework (Reichwald et al. 2000)

**Characteristics of the telework:** We need to differentiate between the workplace being at home (home-based telework), at telecenters close to the home (center-based telework), "on site" at the customer or supplier's location (on-site telework) or location-independent (mobile telework). Although Olsen (1983) already suggested a differentiation along these lines in the 1980s, for a long time only the extreme form of (usually isolated) telehomework was implemented in practice. With telehomework, the workplace was completely relocated to the home. In the interim, the advantages offered by the various forms of telework have been recognized.

**Characteristics of the working hours and schedule:** One needs to clarify whether the work is carried out in a decentralized workplace (permanent telework in a satellite office), in variable forms (alternating telehomework, with a part of the week spent at the home workplace and the remaining time on site at the company's location), or in freely chosen locations and time. Moreover, one needs to decide if a teleworker works fixed working hours, flextime, or is fully independent with regard to time.

**Characteristics of the form of the contract:** They are closely linked to the teleworker's legal status: Is this a telework employee who is contractually employed by means of a full-time employment contract or by means of self-employment (teleentrepreneur and / or freelancer)? There is a spectrum of various possibilities between these two extreme forms of work.

**Characteristics of the technical infrastructure:** The deployment of information and communication technology infrastructures is a constituting element of telecooperation. Establishing teleworkplaces therefore requires decisions about the type of technical connection to these decentralized workplaces. Fundamentally, we differentiate between asynchronous offline work and synchronous online work. With offline work, reconciliation and information exchange is only possible at specific synchronization points in time. With synchronous online work, the various locations are permanently connected. Here too, various types of connections and arrangements are possible.

There is no specific favorite form of telework that can be identified from the variety of possible forms. In practice, telecooperation is presented as a combination of different implementation forms. In keeping with the task, work phase, and / or specific project demands, certain telecooperative forms may offer spatial, temporal, contractual or technical advantages.

### Deployment and Application Conditions of Telecooperative Work Forms

It is still unclear which organizational form is best suited to specific telework conditions and applications. In the early stages of coming to terms with these new work models, telework was employed for simple supportive tasks with well defined structures, lines of demarcation, and, above all, limited communication intensity (e.g., text and data acquisition). A study by the German Trade Union (Deutscher Gewerkschaftsbund or DGB) revealed that relocating firms' workplaces to domestic areas is appropriate for work with a high degree of autonomy in managerial and creative areas, as well as with result-oriented characteristics. This is found to be appropriate for employees in professions with relatively higher qualification levels (Fischer et al. 1993). However, both these recommendations pertain only to the extremes of home-based telework, revealing various contradictions and unanswered questions that need to be addressed.

These design recommendations reveal various paradoxical situations: The required division of labor in telecooperative work models tends to clash with organizational suggestions for the integration of tasks (Picot / Reichwald 1987). Recent trends towards the comprehensive implementation of teamwork concepts seem not to be compatible with autonomy-oriented individual work in telecooperative work arrangements (Ulich 1991; 1994). The latest proposed solutions that try to solve these contradictions and reap the benefits of teamwork are, however, equally controversial (e.g., Ulich 1994, p. 188) despite tendencies towards spatial decentralization: The concept of teamwork in satellite offices (Ulich 2001) organizes team members in decentralized units, making the maintenance of direct personal interactions between parties of major interest. On the other hand, the concept of virtual teams (e.g., Savage 1997) takes spatial distance between team members for granted; electronic networks should therefore support cooperative relationships (see Oberquelle 1991).

When addressing these problematic areas and considering solutions, we must differentiate between telework's design models and their incorporation into the surrounding labor system. Choosing a particular cooperative telework configuration can only be meaningfully accomplished in this context when larger, supraordinate work-related conditions and circumstances are considered.

Numerous projects have been undertaken for the exploration and evaluation of this new work form with some poor, some medium and some very successful results. What has, however, been missing are results with sufficient penetrating power or "critical mass". This will only become possible when competitive and strategic utility can be empirically verified through unambiguous transparency (Reichwald / Möslein 2000).

### 8.2.1.3   Telemanagement in the Context of Locomotion and Cohesion

Telecooperative work models make new demands on coordinating task accomplishments. They change management and work processes substantially, yet they also require inventive forms of self-organizing and self-coordinating from dispersed employees. Telemanagement, the generic expression for all media-supported forms of dispersed coordination of tasks, comprises patterns of both self-coordination and extraneous coordination. The following paragraphs mainly focus on management processes. For more information on aspects of self-organization and self-management, see Probst (1992).

Pan-organizational linkages, decentralization, and the globalization of companies make new demands on management strategies. Empirical surveys of transnational enterprises have demonstrated (Bartlett / Goshal 1991; Pribilla / Reichwald / Goecke 1996; Reichwald / Möslein 2001) that linking, decentralizing, and internationalizing go hand-in-hand with increased travel activities and the intensified use of telecommunication media by management. Despite the availability of mobile communication media, management personnel's travel activities will presumably increase in the future and not, as often presumed, decrease (telecommunication paradox).

Managing "invisible workers" presents a new challenge for managers. If possibilities for personal supervision diminish due to telecooperative arrangements, behavior-oriented management models will inevitably also fail. This, however, need not necessarily be a disadvantage: If managers learn how to supervise without observing employees constantly at their workplace, they will be free to focus on actual performance (Collins 1986, p. 25; Godehardt 1994). Dispersed task accomplishment therefore replaces the result-oriented supervision of management by objectives (Di Martino / Wirth 1990) with behavior-oriented management. Management by (agreed upon) results, as well as management measures such as managers' frequent discussions with employees, personal qualification, career, and development processes can be a partial substitute for direct management. The degree to which management without personal supervision can succeed, mostly depends on the mutual trust between the employees and manager, the employees' motivation and qualification, as well as the type of planning and the structuring of tasks (Reichwald / Bastian 1999).

Empirical research on the influence of telemedia on management processes reveals (Grote 1993) that there is no technical communication form that can fully substitute the confidence and motivation building of face-to-face communication. Following this line of thinking, the supervision of employees in dispersed work locations has restrictions. These restrictions have far-reaching consequences for organizational conditions under which telecooperative work models are effective and efficient. The support of specific management tasks through electronic media is of particular importance.

Besides task-oriented group activities (locomotion function), an essential element of management is personal interaction, i.e. the building and nurturing of individual relationships (cohesion function). Depending on the chosen communication form, social presence is developed to a greater or lesser extent (Kiesler / Siegel /

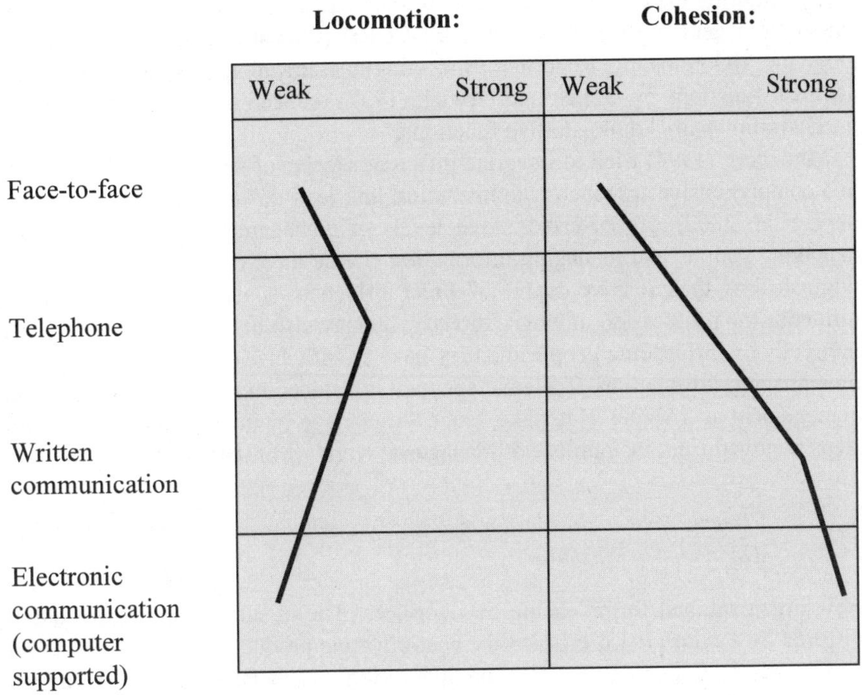

**Fig. 8.5.** Effects of electronic communication on management processes (based on Grote 1994)

McGuire 1984). The limitations of electronic communication media with regard to providing social presence encourage a business-like style of communication (Sorg / Zangl 1986). Electronic communication media are therefore not considered appropriate for all management tasks (Grote 1993): The use of telecommunication media for communication between managers and employees is considered rather appropriate for supporting group tasks and goals (locomotion).

On the other hand, according to empirical studies, computer supported communication forms like electronic mail (e-mail) are less useful for promoting social relationships (cohesion) between employees and managers (see figure 8.4). Accordingly, the choice of a technical communication form may influence the content, task-related, and social relationships of communication partners. Research indicates that locomotion-oriented management behavior correlates positively with group performance and cohesion-oriented management patterns, and is positively associated with team members' work satisfaction.

New ways of accomplishing telecooperative tasks may require a new understanding of the relationship between a manager and employee (see chapter 9). This is important, since the development of the management of organizations and the role of managers in organizations is directly connected to the development and improvement of the organization itself. Management as a distinct profession first emerged during the course of industrialization (e.g., Staehle, 1994). Fayol's (1916) classic management theory and the POSDCORB (Planning, Organizing, Staffing, Directing, COordinating, Reporting, Budgeting) classification of fundamental management functions by Gulick and Urwick (1937) reduced the role of manager to purely rudimentary administrative functions.

Mintzberg (1994) tried to integrate different aspects of successful management in a comprehensive approach with his "think-link-lead-do" model (see also Mintzberg et al. 2002). He describes three levels of management: Managing action, managing people, and managing information. These three different levels are distinguished by their relative degree of direct influence: A manager may be able to influence the progression of events directly; he may also be able to control actions indirectly by influencing people and may have an influence on individuals' actions by managing information. If telemanagement is reduced to managing information, management as a whole is at stake, since "to manage by information is to sit two steps removed from the purpose of managerial work" (Mintzberg 1994, p. 16).

### 8.2.1.4    Teleservices in the Customer Proximity and Resource Dependency Paradox

New organizational forms enable new services. The manufacturing organization inspired by Taylor (1913) enabled the cost-effective production of mass-produced goods, whereas today's modular manufacturing concepts, which are based on flexible manufacturing systems, enable the individualization of these industrial mass-produced goods (mass customization, see Pine 1993; Piller 1998a, 2001). Similarly, telecooperative organization designs based on a productive information infrastructure (Diebold 1994) offer the key to a new product class, i.e. teleservices (Reichwald and Möslein 1997b, 1998; Reichwald et al. 2000).

Teleservices are information products that can be offered, asked for, and exchanged via new telecommunication largely focused on the problems of designing fundamental technical infrastructure, i.e. the National Information Infrastructure (NII), as well as the Global Information Infrastructure (GII) (e.g., Benjamin / Wigand 1995; Wigand 1996). However, very few issues concerning the potential products, their markets, and the organizational forms required to produce such products have been researched satisfactorily. An extensive survey, initiated by the French government (Breton 1994b), analyzed the applicability of teleservices and compared the country's supply and demand structures internationally. Selected extracts from this survey, which provide an overview and introduction, are presented to familiarize the reader with the field of teleservice.

The product range of teleservices can be divided into seven segments. Figure 8.6 depicts selected applications and their respective teleservices.

These application segments provide only a one-dimensional and rough classification. Positioning the identified teleservices qualitatively with regard to relevant

| Application segment | Teleservices |
|---|---|
| **Functional teleservices** | • Teleconsulting<br>• Telesecretarial services<br>• Teletranslation<br>• Teleinterpretation |
| **Computer-related teleservices** | • Teleprogramming<br>• Teleinstallation and system maintenance<br>• Teleengineering<br>• Telesystems support<br>• Teledata security and archiving |
| **Teleservices in information processing and information transmission** | • Travel and airline bookings<br>• Electronic banking<br>• Electronic brokerage<br>• Electronic catalogues<br>• Electronic ordering and delivery systems |
| **Telelearning** | All forms of media-supported education and qualifications<br>• Teleinstruction<br>• Telelecturing<br>• Teleeducation |
| **Telemedicine** | General medical and specialist medical teleconsulting, teletreatment and telecare<br>• Telediagnosis<br>• Teleconsulting-hours<br>• Medical image processing and transmission |
| **Telesurveillance of sites, infrastructure installations and processes** | Telesurveillance of, e.g., buildings, elevators, alarm installations, air conditioning plants, supply sites, transport routes, production,... |
| **Teleservices for private end-users** | • Pay TV<br>• Video-on-demand<br>• Teleshopping<br>• ... |

**Fig. 8.6.**   The product range of teleservices (based on Breton 1994b, p. 20; Reichwald et al., 2000)

supply and demand assessment criteria provides a detailed depiction of potential use. Figures 8.7 and 8.8 display the resulting portfolios that systematizes tele-services into:

- The service delivery's capital and qualification intensity for the provider (supplier);
- The services supply's depth of performance (single step, partial process, to-tal process) and the specificity of service customers (buyers).

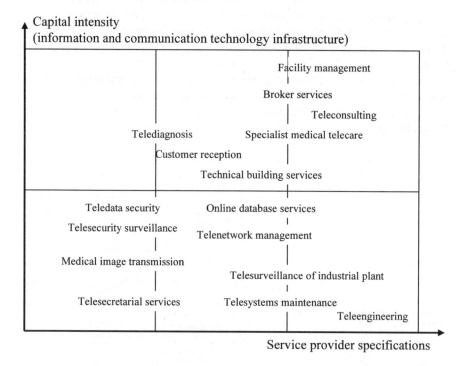

Capital intensity
(information and communication technology infrastructure)

Facility management

Broker services

Teleconsulting

Telediagnosis          Specialist medical telecare

Customer reception

Technical building services

Teledata security       Online database services

Telesecurity surveillance

Telenetwork management

Medical image transmission

Telesurveillance of industrial plant

Telesecretarial services    Telesystems maintenance

Teleengineering

Service provider specifications

**Fig. 8.7.**   Capital and qualification intensity of the supply side (based on Breton 1994b, p. 26)

The illustrated spectrum of useful teleservices clearly demonstrates that the poten-tial of telecooperative task accomplishment reaches far beyond opportunities for the spatial decentralization of workplaces. Basically, telecooperation allows all types of information products to be offered in the form of professional services. This has far-reaching consequences on decisions whether to make or buy informa-tion services, the centralization vs. decentralization of service delivery, as well as the international division of labor within the information production area.

In respect of teleservices, Breton's study considers only services that are ex-changed between firms. Intra-organizational services as a form of work relation-ships are not considered. This restriction in respect of the service provider's legal

**Performance quality
of external services**

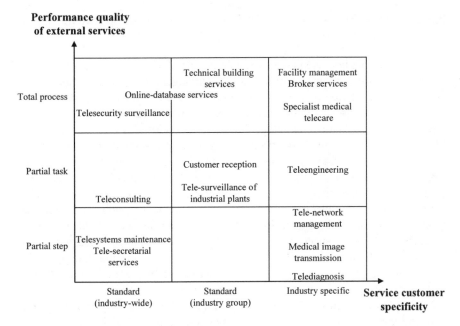

**Fig. 8.8.**    Depth of performance of service providers and specificity of service recipients (based on Breton 1994b, p. 28)

status seems to be unnecessarily narrow and is reminiscent of the previous restrictions that only allowed the use of the term telework in respect of conventional employees. We may, however, assume that the tendency towards increased dispersed service provision can often appropriately replace office and administrative tasks that have to date been done internally.

With regard to the risks and potentials of teleworking, the study (based on the restricted terminological definition) concludes that:

- The greater the willingness to outsource, as well as the willingness to accept advanced information technology, the greater the expected development potential of teleservices.

- The greater the willingness to outsource as well as the degree of internationalizing, the higher the potential for the relocation of service delivery to a foreign country.

The deployment of mobile information and communication technology expands the possibilities of location-independent telecooperative work forms with regard to their location-independent dimension. Telework, telemanagement and teleservice are equally impacted by this dimension of mobility. They confront business administration research and management practice with new tasks and pose new challenges, but they also offer new opportunities.

## 8.2.2  Virtual Enterprises as an Outcome of Telecooperative Work Models

Advanced information technologies enable the dissolution of temporal and spatial dependence as constraints of organizational arrangements. What are the advantages of the dissolution of such organizational boundaries for various institutions? Are classical hierarchies with fixed locations going to be replaced by location-independent "electronic hierarchies"? (Benjamin / Wigand 1995; Malone 1994; Malone / Yates / Benjamin 1986) Will the opportunities that dispersed locations present promote the trend towards partially dissolved hierarchies and encourage the establishing of cooperative structures between markets and hierarchies? Or do hybrid cooperative structures only represent a temporary transition between the two ideal types, i.e. market and hierarchy? From an institutional and economic point of view (see chapter 2), a coordination form that lies in the spectrum between the market and hierarchy will always succeed in respect of the accomplishment of tasks based on the division of labor. This is due to such a coordination form minimizing the total cost of the production of goods and services (as the sum of the production and coordination costs). Media support basically provides all coordination forms based on the division of labor with new points of departure by enabling (telecooperative) solutions. How the increased adoption of telecooperative work models will influence institutional arrangements' relative advantages in the long run is only beginning to be understood (e.g., Benjamin / Wigand 1995; Ciborra 1993; Picot / Ripperger / Wolf 1999).

One organizational form that is gaining importance in theory and in practice as a result of information and communication networks' increasing influence is the virtual organization (see chapter 4, as well as Davidow / Malone 1996; Ettighofer 1992; Szyperski / Klein 1993; Mertens 1994; Bleicher 1996b; Reichwald / Möslein 1996a; Picot / Reichwald 1999; Reichwald et al. 2000). The virtual organization is the result of the targeted deployment of new telecooperation possibilities and describes the adept combination of different organization design strategies, thus simultaneously enabling efficiency and flexibility.

If we regard the term "virtual" in the sense of "not real," the justification for this organizational form is not immediately explicit from an economic standpoint. If the virtual enterprise is both internally and externally interpreted as a "shapeless structure" (Davidow / Malone 1996; Mertens 1994), it is at best different from the traditional enterprise. This difference, however, does not necessarily improve the enterprise. It is certainly not the much heralded cure all: "**The virtual corporation** will, we believe, for the first time tie all of these diverse innovations together into a single cohesive vision of the corporation of the twenty-first century. ... the virtual corporation, that results from integrating these components is so extraordinarily adaptable and fast moving as to almost overnight leave traditionally organized competitors far behind" (Davidow / Malone 1996, p. 17; emphasis in the original). Exaggerated euphoria is, of course, not advisable: Contingency theory clearly demonstrated that there cannot be "one best way" of organization design (e.g., Hill /

Fehlbaum / Ulrich 1998; Kieser / Kubicek 1992; Kieser 1998; Picot 1999). Numerous attempts to deduce universal design principles from early organizational and theoretical approaches failed in the past. Consequently, today's organization theory focuses on the conditions under which forms of organization design are observable (descriptive approach) and / or can be recommended (normative design approach). This design aspect is the focus of attention in our discussion of the virtual organization.

Based on their changed legal and technological conditions, virtual organizations may be viewed as a further development of hybrid coordination forms within the spectrum between market and hierarchy (see chapter 2). They are linkages between firms that are based on the division of labor. Symbiosis as a fundamental idea is therefore of vital importance for their existence. Chapter 6 viewed symbiotic organizational networks as long-term enterprise linkages. Where, however, do the differences lie between enterprise networks and a virtual organization? Although an unambiguous boundary cannot be delineated, it is possible to characterize a virtual organization according to unique features and characteristics. Accordingly, four main questions can be addressed (Reichwald / Möslein 1996a; Reichwald et al. 2000):

- What is the theoretical basis of the virtual organization concept?

- What are typical characteristics and design principles of virtual organizations?

- Which design goals are pursued by means of these design principles?

- Under which conditions are the development of design goals meaningful?

*8.2.2.1 Virtuality as a Performance Improvement Concept*

In various ways, the concept of virtuality is important for architectural principles in the information systems and science area (e.g., Jessen / Valk 1986; Siegert 1991). Hardware architecture's capacity and flexibility limitations should be overcome through the conceptual differentiation between physical and logical computer components. The concept of virtual system components allows, for example, numerous "clients" of a single system to be given the impression that they are the sole users. The "client" is only aware of the logical system, but is not aware that his requirements are ultimately fulfilled by means of a dynamic transfer from logical to real system components.

The virtuality concept in the area of computer memory architecture is probably the most suitable and most cited example of virtual organization architecture. The creation of swappable virtual memory is based on the trade-off between the speed, cost, and capacity of the storage media. High-speed memory is relatively expensive and, consequently, is acquired only sparingly. In contrast, low speed memory is comparatively cheap. Theoretically, it is almost limitlessly at one's disposal. If an order has to be filled that needs to be carried out quickly in spite of great capacity requirements, the logical overall memory assigns it to a small, but fast real memory.

Through a clever combination of heterogeneous components with varying performance characteristics (e.g., speed, high capacity, low costs) inside the system, a certain impression can be created externally, (depending on the demands that the system is able to perform, e.g., almost as fast, as the fastest; as big, as the biggest; as cheap, as the cheapest). With the help of virtual concepts, each specific system component does not have to accomplish all demands optimally and simultaneously, even if the goals are partly contradictory. The concept's function goes back to the 1950s' "idea of sampling extraction", which means: If only one particular snapshot of the world (i.e. the overall memory) is in use at a specific time (or period of time) within task processing, the whole system can be optimized by creating an appropriate snapshot (extraction) of the world. Dynamic storing processes swap in and out of the core memory and can therefore influence the allocation of resources within the system.

It is obvious that this technical concept, created to increase computer architecture performance, cannot be entirely transferred to social systems and the architecture of organizations. However, there are several analogies that can be currently identified that represent virtual units within enterprises. Translation agencies, collaborating with others, independent translation agencies (and/or freelance translators) on an international basis are all a concrete example of this virtual enterprise concept that is actually a worldwide network. Such an agency therefore forms a virtual organization that operates worldwide. It is able to provide translations by qualified professional translators in (almost) every language and in (almost) any field. Each contract or assignment makes use of only specific extracts of the entire system. This small extract is the "organization," that configures and reconfigures itself, depending on the specific assignment. This short-term organization dissolves after completing the purpose for its existence. All the actors contribute their specific performance and qualification profiles to the virtual enterprise. Each can be a member of different, entirely independent, as well as concurrent "organizations." Task accomplishment does not occur in static, pre-defined structures, but as a problem-oriented, dynamic networking of real resources to tackle concrete tasks.

Analogous to the virtual concept of computer memory architecture, a virtual enterprise is equipped with much more capacity than a traditional, legal organization unit with its human, technical, infrastructural or financial resources available in its core areas. In a virtual organization, company performance conditions and traditional organizational boundaries lose their importance. Telecommunication technologies make it mostly possible to perform tasks regardless of time and space. Consequently, creating communication networks with business partners in all functional areas can extend spatial capacity limits. Linkages with suppliers and/or customers can extend the development potential; linkages with market partners can extend the range of products and services. Even linkages with competitors are important at times when a temporarily extended production capacity becomes available (e.g., to accomplish large-scale orders such as the construction of a major airport that cannot be handled by one company only). An expansion of temporal capacity boundaries occurs when an enterprise has dispersed its work locations over numerous time zones. Thus, a globally operating company can provide services like consulting, remote diagnosis, maintenance or provide order status information around the clock through the use of telecommunications technologies (Wigand 1996). The customer's inquiry is forwarded to the work location on duty in a particular time zone. The inquirer or customer is not even aware of the real location that provides the information. Ignoring time limits is already part of today's internationally operating airlines, security services, software development firms, high-tech services, and others.

Virtual enterprises develop through a network of physically dispersed organization units, participating in a coordinated, value-added process based on the division of labor. A multitude of persons, who are in varying degrees 'organized' into the organization units, form the professional core areas. These persons accomplish their enterprise missions internally or externally and, in addition, they themselves are associated through various cooperative arrangements with other persons. Even the professional core may consist of organization units that are either physically dispersed or in a fixed location. Virtual organizations are considered an alternative to organizational forms with long-term internally and externally defined boundaries, a stabile location, and relatively durable resources. Such an enterprise is able to improve its performance through the dissolution of traditional temporal and spatial limits and structures beyond the point that would be possible through traditionally available resources. In reality, however, the virtual organization concept can only be realized when the necessary resources, especially the qualified human resources, are actually available. For a discussion of these possibilities, as well as the conditions and limits of access to qualified human resources, the reader is referred to chapter 9.

### 8.2.2.2   Characteristics and Design Principles of Virtual Organizations

The virtual organization as an architectural concept of information systems and science was broadly discussed in the previous section and analogies of entrepreneurial organizations were presented. Apparently, this organizational concept of virtuality, created to increase performance, can be transferred to the architecture of organizations. However, the implementation of concepts always requires tangible applicability. Consequently, multiple strategies have recently been developed to design computer memory architecture. These strategies have turned out to be advantageous to a certain degree, depending on the definition of the requirements and task. It is still too soon to discuss virtual enterprises' specific design strategies and their particular advantages. It therefore seems more meaningful to highlight the characteristics and fundamental design principles of virtual enterprises (Reichwald et al. 2000).

Virtual enterprises manifest themselves as dynamic networks of organization units. Single network nodes can be set up by authorized individuals, organization units or organizations. The connections between single nodes are established dynamically and in a problem-oriented fashion. Task-oriented assignments therefore determine a virtual enterprise's structure at a given point in time. In spite of its fleeting nature, this organization structure is not shapeless, as performance increases through virtuality are only attainable within systems if the fundamental components can meet the demands of specific basic tasks appropriately. Accordingly, we can isolate characteristics that are essential for virtual enterprises and their goal attainment (see figure 8.9):

| Characteristics | Implementation principles |
|---|---|
| • Modularity<br>• Heterogeneity<br>• Time and spatial distribution | • The open-closed principle<br>• Complementarity principle<br>• Transparency principle |

**Fig. 8.9.**    Characteristics and implementation principles of virtual organizations (Reichwald et al. 2000)

Modularity: Modular units are the building blocks of a virtual enterprise, i.e. relatively small but manageable units with decentralized decision-making competence and responsibilities (see chapter 5). While chapter 5 interpreted the creation of modules as an internal structural concept, virtual enterprises also require "virtual modules" for their realization. These are units consisting of clients and customers, who can belong to different legal institutions. There is no efficient and dynamic way of reconfiguring a system, if its components do not have a high degree of modularity, as well as internal consistency and external openness.

Heterogeneity: The building blocks of a virtual enterprise have varying performance profiles with regard to strengths and competencies. A targeted focus on core competencies creates the necessary prerequisites for the formation of a symbiotic relationship (see chapter 6). Without the qualitative variation of the components, the system's dynamic reconfiguration is limited to a purely quantitative order of magnitude. It follows that the hoped for realization of performance goals, for example, with regard to quality and flexibility, will be lost. Moreover, advantages gained over other organizational forms are questionable.

Time and Spatial Distribution: The building blocks of virtual enterprises are spatially distributed, i.e. they depend on dynamic reconfiguration (see chapters 4 and 7). The possibilities of telecooperative task accomplishment therefore constitute the emergence of virtual enterprises. Information and communication technology infrastructures, however, also define the system's boundaries and limitations.

The three characteristic features of virtual enterprises, as illustrated above, are directly linked to fundamental design principles, which constitute a virtual enterprise's very essence:

The Open-Closed Principle: The open-closed principle is based on the virtual enterprise's modularity. Owing to their modular construction, virtual organizations appear on the market cohesively while simultaneously also manifesting open and dynamic structures. A customer places an order with a company that he / she trusts and which seems to be optimally tailored to his / her needs. The visible "envelope" of such an enterprise presents itself to the customer as a cohesive unit. However, the actual custom-built organization, which has to carry out the order, does not construct itself until the process of task accomplishment has been initiated. The internal structure (the content of the envelope) forms the open system.

The Complementarity Principle: This principle is based on the heterogeneity of the nodes that constitute a virtual enterprise. Modular units with varying performance profiles enhance one another through complementary competencies in the sense of symbiotic organizational configurations.

The Transparency Principle: The transparency principle refers to a virtual enterprise's temporal and spatial distribution. Consequently, the user can regard the entire virtual enterprise as a black box. Furthermore, the user only recognizes the envelope and is not concerned with the exact location where performance per se occurs. In spite of and / or especially because of this permanent reconfiguration, the enterprise appears to be especially tailored to the user's needs at any time.

At first, the described characteristics and design principles seem to be very abstract. The translation agency example, however, puts these characteristics and principles into more concrete terms. In addition, the "Worldwide Group" scenario (see the beginning of this chapter) presented a visionary form of virtual enterprise that contained all the features just discussed. These fundamental characteristics and basic principles help us to judge to what extent virtual enterprises are indeed able to increase their performance as an organizational concept by means of virtuality. The design of virtual enterprises is additionally enabled by already known, common organization design strategies. Moreover, the demarcation of virtual enterprises' organizational characteristics allows the scope of their applications to be determined. The following section focuses on the goals that can be pursued by these design principles and the task-oriented conditions and settings under which their application is appropriate.

### 8.2.2.3  Perspectives of Organization Design

Flexibility is the main goal when forming virtual organizations. It describes an organization's capability to dynamically adapt to changes in the environment. While stabilizing strategies maintain organizations' internal stability with regard to external forces, flexibility strategies try to achieve adaptability and the capability to process change actively (Klimecki / Probst / Gmür 1993). As a rule, stabilizing strategies are more efficient if there are only few environmental changes and / or little variability in demands. However, the more turbulent the environmental conditions and / or the higher the demand variability, the more successful a flexibility strategy will be. Flexibility strategies were long considered a waste of resources and efficiency in organization theory, for example, the formation of organizational slack, the development of redundant structures, and the creation of loose couplings (see Staehle 1991). These strategies mainly represent an intra-organizational application to increase flexibility (Reichwald / Behrbohm 1983; Kaluza / Blecker

1999). The organization itself continues to exist, but its internal potential to cope with and process environmental change is increased.

The flexibility approach of virtual organizations is, however, perceived differently. It questions the very existence of all organization structures. In other words, virtual organizations configure themselves along a task orientation, for which they use information and communication technologies' flexibility potential. For many years, enterprises' use of technology was determined by efficiency perspectives. In fact, advanced technologies increased productivity, but always at the expense of flexibility. Competing goals developed, as well as an incompatible trade-off between the productivity and flexibility concepts (Wigand 1995d). More recently, modern information technology has allowed lost flexibility to be partially recovered (see figure 8.10; Klimecki / Probst / Gmür 1993).

It has therefore had an enormous influence on organizational flexibility. Nevertheless, this influence does not always seem to be completely beneficial. Lucas and Olson (1994) emphasize the immense flexibility potential that information

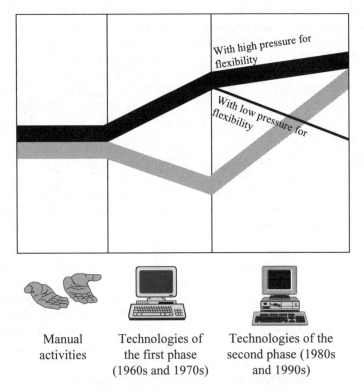

**Fig. 8.10.**     Technical developments in work environments regarding flexibility and productivity (based on Klimecki / Probst / Gmür 1993)

technology utilization can bring about. They address flexibility improvements in three primary areas:

- Changing the temporal and spatial dimensions of performance;
- Increasing performance speed; and
- Improving enterprises' response time to market changes.

The authors moreover point out the flexibility paradox when information technology is deployed. This is based on the differences between organizational and technical flexibility. Basically, information technology can increase the degree of organizational flexibility. Flexibility can change over time, triggering an opposite effect, i.e. resulting in organizational rigidity and inflexibility. This phenomenon is based on the inherent inflexibility often embedded in an aging technical infrastructure.

How can a virtual organization become flexible? This cannot be achieved by only focusing on the flexibility potential provided by the technical infrastructure. The infrastructure is only the foundation that allows organizational problems to be partially reduced (Möslein 2001). Therefore, virtual organizations aim at:

- Achieving "virtual largeness" despite "actual smallness;"
- Taking advantage of centralization within a decentralized structure; and
- Eliminating the contradiction between generalization and specialization.

Figure 8.11 provides an overview of the expected positive and negative flexibility effects of the first and second order.

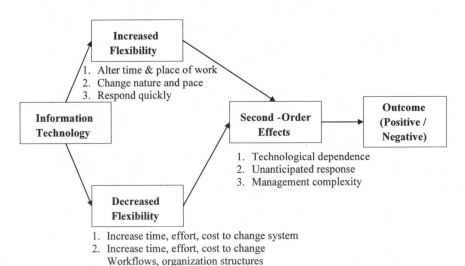

**Fig. 8.11.**   Information technology and organizational flexibility (based on Lucas / Olson 1994)

**"Virtual largeness" despite "actual smallness":** Today's global trade and investments in technology and innovation demand largeness. Growth and largeness are considered relevant for companies' success on the market and for competition. Largeness is, however, also considered a synonym for sluggishness. Inflexibility and inefficiency that are associated with largeness should therefore be avoided. Until recently, economic goals such as economies of scale or economies of scope could only be achieved by solid economic growth. In today's world, however, the impact of information and communication technologies does not only favor small companies (see Scott Morton 1992; Brynjolfsson / Malone / Gurbaxani / Kambil 1993; Wigand 1995d), but they gain the potential to grow to virtual largeness (Gurbaxani / Whang 1991). Virtual organizations' open-closed principle and their dispersion lead to their noticeable largeness on the market. Largeness is achieved through symbiotic cooperation structures as a result of the shared use of resources and / or financial means. Vertical integration strategies are very often associated with the disadvantages of competition, while the visible shift towards outsourcing and downsizing also leads to vertical disintegration. Conversely, however, virtual organizations take advantage of virtual integration concepts through the multiple linkages between independent units (e.g., Voskamp / Wittke 1994). This concept results in virtual organizations experiencing an "insiderization of outsiders" (Peters 1994), which refers to the breakdown of formal organizational boundaries between the inside and the outside.

**Centralization despite decentralization:** When deciding between centralization and decentralization, organizations have to decide which instruments from the market-hierarchy continuum they want to use to coordinate economic activities and under which conditions (see Picot / Neuburger 1997a; Picot 1999). Complete centralization means self-sufficiency; complete decentralization implies the transfer of all tasks to independent entrepreneurs. To what extent should firms take advantage of centralized (i.e. hierarchic) or decentralized (i.e. market) organizational forms to accomplish their tasks? There are, unfortunately, no ready-made solutions and either-or answers. It is therefore essential to find an intermediate solution that combines an appropriate mixture of centralization and decentralization. Centralization and decentralization's extreme positions are, however, often perilous. Complete centralization could trigger a breakdown due to too many demands made of the central authority. On the other hand, a decentralized solution cannot work if there are no appropriate centralized frameworks, infrastructures, etc.

**Generalization despite specialization:** Generalization requires sufficient redundant resources for entrepreneurial organizations, as well as for organization units and individuals (Staehle 1991). In the accomplishing of a single, specific task, generalists inevitably cause higher costs and lower efficiency than a specialist who is specifically assigned to this task. However, the specialists' advantage disappears immediately if the accomplishment of tasks bundles occurs in a dynamic and uncertain environment. Figure 8.12 illustrates this relationship. The advantages (degree of fit) of a specialist (B) lie in the interval of low environmental variability (n, m), while the advantages of this interval's external generalization become clear. Through their modularity and heterogeneity, virtual organizations can simultaneously achieve a generalized external appearance (e.g., performance offer) and exploit cost advantages through single components' internal specialization (Reiss 1992b). Again, we remind the reader of the translation agency example, as it illustrates the generalizing strategy despite specializing. Each translator is a specialist in a specific combination of languages and in a particular field. The virtual enterprise "translation agency" is able to offer the market a whole range of languages and subjects by combining individuals' skills in a symbiotic network.

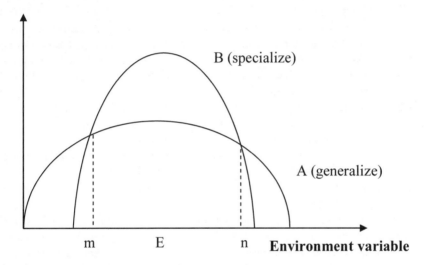

**Fig. 8.12.** Generalization versus specialization (Hannan / Freeman 1977, p. 947; cited by Staehle 1991, p. 341)

The question still remains when and under what circumstances it makes sense to utilize a virtual organization, including all of its flexibility potential. A virtual organization is only the appropriate organizational form if there is a need for a high degree of flexibility. If a task is characterized by a high degree of product complexity and high market uncertainty, this situation requires the formation of temporary task-related cooperative structures (to control uncertainty) in which competencies complement each other well (to control complexity). Accordingly, this type of organization lends itself to an organizational innovation strategy with which to accomplish complex, highly variable problems, or for tasks reflecting a high degree of novelty in an uncertain environment.

## 8.3 Explanatory Approaches for Dispersed Organizations

### 8.3.1 Virtualization from a Competitive and Strategic View

As discussed so far, organization design goals enable the virtual organization to realize a very high degree of flexibility. However, what are the conditions under which an organization can meaningfully deploy these ideas? A virtual organization is only a suitable organizational form when the performance characteristics associated with virtualization are truly required (see chapter 5). While the traditional hierarchy will continue to be a suitable organizational form in terms of economic efficiency, uncertain market conditions and complex product characteristics make different demands. Under conditions of increasing product complexity, there is an increased need for modular organization structures. The need for organization interconnectedness (see chapter 6) increases, however, under conditions of increasing market uncertainty. If a task situation is characterized by both high product complexity and prevailing market uncertainty, this suggests the formation of temporary, task-related cooperative structures (in order to control uncertainty), in which complementary competencies enhance each other as much as possible (in order to control complexity). The virtual organization thus presents itself as an organizational innovation strategy for the control of complex, high-grade variable task generation, or for tasks with high levels of innovation in an uncertain world (Reichwald/Möslein 2000).

The virtualization strategy unifies aspects of organizational boundaries' dissolution in the internal (modularization) and external relationship (network formation) of the enterprise. Accordingly, virtualization has become an organizational form that expands traditional organizational boundaries. Nevertheless, it still very emphatically requires rules to coordinate dispersed collaboration: Technologies and tele-cooperation systems are a constituting element of such virtualization. Current approaches in organization theory are focused on team structures and modularization, organization network concepts, and symbioses. Organizational solutions are sought that will enable the efficient coordination of the delivery of goods and services in a turbulent environment or when there are complex demands. In the final analysis, it is the task that determines which solutions are economically efficient.

Virtualization as an organization strategy was already addressed by Mowshowitz's (1991) theoretical architecture concept of organization virtualization. Ettighoffers' (1992) model of future work in his book "L'Entreprise Virtuelle ou les Nouveaux Modes de Travail" ("The Virtual Enterprise of the New Work Forms", translation by the authors) is especially vivid. This practice-oriented design for a virtual organization also examines the concepts, implementation, and development trends of dispersed forms of work analytically. Many practical examples and insights identify dispersed forms of work, but they also identify wrong tracks taken and failures. For Ettighoffer, dispersed work is therefore not – as so often with other authors – an end in itself but an organizational necessity. It forms the basis for the implementation of innovative organization strategies (Eurotechnopolis Institut 1994).

For Ettighoffer, the virtual enterprise is a new form of a post-Tayloristic company organization. It does not substitute traditional and work organizational forms, but symbiotically complements them through its coexistence, thus also influencing and changing them. Ettighoffer emphasizes three key peculiarities of the virtual organization (1992):

- "L'ubiquité" – ubiquity (i.e. location or site independence): This is increasingly enabled by the technical feasibility concept of telepresence and manifests itself in the improved possibilities to utilize external expert knowledge, to utilize distant management resources, as well as the viability of maximum market proximity.

- "L'omniprésence" – omnipresence (i.e. time independence): It is being increasingly improved by the new possibilities of flexible automation, such as the automatic acceptance or transmission of orders. This results in a more intensive utilization of the equipment and assets (and thus an improved capital productivity), improvement of the service quality, and availability, as well as an increasingly closer integration of customers and suppliers.

- "Neuroconnexion" – the integration of knowledge resources: It is enabled by new information and communication technologies and manifests itself in the increased building of specialist networks.

Ettighoffer's design illustrates that the real economic potential can be found in the combination of technical and organizational virtualization. If, with continuing technological development, space and time become less important as boundaries of organization design, the advantage gained from alternative organization strategies will also change. Even complex coordination mechanisms will then be viable. Networks in which complex, multilateral coordination processes substitute simple, hierarchical instruction and control mechanisms are becoming increasingly important. The architectural concept of virtualization is thus becoming a sustainable competitive strategy for companies (Möslein 2001).

Virtual enterprises arise through the task-specific integration of distributed organization units that are part of a coordinated, value-adding process based on the division of labor. Around the professional core are a multitude of actors linked in ad hoc cooperational forms that are also linked to other such cooperations and actors. Virtual organizations are thus an alternative to existing organizational forms with long-defined boundaries between inside and outside, which are tied to a particular location and have a relatively long-lasting resource allocation. Through the dissolution of local and temporal boundaries and in conjunction with the dissolution of traditional enterprise limits and structures, an enterprise may deliver more goods and services to the market than would have been possible through immediately available resources (Reichwald / Möslein 1996a).

## 8.3.2  Virtualization from an Institutional Economics Perspective

From an Institutional economic perspective, we need to answer two questions with regard to virtualization: How can one ensure that all virtual organizations have incentives for all partners to make decisions efficiently? Furthermore, how does one know under which conditions a virtual organization is the most efficient organizational form? Virtual organizational forms are only sustainable when they are staffed with motivated and qualified actors. Consequently, the management of virtual organizations faces the following demands:

- The development of trust;
- Cooperation and a relationship orientation;
- Co-worker orientation;
- Customer orientation.

Room for maneuvering is expanded and / or created by the minimum contractual certainty, a potentially frequent change of partners, the coordination of location-dispersed modules, as well as the shifting and overcoming of spatial and organizational boundaries. Moreover, co-workers and cooperation partners' behavior in markets can no longer just be controlled by conventional (hierarchical) control measures requiring a personal presence or through complete contracts. This requires the development of trust-based relationships. In addition, institutions are required to ensure the functionality of the trust mechanism (Ripperger 1998).

The flexible incorporation of internal and external partners and modules, the swiftly changing collaboration configuration of the virtualization partners, as well as the associated swift dissolution of the virtual organization ultimately demand that management displays stronger cooperation and relationship orientation (see section 8.3.3). While the care of relationships and relationship management are of primary concern to static networks, dynamic networks are more concerned with the actual configuration and interface management in operational processes. Intrinsic and extrinsic incentives should also be designed so that co-workers are motivated to deliver good performances. Consequently, the relationship between co-worker satisfaction and customer orientation needs to be taken into consideration (Heskett et al. 1997; Picot / Neuberger 1998a; Kreis-Engelhardt 1999).

Within the context of an institutional economic concept, virtual enterprises can be regarded as efficient organizational forms (Picot / Neuburger 1998a). Virtualization offers companies the opportunity to react efficiently and quickly to changing market conditions. Consequently, opportunities arise for the development and application of numerous organizational ideas. The competition between various organizational forms forces each of them to function at maximum capacity, as well as to develop efficiency-based incentives for the virtualization partners. Consequently, given that their communication and coordination function effectively, organizations become more capable than when they merely compete among themselves (i.e. with their peers) (Picot / Wolff 1995).

## 8.3.3  Virtualization from a Communication Theory Perspective

In spite of the multitude of current concepts of virtual organizations, there is one point of consensus: Virtual organizations make special demands on communication (see chapter 3). Since partners are mostly not together or close to one another, a tight and flexible communication link is crucial. This not only serves to generate and exchange new ideas, to provide feedback or to coordinate, but also to enable easy and quick access to joint databases and project documents and records. The economic feasibility of virtual enterprises therefore requires an especially flexible communication infrastructure that connects the cooperation partners via individually tailored, quickly configurable, and yet transparent communication services. It is the nervous system of virtual organizations.

Organization and communication are inseparably linked. Communication within and between organizations has taken on many forms: Depending on the task, structures, and basic economic conditions, formal and informal channels are utilized for communication exchange between task bearers. Media support of the communication processes in organizations is therefore based on the division of labor and coordination in companies and markets. We therefore next focus on communication research's most important insights in order to better understand the rules of human communication as a key factor of the future working world (Reichwald 1993; Möslein 1998; Picot 1999; Reichwald et al. 2000; Wigand / Picot / Reichwald 1997).

Communication is an essential component of human existence and is a prerequisite for division of labor and coordination to function in companies and markets. Human communication is therefore also the key factor for virtualization. The insights that communication research offers, allow us to understand virtual enterprise structures better, and to recognize their advantages but also their pitfalls. The term communication is, however, regarded very differently by the various sciences (see chapter 3). In communications engineering, communication is understood as the process of transporting information, coding, physical transmission, and decoding of information. Aspects of understanding, interpretation, and the attribution of meaning, which all occur when humans communicate, are not taken into consideration. From a social science perspective of the term, however, understanding what is communicated is the focal point. From a business management perspective, the relationship between communication and task accomplishment is the most important: It is concerned with human understanding when tasks are executed.

Virtualization has effects on company leadership and also changes management's work. While traditional hierarchical organizational forms are mainly associated with centrally directive leadership mechanisms, the new organizational forms of virtualization make specific new demands on the leadership. The results of case study research (Pribilla / Reichwald / Goecke 1996) give rise to the assumption that new and partially very incompatible demands have emerged in respect of managers' work due to market-relevant, basic organizational business conditions, as well as global competition changes. These demands comprise the increasing need for intensive communication with a growing number of geographically distributed partners, but also the necessity of having to make ever more complex decisions while under increasing time pressure. Consequently, management's work situation is becoming increasingly acute with regard to pressures and demands.

Schreyögg and Hübl (1992) suggest that in the upper management levels, managers' situation intensifies continually in terms of its hectic pace, increasing volume of activities, and interruptions. Globally acting managers often find themselves within a time trap. Signs of this are increasing time pressure and a high volume of tasks to be accomplished, the need to react quickly to critical situations and compulsory public relations, internal leadership, and external networking. These managers have to complete a level of activities that is nearly double what it was 25 years ago. Although the various telemedia are co-contributors to this increasing time pressure, task-appropriate media utilization is also a problem solver. It offers scope for better time management, for screening, and reduces various burdens.

Communication and cooperation are tightly interlinked with each other. From management research, we know how tightly management is usually integrated into a network of cooperative relationships. Whether we are concerned with information acquisition, decision-making processes, planning changes or whatever the underlying tasks may demand, management coordinates, delegates, receives preliminary work from subordinates, and usually depends on cooperation partners' contributions. One of the main stumbling blocks for uninterrupted internal cooperation and communication is managers' unavailability. Via telemedia, it is possible to maintain the information flow between management and their immediate work environment (secretarial offices, personal co-workers, internal partners).

Coordination and management costs in virtual organizations are tightly linked to the overcoming of the boundaries and barriers of telemanagement. Communication costs primarily arise through face-to-face communication contacts with distant partners. When considering top management's high traveling costs in respect of personal meetings, the resultant costs are mainly in the areas of personnel, travel, and opportunity costs. While the use of telecommunication media is regarded as quite suitable for communication between executives and co-workers in order to decrease the coordination costs of task support, these media are still regarded as less suited to foster social relationships (the cohesive function of leadership, see section 8.2.1.2). The more important the development and maintenance of relationship aspects are in interactive processes (co-worker relationships, customer relationships), the more efficient and cost effective face-to-face communication is. The more mere communication of content affects executive processes (e.g., the coordination of documents), the easier costs can be reduced by the deployment of telecommunication media – also across spatial distances (Reichwald et al. 2000).

### 8.3.4  Limits of Telecooperative and Virtual Organizational Forms

With regard to telecooperative and virtual organizational forms, we need to ask ourselves which fundamental forms of spatial flexibility are easier to implement and which ones more difficult. Moreover, which organizational forms promise strategic advantage for companies or meet the demands and expectations of co-workers most readily; which offer ecological and traffic-flow-enhancing problem solutions, or support regional or structural policy aims? (Reichwald et al. 2000; Englberger 2000) The implementation barriers in respect of telecooperative work forms are lowest where telecooperation is directly related to a company's competitive and strategic alignment, where customer loyalty, customer integration, flexibility, and efficiency are supported, and where business and co-operation partners' integration and availability are improved. Mobile telework and / or on-site telework at the customer, supplier or value-adding partner's location are therefore an especially effective work form. There is, however, very little empirical research evidence concerning these work forms. Their use, however, occurs without much furor, planned piloting or scientific monitoring or associated research efforts, but with much apparent success.

Telecooperative work forms face high implementation barriers when such an implementation has advantages for individual co-workers or the company as a whole. These advantages do not, however, have calculable or (in some way) assessable efficiency or cost effective advantages for the company. Telework at home, work at locations near one's residence, and customer-near telecenters are currently affected by the lack of verifiable evidence of their cost-accounting utility for the company. The best evidence is found where telework is practiced in the form of pilot projects.

Virtual organizations also manifest themselves across many boundaries: Across defined temporal and spatial boundaries, across boundaries of the legally defined inner and outer organization, or extending beyond long-range contractual boundaries as far as the organization participants' membership or non-membership is concerned. However, even this organizational form has its limits. On the one hand, these are the limits and boundaries of the technical infrastructure, which is an enterprise's nervous system and determines whether participation is possible (Jarvenpaa / Ives 1994). There are, however, also boundaries and limitations imposed on institutions by human behavioral patterns (see chapter 2; e.g., limited rationalism or opportunism). The theoretical bases of the role of information in respect of markets and firms – as developed in chapters 2 and 3 – as well as insights gained into communication and information behavior enable us to discover initial problem areas regarding virtual organizations' "boundarylessness." Just a few are briefly addressed here (see also Reiss 1996; Reichwald 1997a; Picot 1998a; Englberger 2000; Reichwald et al. 2000).

- Improved possibilities for the support of economic activities by means of modern information systems are a promising strategy for the extension of human performance limits. Human beings only have a limited capacity to process information (see chapter 3). We try to compensate for this through the use of information systems. It is possible, for example, to carry out invitations to tender at low costs and almost no waste of time, as well as to offer services and products online worldwide (Benjamin / Wigand 1995). Consequently, the costs of economic transactions are decreasing. The limits of dynamically built appropriate technical arrangements no longer depend on the costs of such arrangements, but on the quality of the electronically available information. Virtual organizations' practicality depends on the willingness to provide information and on the readiness to use the available information. Nevertheless, "No technology has yet been invented that can convince unwilling managers to share information or even to use it" (Davenport et al. 1992, p. 56; cited by Jarvenpaa / Ives 1994). What are the consequences for a virtual organization as an institution for the processing of economic activities?

- Trust is a crucial coordination mechanism for virtual organizations (Handy 1995). Opportunistic human behavior, in the sense of pursuing self-interests at other persons' expense, usually favors risk taking. The principal-agent theory is helpful in describing how opportunistic usage of asymmetrical information influences the relationship between a buyer and seller (see chapter 2, 'Principal-Agent Theory'; Picot 1993). Asymmetrical information can cause a delegation risk. The higher the behavioral uncertainty and the higher the risk of sustaining a loss, the more one requires safeguards. Likewise, the more complex and strategically important a performance is, the higher the interest in contractual guarantees (see chapter 7). Contracts are also traditionally used to provide performance guarantees. However, virtual organizations mostly avoid contractual guarantees in order to preserve their dynamic features. Trust is therefore their constituting element (e.g., Luhmann 1994, 2000; Fukuyama 1995; Kramer / Tyler 1996; Ripperger 1997). Consequently, contracts are based on trust (Luhmann 1989, 1994). Nevertheless, blind trust is definitely not recommendable. Virtual organizations based on trust are short-lived and dynamic and therefore require a long-term, stable and informal relationship, generally accepted reputations, and reliable certifications or "rules of the game." Only the long-range stability of the rules of the game guarantees an organization's flexibility (see Bonus 1994).

Virtual organizations are therefore concerned with cooperative problem solutions between loosely linked cooperation partners. The structures within which such cooperative relationships occur are dynamically configured and are only temporary. What does a suitable supply of information for such organizations look like and what incentive problems need to be considered? How are commercial law and power of decision distributed within such structures and how are they assigned? How can we appropriately and effectively address the fundamental problems of the principal-agent relationship between the contractor and agent (hidden characteristics, hidden action, hidden intention) in this organizational form? How should the contractual relations be structured so that sufficient flexible and discretionary action is possible, but the risk of opportunistic exploitation (with regard to the problems of incomplete and / or implicit contracts, see chapter 2) is limited?

There are no definitive answers to these questions. However, the set of problems that the questions address point toward one issue: The boundaries of virtual enterprises as a reputed "boundaryless" organizational form do not solely lie within the realm of technical feasibility. Adequate information and communication-technical infrastructures are indeed a necessary, but not a sufficient, prerequisite for the successful realization of this innovative organization strategy.

### 8.3.5   General Framework for the Global Dispersion of Organizations

Information and communication technologies are already generating a new industrial revolution globally. Technological progress enables us to exchange information at high speed and retrieve information in whatever form from databases. Today, various advanced work forms are already in many ways colliding with legal norms and current policies. Consequently, this information-based revolution requires an adjustable legal framework to make further technological developments possible, as these policies and laws were established under different circumstances and thus require further development and amendment. The intercontinental shipment of books, for example, requires customs formalities to be taken into consideration. The transfer of exactly the same information (i.e. the content of these books) via electronic data exchange can be carried out without delay or any additional formalities. Information and knowledge, as well as available human resources are becoming progressively important, although enterprises' balance sheets still focus on fixed and current assets.

In financial accounting, transfers of goods and money are entered into the books, but the exchange of information within or between organizations is not reflected. Information in particular is considered a key ingredient in the service sector and is often viewed as the primary production factor (Picot 1997b). It is, nevertheless, difficult to measure information quality, to determine its value or guarantee its protection. Organization theory and business practice still ignore the importance of information as a valuable resource (e.g., Wigand 1988a). If information is to truly play the important role in the future firm that is currently being predicted, what role does organization theory and business practice play?

The outcome of the 1995 G8-meeting, which is comprised of the most powerful industrialized Western countries, underlined the need for the global liberalization of telecommunication markets. Since then, the creation of a global information infrastructure (GII) as a prerequisite for the predicted information society is no longer just a vision. There are, however, numerous barriers that hamper the transition towards an information age: Strengthening existing network infrastructures and accelerating the construction of new ones; creating a clear and stable regulatory, as well as a legal framework; and discussing different international priority programs. Stimulating awareness, reducing fears, and coping with risks are crucial efforts that are required for development and advancement. It should be noted that similar and often parallel initiatives have been initiated throughout the world.

In December 1993, the European Commission presented future perspectives with the "White Paper on Growth, Competitiveness and Employment: The Challenge and Ways Forward into the 21st Century". Information and communication technologies, services, and applications were to be stimulated and ensure steady economic growth, augment competitiveness, as well as create new jobs, leading to an improvement in the quality of life. The US spared no effort to create an Information Highway and the already mentioned GII. Europe's step into the information society formally started with the Bangemann Report (1995).

The industrial age developed a new framework. In the information age, the world of work also requires a new framework. Currently, however, there are legal constraints that have to be updated in labor law, tax law, and laws pertaining to competition. Economic policies also require adjustments and extensions. However, these adjustments can no longer be made by individual nations alone, as the great diversity of legal systems influences questions pertaining to the distribution of workplaces and firms' cooperation decisions to an increasing extent. Europe is therefore trying to harmonize its differing systems deliberately and carefully. However, whether the diversity of national legal systems is ultimately a facilitator or barrier for firms, customers, workers, as well as society and the environment still remains to be answered.

## 8.4   The Role of Communication and Information Technology

Collaboration across location boundaries demands suitable communication and information infrastructures, since overcoming the boundaries of space and time is primarily a communication problem. In many areas, recent technological developments help to defuse this communication problem and thus improve collaboration between spatially dispersed partners (e.g., Reichwald / Englberger 1998a). If, for example, advice is required from specialists not available locally (teleconsulting), the phone limits the possibilities to express oneself and to demonstrate one's points in providing such advice. Consequently, additional video channels, or the integration of different media (text, data, voice, freeze-frame or moving pictures) within multimedia applications offer obvious improvements. These possibilities can, however, only be realized if effective communication infrastructures are available.

In the context of the BERKOM Project (1986 – 1991), numerous empirical studies were undertaken in Germany that assessed the market potential of digital broadband networks' future use (Kanzow 1991; Bierhals / Nippa / Seetzen 1991; Reichwald 1991). Eight general types of communication and information technol-

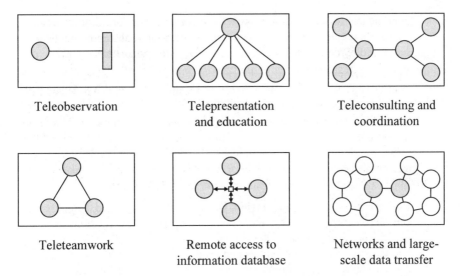

| | | |
|---|---|---|
| Teleobservation | Telepresentation and education | Teleconsulting and coordination |
| Teleteamwork | Remote access to information database | Networks and large-scale data transfer |

**Fig. 8.13.**   Basic types of broadband application deployment (based on Bierhals / Nippa / Seetzen 1991; Reichwald 1991a)

ogy applications emerged from approximately 1,000 applications. Based on communication theoretical considerations, these eight types of application can, in turn, be assigned to six basic structural types. Figure 8.13 depicts these six basic types.

To identify the deployment types, the BERKOM market analysis identified the following potential and application focal points (Reichwald 1991a):

- **Teleobservation:** Teleobservation allows procedures and processes to be controlled and regulated without anyone being specifically physically present at the actual location of the event. Regardless of the location, certain problems can therefore be analyzed and solved around the clock.

- **Telepresentation and Teleeducation:** Telepresentation and teleeducation comprises multimedia-based information processing from an information center to many participants in the communication process. Based on efficient network infrastructures, interactive communication becomes a communication process participant, for example, in the form of the joint processing of documents with parallel voice and video communication. This provides new ways of offering seminars and continuing education sessions, and makes it possible to offer co-workers or customers the existing knowledge potential directly, regardless of the time and location.

- **Teleconsulting and Telecoordination:** Teleconsulting and -coordination include the location-independent communication between a small number of individuals or just two. Being able to rapidly access multimedia documents and uncomplicated contact initiation with organization-internal information carriers can support this. The location-independent availability of

documents, as well as the possibilities for feedback and information retrieval, is unquestionably a significant application feature that needs to be
supported by communication and information infrastructures.

- **Teleteamwork:** Teleteamwork explores new forms of cooperation between
  work groups at geographically dispersed locations. In contrast to teleconsulting and cooperation, more participants are usually involved in teleteamwork. The possibility of interactive multimedia communication provides
  the potential for spontaneous reactions and the direct translation of new
  ideas. In conjunction with technical and cross-company cooperative efforts
  and alliances, teleteamwork therefore holds the promise of increased flexibility, a quicker response capability, and improved efficiency.

- **Remote Access to Information Databases:** Jointly used databases are
  central to the trends toward the globalization of business relationships (e.g.,
  worldwide research and development, international financial markets),
  mass customization of products and product-related services, as well as the
  completion of qualification requirements in the continued education sector.
  Infrastructures with sufficient bandwidth are required to enable the integrated archiving of multimedia documents so that they can, on demand, be
  retrieved from distant locations. Such knowledge pools also constitute the
  starting point of the emergence of self-reliant information markets (see chapter 7). Multimedia information may therefore be offered as an independent
  service and, based on supply and demand, may continue to develop quantitatively and qualitatively.

- **Networks and Large-scale Data Transfer:** The formation of computer
  connections and linkages with other computers enables the use of distant
  computing capacities (e.g., high-performance or specialized computers).
  The utilization of distant capacities is always important when extreme performance demands are at stake that cannot be delivered locally.

The discussed innovative areas of efficient communication and information infrastructure application should not, however, overlook the following: On the one
hand, the newest technologies are perceived as drivers of development. Videoconferencing systems, groupware and work-flow technologies, multimedia applications based on efficient traffic networks, mobile communication, and mobile computing form the infrastructural basis of innovative telecooperative concepts. On
the other hand, successful, practical deployment of such systems is still limited.
Their areas of application are still largely to be found within the high technology industry (e.g., multimedia industry) and / or in highly technical research and development sectors (Reichwald 1919b; Reichwald et al. 2000). Actual telecooperation
within other manufacturing and service industries is still limited to individual applications, as well as to communication via telephone, fax, electronic mail, simple data
transmissions, and terminal emulation (IDATE 1994). These technology building
blocks that have to date been isolated are, however, gradually growing together
into an integrated support system.

## 8.5 Implications for Management

New information and communication technology developments help to surmount traditional temporal and spatial boundaries. The dispersion and/or dissolution of locations are supported by advanced communication technologies. The mere distribution of locations does not, however, provide a company with a competitive advantage. The dispersion and/or independence of locations, (1) as a result of a specific time/space management in order to take advantage of specific locations, and (2) as a reaction to new demands in an environment whose complexity and dynamics are obviously increasing, lead to lasting advantages being realized in global competition.

### Disintegration of the Value Chain and Dispersion of Locations

Value linking and competence advantages are the result of dispersing a company's location. As mentioned above (see section 8.1.3), knowledge, skills, and abilities are heterogeneously distributed across the globe. By purposefully combining varying regional and national strengths, the entire organization's performance capacity may be improved. Griese (1992) refers to organizational opportunities that arise from global information and communication systems for networks and firms operating on a worldwide basis. He believes that the transition from a "real" to a "virtual" enterprise is linked to the systematic dissolution of the value chain: "The value chain is not actually fully present in all countries, however, within the firm, as well as from the customer and supplier's perspective, the firm and the entire value chain have a 'virtual' presence" (Griese 1992, p. 170 (translation by the authors); Griese 1993;

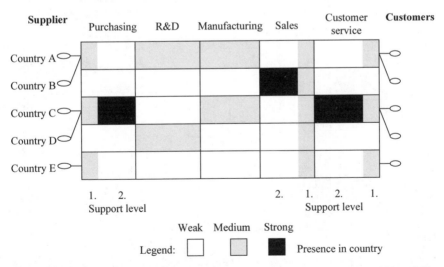

**Fig. 8.14.** Schematic interpretation of the disintegrating value chain (Griese 1992, p.171)

Mertens 1994). According to Griese, figure 8.14 depicts a schematic interpretation of the disintegrating value chain.

Simon, Bauer and Jägeler (1993) think that European management advantages lie in the targeted use of heterogeneity. They do not find advantages for European firms in the search for common ground, but in exactly identifying their differences and utilization: "A trouble-free combination of, for example, French communication capabilities, German organizational talent, and Italian flexibility and / or talent for improvisation, opens a European perspective that may create an almost unbeatable competitive advantage on their global market. A condition for this, however, would not only be mutual understanding and tolerance, but also a high sensibility to cultural and structural change, as well as to their strengths and weaknesses" (Simon / Bauer / Jägeler 1993, p. 119; translation by the authors). With their analysis of management cultures, structures and success factors in Germany, England, France, Italy and Spain, the authors present a model of a European-wide, work-location-dispersed firm in which "all functions and positions are filled in keeping with each country's strengths." Figure 8.15 depicts the working model of such an idealized "European enterprise."

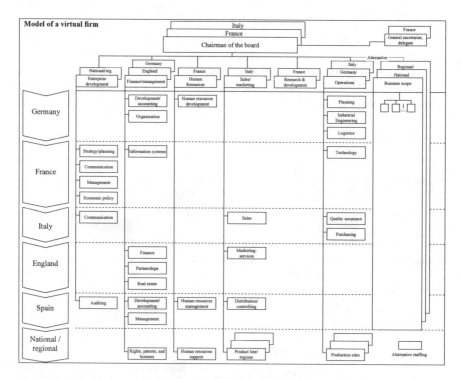

**Fig. 8.15.**   Working model of an idealized "European enterprise" (based on Simon / Bauer / Jägeler 1993, p. 262; Reichwald / Möslein 2002)

**The Virtual Organization: On the Way to a Cognitive Division of Labor**

In our discussion of virtual organizations, we presented a competence and task-oriented approach of organization design: Jurisdictional delineations and relative durable assignment of competence and responsibility are relinquished in favor of dynamic, demand-specific competence allocation. Consequently, abstract assignments are transformed into concrete combinations of problem-solving competences.

Moati and Mouhoud (1994, p. 52) interpret this scenario as a fundamental change from traditional forms of the division of labor to competence and quality-oriented forms of the division of labor. Division of labor seems to be increasingly dominated by cognitive rather than technical aspects.

Their arguments can be summarized as: Information itself has no value. Value is only created when information is transformed into knowledge and put to use in the company. Transforming and using knowledge do, however, require competence. The extraordinary expansion and growth of data, information, and knowledge have led to a constant increase in specialization, and, has therefore triggered an organizational dilemma: Not only do the basic conditions currently require tendentious approaches to coping with tasks, but the growing task complexity also requires an expansion of specialization ("hyperspecialization"). Consequently, the entire enterprise transforms from a traditional location of production into a location of allocated competence: Production is no longer divided into numerous sequences in line with the Tayloristic model; the division of labor depends on employees' knowledge and competence. Moati and Mouhoud (1994) call the resulting form a cognitive division of labor. This form of the division of labor comes close to the pre-industrial division of labor in handcraft-based production structures.

The attainable spectrum of competence and knowledge that an enterprise can provide often restricts performance range. Know-how barriers, found in the model for optimizing performance range (Picot 1991b), increasingly restrict the internal accomplishment of specific or strategically important tasks. If performance specialization is increasingly associated with knowledge specialization (with highly variable requirements), the internal accomplishment of tasks increasingly fails as a result of the prohibitive costs of the internalization of knowledge: "Often the problem does really not lie in finding out whether or not it is more economical to accomplish tasks oneself or in letting someone else do the work. One simply has to have the work done by someone else because one is unable to do the work oneself" (Moati / Mouhoud 1994, p. 60; translation by the authors).

Reflections on the cognitive division of labor are appropriate when distributing tasks in virtual organizations, as this distribution is a dynamic separation, division, and allocation (Reiss 1992) of problems by highly specialized problem-solvers. Reflections on an enterprise's depth of knowledge clarify the task areas for which virtual organizations could be responsible. Highly specific tasks and those of strategic importance whose internalization could fail due to barriers to know-how are suited to the virtual organization concept described in section 8.3.2.

We once again use the translation agency example to explain. We examine the adapting and translation of software and the associated documentation for targeted markets. A US software firm has to decide whether to produce a product for the European market itself or to outsource the order. The software product must be available on the European market shortly after its release on the US market. The high degree of interdependence between the different tasks indicates internal processing. The highly specific knowledge that is required, as well as the software product's strategic relevance has to be taken into account. Internalization nevertheless fails due to know-how barriers. Only well chosen specialists, who are both familiar with the particular market and with all the product details, as well as having the necessary background knowledge, can accomplish the task with the required quality. The higher the complexity and the volume of the software products, the more these types of problems arise (e.g., localizing multimedia encyclopedias). In this case, a virtual integration of the required competencies is the most suitable procedure.

## Realistic Premises for Realistic Design Strategies

Economic thinking is still influenced by the premises that emerged in an earlier time under different circumstances. In that period of time, this way of thinking was appropriate and it can still be, if the particular task is embedded in a stable environment with a low degree of variability and a high degree of repetition, i.e. conditions characteristic of mass production. Lutz (1996) presents six design principles (principles of common wisdom) for this environment (see also Reichwald / Möslein 1995; also see chapter 1):

- The principle of maximum planning of organization processes;
- The principle of the clear demarcation of responsibilities;
- The principle of the preference for organization-internal solutions;
- The principle of the maximum exploitation of economies of scale;
- The principle of market control through incremental product innovation;
- The primacy of labor-saving investments.

Unfortunately, these principles' premises are currently no longer valid in many areas of business, as they emerged in a different time under different conditions. Changing conditions require new premises. New premises therefore call the current principles into question and demand the verification of working models established on these principles. It is still unclear which further steps have to be taken in order to cope with a turbulent and variable environment. Moreover, it is uncertain how changed premises regarding economic explanation and design approaches will affect future working models. Today, we are still at an experimental stage. Greiner and Metes's (1992) approach "simultaneous distributed work (SDW)" stimulates new concepts and experimentation. Four (unconventional) assumptions regarding the reality of distributed collaboration ("working together apart") are the basis of this approach:

- Change is constant.
- All work is distributed.
- Knowledge is the critical resource.
- There will never be enough time.

Virtual organizations should be studied on a trial basis by accepting these conditions of reality and accordingly designing and shaping organizations in novel ways.

Telecooperative work forms are interesting starting points for a reorientation in a changed business world. We should, however, note that telecooperation possibilities might also be used to support traditional entrepreneurial leadership principles. Nevertheless, their effectiveness remains narrowly delimited to largely stabile tasks with a high degree of repetition. This application pattern corresponds to traditional rationalization or economization. When telecooperative work forms are deployed in the context of organizational innovation strategies, that far-reaching effectiveness can be realized. Subsequently, telecooperative systems improve organizations' ability to cooperate internally and externally and enable them to embrace a quick and permanent market orientation (see figure 1.2). Virtualization as an organization innovation strategy based on telecooperation offers the strategy of choice, especially under conditions of high product complexity and uncertain markets (see figure 5.16).

*Chapter 9*

# People in the Boundaryless Organization: New Demands on Employees and Managers

## 9.1 People in the Boundaryless Organization

Overcoming an organization's technical, organizational, legal, market, and spatial boundaries (see chapters 4 through 8) can significantly impact the working environment of managers and employees. It creates new challenges (required competencies, abilities, qualifications), as well as new possibilities (the development of personality, efficiency, and responsibility potentials).

New organizational concepts such as modularized, networked, and / or virtual structures imply a paradigm shift in terms of the image of humankind (Hesch 1997): Holistically, people play a vital role in the new work structure. Changing competitive environments and new work structures are the primary reasons for individuals being rediscovered as a primary resource in the boundaryless organization.

### 9.1.1 The Importance of Individuals in the Changing Competitive Environment

In response to growing competitive pressures, organizations increasingly view individuals or 'human resources' as a more important strategic potential for gaining competitive advantages than traditional factors such as product and process technologies, economies of scale, financial resources or protected and / or regulated markets (Schreyögg 1993; Pfeffer 1994; Backes-Gellner / Lazear / Wolff 2001).

There are two primary reasons for this development. First, qualified and innovative employees are becoming a bottleneck factor for successful organization change. In practice, it has frequently been observed that employees themselves are often the greatest barriers to reorganization. Fear of failure, disorientation, and the fear of losing power often lead to significant resistance to changes within an organization. Organization change can only occur if there are enough employees who support these changes and carry them through. Current basic conditions make the organization more dependent than ever on its employees' creativity and innovation. This makes the development of appropriate human resources a determining factor for competitive success and creates new management challenges.

Second, the importance of people is increasing in relation to customers and relevant markets. The pressure to remain competitive makes the development of long-term customer relationships a primary goal for every organization. In many markets, business success is increasingly determined by the ability to generate incremental customer benefit through products that are tailored to individual customer needs. However, no other resource is more vital for developing relationships with customers and for solving complex customer problems than people. Newer research results confirm this (e.g., Reichwald / Bauer / Lohse 1999; Reichwald / Bastian / Lohse 2000).

Technology-based systems still cannot provide the flexibility required to meet customer requirements that people can. These systems do not foster the same level of trust and personal responsibility in a business relationship nor do they have the

ability to solve complex problems. They also do not meet the need for social interaction and informal exchange between customers and sales professionals, which is
especially relevant, since this personal interaction can uncover latent customer requirements and can directly or indirectly influence buying decisions.

Personal relationships between suppliers and customers will continue to play a
key role in the decisive step of turning satisfied customers into long-term, loyal customers. When automated platforms reach the limits of their communication potential
and flexibility, people and personal consultation remain the only differentiating factor for business success (e.g., Reichwald/Bauer/Lohse 1999; Piller 2001).

There is growing awareness that people are the defining factor for a strategically
important competitive advantage that would be difficult to replicate. This focuses attention on new ways to effectively utilize human capital (von Rosenstiel 2002;
Macharzina 1999; Manz/Sims 1993). The employee is no longer regarded as a cost-
factor to be reduced, but as an investment to be treated with care (Manz/Sims 1993;
Reichwald 1992b). With this aspect in mind, the traditional roles between managers
and employees need to be re-examined and adjusted. The manager allows the employee to evolve from someone carrying out instructions to a key player who has to
make independent decisions and accept responsibility. The manager evolves from
being an instructor and controller to supporter and coach.

## 9.1.2   New Work Structure Models Within the Boundaryless Organization

The changing competitive environment and the development of information and
communication technologies have made organization strategies, such as modularization, network building, and virtualization, not only possible but also imperative (see chapters 5, 6, and 8). These new organization models profoundly impact
the way work is structured. New work structure models are replacing hierarchically oriented and heavily departmentalized organizational concepts. In the context of transforming the value-added chain of boundaryless organizations, three
work structure models will be essential in shaping the future nature of work: Team
concepts, networking, and telecooperation.

**Team Concepts**

Modularization concepts are based on restructuring into small, easily managed
units that are empowered to make decentralized decisions and are responsible for
their own business results (see chapter 5). Work in these units is characterized by
high complexity and relatively low variability. These tasks require direct and spontaneous communication; examples are the development of complex and high-quality
products, or highly innovative and time-sensitive processes with strong market
relevance entailing a high degree of flexibility (Picot/Reichwald 1991; Lawler
1992). Successfully accomplishing such tasks also demands leeway for interpretation and creativity, which can be achieved by combining separate tasks into a

holistic task structure (vertical task integration) and by assigning decision-making flexibility and authority. Consequently, employees enjoy greater managerial flexibility, have more opportunities to influence their work and their results, and are better motivated (Reichwald / Nippa 1989; Manz / Sims 1993; Rothhaar 2001). This makes team structures especially well suited for these types of tasks.

There is a high degree of variability in how teams are defined (see also Boyett / Conn 1992; Lawler 1992; Manz / Sims 1993; Parker 1994; Staehle 1999). These variations can be reduced to a few core characteristics as reflected in the following approach to team definition by Katzenbach / Smith (1994):

- Shared tasks and goals are the basis for creating team spirit, which will lead to top performances by individual team members.

- Mutual problem-solving and decision-making capabilities, as well as team members' complementary professional and social qualifications.

- Team members have a reciprocal sense of responsibility. Each team member supports and defends other team members and the group as a whole.

- Motivation plays a decisive role in team success. The ability to influence each team member, joint decisions, and common group results increase motivation.

- Each team is equipped with the resources and responsibility to produce entire products and / or services or essential components thereof.

- Instead of clearly defined performance goals, teams have a "mission" to serve customers or customer categories either internally (e.g., other teams) or externally (users, buyers).

- The team elects the team leader or they take this role on in turn. Team leaders coordinate the teams, moderate team meetings, and take care of team members.

These comprehensive prerequisites for the formation of a team illustrate that not every task-oriented grouping of employees can automatically be characterized as a true team in practice. In many instances, team spirit remains wishful thinking rather than being reality or does not live up to the other requirements listed above. In such cases, the potential for performance increases – often ascribed to team structures – is not fully utilized.

Parker (1994) categorizes teams along three dimensions: purpose, duration, and membership. Team purposes can include, for example, product development, systems development, quality improvement, problem-solving processes or re-engineering processes. Team duration can be longer term or short term. Permanent teams within the actual organization structure are, for example, departmental teams for specific task areas. Teams with a shorter duration are, for example, project teams, problem-solving teams, and task forces. These serve to develop, analyze, and research certain entrepreneurial tasks. According to Parker (1994, p. 35 ff.), the most commonly encountered teams in today's business environment are:

- **Functional Teams**: These consist of a supervisor and direct subordinates. They are the classic team form in the modern business world. All development engineers within a company can, for example, form a functional team. The team's purpose is often similar to the tasks of its members in the organization. Functional teams are mostly formed for the long term and are also found in hierarchical organizations in relatively stable markets.

- **Cross-functional Teams**: These teams utilize the knowledge of various employees from different departments and areas of expertise. A classic example is the product development team in companies that respond quickly to rapidly changing markets such as computer and/or telecommunications markets. The duration of such teams can vary.

- **Self-directed Teams**: This category describes teams that are responsible for an entire business process, which, in turn, delivers a product and/or service to company-internal and/or company-external customers. Members of self-directed teams continuously improve their work processes, solve problems independently, and plan and/or control their own work. The duration of such teams depends on the type of business and the volatility of its competitive environment. Self-directed teams are mainly suitable for firms doing business in young, dynamic areas and, consequently, integrate their employees closely into entrepreneurial processes.

The introduction of teams embeds employees in decision-making and accountability processes. This creates opportunities to increase the productivity and quality of value-added business processes. Team concepts promote employee flexibility and autonomy in the work place, which are essential for new organization structures. Employees are able to develop and apply their creative potential and positively impact the organization's overall productivity and competitiveness (Pinchot/Pinchot 1993). Teams facilitate work structure forms, such as job enlargement, job enrichment, and job rotation. They also reduce monotony and increase employees' sense of responsibility for one another and for the process as a whole (Gottschall 1994).

The success of team concepts depends on several factors. The most important prerequisites are the acceptance and support of management, team-oriented information systems, and the adaptation of bonus and reward systems to encourage teamwork and reward results achieved cooperatively.

In addition, team structures create new roles for employees and management, which demand certain qualifications (see section 9.2). This requires comprehensive team-building policies and training to increase teamwork skills. Patience and realistic expectations with regard to team implementation reduce the risk of disappointment and resignation. Overcoming resistance to team concepts and building productive teams can, however, be a time-consuming process. The changes necessitated by the implementation of team concepts are evolutionary in nature and time frames of up to ten years are not unusual (Manz/Sims 1993). These requirements also illustrate the complexity of implementing a team organization.

## Networking

Dissolution tendencies within organizations have led to a new type of work structure, called networking. Networks can be regarded as an intermediary means of coordination between the market and the hierarchy. They are characterized by complex, yet relatively stable and cooperative relationships between organizations and organization units (Sydow 1995).

There are many types of networks between competitors, customers, suppliers, as well as foreign organizations. They serve to optimize performance and / or bridge resource gaps, which involve inter-organizational ties that present specific challenges, especially for management. Networking helps develop and expand relationships with cooperation partners. It also encompasses the division of labor of the production of goods and services, as well as the coordination of independent, external organization partners.

Such relatively complex individual and project-related tasks require quick access to extensive information resources, as well as undisturbed and targeted communication with highly qualified and frequently changing communication partners (Bellmann / Wittmann 1991). Furthermore, networking should encompass all aspects of the coordination of autonomous teams within an organization (see chapter 5). Autonomous teams primarily work together in the form of a network and require a high level of cooperation.

## Telecooperation

The third type of work structure can be summarized as telecooperation (see chapter 8, as well as Reichwald et al. 2000). Networks and virtual organizations require decision makers and / or organization units to work on the same tasks or develop goods and services together but at different locations and at different times. This requires the production of goods and services, coordination, and communication to be supported by telemedia.

Telecooperation is especially well suited for those tasks that allow a high degree of autonomy, involve management, as well as creative aspects, whose contribution to the bottom line can be measured, and which are carried out by employees with a relatively high level of professional qualification (Reichwald et al. 2000). Telecooperation provides flexible ways of leveraging the advantages of distributed locations if the social relationships between the participants are relatively trouble-free, the information requirements are predictable, and tasks can mostly be accomplished independently (Bellmann / Wittmann 1991).

The organizational strategies of the boundaryless organization and the resulting new work forms create new challenges for employees and management, as their roles have to be newly defined. This will be discussed in the following sections.

## 9.2    New Roles of Customers, Employees, and Managers in the Boundaryless Organization

### 9.2.1    The New Role of the Customer

As the borders between an organization and its environment, suppliers, and markets become less clearly defined, the customer's role also needs to be redefined. Increasing competition and the possibilities offered by information and communication technologies, as well as by new forms of media require that the customer's individual requirements and wishes be considered. Markets can no longer be regarded as an anonymous or primarily homogeneous segment but, at best, as a subset of that segment. Approaches such as mass customization (Piller 1998a, 2001) or relationship marketing (Bruhn/Bunge 1994; Reichwald/Piller 2002a, 2002b) are some of the possibilities.

Furthermore, segmenting organizations into small, relatively autonomous subunits, the networking of organizations, and virtualization create a new type of customer – the internal customer. New customer-supplier relationships develop when several units develop services collaboratively and partially completed tasks have to be handed to other sectors by means of defined interfaces.

The customer has become more specific and more diverse. The term "customer" can refer to an end user, a value-added partner in networks, sales partner or the next module in the process chain. All of these have one point in common: The customer is increasingly integrated into the organization's value-added chain and becomes a partner instead of a "foreign entity." This offers a key advantage in increasingly competitive environments in which customer loyalty is essential. Long-term relationships with partners create trust and can lower transaction costs on both sides. Additionally, the experience of many organizations shows that winning new customers costs considerably more and is more time-consuming than maintaining and expanding relationships with existing customers. It has been said that the average effort/cost of acquiring a new customer is about five times the effort/cost of retaining an existing customer.

Intensive communication and cooperation with the customer are essential prerequisites for the individualization of products and services, as well as for the bundling of solutions in response to specific customer requirements. This leads to the organization's customer information gaining a new quality, which drives innovation and change in the services offered to customers. The customer becomes the focal point for the organization. The internal focus of previous generations is being replaced by a stronger external, customer-oriented focus (Bauer 2000).

### 9.2.2    The New Role of Employees

New organization strategies and work structures are changing the employee's role. New work structures are primarily increasing the integration of management-related and non-management tasks, which leads to the shifting of decision-making and responsibility from managers to employees. When, for instance, management assigns the responsibility for an entire business process to a team, it also needs to empower the team to make the relevant decisions that arise from this task (Hammer/Champy 1995). This makes sense because employees – through their proximity to customers and the process – frequently have substantial information on how to optimize work processes and meet customer requirements (Hoffman 1994). The extent to which the importance of management's authoritarian and directing role decreases, is equal to the extent to which employees supervising themselves replaces traditional management supervision (Büssing 1988). Consequently, these processes result in the greater empowerment of employees. Employees are therefore trusted to carry out their work in line with the organization's goals and thus feel that their dedication, competence, and creativity are key ingredients in the organization's business success (Boyett/Conn 1992; Pinchot/Pinchot 1993; von Rosenstiel/Regnet/Domsch 1998). The role of empowered employees in these new organizations is illustrated in figure 9.1 and described below.

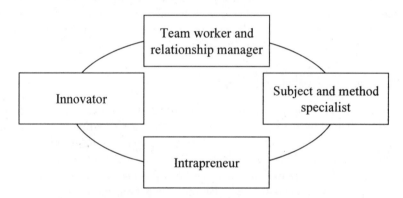

**Fig. 9.1.**    New roles of employees

### 9.2.2.1    Employees as Team Workers and Relationship Managers

The most important requirement in transforming a traditional hierarchical organization into new organizational concepts is the increased demand for cooperation and relationships. While employees may previously have been responsible for a small area that they could control and in which they could work in relative isolation, new organizational concepts have now made this almost impossible. The complexity of tasks and processes, the requirement for rapid market proximity and flexibility, as well as the variability of tasks due to increasingly individualized customer requirements have created tasks that can only be managed by teams and/or by means of cooperation. Networks and telecooperation build on successful cooperation and relationship management realized across spatial and temporal boundaries. In addition, cooperation is a vital prerequisite for customer loyalty and integration strategies (Reichwald / Piller 2002a).

What are the characteristics required of the new employees who act as team workers and relationship managers? Their primary characteristic is social competence, which encompasses access to and appropriate use of active, cognitive, and emotional behavior for effective social interaction (Doepfner 1989). Communication skills are a part of this ability. These employees can communicate their thoughts, wishes, and goals but can also consider the thoughts, wishes, and goals of their interaction partner. They are good listeners. Furthermore, they have the ability to build appropriate relationships with cooperation partners, team members, and customers to facilitate professional cooperation. It also helps if they are open, communicative, and trustworthy, which means they can face conflicts and try to resolve them constructively.

These employees have learned to respect their communication partner's personality. They are willing to protect and support their cooperation partners and to place the team's goals ahead of their own. They actively model ("live") the shared responsibility, goals, values, and norms (Kets de Vries 1999). These basic attitudes also help them in their working relationships with external partners in the context of networks and virtual organizations.

### 9.2.2.2    Employees as Intrapreneurs

Employees who no longer wish to just take orders and begin to make their own decisions on behalf of the organization will also have to be willing to take responsibility for their decisions and to acknowledge their contributions to the organization's market success without being instructed to do so. As a result of vertical task integration, employees within non-hierarchical teams are faced with responsibilities in the areas of problem solving, planning, budgeting, hiring and firing, team discipline, assessments, and performance control.

"Empowered" employees act far more independently and confidently, are aware of their significance for the organization and feel qualified to make decisions on behalf of the organization (Quinn / Spreitzer 1997). In the context of relationship networks, these employees can communicate their needs and wishes, obtain feedback on their performance and can negotiate mutually acceptable performance quality standards (Orsburn et al. 1990). They often appoint themselves as customer advocates in respect of the organization's internal sectors. This is especially true when the customer has various needs that need to be met quickly and flexibly.

During their daily work, these employees again and again identify new business opportunities and development potential. They discuss these with the team and then forward them to the appropriate department within the organization. They care about the success of the team and the organization as a whole. They are entrepreneurs within an organization – intrapreneurs.

### 9.2.2.3  Employees as Subject and Methods Specialists

Employees can only step into their role as intrapreneurs if they have the necessary qualifications to provide competent customer service, make appropriate decisions, and adequately assess opportunities and risks. This not only requires greater expertise in their area of specialty, but also a broader perspective beyond their own area of expertise.

Within a team, the areas of expertise must complement one another appropriately. If employees do not have the required knowledge or expertise, they can nevertheless revert to sound methods to analyze the problem, or they know where to locate the required expertise within the organization. Among the methods that they can competently employ, is the ability to systematically identify problems and opportunities, to assess alternatives, and to make sound decisions based on this ability. They contribute the highest degree of professional expertise, competency, and service-provider orientation to their interactions with customers. In addition, these employees are able to manage, motivate, discipline, and control themselves. They are also proficient in the use of new information and communication technology. When it is their turn to lead a team within a rotating team leadership model, they know how to present and moderate team meetings.

### 9.2.2.4  Employees as Innovators and Self-Starters

Ultimately, employees within the boundaryless organization are prepared for innovation and change. They are eager to search out and try new ideas, to experiment and, consequently, to develop themselves. Their expertise should be constantly updated, since technology cycles are constantly decreasing. They are therefore open to new technologies and are willing to learn.

Such employees regard change as positive. They work on perfecting their own abilities by observing themselves, by reflecting on their actions, by welcoming feedback, and using it as a self-improvement resource. Innovative employees also feel a sense of responsibility for the team and for team processes. They continuously make suggestions for improvements within the team and are never satisfied with the status quo. They regard development and new experiences as great challenges.

### 9.2.2.5  Conclusions Regarding the New Roles of Customers, Employees, and Managers

At first sight, the requirements for the employee of the future seem to describe a superhuman. Drumm (1996) calls this description of employees who are highly motivated, voluntarily pursue professional development, and act independently and entrepreneurial: The "organizational blueprints for archangels." At a second glance, it is, however, clear that the core of employees' new role is truly realistic. Their role is primarily characterized by increased expectations regarding decision-making and the acceptance of responsibility for complete, customer-oriented processes, as well as for team, communication, and innovation skills (e.g., Murphy / O'Leary 1994).

There is a definite trend towards higher qualified employees. The need for un-skilled employees and / or employees with lower levels of qualification is expected to decrease further within the context of new organizational concepts. Value-added work is increasingly replacing unskilled and / or non-professional work based on formalized routine processes.

Current organizational practice nevertheless indicates that these new roles have not yet been fully implemented. Many employees are not fully integrated into the decision and responsibility process, and the practice of empowerment is still in its infancy. The potential of team concepts to increase employee performance is also still underutilized. The number of employees who are part of a team concept, as described above, is still relatively small.

There is therefore a significant gap between the theoretical ideals and reality. This gap is partially due to the new roles that management has to play. Neverthe-less, these roles are also not widely accepted and / or fully utilized, as the next sec-tion will show.

### 9.2.3   The New Role of Managers

Flat organizations and task integration within the context of team concepts are shifting responsibility, actions, and decision-making from managers to employees. Simultaneously, management is being relieved of some of its traditional manage-ment tasks. This raises the question: Which tasks remain for managers within the new organizational concepts? One could even assume that the roles of employees and managers are becoming increasingly intertwined or are even merging.

The role of managers is not, however, made redundant in the new organiza-tional concepts. Instead, there is a fundamental shift in their task priorities. Man-agers no longer focus on instruction, control, and decision-making, but on per-sonal support and mentoring of the "empowered" employee, on external network-ing and relationship management, the drafting of visions, the implementation of changes, and on the architecture and design of the organization and its potential (see figure 9.2).

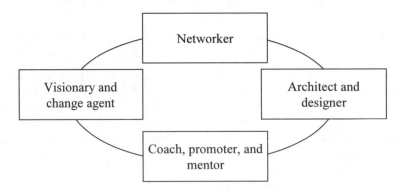

**Fig. 9.2.**   New roles for management

### 9.2.3.1  Managers as Coaches, Promoters, and Mentors

In many traditional organizations, the unwritten rule prevails that supervisors only lead part of the time and primarily concern themselves with important tasks, opinion building, and decisions that cannot be assigned to employees (Kunz 1999). Providing leadership is often viewed as being of secondary importance.

In the new organizational concepts, managers are not primarily concerned with important tasks or involved in operational business. Their primary goal is to "lead" and "promote." They become a service provider for the employees. When management tasks are transferred to individual employees and teams, management is therefore responsible for ensuring that these employees and teams are able to complete their tasks in the best possible way. Managers, who are still responsible for their business unit's results, have to get their employees and teams "into shape" for their daily tasks and challenges.

This view of the manager as a coach is taken from professional sports to symbolize that coaching relationships are based on a professional division of labor. The coach is responsible for the fitness and performance of the employee, who can then go out on to the "playing field" and operate successfully (Bauer 1995; Cranwell-Ward / Bacon / Mackie 2002). Often, however, the fact that employees or supervisors need to be helped is regarded as "helplessness" or "weakness." The coaching image can help to overcome this view.

What characterizes managers in their role as coach, promoter or mentor? For managers, the role of coach implies a completely different approach towards employees. They recognize employees' professional expertise and capabilities with regard to accomplishing their tasks and accept their personalities. Manager and employee are therefore on an equal level. Managers have to advise employees with regard to their decision-making, have to offer directions and point out alternatives, discuss problems, and develop their abilities. As coaches, managers have to adapt their own behavior to focus on the information needs and problems of each employee (Bauer 1995; Schreyögg 1996; Bucking / Coffman 1999; Whitmore 2002).

Coordination is increasingly achieved by means of management by objectives (Latham / Locke 1995). The manager takes time for assessment and goal discussions, develops mutually acceptable annual goals, and takes employees' objections and suggestions seriously. Goals should be challenging but also realistic (Kunz 1999). Quantitative goals are increasingly complemented by individual qualitative goals that are based on the personal abilities or specific work situation of employees. The main goal is to help employees attain enduring success that they can attribute to themselves. In distributed locations, goal-setting techniques are especially suitable for the management of employees who cannot be directly observed (Sachenbacher 2000).

Teams and working groups specifically require managers' support and coaching (e.g., Manz / Sims 1995; Holling / Lammers 1995). Every team experiences different phases in its development, which create situation-specific problems. In the beginning phases, managers can help to orient the team. As the team develops, they can reveal conflicts and find constructive solutions. Once the team has matured, managers can prevent the development of negative group behavior, such as group think (Moorhead/Neck 1995). The main goal is to develop the team so that it can increasingly complete its task autonomously and competently.

Above all, managers should have social skills to fulfill their role as coach, promoter, and mentor. Gollman (1999) describes these "soft" skills – such as social competence, self-reflection, self-control, emotion, and empathy – as "emotional intelligence." His research shows that these skills are increasingly becoming a requirement for successful leadership. Managers should furthermore master non-directive conversation techniques and have a profound knowledge of the cognitive and behavior-oriented aspects of motivation and how to apply them to motivate employees to change their behavior.

Transitioning from a task-oriented decision maker and "mover" to the role of relationship specialist and coach requires substantial time and effort and creates significant problems for many managers. Expertise in the area of employee leadership (conversation management, psychological expertise, goal setting techniques), as well as the willingness to change is often lacking.

### 9.2.3.2   Managers as Architects and Designers

Senge (1990b) uses a metaphor to explain that a manager's role is similar to that of an architect or designer. He compares managers to a shipbuilder and not, as many would expect, to a captain, navigator or helmsman. It would, after all, make no sense if the captain were to order the ship to turn 30 degrees portside and the ship's rudder cannot handle this kind of turn. Ultimately, the shipbuilder decides what the ship is capable of. The captain can only deal with the circumstances.

With this metaphor, Senge suggests that managers should be increasingly involved in the design and architecture of their organizations. Managers are responsible for designing processes that enable employees to complete their tasks, ensure that processes are successfully coordinated, and create appropriate reward systems – such as performance assessments and compensation systems – to motivate employees (Hammer/Champy 1995). This design task also encompasses influencing non-material components and the unwritten rules of the organization – the organization's culture.

The organization's culture is a system of values and norms formed through social interaction in a long-term process that is constantly changing (Schein 1992). The complex nature of this process has led to skepticism about the degree to which an organization's culture can be methodically influenced or changed (Schreyögg 1992). Whatever the case may be, designing an organization's culture is a delicate task. There is, however, consensus that management actions noticeably impact this culture, even if there are no obvious cause-effect relationships, which means that no general recommendations can be offered with regard to action to be taken. Ebers (1995) describes an organization's culture as the "coagulated result of leadership interactions."

One cannot, of course, assume that there is an ideal culture, in the sense of one best way (Schein 1991). There are, nevertheless, certain fundamental attitudes and values that can benefit new organizational concepts. These are, above all, trust and openness, recognition and fairness, communication and cooperation, as well as learning and innovation.

Whatever the circumstances are, managers must increasingly deal with the informal rules of the game and with existing values and norms – the organizational culture. Developing sensitivity to the organizational culture is an important prerequisite for influencing it later. Managers can cumulatively influence the system through their own actions and values ("walk the talk"), through organizational rules and the use of multifaceted symbols (von Rosenstiel 1998) or artifacts (Schein 1995). In every organization and in every organizational culture, symbols can be interpreted in different ways. It is up to managers' skill and sensitivity to employ appropriate tools to achieve their goals.

In contrast to the traditional management style based on control and the achievement of (short-term) fame and status, the outcome of these designer tasks only becomes apparent over time. This type of leadership is subtle and hidden, but according to Mintzberg (1999), it is a sensible way to lead the "empowered" employee.

### 9.2.3.3  Managers as Networkers

In the context of managing decentralized network structures, managers take on boundary-spanning tasks in their networker role (Sydow 1992b). These tasks help to overcome the differences between network partners and build "bridges" that maintain the network. As networkers, managers look for information within and outside the network and pass it on. When required, managers also represent the network in the outside world, negotiate contracts, and monitor their compliance. Managers coordinate task completion within the network team and the organization, and coach employees entrusted with boundary-spanning tasks.

In order to carry out these and other tasks, managers develop and maintain personal networks that go beyond the boundaries of individual, institutionalized network organizations. Informal communication and coordination take on special importance in the networking context. The task of stabilizing interorganizational relationships by balancing the diverse and often changing interests in the network, as well as developing a foundation of trust, creates additional management challenges. This also entails negotiations to define the boundaries of networks and the work to be performed within the organization. Furthermore, strategies can no longer be enforced as they are in traditional hierarchical structures. Due to the network organization's relative autonomy, strategies now have to be implemented by means of consensus processes (Sydow 1992b).

The ability to negotiate, resolve conflicts, and build consensus has thus become a key management skills. Managers therefore require social competence, integration skills, and cognitive abilities such as quick perception and the ability to recognize essential connections. Recent management research has also indicated the importance of these requirements (e.g., Mintzberg 1994; Reichwald / Goecke 1995; Neuberger 2002).

### 9.2.3.4    Managers as Visionaries and Change Agents

As visionaries and change agents, managers need to recognize changes in the environment, develop visions, and translate these into strategies (Hinterhuber/Krauthammer 2001; Bartlett/Goshal 1998). Visions provide orientation and context. They are the basis from which managers can identify the organization's core tasks, core competencies, and core products (Bradford/Cohen 1998; Hinterhuber/Krauthammer 2001). As visionaries, managers know how to get employees to buy into their vision and how to help them make sense of and get excited about the vision. They have excellent communication skills and know how to explain complicated subjects through the use of metaphors, symbols, and pictures and thus make them comprehensible for all employees. Managers "walk the talk" with regard to the vision and the strategies derived from the vision, and know how to win employees' commitment (buy-in).

Furthermore, managers act as change agents. They understand human resistance to change and have the ability to overcome this resistance through communication and enthusiasm. They are also familiar with the success factors for the realization of change processes and involve appropriate stakeholders in the process (Picot/Freudenberg/Gaßner 1999). These tasks also require analytical abilities, creativity, and networked thinking along with social competence and/or emotional intelligence.

### 9.2.3.5    Conclusions Regarding the New Role of Managers

Managers' new role has shifted from a focus on tasks and operational decisions to personal employee leadership and strategic tasks. Managers specifically need to take advantage of new tools and methods within the context of employee leadership. Coaching and mentoring of employees have replaced directives and control. In the new organization, which is principally characterized by distribution and decentralization, management's key tasks are integration, relationship management, and trust building.

## 9.3    How Communication and Organization Change Affect People

The previous sections elucidated that for new organizational forms to have a positive impact on effectiveness and efficiency, employees' and managers' roles need to change substantially in the context of new organizational strategies. What prompted this change in roles?

The discovery of the "human" resource has evolved over several decades. During this process, different factors have influenced people's importance within the organization. In business theory and practice, the image of people as having created the implicit basis for the design of organization and leadership models has undergone transformation.

This transformation was influenced by a similar change in our society's basic values, as well as by the environment that constantly demands change and the realization that an organization can only create change through communication. Finally, it became obvious that distributed organizations can only function well when the organization's culture and common norms and values are truly valued. Theoretical approaches have also been developed that help to explain the changes in roles within the boundaryless organization.

## 9.3.1  The Rediscovery of the Human Resource

### *9.3.1.1    The Image of the Individual and Organization*

The image of the individual is a general assumption about humans' character, motives, and goals. These are the foundation of economic concepts that touch on areas in which people play an important role. Various organization theory approaches are also partially based on and characterized by different images of the individual.

**Homo Oeconomicus**

At the beginning of the 20th century, business theory was strongly influenced by scientific management ideas. This school of thought was founded by Frederick W. Taylor (1913). Taylor assumed that employees strive for the highest possible wage, while the employer seeks to produce goods and/or services at the lowest possible costs. Taylor's approach was implicitly based on the assumption that the working person is an income maximizer (Kanigel 1997).

This assumption is also found in the image of the individual and the employee as perceived in the 18th century's national economy – **homo oeconomicus** (Smith 1776). Based on this image, Taylor championed the introduction of a new type of scientific factory management aimed at achieving productivity improvements through the optimization of manufacturing processes (see Reichwald/Hesch 1993; Hesch 1997; as well as chapter 5). Its goal was to increase the profitability of industrial manufacturing for both the employer and employee. In order to stimulate workers towards better performance, a program was established of rewarding the individual with high wages for high production.

Taylor (1913, p. 37) basically developed three principles:

- The separation of management and the tasks to be implemented;
- Work segmentation and division of labor of delegated work;
- Removal of all planning and controlling activities from the production process.

Taylor's interpretation of human work led to human resource integration into the manufacturing process like any other production factor. Humans were viewed as a machine-like mechanism that could be controlled and planned for just like any other components of the production processes.

Henry Ford applied Taylor's principles by establishing mechanized mass-production using assembly lines. In this Fordism, personal supervision of workers, which was originally conducted by superiors, was replaced by mechanical systems and forced coordination via a technical transport system, the assembly line. This established the basic prerequisites for progressive automation, with all its side effects like the objectification and depersonalization of work (Hill / Fehlbaum / Ulrich 1992, p. 411).

**The Social Person**

Taylor's concepts came under increasing criticism during the 1920s and 1930s and gave rise to a human relations movement that emerged from American industrial psychology and sociology (Kanigel 1997). It was sparked by the work of Mayo and his co-workers, who conducted the now famous Hawthorne Experiments (1924–1932), which examined human behavior at the Western Electric Company's Hawthorne plants in Cicero, Illinois (Roethlisberger / Dickson 1939; Mayo 1945).

These experiments were conducted to analyze how technical working conditions influence productivity. Mayo, for example, examined how lighting and ventilation affect industrial workers' performance. Interestingly, it turned out that the connection between technical working conditions and productivity did not sufficiently explain human working behavior.

Four broad conclusions can be drawn from the Hawthorne studies:

- Individuals' aptitudes are imperfect predictors of job performance. Although they suggest some of the worker's physical and mental potential, the quantity is strongly affected by social factors.

- Informal organization impacts worker productivity, i.e. it was discovered that workers have a group life. Moreover, the relations that workers developed with supervisors influence the way in which workers carry out directives.

- Work-group norms influence productivity. Although the Hawthorne researchers were not first to recognize that work groups arrive at norms of what is "a fair day's work," they offered the best systematic description and interpretation of this phenomenon.

- A workplace is part of a social system. The workplace was regarded as a social system comprised of interdependent parts.

This led to recognition of the importance of social relationships between workers, as well as the phenomenon of internal teams and their role in how organizations function. Informal teams emerge alongside formally defined group structures. They have their own rules and norms, which can stimulate individual performance to a higher degree than, for example, the prospect of wage increases. In what came to be known as the *Hawthorne effect*, the productivity was itself influenced by the empirical survey and the focus on the specific group chosen for the survey influenced. These results contradicted Taylor's claims that workers are income maximizers. Consequently, the social and psychological conditions in which people work became the focus of attention (Reichwald / Hesch 1993) and resulted in a revision of the image of the individual. The Hawthorne studies were reanalyzed using the original data, leading to significantly differing findings that have not yet received wide coverage in the management literature (e.g., Franke / Kaul 1978; Jones 1992), suggesting that social science may have been much too eager to embrace the original Hawthorne interpretations.

The key ideas of the human relations movement were taken into account when revising the image of the individual. The working human being was no longer viewed as a rational individual acting in isolation and motivated only by monetary incentives, but as a social entity, whose behavior is primarily influenced by affiliation with groups and the specific rules and norms that develop within these groups (Wunderer / Grunwald 1980, p. 96).

**The Self-Actualizing Person**

Later research in the fields of organizational and industrial psychology discovered another factor that influences employee motivation. This factor is not so much based on the general conditions of employment (such as wage and social relationships) as on work structure and content. The key role that work structure plays with regard to motivation was documented in a study in which 1,000 employees were asked to name ten factors (such as wages, job security, etc.) that they regarded as closely linked to their work performance and to rank these. It is interesting to note that working assignments and content were some of the highest ranked factors (Kenneth 1987).

Maslow's studies build on this work and assume that there is a hierarchical order of needs. Within this order, there are deficit motivations (such as psychological needs, the need for safety, social contact, and recognition) and growth motivations (such as the need for self-actualization, which only intensifies rather than diminishes with increased satisfaction). This leads to a desire for meaningful work and motivating and interesting work content.

Based on this image of the individual, organization researchers asked the question: "What does motivating or interesting work look like?" The options model offers one systematic approach (Ulich / Groskurth / Bruggemann 1973; as well as figure 5.9). This model contains a horizontal dimension (implementation options as a measurement of task variability) and a vertical dimension (decision-making and control options as characterized by planning and controlling authority, as well as room for autonomous action). Based on these two dimensions, several possibilities were developed for the creation of motivating work tasks:

**Job enlargement** targets the horizontal merging of structurally similar working processes into one job description. This is designed to increase motivation by creating more challenging and diversified working conditions. Job enlargement increases the diversity of tasks, but does not affect decision-making and the span of control.

**Job rotation** is designed to expand work content by assigning the employee to different jobs through planned rotation. This type of task structuring motivates by varying and expanding the levels of work and responsibility. The employee develops a better understanding of organizational processes and is better prepared to take on responsibility. If job rotation encompasses structurally different tasks, it can also provide opportunities for developing additional professional qualifications, which can also be a motivating factor.

**Job enrichment** is based on a structural work content change. By combining management, planning, implementation, and controlling tasks, the employee gains work options, as well as increased responsibility and range of control. Job enrichment is often combined with teamwork in which team members determine their own tasks and control their own results.

Based on these general possibilities for designing individual jobs, concrete restructuring principles were also developed for teamwork (Robbins 1994). This led to the creation of concepts for integrated and autonomous work groups that not only assigned responsibility for individual tasks to the group, but also the responsibility for a task package. The group decides which group member will work on which task. The principle of job rotation is applied in the integrated group context. The position of "supervisor," who assigns tasks and oversees group activities, is specific to the integrated group.

In contrast, autonomous groups practice the principle of job enrichment. The group is given a specific goal and can autonomously decide how this goal will be reached. In this form of group work, the supervisor role does not generally apply. In addition to the motivational aspects of the job concepts, group work also fills the need for social contact at work. This approach is based on the assumption that people strive for self-improvement and actualization, but that these can only be achieved through the communicative self-determination of their social responsibilities and obligations (Oechsler 1997).

### The Complex Human Person

In addition to the already discussed images of the individual in management science, Schein (1980) suggests one more image: The complex person. This image reflects a situational view of people. Schein assumes that people do not just have one dominant need, but that their action may be determined by needs that vary with their situational factors, such as personality, living situation, work situation, etc.

These motives change over time. The employee is regarded as a changing and learning being. For management and the organization, this means that the design of appropriate organization structures and their supporting framework can only occur once an analysis has been made of individual employees' situation and motivation. There is no "one best way" to organize and to motivate. There is only the suggestion that organizations should be adapted to employees and the environment's needs.

The summary of the images of the individual in figure 9.3 clarifies that business administration's mainly technical view needs to be replaced by a consistent socioeconomic view. People and their behavior are increasingly becoming the main focus of business administration (Reichwald/Hesch 1993).

To some extent, this change in the individual's image also explains the change in the roles of employees and managers. When the focus is no longer on reducing employees' motives to a few simple need dimensions, implications automatically emerge for work structures and role assignment. Employees take on more holistic tasks: They plan, direct, and coordinate their own processes and take on diverse roles. Managers provide optimal framework conditions so that employees can carry out their work successfully. They analyze each employee's motivation, provide incentives, promote personal employee development, and ensure that employees have assignments that are in line with their skills and motivation.

| Image | Assumptions |
|---|---|
| Homo oeconomicus | • Employee as rational income maximizer<br>• Employee is passive and needs to be manipulated, motivated and controlled by the organization.<br>• Individual as a "production factor" |
| Social being | • Employee is motivated by social needs<br>• Employee is influenced more by social norms than by management incentives and controls<br>• Work productivity can be increased by meeting social needs |
| Self-actualizing individual | • Human needs are hierarchical<br>• When hierarchically lower needs are met, individual strives for autonomy and prefers self-motivation and self-control |
| Complex individual | • Employee can change and learn<br>• Motivations and need preferences can change<br>• Different systems result in different motivations (assumption of situational theory) |

**Fig. 9.3.** Images of individuals in business administration (based on Schein 1980)

### 9.3.1.2 Change in Values and Cultural Change

The images of the individual as described above do not suffice to explain the change in the roles of employees and managers. Changes in societal and organizational values and norms also substantially influence this role change. As a representation of what a society deems important, social values are bound to change. This means that values can become more or less important in relation to one another (von Rosenstiel 1994).

Since the beginning of the 1970s, there has been a growing trend away from material values and towards non-material ones. Since then, this trend seems to have reached equilibrium. In the workplace, there appears to be equilibrium between the importance of diligence and industriousness and that of quality of life and leisure time (Opaschowski 1997).

A newer generation of employees who have grown up with sufficient and adequate time, money, education, and affluence is entering the workforce. This generation places much higher value on work quality and creative freedom in the workplace. Work autonomy and achieving one's career dreams and goals re important new values. Enjoyment, meaningful work, and leisure time have become more important incentives than money and status. These social values influence the values of the organization as a sub-system of society. A newer generation of employees is turning away from values like obedience and subordination in favor of independence, creativity, and initiative (Opaschowski 1997).

This change in values significantly influenced the socio-political humanization debates of the 1970s. Signs of changing values include increasing criticism of Tayloristic work structures and the search for higher values and more meaningful work because material needs have been satisfied. At the core of this development is the general demand for self-actualization within the workplace (Kreikebaum / Herbert 1988). The humanization debates also address the implications of the practical development of humane working structures, which was derived from Herzberg's two-factor theory (see section 9.3.2.2). They furthermore consider the emphasis on work content and work structures as the most important motivational factor.

The working person's leeway will be expanded through the application of new work structuring principles such as job rotation (task rotation), job enlargement (task expansion) and job enrichment (task enrichment), and the formation of partially autonomic work groups (see section 9.3.1.1). Tayloristic specialization will consequently be limited and the development of each employee's personal character and qualification will be fostered (e.g., Ulich / Groskurth / Bruggemann 1973; Gaugler / Kolb / Ling 1977; Ulich 2001).

It has been generally accepted that employees' true identification with and motivation in respect of the future organization require recognition of and support for their "subjective wellness" (von Rosenstiel 1994). Recent research trends suggest that employees want to take on new roles and responsibility and make independent decisions (Opaschowski 1997). The most important need is, however, for a meaningful life and work. An activity only becomes meaningful when its overall context and the reason for it being done, are understood. The employee's search for meaning gives rise to managers' new role as visionaries and change managers (see section 9.2.3.4) and brings to the fore a new management task: Symbolic leadership, creating meaningful work, and emphasizing purpose and goals. Communication is the key.

### 9.3.1.3   Organization Change as a Communication Process

Over time, a new organizational perspective has emerged. Many authors continue to view organization as a tool with which to direct employees' activities, or as a system of rules that helps its members reach a certain goal (Frese 2000). Other authors, however, conclude that organization occurs in the employee's mind, and that re-organization can only be achieved through communication (Kiese et al. 1998).

The view of organization as the creation of rules is based on the assumption that employees will follow these rules and fully understand them. In practice, however, many failed organizational redesign projects show that formal rules and changes in rules do not always translate into desired employee actions. Change does not fail due to a new organization's formal concepts, but rather due to a lack of understanding and acceptance of new structures. The individual's behavior is not based on mindlessly translating rules into actions, but on the interpretation of these rules (Wollnik 1992).

Formal rules are never so complete that they leave no room for interpretation. One rule can indeed be interpreted very differently. This is because rules and changes are viewed in the context of existing mental theories and models. Employees therefore interpret them against the backdrop of their own personal experiences and expectations, which vary from individual to individual. Implicit theories and mental models develop automatically in organization members' minds, helping them to understand and compartmentalize experiences and situations and offering orientation for appropriate behavior (Kieser et al. 1998).

In order for organizations to act in a coordinated way regardless of individual interpretations, employees have to communicate their interpretations. Management, for example, can repeat certain rules, emphasize certain aspects, give feedback on successful behavior, and thus create consensus for individual employees

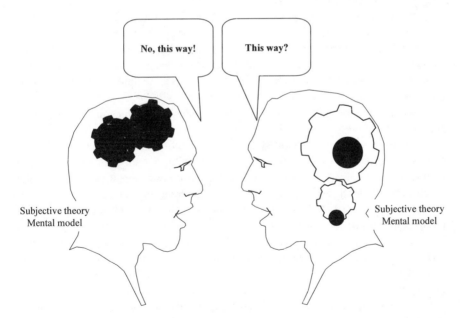

**Fig. 9.4.**   Communication to interpret rules – organization occurs in people's minds (Kieser et al. 1998)

on the interpretation of new rules (Kieser et al. 1998). Between employees, there will, however, still be negotiation about common meanings and interpretations. The key is communication (see figure 9.4).

One can also assume that most of an organization's rules are in the employees' minds and that these rules are regularly updated there. Actually, only very few rules are written down. Formal organization structures thus only describe a small part of sets of rules and regulations that are actually implemented on an organization's working level.

The real challenge for successful organization change is to go beyond redesigning structures and successfully replace the old models and behavior models in employees' minds with new ones. For this to happen, the key tool is communication. Since old patterns within the organization are socially implemented and maintained by communication, new ways of thinking also require communication to successfully replace old patterns (Kieser et al. 1998). Communication needs to be enacted with the aid of theoretical tools. Metaphors, stories, visions, and goals are thus effective tools that the manager, as a visionary and change agent, can skillfully use. Symbolic leadership is also becoming increasingly important and impacts the image of the manager's role as a communication specialist for organization change.

### 9.3.1.4    New Organization Structures and Value Management

Besides the behavioral norms stored in employees' minds, there are also more deeply rooted values and norms within organizations that make up the core of the organization's culture. These values and norms contribute significantly towards coordination, as they help individual employees orient themselves in unstructured and new decision-making situations. It is, however, impossible to design rules that work for every complex, highly variable task. This makes value-based orientation guidelines increasingly important, because they provide employees with the flexibility to coordinate their actions with one another.

Enabling this coordination requires these underlying values and norms to be clearly understood and shared by the organization members. This happens when norms and values are continuously negotiated in communication and interaction processes. However, what happens when the possibilities for communication and interaction are limited? This often occurs in new organization structures when the organization is divided geographically and by different time zones.

Research on distributed work and organization structures has demonstrated that the outsourcing of jobs results in a decrease in informal communication, social integration, and cooperation within the organization (Reichwald/Bastian 1999a, 1999b). When employees are no longer located in a shared location inside the organization and can only communicate through different forms of media rather than face-to-face, there is a risk that the integration and coordination effect of common norms and values will decrease. The model of task-appropriate media selection (Picot/Reichwald 1987; Reichwald 1999; Möslein 1999), as well as media richness theory (Daft/Lengel 1994) indicate that multimedia communication is of limited value for supporting the transmission of meaning, purpose, values, and norms as a complex communication task.

In distributed organizations, there is a specific need to provide opportunities for face-to-face communication and for participating in the organization's culture. This includes regular meetings (despite geographical distances), joint activities beyond regular work tasks, joint personnel and team building measures, as well as memorable events and office gatherings that create a feeling of belonging to the company culture.

Management needs to place additional emphasis on "value management" and ensure sufficient opportunities for communication and interaction between the members of the organization. More so than hierarchical organizations, distributed organizations require symbolic actions and communication to ensure continued organizational unity. Within network structures and virtual organizations, employees are confronted with changing cooperation partners and need to repeatedly negotiate interpretations and common values, such as trust, dependability, and fairness. This requires continuous communicative efforts from employees and managers.

## 9.3.2   Approaches to Role Changes

In addition to the environment changes that impact organizations, such as changes in the image of mankind within the organization, changes in social values, and the growing importance of communication and values, theoretical approaches too can explain people's special value and their changing roles. Macro-economic approaches, as well as theories developed by motivational, behavioral, and communication research, provide fascinating insights.

### 9.3.2.1   Institutional Economics Approaches

The introductory chapters of this book present new organizational concepts by means of institutional economics approaches (see chapter 2). The application of information and communication technologies within the value-added chain can reduce the cost of information and communication. This leads to potentially more economic coordination forms, if the specific task is the same (see chapter 6), which leads to the creation of networks, cooperation webs, virtual structures, and even modular organizations as coordination forms between the organization and the market.

At the same time, the relevance of the principal-agent problems (see chapter 2) increases within distributed structures. The flattening of hierarchies and decline of hierarchical monitoring and control systems, along with the simultaneously intensified delegation of and increase in responsibilities, create a vacuum between the limited means of control and agents' increased responsibilities (Ripperger 1997). Employees become "invisible," cooperation partners are in different locations, and can often only be reached via media. This creates increased potential for the opportunistic exploitation of information advantages by employees and cooperation partners.

Furthermore, the cost of monitoring (controlling) distributed location also increases. In other areas, monitoring in its classic sense becomes impossible.

Results-oriented management techniques (such as management by objectives) provide an approach to monitoring that has the advantage of being well suited for application in distributed organizations (see also section 9.2.3.1 and chapter 10). The development of suitable incentive and bonus systems, designed to align the goals of employees and / or cooperation partners with those of the organization, can help decrease the risk of moral hazard. This requires managers who can apply goal negotiation techniques and who can accurately assess an employee's goals and adjust incentives accordingly (see section 9.2.3.1). However, such systems can never be complete. They need to be reinforced by new management and relationship management mechanisms such as trust and implicit contracts.

Trust remains the basis of and necessary prerequisite for the existence of new organizational forms (Powell 1996; Picot / Dietl / Franck 2002), which institutional economists now largely accept, because wherever comprehensive control is no longer possible or too costly, trust offers an alternative. The main characteristic of trust is that the actor voluntarily offers a risky 'advance' without the use of any contractual safety or control measures to guard against opportunistic behavior (Ripperger 1997). A manager, for example, communicates information to an employee that may be confidential and important for this employee's work. The manager expects the employee to voluntarily keep this information confidential and not fall victim to opportunistic behavior, even if this could result in advantages just for the specific employee. Trust thus reduces complexity and insecurity while excluding opportunistic behavior beforehand.

It is fairly obvious that this method can create more efficient working processes, because the employee can make better decisions based on information received. At the same time, this method can reduce transaction costs, since the manager does not need to employ sanctions or monitor the employee to check whether information was passed on.

Research confirms this theory (Frank 1988; Jones 1995) and other positive effects of trust. Trust facilitates cooperation (Mayer / Davis / Schoorman 1995; Smith et al. 1995), promotes smooth and efficient market exchanges (Arrow 1974; Smith 1981), and provides greater adaptability to change (Korsgaard / Schweiger / Sapienza 1995; McAllister 1995). Trust cannot, of course, be recommended without reservations, as it would expose organizations to substantial risk.

In long-term relationships characterized by repeated interaction and interdependence, trust can be a low risk approach to making interactions mutually more efficient, as violations of such trust become difficult and can be sanctioned (Sjurts 1998). This often applies to networks, strategic alliances, and virtual organizations. Simultaneously, the advantages of trust as the basis of relationships define the new roles of and requirements for employees and managers. The ability to show trust and build relationships based on trust becomes a key factor.

When precise directions and expectations become impossible and inefficient, interest focuses on implicit contracts between management and employees and / or with cooperation partners. While explicit contracts are based on precisely defined agreements, implicit (relationship) contracts are based on unwritten expectations with regard to give and take between the parties. These expectations are formed in the minds of both parties before and during a contract relationship. Implicit contracts with an employee may define work beyond explicit work contracts, loyalty towards the organization, and other service dimensions that are difficult to formulate. The employee, on the other hand, will develop expectations in return. Employees who are expected to make a full commitment to the organization will live up to their responsibilities as long as the other side (the organization) abides by the implicit contract. If, for example, employees do not get the recognition that they need from a supervisor, or if their supervisors do not demonstrate full commitment, they will not feel obliged to abide by the implicit contract in the long run.

The importance of implicit contracts has implications for the new roles of employees and managers. Managers need to model loyalty and commitment in their daily work to create obligations and demonstrate the dimensions of implicit contracts. Communication is essential for reaching an understanding on implicit contracts. Many aspects of employees' new role, such as an entrepreneurial spirit, accepting responsibility, and personal development, are difficult to put into words and become the subject of implicit contracts.

Implicit contracts do not take effect until management agrees to its new role. This includes dealing with the unwritten laws of the organization and the organizational culture, modeling performance standards and providing a positive example to others, developing visions, infusing purpose, coaching, mentoring, and consulting in partnership with the employee (see section 9.2.3)

### 9.3.2.2 Approaches from Motivation Theory

Motivation research confirms the conclusions of the principal-agent theory, i.e. specifically its perspectives on the positive effect of the role change between management and employees. This theory tries to explain how human behavior is determined. It explores (depending on the theoretical approach) the direction, intensity, and longevity of building, maintaining and reducing behavior (Staehle 1999). Motivation theories are of vital interest for management and especially for personal leadership, because they contain useful indications for increasing goal-oriented and performance-oriented behavior.

Generally, motivation theory approaches can be divided into content and process theories. Content theories try to find reasons for what causes humans to behave in a certain way, and what maintains this behavior. Well-known content theory approaches are Maslow's hierarchy of needs, as well as Herzberg's two-factor theory.

Process theory, on the other hand, looks at how behavior happens. It examines what happens before, during, and after the development of new behavior. This will be illustrated with a brief discussion of the approaches developed by Vroom and Porter, as well as by Lawler. Equity and attribution theories are also commonly associated with process theories and will be introduced by a discussion of the approaches developed by Adams and Weiner.

## Maslow's Hierarchy of Needs

The most famous content theory model is Maslow's hierarchy of needs (1954), which explains the structure and dynamics of human needs as the reason for motivation and behavior. In this hierarchy, striving for self-actualization is the highest-ranking goal (see figure 9.5).

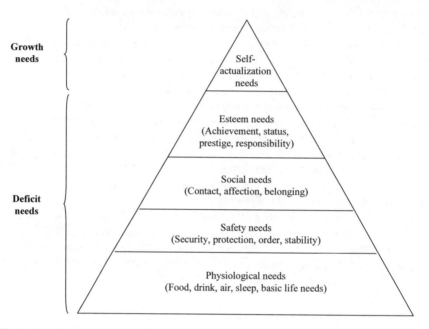

**Fig. 9.5.**    Hierarchy of needs (based on Maslow 1954)

Maslow's (1954) hierarchy is based on the five basic needs that all humans share. They are presented as a pyramid, with the most basic needs at the bottom. Maslow assumes that higher needs will only affect behavior once all the lower needs have been satisfied. He also suggests that, unlike lower needs, the need for self-actualization cannot be satisfied (growth motivation). If this motivation is satisfied, it only becomes stronger, while physical needs arise from a deficit (such as hunger, thirst, etc.), and decline when they become satisfied.

Maslow's hierarchy of needs is a systematic, theoretical approach that does not claim empirical validation. In many areas, it is, however, regarded as empirically plausible. The increased affluence after World War II, for example, led to a change in many employees' motivation structure and to a steady increase in the need for recognition and status, self-actualization, creativity, responsibility, and inclusion in decision-making processes. Similar to the way that scientific management was overtaken by the shift from material to social needs as a dominant motivator, the human relations approach was surpassed by the dominance of higher-level growth motivators (Hill / Fehlbaum / Ulrich 1994).

## Herzberg's Two Factor Theory

Herzberg developed Maslow's theory of motivation further and revealed that the work environment is not the only source of employee motivation, but that work content is also of great importance. In his job satisfaction theory, which is based on empirical research, Herzberg assumes that there are two major factors that influence the range between job satisfaction and job dissatisfaction (Herzberg / Mausner / Snyderman 1959; Herzberg 1968):

- Motivators are factors that can create satisfaction. They pertain to work content such as performance, acknowledgment, interesting work, responsibility, and promotion.

- Hygiene factors prevent dissatisfaction, but do not produce satisfaction. They mainly pertain to the working environment such as organizational politics, working conditions, remuneration, and social relationships.

Motivators serve to create job satisfaction and hygiene factors prevent job dissatisfaction (see figure 9.2). In Herzberg's opinion, job content is the primary determinant of job satisfaction and, therefore, of motivation. Like Maslow, he emphasizes that humans strive for self-actualization. He developed a canon of recommendations for management that is based on his empirical research. He recommends, for example, avoidance of negative hygiene factors and concentrating exclusively on motivators (Staehle 1999). According to Herzberg's theory, it would be wrong to try to motivate people with money. Motivation only results from the quality of the work itself (job-related motivators).

## VIE Models by Vroom, as Well as Porter and Lawler

Vroom's (1964) VIE (valence, instrumentality, and expectancy) theory is a more complex approach to explaining workplace motivation. This theory describes the cognitive processes that motivate individuals and is viewed as a basic model for more recent motivation process theories. Vroom's model is based on the assumption that individuals pursue goals to which they assign value (valence). Individuals differ in their rating of the attractiveness of certain outcomes and rewards. Individuals' choice when acting on available options is therefore based on their confidence that the effort will lead to successful performance (instrumentality). Ultimately, individuals estimate the probability that their efforts will lead to successful performance (expectancy) (Staehle 1990, p. 211; Kupsch / Marr 1991, p. 741). This assessment of valence, instrumentality, and expectancy determines which action the individual will take.

Porter and Lawler (1968) have a similar view of the cognitive process of behavior development. They incorporate some elements of Vroom's approach (valence, estimation of reward and one's own capabilities). In addition, they indicate additional factors that influence behavior and / or are connected to outcomes, satisfaction, and future behavior choices.

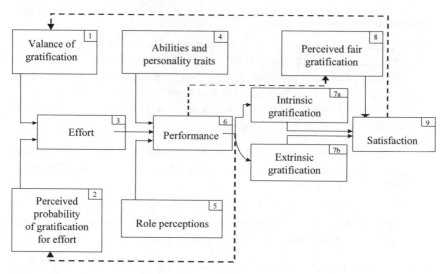

**Fig. 9.6.**   Motivation model by Porter and Lawler (1968)

The concept of valence and expectancy offers the following conclusions for management: In order to motivate the employee towards improved performance, managers can try to change the valence of goals, emphasize the instrumentality of certain behaviors, increase the perceived probability of the success of certain behavior through information and qualification, and reward performance and behavior (von Rosenstiel 1998). This reconfirms managers' new role as analysts, coaches and mentors, and as motivation and leadership specialists.

### Adams's Equity Theory

In addition to these comprehensive valence and expectancy models, Adams (1965) offers the equity theory as another perspective on human behavior within organizations. Adams assumes that there is a general desire for equity. The perception of inequity releases motivational potential directed towards restoring equity (Staehle 1999).

In working organizations, a sense of inequity results when the organization members perceive their performance and received rewards as not being in proportion compared to the input and output of others in the same or similar work situations.

People try to balance this imbalance by adjusting their input (performance) or output (results). If, for example, employees feel that they earn less than co-workers for the same amount of work, there is a significant risk that those employees will reduce their performance. The relationship between managers and employees can also be regarded as an exchange process, in which the input and output have to be balanced (Graen 1976). Equity theory presents important considerations with regard to designing reward systems and performance-based bonuses. It also offers conclusions with regard to the relationship between managers and employees.

**Approaches in Attribution Theory**

More recently, attribution theories have become important as an approach to analyzing performance motivation (Weiner 1994). The fundamental assumption of attribution theory is that people try to discover the causes of certain events. This need to attribute causes to observable experiences or events is a basic motivation because it becomes a basis for subsequent behavior and reactions. In a certain situation, for example, successful behavior can be attributed to one's own abilities and performance (internal attribution), to coincidence, to low task complexity or to external factors (external attribution). Subsequent behavior is determined by attributing previous success or failure to internal or external factors.

People who are, for example, strongly motivated by performance attribute their success or failure to their own abilities, while those who are less motivated by performance generally attribute their success or failures to environmental conditions.

In addition to attributing causes to one's own performance, people also attribute them to others' success and failure. Research shows that management and employees tend to make contrary attributions concerning employee performance: While managers attribute the employees' success to environmental conditions, employees attribute it to their own abilities. This can cause tension that hampers a supportive relationship between managers and employees. Diverging attributions should therefore be avoided.

Managers can avoid divergent attributions by deepening their understanding of employees' personalities, tasks and, the situational conditions. Green and Mitchell (1979) posit that the shorter the psychological distance to the employee is, the more realistic attributions are. This underscores the new role of managers as coaches and mentors, which implies that managers spend sufficient time dealing with and understanding employees as persons. In their role as coach, managers can use communication to try to influence negative attributions that hamper an employee's performance. New organizational concepts that rely on a high degree of delegation and the transfer of increased responsibility and autonomy to the employee can help prevent unjustified external attributions of employee success to the manager and unjustified attribution of failure to the employee.

### 9.3.2.3 Behavioral Research Approaches

Behavioral research also adds to the understanding of management's new roles by making basic assertions about leaders and followers' behavior in the cooperative task completion context. One branch within behavior research is dedicated to leadership style, which is defined as a leader's long-term, relatively stable, situation-invariant behavior pattern. This pattern of behavior is determined by the manager's basic attitude towards the employee (Neuberger 1977).

Based on empirical observations, Tannenbaum and Schmidt (1958) developed a continuum of authoritarian and cooperative leadership styles (see figure 9.7). They assert that the "right" leadership style is determined by the specific characteristics

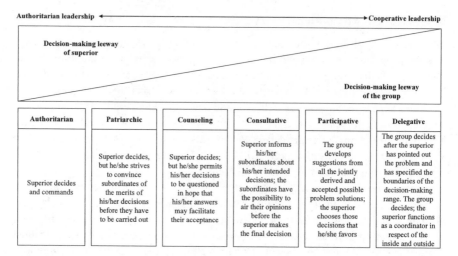

**Fig. 9.7.** Authoritarian and cooperative leadership styles (Tannenbaum / Schmidt 1958)

of the manager, the employee, and the situation. There is no such thing as a single "right" leadership style. The ability to correctly assess the factors influencing a given situation and the flexibility to adjust one's leadership style to that situation is the key to successful leadership (Staehle 1999).

The Ohio Studies (since 1945), the Michigan Studies (since 1947) and the Group Dynamics Studies (1960) identified two distinct characteristics of leadership behavior. These can be summarized as employee orientation and task orientation (Staehle 1999; Goecke 1997). Employee orientation describes a leadership style that emphasizes the special significance of interpersonal relationships for task performance. The employee's individual needs and goals are taken seriously and personal development is encouraged. Task orientation, on the other hand, emphasizes a task's performance aspects. The manager views the employee as a tool with which to achieve organizational goals.

In addition to describing the basic dimensions of leadership behavior, these studies examined leadership style. In their original version of the managerial grid (see figure 9.8), Blake and Mouton (1985) stated that optimal leadership behaviors are characterized by a high concern for tasks and relationships (people and production). Later, this description of a "one best way" style of leadership was again dismissed by these authors and modified by Reddin (1977) and by Hersey and Blanchard (2001), who view the efficiency of a leadership style in the context of a given situation.

Within the context of group dynamics studies, Cartwright and Zander (1968) interpreted leadership dimensions normatively as the functions of leadership. Lukasczyk (1960) first used the term "locomotion function" in respect of ensuring goal achievement and "cohesion function" in respect of maintaining group cohesion. These terms were later picked up in leadership research by, for example, Grote (1994).

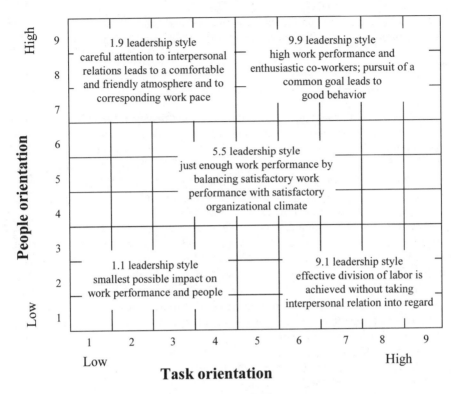

**Fig. 9.8.**    The managerial grid (Blake / Mouton 1968)

The new work and organizational forms influence leadership behavior and / or its task focus. Distributed structures require information, communication, and leadership processes for successful task completion. There is a demand for decision-making responsibility to be distributed to the dispersed units, for increased independence and for support for the autonomy of dispersed units and employees (Boyett / Conn 1992). Within such a framework, true authoritarian leadership styles become problematic. Cooperative leadership styles, on the other hand, are more promising for success.

Since managers are being increasingly divested of work-oriented responsibilities, their focus shifts to relationship-oriented tasks. Another factor impacting this development is telecommuting. Surveys of telecommuters have indicated that employees working in distributed organizations frequently participate less in team decisions. They also perceive a decline in the cooperative climate and a substantial decrease in social contacts (Reichwald / Bastian 1999a, 1999b).

Distributed work appears to inherently bear the risk of losing cohesion effects. This phenomenon can be compared to the "centrifugal forces of decentralization" described by Nerdinger and von Rosenstiel (1996) in the context of decentralization discussions. The main challenge for the management of distributed organizations is to maintain cohesion within teams, within the organization as whole, as well as within the framework of inter-organizational cooperation. This task is in keeping with management's new roles.

### 9.3.2.4   Communication Theory Approaches

Communication plays a vital role in employees and managers' new roles. Empirical studies on the communication of managers have demonstrated that managers spend up to 90% of their workday involved in communication activities (Pribilla / Reichwald / Goecke 1996). Employees within distributed organizations also experience increased communication activities when viewed within the context of new work structures such as teamwork and networking. Communication theory offers some explanations for these developments (Moeslein 2000).

The importance of communication becomes evident if one assumes that observable facts in the environment are never absorbed and transformed into human behavior completely unfiltered, but are instead interpreted by the individual and compared to previous experience and existing mental rules and regulation. According to this basic assumption (which is based on radical constructivism), the minds of humans do not contain objective perceptions of reality but rather interpretive perceptions that are more or less suitable for every day life (Kieser et al. 1998; Weick 1985; Wollnik 1992).

Observable facts in the environment, such as formal organization structures, may be reflected quite differently in the organization members' minds. This can lead to the members' conclusions impacting decisions that they may make, thus contradicting the observable facts. An organization therefore requires communication for it to act in a coordinated way. Communication enables the organization members to negotiate a shared interpretation of facts – they thus construct their shared reality.

Common basic assumptions and rules can help to reduce the time spent on agreements, as well as simplify or speed up tasks completion. This is especially true for complex and highly variable tasks that need to be divided among members of the organization. Teamwork is viewed as performance enhancing because it compels communication between team members and thereby encourages the development of common mental structures.

Managers who want to coach, develop, mentor, and support their employees also need to coordinate their interpretation of facts with that of their employees. As previously discussed in section 9.3.1.3, communication is a decisive factor for initiating organizational transformation and for changing mental structures. This is a task that the manager, as change agent, needs to take on.

According to the pragmatic communication approach (Watzlawick et al. 1990), every form of communication has a content aspect and a relationship aspect (see chapter 3). The content aspect refers to the transmission of facts. In contrast, the relationship aspect refers to the interpersonal relationship between the communication partners, and therefore offers a starting point for the interpretation of pure content.

The less complicated the relationship between the communication partners, the more easily they can share factual information. In the context of increasingly complex and more variable tasks and factual information, good relationships become crucial for successful completion, especially if this takes place in different locations and time zones. This explains the role of the manager as a networker and the role of the employee as a relationship manager whose job it is to build relationships through communication.

Media choice theories support the special role that personal communication plays in new organizational concepts. The communication media model's task-oriented choice (see Reichwald 1999) recommends verbal and synchronized communication tools for complex communication tasks and points to the importance of spatial proximity between communication partners. Media richness theory takes a similar direction (Daft/Lengel 1984; Rice 1992). This theory assumes that diverse forms of communication can vary in their degree of "richness". Richness is determined by factors such as opportunities for feedback, the number of channels used, interpersonal (and/or impersonal) contact or type or variety of communication possibilities (such as body language).

Daft and Lengel (1984) believe that face-to-face communication is the richest form of communication. Media richness theory provides a communication model for effective communication, depending on the complexity of the communication task. It also recommends rich communication tools for complex tasks. Grote's (1994) empirical research indicates that electronic media are of limited value in supporting management's cohesion function (relationship and community building).

If one assumes that in boundaryless organizations, management's tasks are becoming more and more complex, then these models explain interpersonal communication's strong relevance. There are still, of course, factual tasks that are less complex and highly structured and that can therefore be accomplished by means of less rich communication channels. However, the new focus on tasks such as relationship building, networking, initiation of change, and the intensive support of individual employees is characterized by complexity. This makes interpersonal communication the center of attention.

## 9.4   Tackling the Future Organization and Its Challenges for People

### 9.4.1   Qualification and Employee Development

Qualifications and employee development are proving to be the key to the successful change and subsequent adoption of new roles when viewed against their background, the increased challenges for management and employees, and taking the obstacles and barriers to practical application into consideration.

Qualification describes an employee's total competence to meet both present and future challenges. Together with professional expertise, social competence and creativity are also becoming more important to successfully implement and realize new organizational concepts. The importance of professional expertise is therefore decreasing in favor of the other two partial qualifications (Höfer 1997).

This argument is based on social competence and creativity enjoying more longevity than specialized technical know-how (especially in technical areas), which tends to quickly become outdated in the face of continuous technological advancement (Lawler 1994; Underwood 1993). This does not, however, imply that the acquisition of professional skills and expertise can be dispensed with. In the future, too, it will be necessary to acquire and teach professional expertise and skills (Pawlowsky 1992). New incentives and reward systems ensure the goal-oriented transfer of new expertise as well as continued education (life-long learning) and ongoing qualification improvements for employees (see chapter 10).

### 9.4.1.1  Teaching Social Competence

Social competence, social abilities and social intelligence are all skills that help to ensure groups' optimal functionality. They all encompass the ability (von Rosenstiel / Regnet / Domsch 1998) to communicate (speaking and being able to listen) as well as the ability to:

- Show empathy;

- Clearly communicate one's thoughts and feelings;

- Communicate openly and directly;

- Provide feedback;

- Be authentic; and

- Behave in a way that does not increase conflict.

These abilities help to ensure a proper exchange with others (colleagues, customers, supervisors, subordinates, etc.), as well as ensuring and facilitating integration into a social context.

Various methods have been utilized to convey social competence. Each author has used a different systemizing scheme (Conradi 1983; Thom 1987; Neuberger 1994). The following discussion uses von Rosenstiel's scheme (1992, p. 96 ff.), which is largely oriented toward Neuberger (1991). Von Rosenstiel clusters the methods for the conveyance of social competence into content and process-oriented measures. Figure 9.9 provides a summary of possible content and process-oriented qualification measures to convey social competence.

Content-oriented measures (lectures, presentations, films, and videos) refer to qualification by conveying factual information without the participants' active participation. They are of limited value in conveying social competence. For content-oriented measures to be suitable tools for teaching social competence, they need to be combined with visualization (such as a video that models appropriate social behavior).

| Measures | Examples |
|---|---|
| **Content-oriented measures** | • Presentation<br>• Video |
| **Process-oriented measures** | **Non-structural measures**<br>• Learning discussion, panel<br>• Discussions<br>• Role playing<br>• Case studies<br>• Entrepreneurial planning games<br>• Group-dynamics training<br>• Team formation<br>**Structural measures**<br>• Quality circles<br>• Project work<br>• Network information |

**Fig. 9.9.**    Methods for conveying social competence

Process-oriented measures may range from a simple instructional talk to long-range, structural organization change and actively involve the participants in this process. There are numerous trends that have each enjoyed popularity. Among these are role-playing, the use of case studies, group dynamics training, and others. Process-oriented measures may be divided into non-structural and structural measures. Non-structural measures convey social competence without involving organization change, whereas structural measures do. Structural methods are regarded as having a more sustained impact because they are usually designed to span longer periods of time.

### Non-structural Measures

The simplest form of non-structural measures is forums or plenary discussions as a part of seminars, with the participants contributing their own experiences and presenting their problems for review by colleagues.

In comparison, role-plays are characterized by a higher degree of instrumentalization. They offer the possibility to practice appropriate or alternative behavior with the help of supplied materials and information generated from current situations or problems. The participants receive feedback from the other participants or the trainer. Another possibility is for the trainer or a skilled actor to assume the partner role of the person being trained.

The use of case studies tends to involve more complex requirements (Domsch / Regnet / von Rosenstiel 2001). They are designed to transfer theoretical knowledge to daily practice by means of concrete cases. With computer support, complex case studies can develop into management games that can run for several days. Based on certain requirements, participants are therefore assigned different roles, and the computer program offers feedback on the decisions made by individuals or groups. During the assignment, the participants are also given the opportunity to receive specific feedback on their behavior from trained observers. In addition, management games offer the opportunity to take part in the processes of group dynamics. Within the traditional framework of group dynamics training, these processes can also be practiced outside role specifications.

During group dynamics training, approximately twelve people meet over the course of several days. The participants are informed that they are only allowed to talk about things that occur during the training. The main characteristic of the classic group dynamics training is the generally uncensored feedback from the other participants (Gebert 1972). However, transfer of the knowledge and insights gained in this type of training to the everyday business environment can prove difficult. The way to deal with this in practice is to employ group dynamics methods with existing groups within an organization. Such team-building sessions require the implementation of very specific rules and a well-qualified trainer who plays a decisive role in directing and interpreting the training.

Team building and inter-teamwork also employ role clarification and/or role negotiation. The goal of this method is to allow all participants to recognize their role in a social context under the guidance of a process advisor. This is achieved in that all the participants negotiate their role interpretation with another employee with whom they need to cooperate but are at odds with.

## Structural Measures

A quality circle is a limited number of participants who meet with a trained moderator and use problem-solving methods to develop suggestions for improvements (von Rosenstiel 1992; Zink/Ritter 1992). These meetings occur regularly, are voluntary (either during or after work), and take place over longer periods of time. The following are similar to quality circles: Problem-solving groups, suggestion groups, shop floor fora, etc. Quality circles do, however, entail some potential problems: The implementation of the solution proposals that they develop often takes too long. Likewise, there is often a lack of commitment on the part of higher-level management and staff, which is understandable, as these projects often impact their own areas of responsibility. However, because quality circles are not led by trained professionals and employees are not trained in active participation, they are usually occasions for learning by doing. In the process of solving a problem, the participants develop the competence that they require to accomplish the task they set out to do (Neuberger 1994).

Project work is generally directed at specialized goals. Various specialists therefore get together for a limited period of time to complete or solve a task in a coordinated way. A certain amount of social competence is required, but it will also be improved through these measures (von Rosenstiel 1992). There are different types of project work, depending on whether they are organized by a staff function or take place in an established project team or in a matrix organization (Neuberger 1994). Since projects tend to be of limited duration and new groups are frequently set up, project work tends to primarily develop individual social skills (such as flexibility, powers of persuasion, and social adaptability). The development of social relationships is usually a secondary achievement.

Personal, intra-organizational network building is based on the fact that interpersonal relationships are key within every organization. The main goal of network building is the resolving of conflicts between departments and / or different areas, and there are many ways of promoting it (Neuberger 1994). The basic idea of the multiplier concept is to use qualified internal specialists as trainers to combine subject expertise with specific implementation experience. The advantage of these "multipliers" compared to that of external consultants is that they are aware of the organization's formal and informal rules and regulations and therefore generally generate less resistance from those being trained.

Learning communities are a type of self-development. Different employees, who would like to study the same subject or learn a new procedure, divide a task between them. This reduces individual employees' efforts, takes individual needs into consideration, as well as each participant's learning strengths and weaknesses. Learning communities also teach social skills.

With a peer review, a group of employees gets together to discuss practical problems and to benefit from each participant's specific experiences and perspectives. First, an actual case or problem is presented. The other participants obtain additional information by asking questions and receiving feedback, thereafter suggesting possible solutions or sharing similar experiences. A successful peer review requires a conversational climate characterized by trust, mutual respect, and supportiveness.

## 9.4.1.2   Qualifications for Innovation and Creativity

Employees' creativity and innovation strength is increasingly becoming a decisive success factor. The ability to recognize opportunities of relevance to the organization, together with the ability to produce innovative products, processes, methods, concepts, and strategies is of growing importance. Of equal importance is management's ability to appropriately direct and support innovation processes without limiting employee creativity (Brockhoff 1996; Staudt 1986; Rogers 1995).

When applied to the individual, important factors for the innovation process are employees' capacity (creativity) and will (innovation readiness) to deliver innovative performance. While the readiness to innovate may be influenced by innovation-enhancing incentive systems, creativity requires a mix of personal and organizational measures (Corsten 1989). Schlicksupp (1992, p. 43) developed an approach to enhance creativity that combines personal and organizational factors. He views the capacity for creative behavior and / or creative work processes as essentially consisting of three elementary components (see also figure 9.10), which comprise:

| Design elements of the firm / Components of creativity | Knowledge | Conceptual rules | Psychological drivers |
|---|---|---|---|
| Structural organization | 1 | | |
| Process organization | 2 | | 11 |
| Standardization | 3 | | |
| Division of labor | 4 | | 12 |
| Leadership behavior | 5 | 8 | 13 |
| Human resources development | 6 | 9 | 14 |
| Information and communication relationships | 7 | 10 | 15 |

Examples of creativity-enhancing measures

1 Matrix organization
3 Minimizing of bureaucratic processes
4 Job rotation
5 Dissemination of fundamental information to employees (expanding the view of the enterprise as a whole)
6 Choice of training and further education
7 Free access to relevant information; open communication
8 Encouragement of unconventional thinking; openness toward innovations

9 Creativity training
10 Cooperative, prejudice-free collaboration
11 Autonomy in processing
12 Delegation of responsibility
13 Employee-oriented leadership
14 Promotion guidelines that are, e.g., also oriented toward social abilities and attitudes
15 Permitting new ideas to enter and disseminate in the organization

**Fig. 9.10.** Internal endorsement of creativity and primary components of creativity development (based on Schlicksupp 1992)

- Available information (including the reorganization of known knowledge elements);
- Mechanisms of knowledge processing (thinking principles, methods, and degree of freedom in the thinking process);
- Psychodynamic driving forces (trigger mechanisms for creative thinking, e.g., degree of inquisitiveness).

Consequently, creativity cannot only be developed with individuals, but also needs to be developed in the environment surrounding the individual. The development of creative reserves within the organization should therefore be directed towards three goals:

- Making the required knowledge available so that creativity can flourish, for example, through job rotation, the encouragement of teamwork and project work in general, the organization of contacts and information exchange within the organization, and the promotion of cross-functional contacts in the organization (e.g., cross-functional teams or networked work groups).

- Creating working conditions that trigger creativity (e.g., delegation, employee-oriented leadership, an open and generous flow of relevant information from management to employees, promotion guidelines with regard to innovations, and emphasis on team-orientation).

- Encouraging creative knowledge processing (e.g., project work using interdisciplinary teams, the introduction of a suggestion system, the creation of a staff function to provide innovation assistance to all organization units, and the possibility for employees to spend a certain portion of their time pursuing individual interests).

## 9.4.2  The Concept of Organizational Learning

The concept of organizational learning goes beyond the challenges of individual learning that the organization faces. Key to organizational learning is that not only that each organization member should learn, but that the organization as a whole should be in a position to cope with its new environment. Organizational learning is a tool that can be used to overcome old organization structures, can allow new structures to evolve, and / or enable existing new structures to adapt to changing environmental conditions.

### 9.4.2.1  The Connection Between Individual and Organizational Learning

Different disciplines explore the subject of organizational learning and focus on different aspects. Psychology, for instance, tends to explore individual learning processes, while systems theory tends to look at the system, such as the organization as a whole. These seemingly contradictory positions raise the core question: What differentiates organizational learning from individual learning? The fact that individuals can learn is undisputed. It is harder to judge the learning ability of an organization as a whole. An organization always acts (and learns) through its members. An organization's performance, as well as its ability to learn, depends on its members' learning ability and on its organizational interconnections (Reber 1992).

Probst and Büchel (1997) provide the following example of organizational learning by means of recording information independently of the organization members: An employee in the payroll department who processes the payroll according to the rules defined by management may, through trial and error, discover a more effective way of processing the payroll. If the organization registers and implements this new approach, the organization has gained new knowledge that now exists independently of the individual organization members.

Individual learning is a prerequisite for organizations to learn. By recording knowledge, the organization simultaneously becomes independent of its members' individual knowledge (Matsuda 1993). By storing individual knowledge within organizational knowledge systems, responsibilities are gradually abstracted and implemented within the organizational system. While organizations do not have a brain to store knowledge, they do have storage systems such as guidelines, work directions, myths, and cultures at their disposal (Pawlowsky 1992, p. 202). Individuals may leave an organization, but strategic guidelines, leadership principles, goals, values, norms, and knowledge about specific processes outlast most personnel changes.

But what exactly differentiates individual from organizational learning? What characterizes the transition from one level of learning to the next, and how can it be achieved? We first provide a brief definition of individual learning to facilitate its differentiation from organizational learning. Bower and Hilgard (1983, p. 31, translation by the authors) define individual learning as "… a change in behavior or behavior potential … with regard to a certain situation that relates back to repeated experiences in this situation, provided that this behavior change cannot be explained by innate reaction tendencies, maturation or transitional circumstances." This definition of learning implies individual rationality, dependence on personal experiences, linkages with individual needs and motivation, as well as interests and value positions, the difficulty of the subject matter to be learned, and manifestations within many behavioral changes.

In contrast, organizational learning depends on collective rationality and a collective frame of reference. Its emphasis is not on individual motives, needs or values, but on the supra-personal experience worlds, collective decision-making procedures, normative order, and agreement reached through a majority-based decision. Organizational learning not only encompasses adaptation of the organization to changing environmental conditions, but also changing intra-organizational conditions such as its members' motives, needs, interests, goals, values, and norms (Probst / Büchel 1994, p. 20).

Klimecki, Probst and Eberl (1994) demonstrate how organizations might move from one learning level to the next, bridging individual and organizational learning, by meeting the following three transformation conditions:

- Communication, as individual knowledge cannot be made available to the organization without it nor can collective argumentation and organization processes be triggered.

- Transparency with regard to the course and result of communication processes, which storage media may create in respect of knowledge resources and symbolic values, such as a leitmotiv in the form of leadership principles, models, stories, and other forms of symbolism.

- The integration of collective bargaining processes into the entire system.

### 9.4.2.2   Action Theories as Explanatory Aids of Organizational Learning

Each individual has access to a reservoir of knowledge and behavioral possibilities on the personal and the organizational level. This implied action theory provides the framework for actions within the system and makes it possible for the individual to learn within a professional context. The term "theories of action" was first used by Argyris (1964) to denote the reservoir of organizational knowledge. Action theories define expectations about the consequences of certain behavioral patterns under specific conditions. They include strategies, images, goals, cultures and structures, and constitute a frame of reference for the organization's continuity, as well as characteristics that are essential for its survival. Argyris and Schön (1978) undertook the divisioning of this organizational knowledge base in 1978 (see also Probst/Büchel 1994, p. 22). Action theories may be applied as espoused theories or as theories-in-use:

- Espoused theories, or official action theories, form the organizational framework that determines the enterprise's shared image. These theories are expressed as an enterprise's images, strategies, goals, values, norms, and structures.

- Theories-in-use arise from the separation of individual and collective experiences and from their reciprocal effects, as well as by comparing these experiences with the institutional framework.

Espoused theories and theories-in-use do not always have to be compatible within an organization. This incompatibility, which is often not revealed (because theories-in-use are not explicitly expressed or because the organization often has more information than it is aware of), serves as a starting point for organizational learning. Organizational learning is sparked by resolving cognitive conflict or by revealing the action theories practiced by the organization (Ulrich 1993).

### 9.4.2.3    How Does Organizational Learning Occur?

Learning is always directed toward a change in knowledge. Argyris and Schön (1978, p. 18) describe the following three possibilities regarding how knowledge may change and learning may occur (Schanz 1994, p. 433):

- Single-loop learning occurs when the organization members respond to internal or external changes (Hedberg 1981). Deviations or errors in the theories-in-use are uncovered and actions are taken to correct them in a way that preserves the essential characteristics of the official action theories. Optimization is limited to structures and processes, and the norms and goals of the organization are not questioned.

- Double-loop learning becomes important when environmental observations have confirmed a change in context that demands a modification of the official action theory. At this level of organizational learning, a confrontation occurs between organizational hypotheses, norms and directions, and environmental observations. This creates feedback loops from these observations to the framework (knowledge system) of organizations (Pawlowsky 1992, p. 207). The feedback process may result, for example, in the pursuit of a new strategy or in a change in the organization's norm system. Single-loop learning therefore manifests itself in reactive, incremental change, whereas double-loop learning manifests in proactive, radical change (Ulrich 1993). This reorientation requires a capacity for organizational "unlearning" and for the implementation of new behavioral models (Hedberg 1981).

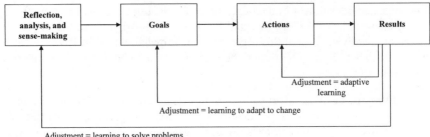

**Fig. 9.11.** Types of learning (based on Probst / Büchel 1997)

- Problem-solving learning (Pawlowsky, 1992, p. 209), labeled by Argyris
  and Schön as "deutero learning," describes improvement in the capacity to
  learn as an organization, while this in itself is the subject of the learning
  process. This learning type is especially useful to ensure creativity, innovation, and the ability to change (Müller / Stewens / Pautzke 1991, p. 198).
  The process of "learning to learn" is based on the recognition of the underlying single-loop and double-loop learning.

Senge (1990a) identifies three other stages of learning: "practice learning," "principle learning," and "essence learning." The highest level ("essence learning") includes a holistic understanding of practices, principles, and system relationships.
This includes recognition of the underlying purpose of these practices and principles. It is therefore no longer only the organization's norms and rules that determine behavior, but the understanding of and insights into the organization's purpose and meaning. All organization members therefore achieve an understanding
stage that is otherwise only achieved by persons or groups with a substantial
knowledge of detail (Senge 1990a, p. 374).

These definitions are just two possibilities found in the literature and are included here to provide some insight into this subject's scope and range. Despite
the large number of definitions to be found in the area of organizational learning,
they share certain characteristics. This conclusion also forms the basis of the subsequent discussion. According to Pawlowsky (1992), organizational learning is a
process that:

- Includes a change in the frame of reference of the organizational knowledge
  base;

- Occurs as an interplay between the individual and the organization;

- Occurs through interaction with the internal and / or external environment;

- Refers to existing action theories within the organization; and

- Is designed to facilitate adaptation to the internal and external environment
  and / or the system's increased problem-solving capacity.

### 9.4.2.4  Starting Points for the Nurturing of Organizational Learning

How can organizational learning be nurtured? Measures that promote organizational learning usually make several assumptions. One example of a systematized approach is the "magic square" by Probst and Büchel (1997). It shows the four development areas: Strategy, structure, culture, and employee development (see Figure 9.12).

**"The Magic Square"**

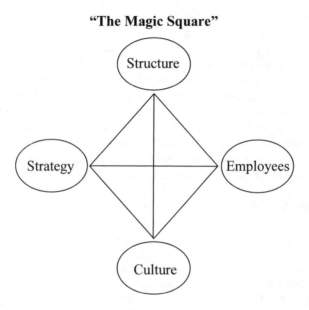

**Fig. 9.12.**  Approaches for the nurturing of organizational learning (Probst / Büchel 1997)

The following are examples of advancement measures in the area of strategy development: Computer-supported management games that enable the simulation of complete business processes; a scenario analysis forecasts future developments inside and outside the organization, while strategic controlling is aimed at the key role of feedback on examined processes. Actions, measures, behaviors or goals can be subsequently corrected by means of the information that has been fed back. In this context, it is important that the organization's lower levels are largely able to participate in the strategy development process. This can, for example, be achieved by the management moderating and structuring emerging strategy development processes (Ulrich 1993). If this is not possible, then the strategies that management develops should be made transparent on all levels.

In the area of structural development, the advantages of the three organizational forms of project organization, network organization, and cooperation are emphasized in the context of the organizational learning concept. In all of these structures, several organization members from varying hierarchical levels and areas work together. Horizontal connections are developed to create opportunities for innovation and creativity by solving problems, recognizing opportunities, accomplishing tasks holistically, and enabling employees to participate in decision-making (Reichwald / Koller 1996a).

Within the framework of culture development, Probst and Büchel (1997) emphasize the process of developing models as a frame of reference for employees' view of themselves and their behavior. They furthermore emphasize communication forums for the development of codes to facilitate the questioning of existing values and norms. Open vertical and horizontal information flows also contribute to a positive learning culture in the enterprise. Internal and external image analyses for the positioning, questioning, and early recognition of changes, as well as the initiation of corrective measures are also mentioned.

The fourth cornerstone within the magic square of measures for advancing organizational learning is human resources development. Concepts of participatory, group-oriented learning are especially emphasized. A particularly useful effect is attributed to learning-partner relationships (such as coaching, mentoring, personal development alliances), workplace-based interventions (such as rotation principle, project work, suggestion systems), and creativity techniques (such as mind-mapping). While learning-partner relationships and creativity techniques are mainly used in the questioning of values and norms, workplace-based interventions are mainly geared toward the integration of learning and work.

### 9.4.2.5  New Demands on Employees Involved in Organizational Learning

In addition to the great many interpretations of the term organizational learning, there is another reason why so few concepts of organizational learning have been applied in practice. One explanation is certainly the misunderstanding of the new roles of employees and managers (Senge 1990b, p. 8), since the organization's ability to learn is substantially determined by its members' individual behavior.

The learning capacity of an organization depends largely on its members' individual behavior. It is only when individuals learn that the organization as a whole experiences further learning. Senge (1990) mentions five "disciplines" that, when combined, may lead to organizational learning:

1. Personal mastery;
2. Mental models;
3. Shared vision;
4. Team learning;
5. System thinking.

System thinking integrates the other four disciplines because it provides a framework for the other four disciplines. At the same time though, system thinking also requires the other disciplines to unfold its full potential (Senge 1990a, p. 12). The five disciplines are described below.

**Personal Mastery**

Personal mastery does not refer to gaining power over people or things, but to a specific type of self-motivating ability. Individuals who strongly exhibit this trait are capable of consistently achieving expected results over the long term. Their achievement is based on life-long learning. Personal mastery includes the following capabilities:

- Continuous clarification of one's goals and scrutinizing of one's achievements;
- Bundling of one's energies;
- Development of patience; and
- An objective view.

Very few enterprises invest in developing such abilities in their employees. Usually, highly motivated individuals with a high level of expert knowledge join an enterprise. Over time, two kinds employees emerge: Those who move up the career ladder quickly and those who merely "do their time," with their main attention focused on matters outside work. They lose their link to the organization and no longer perceive the deeper meaning of their work. Furthermore, they no longer perform their work with the same excitement as at the beginning of their career (Senge 1990a, p. 7).

**Questioning Mental Models**

Mental models are deeply rooted assumptions, generalizations or images that influence how people view the world and how they react to it. People connect observations with their mental models and draw conclusions about (non-observable) facts, perhaps because these facts always occurred in this manner in the past and have been stored as mental models. Based on existing mental models, one assumes certain outcomes, even though it is not at all clear that these outcomes will occur as assumed. Unreflected mental models are not to be underestimated in professional daily life. For example, the opening of new markets or the introduction of newer organizational forms may fail because of employees' prevailing mental models. The more organization members share such mental models, the more organizational learning will be hampered, if not prevented all together.

How can mental models then be used to advance organizational learning? Senge suggests that overcoming mental models that inhibit organizational learning requires the organization members to reflect on and discover their own mental models, to bring them to the surface, and examine them. This requires the ability to lead learning-enhancing discussions in which a balance needs to be found between the accusative ("This is wrong, because …"), and defensive ("I did this because …"). Employees must be able to present their own thoughts and open themselves to others' influence. They should not cling to their own mental models, but be able to revise them by being aware of them and by reflecting on their appropriateness.

**Anticipating Shared Vision**

It is a generally accepted fact that organizations are especially successful when there are goals, values, and norms that are shared and implemented by all employees and through which individual employees' activities can be directed towards a common goal. Senge (1990b, p. 9) views such visions as an essential starting point for influencing organizational learning. According to Senge, people do not learn because they are required to learn, but because there is a common vision within the organization, to which they voluntarily align their learning. An organization-specific vision gives employees a common identity and a sense of belonging.

The difficulty with constructing such visions is the transformation of individual organization members' goals, values, and norms into a shared, organization-wide vision. There are no generally applicable formulas for accomplishing such visions, only a set of principles and directions that needs to be adapted to specific situations (see Senge, 1994, p. 295). For this vision to be shared by all employees, it should be created in a participatory way and all employees should be invited to participate in identifying relevant visions for the future. It is only through this participatory procedure that a shared vision can emerge that also forms the employee's true link to the organization.

**Team Learning**

Each organization is divided into sub-groups or teams that have jointly utilized techniques or specific forms of learning, their own goals, values, and norms and are therefore differentiated from other groups or teams. In order for an organization to learn, all sub-groups must be coordinated (Schein 1992, p. 41).

Schein (1992, p. 40) refers to the use of dialogue as a tool to support successful learning in and between groups. He argues that organizational effectiveness is largely dependent on communication beyond group boundaries and that dialogue is therefore the most suitable coordination tool. Dialogue is aimed at solving problems and finding consensus with regard to a choice of alternative conflict solutions. Through dialogue, it is possible for group members to rid themselves of prejudices and develop a true team spirit. Dialogue enables group members to recognize interaction patterns, including defensive behavior, within and between groups in the way in which cooperation (or the lack thereof) occurs. Defensive patterns are often deeply rooted and, if not recognized, can undermine learning. If brought to the surface, however, defensive patterns can actually speed up learning. This usually occurs in group meetings in which – depending on the problem to be resolved – either all members of a group or members of different groups participate.

**System Thinking**

The discipline of system thinking integrates the four previously described components of a learning organization. Senge (1990a, p. 6) uses the following example

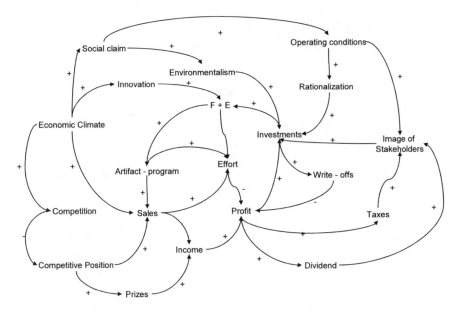

**Fig. 9.13.**  The organization as a schematic network with positive and negative feedback
loops (based on Probst / Gomez 1991)

to illustrate system thinking: When clouds arise and the sky darkens, we know that
it will soon rain. We also know that after the thunderstorm, rain will trickle into
the ground water, and the sky will be clear again by the next day. All of these events
occur at a different time and location, yet all of them are connected by the same
pattern. Each event influences the others. This influence usually remains invisible.
The system "thunderstorm" can only be understood when we observe the entire
system and not just one individual part of the model.

Figure 9.13 exemplifies the organization as a networked system. As this system's complexity is clearly visible, events do not always occur as planned, because it is hard to judge individual cycles and their interconnectivity in advance.
This means that it can be years before the individual structural parts of respective organizations work together in a way that takes full advantage of connectivity effects.

Since the individual employee is a part of this system, it is very difficult to recognize the system as a whole. Humans tend to take "snapshots" of isolated parts of
the entire system. In order to work successfully in the future, each employee will
have to be capable of thinking in a networked context and of recognizing the individual elements (co-workers, work groups, departments) and the activity between
the elements of the system "enterprise." Individually, all employees need to judge
the effects of their actions on other employees who are connected with their workplace and act accordingly (Senge 1990a).

## 9.5    ICT and the New Role of People Within Boundaryless Organizations

The new information and communication technologies have also contributed to the new role of people within organizations. Simultaneously, they have the potential to effectively help managers and employees to prepare for their new roles. The newest generation of these technologies enables a degree of data integration that can support new organizational concepts in their evolution from functional work distribution to operation and process integration. They also enable horizontal task integration (integration of different types of tasks at the implementation level), as well as vertical task integration (inclusion in planning, decision-making and controlling tasks). All systems access a common integrated database, which enables the combined use of the same data by different operational functions (Picot/Reichwald 1991).

Process-oriented interweaving of operational procedures through shared data requires different areas to work together extensively and produces an integrated view of operational functions. In addition, vertical task integration is closely tied to organizational decentralization with increased decision-making, participation, and information privileges. This means that task integration leads to a flatter organization structure.

Computer-supported production planning systems (PPS) for industrial manufacturing, concepts for the process of quality assurance, as well as the widely accepted view of the enterprise as a process-oriented, value-added chain (all popular in the 1980s) led to a reversal of Taylor's ideas on separating management and implementation tasks in industrial production. This created additional options for the reintegration of distributed work processes.

Organizational learning and development processes can be promoted with new information and technology and can also be stored for future use. Successful learning organizations can transform information into important know-how for the organization by combining technologies that support individual and group learning, as well as problem-solving activities. One component of this transformation is the design of an appropriate technology architecture comprising user support, integrated technology networks, and information tools designed to enable information to be accessed and exchanged. Among such tools are electronic tools, of course, but also advanced learning methods such as computer conferencing, simulations, and data-processing tools for computer-supported cooperative work. Marquardt and Reynolds (1994, p. 63) state that the goal here is the creation of "knowledge freeways."

These methods of telelearning or e-learning differ from computer-based training (CBT). CBT usually refers to commercial learning programs in which the user cannot interact with other fellow-learners or with an instructor (Sippel 1994).

Artificial intelligence can also be employed as a learning tool. This technology aims at modeling the human brain's thought processes. Potential users (learners) are then supervised, guided, and coached with the help of artificial intelligence. Instructions can also be modified in keeping with the learner's responses. The artificial intelligence system adapts to each user's learning style and the assistance provided is always user oriented. This makes continued education more interesting, practicable, and motivating, since the information provided is only focused on what the user really needs.

Information is key to organizational learning. Within organizations, information can be acquired, distributed, given meaning, stored and located (Marquardt/Reynolds 1994). For organizations to learn effectively and efficiently, these forms of information-handling should be systematically linked to one another.

The use of information and communication technology for training is expected to increase even further in the future. The following solution approach illustrates these technologies' potential applications in support of organizational learning. The goal of this approach is the development of organizational memory for frequently asked questions and their respective answers. The application system "Answer Garden," developed at MIT (see Ackerman 1992, 1994), is designed to change organizations' information search behavior, to develop organizational memory, and improve the coordination and management of intellectual capabilities within the enterprise.

With the assistance of a branching network of diagnosing questions, "Answer Garden" offers specific support with the search and retrieval of information. If an answer is not available in the database, the system automatically directs the question to the expert in charge of this area. Figure 9.14 depicts an inquiry's processing procedures by means of "Answer Garden."

The examples discussed here only offer a glimpse of the teletraining and/or e-learning area. The development trends can, however, be summarized as follows:

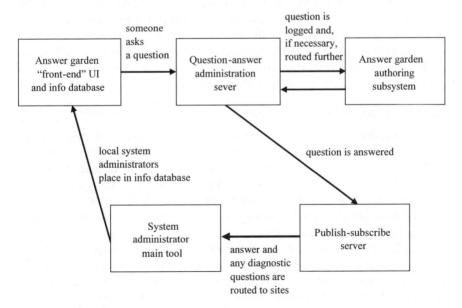

**Fig. 9.14.** "Answer Garden" inquiry process (Ackerman 1992)

There are efforts underway to encourage the increased use of these technologies to support individual as well as organizational learning processes. The main focus at this time is still on individual learning processes (Beck / Bendel / Stoller-Schai 2001).

## 9.6    Implications for Management

The models and theories discussed in this chapter have demonstrated that distributed work and organization models, networks, and virtual organizations have created new roles for management and employees. Fulfillment of these roles is an important requirement for the success of new organizational concepts. Section 9.3 of this chapter explored and justified these new roles from different theoretical perspectives.

### New Roles and Challenges for Employees

Holistic task completion results in most operational autonomy and decision-making responsibility being transferred to employees and employee teams. Employees have more freedom, more influence on their work, and have a greater responsibility for their work results. Altogether, these processes constitute empowerment. Elements of the new roles of employees are: Team work and relationship management, specialty and method expertise, organizational thinking and behavior, as well as learning and development.

This multitude of roles creates new challenges for the employee in the areas of expanded specialty expertise and method competence, but even more so in respect of social competence, creativity, innovation, and the ability to self-manage. These new challenges require higher levels of qualification than those required from the traditional employee in the past, and this trend towards higher-level qualification is clearly noticeable. This also means that the need for untrained or less qualified employees will continue to decrease substantially.

### New Roles and Challenges for Managers

Due to this new "empowerment" of employees, the manager's tasks are changing significantly. The manager's job is no longer dominated by giving directions, controlling, and decision-making but by personal leadership and support of the "empowered" employees and teams, networking, external relationship management, the design of visions, and the implementation of changes, as well as the architecture and design of the organization and its potential. Greater emphasis is placed on the relationship aspects of leadership.

The challenges arising from this new form of employee management for managers are primarily in the areas of social and communication skills, integration capability, negotiation skills, and the ability to build trust. Employees' potential to develop and perform depends on the abilities of managers. These new forms of personnel management therefore become models for new innovation strategies.

**New Forms of Qualifications**

With their increased emphasis on social skills and creativity rather than specialization, employees and management's new challenges also require new forms of qualification. There are limits to the potential for developing creativity with just an individual. Developing creativity also involves the creation of an organizational framework, such as access to information required for creative performance, the promotion of creative information processing in the context of operational suggestion systems, and / or creative freedom for the generation of new ideas.

**Organizational Learning as a Concept for Coping with Change Processes**

Organizational learning is a useful tool for enterprises when developing new organizational forms. It is designed to break through traditional organization structures and enable the organization to adapt to changing competitive conditions, as well as to changing intra-organizational conditions, such as the organization members' changing needs and values.

Above all, organizational learning occurs through the recording of knowledge. This makes the enterprise independent of the individual knowledge held by individual employees. The enterprise's essential knowledge base includes shared strategies, guiding images, goals, as well as the organization's culture as a whole. These factors usually outlast changes in employment and provide a frame of reference for individual actions within the enterprise, as well as for employees' individual learning on the job.

Ultimately, an organization always learns and acts through its employees. Only when these employees learn does the organization as a whole experience far-reaching learning. Network thinking, i.e. recognizing the individual elements of the system "enterprise" (such as the employees, teams, and networks) and their reciprocal relationships, are becoming increasingly important. Employees must be able to predict the impact of their actions on other employees within the value-chain process and adjust their actions accordingly. Managers, above all, have the task of nurturing the development of the enterprise culture.

# Controlling the Boundaryless Enterprise: Strategies and Control Systems

# Case Study Chapter 10: The Virtual Factory of North West Switzerland / Mittelland

The following example explains the controlling challenges faced by a boundaryless organization. First, the Virtual Factory of North West Switzerland / Mittelland (*Virtuelle Fabrik Nordwestschweiz / Mittelland*) (VFN) is presented as a type of corporate network. Thereafter, the controlling tools that the VFN uses are described in respect of specific order-related activities, as well as order-spanning activities (Hess 2002).

The VFN network is a business network comprising small and mid-sized industrial enterprises, each of which has between 10 and 300 employees. The purpose of this association is to have the plant, instruments and mechanical engineering, tool-making, mold and die construction sectors, as well as the handling and automation sectors provide customer-oriented, complex, and complete solutions and services. Most of the enterprises in this association joined the VFN network due to capacity and / or competence bottlenecks. The cooperating businesses hope that the resources available within the association will enable them to adapt more rapidly and flexibly to changing market conditions and that they will gain competitive advantages. Another motive for participation are the investment and cost advantages gained through joint procurement and the dispersion of risks.

The virtual factory was established in 1995 with the support of the Institute for Technology Management at the University of St. Gallen, Switzerland. In 2000, approximately 30 enterprises in the Swiss Mittelland region, whose skills and expertise overlap to some degree, were equal partners in this network. By the summer of 2000, about 200 orders with a total volume of approximately US$ 10 million had been processed through the VFN network, including one large order for about US$ 2.1 million. The partners nevertheless realize only about 20% of their respective sales through the network.

There are various roles within the network: The broker and the coach share those network tasks that are unrelated to customer order activities. While the broker is mainly responsible for marketing and contacting external parties, the coach is responsible for the continuous development of the pool of partners and the infrastructure. The broker and the order manager jointly plan an order. Only the order manager, who usually also acts as the contracting party for customers, is responsible for its execution. The firm that has the largest share of the order often assumes the order manager role. Within the network, an accountant acts as the auditor. The steering body, consisting of five representatives from the cooperating businesses, heads the network. Each of these five members has a functional work focus. Orders are divided into sub-tasks and put out for bidding within the network via the intranet, providing more than 20 criteria that cover the customer's quality, temporal and logistics requirements. Based on a database of the cooperating businesses' capabilities, the order manager directly contacts suitable partners via e-mail. The decision regarding where the order should be placed, depends on the prices that the bidding companies propose. Within the context of order-related controlling, each firm in the association calculates the partial performance that it has to render and / or has already rendered as it sees fit. This is applicable to all financial considerations; therefore, also applying to the profit surcharge structure and depreciation rates, as well as to determining what the specified costs will be. The partners consequently add variable and / or fixed costs to their partial performance calculation, depending on the conditions of the order. There has been no effort to standardize this process yet. In the meantime, the network has set up a work group to systematically address this issue.

The costs of partial performance, which are defined as described above, are aggregated. The partner with the largest share in the total performance then negotiates the final price with the customer on behalf of all the partners. Occasionally, individual partners will mention their minimum prices. Each cooperating partner pays an annual lump sum amounting to about US$ 1,500 for corporations with up to five employees and about US$ 7,750 for corporations with more than 100 employees for general, order-spanning activities. This amount is also payable when a corporation joins the network. Expenditures on specific activities, for example, a joint appearance at a trade fair, are billed as incurred. Separate remuneration is likewise paid for winning an order. At present, the company winning the order receives three percent of the order's sum as a bonus.

In 2000, the issue of controlling order-spanning activities successfully was addressed for the first time. Each partner in the association was asked to name three to five of the most important goals linked to its involvement in the network and to describe these in terms of priority, measuring criterion, and deadline for meeting them. The aim of this action was to define three to five network goals that would serve as criteria for the network's strategic orientation. The intention is to conduct this kind of examination at regular intervals. Basic issues concerning the network's strategic position will in fact be examined annually in the future. Moreover, the network intends recording the results of this analysis in a business plan, regularly checking whether they are complied with. In addition, specific work groups that have to coordinate marketing, production, and other areas have been set up.

Software tools support the selection of new cooperating businesses for the pool. Potential partners apply by writing to the VFN, and are required to give a very specific description of the objective of their cooperation. This formal application is usually preceded by contact with one of the network partners. The network coach conducts an interview with the candidate, who is characterized on the basis of a predefined catalog of criteria, which usually consists of eight pages. With the aid of these criteria, the information gathered is condensed into a profile of the candidate. If the network coach considers the potential partner to be suitable, the candidate is invited to a partners' meeting where a decision is made regarding acceptance into the network.

## 10.1  Strategic Challenges for Boundaryless Organizations

Boundaryless organizations are created by a task and/or problem-related alliance between various corporations, business units and/or work places, which are often located at different sites, have different legal constellations, and work at different times. These circumstances dissolve temporal, geographical, hierarchical, legal, and economic boundaries.

In the course of the previous discussion, it became apparent that:

- The potential inherent in information and communication technology not only supports this development but is also an essential requirement for boundaryless organizations to function well (chapter 4);

- The boundaryless organization concept masks a variety of specific organizational forms (chapters 5 – 8), and

- New personnel and employee-related demands and expectations have to be taken into consideration (chapter 9).

This chapter focuses on the consequences of the above for the management of boundaryless organizations. These consequences are less concerned with what is required from a modern corporation's managers, as discussed in section 9.2.3, than with the actual instruments that management-oriented controlling functions employ to support boundaryless corporation management. Controlling is consequently a means of steering, monitoring and governing. While management defines goals, strategies, and organization structures, controlling steers the ongoing process as an integral function of the management process (Picot/Böhme 1999). Certain instruments and methods are available for this purpose. However, before describing which controlling methods are required for the new demands in the following section, the change in what is understood by strategy and corporate strategy creation will be discussed first as a starting point and as a point of reference.

First and foremost, corporate strategies build entrepreneurial success potentials, achieve competitive advantages, and improve a firm's competitive position. These objectives provide the firm with a unique (and relative) advantage compared to that of its competitors. This competitive advantage must be sufficiently superior to that of the competition by offering to provide a reaction-free (i.e. more or less monopolistic) autonomy characterized by little elasticity in demand (Corsten 1998). To achieve this position, a firm analyzes the prevailing competitive structure. It then bases a decision with regard to its behavior in the market on this analysis.

According to Porter (1980, 1996), this behavior is realized by adopting one of the three following generic competitive strategies: Cost leadership, differentiation strategy, and focusing on key elements (Fleck 1995). Each strategy requires different (internal) activities, as well as the harmonized coordination of external interfaces, which Porter explains by means of the value chain concept. The different degrees of success that firms in a sector achieve are thus attributed to a firm's correct assessment of its competitive position in its sector and its ability to derive an adequate response to this assessment within a dominating market structure.

A competitive advantage must have a performance characteristic that is important to customers, one of which they are actually aware of, and should be quite constant (Simon 1988). In recent years almost all popular management approaches (total quality management, benchmarking, time-based competition, outsourcing, re-engineering, change management) have emphasized the importance of productivity, quality, and speed as conditions for competitive advantage. This operational effectiveness (Porter 1996) nevertheless only creates a necessary but inadequate condition for lasting corporate success. Operational effectiveness means executing comparable activities better than one's competitors, i.e. making better use of the production factors employed, for example, by reducing production errors and / or accelerating the development process (establishing best practices). This was precisely the reason for Japanese firms' superior position in the 1980s: They were able to offer inexpensive, high-quality products because of their significant productivity advantages. Today, the principles learned from the Japanese, such as Kaizen, ongoing improvement, change management, and the learning enterprise, should ensure that western corporations' operational effectiveness also continues to improve in the sense of new best practices being realized. These best practices are, however, rapidly becoming an industry standard due to the growing importance of benchmarking in practice.

To achieve a truly unique competitive position, a corporation must have more new activities than its rivals: "Competitive strategy is about being different" (Porter 1996, p. 64). A unique strategic position does not, however, suffice if the innovative combination of the value-based activities can be easily imitated. Porter (1996) mentions three conditions that should lead to permanent competitive advantages (see also Milgrom / Roberts 1995; Piller 2001):

- Ensuring the corporation's unique position through a set of activities that differs from those of all its competitors.

- Creating complementarities between each of the corporation's activities by ensuring that they fit closely and are harmonized. It is particularly important for a corporation to create its own innovative interconnections. The generic interconnections found in many corporations do not suffice.

- Coping with the conflicts (trade-offs) between the corporation's activities that arise, for example, from inconsistencies in its image, from factors in the process technologies applied, and / or from technical dependencies. A corporation must be aware of the prevailing trade-offs in competition. Strategic decisions must select bundles of activities that take existing trade-offs into consideration and better combine conflicting goals than competitors' concepts would allow. The task is not, however, to reduce conflicts between goals (since controlling these conflicts guarantees a firm's competitive advantage): "The essence of strategy is choosing what not to do" (Porter 1996, p. 70).

According to Porter (1996), these three aspects are strategically decisive for achieving a unique and superior competitive position. As a consequence an orientation toward certain processes' best practices is of great importance to ensure survival in a market, as they ensure the required efficiency. Furthermore, the continual expansion of the fit between a firm's own activities and its concentration on mastering its trade-offs is of crucial importance for maintaining a permanent and superior competitive position. Managers who confuse operational efficiency with strategic orientation only gain a temporary competitive advantage, which soon changes into an expected conditional requirement since the competition has caught up.

What implications arise from these requirements for formulating competitive strategy due to companies' increasing networking and modularization? To date, competitive strategy has been based on a strategic triangle that, from customers' perspective, compares a corporation's performance with that of its competitors. Today, however, the boundaryless organization concept is rather an issue of an individual corporation and its core competencies joining forces with other partners to form an alliance to competitively offer a product and / or service package that has been tailored to customer needs (Blecker 1999). The more individual companies join forces to provide a complex, customer-related product and / or service, the less the customer's evaluation of the utility of these products and / or services is related to their separate parts and the more to the overall result. The competition between individual corporations thus changes into competition between corporate alliances. This has lasting effects on what we regard as strategy and demands that familiar approaches to competitive strategy are modified and expanded. Competitive strategy now includes the following new tasks:

- **The definition of core competencies and core processes:** If an increase in the value of product and / or service packages and complex systems is a focal consideration of boundaryless organizations, it becomes more important that each company involved should define its core competencies and processes, and concentrate its corporate activities on them (Prahalad / Hamel 1990). It is especially important that the defined core competencies are marketed as such and are perceived as unique. When defining core competencies, the three above-mentioned conditions for ensuring a permanent competitive advantage (unique positioning, creating complementarities, establishing and mastering trade-offs) are therefore essential. Each partner should not only ensure its own unique expertise compared to that of the other network members and external suppliers, but should especially realize the importance of continually extending the fit between its own activities and those of the alliance as a whole (creation of complementarities).

- **Creating a unique cooperation network:** A logical consequence of concentration on core competencies and specialization is the need to increasingly collaborate with third parties. The interfaces between each of the companies are therefore especially important. Interfaces not only entail problems (delay, distortion, and loss of information), but may also be the source of a competitive advantage. Their goal-oriented design and coordination become a unique feature of the competitive strength of a corporate alliance. It is not the alliance that excels due to the superiority of its individual products or services that gains an advantage above others, but rather one that is most successful at combining individual products and / or services to form a unique package that is exactly tailored to meet buyer requirements. The objective is therefore not to eliminate all interfaces: If advantages are to be derived from an integrated combination of core competencies and technical specialization, it is essential to distinguish between specialized sub-areas within an organization structure and to develop interfaces between these areas.

It is particularly important to structure the coordination of these interfaces. Formulating a competitive strategy regarding this issue faces the challenge of new demands and, consequently, appropriate management instruments for management-oriented controlling as well. Entrepreneurial skills such as cooperation orientation and relationship management, as well as the ability to flexibly assemble suitable partners in keeping with customer requirements and working with them at many different levels if required, therefore play a greater role than in a traditional, hierarchically structured company. Even more importantly, however, these skills create this kind of a corporate alliance's unique competitive advantage.

- **Promoting customer and market orientation:** Closer cooperation also refers to the customer. To ensure a flexible response to customer requests and to configure the requested product and / or service package, customer problems and requests have to be identified and determined at an early stage. Regarding the customized development of specific solutions, the existing resources and / or human resources and machine capacities are less relevant than the customers and their problems. A new level of customer and market orientation has been added: Individual companies were previously required to satisfy external customers. Now, there are also "internal network" customers, i.e. the other companies (modules) in the network. If there are several suppliers of a certain service or product component within the potential network companies, they compete for an (internal) order and are required to not only tailor their competitive activities toward the end customer, but also toward the network coordinator. The same holds true for modular structures within a corporation where individual profit centers frequently compete with external suppliers to create specific products and / or services for other modules within the corporation. This has consequently created a new level of customer orientation.

A business unit and / or a network company can achieve an excellent competitive advantage in such a situation if its products and / or services – in keeping with classic theory of competition (good quality, highly innovative, etc.) – are not only particularly inexpensive or differentiated but also display special complementarities with regard to other products and/or services in the network. The modules that display the greatest fit between their products and/or services and other network activities and thus contribute to the entire product and/or service package's unique position, are especially successful as far as competitive strategy is concerned. Here, again, it is obvious that competitive strategic action is more than just an orientation toward best practices.

- **Promoting entrepreneurship and innovation capability:** Closely connected to the above is the necessity of promoting entrepreneurship and innovative ability. In chapter 2, entrepreneurship was defined as the creative bridging of areas of information (information on procurement and sales markets). This is particularly relevant in the case of boundaryless organizations. They have to know which resources are available in the value-added network in order to create and provide innovative solutions, such as innovative service configurations, that also provide a form of entrepreneurial bridging. To ensure that this endeavor is successful, business units specialized in core competencies and/or core processes must know customers' problems and foster their own development accordingly. Entrepreneurial thinking and innovative ability must therefore be promoted at all levels and in all the involved units. Well-functioning knowledge and information management throughout the corporate network forms the basis of such promotion.

By realizing these success factors, the classic strategic choice between cost leadership and differentiation is, as postulated by Porter's alternative hypothesis, no longer required in boundaryless organizations. According to this alternative hypothesis, a company has to adopt one clear strategic focus for each product group: "A company that adopts each type of strategy, but is unable to adopt even one, is 'stuck in the middle': It does not have a competitive advantage. This strategic position usually leads to below average performance." (Porter 1992, p. 38). Porter explains the alternative hypothesis by means of the various inconsistencies between cost leadership and differentiation (Fleck 1995; Proff/Proff 1997): On the one hand, there is an inconsistency in the various market share requirements of strategies, which is based on the traditional trade-off between variant diversity (flexibility) and production costs (productivity) *(convexity principle)*. On the other hand, clearly positioned companies can align their internal coordination, which is characterized by conflicts between goals, more efficiently. If a mixed strategy is adopted, the company will always encounter a competitor that is better at a value-creating activity because it is completely focused on this goal *(consistency principle)*. All actions (in respect of resources, organization structures, incentive systems, functional strategies) must be concentrated on the chosen strategy to gain a leading position.

Criticism of this alternative hypothesis, however, has been growing (Corsten/Will 1995; Fleck 1995; Kaluza/Kremminer 1997; Piller 1998a, 1998b). Under today's competitive conditions (see chapter 1), there are obvious risks attached to a market position with only one generic strategy option. Many sectors are at an advanced stage of their life cycle and thus have similar cost structures. If experience curve effects have only a marginal impact, there is no new, significant cost-cutting potential. This means that often a strategy based purely on cost leadership has no solid basis for success because above-average profits are only guaranteed if there is one clear cost leader. Conversely, customers currently no longer appreciate the value added that a strategy based solely on differentiation offers. In addition, measures taken by competitors can decrease customers' willingness to pay higher prices for an additional differentiation. Simultaneously, buyers' demands are increasing in many sectors. The worldwide provision of solutions and access to electronic markets via information and communication technologies are leading to more selective purchase decisions. The price-performance relation has thus shifted to such an extent that even if the selling price is low, buyers still have relatively high expectations with regard to quality, service, exact fit, and functionality or, vice versa in respect of a product's marked differentiation, have certain minimum requirements concerning the price. A corporation is therefore required to constantly adapt to changes in customer requirements in both dimensions.

In addition to a wealth of potential benefits from the new information and communication technologies (Piller 2001), it is specifically boundaryless, modular corporate structures that support and enable alternative hypotheses. If one takes into account that market size determines the degree of specialization, networking with globally operating, value-creating partners provides new opportunities for specialization. At the same time, a flexible configuration of differentiated, customized market services is made possible by increased customer orientation in combination with a network of specialized providers. Through specialization, it is also possible to create these market services inexpensively. This means that a connection can be created for boundaryless organizations between the basic strategies − cost leadership (in the sense of specialization) and differentiation (in the sense of customized configuration) − that have to date been regarded as contradictory. Indeed, this connection has already been established by the concept of customer-oriented networking of specialized business units. Today, traditionally conflicting goals and a greater degree of realization can be achieved simultaneously. Subsequently, through modern restructuring approaches, corporations continue to shift the boundaries of existing goal conflicts by developing integrated, customer-oriented processes that are implemented by relatively small, easily manageable units (process modules) and are harmonized with one another by decentralized, non-hierarchical forms of coordination.

The principles of the boundaryless organization likewise expand the scope of competitive strategy. In contrast to the alternative hypothesis, the simultaneity hypothesis requires a simultaneous realization of cost leadership and differentiation as a promising way of establishing a permanent competitive advantage (Fleck 1995; Picot/Scheuble 1999a; Piller 2001). Boundaryless enterprises must understand that a concentration on core competencies, as well as the formation of alliances and partnerships is a strategic element that needs to be implemented as a comprehensive strategy. The task of company management is to realize the requirements and tailor all corporate activities to achieve the competitive strategy's goals. This requires the coordination of all of the company's individual contributors, which is the task of a modern controlling concept. The tasks to be solved in this respect and the various methods are the focus of the following discussion.

## 10.2 Controlling Challenges in Boundaryless Organizations

As an essential element of business management concepts, controlling is a comparatively recent development. Although "controlling" was initially regarded with skepticism and only reluctantly accepted as an independent discipline, there is at present an intense debate on this issue. This is demonstrated by the steadily growing number of publications on the theory and practice of controlling, as well as by the increasing institutional anchoring of controlling functions in entrepreneurial practice, for example, in the form of separate controller positions and departments and/or autonomous management boards (Kieser/Hegele 1998; Weber/Kosmider 1991). Controllers are, nevertheless, not always very popular in a corporation: Derogatory names such as "snooper" or "bean counter" lead one to assume that controlling does not always perform tasks in accordance with the firm's goals or to the satisfaction of all employees. A glance at the history of controlling and the focal points of its functions and tasks helps to analyze the problems, conflicts, and dissatisfaction that are frequently associated with controlling (Lingnau 1998).

- The development of controlling functions started with business accounting. In early accounting-based approaches, controlling is viewed as an operations-based instrument that supports the firm's day-to-day control by means of accounting data.

- With controlling now largely established in business practice, a partial change is evident in how information-based controlling approaches have been conceived. The coordination of information needs and information procurement is regarded as their main task. Although this view is based on accounting-oriented approaches, it expands them toward a comprehensive information economy, particularly in the light of the increasing support provided by information and communication technology.

- Influenced by the increasingly theoretical contemplation of this topic, the understanding of controlling is again changing – especially in the field of business research – to management-based controlling with its own place in the management system. This point of view is largely based on the fact that the quantity and complexity of managerial tasks usually exceed the capacities of a (more or less) monolithic, central management system and, indeed, the capacity of any one "patriarchal" leader (see chapter 3 on the limited capacity to process information). This is especially true of innovative forms of work and organization. It is therefore necessary to divide the management system into sub-systems that are more or less autonomous. Consequently, a need is developed for reciprocal coordination.

Management-based approaches form the basis of the coordination-based controlling concept development that prevails in the current controlling literature. These approaches view the coordination of specialized management sub-systems as a key function of controlling (e.g., Weber 2002; Küpper 2001). "This concerns a discrete task that has become more important. It therefore appears … warranted to introduce a new and special term for this function. If controlling is to be more than just a new name for familiar management aspects or areas, the problem lies in the coordination of the management system because this function was first created by and only became important through the systematic expansion of a structured management system" (Küpper 2001, p. 19, translation by the authors). Greater importance is thus attached to controlling than to other concepts and it is assumed to have a larger range of tasks and instruments.

Controlling is often interpreted as a system for the "management of the management system" (see Stoffel 1995 on this "meta management"; for a critical review see Horváth 2002). Controlling is also interpreted as a management service function. Here, the emphasis is primarily on controlling's capacity to support management in its development, selection, and use of suitable methods for steering and coordination, thus providing "management assistance" (Küpper 2001). This view forms the basis of the following discussion.

In accordance with the coordination and service-oriented concept, controlling is understood as an ongoing, process-accompanying steering and coordination of the value-added processes within the corporation (Picot 1997; Picot/Reichwald 1999). In the context of the forms of work and organization discussed here, this view appears to be much more useful than an ultimately hierarchy-based, meta management system.

However, those who do implement such sophisticated and centralized forms of controlling find that the system increasingly fails to meet the requirements for the comprehensive controlling and coordination of value-added activities and ultimately leads to deficiencies in controlling's effectiveness and efficiency. In this context, there are two specific problem areas (Reichwald/Koller 1996; Kinkel 1997):

- **Orientation of traditional controlling toward cost accounting:** There are often complaints that controlling is strongly oriented toward business accounting, particularly to cost and revenue accounting. This leads to a short-term, operative view and a strong focus on the production area aimed at recording more or less precisely historical costs, but not proactively influencing or steering them. It is doubtful whether controlling can be effective in this sense: A large share of the costs is already determined in upstream areas such as R&D, construction or design and can rarely be influenced at a later stage. Moreover, costs are accruing in indirect, production-remote areas to an increasingly greater degree (Johnson/Kaplan 1991). In practice, these problems manifest themselves in opaque cost structures with largely undifferentiated overhead surcharge rates that often exceed the rate of the surcharge basis – the direct production costs of a unit of performance – several times over. Furthermore, this exclusively monetary orientation of controlling contributes to a lack of transparency. Non-monetary variables such as time, quality, flexibility and the human situation are not usually incorporated in the controlling system even if highly sophisticated instruments are available for recording and allocating the various types of costs and revenues. These factors are, however, not only of great importance for a longer-term and comprehensive assessment of corporate restructuring measures (Reichwald/Höfer/Weichselbaumer 1996), but they also lay the foundation for a hybrid competitive strategy that is distinguished by more than its positive cost position.

- **Orientation of traditional controlling toward hierarchical structures:** Controlling was already developed as an effective instrument for the steering and controlling of strictly hierarchical, Tayloristically based large corporations focused on mass production at an early stage. The consequences are still obvious: "By 1925 virtually all management accounting practices used today had been developed …. At that point the pace of innovation seemed to stop" (Johnson/Kaplan 1991, p. 12). Whilst a centralized and highly standardized controlling system was useful at that time due to the almost unchanging and highly structured tasks, controlling's excessive centrality and static state are often criticized today. In a dynamic environment, this can lead to sub-optimal decisions being made because controllers have no real contact with the business in question and are too inflexible in their behavior toward specific cases. In addition, there is a risk that controlling will not be fully accepted in a corporation due to its image as an omnipresent and impersonal monitoring system.

In hierarchical structures, traditional controlling established itself as a purely internal steering and control system. However, this strong internal orientation has a detrimental effect on a stronger market orientation. At best, traditional controlling supports longer term decisions on enterprise configuration and enterprise boundaries (e.g., with regard to performance depth and the increase in or reduction of fixed cost areas) by providing short-term cost comparison data, although it largely disregards strategic enterprise arguments. The deficiencies of traditional controlling, which are associated with the implementation of new forms of work and organization, with internal modularization and cross-company networking efforts (see chapters 5 and 6), with the tendency toward an increasing marketing of service relationships (see chapter 7), and with the trend toward the virtualization of value-added processes (see chapter 8), are particularly noticeable. In these forms, traditional controlling as a "product of a division of labor in hierarchical organizational structures" (Horváth 1995, p. 261; translation by the authors) is often more a restraint on innovation than an effective management service. Thus, there are still considerable discrepancies between the capability and performance profile of traditional controlling and the requirements that a boundaryless enterprise demands from the controlling and coordinating efforts of its value-added activities.

The following discussion is therefore concerned with how effective and efficient controlling should manifest itself in boundaryless organizations and what functions and tools are available for this purpose. The ideas are based on an understanding of controlling as a coordination-based and management-related function. In the following sections, selected controlling functions within boundaryless organizations are presented in respect of a few management sub-systems. Original controlling areas that do not specifically concern boundaryless enterprises (e.g., cost variance, gap or portfolio analyses) will therefore not be discussed in any depth. Instead, the focus is placed on the particularities of enterprise networks. Most of the discussions therefore prioritize the specific controlling systems of controlling, which are the focus of attention in section 10.5. However, first of all, interface coordination as an essential task (section 10.3) will be considered in greater depth, as will the relation between direct and indirect management as a main area of controlling tension (section 10.4) in the boundaryless organization.

## 10.3  Interface Coordination in the Boundaryless Organization

Interfaces are created in companies whenever there are interdependencies between organization units that have their own decision-making powers and, as a result, a mutual need for coordination arises. The overall coordination of a corporation or network with specialized sub-areas occurs at these points. At the same time, interfaces may also harbor problems: Information is transported via them, which means that this information sometimes needs to be transformed (e.g., into other data formats or media). This not only causes transaction costs, but also carries the risk of information being delayed, distorted or even lost (Horváth 1991). Avoiding such interface problems as far as possible is an important goal of new organization strategies such as modularization, networking, and virtualization. Although a large number of interfaces are unavoidably created between highly specialized functional areas, as well as between management and operating levels in hierarchical, Tayloristic structures, the new concepts endeavor to define interfaces more precisely and to reduce them. This is attempted by means of an extensive object-oriented integration of tasks and a decrease in hierarchically superior and subordinate relations. In principle, however, the complete eradication of all interfaces is impossible: If advantages are to be gained from the pooling of core competencies and technical specialization, it is impossible to avoid differentiating between the specialized sub-areas of an organization structure and thus creating interfaces between these areas.

To minimize the risks of such interfaces, approaches are currently being discussed that enable specifically targeted interface management and interface controlling. From the boundaryless organization's point of view, interface management is specifically related to two areas: (1) Within the context of configuration management, its task is to identify suitable organization units for cooperation and to combine these to form a working alliance. (2) Process-oriented interface management subsequently ensures that the collaboration in the alliance is as efficient as possible.

## 10.3.1 Coordinating the Configuration

An important prerequisite for the creation of efficient interfaces is selecting suitable partners who cooperatively produce goods or services. These partners can be internal units, as well as independent individual actors or an entire corporation. The configuration, i.e. the purposeful combination of these partners, must satisfy the criteria for system and social integration: The partners' potentials must be coordinated in respect of their ability to perform the required (sub-)tasks, as well as in respect of their social acceptability and compatibility with the other cooperating partners. A step-by-step procedure has shown to be useful in this context (Steinle / Kraege 1998; Picot / Reichwald 1999).

### Strategic Initiation Stage and the Search for and Evaluation of Partners

The first configuration stages occur irrespective of a specific customer order and serve to introduce the basic potential available. Sections 5.2, 6.2, 7.2 and 8.2 presented driving forces that accelerate the development of new forms of cooperation. Prior to the actual realization of such cooperations, a basic concept needs to be drafted for later collaboration during the strategic initiation phase. Consequently, the characteristics of the driving forces that are relevant for cooperation must be verified in specific cases through, for example, analyzing the competition. Such an analysis comprises a general environmental analysis and a specific sector analysis. Furthermore, the future development of such forces needs to be predicted. This can be done through, for example, scenario methods, a life cycle analysis or a survey of experts based on the Delphi method. The next task is to derive significant competencies and resources from these data for the future or for the processing of a specific task.

The information gained lays the foundation for the partner search and evaluation phase (Hess et al. 2001). The identified competencies and resources are then compared with the actual potential of possible cooperation partners. Here it is essential to identify their core competencies. The methods for gathering data for an extensive evaluation of possible cooperation partners range from analyses of the goods and services that they create, questioning their reference customers, audits and benchmarking analyses, to conducting interviews with key people (Eickhoff 1998). In addition, experience gained in previous alliances is of great importance for gathering relevant data during a partner search and evaluation. It is a great advantage if businesses can be recruited from a "pool" of tried and tested partners, especially in respect of short-term cooperation (of which the virtual organization is an extreme example). In this regard, a regular *evaluation* can be established in the form of generally accessible and transparent evaluations of competence and trust that have been accumulated through previous alliances and verify the reputation of possible cooperating partners (Picot 1999).

**Cooperation Decision and Set-up**

Upon the receipt of a specific customer order, or upon discovery of a specific market opportunity (preparation of an offer, participation in a bidding process), the most suitable partners are selected from the total number of possible cooperating partners analyzed in the partner search and evaluation phase. They are then combined to form a cooperating alliance. At this stage, money-based procedures usually predominate, such as a cost-benefit analysis or investment analysis methods. There is, however, a growing awareness that making a decision on cooperation that is purely based on monetary aspects (e.g., on the basis of the (internal) prices demanded for partial tasks) is becoming less important. Conversely, factors such as adaptability, guaranteed future provision of goods and services (degree of service), and a willingness to use common resources in a flexible way (Wildemann 1997) appear to be of greater importance. Estimating the total utility gained from the collaboration and how it should be distributed between the partners involved is another important task in the cooperation decision and set-up stage. "When calculating the advantages and disadvantages of a cooperation, it is important that the basis of the 'assessment key' is understood and can be flexibly transferred and put into practice in alternative environmental conditions. The analytical decomposition of the total utility into its constituent parts and impacting determinants also satisfies the basic requirement for targeted design and implementation" (Steinle/Kraege 1998, translation by the authors).

## 10.3.2 Process-Oriented Interface Management

The partners involved in an alliance and their specific contributions to the products and services are determined by configuration management. Conversely, the task of controlling the continual information and service flows between partners is the responsibility of a process-oriented interface management. It has to ensure that information needs resulting from the interdependencies between partners are identified and that relevant information is not only exchanged with as few distortions, delays and losses as possible, but also with as little effort as possible. According to Frese (1995), interface management may adopt two theoretically extreme strategies for this purpose:

- No reciprocal coordination of interdependencies is undertaken at all. The autonomy costs (the opportunity costs of a sub-optimal overall result) that arise are accepted in the light of the savings on coordination costs. Interfaces therefore transmit merely unilaterally the basic conditions determined by one unit to the unit affected by them. A purchasing department can, for example, autonomously implement an optimum purchasing program and simply notify the production department of the ensuing availability of materials as a basic condition requiring compliance, without the latter being able to exert any influence. This strategy only appears feasible if the working relations are of such low complexity that they enable the effects of decisions to become transparent and if there are incentives to avoid negative effects outside one's own sector.

- An attempt is made to completely dissolve the interdependencies, and thus the interfaces, between two cooperating partners by decisions being considered and solved on a cross-unit basis (e.g., in a central planning department). In the example above, simultaneous purchasing and production planning would be necessary. In principle, however, this strategy destroys the advantages of autonomizing sub-areas and decentralizing decision-making powers. The high level of complexity and low flexibility of even the simplest integrated planning models demonstrate that this procedure is only possible in a very limited number of exceptional cases (e.g., simultaneous purchasing and production planning for an important special order).

In a real corporation, neither of the strategies described appears practicable in their extreme form. As a rule, realistic interface management must steer a middle course between the mere transmission of already fixed data and an attempt to achieve full transparency and coordination of units. Although the first alternative would establish total decision-making autonomy in each of the areas, it would lead to sub-optimal solutions on the whole. In contrast, the second alternative enables optimum decisions in theory, but in practice entails decision-making complexity and, thus, inflexible decision-making processes that are extremely difficult to manage. The key to efficient process-oriented interface management therefore lies in determining the correct degree to which information should be exchanged. Baldwin / Clark (1998) suggest an approach to this issue that differentiates two classes of information:

Hidden information primarily relates to the internal processing in a sub-area. It does not influence the entire alliance and is thus irrelevant outside the unit. This information can be directly processed "on site" as part of self-controlling without any need for external coordination.

- Open information concerns the overriding goals of the entire alliance, which have to be transparent to all partners. The processing and exchange of this information should be steered via a central unit (e.g., a hierarchically higher ranking controlling unit or coordination committee) to ensure consistency. This "external controlling" must not, however, unnecessarily limit the autonomy of the partners and must be minimized.

Process costing is viewed as having a major potential to make open information transparent, at least with regard to cost targets (Mayer 1991). The development of this instrument started with the finding that allocating costs to products based on their use is becoming increasingly difficult since "production-remote" overheads have increased in enterprises with traditional, cost-center-based and, thus, area-oriented, accounting systems. Undifferentiated overhead surcharges of several hundred percent that can be directly attributed to prime product costs shed little light on the structure of and reasons for the accrual of overhead costs. In process costing, an attempt is made to define cross-unit processes and – through the aggregation of each of the sub-processes occurring in the areas – to assess these as costs (process cost rates). Overhead areas are explicitly included (e.g., costs in respect of administration, purchasing, sales, service, etc.). Depending on how these processes are used, process cost rates can be allocated to the product.

This method can provide effective support for process-oriented interface management (Mayer 1991): Even the implementation of a process-costing system requires reciprocal coordination. When identifying cross-unit processes, all the units involved must cooperate in determining the process structure, the reciprocal interactions between each of the sub-processes, and the relevant cost rates.

This creates transparency and fosters the optimization of process interfaces. When applied, process costing clarifies the consequences that the costs of decisions made in one area have on other areas. For example, the effects that the introduction of new product versions or the utilization of special components have on areas such as production or warehousing are already transparent in the R&D department.

Target costing is an important complement to process costing. It changes cost accounting's traditional focus on the (subsequent) billing of incurred costs to the proactive influencing of costs to achieve a cost target predetermined by the sales market. This is especially important for a firm's continued existence in fiercely competitive buyers' markets over the long term. "A basic question of target costing is not 'What will a product cost us?' but 'What may a product cost us?' Target costing is therefore strictly market-oriented cost management, which ensures ... the cost-oriented coordination of all corporate areas" (Seidenschwarz 1991, p. 193, translation by the authors). In this case, process-oriented interface management is specifically supported by the obligation to jointly align all the units to the set goal, i.e. adherence to the target costs determined by customers.

## 10.4 Area of Tension Between Direct and Indirect Management

The contrast between direct and indirect management is a major area of tension for a modern controlling concept for the boundaryless organization. Both management concepts are equally supported by the new technical and organizational innovations in information and communication technologies. This means that an enterprise needs to deliberately dissolve this area of tension, as information and communication technologies open up new potentials to directly monitor and steer work processes at comparatively low monitoring costs.

Technical monitoring systems, for example, enable person-driven steering and control of those responsible for task completion (task managers) at different locations. Traditional hierarchical coordination mechanisms can therefore be largely replaced by information and communication technologies. However, information and communication technologies, in conjunction with new organization structures, are also responsible for creating the potential to reintegrate work processes, notably internal and external modularization, cross-company networks or forms of telework and telecooperation. This means that there are new decentralized degrees of autonomy. Task managers can therefore deal directly with most of the coordination tasks.

Here, however, an area of tension is created for the management of boundaryless organizations: Not only do information and communication technologies make direct monitoring methods possible, but indirect management methods are particularly crucial in boundaryless enterprises to support the self-coordination required of task managers. An important challenge for managerial staff is thus to combine – humanely but at the same time efficiently – indirect management methods with direct monitoring systems, depending on the underlying tasks, incentive systems, personalities, and the corporate culture. There are specific recommendations for action in this regard, for example, principal-agent theory (see section 2.3.4), which proposes controlling strategies that are suitable for specific situations, depending on the agent's ability to influence events, as well as on the principal's ability to observe the agent's actions (see figure 10.1).

## 10.4.1 Possibilities of Direct Management

In hierarchical companies, coordination is mainly conducted by explicitly controlling the behavior of task managers toward an "ideal behavior" that should guarantee the optimum performance of tasks. Behavior can be steered by giving personal orders and by monitoring, by a "compulsory coordination" related to production engineering as found in Taylorism and Fordism (see section 9.3), and by impersonal bureaucratic steering and control (Sandner 1988).

The prerequisite for these mechanisms to function is, however, that it is possible to monitor behavior on an ongoing basis, to comply with an order, to perform certain activities on the assembly line, to observe official regulations and procedural rules, etc.: "Despite the development of global organization, remote work technologies, and telecommunication-based coordination, management practice remains tradition-bound. It relies on two forms of control: rules and visual observation of the work process. Rules tell workers what to do and observations confirm how well they do it" (Kugelmass 1995, p. 6).

In the boundaryless enterprise, the direct observation and monitoring of behavior seems less feasible due to the greater autonomy and / or a geographical distribution of task managers. Today, however, information and communication technology offers many ways in which such restricted, direct monitoring of behavior

**Principal's ability to observe the actions of the agent**

|  | | Fairly<br>high | Fairly<br>low |
|---|---|---|---|
| **Agent's ability to<br>influence events** | Fairly<br>high | **(1) Direct management**<br><br>Controlling of the agent by the principal | **(2) Indirect management**<br><br>Self-controlling of the agent. Management via agreement on targets, incentive systems, and reputation |
|  | Fairly<br>low | **(3) Central monitoring:<br>Focus on process**<br><br>Controlling by the principal, supported by staff | **(4) Central monitoring:<br>Focus on result**<br><br>Controlling by the principal, supported by staff |

**Fig. 10.1.** Controlling strategies of the principal-agent theory (Picot / Böhme 1999, p. 7)

can be substituted (Sewell 1998). From a purely technical point of view, the following are examples of possible approaches:

- recording log-in times, measuring the operating periods of hardware components or measuring the time required for specific performances (e.g., the duration of contact with a customer in telephone sales, or the time required to enter a data record);

- measuring the frequency of keyboard strokes or supervising work via video systems;

- monitoring the task-related flow of information, for example, by recording the use of e-mails or the WWW;

- systematic, automatic saving and evaluation of collected behavior-related data and the creation of user and capability profiles.

These approaches to monitoring the behavior of task managers are based on the assumption that the extent and quality of task completion can be deduced from the ability to observe certain activities. These deductions are, however, problematic (Becker 1998). Monitoring is, for example, frequently restricted to one or just a few sub-areas that are easy to record technically. In an ideal case, this produces a specific normal behavior profile. It is, however, impossible to deduce such normal behavior with respect to activities that are largely information-based and have creative components (knowledge working).

On ethical and moral grounds, as well as for motivational reasons, intensive electronic surveillance is also unacceptable from the employees' point of view.

Monitored employees feel that their freedom of action is restricted, which should be viewed as especially negative. In an extreme case, the perceived freedom of action is reduced to the process cycle determined by the monitoring technique (Bogard 1996). Damaging employees' sense of self-worth and their privacy will demotivate them, cause resistance and lasting damage to trust relationships (Thieme 1982). If employee behavior truly needs to be directly monitored by means of information and communication technology, this should be restricted to well-structured, fairly straightforward tasks with an unambiguous link between input and output. The traditional, Tayloristic-type corporate hierarchy with its extensive decomposition of jobs and formalized cooperation relationships resembles this procedure most. However, any form of electronic surveillance means that it will no longer be possible to utilize the new technology for organizational innovation and, thus, to adapt in a sustainable way to the new competitive conditions.

## 10.4.2  Methods and Instruments of Indirect Management

Innovative organization strategies such as modularization, networking, and virtualization require management methods that take the characteristics of such strategies into account: On the one hand, the utility potential created by the cooperating partners' stronger decentralization and autonomization must not be restricted again. On the other hand, one of the vital tasks of management is to prevent the uncontrolled and dysfunctional dissolution of value-added structures by providing a uniform coordination framework (Reichwald / Koller 1996) to ensure that there is a unique, coordinated fit between all of the network's activities. This fit forms the basis of an excellent competitive position. Next we provide a description of indirect management and controlling instruments, which satisfy these requirements by performing this basic function. They therefore guarantee the comprehensive coordination and controlling of value-added activities (see also Küpper 2001).

Figure 10.2 provides an overview of the key instruments employed for coordination-related controlling. While centralist management systems are mainly based on the strategy of directly monitoring behavior and direct management methods, the non-hierarchical, indirect coordination of equal cooperation partners is based on budgeting and target systems, as well as on internal transfer and control price systems. The latter must be further supplemented by the evaluation of additional qualitative factors (see section 10.3.1).

The coordination between equal partners becomes increasingly non-hierarchical with the transition from centralist management systems to indirect management. This is revealed by the progressive delegation of decision making, increased reciprocal planning, as well as by the growing need for a cooperative leadership style. The behavior-oriented monitoring of direct management gives way to a greater profit orientation. In centralist management systems, an immediate superior, who directly influences an employee's behavior, carries out work processes, but only a few, highly aggregated operating results variables are the controlling yardstick for

| | Centralist management systems | Budgeting systems | Target systems | Internal and steering price systems |
|---|---|---|---|---|
| Degree of delegation | | | | |
| Reciprocity of planning sequence | | | | |
| Degree of cooperation of leadership style | | | | |
| Segmentation of corporate accounting | | | | |

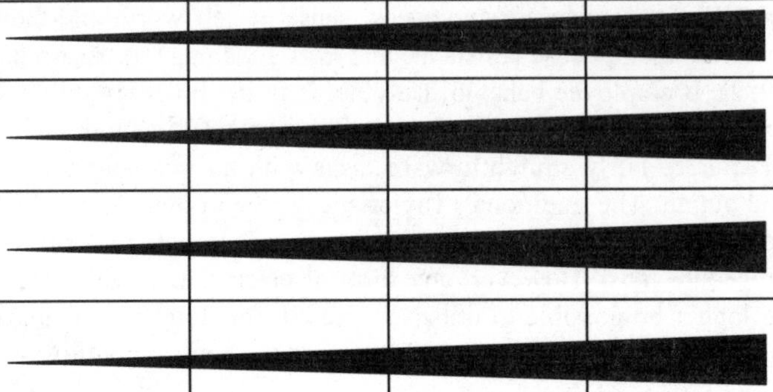

**Fig. 10.2.** Controlling methods for the coordination of work processes (based on Küpper 2001)

an organization unit's budgeting, ratio, target, and internal price systems (see section 10.5.1 with regard to the set-up and functioning of these instruments). Due to this focus on results, decentralized units have decision-making and action-taking autonomy as far as the design of their work processes is concerned.

However, this autonomy also increases the risk of opportunistic abuse that contradicts corporate goals. There are, however, deficiencies on several levels (Pfohl / Stölzle 1997):

- By using budgeting systems, business sectors may attempt to decrease budget observance by building up budgetary slack. When, for instance, negotiating and defining budgets, information such as the difficulty of tasks or basic conditions is specifically filtered or distorted, or corporate processes are initiated by, for example, bringing personal contacts into play. Such "budget games" appear to be particularly "promising" for strongly networked and uncertain work processes (non-separability problem).

- When performance measurement systems are used, there is a risk that task managers will only base their work behavior on the optimization of performance indicators. They could thus lose sight of the actual corporate goals (e.g., short-term profit optimization at the expense of required long-term investments, a business sector's egotistical conduct, overemphasis of quantitative goals, etc.) due to the condensed and simplified depiction of company-relevant facts. This is particularly valid if the performance measurement system is linked to an incentive system. Performance indicators can only provide a rough depiction of very complex work structures.

- When employing internal transfer and control price systems, unilateral dependencies may be exploited for opportunist reasons, particularly with regard to highly specialized goods and services. Excessively high prices might also be demanded, for example. This can lead to the dependent business areas avoiding this situation by creating these goods and services themselves (Reichwald / Koller 1996). This fragmentation of work processes is, however, undesirable when viewed from the perspective of the company as a whole.

In the light of these examples, controlling faces a dilemma: Specific, complex, uncertain, and network goods and services characterize new organizational forms. They dispense with detailed controlling of behavior, the maintenance of decentralized autonomy, and a stronger profit orientation to fully exploit the creativity, motivation and self-coordination of decentralized units. This, however, creates room for dysfunctional, opportunistic behavior that cannot be completely eradicated by merely controlling the verification of results. Consequently, "recordable output is not a suitable indicator for measuring performance" in respect of specific, complex, uncertain, and networked services (Rössl 1996, p. 319, translation by the authors) and cannot serve as the sole basis for controlling and coordinating the underlying work processes.

An attempt to eliminate any freedom endangered by opportunism will in turn entail an increase in monitoring methods, or result in an overpowered, central controlling function. It will certainly not solve the above-mentioned dilemma of centrality and rigidity versus the abuse of autonomy. It therefore appears far more promising to just leave the existing room for maneuvering as it is and to ensure that tendencies towards opportunistic behavior simply do not occur at all.

This is where management and leadership theories, which at an early stage already recognized that successful work process coordination is based on two pillars, come into play (e.g., Blake / Mouton 1968). While the function of task-oriented management is to coordinate the work process specifically and logically, employee-oriented management ensures that there is consensus regarding joint action. This is also emphasized by numerous new business administration approaches such as the establishment of trust organizations (Bleicher 1985), the creation of positive corporate cultures (Schein 1995), the reciprocal commitment of employees (Rössl 1996), and their socialization through organizational learning measures (see section 9.4.2). All these approaches have in common that they endeavor to create an alignment between corporate goals and the individual employee's targets. They all therefore endeavor to reduce the tendency toward opportunistic behavior by creating or strengthening jointly accepted standards, values, and motives.

The objective of the controlling functions of boundaryless enterprises can therefore no longer be to record and evaluate all available information as fully as possible. Rather, a relatively simply structured, transparent controlling system that provides units with sufficient autonomy for decentralized self-coordination should be developed. This relatively loose framework, which can certainly be created with the aid of instruments such as budgeting systems, performance measure, and target systems or internal account settlement and price control systems, needs to be complemented with social integration measures that prevent the existing autonomy from being exploited by opportunistic behavior. This employee and partner-related management is the basic change that has occurred in the roles and tasks in modern controlling functions. However, in many corporations this transformation is currently only in its infancy.

## 10.5   Controlling Systems

After pointing out the areas of tension and the resulting demands faced by a modern controlling concept for the boundaryless organization in the previous sections of this chapter, specific controlling systems will now be presented. This specifically concerns:

- Financial controlling instruments (section 10.5.1);

- Human resource controlling instruments (section 10.5.2);

- Information and knowledge management instruments and methods (section 10.5.3);

- Comprehensive, cross-company-spanning controlling systems for the integration of the various planning and management levels (section 10.5.4).

### 10.5.1 Financial Controlling Instruments

One of the major objectives of controlling in a boundaryless enterprise is the coordination of each of its divisions. A business management area, which is also widely found in practice, can be regarded as a typical boundaryless enterprise. The economic success of this kind of structure depends largely on the extent to which the organization succeeds in demarcating the right business segments, in defining suitable evaluation criteria for the business management area and in efficiently billing internal prices for supplies and services between business areas (Picot / Dietl / Franck 2002). As the first point concerning the boundaries of business areas has already been dealt with in section 10.3.1, the next two points will be the focus of the following discussion. The analysis of business areas can also be transferred to other modular units.

The assessment of the business management area (profit centers, enterprise segment, and enterprise module) aims at coordinating the business management area's autonomy so that it is in line with the interests of the enterprise as a whole. To limit the moral hazard arising from the principal-agent relationship (see chapter 2) between the company management (principal) and the business management area (agent), the agent is mostly given a share in the profits. A prerequisite for this is, however, that the business area's operating result has to be determined. It is often assessed on the basis of traditional criteria, for example, the business area costs as determined by traditional methods, its profit, its return on total investment (ROI) and / or its return on equity (ROE). However, market-value-based evaluation criteria are increasingly applied in line with market-oriented thinking, on the one hand, and the necessity to coordinate all business areas to achieve the most important overall corporate goals on the other. These criteria assess a business area's performance on the basis of its contribution to the change in the entire corporation's market value (Picot / Dietl / Franck 2002). The market value added (MVA) for listed corporations and / or business segments or the economic value added (EVA) are examples of such statistical parameters. These will be examined in closer detail below.

The condition for suitable evaluation criteria selection is invariably the extent to which the company management delegates decision making to the business management area. Only criteria that fall within the examined unit's sphere of influence and decision making may be used for evaluation. A cost center cannot, for example, be measured on the basis of its profit contribution if it is only responsible for costs. In such a case, management-oriented controlling usually employs budget targets.

### 10.5.1.1 Budgeting Systems

A budget is a planned entity assessed in monetary units (e.g., sales, expenditure or cost budgets). This planned entity is binding on an organization unit (e.g., an individual post, a module or a partner within an enterprise network) for a given period (often one year or less). The organization unit is thus responsible for adhering to the budget during the period. Budgeting systems are specifically employed in boundaryless enterprises if a unit (business area, enterprise module) is only responsible for costs, but not for the operating result. The management of a business area is consequently specifically assessed by whether it succeeds in adhering to certain cost budgets. Budget overruns lead to sanctions, while budget underruns are rewarded. Profit centers can also be managed via profit targets (profit budgets).

Budgeting merely defines each area's leeway. Within this context, there is extensive discretionary scope within which to realize specific measures. Compared to centralist management systems with their stronger focus on task manager behavior, budgeting systems have a greater orientation toward business areas and operating results (Eichenseher 1997) and are thus more suitable for modularizing enterprise structures. In this context, budgeting systems have a coordinating effect at two levels: First, management is not required to prepare a complex, detailed action plan. Its main task is to plan and specify aggregated budgets. By coordinating the budgets of each area of accountability, it is possible to steer the mutual collaboration (allocation function) and monitor by comparing the budgeted target variables with the actually realized variables (control function). Second, increased autonomy provides the areas of accountability with opportunities to develop initiative by assuming responsibility for the planning, steering, control, and coordination of task completion in the form of self-control (motivation function).

Budgeting systems continue to have a certain hierarchical character, since a decision regarding the amount and distribution of budgets is usually made by higher-ranking organization units. Despite the units' relatively high degree of autonomy, a budgeting decision is therefore not the outcome of reciprocal coordination between equal areas of responsibility. Whether defined budgets lead to greater or less efficiency in respect of the management of business areas depends primarily on whether suitable budget specifications are found. A well-structured, standardized task assignment with relatively unambiguous input and output relationships allows production and cost functions to be used to derive budgets quantitatively. Such problem-oriented budget specification techniques are specifically supported by standard costing methods. Conversely, the unclear input and output relationships make it difficult to adopt these approaches for unstructured work processes with little standardization possibility. In procedure-oriented budget specification techniques, the input and/or output are consequently examined individually. The input-oriented value-analytical specifications or prior year data (incremental budgeting) are applied, with the latter being the most prevalent technique in practice. In the case of prior year data, however, undesired incentives for action are created in the long term. If a manager stays below budget in one year, it usually leads to a reward in the next. Since the area management anticipates an adjustment of the budget in the following year and an ensuing reduction of its autonomy, it will endeavor to meet budget targets as exactly as possible and not fall short of them.

### 10.5.1.2 Market-Value-Based Indices

Controlling by means of profit sharing should overcome the disadvantages of budgeting and cope with the delegation of decision-making powers. Various indices are applied to determine an area's results. Such indices depict company-relevant facts, which are generally measurable as quantities, as numerical quantities. In this context, facts and their mutual interrelationships are usually presented in a condensed and simplified form (Reichmann 1997). Such indices may be absolute variables (e.g., balance sheet total, time-to-market), as well as index variables by means of which two variables are related to one another (e.g., profit / equity capital (ROE)).

As a pure information instrument, indices depict real facts and thus provide task managers with relevant information. In the context of non-hierarchical coordination processes, however, their use as a controlling and coordination instrument is of special importance. An index has a two-fold function here. Firstly, it depicts a target variable as a desired value, and thus has the function of specifying a performance target and acting as a yardstick. Secondly, it quantifies a company's real state of affairs retrospectively. The ongoing comparison between the budgeted index and the actually realized index steers and controls this situation purposefully. It is possible to achieve a comprehensive coordination of value-creating processes in an enterprise by means of a harmonized index and target system. In contrast to budgeting systems, coordination by means of index and target systems is not carried out by restricting basic conditions, but by setting specific targets that are directly related to the organization units and their tasks.

In many enterprises, balance-sheet-based controlling variables are still the focus of attention. DaimlerChrysler, for example, steered its industrial business areas according to its return on net assets (RONA). It is calculated as a quotient of the operating profit before taxes (operating profit according to US-GAAP (Generally Accepted Accounting Principles)) and the net assets (taken from the balance sheet). According to enterprise management, it must amount to at least 15.5% (Ballwieser 2000). These balance-sheet-based variables – as well as the ROI (return on investment) and ROE (return on equity) – are, however, viewed with growing skepticism since they fail to take the market perspective into account and are based on historical figures (e.g., Rappaport 1986; Günther et al. 2000).

Consequently, market-value-based ratios should better assess the effect of business area decisions on the current market value of the company as a whole. Although this kind of value-based corporate management is not a new idea (Ballwieser 2000), it regained prominence with Rappaport's book (1986) on shareholder value. Rappaport argues against using historical accounting ratios and in favor of using discounted cash flow (DCF), which corresponds to the capitalized value known from investment theory. As a cash value of payments to owners, DCF is an asset variable that is very well suited for controlling purposes in enterprises without agency problems. However, in decentralized, boundaryless organizations, the utilization of this variable leads to problems with incentives and coordination: The headquarters and units can use different interest rates and planning horizons for the same project. One cannot guarantee that the determination of DCF can be verified either, as expected variables flow into it. Consequently, if there are changes to the DCF, the events that the management can justify must be separated from those that the business management area cannot justify. There are, however, no reliable methods for doing so (Ballwieser 2000). Consequently, alternative approaches —market value added and economic value added – will be discussed (see also Picot / Böhme 1999).

**Market value added (MVA):** From a market-value-based view, the value of an enterprise is measured by the discounted future payment surpluses that the enterprise generates for its owners. The market capitalization value (share price x number of shares issued) can be best used for this purpose. Since the share value reflects the ability of all capital market operators to pay, it can bypass the problem that arises from forecasting the future market value resulting from current business activities. Market participants' ability to pay off capital market operators (shareholders and those willing to buy stocks) is based on the current value of future dividend payments, price increases, and capital repayments, as well as on entrepreneurial risk. The market value added (MVA) is applied as a ratio for this market-value-related evaluation of listed enterprises and / or business areas. This ratio's task is to depict the future potential. It is calculated as the difference between an enterprise's (division's, business area's) market value and the invested capital (Picot / Dietl / Franck 2002). If, for example, an enterprise is shown as having a total market value of $15 million in the year under review, and if investors have provided a total of $9 million in capital, the company has an MVA of $6 million. The corporation has thus converted an investment of $1 into a value of $1.66. In a boundaryless organization, the concept of the valuation of an enterprise as a whole by means of MVA can be transferred to the valuation of each of the business areas. The MVA of a business area then serves as a controlling and valuation variable within the context of management-based controlling. However, in the profit center concept, for example, the problem often arises that a theoretical determination of a business area's market value is only possible if this is a legally independent unit whose market value has been validated on the capital market. This will only be feasible in a few corporations.

**Economic value added (EVA):** Since the stock market listing of many corporations' individual business areas will not take place, other indices must be used. Consequently, various consulting and auditing companies have developed competing indices (see the "metric war" in the consultancy practice (Myers 1996)). Stern Steward's economic value added (EVA) (Steward 1991; see also Fisher 1999; Young 1999; Günther et al. 2000) is the most widespread index used in this context, also outside the US business practice. EVA is one of the residual variable-based indices applied to the analysis of the difference between a profit variable (or cash flow variable) and capital costs. The EVA arises from the net operating result after taxes less capital costs. The specific business area risk is considered as being covered by he capital costs. The assumption behind this is that the capital market only finances risky business activities with appropriate surcharges. Allowing for capital costs also expands EVA to its predecessor, i.e. residual income. Put in simpler terms, EVA corresponds to the net profit after taxes less the minimum profit that has to be generated to justify the risk entailed in the business activity (e.g., compared to an investment in capital market funds). A corporation, for example, acquires business premises and machinery at a cost of $300,000. Forty percent tax is then levied on the resulting profit before tax of $200,000, leading to a net profit after tax of $120,000. Next, EVA is calculated by first deducting the interest payments on the one million dollars, for example, 4% ($40,000). However, a supplementary percentage rate is added, which allows for risks entailed in the business activity under review (e.g., 6%). If a total of 10% capital costs are thus taken into consideration, this finally results in an EVA of $20,000 ($120,000 after taxes less capital costs of $100,000).

By means of the profit and loss account's net operating result, it is possible to calculate EVA without much effort by basing it on US accounting requirements (see, e.g., Young 1999 for further details). In modular corporate structures, however, internal working relationships should be taken into account when determining a business area's operating income. Internal price systems are usually applied for this purpose, which will be more closely examined in the next section.

The advantage of controlling unlisted business areas by means of EVA is giving strategic investments a sense of responsibility. EVA's historical basis and its inability to show any explicit future values are, however, a problem (see Ballwieser 2000, p. 163f. for further details). There is also no standardized methodology for calculating EVA, since capital costs, risk assessment and, above all, the required adjustment accounting may be based on various company accounting standards. Business areas and / or companies have specific autonomy in this respect. Moreover, in addition to the problems entailed in defining the contents, criticism is also often directed at the single period review and the consequently restricted cross-period controlling perspective (Fischer 1999).

In the meantime, there are a growing number of people who believe that market-value-based indices alone are not sufficient to determine the operating result. The increasing importance of intangible resources in modern enterprises specifically requires a reorientation and / or expansion of capital-based valuation approaches. An increase in employee-oriented approaches is, for example, found in start-ups and innovative technology firms. Just as Porter's 1980s writings on the value chain emphasized the strategic importance of processes but could not determine the process costs of controlling, it is currently also impossible to provide suitable monetary values for investments in business relations, networks or management competence (Bausch / Kaufmann 2000).

Consequently, resources that are required for the sustained creation of value in an enterprise are combined under the umbrella term "intellectual capital" (Fischer 1999; Mourtisen 1998; Deking 2002). Intellectual capital comprises the value of human capital, customer relations, and all other process-related and innovation-related organization competencies. To increase value, the components of intellectual capital must be influenced by means of non-financial index targets. Employee satisfaction, sick days and / or fluctuation behavior would, for example, be suitable variables for human capital, whilst customer satisfaction and / or the number of regular customers are appropriate variables for customer capital. Controlling's objective must ultimately be to establish return on intangibles which, in turn, can be partitioned into its respective impact factors. Investments in intangible resources can be interpreted as option purchases, implying that variables based on shareholder value and capital markets can be determined by real option value, as well as by statements on real option portfolios in the sense of an "enterprise as a stock of optional actions." The balanced scorecard concept (see section 10.5.4) is an example of an approach that systematically combines monetary and non-monetary ratios to implement these requirements.

### 10.5.1.3 Internal Transfer and Control Price Systems

In the previous two sections, we focused on individual business areas' coordination from the viewpoint of the enterprise as a whole. A further important task in the boundaryless organization is controlling the reciprocal working relations between the business areas and / or central departments. In this context, each unit should be aligned with the overriding enterprise goals and managed with as little intervention as possible. In the context of the examined non-hierarchical forms of coordination, the coordinating effect of internal transfer and control price systems is of special importance. Internal transfer and control prices are prices fixed by an enterprise for the internal exchange of supplies and services. This is an attempt to also utilize the market coordination mechanism between independent economic units for the exchange of supplies and services between more or less independent units within a corporation. As scarcity indicators, internal prices contribute to existing resources being utilized in the most profitable way possible. They are also used to determine a business area's success (performance evaluation function) – a basis for the determination of value-based indices.

Various valuation bases can be used as a yardstick of internal transfer and control price levels, depending on the billing targets and the valuation situation. An overview of these valuation bases is provided in figure 10.3 (Ewert/Wagenhofer 2000). In respect of a market-based derivation, the price of an internal service is based on external market prices (Hess 2000). This is nonetheless only possible if a similar service is available and traded outside the company or network (both in terms of direct product characteristics and in terms of procurement periods, available quantities, longer term transport and supply security, etc.). From the transaction cost perspective, however, only highly specific services, for which there is no external market, are carried out within an enterprise. It is therefore impossible to price these services according to market prices. Consequently, the internal price is derived in a cost-oriented way. While only marginal costs (variable costs) are determined from a short-term perspective, fixed costs (full-cost-based prices) and possibly profit surcharges (cost-plus approaches) must also be taken into consideration for a longer-term perspective. In both cases, it should be discerned whether operational bottlenecks (capacity bottlenecks) influence the determination of internal transfer and control prices. If a (scarce) service can be used for various alternative purposes, this service's opportunity costs and not its variable costs are relevant when pricing a service exchange. These costs correspond to the assessed utility that the allocated service would have provided in the best possible alternative use (Picot/Dietl/Franck 2002).

| Valuation rates for internal transfer prices | External market available | No external market available | |
|---|---|---|---|
| | | No internal bottlenecks | Internal bottlenecks |
| Control function | Market price | Short-term management: marginal costs Long-term management: Full costs | Short-term management: opportunity costs Long-term management: Full costs |
| Income calculation function | Market price | Simulated market prices (Full costs + appropriate share in net value creation) | Simulated market prices (Full costs + appropriate share in net value creation) |

**Fig. 10.3.** Valuation rate for internal transfer prices based on internal transfer goals and valuation situation (Picot/Dietl/Franck 2002)

In practice, however, the implementation of theoretically based valuations is often difficult. In-depth knowledge of the cost structure and, in respect of bottlenecks, of the value-creating structure is required. The relevant business area will usually endeavor to attain the highest internal price possible, thus tending to present its cost structure unfavorably. Consequently, a higher-ranking organization unit often fixes internal transfer and control prices centrally, which contrast strongly with the completely free negotiation of prices between equal ranking units. The latter does, however, often threaten to degenerate into a transaction-cost-intensive dispute about the net value added. An interim solution is to initially fix prices through negotiations. If, however, there is a risk of unfavorable joint solutions (e.g., due to the opportunism or the negotiating parties' limited rationality), the headquarters should be included in the procedure as a higher-level organization unit, or it should restrict the negotiating range of the units involved early on. The latter solution is possible by determining price-fixing rules or by stipulating the upper and lower limits of prices.

At first glance, coordination on the basis of internal transfer prices appears to be "enticing because the groups are largely autonomous, yet have to design their services attractively in order to offer them successfully on an internal market. This fosters employees' entrepreneurial, success-related thinking and action" (Reichwald/Koller 1996, p. 118, translation by the authors). However, it must never be forgotten when applying internal transfer prices that perfect market conditions are required for this instrument, which is based on the market coordination principle, to function optimally (see chapter 2 on the market's "invisible hand"). These conditions are not usually found in a company or in a well-established enterprise network. At this point, the self-organization of the internal market must be supplemented by the targeted intervention of the company management (Koch 1997). This is the task of the human resources controlling instruments considered below.

## 10.5.2 Human Resources Management Instruments

### 10.5.2.1   Design of Incentive Systems and Human Resources Development

So far, the described controlling tasks and methods in new organizational forms have been related to the reciprocal coordination of the individual internal and external modules. The controlling and coordination tasks required for this purpose should be managed by means of suitable support systems. Controlling at employee-level complements these tasks and aims to motivate employees to deal appropriately with first-level controlling measures. Suitable incentives play a key role in this regard. The following discussion is presented from the perspective of the individual employee. When providing incentives at a modular level, it is also important, however, to guide the module towards behavior that can create permanent competitive advantages for the company as a whole and/or the network. If this is to be achieved, the incentives presented below must be utilized.

Incentives are necessary to trigger action. To achieve this, there must already be a latent willingness to take action, which, in turn, is determined by the acting person's motives. Working people have a large number of motives, of which only some can be activated by incentives to actually perform a specific act. Motivation is the total number of motives activated by incentives. Work motivation therefore comprises all the motives activated in work situations (Oechsler 1997). It is, nevertheless, not only motives and incentives in work situations that are relevant, as they are complemented by motives in other areas (family, free time, etc.) (Lawler 1994). In the following, however, only the motives that can be influenced by the organization will be considered. Monetary incentives (e.g., fixed pay, profit-sharing plan for employees, company social benefits, etc.) and non-monetary incentives (e.g., work content, possibilities of gaining qualifications, promotion opportunities, workplace design, regulations regarding hours of work and breaks, etc.) serve to activate motives. A rough distinction can be made between time rate, piece rate, and time rate plus bonus as traditional forms of remuneration (Hentze 1995). Time rate entails a specific wage rate fixed for a unit of time in which work is performed for the enterprise. In contrast, piece rate and time rate plus bonus are performance-related forms of remuneration. Piece rates are paid as a fixed monetary value for an output unit irrespective of the actual hours of work required. The amount of pay thus increases proportionally to the quantity of output units produced. Time rate plus bonus comprises a basic wage (e.g., collectively agreed wage) and a bonus, the level of which depends on increased output, which can be influenced by co-workers. Bonuses can, for example, be granted as a quantity or quality bonus, as a savings bonus or a bonus for degree of utility. These types of bonuses can also be applied in combination and as an individual or group bonus.

These traditional forms of remuneration are based on a strictly hierarchical organization structure. Each job is classified in the enterprise's wage structure through job rating. This involves rating the requirements of a job in relation to other jobs on the basis of a standard yardstick. Various methods are first applied to determine the requirements of a job, which are then weighted according to their importance for the best possible performance of the task as a whole. This procedure results in a job description, with the aid of which each job is unambiguously classified in the enterprise's existing job structure. "... through a series of subjective decisions, an organization can translate the tasks it asks individuals to perform into an 'objective' quantified result and a pay level ..." (Lawler 1992, p. 145). This procedure's informational value should, however, be assessed critically. The complicated calculations frequently convey only an apparent objectivity in respect of the job rating. Other disadvantages are the lack of market orientation, the inflexibility of employees in respect of restructuring, a focus on hierarchy-based career planning only, and the tendency to build "kingdoms." Added to this is the great effort required by job rating, which is unacceptable for modular organizational forms as they constantly conduct task-related reconfiguration of the organization structure. Furthermore, too little importance is attached to the continually growing importance of the factor "knowledge." The following sections discuss the necessity of new remuneration concepts with regard to the implementation of new organizational forms: The level of pay can either be based on employee qualifications, or employee and company interests can be more strongly aligned toward achievement and value-oriented forms of remuneration.

## Qualification-Based Remuneration

Qualification-based remuneration (see, e.g., Orsburn 1990; Boyett/Conn 1992; Lawler 1992) is based on the principle of paying employees according to the potential of their qualifications and capabilities, thus irrespective of the work activities that they currently undertake. This kind of remuneration system is usually implemented in stages (Lawler 1992):

- First of all, the tasks required for the goods and services are identified and the required qualifications are determined. At the same time, employees are tested to determine whether they have these capabilities.

- Next, the number and type of capabilities are specified that employees should acquire. This determines the structure of the later remuneration system. Simultaneously, the qualification requirements are aligned with the organizational form, business strategy, and the enterprise's core competencies.

- The employees are informed of the capabilities that they still have to acquire to perform their tasks and how these capabilities influence their remuneration.

Paying employees on the basis of their qualifications does not rule out the above-mentioned traditional forms of remuneration. On the contrary, this form is usually based on bonus remuneration systems in which the bonus is partly dependent on the individual employee or group's qualifications and partly on their performance (e.g., Boyett/Conn 1992). The great advantage of qualification-based remuneration is the possibility of motivating employees to learn various skills by promising higher remuneration. This is important, since the future success of many enterprises is increasingly dependent on their employees having a broad diversity of skills and capabilities. There are, nevertheless, also some disadvantages entailed in introducing this kind of pay system. As all employees have to have an opportunity to permanently continue their education, this requires high investments. Moreover, after further training measures, performance will initially still be poor. In addition, the administration of this remuneration system is fairly complex, since employee remuneration may change frequently – whenever a new qualification is learned. Finally, there is a possibility that an employee may fully exploit all possible qualification potential and be frustrated at having no further incentives.

## Achievement and Value-Based Remuneration

Remuneration based purely on qualifications is not a sufficient incentive for market and customer-oriented employee behavior. At the beginning of this chapter, this kind of behavior was, however, identified as an essential success factor for permanent competitive advantage. A modern remuneration system must therefore create the right incentives in this respect, too. This task is specifically faced when determining a reasonable level of remuneration for company management. On the one hand, merely providing a livelihood that is only slightly better than one based on time rates offers little direct incentive to perform well. Conversely, due to the diversity and complexity of managerial tasks it is very difficult to find suitable, direct reference values (output units) for performance-oriented remuneration (Pribilla / Reichwald / Goecke 1996). Qualification-based remuneration also reaches its limits here: The diversity of key qualifications required for successful management (see section 9.2) cannot really be described in a formal system. In addition, it is almost impossible to measure and quantify someone's "soft skills." Principal-agent theory offers a possible solution: The remuneration of managerial staff – and increasingly also that of other employees – creates the desired incentive effect and, thus, behavior oriented toward the enterprise goals, if it is linked to the company's success. The interests of the corporation and its employees are thus aligned. Consequently, a part of the remuneration is granted variably, thus depending on the business success.

If relatively short-term variables such as the profit or revenue within a given period are chosen for this purpose, a direct connection can be established between actions and effects. In line with the movement toward market-value-based company management, the financial indices MVA and EVA (see section 10.5.1.2) are currently included in incentive systems as a basis of assessment (Fischer 1999). The EVA concept specifically enables the measurement of individual areas or projects' contributions to the value added (e.g., the level of a bonus payment). EVA combines the capital-market-oriented view with the company's internal view and is thus well suited for company management based on shareholder value.

However, since there is an increasingly rapid change of personnel in managerial positions today, the problems of short-term optimization affect strategic goals negatively. Consequently, long-term incentives are often preferred in the field of management. Interests are usually aligned through participation in the enterprise's capital stock. In the case of listed companies, this ultimately results in remuneration being oriented to the company's market value and long-term success. "Greater identification with the corporation, more motivation to assume responsibility, a higher cost awareness, and better insight into entrepreneurial interrelationships are the essential effects that capital and profit sharing promise" (Koller 1998, p. 91, translation by the authors).

These value-oriented remuneration concepts are usually realized in the form of stock option plans. Instead of a direct remuneration, employees are granted options to a certain number of company shares. These stock options entitle employees to buy shares at a fixed subscription price during a given period of time (usually long term, up to 15 years). This means that option recipients become a company's (potential) equity suppliers. One can expect them to focus their actions more strongly to ensure a long-term increase in the earning power and market value of the company, because this would result in an increase in the value of their options. Systems that only grant options on the condition that certain target variables (e.g., growth targets) are attained over the long term (performance share plans, see Becker 1990) are one version of the stock option plans. There is some controversy regarding how effective stock option plans actually are. The generation of suitable incentive effects is doubted, particularly in two areas (Winter

1998): Share prices that determine the value of the options and, thus, the level of incentive, depend strongly on external, macro-economic developments (e.g., economic activity in a specific industry, political developments, speculative influences, etc.). However, the recipients of incentives have no influence on these developments. In the worst possible case, an employee could receive no reward at all, despite great personal commitment. To compensate for these external influences, refined procedures have been developed to determine the subscription price. In market indexed stock option plans (MISOP), an attempt is made to remove external influences arising from share price fluctuations from the calculation. In spite of great efforts, it is not possible to exclude these influences accurately, although a satisfactory approximation is often possible. A further problem is that the share price, as a highly aggregated overall evaluation of a company, barely reflects employees' individual contributions. A manager can, for example, profit from others doing good work, while his work also benefits others. This does not, however, ensure an adequate level of performance. "The free rider problem with regard to shareholders is merely added to a free rider problem with regard to colleagues" (Winter 1998, p. 1129, translation by the authors). Such a system should therefore not be applied in isolation, but be supplemented by more strongly individualized incentive systems.

### Controlling Between Individualization and Transparency

As people have many motives, incentive systems should entail several components. As an entity for the ongoing controlling and coordination of a company's value-creating processes, controlling has a decisive influence on the development, coordination and "operation" of such an incentive system. In this context, it is necessary to satisfy two requirements (Weber 2002):

- The effect of incentives depends on the extent to which they address an employee's motives, i.e. what power these incentives have for the employee. The more flexible and multi-dimensional an incentive system is, the greater the chance that an individual's specific motives will be targeted. A high level of individuality thus increases the effectiveness of an incentive system. Ideally and figuratively speaking, "… incentive systems are always tailor-made suits" (Koch 1997, p. 314, translation by the authors).

- The incentive system should also be as transparent as possible for employees. It should be possible to clearly identify both the type and quantity of possible incentives, as well as the correlation between actions and the granting of incentives (instrumentality). Such high transparency is, however, only guaranteed in incentive systems that are not complex. "People's limited ability to process information … sets relatively narrow limits in respect of the number of individual incentives and their combined effects" (Weber 2002, p. 260, translation by the authors).

In respect of controlling, this reveals a dilemma between ensuring individuality, as well as transparency. On the one hand, the differences between individual employees must be taken into account to fully develop the human resources available, particularly in new forms of organization. This means that incentive system design has to be highly flexible and be able to individualize. On the other hand, the system then inevitably becomes more complex and less transparent. A barely transparent incentive system runs the risk of not being accepted by employees, of running counter to their sense of fairness, and of becoming less effective. It is therefore controlling's task to ensure that an incentive system's structure lies between these extreme and that a reasonable compromise is found between individuality and transparency.

### 10.5.2.2  The Role of Trust

In its traditional form, controlling is frequently viewed as a main source of distrust in an enterprise. This is due to its control focus, which is an outdated view that dominates a controller's work, as well as due to the clear discrepancy between the power of information and the responsibility of controlling (Krystek / Redel / Reppegather 1997). However, the function and significance of controlling are undergoing a radical change in the context of new forms of organization. Owing to indirect management support, the coordination of interfaces, and the provision of suitable incentive systems, the strongly emphasized "hard" control function in traditional controlling, which evidently promotes distrust, is receding in favor of a proactive organization, management, and control of value-creating processes.

Can controlling completely dispense with control? Recently, the role of trust as a substitute for control has been discussed quite frequently, particularly in connection with new forms of organization. With their re-integrated tasks, decentralized structures, and the high degree of autonomy that their top performers enjoy, traditional forms of control suit them less. Establishing relations based on trust (Ripperger 1998 and section 3.6) appears to be an important part of coping with complexity and uncertainty: In trusting relationships, alternative courses of action resulting in a one-sided benefit at the expense of the trusting party are ruled out, as this would normally lead to an undesired end to the trusting relationship.

The risks of receiving incomplete information, which arises from high complexity and uncertainty, and poor protection against opportunistic action, are compensated by trusting that the cooperating partner's actions are meant well (Sjurts 1998). The ensuing reduction in "possible" alternative courses of action results in the decision complexity being reduced. Trust therefore "... not only represents a cost-efficient way of handling exchange relations, it is also the only possible form of coordination for complex transactions that cannot be steered by means of 'hard contracting' ..." (Rössl 1996, p. 326, translation by the authors).

By creating trust, the coordination of value-adding processes can therefore be effectively supported in new organization structures (see also section 3.6). However, creating trust is usually a long-term process strongly bound to personal relationships between individuals. A paradoxical situation arises here: The more dynamically cooperative work is processed and the shorter the term in which it is done, the more likely traditional control mechanisms are to fail and the greater is the need for protection through trust. At the same time, however, the opportunity to establish long-term trust, especially in these structures, is increasingly diminished due to the rapid change of and frequent fluctuation of interaction partners (Sydow 1996; Reichwald et al. 2000).

In respect of the extreme case of a virtual corporation, Handy (1995) argues: "Paradoxically, the more virtual an organization becomes, the more its people need to meet in person." Sydow (1996) mentions a trust dilemma in this regard. This is a further area of tension for controlling in a boundaryless organization.

## 10.5.3 Information and Knowledge Management

### 10.5.3.1  Information Management Between Centralization and Decentralization

In conjunction with networking, virtualization, and the development of boundaryless organizations, two further human resource management instruments play a progressively important role: Information management and knowledge management. The two approaches are closely connected, but are based on different concepts and pursue different goals due to the differing importance of information and knowledge. If knowledge is regarded as meaningful signs that are required to attain a goal, the task of information management is to efficiently and effectively supply all organization units with the information required by each of them.

Chapter 4 explained into which levels and into which tasks information management can be further differentiated. Information lays the foundation for knowledge management. Knowledge can be regarded as the combination of information that permits the carrier to build action assets and to start actions. Knowledge can be explicitly available, for example, in databases, or be implicitly hidden in the minds of employees (see also chapter 3). Knowledge management has the task of recording, systematizing, and maintaining this knowledge. Both concepts play an increasingly important role in boundaryless organizations and will therefore be dealt with in greater detail in the following sections. Proceeding from a holistic, value-added chain, the boundaryless enterprise is based on the forming of process-oriented units that are either managed as internal modules (chapter 5) in cooperation with external partners (chapter 6), or via (electronic) markets (chapter 7). Modularization, concentration on core competencies and / or core processes, and the integration of the remaining competencies through alliances are essential principles. An efficient coordination between modules can only be attained if the underlying flow of information runs smoothly. This is particularly true if the modules are located at different sites or if they operate in a mobile way (see chapter 8).

Information and communication technology networking lays the foundation for networking between enterprises and the associated creation of boundaryless organizations ("the network is the factory"). This expands information management's range of tasks (chapter 4). Apart from supplying internal task managers, as well as organization units with the necessary information, a particularly important information management task in boundaryless enterprises is implementing the required information flow and communication between all internal and external modules involved.

Information management therefore gains complexity. When tasks are largely shifted to the intercompany area, different processes, systems, standards, applications, and perhaps also techniques have to be taken into account. The complexity of information management increases even further when the phase model is taken into consideration. This often serves as a basis for boundaryless or virtual enterprises (e.g., Mertens / Griese / Ehrenberg 1998). According to this model, virtual companies are based on several phases (configuration, control and dissolving), each of which makes different demands on the underlying information management.

Depending on the specific life cycle, various information and communication systems must be available to provide support. In addition, there are instruments for cross-phase tasks such as communication systems, document and work flow management systems, as well as project management systems (see figure 10.4 for an overview). During the actual implementation of this phase-related information management organization, the question arises as to who assumes responsibility for information management and, for example, decides:

- Which specific information and communication systems should be used;

- How the interfaces between systems should be defined; and

- Which specific data and data types should be exchanged.

The allocation of responsibility for information management as a controlling instrument is clearly more difficult and complex in respect of boundaryless (virtual) enterprises than of hierarchical corporations. Information management is progressively changing into a coordination instrument that has to take diverging interests

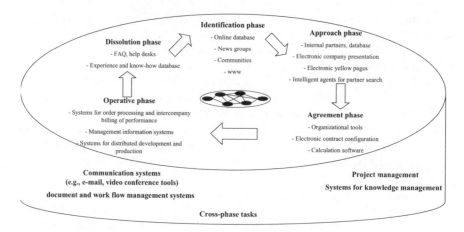

**Fig. 10.4.**   Information and communication systems for virtual companies (Mertens / Griese / Ehrenberg 1998, p. 54)

into consideration, but must nevertheless implement a smooth and interface-free information and communication technology infrastructure. In the sense of efficiently and effectively coordinating the supply of specific information that each organization unit requires, information management thus becomes a major task of controlling functions in boundaryless organizations. The key question in this respect is which of the tasks involved in information management (see section 6.3) has to be handled by a central, superior unit and which ones can be dealt with by decentralized individual units.

If all information management tasks are decided and predetermined centrally, a (central) module must be responsible for the realization of a functioning infrastructure. This not only makes the consistency of transmitted information easier to guarantee, but it also provides an overview of all of the network's information links. A central solution is also more likely to offer the possibility to integrate new partners flexibly into the problem solution. However, this solution becomes problematic if an association of legally independent enterprises – which is typical of a virtual company – has to be coordinated with its own processes, information and communication systems and solutions. Separate companies only reluctantly respond to centrally specified requirements. This problem is also encountered in large groups with several regional companies. In practice, it has repeatedly been problematic to make certain processes and procedures mandatory for decentralized regional companies that already have established structures, due to the costs that each company incurs when giving up tried and tested systems and operational structures. This not only affects the level of the information and communication technology infrastructures, but also requires the organization and its processes to adjust. A further problem is the issue of choosing the module that has to assume the task of stipulating central requirements. Conversely, in a decentralized solution, every module is responsible for its own information management tasks and decides which information and communication systems to use. The greatest advantage is that the effort involved in central coordination is reduced. Interface problems are more likely to occur, however, since smooth communication is no longer guaranteed. This happens, for example, if two firms use different enterprise resource planning (ERP) systems that do not communicate with each other and thus cannot exchange data. Many interorganizational alliances have failed in the past and still fail today, as the implementation of different information systems entails excessively high transaction costs (Thome 1998, 1999).

A combination of a central and decentralized solution therefore appears advisable. As a basic rule, every unit is responsible for its own information tasks and decides which applications, systems, and procedures should be applied and how internal information flows should be organized. However, a central information management guarantees the flow of information between the units by observing certain basic requirements. These include, for example, responsibility for and maintenance of the underlying network, the stipulation of interfaces and standards for the transmission of data between units, and the stipulation of services for rapid and trouble-free access to information and communication flows. The idea behind this solution is a mental separation of information management tasks from those concerning the overall information flow and those processed within a module. Consequently, central information management has to pay specific attention to the underlying infrastructure and define "sockets" for trouble-free integration. Electronic data exchange (EDI) standards are examples of typical "sockets." All information management tasks that only concern the decentralized units can be transferred to these sockets.

A further issue concerning coordination is allocating central information management tasks to a specific task manager, which then becomes responsible for these tasks. This might be a network enterprise module or a legally independent company. Apart from the possibility of integrating a central module, which has "information management" as its core competence, into the alliance as the unit responsible for the network configuration, a broker and/or the unit that configured the boundaryless organization could also define central requirements for information management. This unit's range of tasks is thus expanded: It is also responsible for information management and not only for the interface with the customer and the configuration of the required modules. A third solution is to call in external service providers that are specialized in handling information management between a network's units. This could, for example, be a service provider that, within the context of a Web EDI system, assumes the task of translating the data between a traditional EDI solution and another partner only connected via a WWW browser.

### 10.5.3.2  Set-up of a Knowledge Management System Within and Between Companies

A smooth information flow merely lays the foundation for efficient cooperation. Knowledge is the crucial success factor for boundaryless organizations. In traditional industrial and factory structures, potential factors such as buildings, machinery, production plants, vehicle fleets, etc. were viewed as success factors. Human labor was combined with physical capital. This has changed. The problem-oriented combination of know-how and expertise is becoming more important. In the light of knowledge of customer problems and knowledge of the resources available, boundaryless enterprises have to find the right recipe to combine them. Products and services as end-products are becoming more and more knowledge intensive.

Textile enterprises are a good example of this. Today, their services increasingly consist of translating knowledge of customer requirements into the product design and of making the production process, which often involves different (external) production sites, as efficient as possible (Grandke 1999). It is therefore essential, particularly for boundaryless organizations, to record, systematize, make available, and nurture existing and essential knowledge. The literature proposes a variety of concepts for such knowledge management.

Knowledge management can be regarded as a process involving various phases that range from knowledge identification and knowledge structuring to knowledge

reduction. This process is supplemented by rules for the access, nurture, and protection of knowledge (e.g., Probst/Rau/Romhardt 1999). As boundaryless organizations are by definition concerned with flexible forms of organizations occurring in different and variable constellations, these phases cannot be directly
transferred. Another approach has therefore completely disengaged from this line
of thought on processes and deals with knowledge management tasks in three
stages (see figure 10.5): Creation of technical competencies and creation of internal and external structures to improve the transfer of knowledge within and between companies (Picot/Scheuble 1999b). The task thus becomes the focus of attention and can only be accomplished by searching for appropriate competencies
and creating appropriate structures.

At the development, utilization, and nurturing of competencies stage (stage 1 in
figure 10.5), the configuration phase is concerned with defining the competencies
required for the task (knowledge identification).

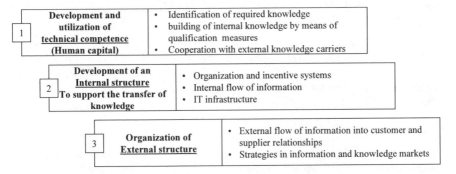

**Fig. 10.5.**   The stage concept of knowledge management (based on Picot/Scheuble 1999b)

It is furthermore concerned with the issue of where which internal and external
competencies are available and how these can be acquired through alliances with external parties and/or through internal employees' appropriate qualification measures
(knowledge acquisition). Controlling boundaryless organizations requires an efficient exchange of information between all corporate units involved to further develop existing competencies and to ensure access to the required internal and external knowledge (knowledge distribution and utilization). In the dissolving of the
boundaryless enterprise phase, existing experience and results must be saved and
processed further to continue the development of competencies (knowledge pres-
ervation). In the context of the creation of internal structures (stage 2 of the
knowledge management concept), infrastructures and rules are provided, which
helps to identify, represent, communicate, and transfer the required knowledge.
Central in this regard is the deployment of information and communication technologies, notably standardized databases, workflow systems, and intranets (Mer-
tens/Faisst 1997). A well-maintained database of partners can therefore help to

find the required competencies and partners in the configuration phase. The controlling phase supports, for example, telecooperation systems.

In the light of the underlying tasks and the existing competencies, the external knowledge sources that are required and how these can best be integrated must be taken into consideration during the creation of external knowledge structures (stage 3). Basically, the measures mentioned in connection with internal structures can also be transferred to this stage, since it is often quite difficult to differentiate between internal and external structures in boundaryless organizations. From the perspective of individual corporations, for example, a supplier relationship is an external relationship, but from the perspective of the boundaryless enterprise, it is an internal relationship. Customers, who are an important external source, are, however, an exception to this rule. During configuration, their needs must be identified and a solution found, during controlling they must be integrated into the solution at an early stage; in the separation phase, an after-sales service must be ensured even after dissolving has occurred. The specific design of internal and external structures ultimately depends on whether tacit (implicit) or explicit knowledge form the basis of the design (see chapter 3; Scheuble 1998).

Explicit knowledge is easily communicable and is reflected, for example, in an architect's drawings, technical information, and reports. In contrast, implicit knowledge is subjective, based on experience, and difficult to articulate. Both knowledge components play an important role in controlling the boundaryless organization. Knowledge management infrastructure must therefore take both knowledge categories into account. By definition, implicit knowledge cannot be verbalized or codified; therefore, it can only be entered into and be represented in technical systems to a limited extent. Consequently, it is sensible to check whether face-to-face communication or communication supported by telecommunications is preferable, whether and to what extent the knowledge of certain experts can be codified, and whether knowledge brokers should be used. The latter are responsible for conveying the relevant range of knowledge and often assume the task of preparing and updating the contents of knowledge databases.

## 10.5.4 Comprehensive Controlling Systems

In the following sections, new approaches will be presented that are based on the discussions above and meet the requirements for modern controlling functions in a boundaryless organization more so than many of the instruments still used in practice. Traditional controlling is predominantly based on figures; qualitative aspects are hard to find in the business controlling of enterprises. Direct market and customer perspectives are rarely considered deliberately, for example, by taking customer satisfaction values into account. In addition, many common controlling concepts are function-oriented, with productivity processes thus forming the focal point of manufacturing. This means that processes primarily based on personal production forms, such as the creation of services, are more difficult to control and support.

Currently, controlling is rather applied as a set of centrally controlled planning and controlling instruments, which no longer meets the requirements of modern organizational forms – particularly not those of the boundaryless organization.

Methods and concepts are required that can support decentralized coordination and take linking and network effects into account. Individual employees should be more closely integrated into the controlling and planning process, since people working in decentralized organization units are often actually those with the knowledge. This is the only way that they can fulfill their new roles as intrapreneurs and innovators (see chapter 9). The management must also be supported by suitable controlling instruments in respect of empowered employees' personal management and support, networking and relationship management with external parties, change management, and the architecture and design of the enterprise and its potentials. Consequently, modern controlling methods for the boundaryless organization must be holistic and integrative. This includes a multi-dimensional pursuit of goals, the explicit integration of qualitative aspects and indices (particularly the customer and market perspectives), and a stronger integration of the various functional areas. To elucidate the new view adopted by controlling, two concepts that take the integrated controlling notion into account are presented in the following sections: The expanded efficiency concept and the balanced scorecard concept.

### 10.5.4.1 Expanded Efficiency Concept

The expanded efficiency concept was originally developed to evaluate reorganization measures in the field of information and communication technology (Reichwald / Höfer / Weichselbaumer 1996; see also section 4.3.6). However, it also serves as a general controlling instrument to evaluate investment projects both in advance and retrospectively and is a reliable decision-making aid for management. This concept also covers the evaluation of cooperative projects or the design of boundaryless organizations.

On controlling and evaluating such projects, it is again possible to detect a general tendency toward an "escape into figures" in current business practice. The new availability of figures, due to modern information and communication technologies, is regarded as a reason for such an "escape into figures." In recent years, the production, distribution, and utilization of figures have increased drastically in conjunction with IT-aided evaluation procedures in controlling functions. Experience has, however, also often revealed that restricting evaluation to purely quantitative monetary variables in order to support controlling decisions, entails a great risk of controlling failures. The expanded efficiency concept endeavors to overcome this "unquestioning faith in figures" and assumes that economic efficiency need not just be expressed in terms of purely monetary input-output relations (Reichwald / Höfer / Weichselbaumer 1996).

A forerunner of the concept is the three-stage procedure for the evaluation of work systems according to Zangemeister (1993). In addition to monetary costs and revenue variables, which can be recorded directly, this procedure also incorporates indirectly inferable qualitative aspects. These include, for example, individual employees' quality, flexibility and job situation (see figure 10.6). All these variables have an effect on a company's long-term competitiveness, which is realized by key success factors such as customer and employee satisfaction and social acceptance.

The expanded efficiency concept starts with this comprehensive evaluation of goals and then structures it further. In order to do justice to the decision area's complexity, various perspectives are taken into consideration, which is integral to this approach. Any change to a corporation due to individual decisions should therefore be evaluated and compared from several perspectives (multi-level evaluation). Various goal categories are dominant in such an evaluation, depending on the perspective that the observer has adopted (see figure 10.7).

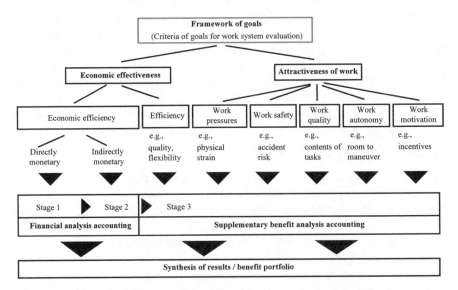

**Fig. 10.6.** Three-stage procedure for the evaluation of work systems (based on Zangemeister 1993)

From an employee perspective, human goals are predominantly considered, such as goals that have a direct impact on the satisfaction of employees. This also includes the leeway that an individual employee has in respect of decision-making powers or creative cooperation on a team. From a corporate perspective, however, productivity indices, such as the time required by a sales team to service a particular customer segment, or the costs arising from all of a firm's marketing measures, are frequently the focus of attention. The third level evaluates external effects that must be taken into account from a social perspective. Currently, these tend to play a subordinate role in corporate practice. Environmental damage caused by, for example, freight transport is only included in the decision-making process if costs arise from it.

Experience shows that although decision-relevant information is available in a company, it is not available in a suitable form at the right place. Information holders in the company are employed in various functional areas and at various hierarchical levels. Thus, to evaluate alternative actions with regard to decision making, such information holders from all levels have to be incorporated. In a guided group process, the positive and negative effects of alternative actions are evaluated by all of those involved. In certain decision-making situations, it may also be necessary to generate additional information and to make this available to an evaluation group. This information might be available within the company, such as data from the production or research and development department, or could be information specifically gathered for the situation, for example, by means of a customer survey. For specific issues, however, customers and suppliers must be directly integrated into the process.

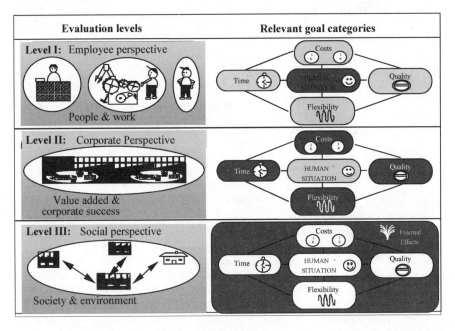

**Fig. 10.7.**  Multi-level model of expanded economic efficiency (based on Reichwald / Höfer / Weichselbaumer 1996)

In guided sessions, the evaluation process is structured into several stages (see figure 10.8). First, a comprehensive, individual taxonomy of goals must be generated, starting with global goals for each of the levels and going up to specific sub-goals. A list of criteria, which provides a number of reference points for the goal-setting process, supports this process stage. These sub-goals are then operationalized by company-specific variables and made measurable. In several learning loops, individual goals and measured variables are checked for interdependencies, redundancies and gaps, and adjusted if necessary. In keeping with the goal definition, appropriate measures are developed to provide appropriate solution measures. The generated measures are in turn checked for their compatibility with one another and combined to form a bundle of measures. In a final benefit analysis and/or scoring model, all the decision-makers involved evaluate whether the goals that have been set can be achieved by means of the bundles of measures. With the aid of this group process, various alternative solutions can be compared in terms of their specific enterprise utility potential. The management thus receives a reliable decision-making basis on which consensus should be reached by including all impacted employees.

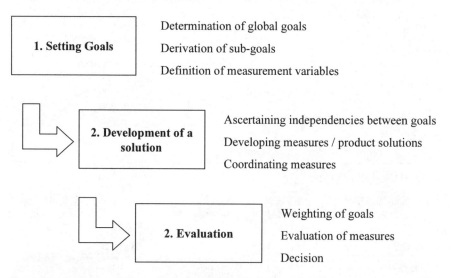

**Fig. 10.8.** Sequence of phases in the expanded efficiency analysis

The expanded efficiency concept is an integrated controlling concept that incorporates the notion of efficiency expanded by strategic and qualitative aspects. This concept overcomes the short-term, quantitative perspective of traditional controlling. It is now possible to support decisions for which relevant information is not available in one place, but is spread throughout the company. This concept also takes into account that decision-making situations are never identical and that the approach must be tailored to various evaluation situations (Reichwald/Bauer/Weichselbaumer 1997).

These advantages can be summarized by means of the fundamental principles of the expanded efficiency concept (Deking/Meier 2000). All of the following principles are closely connected to the various characteristics of the boundaryless enterprise as described in the previous sections.

- **Strategy orientation**: The expanded efficiency concept not only takes input-output relations into consideration, but also variables that lead to a quantitative result. Drivers of customer satisfaction such as flexibility, time and quality, which are a part of many marketing strategies today, are explicitly included in the evaluation. Owing to its market orientation, it takes the new internal and external roles of customers into account.

- **Participation orientation**: The advantages gained from employee participation in planning, steering, and controlling are transparency and acceptance of the decisions made. Employees are required to assume responsibility and can also contribute their decentralized knowledge to the decision-making process. At the same time, this creates a foundation for profit-oriented pay and management by objectives is supported.

- **Consideration of networking and linking effects**: Each activity that an employee performs in each functional area creates a link to upstream or downstream value-creating processes inside and outside the corporation. These linking effects are revealed by the expanded efficiency analysis and taken into account. Mutual dependencies on and between other partners of an enterprise alliance can also be depicted in the same way.

- **Human goal orientation**: Psychological findings indicate that work tasks can give people the opportunity to develop themselves and to be appreciated by others. This means that an individual's goals can be coordinated with the goals of the firm. Consequently, the method has a human focus and not a technical focus.

- **Instrumental support for evaluation processes in autonomous group organizations**: The problem with coordinating widely dispersed organizations is the relatively decentralized and modular structures of the organization units. Consequently, instrumental support is fostered in terms of what is referred to as self-controlling. The expanded efficiency approach, supported by modern information and communication technologies, not only offers good prerequisites for the incorporation of dispersed units into cross-area decisions, but it is also an instrument that can be deployed within dispersed units to support decision making.

### 10.5.4.2  Balanced Scorecard Concept

While the expanded efficiency analysis is primarily applied for a non-recurring consideration of reorganization processes and/or in individual cases as a method for project monitoring, a balanced scorecard is a continual, comprehensive instrument for directing and controlling entire companies and/or corporate units (Kaplan/Norton 1997). The starting point is a widespread problem: Controlling systems in companies are often historically based, focused on a unilateral analysis of financial figures, and not uniform in all corporate areas. Controlling functions have, for example, not yet coordinated sales tasks with those of production or purchasing (Deking 2002). To overcome this gap and to apply an integrated controlling concept based on the corporate strategy, an increasing number of companies have applied the balanced scorecard. This central controlling instrument is in widespread use, especially in the US, where the vast majority of Fortune 1000 corporations are using it in some form. The range of users extends from mid-sized corporations and large conglomerates to governments.

The balanced scorecard represents a holistic index and measuring system that breaks down and depicts the corporate strategy (performance measurement system according to Kaplan / Norton 1997). The basic idea consists in operationalizing a company's vision and strategy by means of qualitative and quantitative goals and then converting these into measurable variables. The management is obliged to develop specific strategic targets and to coordinate these throughout the enterprise. The intensive involvement of employees from each of the functional areas and corporate levels in the conception and implementation of the system ensures their strong identification with company goals (Butler / Letza / Neale 1997). The concept not only includes the new role of employees in boundaryless organizations, it also explicitly takes the strategic orientation of management-based controlling functions into account (see section 10.1).

The core of the balanced scorecard concept consists of depicting the strategy by means of four different perspectives. Figure 10.9 presents an example of a few enterprise goals:

- The **financial perspective** indicates whether the strategy and its operational implementation of an enterprise are also ultimately economically successful. Profit-level indicators and market value increases are specific target variables in this regard. The indices and targets of other perspectives flow into the financial indices. Finances are thus the final element in the chain of the cause-and-effect relations of the balanced scorecard.

- The **learning and development perspective** focuses on an enterprise's infrastructure analysis in the areas of information systems, employee training and qualification, as well as innovation management. In practice, employee satisfaction figures are often also considered in this perspective.

- The **internal processes perspective** includes fundamentals with which to achieve the goals of other perspectives. How efficiently does the corporation work? How well is strategy implementation supported by the organization? Answers to these questions serve to supply measurement values such as development, throughput, and processing times.

- Great importance is attached to the **customer perspective** in this concept. This view focuses very strongly on all areas of customer interaction and is closely related to the marketing control already established in many corporations. Typical variables are customer satisfaction values or market share variables. A corporation that consistently works with a balanced scorecard also automatically deals with customer orientation.

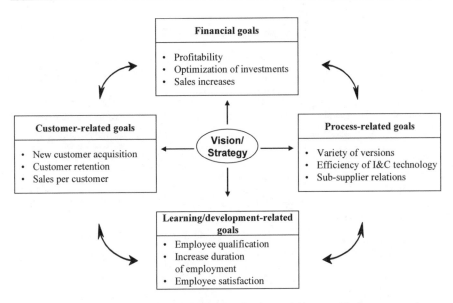

**Fig. 10.9.**  The four perspectives of the balanced scorecard (the specific items are only examples)

In addition to the individual goals, the balanced scorecard and / or its various levels contain relevant indices, projections (budgets), and specific action plans. Each of the different perspectives should not, however, be viewed as generally acceptable. Instead, they should be explicitly tailored to suit each company's strategy. Some corporations, for example, use five areas instead of the customary four. Analogous to their corporate philosophy, these firms place greater emphasis on the human resources aspect and create a separate employee perspective (Ewing 1995, Seidenschwarz 1999a). On the whole, the variety of perspectives has supported the move away from purely considering financial controlling variables. Instead, variables are included that drive a company's financial results. The balanced scorecard thus achieves a good balance between income indices and performance drivers. In all four levels of analysis, the utilization of suitable output variables is, however, important. The number of seminars attended by a sales employee, for example, has little informative value. Only improved customer satisfaction values or cross-selling rates as the output of this employee's increase in knowledge, or the improvement of this individual's sales capabilities are relevant measurement variables (Deking 2002).

How is the concept of the balanced scorecard implemented in a company? Figure 10.10 provides an overview of the implementation and communication process (Kaplan / Norton 1996). Introducing a balanced scorecard starts with the management, aided by a project team (often complemented by external consultants), assuming responsibility. The first step is to determine the strategic orientation as exactly as possible (visioneering). Consequently, consensus has to be reached within

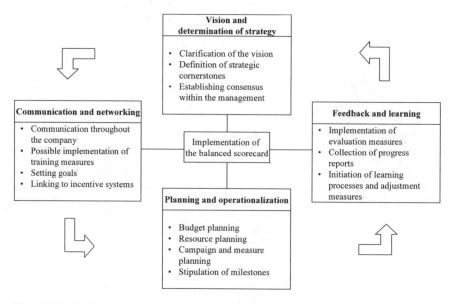

**Fig. 10.10.** A balanced scorecard implementation process

the management and the most important strategic cornerstones have to be defined (Lazere 1998).

The next step requires the adopted orientation to be communicated throughout the company. Furthermore, the project team, together with the affected employees, must develop specific, operational goals in respect of departments or functional areas. In many companies, however, many employees do not understand or know the corporate strategy, which is a problem. According to a study carried out by the business consultants Renaissance Worldwide, only 71% of executive staff in the US, and only 59% in Great Britain understand their company's vision. This share falls to 40% in respect of middle management and to 10% in respect of "normal employees" (Gentia 1998). Training measures are required to overcome this "vision barrier" and to familiarize each employee with the newly introduced vision. The goals created must be allocated to those responsible, and performance indices must be linked to the existing and / or to-be-adjusted incentive system to emphasize its importance, as well as to provide employees with incentives. Next, suitable measures such as the definition of budgets, target values, and the distribution of resources can be generated from the requirements of the goals.

With the aid of feedback processes, in which the conceptual overview is reviewed, feedback is given of decisions and actions. In contrast to normal feedback processes, this also takes place at a strategic level, not only at an operative level. The balanced scorecard is thus designed as a dynamic set of instruments. Loops, which permit learning on an ongoing basis, arise due to employee feedback and regular progress reports. Top management is also required to continually undergo self-reflection to recognize and initiate any required strategy changes.

This process can be further institutionalized by a survey of the employees affected, using the critical incident technique to gather critical (positive and negative) suggestions. Employee and customer satisfaction values can also be collected through this method. The advantages of this method, which Flanagan already developed in 1954, are that it reflects specific incidents, employees' and customers' ways of thinking, and that, qualitatively, it enables the most meaningful insights to be gained (Flanagan 1954). The disadvantage is the great effort involved in the evaluation. In the future, modern information and communication technologies will support the evaluation and increase its efficiency. This also applies to the survey process, which some corporations conduct by e-mail. The electronic form considerably facilitates implementation, particularly with regard to dispersed organizations (see Englberger 2000).

The balanced scorecard will have a company-wide effect if not just one scorecard is developed for the entire enterprise, but if "sub-scorecards" are derived from the original for the separate business units or units of responsibility (Horstmann 1999). Some corporations break scorecards down to the individual employee level. Every single scorecard lists the most important 10 to 20 variables in respect of the specific task field, with which desired corporate activities can then be measured and controlled. This allows responsibilities to be allocated exactly, allows a high degree of operationalization, and allows employees to largely identify with the system.

This system ensures that just those performance indices are used for each functional area that is relevant for its direction and control. Scorecards are interlinked and based on one another, which is achieved by top-down implementation. It would be counterproductive if all scorecards were not dependent on one another, as it would then not be possible to guarantee strategic orientation. Instead, the interlinking of scorecards fosters a continual communication and learning process in a horizontal and vertical direction. Employees subsequently recognize that their actions and achievements are very strongly influenced by other departments. This reduces egotistical conduct by particular areas, since employees are also measured by their respective contribution to the company as a whole. Incentives are, for example, provided for a sales employee to cooperate with other units of responsibility, such as the R&D department or production areas. The balanced scorecard thus creates a good basis for not only linking the variable compensation of executive employees to financial variables such as revenue. Figure 10.11 presents an example of the implementation of a balanced scorecard.

The example demonstrates how the balanced scorecard can be tailored to a particular firm. The cause-and-effect relationships between individual variables are specifically emphasized. Qualitative variables are related to quantitative variables and are depicted and measured via operationalizable values. Causal connections must be ascertained as precisely as possible, as they explain to employees how important cooperation throughout the company as a whole is. The interlinking of scorecards can be improved by taking variables into account that have an interface to upstream or downstream scorecards.

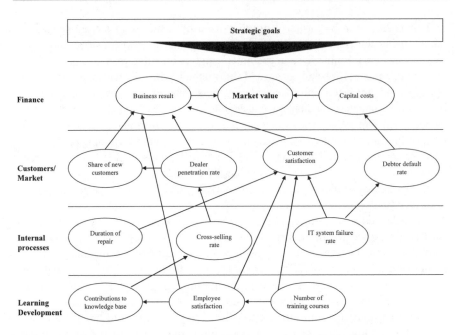

**Fig. 10.11.** Example of a balanced scorecard and its cause-and-effect relations

### 10.5.4.3  Appraisal of Approaches

On the whole, the described approaches present possibilities and opportunities while taking the holistic notion of control functions into account. The expanded efficiency and balanced scorecard concepts can be key controlling methods of a boundaryless organization and contribute to the overall coordination of an enterprise. Both approaches are output and/or market-oriented and focus on the value – a control variable – which an enterprise creates for its internal and external customers at a wide variety of levels. In addition, both concepts support the organizational modularization of value added processes – the basis of the boundaryless organization concept – since they can depict and evaluate cooperative task completion. There are, nevertheless, still major differences between these methods. The application of the expanded efficiency analysis can be regarded as a proactive evaluation procedure supporting decision making used to select alternatives. Owing to the high degree of effort involved, this is especially advantageous for strategic decisions in special and specific cases. Conversely, the balanced scorecard, whose implementation also entails a huge effort, can be regarded as a continual governing and control instrument that is used for strategic, as well as operative control tasks.

The methods are not incompatible – they complement each other. The implementation of a balanced scorecard is implicitly based on the notion of an expanded efficiency analysis (Deking 2002). In turn, both procedures should be complemented with the specialized controlling tools presented in sections 10.5.1 to 10.5.3.

The implementation of the concepts presented is not always easy in practice. The great effort involved is a specific point of criticism. Not every decision-making problem is, for example, tackled with the aid of a complete efficiency analysis process – the complex group process can only be justified in respect of large investment projects. In addition, the effort entailed to introduce a balanced scorecard is frequently underestimated. A year or more may be required, especially if it is introduced beyond a business unit's boundaries (e.g., implementation within the company's own call center). Furthermore, the original concept does not explain the exact procedures regarding goal setting and decision making – key success factors for the balanced scorecard (Weber / Schäffer 1998). The issues of how employees react if specified strategies are often questioned, or untargeted control elements occur due to group dynamics, are left open. The strategic analysis also fails to consider the competition whose actions undoubtedly have a major impact on enterprise actions. One of the main points of criticism is the lack of a methodical procedure to derive the "right" goals and measurement variables from strategic performance targets. It is thus left up to companies to develop the relevant instruments and processes with which to generate the desired indices.

The success of holistic controlling concepts depends above all on their implementation and daily use (Mountfield / Schalch 1998). Frequent errors and / or difficult problems encountered in practice during implementation are due to the lack of connection between the strategy and unambiguous performance drivers. Furthermore, the complete and valid depiction of cause-and-effect relations (among the indices) is often left to intuition, and thus remains a source of error. Nor are these concepts particularly promising if they are insufficiently tailored to the company or too strongly oriented to top management. Neither the balanced scorecard nor the expanded efficiency analysis is a cure-all. Through their underlying concepts, they are, however, appropriate for cultivating strategic ways of thinking and acting in all enterprise areas and for depicting the new principles of successful management in a modern controlling concept, which characterize boundaryless organizations in our information age.

## 10.6  Implications for Management

In a progressively digitized and networked world, managers must change their way of thinking and direct their attention to changes in success factors, strategies, and controlling systems. This does not, however, mean that traditionally tried and tested instruments in traditional enterprises are not important. There will always be environmental conditions in which traditional enterprises and their managerial instruments will present an efficient organizational solution. Nevertheless, new competitive conditions increasingly require traditional and time-tested structures and processes to be adjusted and restructured. In many cases, new information and communication technologies form the basis for innovative organization structures. Despite all their capabilities, they are nevertheless just a tool. At the center of boundaryless organizations are also working, decision-making, networking, trusting, motivated, as well as opportunistic people. More than ever before, they are the crucial factor of successful entrepreneurial action. This is why there are no prefabricated organizational "best practice" solutions. Only their creativity, uniqueness, and originality can provide permanent competitive advantages. This book has described approaches to unlock these advantages. The task of implementing the approaches is left to managers and employees.

Boundaryless enterprises are based on different concepts and success factors than traditional companies. This inevitably has an impact on strategic success factors and the design of important management systems. From the perspective of competitive strategy, it is therefore crucial that management concentrates on particular core competencies, utilizes its ability to cooperate with other partners as a source of competitive advantage, and fosters factors such as market and customer orientation and entrepreneurship. In this regard, the target is increasingly to implement hybrid competitive strategies that overcome the alleged traditional contradiction between cost leadership and differentiation, and to simultaneously realize cost leadership and differentiation as a promising way of establishing a sustainable and ultimately permanent competitive advantage. Consequently, the design of management instruments, such as controlling and information management, must place greater emphasis on coordination. This means integrating direct and indirect management into controlling methods and establishing knowledge management that focuses on building competencies, as well as knowledge structures within and between companies.

# References

Achleitner, A.-K./ Thommen, J.-P. (2001): Allgemeine Betriebswirtschaftslehre: Umfassende Einfuehrung aus managementorientierter Sicht, 3rd edn., Wiesbaden: Gabler, 2001.

Ackerman, M.S. (1992): Answer Garden: A Tool for Growing Organizational Memory, MIT Working Paper, Cambridge, MA, 1992.

Ackerman, M.S. (1994): Answer Garden and the Organization of Expertise, MIT Working Paper, Cambridge, MA, 1994.

Adams, J.S. (1965): Inequity in social exchange, in: Berkowitz, L.(ed.): Advances in experimental social psychology, Vol. 2, New York, NY: Academic Press, 1965, pp. 267–299.

Adstead, S./McGarvey, P.(1997): Convergence in Europe. The New Media Value Chain, London: Financial Times Management Report, 1997.

Akerlof, G.A. (1970): The Market for 'Lemons': Quality Uncertainty and the Market Mechanism, Quarterly Journal of Economics, Vol. 84, No. 3, 1970, pp. 488–500.

Albach, H. (1969): Informationswert, in: Grochla, E. (ed.): Handwoerterbuch der Organisation, Stuttgart: Schaeffer-Poeschel, 1969, pp. 720–727.

Albach, H. (1980): Vertrauen in der oekonomischen Theorie, in: Zeitschrift fuer die gesamte Staatswissenschaft, No. 1, 1980, pp. 2–11.

Albers, S. (1999): Was verkauft sich im Internet? – Produkte und Inhalte, in: Albers, S. et al. (eds.), eCommerce. Einstieg, Strategie und Umsetzung im Unternehmen, Frankfurt/Main: FAZ-Institute, 1999, pp. 21–34.

Albers, S./ Peters, K. (2000): Wertschoepfungsstrukturen und Electronic Commerce – die Wertschoepfungskette des Handels im Zeichen des Internet, in: Wamser, C. (ed.): Electronic Commerce, Verlag Vahlen: Munich, 2000, pp. 185–196.

Albers, S./Clement, M./Peters, K./Skiera, B. (eds., 2000): eCommerce. Einstieg, Strategie und Umsetzung im Unternehmen, 2nd edn., Frankfurt/Main: FAZ-Institut, 2000.

Albers, S. et al. (2001): Produkte und Inhalte, in: Albers, S./Clement, P./Peters, K. (eds.): Marketing mit interaktiven Medien. Strategien zum Markterfolg, 3rd edn., Frankfurt/Main: IMK, 2001, pp. 267–282.

Albers, S./Panten, G./Schaefers, B. (2002): Die eCommerce-Gewinner. Wie Unternehmen im Web profitabel wurden – 10 Erfolgsgeschichten aus erster Hand, Frankfurt/Main: FAZ-Institute, 2002.

Alchian, A.A./Demsetz, H. (1972): Production, Information Costs and Economic Organization, American Economic Review, Vol. 62, No. 5, 1972, pp. 777–795.

Aldrich, H.E. (1972): Technology and Organization Structure: A Reexamination of the Findings of the Aston Group, in: Administrative Science Quarterly, No. 17, 1972, pp. 26–43.

Allen, T.J./Scott Morton, M.S. (eds., 1994): Information Technology and the Corporation of the 1990s, New York, NY: Oxford University Press, 1994.

ANSI/SPARC (1975): Study Group on Data Base Management Systems: Interim Report, FDT 7:2, New York, NY: ACM, 1975.

Aoki, M./Gustafson, B./Williamson, O.E. (eds., 1990): The Firm as a Nexus of Treaties, Swedish Collegium for Advanced Study in the Social Sciences series, Newbury Park, CA: Sage, 1990.

Applegate, L.M/Holsapple, C.W./Kalakota, R./Radermacher, F.J./Whinston, A.B. (1996): Electronic Commerce: Building Blocks of New Business Opportunity, in: Journal of Organizational Computing an Electronic Commerce, Vol. 6, No. 1, 1996, pp. 1–10.

Arbeitskreis Organisation der Schmalenbach-Gesellschaft (1996): Organisation im Umbruch, in: Zeitschrift fuer betriebswirtschaftliche Forschung, No. 6, 1996, pp. 621–665.

Argyris, C. (1964): Integrating the Individual and the Organization, New York, NY: Wiley & Sons, 1964.

Argyris, C./Schoen, D. A. (1978): Organizational Learning: A Theory of Action Perspective, Reading, MA: Addison-Wesley, 1978.

Armstrong, A./Hagel, J. (1996): The Real Value of On-Line Communities, in: The McKinsey Quarterly, No. 3, 1995, pp. 127–141.

Arrow, K.J. (1962): Economic Welfare and the Allocation of Ressources for Invention, in: Nelson, R. R. (ed.): The Rate and Direction of Inventive Actitvity: Economic and Social Factors, New York, NY: Princeton University Press, 1962, pp. 609–625.

Arrow, K.J. (1974): The Limits of Organization, New York, NY: Norton, 1974.

Austin, J.L. (1989): Zur Theorie der Sprechakte, 2nd edn., Stuttgart: Reclam, 1989.

Axelrod, R. (1997): The Evolution of Cooperation, New York, NY: Basic Books, 1997.

Backes-Gellner, U./Lazear, E./Wolff, B. (2001): Personaloekonomik. Fortgeschrittene Anwendungen fuer das Management, Stuttgart: Schaeffer-Poeschel, 2001.

Backhaus, K. (1997): Relationship Marketing – Ein neues Paradigma im Marketing?, in: Bruhn, M./Steffenhagen, H. (eds.): Marktorientierte Unternehmensfuehrung, Wiesbaden: Gabler, 1997, pp. 19–35.

Baier, A. (1986): Trust and antitrust, in: Ethics, Vol. 96, 1986, pp. 231–260.

Bailey, J.P./Bakos, Y. (1997): An Exploratory Study of the Emerging Role of Electronic Intermediaries, in: International Journal of Electronic Commerce, Vol. 1, No. 3, Spring 1997, pp. 7–20.

Bakos, Y. (1991): A Strategic Analysis of Electronic Marketplaces, in: MIS Quarterly, Vol. 15, No. 3, September 1991, pp. 295–310.

Bakos, Y. (1998): The Emerging Role of Electronic Marketplaces on the Internet, in: Communications of the ACM, August 1998, Vol. 41, No. 8, pp. 35–42.

Bakos, Y./Brynjolfsson, E. (1999): Bundling Information Goods: Pricing, Profits and Efficiency, Working Paper Series, MIT Sloan School of Management, 1999.

Baldwin, C.Y./Clark, K.B. (1998): Modularisierung: Ein Konzept wird universell, in: Harvard Business Manager, No. 2, 1998, pp. 39–48.

Ballwieser, W. (2000): Wertorientierte Unternehmensfuehrung, in: Zeitschrift fuer betriebswirtschaftliche Forschung, No. 3, 2000, pp. 160–166.

Bamford, R.S./Burgelman, R.A. (1997): Netscape Communications Corporation in 1997, Stanford Graduate School of Business Case SM-42, Stanford, CA: Stanford Graduate School of Business, 1997.

Bangemann, M. (1995): Europas Weg in die Informationsgesellschaft, Eroeffnungsrede auf dem 13. Weltkongress der International Federation for Information Processing am 29. August 1994 in Hamburg, in: Informatik Spektrum, No. 1, 1995, pp. 1–3.

Barber, B. (1983): The logic and limits of trust, New Brunswick, NJ: Rutgers University Press, 1983.

Barley, S. (1986): Technology as an Occasion for Structuring: Evidence from Observation of CT Scanners and the Social Order of Radiology Departments, in: Administrative Science Quarterly, Vol. 31, 1986, pp. 78–108.

Barley, S. (1990): The Alignment of Technology and Structure Through Roles and Networks, in: Administrative Science Quarterly, Vol. 35, 1990, pp. 61–103.

Bartlett, C.A./Goshal, S. (1992): What is a Global Manager?, in: Harvard Business Review, September/October 1992, pp. 124–132.

Bartlett, C.A./Goshal, S.(1998): Wie sich die Rolle des Managers veraendert, in: Harvard Business Manager, No. 6, 1998, pp. 79–90.

Bartoelke, K./Kappler, E./Laske, S./Nieder, P. (eds., 1978): Arbeitsqualitaet in Organisationen, Wiesbaden: Gabler, 1978.

Bauer, F.L./Woessner, H. (1981): Algorithmische Sprache und Programmentwicklung, Berlin et al.: Springer, 1981.

Bauer, R. (1995): Coaching, in: Kieser, A./Reber, G./Wunderer, R. (eds.): Handwoerterbuch der Fuehrung, 2nd edn., Stuttgart: Schaeffer-Poeschel, 1995, col. 200–211.

Baumgarten, B. (1996): Petri-Netze: Grundlagen und Anwendungen, 2nd edn., Mannheim et al.: BI Wissenschaftsverlag, 1996.

Baumgarten, U. (2002): Technische Infrastruktur fuer das Mobile Business, in: Reichwald, R. (ed.): Mobile Kommunikation – Wertschoepfung, Technologien, neue Dienste, Wiesbaden: Gabler, 2002, pp. 101–112.

Baur, C. (1990): Make-or-Buy-Entscheidungen in einem Unternehmen der Automobilindustrie – Empirische Analyse und Gestaltung der Fertigungstiefe aus transaktionskostentheoretischer Sicht, Munich: VVF, 1990.

Bausch, A./Kaufmann, L. (2000): Innovationen im Controlling am Beispiel der Entwicklung monetaerer Kennzahlensysteme, in: Controlling, No. 3, 2000, pp. 121–128.

Beam, C./Segev, A. (1997): Automated Negotiations: A Survey of the State of the Art, CMIT Working Paper 97-WP-1022, May, 1997.

Beam, C./Segev, A. (1998): Auctions on the Internet: A Field Study, CMIT Working Paper 98-WP-1032, May, 1998.

Beck, A./Bendel, O./Stoller-Schai, D. (2001): E-Learning im Unternehmen: Grundlagen – Strategien – Methoden – Technologien, Zuerich: Orell Fuessli, 2001

Becker, F.G. (1990): Anreizsysteme fuer Fuehrungskraefte – Moeglichkeiten zur strategisch-orientierten Steuerung des Managements, Stuttgart: Schaeffer-Poeschel, 1990.

Becker, F.G. (1998): Grundlagen betrieblicher Leistungsbeurteilungen. Leistungsverstaendnis und -prinzip, Beurteilungsproblematik und Verfahrensprobleme, 3rd edn., Stuttgart: Schaeffer-Poeschel, 1998.

Becker, J. (1995): Der grosse Kabelsalat, in: Zeitmagazin, No. 10, 3rd edn., March 1995, pp. 20 – 22.

Beckurts K.H. / Reichwald, R. (1984): Kooperation im Management mit integrierter Buerotechnik, Muenchen: CW-Publikationen, 1984.

Bellmann, K. / Wittmann, E. (1991): Modelle der organisatorischen Arbeitsstrukturierung: Oekonomische und humane Effekte, in: Bullinger, H.-J. (ed.): Handbuch des Informationsmanagements im Unternehmen, Vol. 1, Munich: Beck, 1991, pp. 487 – 515.

Benchimol, G. (1994): L'Entreprise Délocalisée, Paris: Editions Hermès, Collection Systèmes d'information, 1994.

Benjamin, R. / Wigand, R. T. (1995): Electronic Markets and Virtual Value Chains on the Information Superhighway, in: Sloan Management Review, Winter 1995, pp. 62 – 72.

Bennis, W. (1993): Beyond Bureaucracy: Essays on the Development and Evolution of Human Organization, San Francisco, CA: Jossey-Bass, 1993.

Berger, P.L. / Luckmann, T. (1967): The Social Construction of Reality, New York, NY: Doubleday, 1967.

Bernstein, L. (1990), The choice between public and private law: the diamond industry's preference for extra-legal contracts and a private law system of dispute resolution, Discussion Paper No. 72 of the Program in Law and Economics, Harvard Law School, Boston, MA: Harvard University, 1990.

Besen, S.M. / Saloner, G. (1988): Compatibility Standards and the Market for Telecommunications Services, Rand Corporation Paper P-7393, Management in the 1990s, Sloan School of Management, Cambridge: Massachusetts Institute of Technology, 1988.

Besen, S.M. / Saloner, G. (1989): The Economics of Telecommunications Standards, in: Crandall, R.W. / Flamm, K. (eds.): Changing the Rules: Technological Change, International Competition, and Regulation in Communications, Washington, DC: Brookings Institution, 1989, pp. 177 – 220.

Beuermann, G. (1992): Zentralisation und Dezentralisation, in: Frese, E. (ed.): Handwoerterbuch der Organisation, 3rd edn., Stuttgart: Schaeffer-Poeschel, 1992, col. 2611 – 2625.

Bichler, M. / Segev, A. (1998): A Brokerage Framework for Internet Commerce, CMIT Working Paper 98-WP-1031, Berkeley, 1998.

Bieberbach, F. (2001): Die optimale Groesse und Struktur von Unternehmen: der Einfluss von Informations- und Kommunikationstechnik, Wiesbaden: Gabler, 2001.

Bieberbach, F. / Hermann, M. (1999): Die Substitution von Dienstleistungen durch Informationsprodukte auf elektronischen Maerkten; in: Scheer, A.-W. / Nuettgens, M. (eds.) Electronic Business Engineering – 4. Internationale Tagung Wirtschaftsinformatik 1999, Heidelberg, 1999.

Bierhals, R. / Nippa, M. / Seetzen, J. (1991): Marktpotential fuer die zukuenftige Nutzung digitaler Breitbandnetze, in: Ricke, H. / Kanzow, J. (eds.): BERKOM: Breitbandkommunikation im Glasfasernetz. Uebersicht und Zusammenfassung 1986 – 91, Heidelberg: R.V. Decker, 1991, pp. 39 – 50.

Billinghurst, M. / Weghorst, S. / Furness, T. (1998): Shared Space: an augumented reality approach for computer supported cooperative work. Virtual Reality: research development and application, 1998.

Bittl, A. (1997): Vertrauen durch kommunikationsintendiertes Handeln: eine grundlagentheoretische Diskussion in der Betriebswirtschaftslehre mit Gestaltungsempfehlungen fuer die Versicherungswirtschaft. Wiesbaden: Gabler, 1997.

Bjørn-Andersen, N. / Eason, K. / Robey, D. (1986): Managing Computer Impact, Norwood, NJ: Ablex Publ., 1986.

Blake, R.R. / Mouton, J.S. (1968): Verhaltenspsychologie im Betrieb, dt. Uebersetzung von Blake / Mouton: The Managerial Grid, Houston, TX: Gulf, 1964, Duesseldorf et al.: Econ, 1968.

Blake, R.R. / Mouton, J.S. (1985): The Managerial Grid III, 3rd edn., Houston, TX: Gulf, 1985.

Blankart, C.B. / Knieps, G. (1995): Kommunikationsgueter oekonomisch betrachtet, in: Homo Oeconomicus, No. 3, 1995, pp. 449–464.

Blau, P. / McHugh-Falbe, C. / McKinley, W. / Phelps, T. (1976): Technology and Organization in Manufacturing, in: Administrative Science Quarterly, No. 21, 1976, pp. 20–40.

Blecker, J. (1999): Unternehmen ohne Grenzen – Konzepte, Strategien und Gestaltungsempfehlungen fuer das strategische Management, Wiesbaden: Gabler, 1999.

Bleicher, K. (1985): Meilensteine auf dem Weg zur Vertrauensorganisation, in: Texis, No. 4, 1985, pp. 2–7.

Bleicher, K. (1992): Der Strategie-, Struktur- und Kulturfit Strategischer Allianzen als Erfolgsfaktor, in: Bronder, C. / Pritzl, R. (eds.): Wegweiser fuer strategische Allianzen: Meilen- und Stolpersteine bei Kooperationen, Frankfurt / Main: Campus, 1992, pp. 267–292.

Bleicher, K. (1995): Vertrauen als kritischer Faktor einer Bewaeltigung des Wandels, in: Zeitschrift fuer Organisation, No. 6, 1995, pp. 390–395.

Bleicher, K. (1996): Der Weg zum virtuellen Unternehmen, in: Office Management, No. 1–2, 1996, pp. 10–15.

Blohm, H. / Lueder, K. (1995): Investition, Schwachstellen im Investitionsbereich des Industriebetriebes und Wege zu ihrer Beseitigung, 8th edn., Munich: Vahlen, 1995.

Boecking, S. (1997): Die Zukunft des Internet – Fakten und Visionen, in: Vernetzte Systeme – Vernetzte Welt, Nymphenburger Gespraeche vom 25.6.1997, pp. 4–26.

Bode, A. (ed., 1990): RISC-Architekturen, 2nd edn., Mannheim et al.: BI Wissenschaftsverlag, 1990.

Bode, J. (1997): Der Informationsbegriff in der Betriebswirtschaftslehre, in: Schmalenbachs Zeitschrift fuer betriebswirtschaftliche Forschung, Vol. 49, No. 5, 1997, pp. 449–468.

Bode, J. (1993): Betriebliche Produktion von Information, Wiesbaden: DUV, 1993.

Boehm, B. (1988): Software Engineering Economics, Englewood Cliffs, NJ: Prentice Hall, 1988.

Bogard, W. (1996): The Simulation of Surveillance: Hypercontrol in Telematic Societies, Cambridge, MA: Cambridge University Press, 1996.

Boehm-Bawerk, E.v. (1909): Kapital und Kapitalzins (I): Positive Theorie des Kapitales, 3rd edn., Innsbruck: Wagner'sche Universitaetsbuchhandlung, 1909.

Boehme, M. (1997): Die Zukunft der Universalbank, Wiesbaden: Gabler, 1997.

Bonus, H. 1998): Die Langsamkeit von Spielregeln, in: Backhaus, K./Bonus, H. (eds.): Die Beschleunigungsfalle oder der Triumph der Schildkroete, 3rd edn., Stuttgart: Schaeffer-Poeschel, 1998, pp. 1–18.

Boerger E. (1992): Berechenbarkeit, Komplexitaet, Logik: Algorithmen, Sprachen und Kalkuele unter besonderer Beruecksichtigung ihrer Komplexitaet, 3rd edn., Braunschweig et al.: Vieweg, 1992.

Borghoff, U.M./Schlichter, J.H. (1998): Rechnergestuetzte Gruppenarbeit. Eine Einfuehrung in Verteilte Anwendungen, 2nd edn., Berlin et al.: Springer, 1998.

Borghoff, U.M./Schlichter, J.H. (2000): Computer-Supported Cooperative Work. Introduction to Distributed Applications, Berlin et al.: Springer, 2000.

Bornschein-Grass, C. (1995): Groupware und computergestuetzte Zusammenarbeit, Wiesbaden: Gabler, 1995.

Bower, G.H./Hilgard, E.R. (1983): Theorien des Lernens, Vol. 2, Stuttgart: Klett-Cotta, 1983.

Boyett, J.H./Conn, H.P. (1992): Workplace 2000: The Revolution Reshaping American Business, New York, NY: Penguin, 1992.

Bradford, D.L./Cohen, A.R. (1998): Power up – Transforming organizations through shered leadership, New York et al.: Wiley, 1998

Breton, T. (1994a): Le Télétravail en France. Situation actuelle, perspectives de développement et aspects juridiques, Rapport au ministre d'État, ministre de l'Intérieur et de l'Aménagement du territoire et au ministre des Entreprises et du Développement économique, Paris: La documentation Française, 1994.

Breton, T. (1994b): Les Téléservices en France. Quels marchés pour les autoroutes de l'information?, Rapport au ministre d'État, ministre de l'Intérieur et de l'Aménagement du territoire et au ministre des Entreprises et du Développement économique, Paris: La documentation Française, 1994.

Brockhoff, K. (1989): Schnittstellenmanagement, Stuttgart: Schaeffer-Poeschel, 1989.

Brockhoff, K. (ed.,1996): Management von Innovation, Wiesbaden: Gabler, 1996.

Bronder, C. (1993): Kooperationsmanagement: Unternehmensdynamik durch Strategische Allianzen, Frankfurt/Main et al.: Campus, 1993.

Bruhn, M./Bunge, B. (1994): Beziehungsmarketing – Neuorientierung fuer Marketingwissenschaft und -praxis?, in: Bruhn, M./Meffert, H./Wehrle, F. (eds.): Marktorientierte Unternehmensfuehrung im Umbruch. Effizienz und Flexibilitaet als Herausforderungen des Marketing, Stuttgart: Schaeffer-Poeschel, 1994, pp. 41–84.

Brynjolfsson, E. (1993): The Productivity Paradox of Information Technology, in: Communications of the ACM, Vol. 36, No. 12, 1993, pp. 7–77.

Brynjolfsson, E./Hitt, L. (1993): New Evidence on the Returns to Information Systems; Center for Coordination Science, Sloan School of Management, CCS Working Paper No. 162, Cambridge, MA: MIT, 1993.

Brynjolfsson, E./Hitt, L. (1995a): Information Technology as a Factor of Production: The Role of Differences Among Firms, in: Economics of Innovation New Technology, No. 3–4, 1995, pp. 183–195.

Brynjolfsson, E./Hitt, L. (1995b): The Productive Keep Producing – Successful companies support good business plans with the right information technologies, in: InformationWeek, 1995, pp. 38–43.

Brynjolfsson, E. / Hitt, L. (1998): Beyond the Productivity Paradox, in: Communications of the ACM, Vol. 41, 1998.

Brynjolfsson, E. / Kahin, B. (eds., 2000): Understanding the digital economy: Data, tools, and research. Cambridge, MA: The MIT Press, 2000.

Buechs, M.J. (1991): Zwischen Markt und Hierarchie: Kooperationen als alternative Koordinationsform, in: Zeitschrift fuer Betriebswirtschaft, supplement No. 1, 1991, pp. 1–38.

Bues, M. (1994): Offene Systeme. Strategien, Konzepte und Techniken fuer das Informationsmanagement, Berlin et al.: Springer, 1994.

Buckingham, M. / Coffman, C. (1999): First, break all the rules, New York: Simon & Schuster, 1999.

Buehner, R. (1987): Management-Holding, in: Die Betriebswirtschaft, No. 1, 1987, pp. 40–49.

Buehner, R. (1993): Die schlanke Management-Holding, in: Zeitschrift Fuehrung + Organisation, No. 1, 1993, pp. 9–19.

Bullen, C.V. / Bennett, J.L. (1990): Groupware in Practice: An Interpretation of Work Experience, Center for Information Systems Research Working Paper No. 205, 1990.

Bullen, C.V. / Johansen, R.R. (1988): Groupware: A Key to Managing Business Teams?, Center for Information Systems Research, Sloan School of Management, Working Paper CISR No. 169, Cambridge, MA: MIT, 1988.

Bullinger, H.-J. (ed., 1991): Handbuch des Informationsmanagements im Unternehmen, Vol. 2, Munich: Beck, 1991.

Bullinger, H.-J. / Seidel, U.A. (1992): Neuorientierung im Produktionsmanagement, in: Fortschrittliche Betriebsfuehrung und Industrial Engineering, No. 4, 1992, pp. 150–156.

Bungert, W. / Hess, H. (1995): Objektorientierte Geschaeftsprozessmodellierung, in: Information Management, No. 1, 1995, pp. 52–63.

Burke, R. (1998): Real Shopping in a Virtual Store; in: Bradley, S. / Nolan, R.L. (eds.): Sense & Respond – Capturing Value in the Network Era, Boston: Harvard Business School Press 1998, pp. 245–260.

Burr, W. (1995): Netzwettbewerb in der Telekommunikation. Chancen und Risiken aus Sicht der oekonomischen Theorie, Wiesbaden: Gabler, 1995.

Burr, W./ Kreis-Engelhardt, B. (1999): Telearbeit und organisatorischer Wandel in Versicherungsunternehmen, Karlsruhe: VVW, 1999.

Business Week (1998): Cyberspace Winners: How they did it, Business Week, June 22, 1998.

Buessing, A. (1988): Kontrollmotivation und Taetigkeit, Universitaet Osnabrueck, 1988.

Butler, A. / Letza, S.R. / Neale, B. (1997): Linking the Balanced Scorecard to Strategy, in: Long Range Planning, No. 2, 1997, pp. 242–253.

Buxmann, P. (1996): Standardisierung betrieblicher Informationssysteme, Wiesbaden: Gabler, 1996.

Buxmann, P. / Gebauer, J. (1997): Internet-based Intermediaries – The Case of the Real Estate Market, in: Proceedings of the 6th European Conference on Information Systems (ECIS'98), Aix-en-Provence, France, June 1998.

Buxmann, P./Weitzel, T./Koenig, W. (1999): Auswirkung alternativer Koordinationsmechanismen auf die Auswahl von Kommunikationsstandards, in: Zeitschrift fuer Betriebswirtschaft, supplement 2, 1999, pp. 133–151.

Cartwright, D./Zander, A. (1968): Group Dynamics: Research and Theory, 3rd edn., New York, NY: Harper & Row, 1968.

Casson, M. (1982): The Entrepreneur: An Economic Theory, Totowa, NJ: Barnes & Nobles, 1982.

Casson, M. (1987): Entrepreneur, in: Eatwell, J./Milgate, M./Newman, P. (eds.): The New Palgrave: A Dictionary of Economics (II), London et al.: MacMillan Press, 1987, pp. 151–153.

Cellular-News, September (2006): 2.5 Billion Mobile Phones in Use. See: www.cellular-news.com/story/19223.php, last accessed on December 18, 2007.

Chandler, A.D. (1962): Strategy and Structure, Cambridge, MA: MIT, 1962.

Chandler, A.D. (1977): The Visible Hand, Cambridge, MA: Belknap, 1977.

Chen, P. (1976): The Entity Relationship Model – Towards A Unified View of Data, in: ACM Transactions on Database Systems, No. 1, 1976, pp. 9–36.

Cheung, St.N.S. (1983): The Contractual Nature of the Firm, Journal of Law and Economics, Vol. 26, No. 1, 1983, pp. 1–21.

Child, J. (1972): Organizational Structure, Environment and Performance: The Role of Strategic Choice, in: Sociology, No. 6, 1972, pp. 1–22.

Choi, S.-Y./Stahl, D.O./Whinston, A.B. (1997): The Economics of Electronic Commerce – The Essential Economics of Doing Business in the Electronic Marketplace, New York et al.: Macmillan, 1997.

Ciborra, C.U. (1987): Reframing the Role of Computers in Organizations – The Transaction Cost Approach, in: Office Technology and People, No. 1, 1987, pp. 17–38.

Ciborra, C.U. (1993): Teams, Markets and Systems. Business Innovation and Information Technology, Cambridge, MA: Cambridge University Press, 1993.

Ciborra, C.U. (1994): The Grassroots of IT and Strategy, in: Ciborra, C.U./Jelassi, T. (eds.): Strategic Information Systems: A European Perspective, Chichester: Wiley, 1994, pp. 3–24.

Coad, P./Yourdon, E. (1991): Object-Oriented Analysis, Englewood Cliffs, NJ: Yourdon Press, 1991.

Coase, R.H. (1937): The Nature of the Firm, in: Economica, Vol. 4, No. 16, 1937, pp. 386–405.

Coase, R.H. (1960): The Problem of Social Cost, in: Journal of Law and Economics, Vol. 3, No. 1, 1960, pp. 1–44.

Codd, E.F. (1970): A Relational Model of Data for Large Shared Data Banks, in: Communications of the ACM, Vol. 13, No. 6, 1970, pp. 377–387.

Cohen, D.I. (1991): Introduction to Computer Theory, New York, NY: Wiley, 1991.

Cohen, D./Prusak, L. (2001): In Good Company. How Social Capital Makes Organizations Work, Boston, MA: Harvard Business School Press, 2001.

Coleman, J.S. (1990): Foundations of Social Theory, Cambridge, MA: Belknap Press, 1990.

Collardin, M. (1995): Aktuelle Rechtsfragen der Telearbeit, Berlin: E. Schmidt, 1995.

Colliers. See: http://www.colliers.com/Corporate/About/, last accessed on December 18, 2007

Collins, E.G. (1986): Eine Firma ohne Buero. Steve Shirley im Gespraech mit Eliza E.G. Collins, in: Harvard Manager, No. 3, 1986, pp. 23–26.

Collis, D.J./Bane, P.W./Bradley, S.P. (1997): Winners and Losers: Industry Structure in the Converging World of Telecommunications, Computing, and Entertainment, in: Yoffie, D.B. (ed.): Competing in the Age of Digital Convergence, Boston, MA: Harvard Business School, 1997.

Conradi, W. (1983): Personalentwicklung, Stuttgart: Enke, 1983.

Corsten, H. (1989): Ueberlegungen zu einem Innovationsmanagement, in: Corsten, H. (ed.): Die Gestaltung von Innovationsprozessen: Hindernisse und Erfolgsfaktoren im Organisations-, Finanz- und Informationsbereich, Berlin: E. Schmidt, 1989, pp. 1–56.

Corsten, H. (1998): Grundlagen der Wettbewerbsstrategie, Stuttgart et al.: Teubner, 1998.

Corsten, H./Will, T.(1995): Das Konzept generischer Wettbewerbsstrategien, in: Corsten, H. (ed.): Produktion als Wettbewerbsfaktor, Wiesbaden: Gabler, 1995, pp. 119–129.

Crowston, K./Sawyer, S./Wigand, R. T. (2001): Investigating the interplay between structure and technology in the real estate industry, in: Information, Technology and People, Vol. 14, No. 2, 2001, pp. 163–183.

Crowston, K./Wigand, R. T. (1999): Real estate war in cyberspace: An emerging electronic market?, in: International Journal of Electronic Markets, Vol. 9, No. 1–2, 1999, pp. 1–8.

Cranwell-Ward, J./Bacon, A./Mackie, R. (2002): Inspiring Leadership – Staying afloat in turbulent times, London et al.: Thomson Learning 2002.

Creed, D.W.E./Miles, R.E. (1996): Trust in organizations: A conceptual framework linking organizational forms, managerial philosophies, and the opportunity costs of control, in: Kramer, R.M./Tyler, T.R. (eds.): Trust in organizations: frontiers of theory and research, Thousand Oaks, CA: Sage, 1996, pp. 16–38.

Cusumano, M.A./Yoffie, D.B. (1998): Competing on Internet Time: Lessons from Netscape and Its Battle with Microsoft, New York, NY: Free Press, 1998.

Cyran, R./Hutchinson, M. (2007): Razr Thin Handset Profits, in: Wall Street Journal, Vol. 6, January 2007, p. B14.

Daft, R.L./Lengel, R.H. (1984): Information Richness: A New Approach to Managerial Behavior and Organization Design, in: Staw, B.M./Cummings, L.L. (eds.): Research in Organizational Behavior, No. 6, 1984, pp. 191–233.

Daft, R.L./Lengel, R.H. (1986): Organizational Information Requirements, Media Richness and Structural Design, in: Management Science, No. 5, 1986, pp. 554–571.

Daft, R.L./Lengel, R.H./Trevino, L.K. (1987): Message Equivocality, Media Selection and Manager Performance: Implications for Information Systems, in: MIS Quarterly, Vol. 11, 1987, pp. 355–366.

Dahl, O.J./Myrhaug, B./Nygaard, K. (1970): Simula 67: Common Base Language, Publication NS 22, Oslo: Norsk Regnesentral, 1970.

Darby, M.R./Karny, E. (1973): Free Competition and the Optimal Degree of Fraud, in: The Journal of Law and Economics, Vol. 16, pp. 67–88.

Date, C.J. (1999): An Introduction to Database Systems, Vol. 1, 7th edn., Reading, MA: Addison-Wesley, 1999.

Davenport, T.H. (1993): Process Innovation – Reengineering Work through Information Technology, Boston, MA: Harvard Business School, 1993.

Davenport, T.H. (1998): Putting the Enterprise into the Enterprise System, in: Harvard Business Review, July-August 1998, pp. 121 – 119.

Davenport, T.H. / Eccles, R.G. / Prusak, L. (1992): Information Politics, in: Sloan Management Review, Fall 1992, pp. 53 – 65.

Davidow, W.H. / Malone, M.S. (1993): Das virtuelle Unternehmen, Frankfurt / Main et al.: Campus, 1993.

Davidow, W.H. / Malone, M.S. (1996): The Virtual Corporation. Structuring and Revitalizing the Corporation for the 21st Century, 2nd edn., New York, NY: Harper Collins, 1996.

Davis, F.D. (1989): Perceived Usefulness, Perceived Ease of Use, and User Acceptance of Information Technology, in: MIS Quarterly, No. 13, 1989, pp. 319 – 339.

Davis, L.E. / Taylor, J.C. (1986): Technology, Organization and Job Structure, in: Dubin, R. (ed.): Handbook of Work, Organization and Society, Chicago, IL: Rand McNally, 1986, pp. 379 – 419.

Deking, I. (2002): Management des Intellectual Capital: Auf dem Weg zur strategiefokussierten Wissensorganisation, Dissertation, Munich: Technical University Munich, 2002.

Deking, I. / Meier, R. (2000): Vertriebscontrolling – Grundlagen fuer ein innovatives, anwenderorientiertes Verstaendnis, in: Reichwald, R. / Bullinger, H.-J. (eds.): Vertriebsmanagement: Organisation, Technologieeinsatz, Personal, Stuttgart: Schaeffer-Poeschel, 2000, pp. 250 – 267.

Delphi (1998): Studie zur Globalen Entwicklung von Wissenschaft und Technik, Frauenhofer-Institut fuer Systemtechnik und Innovationsforschung im Auftrag des Bundesministeriums fuer Bildung, Wissenschaft, Forschung und Technologie, Karlsruhe: FSI Verlag, 1998.

DeMarco, T. (1978): Structured Analysis and System Specification, Englewood Cliffs, NJ: Prentice Hall, 1978.

Demsetz, H. (1988): The Theory of the Firm Revisited, Journal of Law, Economics and Organization, Vol. 4, No. 1, 1988, pp. 141 – 161.

Denic eG (2002): Wachstum DE-Domains, elektronisch veroeffentlicht: http://www.denic.de/DENICdb/stats/domains_simple.html, Version vom 21.8.2002.

Derlien, H.-U. (1992): Buerokratie, in: Frese, E. (ed.): Handwoerterbuch der Organisation, 3rd edn., Stuttgart: Schaeffer-Poeschel, 1992, col. 2024 – 2039.

DeSanctis, G. / Gallupe, B. (1985): Group Decision Support System: A New Frontier, in: Data Base, No. 2, 1985, pp. 3 – 10.

Deutsch, M. (1960a): The effect of motivational orientation upon trust and suspicion, in: Human Relations, Vol. 13, 1960, pp. 123 – 139.

Deutsch, M. (1960b): Trust, trustworthiness and the Scale, in: Journal of Abnormal and Social Psychology, Vol. 61, 1960, pp. 138 – 140.

Deutsch, M. (1976): Konfliktregelung: konstruktive und destruktive Prozesse, Munich et al.: Reinhardt, 1976.

Deutsche Telekom (1998): Grundlagen und Erfahrungen fuer die Einfuehrung von Telearbeit – Das Pilotprojekt der Deutschen Telekom AG, Bonn 1998.

Di Martino, V. / Wirth L. (1990): Telework: An Overview. International Telework Report, Part I, Genf: International Labour Office, 1990.

Diebold, J. (1994): Wohin fuehrt die Informationsgesellschaft?, in: Der GMD-Spiegel, No. 4, 1994, pp. 27 – 35.

Diesler, P. (1998): Buero der Zukunft: Der unsichtbare Schreibtisch, in: CHIP, No. 3, 1998, p. 212.

Dietl, H. (1993): Institutionen und Zeit, Tuebingen: Mohr, 1993.

Dietl, H. (1995): Institutionelle Koordination spezialisierungsbedingter wirtschaftlicher Abhaengigkeit, in: Zeitschrift fuer Betriebswirtschaft, No. 6, 1995, pp. 569 – 585.

Dietrich, A. (2001): Selbstorganisation: Management aus ganzheitlicher Perspektive, Wiesbaden 2001.

Domsch, M. / Regnet, E. / Rosenstiel, L.v. (eds., 2001): Fuehrung von Mitarbeitern. Fallstudien zum Personalmanagement, 2nd edn., Stuttgart: Schaeffer-Poeschel, 2001.

Doepfner, M. (1989): Soziale Informationsverarbeitung – ein Beitrag zur Differenzierung sozialer Inkompetenzen, in: Zeitschrift fuer paedagogische Psychologie, No. 3, 1989, pp. 1 – 8.

Doerner, D. (1989): Die Logik des Misslingens. Strategisches Denken in komplexen Situationen, Reinbek bei Hamburg: Rohwolt, 1989.

Drucker, P. (1990): The Emerging Theory of Manufacturing, in: Harvard Business Review, May-June 1990, pp. 94 – 102.

Drumm, H.J. (1995): Personalwirtschaftslehre, 3rd edn., Berlin et al.: Springer, 1995.

Drumm, H.J. (1996): Das Paradigma der Neuen Dezentralisation, in: Die Betriebswirtschaft, No. 1, 1996, pp. 7 – 20.

Duelli, H. / Pernsteiner, P. (1992): Alles ueber Mobilfunk: Dienste, Anwendungen, Kosten, Nutzen, 2nd edn., Munich: Franzis, 1992.

Dunnette, M.D. (ed., 1976): Handbook of industrial and organizational psychology, Chicago, IL: Rand MacNally, 1976.

Ebers, M. (1995): Organisationskultur und Fuehrung, in: Kieser, A. / Reber, G. / Wunderer, R. (eds.): Handwoerterbuch der Fuehrung, 2nd edn., Stuttgart: Schaeffer-Poeschel, 1995, col. 1664 – 1682.

Eckardstein, D.v. (1989): Betriebliche Personalpolitik. UEberblick ueber die Grundfragen der Personalpolitik, 4th edn., Munich: Vahlen, 1989.

Eco, U. (1977): Einfuehrung in die Semiotik, Munich: Fink, 1977.

Eeles, P. / Sims, O. (1998): Building Business Objects, New York, NY: Wiley, 1998.

Ehrlenspiel, K. / Ambrosy, S. / Assmann, G. (1995): Integrierter Konstruktionsarbeitsplatz, in: Zeitschrift fuer wirtschaftliche Fertigung und Automatisierung, No. 9, 1995, pp. 410 – 413.

Eichenseher, E. (1997): Dezentralisierung des Controlling, Frankfurt / Main et al.: Lang, 1997.

Eickhoff, M. (1998): Controlling in der "grenzenlosen" Unternehmung, in: Steinle, C. / Eggers, B. / Lawa, D. (eds.): Zukunftsgerichtetes Controlling, 3rd edn., Wiesbaden: Gabler, 1998, pp. 123 – 137.

Endenburg, G. (1994): Soziokratie – Koenigsweg zwischen Diktatur und Demokratie, in: Fuchs, J. (ed.): Das biokybernetische Modell: Unternehmen als Organismen, 2nd edn., Wiesbaden: Gabler, 1994, pp. 135–149.

Engeler, E. / Laeuchli, P. (1988): Berechnungstheorie fuer Informatiker, Stuttgart: Teubner, 1988.

Englberger, H. (2000): Kommunikation von Innovationsbarrieren in telekooperativen Reorganisationsprozessen, Wiesbaden: Gabler, 2000.

Enquete-Kommission "Zukunft der Medien in Wirtschaft und Gesellschaft" (1998): Sicherheit und Schutz im Netz, Schriftenreihe "Enquete-Komission: Zukunft der Medien – Deutschlands Weg in die Informationsgesellschaft", Vol. 7, Bonn: Deutscher Bundestag / Zeitungs-Verlag Service, 1998.

Ettighofer, D. (1992): L'Entreprise Virtuelle ou Les Nouveaux Modes de Travail, Paris: Editions Odile Jacob, 1992.

European Commission (ed., 1994a): Europe and the global information society, Recommendations to the European Council, Bruessel, 1994.

European Commission (ed., 1994b): Europas Weg in die Informationsgesellschaft, Mitteilung der Kommission an den Rat und das Europaeische Parlament sowie an den Wirtschafts- und Sozialausschuss und den Ausschuss der Regionen vom 19.7.1994, Brussels, 1994.

European Commission, Brussels:White Paper on Growth, Competitiveness, and Employment: The Challenges and Ways forward into the 21st Century, 1993

Eurotechnopolis Institut (ed., 1994): Le Bureau du Futur. Les centres d'affaires et de services partagés, Paris: Dunod, 1994.

Evans, P.B. / Wurster, T.S. (1997): Strategy and the New Economics of Information, in: Harvard Business Review, September-October 1997, pp. 71–82.

Eveland, J.D. (1986): Diffusion, Technology, Transfer, and Implementation, in: Knowledge, Creation, Diffusion, Utilization, No. 2, 1988, pp. 303–322.

Ewert, R. / Wagenhofer, A. (2000): Interne Unternehmensrechnung, 4th edn., Berlin et al.: Springer, 2000.

Ewing, P. (1995): The Balanced Scorecard at ABB Schweden – a Management System in a "Lean Enterprise", Proceedings of the EAA-conference, Birmingham, 1995.

Fandel, G. / Hegener, C. (2001): Multimedia in der Lehre: Entwicklungen und Wirtschaftlichkeitsaspekte, in: Zeitschrift fuer Betriebswirtschaft, supplement No. 3/2001, pp. 111–133.

Fama, E.F. (1980): Agency Problems and the Theory of the Firm, in: Journal of Political Economy, Vol. 88, No. 2, 1980, pp. 288–307.

Farrell, J. / Saloner, G. (1986): Standardization and Variety, in: Economics Letters, Vol. 20, No. 1, 1986, pp. 71–74.

Fayol, H. (1916): Administration Industrielle et Générale, Paris, 1916.

Feldman, M.S. / March, J.G. (1981): Information in Organizations as Signal and Symbol, in: Administrative Science Quarterly, No. 26, 1981, pp. 171–186.

Ferstl, O.K. / Sinz, E.J. (1990): Objektmodellierung betrieblicher Informationssysteme im Semantischen Objektmodell (SOM), in: Wirtschaftsinformatik, No. 6, 1990, pp. 566–581.

Ferstl, O.K. / Sinz, E.J. (1991): Ein Vorgehensmodell zur Objektmodellierung betrieblicher Informationssysteme im Semantischen Objektmodell (SOM), in: Wirtschaftsinformatik, No. 6, 1991, pp. 477–491.

Fischer, T.M. (1999): Economic Value Added – Informationen aus der externen Rechnungslegung zur internen Unternehmenssteuerung?, Working Paper No. 27 of the Handelshochschule Leipzig, Leipzig, 1999.

Fischer, U. / Spaeker, G. / Weissbach, H.-J. (1993): Neue Entwicklungen bei der sozialen Gestaltung von Telearbeit, in: Informationen zur Technologiepolitik und zur Humanisierung der Arbeit, No. 18, Duesseldorf, August 1993.

Flanagan, J. (1954): The Critical Incident Technique, in: Psychological Bulletin, No. 4, 1954, pp. 327–358.

Fleck, A. (1995): Hybride Wettbewerbsstrategien, Wiesbaden: Gabler, 1995.

Flichey, P. (1994): TELE – Geschichte der modernen Kommunikation, Frankfurt / Main et al.: Campus, 1994.

Foss, N.J. (2001): Selective Intervention and Internal Hydrids: Interpreting and Learning from the Rise and Decline of the Oticon Spaghetti Organization, DRUID Working Paper No. 01 – 16, Frederiksberg, DK: Department of Industrial Economics and Strategy, Copenhagen Business School, 2001.

Fowler, M. (1999): UML Distilled, Second Edition: A Brief Guide to the Standard Object Modelling Language, Reading, MA: Addison-Wesley, 1999.

Franck, G. (1998): Oekonomie der Aufmerksamkeit, Munich: Hanser, 1998.

Frank, R.H. (1988): Passions within reason: The strategic role of emotions, New York, NY: Norton, 1988.

Franke, R.H. / Kaul, J.D. (1978): The Hawthorne experiments: First statistical interpretation, in: American Sociological Review, Vol. 43, 1978, pp. 623–643.

Frazier, D. / Herbst, K. (1994): Get Ready to Profit from the InfoBahn, in: Datamation, 15th Mai 1994, pp. 50–56.

Frese, E. (1989): Organisationstheoretische Anmerkungen zur Diskussion um "CIM-faehige" Unternehmungen, in: Wildemann, H. (ed.): Gestaltung CIM-faehiger Unternehmen, Munich: gfmt, 1989, pp. 161–184.

Frese, E. (1993): Geschaeftssegmentierung als organisatorisches Konzept: Zur Leitbildfunktion mittelstaendischer Strukturen fuer Grossunternehmungen, in: Zeitschrift fuer betriebswirtschaftliche Forschung, No. 12, 1993, pp. 999–1024.

Frese, E. (1995): Profit Center: Motivation durch internen Marktdruck, in: Reichwald, R. / Wildemann, H. (eds.): Kreative Unternehmen – Spitzenleistungen durch Produkt- und Prozessinnovation, Stuttgart: Schaeffer-Poeschel, 1995, pp. 77–93.

Frese, E. (2000): Grundlagen der Organisation, 8th edn., Wiesbaden: Gabler, 2000.

Frese, E. / Noetel, W. (1990): Kundenorientierte Organisationsstrukturen in Produktion und Vertrieb – Konzeption und ausgewaehlte Ergebnisse einer empirischen Untersuchung, in: Zahn, E. (ed.): Organisationsstrategie und Produktion, Muenchen: gfmt, 1990, pp. 15–58.

Frey, B.S. / Osterloh, M. (eds., 2000): Managing Motivation – Wie Sie die neue Motivationsforschung fuer Ihr Unternehmen nutzen koennen, Wiesbaden: Gabler, 2000, (chap. 9).

Frieling, E. (1992): Veraenderte Produktionskonzepte durch "Lean Production", in: Reichwald, R. (ed.): Marktnahe Produktion, Wiesbaden: Gabler, 1992, pp. 165 – 177.

Fromm, H. (1992): Das Management von Zeit und Variabilitaet in Geschaeftsprozessen, in: CIM Management, No. 5, 1992, pp. 7 – 14.

Fukuyama, F. (1995): Trust: The Social Virtues and the Creation of Prosperity, New York, NY: The Free Press, 1995.

Furubotn, E.G. / Pejovich, S. (1974): Introduction: The New Property Rights Literature, in: Furubotn, E.G. / Pejovich, S. (eds.): The Economics of Property Rights, Cambridge, MA: Ballinger, 1974, pp. 1 – 9.

Gable, R.A. (1993): Inbound Call Centers: Design, Implementation, and Management, Boston et al.: Artech House, 1993.

Gaiser, B. (1993): Schnittstellencontrolling bei der Produktentwicklung, Munich: Vahlen, 1993.

Gaitanides, M. (1983): Prozessorganisation: Entwicklung, Ansaetze und Programme prozessorientierter Organisationsgestaltung, Muenchen: Vahlen, 1983.

Gaitanides, M. (1996): Prozessorganisation, in: Kern, W. / Schroeder, H.-H. / Weber. J. (eds.): Handwoerterbuch der Produktionswirtschaft, 2nd edn., Stuttgart 1996, col. 1682 – 1696.

Gallie, W.B. (1952): Price and Pragmatism, Harmondsworth: Penguin Books, 1952.

Gambetta, D. (1988): Can we trust trust?, in: Gambetta, D. (ed.): Trust: making and breaking cooperative relations, New York, NY: Blackwell, 1988, pp. 213 – 237.

Gates, B. / Myhrvold, N. / Rinearson, P. (1997): Der Weg nach vorn: Die Zukunft der Informationsgesellschaft, Munich: Heyne, 1997.

Gaugler, E. / Kolb, M. / Ling, B. (1977): Humanisierung der Arbeitswelt und Produktivitaet, 2nd edn., Ludwigshafen: Kiehl, 1977.

Gebauer, J. (1996): Informationstechnische Unterstuetzung von Transaktionen: eine Analyse aus oekonomischer Sicht, Wiesbaden: DUV / Gabler, 1996.

Gebert, D. (1972): Gruppendynamik in der betrieblichen Fuehrungsschulung, Berlin: Duncker & Humblot, 1972.

Geihs, K. (1995): Client / Server-Systeme: Grundlagen und Architekturen, Bonn: International Thomson Publishing, 1995.

Gemuenden, H. G. / Ritter, T. (1998): Die netzwerkende Unternehmung: Organisationale Voraussetzungen netzwerkkompetenter Unternehmen, in: Zeitschrift Fuehrung und Organisation, Vol. 67, No. 5, 1998, pp. 260 – 265.

Gentia Software (1998): White Paper, Boston 1998, elektronisch veroeffentlicht. http://www.gentia.com, last accessed on November 29th 2007.

Gerpott, T.J. (1993): Integrationsgestaltung und Erfolg von Unternehmensakquisitionen, Stuttgart: Schaeffer-Poeschel, 1993.

Gerpott, T.J. / Boehm, S. (2000): Modulare Unternehmen, in: Nagel, K. / Erben, R. / Piller, F.T. (eds.): Produktionswirtschaft 2000 – Perspektiven fuer die Fabrik der Zukunft, Wiesbaden: Gabler, 1999, pp. 151 – 174.

Gerpott, T.J. / Thomas, S.E. (2002): Organisationsveraenderungen durch Mobile Business, in: Reichwald, R. (ed.): Mobile Kommunikation – Wertschoepfung, Technologien, neue Dienste, Wiesbaden: Gabler, 2002, pp. 37–54.

Gerpott, T.J. / Winzer, P. (2000): Simultaneous Engineering: kritische Analyse eines Planungs- und Organisationsansatzes zur Erfolgsverbesserung industrieller Produktinnovationen, in: Goetze, U. (ed.): Management und Zeit, Heidelberg: Physica-Verlag, 2000, pp. 244–265.

Gerybadze, A. (1995): Strategic Alliance and Process Redesign, Berlin et al.: de Gruyter, 1995.

Gibbert, M. / Jenzowsky, S. / Jonczyk, C. / Thiel, M. / Voelpel S. (2002): ShareNet – the next generation of Knowledge Management, in: Davenport, T.H. / Probst, G. (eds.): Knowledge Management Case Book, 2nd edn., Erlangen: Publicis Corporate Publ., 2002, pp. 22–39.

Giddens, A. (1979): Central Problems in Social Theory: Action, Structure and Contradiction in Social Analysis, Berkeley, CA: University of California, 1979.

Giddens, A. (1984): The Constitution of Society: Outline of the Theory of Structure, Berkeley, CA: University of California, 1984.

GMD – Forschungszentrum Informationstechnik (1998): AMBIENTE activity: i-LAND, electronically published under: http://www.darmstadt.gmd.de/ambiente/i-land.html, Version of 09.07.1998.

Goecke, R. (1997): Kommunikation von Fuehrungskraeften: Fallstudien zur Medienanwendung im oberen Management, Wiesbaden: Gabler, 1997.

Goldberg, A. / Robson, D. (1989): Smalltalk-80: The Language, Reading, MA: Addison-Wesley, 1989.

Goldhaber, M.H. (1997): Attention Shoppers!, in: Wired Magazine, December 1997.

Goleman, D. (1999): Emotionale Intelligenz – zum Fuehren unerlaesslich, in: Harvard Business Manager, No. 3, 1999, pp. 27–36.

Gomez, P. / Zimmermann, T. (1999): Unternehmensorganisation: Profile, Dynamik, Methodik, 4th edn., Frankfurt / Main et al.: Campus, 1999.

Google Inc. (2001): Google Offers Immediate Access to 3 Billion Web Documents, electronically published under: http://www.google.com/press/pressrel/3billion.html, Version of 21.8.2002.

Goepfert, J. (1998): Modulare Produktentwicklung: Zur gemeinsamen Gestaltung von Technik und Organisation, Wiesbaden: Gabler, 1998

Goetzer, K.G. (1997): Workflow: Unternehmenserfolg durch effiziente Arbeitsablaeufe: Technik, Einsatz, Fallstudien, 2nd edn., Munich, 1997.

Gottschall, D. (1994): Sand im Betriebe, in: Manager Magazin, No. 12, 1994, pp. 234–247.

Gouldner, A.W. (1960): The norm of reciprocity, in: American Sociological Review, Vol. 25, 1960, pp. 161–78.

Graen, G.B. (1976): Role making processes within complex organizations, in: Dunnette, M.D. (ed.): Handbook of industrial and organizational psychology, Chicago, IL: Rand MacNally, 1976, pp. 1201–1245.

Graham, J. (2000): Object Oriented Methods, 3rd edn., Workingham et al.: Addison-Wesley, 2000.

Grandke, S. (1999): Strategische Netzwerke in der Textilindustrie, Wiesbaden: Gabler, 1999.

Green, S.G. / Mitchell, T.R. (1979): Attributional processes of leaders in leader-member interaction, in: Organizational Behavior and Human Performance, Vol. 23, 1979, pp. 429–458.

Greenstein S. / Khanna T. (1997): What does Industry Convergence mean?, in: Yoffie, D.B. (ed.): Competing in the Age of Digital Convergence, Boston, MA: Harvard Business School, 1997.

Greif, A. (1989): Reputation and coalitions in medieval trade: Evidence on the Maghribi traders, in: Journal of Economic History, Vol. 49, 1989, pp. 857–882.

Grenier, R. / Metes, G. (1992): Enterprise Networking: Working Together Apart, Bedford, MA: Digital Press, 1992.

Griese, J. (1992): Auswirkungen globaler Informations- und Kommunikationssysteme auf die Organisation weltweit taetiger Unternehmen, in: Staehle, W.H.v. / Conrad, P. (eds.): Managementforschung 2, Berlin et al.: de Gruyter, 1992, pp. 163–175.

Griese, J. (1993): Informations- und Kommunikationssysteme in international taetigen Unternehmen, in: Management & Computer, No. 1, 1993, pp. 283–288.

Grindley, P. (1995): Standards, Strategy, and Policy: Cases and Stories, New York et al.: Oxford University, 1995.

Groenke, L. (1985): Der Normenausschuss Informationsverarbeitungssysteme (NI) und seine Aufgaben: Verbindlichkeit und Durchsetzbarkeit von Normen, in: Angewandte Informatik, No. 6, 1985, p. 247.

Grote, G. (1993): Schneller, besser, anders kommunizieren?, Stuttgart: Teubner, 1993.

Grote, G. (1994): Auswirkungen elektronischer Kommunikation auf Fuehrungsprozesse, in: Zeitschrift fuer Arbeits- und Organisationspsychologie, No. 12, 1994, pp. 71–75.

Grudin, J. (1991): The convergence of two disciplines, in: Proceedings of the ACM SIGCHI Conference on Human Factors in Computing Systems, New Orleans, LA: April 28 – May 2, 1991, ACM, pp. 91–97.

Gruendler, A. (1997): Computer und Produktivitaet – Das Produktivitaetsparadoxon der Informationstechnologie, Wiesbaden: Gabler, 1997.

Grueninger, C. (1996): Computergestuetzte Gruppenarbeit im Buero. Entwicklung, Nutzung, Bewertung, Frankfurt / Main: Campus 1996.

Gulick, L.H. / Urwick, L.F. (eds., 1937): Papers on the Science of Administration, New York, NY: Institute of Public Administration, 1937.

Guenther, T. / Landrock, B. / Muche, T. (2000): Gewinn- versus unternehmenswertbasierte Performancemasse: Eine empirische Untersuchung auf Basis der Korrelation von Kapitalmarktrenditen, Teil I, in: Controlling, No. 2, 2000, pp. 69–75.

Gurbaxani, V. / Whang, S. (1991): The Impact of Information Systems on Organizations and Markets, in: Communications of the ACM, No. 1, 1991, S. 59–73.

Gutenberg, E. (1965): Grundlagen der Betriebswirtschaftslehre (I): Die Produktion, 11th edn., Berlin et al.: Springer, 1965.

Gueth, W. (1996): Theorie der Marktwirtschaft, 2nd edn., Berlin et al.: Springer, 1996.

Habermas, J. (1976): Was heisst Universalpragmatik?, in: Apel, K.-O. (ed.): Sprachpragmatik und Philosophie, Frankfurt / Main: Suhrkamp, 1976, pp. 174–272.

Habermas, J. (1981): Theorie des kommunikativen Handelns, Vol. 1: Zur Kritik der funktionalistischen Vernunft, Frankfurt / Main: Suhrkamp, 1981.

Habermas, J. (1984): Vorstudien und Ergaenzungen zur Theorie des kommunikativen Handelns, Frankfurt / Main: Suhrkamp, 1984.

Hackman, J.R. (1969): Nature of Task as a Determiner of Job Behaviour, in: Personell Psychology, 1969, pp. 435 – 444.

Haeckel, S. / Nolan, R. (1993): Managing by wire, in: Harvard Business Review, Vol. 71, September-October, 1993, pp. 122 – 132.

Hagel, J. (1996): Spider versus spider, in: The McKinsey Quarterly, No. 1, pp. 4 – 19.

Hagel, J. / Armstrong, A. (1997): Net Gain, Boston: Harvard Business School Press, 1997.

Hagstroem, P. (1995a): Oticon A / S: "Cogitate Incognito" ["Think the Unthinkable"; Otticon A / S Company Motto], Harvard Business School Case No. 9 – 195 – 140, Boston, MA: Harvard Business School Publishing, 1995.

Hagstroem, P. (1995b): Oticon A / S: Project 330, Harvard Business School Case No. 9-195-141, Boston, MA: Harvard Business School Publishing, 1995.

Hahn, D. (2001): PuK, Controllingkonzepte, 6th edn., Wiesbaden: Gabler, 2001.

Hamm, S. (1998a): Jim Clark is off and running again, in: Business Week (European Edition) 19.10.1998, p. 80.

Hamm, S. (1998b): The Education of Marc Andreessen, in: Business Week, 13.04.1998, pp. 84 – 92.

Hammer, M. / Champy, J. (1993): Reengineering the Corporation: A Manifesto for Business Revolution, New York, NY: Harper Collins, 1993.

Hammer, M. / Champy, J. (1995): Business Reengineering, 5th edn., Frankfurt / Main et al.: Campus, 1995.

Hampe, F. / Schwabe, G. (2002): Mobile Customer Relationship Management, in: Reichwald, R. (ed.): Mobile Kommunikation – Wertschoepfung, Technologien, neue Dienste, Wiesbaden: Gabler, 2002, pp. 301 – 316.

Hampe, J.F. / Schoenert, S. (1997): Computer Telephony Integration, in: Wirtschaftsinformatik, No. 3, 1997, pp. 269 – 278.

Handy, C. (1995): Trust and the Virtual Organization, in: Harvard Business Review, May-June 1995, pp. 40 – 50.

Hanker, J. (1990): Die strategische Bedeutung der Informatik fuer Organisationen: Industrieoekonomische Grundlagen des Strategischen Informatikmanagements, Stuttgart: Teubner, 1990.

Hannan, M.T. / Freeman, J. (1977): The population ecology of organizations, in: American Journal of Sociology, Vol. 82, 1977, pp. 929 – 964.

Harrington, J. (1991): Business Process Improvement: The Breakthrough Strategy for Total Quality, Productivity and Competitiveness, New York, NY: McGraw-Hill, 1991.

Hartzheim, (1990): EDI-Anwendungspraxis: Elektronischer Datenaustausch in der Automobilindustrie – EDI in einem multinationalen Konzern: Ford of Europe, in: EWI (ed.): Electronic Data Interchange, EDI 90, Muenchen: Gugath, 1990.

Hasenkamp, U. / Kirn, S. / Syring, M. (1994): CSCW – Computer Supported Cooperative Work, Bonn et al.: Addison-Wessley, 1994.

Hass, B.H. (2002): Geschaeftsmodelle von Medienunternehmen: OEkonomische Grundlagen und Veraenderungen durch neue Informations- und Kommunikationstechnik, Wiesbaden: Gabler, 2002.

Hauschild, J. / Gemuenden, H.G. (eds., 1999): Promotoren – Champions der Innovation, 2nd edn., Wiesbaden: Gabler, 1999.

Hayek, F. A. v. (1945): The Use of Knowledge in Society, in: American Economic Review, Vol. 35, No. 4, 1945, pp. 519 – 530.

Hayek, F. A. v. (1994): Der Wettbewerb als Entdeckungsverfahren, in: Hayek, F. A. von (ed.): Freiburger Studien: Gesammelte Aufsaetze von Hayek, F. A. v., 2nd edn., Tuebingen: Mohr, 1994 [1st edn.: 1968], pp. 249 – 265.

Hedberg, B. (1981): How Organizations Learn and Unlearn, in: Nystroem, P. C. / Starbuck, W. H. (eds.): Handbook of Organizational Design, Vol. 1: Adapting Organizations to their Environments, New York, NY: Oxford University Press, 1981, pp. 3 – 27.

Heinen, E. (1986): Menschliche Arbeit aus betriebswirtschaftlicher Sicht, in: Schubert, V. (eds.): Der Mensch und seine Arbeit, St. Ottilien: EOS, 1986, pp. 307 – 329.

Henderson-Sellers, B. / Edwards, J. M. (1990): The Object-Oriented Systems Life Cycle, in: Communications of the ACM, No. 9, 1990, pp. 142 – 159.

Hennessy, J. L. / Patterson, D. A. (1994): Rechnerarchitektur: Analyse, Entwurf, Implementierung, Bewertung, Braunschweig et al.: Vieweg, 1994.

Hentze, J. (1995): Personalwirtschaftslehre 2, 6th edn., Bern et al.: UTB, 1995.

Hermann, M. (2002): Vom Broadcast zum Personalcast: Oekonomische Potenziale der Individualisierung audiovisueller Medienprodukte, Wiesbaden: DUV / Gabler, 2002.

Hermann, M. / Bieberbach, F. (1999): Das Internet als strategische Herausforderung fuer Informationsdienstleister, in: Information Management & Consulting, Vol. 14, No. 3, 1999, pp. 69 – 73.

Hersey, P. / Blanchard, K. H. (2001): Management of organizational behavior, 8th edn., Engelwood Cliffs, NJ: Prentice-Hall, 2001.

Herstatt, C. (1999): Theorie und Praxis der fruehen Phasen des Innovationsprozesses, in: io-Management, Vol. 68, No. 10, 1999, pp. 80 – 91.

Herzberg, F. (1968): One more time: How Do You Motivate Employees?, in: Harvard Business Review, No. 1, 1968, pp. 53 – 62.

Herzberg, F. / Mausner, B. / Snyderman, B. (1959): The Motivation to Work, 2nd edn., New York, NY: Wiley, 1959.

Hesch, G. (1997): Das Menschenbild neuer Organisationsformen: Mitarbeiter und Manager im Unternehmen der Zukunft, Wiesbaden: Gabler, 1997.

Heskett, J. / Sasser, E. / Schlesubger, L. (1997): The Service Profit Chain. How leading companies link profit and growth to loyality satisfaction and value, New York: Free, 1997.

Hess, T. (2002): Netzwerkcontrolling: Instrumente und ihre Werkzeugunterstuetzung, Wiesbaden: Gabler, 2002.

Hess, T. / Schumann, M. (2000): Durch elektronische Maerkte zu marktorientierten Verrechnungspreisen?, in: Controlling Vol. 11 – 12, 2000, pp. 557 – 562.

Hess, T. / Wohlgemuth, O. / Schlembach, H.-G. (2001): Bewertung von Unternehmensnetzwerken – Methodik und erste Erfahrungen aus einem Pilotprojekt, in: Zeitschrift Fuehrung + Organisation, Vol. 70, No. 2, 2001, pp. 68 – 74.

Hesse, W. / Merbeth, G. / Froelich, R. (1992): Software-Entwicklung: Vorgehensmodelle, Projektfuehrung, Produktverwaltung, Muenchen et al.: Oldenbourg, 1992.

Hickson, D. / Pugh, D. S. / Pheysey, D. (1969): Operations Technology and Organization Structure, in: Administrative Science Quarterly, No. 14, 1969, pp. 378 – 397.

Hill, W. / Fehlbaum, R. / Ulrich, P. (1994): Organisationslehre, Vol. 2, 5th edn., Bern et al.: Haupt, 1994.

Hill, W. / Fehlbaum, R. / Ulrich, P. (1998): Organisationslehre, Vol. 1, 5th edn., Bern et al.: Haupt, 1998.

Hilpert, W. (1993): Workflow Management im Office-Bereich mit verteilten Dokumenten-datenbanken, in: Nastansky, L. (ed.): Workgroup Computing, Hamburg: Steuer- und Wirtschaftsverlag, 1993.

Himberger, A. (1994): Der Elektronische Markt als Koordinationssystem Dissertation, Hochschule St. Gallen, 1994.

Hinterhuber, H. H. / Krauthammer, E. (2001): Leadership – mehr als Management, 3rd edn., Wiesbaden: Gabler 2001.

Hippel, E.v. (1988): The Sources of Innovation, New York, NY: University Press, 1988.

Hippel, E.v. / Tyre, M. J. (1997): The Situated Nature of Adaptive Learning in Organizations, in: Organization science, Vol. 8, No. 1, pp. 71 – 83.

Hoefer, C. (1997): Betriebswirtschaftliche Bewertung von Qualifizierungsinvestitionen: Auswirkungen auf die langfristigen Unternehmensziele, Wiesbaden: Gabler, 1997.

Hoffman, G. M. (1994): Technology Payoff: How to Profit with Empowered Workers in the Information Age, New York, NY: Irwin Publ., 1994.

Holler, M. (1983): Collective Action, Rational Man and Economic Reasoning, in: Quality and Quantity, Vol. 17, No. 2, 1983, pp. 163 – 177.

Holling, H. / Lammers, F. (1995): Beeinflussung von Gruppenprozessen als Fuehrungsauf-gabe, in: Kieser, A. / Reber, G. / Wunderer, R. (eds.): Handwoerterbuch der Fuehrung, 2nd edn., Stuttgart: Schaeffer-Poeschel, 1995, col. 129 – 137.

Hopcroft, J. E. / Ullman, J. D. (1979): Introduction to Automata Theory, Languages and Computation, Reading, MA: Addison-Wesley, 1979.

Hopcroft, J. E. / Ullman, J. D. (2000): Einfuehrung in die Automatentheorie, Formale Spra-chen und Komplexitaetstheorie, 4th edn., Munich: Oldenbourg 2000.

Horstmann, W. (1999): Der Balanced Scorecard-Ansatz als Instrument der Umsetzung von Unternehmensstrategien, in: Controlling, No. 4 / 5, 1999, pp. 193 – 199.

Horváth, P. (1991): Schnittstellenueberwindung durch das Controlling, in: Horváth, P. (ed.): Synergien durch Schnittstellen-Controlling, Stuttgart: Schaeffer-Poeschel, 1991, pp. 1 – 23.

Horváth, P. (1995): Selbstorganisation und Controlling, in: Krystek, U. / Link, J. (eds.): Fuehrungskraefte und Fuehrungserfolg. Neue Herausforderungen fuer das strategische Management, Wiesbaden: Gabler, 1995, pp. 255 – 267.

Horváth, P. (2002): Controlling, 8th edn., Munich: Vahlen, 2002.

Howard, Mickey. 2005 Collaboration and the "3DayCar": a study of automotive ICT adop-tion. Journal of Information Technology, Vol. 20, No. 4, December 2005, pp. 245 – 258.

Hrubi, F. R. (1988): Kommunikationsmanagement, in: Hofmann, M. / Rosenstiel, L. v. (eds.): Funktionale Managementlehre, Berlin et al.: Springer, 1988, pp. 59 – 94.

Hwang, K./Briggs, F. A. (1985): Computer Architecture and Parallel Processing, New York, NY: McGraw-Hill, 1985.

Iacono, S./Wigand, R.T. (2005): Preface to the Special Issue: Information Technology and Industry Change: View from an Industry Level of Analysis, in: Journal of Information Technology, Vol. 20, No. 4, December 2005, pp. 211–212.

IDATE (1994): European Telecommunications Handbook for Teleworkers, A study for the Commission of the European Union, ed. by ExperTeam TeleCom Dortmund and IDATE Montpellier, 1994.

Imai, K./Itami, H. (1984): Interpenetration of Organization and Market, in: International Journal of Industrial Organization, No. 4, 1984, pp. 285–310.

Internet Retailer. 2007. www.internetretailer.com, last accessed on December 18th 2007.

Internet Usage Statistics 2007. www.internetworldstats.com/stats.htm, last accessed on November 29th 2007.

Jablonski, S. (1991): Konzepte der verteilten Datenverwaltung, in: Handbuch der modernen Datenverarbeitung, No. 157, 1991, pp. 1–21.

Jablonski, S./Boehm, M./Schulze, W. (1997): Workflow Management: Entwicklung von Anwendungen und Systemen, Heidelberg, 1997.

James, W. (1962): The Principles of Psychology, New York, NY: Dover, 1962.

Janis, I.L. (1982): Groupthink. Psychological studies of policy decisions and fiascoes, Boston, MY: Houghton Mifflin, 1982

Jarillo, J.C. (1988): On Strategic Networks, in: Strategic Management Journal, Vol. 9, 1988, pp. 31–41.

Jarillo, J.C. (1993): Strategic Networks: Creating the borderless organization, Oxford: Butterworth-Heinemann, 1993.

Jaros-Sturhahn, A./Loeffler, P. (1995): Das Internet als Werkzeug zur Deckung des betrieblichen Informationsbedarfs, in: Information Management, No. 1, 1995, pp. 6–13.

Jarvenpaa, S.L./Ives, B. (1994): The Global Network Organization of the Future: Information Management Opportunities and Challenges, in: Journal of Management Information Systems, No. 4, 1994, pp. 25–57.

Jensen, M.C./Meckling, W.H. (1976): Theory of the Firm: Managerial Behavior, Agency Costs and Ownership Structure, in: Journal of Financial Economics, Vol. 3, No. 4, 1976, pp. 305–360.

Jessen, E. (1996): Die Entwicklung des virtuellen Speichers, in: Informatik Spektrum, No. 4, 1996, pp. 216–219.

Jessen, E./Valk, R. (1987): Rechensysteme: Grundlagen der Modellbildung, Berlin et al.: Springer, 1987.

Johansen, R. (1991): Teams for Tomorrow, in: Proceedings of the 24th Annual Hawai International Conference on Systems Sciences, Los Alamitos: IEEE Computer Society Press, 1991, pp. 520–534.

Johnson, H. T./Kaplan, R. S. (1991): Relevance Lost. The Rise and Fall of Management Accounting, Boston, MA: Harvard Business School, 1991.

Jones, T. M. (1995): Instrumental stakeholder theory: A synthesis of ethics and economics, in: Academy of Management Review, Vol. 20, 1995, pp. 404–437.

Jones, S.R.G. (1992): Was There a Hawthorne Effect?, in: The American Journal of Sociology, Vol. 98, No. 3, November 1992, pp. 451–468

Jost, P.-J. (ed., 2001a): Die Prinzipal-Agenten-Theorie in der Betriebswirtschaftslehre, Schaeffer-Poeschel: Stuttgart, 2001.

Jost, P.-J. (ed., 2001b): Der Transaktionskostenansatz in der Betriebswirtschaftslehre, Schaeffer-Poeschel: Stuttgart, 2001.

Kaluza, B. / Blecker, Th. (1999): Dynamische Produktdifferenzierungsstrategie und Produktionsnetzwerke, in: Nagel, K. / Erben, R. / Piller, F.T. (eds.): Produktionswirtschaft 2000 – Perspektiven fuer die Fabrik der Zukunft, Wiesbaden: Gabler, 1999, pp. 265–280.

Kaluza, B. / Blecker, Th. (eds., 2000): Produktions- und Logistikmanagement in Virtuellen Unternehmen und Unternehmensnetzwerken, Stuttgart: Springer, 2000.

Kaluza, B. / Blecker, Th. (2001a): Produktionsplanung und -steuerung in der Unternehmung ohne Grenzen, in: Bellmann, K. (ed.): Kooperations- und Netzwerkmanagement, Berlin: Duncker & Humblot, 2001, pp. 83–110.

Kaluza, B. / Blecker, Th. (2001b): Produzieren in vernetzten Unternehmen, in: Industriemanagement, No. 5, 2001, pp. 49–52.

Kaluza, B. / Kremminer, J. (1997): Dynamisches Supply Management und Dynamische Produktdifferenzierungsstrategie, in: Kaluza, B. / Trefz, J. (eds.): Herausforderung Materialwirtschaft, Hamburg: Steuer- und Wirtschaftsverlag, 1997, pp. 5–53.

Kanigel, R. (1997): The One Best Way: Frederic Winslow Taylor and the Enigma of Efficiency. New York: Viking, 1997.

Kanzow, J. (1991): BERKOM-Breitbandkommunikation im Glasfasernetz, in: Ricke, H. / Kanzow, J. (eds.): BERKOM: Breitbandkommunikation im Glasfasernetz. Uebersicht und Zusammenfassung 1986–91, Heidelberg: Decker, 1991, pp. 1–9.

Kao, J. (1996): Oticon (A), Harvard Business School Case No. 9–395–140, Boston, MA: Harvard Business School Publishing, 1995

Kaplan, R. S. / Norton, D. P. (1996): Using the Balanced Scorecard as a Strategic Management System, in: Harvard Business Review, January-February 1996, pp. 75–85.

Kaplan, R. S. / Norton, D. P. (1997): Balanced Scorecard. Strategien erfolgreich umsetzen, Stuttgart: Schaeffer-Poeschel, 1997.

Kappich, L. (1989): Theorie der internationalen Unternehmungstaetigkeit, Munich: VVF, 1989.

Kappler, E. / Rehkugler, H. (1991): Konstitutive Entscheidungen, in: Heinen, E. (ed.): Industriebetriebslehre, Entscheidungen im Industriebetrieb, 9th edn., Wiesbaden: Gabler, 1991, pp. 73–240.

Katz, M. L. / Shapiro, C. (1985): Network Externalities, Competition and Compatibility, in: American Economic Review, Vol. 75, No. 3, 1985, pp. 424–440.

Katzenbach, J.R. / Smith, D.K. (1994): The Wisdom of Teams, New York, NY: Harper Business, 1994.

Kaulmann, T. (1987): Property rights und Unternehmungstheorie: Stand und Weiterentwicklung der empirischen Forschung, Muenchen: Florentz, 1987.

Keen, P.G. / Scott Morton, M.S. (1978): Decision Support Systems: An Organizational Perspective, Reading, MA: Addison-Wesley, 1978.

Keller, E. (1992): Management in fremden Kulturen, Stuttgart: Haupt, 1982.

Kelly, K. (1997): New Rules for the New Economy, in: Wired, Vol 5, No. 9, 1997, http://www.wired.com/wired/5.09/newrules.html.

Kenneth, A. K. (1987): What Motivates Employees? Workers and Supervisors Give Different Answers, in: Business Horizones, No. 9/10, 1987, pp. 58–65.

Kets de Vries, M. F. R. (1999): High-Performance Teams: Lessons from the Pygmies, in: Organizational Dynamics, Winter 1999, pp. 66–77.

Kieser, A. (ed., 1999): Organisationstheorien, 3rd edn., Stuttgart et al.: Kohlhammer, 1999.

Kieser, A./Hegele, C. (1998): Die Veraenderung des Controlling und das Controlling der Veraenderung – aus organisationswissenschaftlicher Sicht, in: krp – Kostenrechnungspraxis, special issue No. 1, 1998, pp. 12–14.

Kieser, A./Hegele, C./Klimmer, M. (1998): Kommunikation im organisatorischen Wandel, Stuttgart: Schaeffer-Poeschel, 1998.

Kieser, A./Kubicek, H. (1992): Organisation, 3rd edn., Berlin et al.: de Gruyter, 1992.

Kiesler, S./Siegel, J./McGuire, T. W. (1984): Social psychological aspects of computer-mediated communication, in: American Psychologist, No. 39, 1984, pp. 1123–1134.

Kilian, W./Picot, A./Neuburger, R./Niggl, J./Scholtes, K.-L./Seiler, W. (1994): Electronic Data Interchange (EDI) aus oekonomischer und juristischer Sicht, Baden-Baden: Nomos, 1994.

Kilian-Momm, A. (1989): Dezentralisierung von Bueroarbeitsplaetzen mit neuen Informations- und Kommunikationstechniken, Munich: VVF, 1989.

Kinkel, S. (1997): Controlling – Kontrollinstrument oder Hilfsmittel zur Selbststeuerung, in: Lay, G./Mies, C. (eds.): Erfolgreich Reorganisieren. Unternehmenskonzepte aus der Praxis, Berlin et al.: Springer, 1997, pp. 235–261.

Kirsch, W. (1992): Kommunikatives Handeln, Autopoiese, Rationalitaet: Sondierungen zu einer evolutionaeren Fuehrungslehre, Herrsching: Kirsch, 1992.

Kirsch, W./Klein, H.K. (1977): Management-Informationssysteme, Vol. 2: Auf dem Weg zu einem neuen Taylorismus?, Stuttgart: Kohlhammer, 1977.

Kirzner, I.M. (1973): Competition and Entrepreneurship, Chicago, IL: University of Chicago, 1973.

Kirzner, I. M. (1978): Wettbewerb und Unternehmertum [Competition and Entrepreneurship, 1973], Tuebingen: Mohr, 1978.

Kirzner, I.M. (1979): Knowing about Knowledge: A Subjectivist View of the Role of Information, in: Kirzner, I.M. (ed.): Perception, Opportunity and Profit, Chicago, IL: University of Chicago, 1979, pp. 137–153.

Klages, H. (1984): Wertorientierungen im Wandel. Rueckblick, Gegenwartsanalyse, Prognosen, Frankfurt/Main et al.: Campus, 1984.

Klein, B./Crawford, R.G./Alchian, A.A. (1978): Vertical Integration, Appropriable Rents, and the Competitive Contracting Process, in: Journal of Law and Economics, Vol. 21, No. 2, 1978, pp. 297–326.

Klein, S. (1994): Virtuelle Organisation, in: Wirtschaftswissenschaftliches Studium, No. 6, 1994, pp. 309–311.

Klein, S. / Gogolin, M. / Dziuk, M. (2002): Elektronische Maerkte im Ueberblick, in: Heilmann, Heidi (ed.): Elektronische Marktplaetze, Heidelberg: dpunkt-Verlag, 2002, pp. 7–19.

Kleinaltenkamp, M. (1993): Standardisierung und Marktprozess: Entwicklungen und Auswirkungen im CIM-Bereich, Wiesbaden: Gabler, 1992.

Klimecki, R. / Probst, G.J. / Eberl, P. (1994): Entwicklungsorientiertes Management, Stuttgart: Schaeffer-Poeschel, 1994.

Klimecki, R. / Probst, G.J. / Gmuer, M. (1993): Flexibilisierungsmanagement, Bern: Schweizerische Volksbank, 1993.

Kling, R. / Iacono, S. (1984): Computing as an Occasion for Social Control, in: Journal of Social Issues, No. 40, 1984, pp. 77–96.

Klingenberg, H. / Kraenzle, H.-P. (1983): Kommunikationstechnik und Nutzerverhalten: Forschungsprojekt Buerokommunikation, Muenchen: CW-Publikationen, 1983.

Klotz, K. / Mueller, P. (1998): Digital Signieren: Ein Kapitel fuer sich, in: CHIP, No. 3, 1998, p. 218.

Knoop, C.-I / Appelgate, L.M. (1997): Colliers International Property Consultants: Managing a Virtual Organization, Harvard Business School Case 9–396–080, Cambridge: Harvard Business School Publishing, 1997.

Knuth, D.E. (1997): The Art of Computer Programming, Vol. 1: Fundamental Algorithms, 3rd edn., Reading, MA: Addison-Wesley, 1997.

Knuth, D.E. (1998): The Art of Computer Programming, Vol. 2: Seminumerical Algorithms, 3rd edn., Reading, MA: Addison-Wesley, 1998.

Knyphausen-Aufsess, D. v. (1999): Theoretische Perspektiven der Entwicklung von Regionalnetzwerken, in: Zeitschrift fuer Betriebswirtschaft, No. 5/6, 2000, pp. 593–616.

Koch, H.-D. (1997): Informations- und Controlling-Strukturen in dezentralisierten Unternehmen, in: Picot, A. (ed.): Information als Wettbewerbsfaktor. Kongress-Dokumentation 50th Deutscher Betriebswirtschafter-Tag 1996, Stuttgart: Schaeffer-Poeschel, 1997, pp. 303–314.

Koch, M. / Moeslein, K. / Wagner, M. (2000): Vertrauen und Reputation in Online-Anwendungen und virtuellen Gemeinschaften, Tagungsbeitrag zur GeNeMe 2000 (Gemeinschaften in Neuen Medien), Dresden 5th/6th October 2000.

Koerber, E. v. (1993): Geschaeftssegmentierung und Matrixstruktur im internationalen Grossunternehmen – Das Beispiel ABB, in: Zeitschrift fuer betriebswirtschaftliche Forschung, No. 12, 1993, pp. 1060–1077.

Koller, H. (1994): Die Integration von Textverarbeitung und Datenverarbeitung: Analyse des Bedarfs und seiner Determinanten aus betriebswirtschaftlicher Sicht, Wiesbaden: Gabler, 1994.

Koller, H. (1997): Probleme und Ausgestaltung der Unternehmensdezentralisierung, in: Lutz, B. (ed.): Ergebnisse des Expertenkreises "Zukunftsstrategien", Band IV, Frankfurt / Main et al.: Campus, 1997.

Korb, J.C. (2000): Kaufprozesse im Electronic Commerce: Einfluesse veraenderter Kundenbeduerfnisse auf die Gestaltung, Wiesbaden: DUV / Gabler, 2000.

Korsgaard, M./Schweiger, D./Sapienza, H. (1995): Building commitment, attachment and trust in strategic decision-making teams: The role of procedural justice, in: Academy of Management Journal, Vol. 38, 1995, pp. 60–84.

Kosiol, E. (1968): Einfuehrung in die Betriebswirtschaftslehre: Die Unternehmung als wirtschaftliches Aktionszentrum, Wiesbaden: Gabler, 1968.

Kraehenmann, N. (1994): Oekonomische Gestaltungsanforderungen fuer die Entwicklung elektronischer Maerkte, Hochschule St. Gallen, 1994.

Krallmann, H./Klotz, M. (1994): Grafisches Organisationswerkzeug zur Unternehmensmodellierung, in: Office Management, No. 5, 1994, pp. 34–36.

Kramer, R.M./Tyler, T.R (eds., 1996): Trust in Organizations: Frontiers of strategy and research, Thousand Oaks, CA: Sage, 1996.

Kraut, R./Egido, C. (1988): Patterns of Contact and Communication in Scientific Research Collaboration, in: Proceedings of the Conference on Computer-Supported Cooperative Work, 1988, New York, NY: ACM, 1988, pp. 1–12.

Krcmar, H. (1992): Computer Aided Team – Ein Ueberblick, in: Information Management, No. 1, 1992, pp. 6–9.

Krcmar, H. (2002): Informationsmanagement, 2nd edn., Heidelberg et al.: Springer, 2002.

Krcmar, H./Lewe, H. (1992): GroupSystems: Aufbau und Auswirkungen, in: Information Management, No. 1, 1992, pp. 32–41.

Kredel, L. (1988): Wirtschaftlichkeit von Buerokommunikationssystemen, Berlin et al.: Springer, 1988.

Kreikebaum, K./Herbert, K.-J. (1988): Humanisierung der Arbeit, Wiesbaden: Gabler, 1988.

Kreis-Engelhardt, B. (1999): Kundenorientierung durch Telearbeit – Potentiale und Gestaltungsempfehlungen am Beispiel finanzdienstleistungsorientierter Unternehmen, Wiesbaden: Gabler, 1999.

Kreps, D. M. (1990): A Course in Microeconmic Theory, New York, NY et al.: Harvester Wheatsheaf, 1990.

Krueger, W./Pfeiffer, P. (1988): Strategische Ausrichtung, organisatorische Gestaltung und Auswirkungen des Informations-Management, in: Information Management, No. 3, 1988, pp. 6–15.

Krystek, U./Redel, W./Reppegather, S. (1997): Grundzuege virtueller Organisationen. Elemente und Erfolgsfaktoren, Chancen und Risiken, Wiesbaden: Gabler, 1997.

Kubicek, H. (1990): Was bringt uns die Telekommunikation? ISDN – 66 kritische Antworten, Frankfurt/Main: Campus, 1990.

Kubicek, H. (1992): Die Organisationsluecke beim elektronischen Austausch von Geschaeftsdokumenten (EDI) zwischen Organisationen, Vortrag auf dem 16. Workshop der Wissenschaftlichen Kommission "Organisation" im Verband der Hochschullehrer fuer Betriebswirtschaft "Oekonomische Theorien der interorganisationalen Beziehungen", 2.–4.4.1992.

Kugelmass, J. (1995): Telecommuting. A Manager's Guide to Flexible Work Arrangements, New York, NY: Lexington, 1995.

Kuehl, S. (1998): Wenn die Affen den Zoo regieren: Die Tuecken der flachen Hierarchie, 5th edn., Frankfurt/Main et al.: Campus, 1998.

Kuhlen, R. (1995): Informationsmarkt: Chancen und Risiken der Kommerzialisierung von Wissen, Konstanz: UKV, 1995.

Kuhlmann, T. / Lischke, C. / Oehlmann, R. / Thoben, K.-D. (1993): Concurrent Engineering in der Unikatfertigung, in: CIM Management, No. 2, 1993, pp. 10 – 16.

Kunz, G. (1999): Ziele partnerschaftlich vereinbaren – ein Weg zum Erfolg, in: Harvard Business Manager, No. 2, 1999, pp. 79 – 88.

Kunz, H. (1985): Marktsystem und Information: "Konstitutionelle Unwissenheit" als Quelle von "Ordnung", Tuebingen: Mohr, 1983.

Kuepper, H.-U. (2005): Controlling: Konzeption, Aufgaben und Instrumente, 4rd edn., Stuttgart: Schaeffer-Poeschel, 2005.

Kuepper, H.-U. / Mellwig, W. / Moxter, A. / Ordelheide, D. (1990): Unternehmensfuehrung und Controlling, Wiesbaden: Gabler, 1990.

Kupsch, P.U. / Marr, R. (1991): Personalwirtschaft, in: Heinen, E. (ed.): Industriebetriebslehre: Entscheidungen im Industriebetrieb, 9th edn., Wiesbaden: Gabler, 1991, pp. 729 – 894.

Kyas, O. (1993): ATM Netzwerke. Aufbau – Funktionen – Performance, Bergheim: Datacom, 1993.

Lange, K. (1990): Chancen und Risiken der Mobilfunktechnologien, Diskussionsbeitrag No. 60, Wissenschaftliches Institut fuer Kommunikationsdienste, Bad Honnef: WIK, 1990.

Laske, S. / Weiskopf, R. (1992): Hierarchie, in: Frese, E. (Hrsg.): Handwoerterbuch der Organisation, 3rd edn., Stuttgart: Schaeffer-Poeschel, 1992, col. 791 – 807.

Latham, G.P. / Locke, E.A. (1995): Zielsetzung als Fuehrungsaufgabe, in: Kieser, A. / Reber, G. / Wunderer, R. (eds.): Handwoerterbuch der Fuehrung, 2nd edn., Stuttgart: Schaeffer-Poeschel, 1995, col. 2222 – 2234.

Laux, Helmut (1998): Entscheidungstheorie, 4th edn., Berlin et al.: Springer, 1998.

Lawler, E. E. (1992): The Ultimative Advantage: Creating the High-Involvement Organization, New York, NY: Jossey-Bass, 1992.

Lawler, E.E. (1994): Motivation in Work Organizations, New York, NY: Jossey-Bass, 1994.

Lazere, C. (1998): All together now, in: Chief Financial Officer, No. 2, 1998.

Legrand, G. (1972): Dictionnaire de Philosophie, Paris et al.: Bordas, 1972.

Leimeister, J.M. / Klein, A. / Krcmar, H. (2002): Mobile virtuelle Communities – Chancen und Herausforderungen des Community-Engineerings im Gesundheitsbereich, in: Reichwald, R. (ed.): Mobile Kommunikation – Wertschoepfung, Technologien, neue Dienste, Wiesbaden: Gabler, 2002, pp. 507 – 520.

Liebowitz, J. (1988): Introduction to Expert Systems, Santa Cruz, CA: Mitchell Publishing, 1988.

Liessmann, K. (1990): Joint Venture erfolgreich organisieren und managen: Neue Maerkte durch strategische Kooperation, Muenchen: WRS, 1990.

Likert, R. (1961): New Patterns of Management, New York, NY et al.: McGraw-Hill, 1961.

Lingen, T. v. (1993): Marktgleichgewicht oder Marktprozess: Perspektiven der Mikrooekonomie, Wiesbaden: Gabler, 1993.

Lingnau, V. (1998): Geschichte des Controlling, in: Wirtschaftswissenschaftliches Studium, No. 6, 1998, pp. 274 – 281.

Loose, A. / Sydow, J. (1994): Vertrauen und Oekonomie in Netzwerkbeziehungen – Strukturationstheoretische Betrachtungen, in: Sydow, J. / Windeler A. (eds.): Management Interorganisationaler Beziehungen: Vertrauen, Kontrolle und Informationstechnik, Opladen: Westdeutscher Verlag, 1994, pp. 160 – 193.

Looss, W. (1991): Coaching fuer Manager: Konfliktbewaeltigung unter vier Augen, Landsberg et al.: Moderne Industrie, 1991.

Lucas, H. C. / Olson, M. (1994): The Impact of Information Technology on Organizational Flexibility, in: Journal of Organizational Computing, No. 2, 1994, pp. 155 – 176.

Luce, R.D. / Raiffa, H. (1957): Games and Decisions: Introduction and Critical Survey, New York. NY et al.: Wiley, 1957.

Luhmann, N. (1986): Organisation, in: Kuepper, W. / Ortmann, G. (eds.): Mikropolitik. Rationalitaet, Macht und Spiele in Organisationen, Opladen: Westdeutscher Verlag, 1986, pp. 165 – 185.

Luhmann, N. (1988): Familiarity, confidence, trust: Problems and alternatives, in: Gambetta, D. (ed.): Trust: making and breaking cooperative relations, New York, NY: Blackwell, 1988, pp. 94 – 107.

Luhmann, N. (2000): Vertrauen: Ein Mechanismus der Reduktion sozialer Komplexitaet, 4th edn., Stuttgart: Enke, 2000.

Luhmann, N. (1994): Die Wirtschaft der Gesellschaft, Frankfurt / Main: Suhrkamp, 1994.

Lukasczyk, K. (1960): Zur Theorie der Fuehrerrolle, in: Psychologische Rundschau, 1960, pp. 179 – 188.

Luetge, G. (1995): Starker Glaube, schwache Fakten, in: Die Zeit, No. 13, 24th March 1995, pp. 41 – 42.

Lutz, B. (1996): Einleitung, in: Lutz, B. / Hartmann, M. / Hirsch-Kreinsen, H. (eds.): Produzieren im 21. Jahrhundert. Herausforderungen fuer die deutsche Industrie, Frankfurt / Main et al.: Campus, 1996, pp. 9 – 43.

Lutz, W.-G. (1997): Das objektorientierte Paradigma – Organisationstheoretische Perspektiven der datenzentrierten Modellierung von Software, Wiesbaden: Gabler, 1997.

Maass, S. (1991): Computergestuetzte Kommunikation und Kooperation, in: Oberquelle, H. (ed.): Kooperative Arbeit und Computerunterstuetzung: Stand und Perspektiven, Goettingen: Verlag fuer allgemeine Psychologie, 1991, pp. 11 – 35.

Macharzina, K. (1999): Unternehmensfuehrung: Das internationale Managementwissen, 3rd edn., Wiesbaden: Gabler, 1999.

MacNeil, I.R. (1978): Contracts: Adjustment of Long-Term Economic Relations under Classical, Neoclassical, and Relational Contract Law, in: Northwestern University Law Review, Vol. 72, No. 6, 1978, pp. 854 – 905.

Maier, M. (1990): Theoretischer Bezugsrahmen und Methoden zur Gestaltung computergestuetzter Informationssysteme, Muenchen: VVF, 1990.

Malone, T.W. (1988): What is coordination theory?, CISR Working Paper No. 182, Sloan Working Paper No. 2051 – 88, Cambridge, MA: MIT, 1988.

Malone, T.W. (1990): Organizing Information Processing Systems: Parallels Between Human Organizations and Computer Systems, in: Zachary, W. / Robertson, S. / Black, J. (eds.): Cognition, Computation and Cooperation, Norwood: Ablex Publ., 1990, pp. 56 – 83.

Malone, T.W. / Yates, J.A. / Benjamin, R.I. (1986): Electronic Markets and Electronic Hierarchies, CISR Workingpaper No. 137, Sloan Workingpaper No. 1770–86, Cambridge, MA: MIT, April 1986.

Malone, T.W. / Yates, J.A. / Benjamin, R.I. (1987): Electronic Markets and Electronic Hierarchies, Communications of the ACM, Vol. 30, No. 6, 1987, pp. 484–497.

Malone, T.W. / Yates, J.A. / Benjamin, R.I. (1989): The Logic of Electronic Markets, in: Harvard Business Review, No. 3, 1989, pp. 166–172.

Mandrioli, D. / Meyer, B. (Hrsg, 1992): Advances in Objectoriented Software Engineering, New York, NY et al.: Prentice Hall, 1992.

Manz, C.C. / Sims, H.P. (1993): Business without Bosses: How Self-Managing Teams Are Building High Performing Companies, New York, NY et al.: Wiley, 1993.

Manz, C.C. / Sims, H.P. (1995): Selbststeuernde Gruppen, Fuehrung, in: Kieser, A. / Reber, G. / Wunderer, R. (eds.): Handwoerterbuch der Fuehrung, 2nd edn., Stuttgart: Schaeffer-Poeschel, 1995, col. 1873–1894.

March, J.G. / Simon, H.A. (1958): Organizations, New York, NY et al.: Wiley, 1958.

Margherio, L. et al. (1998): The Emerging Digital Economy, US Department of Commerce, Washington, 1998.

Markus, M.L. (1983): Power, Politics, and MIS Implementation, in: Communications of the ACM, No. 26, 1983, pp. 430–444.

Markus, M.L. (1994): Electronic Mail as the Medium of Managerial Choice, in: Organization Science, No. 4, November 1994, pp. 502–527.

Marquardt, M. / Reynolds, A. (1994): The Global Learning Organization: Gaining Competitive Advantage through Continuous Learning, New York, NY: Irwin Publ., 1994.

Marr, R. / Stitzel, M. (1979): Personalwirtschaft: ein konfliktorientierter Ansatz, Munich: Moderne Industrie, 1979.

Marschak, J. (1954): Towards and Economic Theory of Organization and Information, in: Thrall, R.M. / Coombs, C.H. / Davis, R.L. (eds.): Decision Processes, New York, NY: Wiley, 1954, pp. 187–220.

Maslow, A. H. (1954): Motivation and Personality, New York, NY et al.: Harper, 1954.

Mathews, J. (1994): The Governance of Inter-Organisational Networks, in: Corporate Governance, No. 1, 1994, pp. 14–19.

Matsuda, T. (1993): "Organizational Intelligence" als Prozess und als Produkt, in: t+m, No. 1, 1993, pp. 12–17.

Matthews, R.C.O. (1986): The Economics of Institutions and the Sources of Growth, in: Economic Journal, Vol. 96, No. 4, 1986, pp. 903–918.

Maturana, R.H. / Varela, F.J. (1987): Der Baum der Erkenntnis, Bern et al.: Scherz, 1987.

Mayer, R. (1991): Die Prozesskostenrechnung als Instrument des Schnittstellenmanagement, in: Horváth, P. (ed.): Synergien durch Schnittstellen-Controlling, Stuttgart: Schaeffer-Poeschel, 1991, pp. 211–227.

Mayer, R.C. / Davis, J.H. / Schoorman, F.D. (1995): An integrative model of organizational trust, in: Academy of Management Review, Vol. 20, 1995, pp. 709–734.

Mayo, E. (1949): Probleme industrieller Arbeitsbedingungen, Frankfurt / Main: Frankfurter Hefte, 1949.

McAllister, D.J. (1995): Affect- and cognition-based trust as foundation for interpersonal cooperation in organizations, in: Academy of Management Journal, Vol. 38, 1995, pp. 24 – 59.

McDermid, J. / Rook, P. (1991): Software development process models, in: McDermid, J. (ed.): Software Engineer's Reference Book, Oxford: Butterworth-Heinemann, 1991.

McKnight, L.W. / Bailey, J.P. (1997): Internet Economics, Cambridge / London: MIT Press, 1997.

Medina-Mora, R. / Winograd, T. / Flores, R. / Flores, F. (1992): The Action Workflow Approach to Workflow Management Technology, in: CSCW 92: Sharing Perspectives. ACM Conference on Computer-Supported Cooperative Work, Toronto: ACM Press, 1992, pp. 281 – 288.

Mehrabian, A. (1971): Silent Messages, Belmont, CA: Wadsworth, 1971.

Menger, C. (1923 [1871]): Grundsaetze der Volkswirtschaftslehre, 2nd edn., Wien et al.: Hoelder-Pichler-Tempsky, 1923.

Mertens, P. (1994): Virtuelle Unternehmen, in: Wirtschaftsinformatik, No. 2, 1994, pp. 169 – 172.

Mertens, P. (2001): Integrierte Informationsverarbeitung, Vol. 1: Administrations- und Dispositionssysteme in der Industrie, 13th edn., Wiesbaden: Gabler, 2001.

Mertens, P. / Bodendorf, F. / Koenig, W. / Picot, A. / Schumann, M. (2001): Grundzuege der Wirtschaftsinformatik, 7th edn., Berlin et al.: Springer, 2001.

Mertens, P. / Faisst, W. (1997): Virtuelle Unternehmen. Idee, Informationsverarbeitung, Illusion, 18. Saarbruecker Arbeitstag fuer Industrie, Dienstleistung und Verwaltung, Heidelberg: Springer, 1997.

Mertens, P. / Griese, J. (2000): Integrierte Informationsverarbeitung, Vol. 2: Planungs- und Kontrollsysteme in der Industrie, 8th edn., Wiesbaden: Gabler, 2000.

Mertens, P. / Griese, J. / Ehrenberg, D. (1998): Virtuelle Unternehmen und Informationsverarbeitung, Berlin: Springer, 1998.

Metro Group Future Store, http://www.metrogroup.de/servlet/PB/menu/1009740_l2/index.html (last accessed November 29, 2007).

Meyer, A. / Davidson, H. (2001): Offensives Marketing: Gewinnen mit POISE, Munich: Haufe, 2001.

Meyer, B. (1989): Reusability: The Case For Object-Oriented Design: The Road To Eiffel, in: Structured Programming, No. 1, 1989, pp. 19 – 39.

Meyer, B. (1990): Objektorientierte Softwareentwicklung, Munich et al.: Hanser, 1990.

Meyer, B. (1992): Eiffel: The Language, New York, NY et al.: Prentice Hall, 1992.

Michie, D. (1980): Knowledge-Based Systems, University of Illinois at Urbana-Champaign, Report 80 – 1001, Urbana-Champaign, IL: University of Illinois, 1980.

Milgrom, P. / Roberts, J. (1992): Economics, Organization and Management, Englewood Cliffs, NJ: Prentice Hall, 1992.

Milgrom, P. / Roberts, J. (1995): Complementarities and fit – strategy, structure, and organizational change in manufacturing, in: Journal of Accounting and Economics, No. 2, 1995, pp. 179 – 208.

Mintzberg, H. (1973): The Nature of Managerial Work, Englewood Cliffs, NJ: Prentice Hall, 1973.

Mintzberg, H. (1994): Rounding out the Manager's Job, in: Sloan Management Review, No. 1, 1994, pp. 11–26.

Mintzberg, H. (1999): Profis beduerfen sanfter Fuehrung, in: Harvard Business Manager, No. 3, 1999, pp. 9–16.

Mintzberg, H. et al. (2002): The Strategy Process, Englewood Cliffs, NJ: Prentice Hall, 2002.

Mises, L. v. (1949): Human action: A Treatise on Economics, London et al.: William Hodge, 1949.

Mizuno, S. (1988): Company Wide Total Quality Control, Tokio: Asian Productivity Organization, 1988.

Moati, P. / Mouhoud, E.M. (1994): Information et organisation de la production: vers une division cognitive du travail, in: Economie Appliquée, No. 1, 1994, pp. 47–73.

Monopolkommission (1991): Wettbewerbspolitik oder Industriepolitik, Hauptgutachten 1990 / 1991, Baden-Baden: Nomos, 1991.

Moorhead, G. / Neck, C.P. (1995): Groupthink und Fuehrung, in: Kieser, A. / Reber, G. / Wunderer, R. (eds.): Handwoerterbuch der Fuehrung, 2nd edn., Stuttgart: Schaeffer-Poeschel, 1995, col. 1130–1138.

Moser, P.K. / Nat van der, A. (eds., 1995): Human Knowledge: Classical and Contemporary Approaches, 2nd edn., New York, NY et al.: Oxford University, 1995.

Moeslein, K. (1999): Medientheorien – Perspektiven der Medienwahl und Medienwirkung im Ueberblick, Arbeitsberichte des Lehrstuhls fuer Allgemeine und Industrielle Betriebswirtschaftslehre, Vol. 10, Munich: Technical University Munich, 1999.

Moeslein, K. (2000): Bilder in Organisationen. Wandel, Wissen und Visualisierung, Wiesbaden: Gabler / DUV, 2000.

Moeslein, K. (2001a): The Location Problem in Electronic Business: Evidence from Exploratory Research, in: Sprague, R.H. Jr. (ed.): Proceedings of the 34th Annual Hawaii International Conference on Systems Sciences, HICSS-34, January 3–6, 2001, Maui, Hawaii, Los Alamitos: IEEE Press, 2001.

Moeslein, K. (2001b): Die virtuelle Organisation: Von der Idee zur Wettbewerbsstrategie, in: Wulf, V. / Rittenbruch, M. / Rohde, M. (eds.): Auf dem Weg zur Virtuellen Organisation, Physica: Heidelberg, 2001, pp. 13–31.

Mountfield, A. / Schalch, O. (1998): Konzeption von Balanced Scorecards und Umsetzung in ein Management-Informationssystem mit dem SAP Business Information Warehouse, in: Controlling, No. 5, 1998, pp. 316–322.

Mourtisen, J. (1998): Driving Growth – Economic Value Added versus Intellectual Capital, in: Management Accounting Research, Vol. 9, 1998, pp. 461–482.

Mowshowitz, A. (1991): Virtual Feudalism: A Vision of Political Organization in the Information Age, Deelstudie in het kader van NOTA – Project Democratie en Informatiesamenleving, Amsterdam, 1991.

Mueller-Boeling, D. / Ramme I. (1990): Informations- und Kommunikationstechniken fuer Fuehrungskraefte: Top Manager zwischen Technikeuphorie und Tastaturphobie, Munich et al.: Oldenbourg, 1990.

Mueller-Stewens, G. / Pautzke, G. (1991): Fuehrungskraefteentwicklung und organisatorisches Lernen, in: Sattelberger, T. (ed.): Die lernende Organisation, Konzepte fuer eine neue Qualitaet der Unternehmensentwicklung, Wiesbaden: Gabler, 1991, pp. 183 – 205.

Murphy, C. / O'Leary, T. (1994): Review Essay: Empowered Selves, in: Accounting Management and Information Technologies, No. 2, 1994, pp. 107 – 115.

Myers, R. (1996): Metric Wars, in: CFO, No. 10, 1996, pp. 41 – 48.

Nagel, K. (1991): Nutzen der Informationsverarbeitung. Methoden zur Bewertung von strategischen Wettbewerbsvorteilen, Produktivitaetsverbesserungen und Kosteneinsparungen, 2nd edn., Munich et al.: Oldenbourg, 1991.

Nastansky, L. (ed., 1992): Workgroup Computing, Hamburg: Steuer- und Wirtschaftsverlag, 1992.

Nelson, P. (1970): Information and Consumer Behavior, in: The Journal of Political Economy, Vol. 78, pp. 311 – 329.

Nelson, R.R. / Winter, S. (1982): An Evolutionary Theory of Economic Change, Cambridge, MA: Cambridge University, 1982.

Nerdinger, F. / v. Rosenstiel, L. (1996): Fuehrung und Personalwirtschaft bei dezentralisierten Kompetenzen, in: Lutz, B. / Hartmann, M. / Hirsch-Kreinsen, H. (eds.): Produzieren im 21. Jahrhundert, Frankfurt / Main et al.: Campus, 1996, pp. 295 – 323.

NetNames International Ltd. (2002): Domainstats.com – your complete domain name resource, elektronisch veroeffentlicht: http://www.domainstats.com/, Version vom 21.8.2002.

Neuberger, O. (1977): Organisation und Fuehrung, Stuttgart: Enke, 1977.

Neuberger, O. (1985): Miteinander arbeiten – miteinander reden!, 6th edn., Munich: Bayerisches Staatsministerium fuer Arbeit und Sozialordnung, 1985.

Neuberger, O. (1994): Personalentwicklung, 2nd edn., Stuttgart: Enke, 1994.

Neuberger, O. (2002): Fuehren und fuehren lassen: Ansaetze, Ergebnisse und Kritik der Fuehrungsforschung, 6th edn., Stuttgart: Lucius & Lucius, 2002.

Neuburger, R. (1994): Electronic Data Interchange – Einsatzmoeglichkeiten und oekonomische Auswirkungen, Wiesbaden: Gabler, 1994.

Neuburger, R. (1999): Die EDI-Mauern fallen, in: Computerwoche Spezial – Netze mit Nutzen, No. 1, 1999, pp. 40 – 43.

Nieschlag, R. / Dichtl, E. / Hoerschgen, H. (1997): Marketing, 18th edn., Berlin: Duncker und Humblot, 1997.

Niggl, J. (1994): Die Entstehung von Electronic Data Interchange Standards, Wiesbaden: Gabler, 1994.

Nilles, J. M. (1998): Managing Telework – Strategies for Managing the Virtual Workforce, New York, NY: Wiley, 1998.

Nilles, J. M. / Carlson, F. R. / Gray, P. / Hanneman, G. J. (1976): The Telecommunications – Transportation Trade off, New York, NY: Wiley, 1976.

Nippa, M. (1995): Anforderungen an das Management prozessorientierter Unternehmen, in: Nippa, M. / Picot, A. (eds.): Prozessmanagement und Reengineering. Die Praxis im deutschsprachigen Raum, Frankfurt / Main et al.: Campus, 1995, pp. 39 – 77.

Nippa, M. / Reichwald, R. (1990): Theoretische Grundueberlegungen zur Verkuerzung der Durchlaufzeit in der industriellen Entwicklung, in: Reichwald, R. / Schmelzer, H. J. (eds.): Durchlaufzeiten in der Entwicklung, Muenchen et al.: Oldenbourg, 1990, pp. 65 – 114.

Nonaka, I. / Takeuchi, H. (1985): The Knowledge-Creating Company – How Japans Companies Create the Dynamics of Innovation, New York, NY et al.: Oxford University, 1985.

O'Hara-Devereaux, M. / Johansen, R. (1994): Global Work. Bridging Distance, Culture and Time, San Francisco, CA: Jossey-Bass, 1994.

O'Reilly, C. A. (1983): The Use of Information in Organizational Decision Making: A Model and some Propositions, in: Research in Organizational Behavior, No. 5, 1983, pp. 103 – 139.

Oberquelle, H. (ed., 1991): Kooperative Arbeit und Computerunterstuetzung. Stand und Perspektiven, Stuttgart: Verlag fuer Angewandte Psychologie, 1991.

Ochsenbauer, C. (1989): Organisatorische Alternativen zur Hierarchie, Munich: GBI, 1989.

OECD (1998): Electronic Commerce: Prices and Consumer Issues for three Products: Books, Compact Disks, and Software; Organisation for Economic Co-operation and Development, DSTI / ICCP / IE(98)4/FINAL, Paris, 1998.

Oechsler, W.A. (1997): Personal und Arbeit: Einfuehrung in die Personalwirtschaftslehre, 6th edn., Munich et al.: Oldenbourg, 1997.

Oess, A. (1994): Total Quality Management, 3rd edn., Wiesbaden: Gabler, 1994.

Oestereich, B. (1998): Objektorientierte Softwareentwicklung: Analyse und Design mit der Unified Modeling Language, 4th edn., Munich: Oldenbourg, 1998.

Olson, M. H. (1983): Remote Office Work: Changing Work Patterns in Space and Time, in: Communications of the ACM, Vol. 26, No. 3, 1983, pp. 182 – 187.

OMG (1992): The Common Object Request Broker: Architecture and Specification, OMG Document Number 91 – 12 – 01, Framingham: OMG, 1992.

OMG Common Facilities RFP-4 (1996): Common Business Objects and Business Object Facility, OMG Document 96 – 01 – 04, Framingham: OMG, 1996.

Opaschowski, H. W. (1997): Deutschland 2010. Wie wir morgen leben – Voraussagen der Wissenschaft zur Zukunft unserer Gesellschaft, Hamburg: British American Tobacco 1997.

Oram, A. (ed., 2001): Peer-to-peer: Harnessing the power of disruptive technologies. Sebastopol, CA: O'Reilly, 2001.

Orlikowski, W. J. (1992): The Duality of Technology: Rethinking the Concept of Technology in Organizations, in: Organization Science, No. 3, 1992, pp. 398 – 427.

Orsburn, J.D. / Moran, L. / Musselwhite, E. / Zenger, J. (1990): Self-Directed Work Teams: The New American Challenge, New York, NY: Irwin, 1990.

Osten, H. v. d. (1989): Technologie-Transaktionen: Die Akquisition von technologischer Kompetenz durch Unternehmen, Goettingen: Vandenhoeck & Ruprecht, 1989.

Oesterle, H. (1995a): Business Engineering. Prozess- und Systementwicklung, Vol. 1: Entwurfsmethoden, Berlin et al.: Springer, 1995.

Oesterle, H. (1995b): Business in the Information Age. Heading for New Processes, Berlin et al.: Springer, 1995.

Osterloh, M. / Frey, B. S. / Benz, M. (2001): Grenzen variabler Leistungsloehne: Die Rolle intrinsischer Motivation, in: Jost, P.-J. (ed.): Die Prinzipal-Agenten-Theorie in der Betriebswirtschaftslehre, Schaeffer-Poeschel: Stuttgart 2001, pp. 561 – 579.

Osterloh, M. / Wuebker, S. (1999): Wettbewerbsfaehiger durch Prozess- und Wissensmanagement. Mit Chancengleichheit auf Erfolgskurs, Wiesbaden: Gabler, 1999.

Ottmann, T. / Widmayer, P. (1996): Algorithmen und Datenstrukturen, 3rd edn., Mannheim et al.: BI Wissenschaftsverlag, 1996.

Ouchi, W.G. (1980): Markets, Bureaucracies and Clans, in: Administrative Science Quarterly, No. 25, 1980, pp. 129–141.

Palermo, A. / McCready, S. (1992): Workflow Software: A Primer, in: Coleman, D. (ed.): Groupware '92, San Mateo, CA: Morgan Kaufmann, 1992.

Parker, G.M. (1994): Cross-Functional Teams, San Francisco, CA: Jossey-Bass, 1994.

Pawlowsky, P. (1992): Betriebliche Qualifikationsstrategien und organisationales Lernen, in: Staehle, W.H. / Conrad, P. (eds.): Managementforschung 2, Berlin et al.: de Gruyter, 1992, pp. 177–237.

Perridon, L. / Steiner, M. (2002): Finanzwirtschaft der Unternehmung, 11th edn., Munich: Vahlen, 2002.

Perrow, C. (1967): A Framework for the Comparative Analysis of Organizations, in: American Sociological Review, No. 32, 1967, pp. 194–208.

Perrow, Ch. B. (1970): Organizational analysis: a sociological view, London: Travistock, 1970.

Petermann, F. (1996): Psychologie des Vertrauens, 3rd edn., Goettingen et al.: Hogrefe, 1996.

Peters, T. J. (1993): Jenseits der Hierarchien, Duesseldorf et al.: Econ, 1993.

Peters, T. J. (1994): Liberation Management, New York, NY: Fawcett Columbine, 1994.

Peters, T. J. / Waterman, R. H. (1984): Auf der Suche nach Spitzenleistungen: Was man von den bestgefuehrten US-Unternehmen lernen kann, Landsberg am Lech: Moderne Industrie, 1984.

Pethig, R. (1997): Information als Wirtschaftsgut aus wirtschaftswissenschaftlicher Sicht, in: Fiedler, H. / Ullrich, H. (eds.): Information als Wirtschaftsgut: Management und Rechtsgestaltung, Koeln: Schmidt, 1997, pp. 1–28.

Pfeffer, J. (1994): Competitive Advantage Through People: Unleashing the Power of the Workforce, Boston, MA.: Harvard Business School Press, 1994.

Pfefferkorn, P. (1991): Das "Soziokratie-Modell" – Eine Renaissance des "Linking Pin-Modells"?, Rotterdam: Soziokratisch Centrum, 1991.

Pfeiffer, W. / Weiss, E. (1994): Lean Management: Grundlagen der Fuehrung und Organisation industrieller Unternehmen, 2nd edn., Berlin: E. Schmidt, 1994.

Pfohl, H.-C. / Stoelzle, W. (1997): Planung und Kontrolle. Konzeption, Gestaltung, Implementierung, 2nd edn., Munich: Vahlen, 1997.

Picot, A. (1979a): Rationalisierung im Verwaltungsbereich als betriebswirtschaftliches Problem, in: Zeitschrift fuer Betriebswirtschaft, No. 12, 1979, pp. 1145–1165.

Picot, A. (1979b): Organisationsprinzipien, in: Wirtschaftswissenschaftliches Studium, No. 8, 1979, pp. 480–485.

Picot, A. (1981): Der Beitrag der Theorie der Verfuegungsrechte zur oekonomischen Analyse von Unternehmensverfassungen, in: Bohr, K. et al. (ed.): Unternehmensverfassung als Problem der Betriebswirtschaftslehre, Berlin: Schmidt, 1981, pp. 153–197.

Picot, A. (1982): Transaktionskostenansatz in der Organisationstheorie: Stand der Diskussion und Aussagewert, in: Die Betriebswirtschaft, No. 2, 1982, pp. 267–284.

Picot, A. (1985): Integrierte Telekommunikation und Dezentralisierung in der Wirtschaft, in: Kaiser, W. (ed.): Integrierte Telekommunikation, Berlin et al.: Springer, 1985, pp. 484–498.

Picot, A. (1989a): Der Produktionsfaktor Information in der Unternehmensfuehrung, in: Thexis, No. 4, 1989, pp. 3–9.

Picot, A. (1989b): Zur Bedeutung allgemeiner Theorieansaetze fuer die betriebswirtschaftliche Information und Kommunikation: Der Beitrag der Transaktionskosten- und Principal-Agent-Theorie, in: Kirsch, W. / Picot, A. (eds.): Die Betriebswirtschaftslehre im Spannungsfeld zwischen Generalisierung und Spezialisierung, Wiesbaden: Gabler, 1989, pp. 361–379.

Picot, A. (1990): Organisation von Informationssystemen und Controlling, in: Controlling, No. 6, 1990, pp. 296–305.

Picot, A. (1991a): Oekonomische Theorien der Organisation – Ein Ueberblick ueber neuere Ansaetze und deren betriebswirtschaftliches Anwendungspotential, in: Ordelheide, D. / Rudolph, B. / Buesselmann, E. (eds.): Betriebswirtschaftslehre und oekonomische Theorie, Stuttgart: Schaeffer-Poeschel, 1991, pp. 143–170.

Picot, A. (1991b): Ein neuer Ansatz zur Gestaltung der Leistungstiefe, in: Zeitschrift fuer betriebswirtschaftliche Forschung, No. 4, 1991, pp. 336–357.

Picot, A. (1991c): Subsidiaritaetsprinzip und oekonomische Theorie der Organisation, in: Faller, P. / Witt, D. (eds.): Erwerbsprinzip und Dienstprinzip in oeffentlicher Wirtschaft und Verkehrswirtschaft, Festschrift fuer K. Oettle, Baden-Baden: Nomos, 1991, pp. 102–116.

Picot, A. (1993a): Organisation, in: Bitz, M. / Dellmann, K. / Domsch, M. / Egner, H. (eds.): Vahlens Kompendium der Betriebswirtschaftslehre, Vol. 2, 3rd edn., Munich: Vahlen, 1993, pp. 101–174.

Picot, A. (1993b): Organisationsstrukturen der Wirtschaft und ihre Anforderungen an die Informations- und Kommunikationstechnik, in: Scheer, A.-W. (ed.): Handbuch Informationsmanagement: Aufgaben – Konzepte – Praxisloesungen, Wiesbaden: Gabler, 1993, pp. 49–68.

Picot, A. (1993c): Contingencies for the Emergence of Efficient Symbiotic Arrangements, in: Journal of Institutional and Theoretical Economics, No. 4, 1993, pp. 731–740.

Picot, A. (ed., 1997a): Telekooperation und virtuelle Unternehmen – Auf dem Weg zu neuen Arbeitsformen, Heidelberg: Decker, 1997.

Picot, A. (1997b): Information als Wettbewerbsfaktor – Veraenderungen in Organisation und Controlling, in: Picot, A. (ed.): Information als Wettbewerbsfaktor, Stuttgart: Schaeffer-Poeschel, 1997, pp. 175–199.

Picot, A. (1998a): Auf dem Weg zur grenzenlosen Unternehmung?, in: Becker, M. / Kloock, J. / Schmidt, R. / Waescher, G. (eds.): Unternehmen im Wandel und Umbruch, Tagungsband zur wissenschaftlichen Jahrestagung 1997 des Verbandes der Hochschullehrer fuer Betriebswirtschaft, Stuttgart: Schaeffer-Poeschel, 1998, pp. 25–49.

Picot, A. (1998b): Zusammenhaenge zwischen Innovation und Marktentwicklung durch Telekommunikation, in: Picot, A. (ed.): Telekommunikation im Spannungsfeld von Innovation, Wettbewerb und Regulierung, Heidelberg: Huethig, 1998, pp. 77–98.

Picot, A. (1998c): Die Transformation wirtschaftlicher Aktivitaet unter dem Einfluss der Informations- und Kommunikationstechnik, Freiberger Arbeitspapier 98 (2), Freiberg: Technical University Freiberg, 1998.

Picot, A. (1999): Organisation, in: Bitz, M. / Dellmann, K. / Domsch, M. / Wagner, F. (eds.): Vahlens Kompendium der Betriebswirtschaftslehre, Vol. 2, 4th edn., Munich: Vahlen, 1999, pp. 107 – 180.

Picot, A. / Boehme, M. (1999): Controlling in dezentralen Unternehmensstrukturen, Munich: Vahlen, 1999.

Picot, A. / Bortenlaenger, C. / Roehrl, H. (1995): The Automation of Capital Markets, in: The Journal of Computer-Mediated Communication, URL: http://www.ascusc.org/ jcmc/vol1/ issue3/picot.html, No. 3, 1995

Picot, A. / Bortenlaenger, C. / Roehrl, H. (1996): Boersen im Wandel: Der Einfluss von Informationstechnik und Wettbewerb auf die Organisation von Wertpapiermaerkten, Frankfurt / Main: Fritz Knapp Verlag, 1996.

Picot, A. / Bortenlaenger, C. / Roehrl, H. (1997): Organization of Electronic Markets: Contributions from the New Institutional Economics, in: The Information Society, No. 13, 1997, pp. 107 – 123.

Picot, A. / Dietl, H. / Franck, E. (2002): Organisation: Eine oekonomische Perspektive, 3rd edn., Stuttgart: Schaeffer-Poeschel 2002.

Picot, A. / Franck, E. (1988): Die Planung der Unternehmensressource Information (I), in: Das Wirtschaftsstudium, No. 10, 1988, pp. 544 – 549.

Picot, A. / Franck, E. (1995): Prozessorganisation. Eine Bewertung der neuen Ansaetze aus Sicht der Organisationslehre, in: Picot, A. / Nippa, M. (eds.): Prozessmanagement und Reengineering. Die Praxis im deutschsprachigen Raum, Frankfurt / Main et al.: Campus, 1995, pp. 13 – 38.

Picot, A. / Freudenberg, H. (1997): Neue organisatorische Ansaetze zum Umgang mit Komplexitaet, in: Adam, D. (ed.): Komplexitaetsmanagement. Schriften zur Unternehmensfuehrung, Wiesbaden: Gabler, 1997.

Picot, A. / Freudenberg, H. / Gassner, W. (1999): Management von Reorganisationen: Massschneidern als Konzept fuer den Wandel, Wiesbaden: Gabler, 1999.

Picot, A. / Gruendler, A. (1995): Deutsche Dienstleister scheinen von IT nur wenig zu profitieren, in: Computerwoche, No. 10, 1995, pp. 10 – 11.

Picot, A. / Hass, B.H. (2002): "Digitale Organisation", in: Spoun, S. / Wunderlich, W. (eds.): Medienkultur im digitalen Wandel, Bern: Paul Haupt, 2002, pp. 143 – 166.

Picot, A. / Kreis, B. (1997): Chancen fuer Organisatoren der Kundenorientierung – Telearbeit bei Finanzdienstleistern, in: Office Management, No. 3, 1997, pp. 40 – 45.

Picot, A. / Neuburger, R. (1997a): Der Beitrag virtueller Unternehmen zur Marktorientierung, in: Bruhn M. / Steffenhagen, H. (eds.): Marktorientierte Unternehmensfuehrung – Reflexionen, Denkanstoesse, Perspektiven, Wiesbaden: Gabler, 1997, pp. 119 – 140.

Picot, A. / Neuburger, R. (1997b): Application Potentials of Multimedia Services in the Firm, in: Elixmann, D. / Kuerble, P. (eds.): Multimedia – Potentials and Challenges from an Economic Perspective, Bad Honnef: WIK, 1997.

Picot, A. / Neuburger, R. (1998a): Virtuelle Organisationsformen im Dienstleistungssektor, in: Bruhn, M. / Meffert, H. (eds.): Handbuch Dienstleistungsmanagement, Wiesbaden: Gabler, 1998, pp. 513 – 533.

Picot, A. / Neuburger, R. (1998b): Virtuelle Organisationsformen, in: Spoun, S. et al. (eds.): Universitaet und Praxis, Zuerich: Verlag neue Zuericher Zeitung, 1998, pp. 449 – 468.

Picot, A. / Neuburger, R. (2000): Iuk-Technik und das Firmenkundengeschaeft, Cologne: Bank-Verlag, 2000.

Picot, A. / Neuburger, R. (2002): Mobile Business – Erfolgsfaktoren und Voraussetzungen, in: Reichwald, R. (ed.): Mobile Kommunikation – Wertschoepfung, Technologien, neue Dienste, Wiesbaden: Gabler, 2002, pp. 55 – 70.

Picot, A. / Neuburger, R. / Niggl, J. (1991): Oekonomische Perspektiven eines "Electronic Data Interchange", in: Information Management, No. 2, 1991, pp. 22 – 29.

Picot, A. / Neuburger, R. / Niggl, J. (1994): Wirtschaftliche Potentiale von EDI – Praxiserfahrungen und Perspektiven, in: x-change, No. 2, 1994, pp. 32 – 35.

Picot, A. / Neuburger, R. / Niggl, J. (1995): Ausbreitung und Auswirkungen von Electronic Data Interchange – Empirische Ergebnisse aus der deutschen Automobil- und Transportbranche, in: Schreyoegg, G. / Sydow, J. (eds.): Managementforschung 5, Berlin et al.: de Gruyter, 1995, pp. 47 – 106.

Picot, A. / Reichwald, R. (1987): Buerokommunikation. Leitsaetze fuer den Anwender, 3rd edn., Hallbergmoos: CW-Publikationen, 1987.

Picot, A. / Reichwald, R. (1991): Informationswirtschaft, in: Heinen, E. (ed.): Industriebetriebslehre: Entscheidungen im Industriebetrieb, 9th edn., Wiesbaden: Gabler, 1991, pp. 241 – 393.

Picot, A. / Reichwald, R. (1994): Aufloesung der Unternehmung? Vom Einfluss der IuK-Technik auf Organisationsstrukturen und Kooperationsformen, in: Zeitschrift fuer Betriebswirtschaft, No. 5, 1994, pp. 547 – 570.

Picot, A. / Reichwald, R. (1999): Fuehrung in virtuellen Organisationsformen, in: Nagel, K. / Erben, R. / Piller, F.T. (eds.): Produktionswirtschaft 2000 – Perspektiven fuer die Fabrik der Zukunft, Wiesbaden: Gabler, 1999, pp. 129 – 149.

Picot, A. / Reichwald, R. / Behrbohm, P. (1985): Menschengerechte Arbeitsplaetze sind wirtschaftlich!, Das Vier-Ebenen-Modell der Wirtschaftlichkeitsbeurteilung, Eschborn: RKW, 1985.

Picot, A. / Reichwald, R. / Nippa, M. (1988): Zur Bedeutung der Entwicklungsaufgabe fuer die Entwicklungszeit – Ansaetze fuer die Entwicklungszeitgestaltung, in: Brockhoff, K. / Picot, A. / Urban, C. (eds.): Zeitmanagement in Forschung und Entwicklung, ZfbF-special issue No. 23, 1988, pp. 112 – 137.

Picot, A. / Ripperger, T. / Wolff, B. (1996): The Fading Boundaries of the Firm: The Role of Information and Communication Technology, in: Journal of Institutional and Theoretical Economics (JITE), Vol. 152, No. 1, 1996, pp. 65 – 79.

Picot, A. / Scheuble, S. (1999a): Hybride Wettbewerbsstrategien in der Informations- und Netzoekonomie, in: Welge, M. / Al-Laham, A. / Kajueter, P. (eds.): Praxis des strategischen Managements, Wiesbaden: Gabler, 1999, pp. 239 – 257.

Picot, A. / Scheuble, S. (1999b): Die Rolle des Wissensmanagements in erfolgreichen Unternehmen, in: Mandl, H. / Reinmann-Rothmeier, G. (eds.) Wissensmanagement: Informationszuwachs – Wissensschwund?, Munich et al.: Oldenbourg, 1999, pp. 19 – 37.

Picot, A./Schneider, D. (1988): Unternehmerisches Innovationsverhalten, Verfuegungs-rechte und Transaktionskosten, in: Budaeus, D./Gerum, E./Zimmermann, G. (Hrsg.): Betriebswirtschaftslehre und Theorie der Verfuegungsrechte, Wiesbaden: Gabler, 1988, pp. 91–118.

Picot, A./Sennewald, N. (1997): Die Internet-Technologie als betriebswirtschaftliches Informations- und Kommunikationsmedium, in: Reichmann, T. (ed.): Handbuch Globale Datennetze, Muenchen: Vahlen, 1997.

Picot, A./Wolff, B. (1995): Franchising als effiziente Vertriebsform, in: Kaas, K. P. (ed.): Marketing und Neue Institutionenlehre, ZfbF-Sonderheft No. 35, 1995, pp. 223–243.

Picot, A./Wolff, B. (1997): Informationsoekonomik, in: Gabler's Wirtschaftslexikon, Wiesbaden: Gabler, 1997, pp. 1870–1878.

Piller, F.T. (1998a): Kundenindividuelle Massenproduktion, Muenchen: Hanser, 1998.

Piller, F.T. (1998b): Mit Mass Customization zu echtem Beziehungsmanagement, in: Harvard Business Manager, No. 6, 1998, pp. 103–107.

Piller, F.T. (1998c): Das Produktivitaetsparadoxon der Informationstechnik aus betriebs-wirtschaftlicher Sicht, in: Wirtschaftspolitische Blaetter, No. 6, 1998, pp. 635–645.

Piller, F.T. (2001): Mass Customization: Ein Wettbewerbskonzept fuer das Informations-zeitalter, 2nd edn., Wiesbaden: Gabler/DUV, 2001.

Piller, F.T./Stotko, C. (2002): Der Kunde als Wertschoepfungspartner: Vom Co-Produzenten zum Co-Entwickler, Duesseldorf: Symposion, 2002.

Pinchot, G./Pinchot, E. (1993): The End of Bureaucracy and the Rise of the Intelligent Or-ganization, San Francisco, CA: Berrett-Koehler, 1993.

Pine, B. J. (1993): Mass Customization. The New Frontier in Business Competition, Bos-ton, MA: Harvard Business School, 1993.

Plinke, W. (1999): Grundlagen des Marktprozesses, in: Kleinaltenkamp, M./Plinke, W. (eds.): Technischer Vertrieb: Grundlagen des Business-to-Business Marketing, 2nd edn., Berlin et al.: Springer, 1999, pp. 3–99.

Polanyi, M. (1962): Personal Knowledge: Towards a Post-Critical Philosophy, 2nd edn., New York, NY: Harper Row, 1962.

Polanyi, M. (1985): Implizites Wissen, Frankfurt/Main: Suhrkamp, 1985.

Pomberger, G./Blaschek, G. (1993): Grundlagen des Software Engineering – Prototyping und objektorientierte Software-Entwicklung, Munich: Hanser, 1993.

PonTell, S./Gray, P./Markus, M.L./Westfall, R.D. (1996): The Demand for Telecommut-ing, in: Proceedings of the Telecommuting 1996 Conference, Jacksonville, Florida, 25–26th April 1996.

Porter, L.W./Lawler III, E.E. (1968): Managerial attitudes and performance, Homewood, IL: Irwin, 1968.

Porter, M.E. (1990): The competitive Advantage of Nations, New York, NY: Free Press, 1990.

Porter, M.E. (1992): Wettbewerbsvorteile, 3rd edn., Frankfurt/Main et al.: Campus, 1992.

Porter, M.E. (1996): What is strategy?, in: Harvard Business Review, November-December 1996, pp. 61–78.

Porter, M.E. (1999): Wettbewerbsstrategie, 10th edn., Frankfurt/Main et al.: Campus, 1999.

Porter, M.E. (2001a): Strategy and the Internet, Harvard Business Review, March 2001, pp. 63–78.

Porter, M.E. (2001b): Regions and the New Economics of Competition, in: Scott, A.J. (ed.): Global City-Regions, Oxford: Oxford University Press, 2001.

Porter, M.E. / Fuller, M.B. (1989): Koalitionen und globale Strategien, in: Porter, M.E. (ed.): Globaler Wettbewerb: Strategien der neuen Internationalisierung, Wiesbaden: Gabler, 1989.

Porter, M.E. / Millar, V.E. (1985): How Information Gives You Competitive Advantage, in: Harvard Business Review, July / Aug. 1985, pp. 149–160.

Powell, W.W. (1996): Trust-based forms of governance, in: Kramer, R.M. / Tyler, T.R. (eds.): Trust in organizations: Frontiers of strategy and research, Thousand Oaks, CA: Sage, 1996, pp. 51–67.

Prahalad, C.K. / Hamel, G. (1990): The Core Competence of the Corporation, in: Harvard Business Review, May / June 1990, pp. 79–91.

Pribilla, P. / Reichwald, R. / Goecke, R. (1996): Telekommunikation im Management, Stuttgart: Schaeffer-Poeschel, 1996.

Probst, G. / Raub, S. / Romhardt, K. (1999): Wissen managen – Wie Unternehmen ihre wertvollste Ressource optimal nutzen, 3rd edn., Wiesbaden: Gabler, 1999.

Probst, G. J. (1992): Selbstorganisation, in: Frese, E. (ed.): Handwoerterbuch der Organisation, 3rd edn., Stuttgart: Schaeffer-Poeschel, 1992, Col. 2255–2269.

Probst, G.J. / Buechel, B. (1997): Organisationales Lernen: Wettbewerbsvorteil der Zukunft, 2nd edn., Wiesbaden: Gabler, 1997.

Probst, G.J. / Gomez P. (1991): Die Methodik des vernetzten Denkens zur Loesung komplexer Probleme, in: Probst, G.J. / Gomez, P. (eds.): Vernetztes Denken: ganzheitliches Fuehren in der Praxis, 2nd edn., Wiesbaden: Gabler, 1991, pp. 3–20.

Proff, H. (1997): Moeglichkeiten und Grenzen hybrider Strategien – dargestellt am Beispiel der deutschen Automobilindustrie, in: Die Betriebswirtschaft, No. 6, 1997, pp. 796–809.

Quinn, R.E. / Spreitzer, G.M. (1997): The Road to Empowerment: Seven Questions Every Leader Should Consider, in: Organizational Dynamics, Autumn 1997, pp. 37–49.

Quittner, J. / Slatalla, M. (1998): Speeding the Net: The Inside Story of Netscape and How It Challenged Microsoft, New York, NY: Atlantic Monthly, 1998.

Rappaport, A. (1986): Creating Shareholder Value, New York, NY: Free Press, 1986.

Rawolle, J. / Kirchfeld, S. / Hess, T. (2002): Zur Integration mobiler und stationaerer Online-Dienste der Medienindustrie, in: Reichwald, R. (ed.): Mobile Kommunikation – Wertschoepfung, Technologien, neue Dienste, Wiesbaden: Gabler, 2002, pp. 335–352.

Rayport, J.F. / Sviokla J.J. (1994): Manging in the Marketspace, in: Harvard Business Review November-December 1994, pp. 141–150.

Reber, G. (1992): Lernen, organisationales, in: Frese, E. (ed.): Handwoerterbuch der Organisation, 3rd edn., Stuttgart: Schaeffer-Poeschel, 1992, pp. 1240–1256.

Reddin, W.J. (1977): Das 3-D-Programm zur Leistungssteigerung des Managements, Muenchen: Hanser, 1977.

Reich, R.B. (1991): Die neue Weltwirtschaft – Das Ende der nationalen Oekonomie, Frankfurt / Main: Fischer, 1996.

Reichmann, T. (1995): Controlling mit Kennzahlen und Managementberichten, 4th edn., Muenchen: Vahlen, 1995.

Reichwald, R. (1977): Arbeit als Produktionsfaktor, Munich et al.: Reinhardt, 1977.

Reichwald, R. (1984): Produktivitaetsbeziehungen in der Unternehmensverwaltung – Grundueberlegungen zur Modellierung und Gestaltung der Bueroarbeit unter dem Einfluss neuer Informationstechnologien, in: Pack, L. / Boerner, D. (eds.): Betriebswirtschaftliche Entscheidungen bei Stagnation, Wiesbaden: Gabler, 1984, pp. 197–213.

Reichwald, R. (1991a): Management-Report: Vermittelnde Breitbandkommunikation zur langfristigen Sicherung des Unternehmenserfolges, in: Ricke, H. / Kanzow, J. (eds.): BERKOM: Breitbandkommunikation im Glasfasernetz. Uebersicht und Zusammenfassung 1986–91, Heidelberg: Decker, 1991, pp. 13–39.

Reichwald, R. (1991b): Innovative Anwendungen neuer Telekommunikationsformen in der industriellen Forschung und Entwicklung, in: Heinrich, L.J. / Pomberger, G. / Schauer, R. (eds.): Die Informationswirtschaft im Unternehmen, Universitaet Linz, 1991, pp. 253–280.

Reichwald, R. (ed., 1992a): Marktnahe Produktion, Wiesbaden: Gabler, 1992.

Reichwald, R. (1992b): Die Wiederentdeckung der menschlichen Arbeit als primaerer Produktionsfaktor fuer eine marktnahe Produktion, in: Reichwald, R. (ed.): Marktnahe Produktion, Wiesbaden: Gabler, 1992, pp. 3–18.

Reichwald, R. (1993a): Die Wirtschaftlichkeit im Spannungsfeld von betriebswirtschaftlicher Theorie und Praxis, Arbeitsbericht des Lehrstuhls fuer Allgemeine und Industrielle Betriebswirtschaftslehre, Vol. 1, Munich: Technical University Munich, 1993.

Reichwald, R. (1993b): Der Mensch als Mittelpunkt einer ganzheitlichen Produktion. Innovative Organisationskonzepte aus betriebswirtschaftlicher Perspektive, Arbeitsbericht des Lehrstuhls fuer Allgemeine und Industrielle Betriebswirtschaftslehre, Vol. 2, Munich: Technical University Munich, 1993.

Reichwald, R. (1997a): Neue Arbeitsformen in der vernetzten Unternehmung: Flexibilitaet und Controlling, in: Picot, A. (ed.): Information als Wettbewerbsfaktor, Stuttgart: Schaeffer-Poeschel, 1997, pp. 233–263.

Reichwald, R. (1997b): Ganzheitliche Unternehmensfuehrung und Medieneinsatz im Top-Management. Ergebnisse aus einer empirischen Untersuchung, in: Seghezzi, H.D. (ed.): Ganzheitliche Unternehmensfuehrung, Stuttgart: Schaeffer-Poeschel, 1997, pp. 271–325.

Reichwald, R. (1999): Informationsmanagement, in: Bitz, M. / Dellmann, K. / Domsch, M. / Egner, H. (eds.): Vahlens Kompendium der Betriebswirtschaftslehre, Vol. 2, 4th edn., Munich: Vahlen, 1999, pp. 221–288.

Reichwald, R. (ed., 2002): Mobile Kommunikation – Wertschoepfung, Technologien, neue Dienste, Wiesbaden: Gabler, 2002.

Reichwald, R. et al. (1999): SOHO (Small Office / Home Office) – Haushalte als Anbieter und Nachfrager von integrierten Dienstleistungen, in: PEM 13: Dienstleistungen als Chance: Entwicklungspfade fuer die Beschaeftigung, Goettingen, 1999, pp. 298 -361.

Reichwald, R. / Bastian, C. (1999a): Fuehrung in verteilten Arbeits- und Organisationsformen, in: Egger, A. / Gruen, O. / Moser, R. (eds.): Managementinstrumente und Konzepte: Entstehung, Verbreitung und Bedeutung fuer die BWL, Stuttgart: Schaeffer-Poeschel, 1999, pp. 141–162.

Reichwald, R. / Bastian, C. (1999b): Fuehrung von Mitarbeitern in verteilten Organisationen – Ergebnisse explorativer Forschung, in: Egger, A. / Gruen, O. / Moser, R. (eds., 1999): Managementinstrumente und -konzepte: Entstehung, Verbreitung und Bedeutung fuer die Betriebswirtschaftslehre, Stuttgart: Schaeffer-Poeschel, 1999, pp. 141–162.

Reichwald, R. / Bastian, C. / Lohse, C. (2000): Vertriebsmanagement im Wandel. Neue Anforderungen fuer die Gestaltung der Kundenschnittstelle, in: Reichwald, R. / Bullinger, H.-J. (eds.): Vertriebsmanagement. Entwicklungen in Organisation, Technologieeinsatz und Personal, Stuttgart: Schaeffer-Poeschel, 2000, pp. 3–33.

Reichwald, R. / Bauer, R. / Weichselbaumer, J. (1997): Modernisierung – Eine betriebliche Innovationsstrategie und ihre Bewertung; in: Reichwald, R. / Fritsch, M. (eds.): Modernisierung als Innovationsstrategie, Aachen: Verl. der Augustinus-Buchhandlung: 1997, pp. 9–58.

Reichwald, R. / Bauer, R.A. / Lohse, C. (1999): Electronic Commerce und die neue Rolle des Vertriebs – Implikationen fuer die Gestaltung des Kundenkontakts, in: Industrie Management, No. 1, 1999, pp. 70–73.

Reichwald, R. / Behrbohm, P. (1983): Flexibilitaet als Eigenschaft produktionswirtschaftlicher Systeme, in: Zeitschrift fuer Betriebswirtschaft, No. 9, 1983, pp. 831–853.

Reichwald, R. / Dietel, B. (1991): Produktionswirtschaft, in: Heinen, E. (ed.): Industriebetriebslehre: Entscheidungen im Industriebetrieb, 9th edn., Wiesbaden: Gabler, 1991, pp. 395–622.

Reichwald, R. / Englberger, H. (1998a): Multimediale Telekooperation in neuen Organisationsstrukturen, in: Reichmann, T. (ed.): Globale Datennetze – Innovative Potentiale fuer Informationsmanagement und Controlling, Munich: Vahlen, 1998, pp. 109–133.

Reichwald, R. / Englberger, H. (1998b): Telecooperation – Overcoming the Boundaries of Location? in: Council of Logistics Management (ed.): Logistics Excellence – Vision, Processes, and People. Annual Conference Proc., Anaheim, CA, 1998, pp. 361–371.

Reichwald, R. / Englberger, H. / Moeslein, K. (1998a): Telearbeit & Telekooperation – Evaluierung und Begleitung der Telekom-internen und Berkom-Telearbeitsprojekte. Berkom-Studie, Munich: Technical University Munich, 1998.

Reichwald, R. / Englberger, H. / Moeslein, K. (1998b): Telekooperation im Innovationstest – Strategieorientierte Evaluation von Pilotprojekten, in: Wirtschaftsinformatik, No. 3, 1998, pp. 205–213.

Reichwald, R. / Fremuth, N. / Ney, M. (2002): Mobile Communities – Erweiterung von Virtuellen Communities mit mobilen Diensten, in: Reichwald, R. (ed.): Mobile Kommunikation – Wertschoepfung, Technologien, neue Dienste, Wiesbaden: Gabler, 2002, pp. 521–538.

Reichwald, R. / Goecke, R. (1995): Buerokommunikationstechnik und Fuehrung, in: Kieser, A. / Reber, G. / Wunderer, R. (eds.): Handwoerterbuch der Fuehrung, 2nd edn., Stuttgart: Schaeffer-Poeschel, 1995, pp. 164–182.

Reichwald, R. / Hesch, G. (1993): Der Mensch als Produktionsfaktor oder Traeger ganzheitlicher Produktion? – Menschenbilder im Wandel der Betriebswirtschaftslehre, in: Weis, K. (ed.): Bilder vom Menschen in Wissenschaft, Technik und Religion, Munich: Vahlen, 1993, pp. 429–460.

Reichwald, R. / Hoefer, C. / Weichselbaumer, J. (1993): Anwenderhandbuch zur erweiterten Wirtschaftlichkeitsbetrachtung, AuT-Verbundvorhaben Humanzentrierte CIM-Konzepte, Lehrstuhl fuer Allgemeine und Industrielle Betriebswirtschaftslehre, Munich: Technical University Munich, 1993.

Reichwald, R. / Hoefer, C. / Weichselbaumer, J. (1996): Erfolg von Reorganisationsprozessen. Leitfaden zur strategieorientierten Bewertung, Stuttgart: Schaeffer-Poeschel, 1996.

Reichwald, R. / Koller, H. (1995): Informations- und Kommunikationstechnologien, in: Tietz, B. / Koehler, R. / Zentes, J. (eds.): Handwoerterbuch des Marketing, 2nd edn., Stuttgart: Schaeffer-Poeschel, 1995, pp. 947 – 962.

Reichwald, R. / Koller, H. (1996a): Die Dezentralisierung als Massnahme zur Foerderung der Lernfaehigkeit von Organisationen, in: Bullinger, H.-J. (ed.): Lernende Organisationen: Konzepte, Methoden, Erfahrungsberichte, Stuttgart: Schaeffer-Poeschel, 1996.

Reichwald, R. / Koller, H. (1996b): Integration und Dezentralisierung von Unternehmensstrukturen, in: Lutz, B. / Hartmann, M. / Hirsch-Kreinsen, H. (eds.): Produzieren im 21. Jahrhundert. Herausforderungen fuer die deutsche Industrie, Frankfurt / Main et al.: Campus, 1996, pp. 225 – 294.

Reichwald, R. / Meier, R. / Fremuth, N. (2002): Die mobile Oekonomie – Definition und Spezifika, in: Reichwald, R. (ed.): Mobile Kommunikation – Wertschoepfung, Technologien, neue Dienste, Wiesbaden: Gabler, 2002, pp. 3 – 18.

Reichwald, R. / Moeslein, K. (1995): Wertschoepfung und Produktivitaet von Dienstleistungen? Innovationsstrategien fuer die Standortsicherung, in: Bullinger, H.-J. (ed.): Dienstleistung der Zukunft: Maerkte, Unternehmen und Infrastrukturen im Wandel, Wiesbaden: Gabler, 1995, pp. 324 – 476.

Reichwald, R. / Moeslein, K. (1996a): Auf dem Weg zur virtuellen Organisation: Wie Telekooperation Unternehmen veraendert, in: Mueller, G. / Kohl, U. / Strauss, R. (eds.): Zukunftsperspektiven der digitalen Vernetzung, Heidelberg: Huethig, 1996, pp. 209 – 233.

Reichwald, R. / Moeslein, K. (1996b): Telearbeit und Telekooperation, in: Bullinger, H.-J. / Warnecke, H.-J. (eds.): Neue Organisationsformen im Unternehmen – Ein Handbuch fuer das moderne Management, Berlin et al.: Springer, 1996, pp. 691 – 708.

Reichwald, R. / Moeslein, K. (1997a): Chancen und Herausforderungen fuer neue unternehmerische Strukturen und Handlungsspielraeume in der Informationsgesellschaft, in: Picot, A. (ed.): Telekooperation und virtuelle Unternehmen – Auf dem Weg zu neuen Arbeitsformen, Heidelberg: Decker, 1997, pp. 1 – 37.

Reichwald, R. / Moeslein, K. (1997b): Innovationsstrategien und neue Geschaeftsfelder von Dienstleistern – Den Wandel gestalten, in: Bullinger, H.-J. (ed.): Dienstleistungen fuer das 21. Jahrhundert. Gestaltung des Wandels und Aufbruch in die Zukunft, Stuttgart: Schaeffer-Poeschel, 1997, pp. 75 – 105.

Reichwald, R. / Moeslein, K. (1998): Dienstleistungsoffensive "Telekooperation", in: Bullinger, H. / Zahn, E. (eds.): Dienstleistungsoffensive – Wachstumschancen intelligent nutzen, Stuttgart: Schaeffer-Poeschel, 1998, pp. 143 – 164.

Reichwald, R. / Moeslein, K. (1999a): Management und Technologie, in: Rosenstiel, L. v. / Regnet, E. / Domsch, M. E. (eds.): Fuehrung von Mitarbeitern. Handbuch fuer erfolgreiches Personalmanagement, 4th edn., Stuttgart: Schaeffer-Poeschel, 1999, pp. 709 – 727.

Reichwald, R. / Moeslein, K. (1999b): Telework Strategies: The Diffusion of a Workplace Innovation, in: Proceedings of the Fourth International Telework Workshop "Telework Strategies for the New Workforce", Tokyo 1999, pp. 166 – 175.

Reichwald, R. / Moeslein, K. (2000): Nutzenpotentiale und Nutzenrealisierung in verteilten Organisationsstrukturen. Experimente, Erprobungen und Erfahrungen auf dem Weg zur virtuellen Unternehmung, in: Zeitschrift fuer Betriebswirtschaft, supplement 2, 2000, pp. 117–136.

Reichwald, R. / Moeslein, K. (2001): Pluri-local Social Spaces by Telecooperation in International Cooperations?, in: Pries, L. (ed.): New Transnational Social Spaces: International Migration and Transnational Companies in the Early Twenty-first Century (Transnationalism), New York: Routledge publ. 2001, pp. 115 – 133.

Reichwald, R. / Moeslein, K. (2002): Theoretische Grundlagen der Virtualisierung von international taetigen Unternehmen, in: Macharzina, K. / Oesterle, M.-J. (eds.): Handbuch Internationales Management: Grundlagen – Instrumente – Perspektiven, 2nd edn., Gabler: Wiesbaden, 2002, pp. 1009–1026.

Reichwald, R. / Moeslein, K. / Piller, F.T. (2000): Taking Stock of Distributed Work: The Past, Present and Future of Telecooperation, Proceedings of the ASAC-IFSAM 2000 Conference, July 8 – 11, 2000, Montreal 2000.

Reichwald, R. / Moeslein, K. / Sachenbacher, H. / Englberger, H. (1997): Telearbeit & Telekooperation: Bedingungen und Strategien erfolgreicher Realisierung, in: Zeitschrift fuer Arbeitswissenschaft, No. 4, 1997, pp. 204–213.

Reichwald, R. / Moeslein, K. / Sachenbacher, H. / Englberger, H. (2000): Telekooperation: Verteilte Arbeits- und Organisationsformen, 2nd edn., Berlin et al.: Springer, 2000.

Reichwald, R. / Nippa, M. (1989): Organisationsmodelle fuer die Bueroarbeit beim Einsatz neuer Technologien, in: Institut fuer angewandte Arbeitswissenschaft e.V. (ed.): Arbeitsgestaltung in Produktion und Verwaltung, Koeln: Wirtschaftsverlag Bachem, 1989, pp. 423–443.

Reichwald, R. / Piller, F.T. (2002a): Der Kunde als Wertschoepfungspartner: Formen und Prinzipien, in: Albach, H. et al. (eds.): Wertschoepfungsmanagement als Kernkompetenz, Wiesbaden: Gabler, 2002, pp. 27–52.

Reichwald, R. / Piller, F.T. (2002b): Mass-Customization-Konzepte im E-Business, in: Weiber, R. (ed.): Handbuch Electronic Business, 2nd edn., Wiesbaden: Gabler, 2002, pp. 469–494.

Reichwald, R. / Sachenbacher, H. (1996): Durchlaufzeiten, in: Kern, W. / Schroeder, H. / Weber, J. (eds.): Handwoerterbuch der Produktion, 2nd edn., Stuttgart: Schaeffer-Poeschel, 1996, pp. 362–374.

Reichwald, R. / Schaller, C. (2002): M-Loyalty: Kundenbindung durch personalisierte mobile Dienste, in: Reichwald, R. (ed.): Mobile Kommunikation – Wertschoepfung, Technologien, neue Dienste, 1st edn., Wiesbaden: Gabler, 2002, pp. 263–288.

Reichwald, R. / Schlichter, J. (eds., 2000): Verteiltes Arbeiten – Arbeit der Zukunft, Tagungsband der D-CSCW 2000, Stuttgart et al.: Teubner, 2000.

Reichwald, R. / Weichselbaumer, J. (1996): Rationalisierung und Erfolg – Traditionelle betriebswirtschaftliche Bewertungsmuster im Umbruch, in: Hoss, D. / Schrick, G. (eds.): Wie rational ist Rationalisierung heute? Ein oeffentlicher Diskurs, Stuttgart et al.: Raabe, 1996, pp. 305–318.

Reisig, W. (1990): Petrinetze: Eine Einfuehrung, Berlin et al.: Springer, 1990.

Reiss, M. (1992a): Arbeitsteilung, in: Frese, E. (ed.): Handwoerterbuch der Organisation, 3rd edn., Stuttgart: Schaeffer-Poeschel, 1992, pp. 167–178.

Reiss, M. (1992b): Spezialisierung, in: Frese, E. (ed.): Handwoerterbuch der Organisation, 3rd edn., Stuttgart: Schaeffer-Poeschel, 1992, pp. 2287–2296.

Reiss, M. (1996): Grenzen der grenzenlosen Unternehmung, in: Die Unternehmung, No. 3, 1996, pp. 195–206.

Reve, T. (1990): The Firm as a Nexus of Internal and External Contracts, in: Aoki, M./Gustafsson, B./Williamson, O. E. (eds.): The Firm as a Nexus of Treaties, London: Sage, 1990, pp. 133–161.

Rice, R. (1992): Task Analysability, Use of New Media and Effectiveness: A multi-site exploration of media richness, in: Organization Science, Vol. 3, 1992, pp. 475–500.

Ripperger, T. (1998): Oekonomik des Vertrauens. Analyse eines Organisationsprinzips, Tuebingen: Mohr, 1998.

Ripperger, T. (1999): Die Effizienz des Vertrauensmechanismus bei der Organisation internationaler Transaktionen, in: Herder-Dorneich, P./Schenk, K.-E./Schmidtchen, D. (eds.): Jahrbuch fuer Neue Politische Oekonomie, Tuebingen: Mohr, 1999.

Roach, S. (1991): Services Under Siege – The Restructuring Imperative, in: Harvard Business Review, September/October 1991, pp. 82–91.

Robbins, S.P. (1990): Organization Theory: Structure, Design and Applications, Englewood Cliffs, NJ: Prentice Hall, 1990.

Robbins, S. P. (1994): Essentials of Organizational Behaviour, 4th edn., Englewood Cliffs, NJ: Prentice Hall, 1994.

Rockart J.F (1986): The rise of managerial computing: the best of the Center for Information Systems Research, Sloan School of Management, Massachusetts Institute of Technology, Homewood, IL: Dow Jones-Irwin, 1986.

Roethlisberger, F.J./Dickson, W.J. (1939): Management and the Worker, Boston, MA: Harvard University, 1939.

Rogers, E.M. (1995): Diffusion of Innovations, 4th edn., New York: The Free Press, 1995.

Rohrbach, P. (1996): Interaktives Teleshopping – Elektronisches Einkaufen auf dem Informationhighway, Wiesbaden: Gabler, 1996.

Rolf, A. (1998): Grundlagen der Organisations- und Wirtschaftsinformatik, Berlin et al.: Springer, 1998.

Rosemann, M./Uthmann,, C. v. (1997): Workflowmanagement in der industriellen Produktion, in: Zeitschrift fuer wirtschaftliche Fertigung und Automtisierung, Vol. 92. No. 7–8, 1997, pp. 351–354.

Rosenstiel, L. v. (1992): Entwicklung von Werthaltungen und interpersonaler Kompetenz – Beitraege der Sozialpsychologie, in: Sonntag, K. (ed.): Personalentwicklung in Organisationen. Psychologische Grundlagen, Methoden und Strategien, Goettingen et al.: Hogrefe, 1992, pp. 83–105.

Rosenstiel, L. v. (1994): Mitarbeiterfuehrung und -motivation bei veraenderten Strukturen und Wertorientierungen, in: Milberg, J./Reinhart, G. (eds.): Unsere Staerken staerken, Muenchner Kolloquium 1994, 24./25. Februar 1994, Munich: Technical University Munich, 1994, pp. 305–317.

Rosenstiel, L. v. (1998): Grundlagen der Fuehrung, in: Rosenstiel, L. v./Regnet, E./Domsch, M. E. (eds., 1998): Fuehrung von Mitarbeitern. Handbuch fuer erfolgreiches Personalmanagement, 4th edn., Stuttgart: Schaeffer-Poeschel, 1998, pp. 3–24.

Rosenstiel, L. v. (2002): Grundlagen der Organisationspsychologie, 5th edn., Stuttgart: Schaeffer-Poeschel, 2002.

Rosenstiel, L. v. / Djarrahzadeh, M. / Einsiedler, H.E. / Streich, R.K. (eds., 1993): Wertewandel als Herausforderung fuer die Unternehmenspolitik in den 1990er Jahren, 2nd edn., Stuttgart: Schaeffer-Poeschel, 1993.

Rosenstiel, L. v. / Regnet, E. / Domsch, M.E. (eds., 1998): Fuehrung von Mitarbeitern. Handbuch fuer erfolgreiches Personalmanagement, 4th edn., Stuttgart: Schaeffer-Poeschel, 1998.

Ross, S.A. (1973): The Economic Theory of Agency: The Principal's Problem, American Economic Review, Vol. 63, No. 2, 1973, pp. 134 – 139.

Roessl, D. (1996): Selbstverpflichtung als alternative Koordinationsform von komplexen Austauschbeziehungen, in: Zeitschrift fuer betriebswirtschaftliche Forschung, No. 4, 1996, pp. 311 – 334.

Rotering, J. (1990): Forschungs- und Entwicklungskooperationen zwischen Unternehmen, Stuttgart: Schaeffer-Poeschel, 1990.

Rothhaar, C. (2001): Fuehrung und Motivation im Kundenbeziehungsmanagement, Wiesbaden: DUV / Gabler, 2001.

Rotering, J. (1993): Zwischenbetriebliche Kooperation als alternative Organisationsform, Stuttgart: Schaeffer-Poeschel, 1993.

Rotter, J.B. (1971): Generalized expectancies for interpersonal trust, in: American Psychologist, Vol. 26, 1971, pp. 443 – 452.

Rotter, J.B. (1980): Interpersonal trust, trustworthiness and gullibility, in: American Psychologist, Vol. 35, 1980, pp. 1 – 7.

Royce, W.W. (1970): Managing the development of large software systems: Concepts and Techniques, Proceedings of IEEE WESCON, 1970.

Rumbaugh, J. / Blaha, M. / Premerlani, W. / Eddy, F. / Lorensen, W. (1991): Object-Oriented Modeling and Design, Englewood Cliffs, NJ: Prentice Hall, 1991.

Rupprecht-Daeullary, M. (1994): Zwischenbetriebliche Kooperation, Wiesbaden: Gabler, 1994.

Ryle, G. (1949): The Concept of Mind, London: Hutchinson, 1949.

Sachenbacher, H. (2000): Controlling in telekooperativen Strukturen: Steuerung und Koordination verteilter Zusammenarbeit, Wiesbaden: DUV / Gabler, 2000.

Sager, I. et al. (1998): A New Cyber Order, Business Week, 07.12.1998, pp. 55 – 59.

Sanchez, R. / Mahoney, J.T. (1996): Modularity, Flexibility and Knowledge Management in Product and Organizational Design, in: Strategic Management Journal, Vol. 17, Special Issue Winter, 1996, pp. 63 – 76.

Sander, P. / Stucky, W. / Herschel, R. (1995): Automaten, Sprachen, Berechenbarkeit, 2nd edn., Stuttgart: Teubner, 1995.

Sandner, K. (1988): Strukturen der Fuehrung von Mitarbeitern. Steuerung und Kontrolle beruflicher Arbeit, in: Hofmann, M. / Rosenstiel, L. v. (eds.): Funktionale Managementlehre, Berlin et al.: Springer, 1988.

Savage, C.M. (1990): 5th Generation Management: Kreatives Kooperieren durch virtuelles Unternehmertum, dynamische Teambildung und Vernetzung von Wissen, Zuerich: vdf, 1997.

Schanz, G. (1994): Organisationsgestaltung: Management von Arbeitsteilung und Koordination, 2nd edn., Munich: Vahlen, 1994.

Schanze, E. (1991): Symbiotic Contracts: Exploring Long-Term Agency Structures Between Contract and Corporation, in: Joerges, Christian (ed.): Franchising and the Law: Theoretical and Comparative Approaches in Europe and the United States, Baden-Baden: Nomos, 1991, pp. 68–103.

Scheckenbach, R. (1997): EC-EDI und noch viel mehr, in: edi-change, No. 1, 1997, p. 11.

Scheer, A.-W. (1990): CIM: der computergestuetzte Industriebetrieb, 4th edn., Berlin et al.: Springer, 1990.

Scheer, A.-W. (1994): Wirtschaftsinformatik – Referenzmodelle fuer industrielle Geschaeftsprozesse, 5th edn., Berlin et al.: Springer, 1994.

Schein, E.H. (1980): Organizational Psychology, 3rd edn., Englewood Cliffs, NJ: Prentice Hall, 1980.

Schein, E.H. (1991): Organisationskultur: ein neues unternehmenstheoretisches Konzept, in: Duelfer, E. (ed.): Organisationskultur, 2nd edn., Stuttgart: Schaeffer-Poeschel, 1991, pp. 26–37.

Schein, E. H. (1992): Organizational Culture and Leadership, 2nd edn., New York, NY: Jossey-Bass, 1992.

Schein, E.H. (1995): Unternehmenskultur. Ein Handbuch fuer Fuehrungskraefte, Frankfurt/Main et al.: Campus, 1995.

Scheller, M./Boden, K. P./Geenen, A./Kampermann, J. (1994): Internet: Werkzeuge und Dienste, Berlin et al.: Springer, 1994.

Scheuble, S. (1998): Wissen und Wissenssurrogate, Wiesbaden: Gabler, 1998.

Schlageter, G./Stucky, W. (1983): Datenbanksysteme: Konzepte und Modelle, 2nd edn., Stuttgart: Teubner, 1983.

Schlicksupp, H. (1992): Innovation, Kreativitaet und Ideenfindung, 6th edn., Wuerzburg: Vogel, 1992.

Schmid, B. (1993): Elektronische Maerkte, in: Wirtschaftsinformatik, No. 5, 1993, pp. 465–480.

Schmid, B. (1995): Elektronische Einzelhandels- und Retailmaerkte, in: Schmid, B./Dratva, R./Mausberg, P./Meli, H./Zimmermann, H.-D. (eds.): Electronic Mall: Banking und Shopping in globalen Netzen, Stuttgart: Teubner, 1995, pp. 17–32.

Schmidt, Ch./Weinhardt, Ch./Horstmann, R. (1998): Internet-Auktionen – Eine Uebersicht zu Online-Versteigerungen im Hard- und Softwarebereich; in: Wirtschaftsinformatik Vol. 40., No. 5, 1998, pp. 450–457.

Schmidt-Bleek, F. (1994): Work in a Sustainable Economy: Some irritating Facts, some Questions, and some Hope, in: Proceedings of the European Assembly on Teleworking and New Ways of Working, 3.-4.11.1994, Berlin, 1994, pp. 19–34.

Schmidtchen, D. (1994): OEkonomik des Vertrauens, in: Hof, H. (ed.): Recht und Verhalten: Verhaltensgrundlagen des Rechts – zum Beispiel Vertrauen, Baden-Baden: Nomos, 1994, pp. 129–163.

Schmitz, J. (1987): Electronic Messaging: System use in local governments, paper presented at the International Communication Association, Montreal, Canada 1987.

Schmoeller, A. (1998): Die Version der globalen Kommunikation, Siemens AG ICN, Muenchen 1998.

Schneider, D. (1988): Zur Entstehung innovativer Unternehmen – Eine oekonomisch-theoretische Perspektive, Muenchen: VVF, 1988.

Schneider, D. / Gerbert, P. (1999): E-Shopping: Erfolgsstrategien im Electronic Commerce: Marken schaffen, Shops gestalten, Kunden binden, Wiesbaden: Gabler, 1999.

Scholl, W. (1992): Informationspathologien, in: Frese, E. (ed.): Handwoerterbuch der Organisation, 3rd edn., Stuttgart: Schaeffer-Poeschel, 1992, pp. 900–912.

Scholz, C. (1994): Die virtuelle Organisation als Strukturkonzept der Zukunft?, Saarbruecken: Universitaet des Saarlandes, 1994.

Scholz, C. (1997): Strategische Organisation: Prinzipien zur Vitalisierung und Virtualisierung, Muenchen: Moderne Industrie, 1997.

Schomburg, E. (1980): Entwicklung eines betriebstypologischen Instrumentariums zur systematischen Ermittlung der Anforderungen an EDV-gestuetzte Produktions-, Planungs- und Steuerungssysteme im Maschinenbau, Aachen: RWTH, 1980.

Schoening, U. (2001): Theoretische Informatik kurz gefasst, 4th edn., Mannheim et al.: BI Wissenschaftsverlag, 2001.

Schottlaender, R. (1957): Theorie des Vertrauens, Berlin: de Gruyter, 1957.

Schrader, S. (1990): Zwischenbetrieblicher Informationstransfer: Eine empirische Analyse kooperativen Verhaltens, Berlin: Duncker & Humblot, 1990.

Schrader, S. (1993): Kooperation, in: Hauschildt, J. / Gruen, O. (eds.): Ergebnisse empirischer betriebswirtschaftlicher Forschung – Zu einer Realtheorie der Unternehmung, Festschrift fuer Witte, E., Stuttgart: Schaeffer-Poeschel, 1993, pp. 221–254.

Schreyoegg, A. (1996): Coaching: eine Einfuehrung fuer Praxis und Ausbildung, 2nd edn., Frankfurt / Main et al.: Campus, 1996.

Schreyoegg, G. (1992): Kann und darf man Unternehmenskulturen aendern?, in: Duelfer, E. (ed.): Organisationskultur, 2nd edn., Stuttgart: Schaeffer-Poeschel, 1991, pp. 202–214.

Schreyoegg, G. (1993): Unternehmensstrategie. Grundfragen einer Theorie strategischer Unternehmensfuehrung, Berlin et al.: de Gruyter, 1993.

Schreyoegg, G. / Huebl, G. (1992): Manager in Action: Ergebnisse einer Beobachtungsstudie in mittelstaendischen Unternehmen, in: Zeitschrift Fuehrung & Organisation, No. 2, 1992, pp. 82–89.

Schulte, B. (1997): Organisation mobiler Arbeit. Koordinations- und Motivationsaspekte beim Einsatz mobiler Informations- und Kommunikationstechnologien, Wiesbaden: Gabler, 1997.

Schulz von Thun, F. (1993): Miteinander Reden, part 1, Stoerungen und Klaerungen, Hamburg: Rowohlt, 1993.

Schumann, M. (1992): Betriebliche Nutzeffekte und Strategiebeitraege der grossintegrierten Informationsverarbeitung, Berlin et al.: Springer, 1992.

Schumann, M. (1993): Wirtschaftlichkeitsbeurteilung fuer IV-Systeme, in: Wirtschaftsinformatik, No. 2, 1993, pp. 167–178.

Schumpeter, J.A. (1908): Das Wesen und der Hauptinhalt der theoretischen Nationaloekonomie, Leipzig: Duncker & Humblot, 1908.

Schumpeter, J.A. (1993 [1934]): Theorie der wirtschaftlichen Entwicklung: Eine Untersuchung ueber Unternehmergewinn, Kapital, Kredit, Zins und den Konjunkturzyklus, 8th edn., Berlin: Duncker & Humblot, 1993.

Schwartz, E.I. (1997): Webonomics: nine essential principles for growing your business on the world wide web, New York: Broadway Books, 1997.

Schwarzer, B. / Krcmar, H. (1994): Neue Organisationsformen: Ein Fuehrer durch das Begriffspotpourri, in: Information Management, No. 4, 1994, pp. 20 – 27.

Schwarzer, B. / Krcmar, H. (1995): Grundlagen der Prozessorientierung: Eine vergleichende Untersuchung in der Elektronik- und Pharmaindustrie, Wiesbaden: Gabler, 1995.

Scott Morton, M. S. (1992): The Effects of Information Technology on Management and Organizations, in: Kochan T.A. / Useem, M. (eds.): Transforming Organizations, New York, NY: Oxford University, 1992, pp. 261 – 279.

Searle, J.R. (1993): Ausdruck und Bedeutung – Untersuchungen zur Sprechakttheorie, 3rd edn., Frankfurt / Main: Suhrkamp, 1993.

Searle, J.R. (1994): Sprechakte – Ein sprachphilosophischer Essay, 6th edn., Frankfurt / Main: Suhrkamp, 1994.

Sedgewick, R. (1992): Algorithms, Reading, MA: Addison-Wesley, 1992.

Seeger, H. (1998): Kommerz mit Kommunikation?, in: Global-Online 4, No. 5, 1998, p. 35.

Segev, A. / Beam, C. (1999): Brokering strategies in electronic commerce markets. Proceedings of the First ACM Conference on Electronic Commerce, 1999, pp. 167 – 176.

Seidenschwarz, W. (1991): Target Costing. Schnittstellenbewaeltigung mit Zielkosten, in: Horváth, P. (ed.): Synergien durch Schnittstellen-Controlling, Stuttgart: Schaeffer-Poeschel, 1991, pp. 191 – 209.

Seidenschwarz, W. (1999a): Balanced Scorecard – Ein Konzept fuer den zielgerichteten strategischen Wandel, in: Horváth, P. (ed.): Controlling & Finance – Aufgaben, Tools und Kompetenzen effektiv koordinieren, Stuttgart: Schaeffer-Poeschel, 1999, pp. 254ff.

Seidenschwarz, W. (1999b): Controlling fuer bewegliche Strukturen, Forschungsbericht No. 56 des Lehrstuhls fuer Controlling am BWI der Universitaet Stuttgart, Stuttgart 1999.

Seitz, R. (1995): Computergestuetzte Tele- und Teamarbeit, Wiesbaden: Gabler, 1995.

Senge, P.M. (1990a): The Fifth Discipline: The Art and Practice of The Learning Organization, New York, NY: Doubleday Currency, 1990.

Senge, P.M. (1990b): The Leader´s New Work: Building Learning Organizations, in: Sloan Management Review, No. 1, 1990, pp. 7 – 23.

Senge, P.M. (1994): The Fifth Discipline Fieldbook: Strategies and Tools for Building a Learning Organization, New York, NY: Doubleday Currency, 1994.

Sennewald, N. (1998): Massenmedien und Internet: Zur Marktentwicklung in der Pressebranche, Wiesbaden: Gabler, 1998.

Sewell, G. (1998): The Discipline of Teams: The Control of Team-based Industrial Work through Electronic and Peer Surveillance, in: Administrative Science Quarterly, Vol. 43, 1998, pp. 397 – 428.

Shannon, C.E. / Weaver, W. (1949): The mathematical theory of communication, Urbana, IL: University of Illinois Press, 1949.

Shapiro, C./Varian, H.R. (1999): Information Rules: A Strategic Guide to the Network Economy, Boston, MA: Harvard Business School Press, 1999.

Siegert, H.-J./Baumgarten, U. (1998): Betriebssysteme, 4th edn., Munich et al.: Oldenbourg, 1998.

Simon, H. (1992): Preismanagement, Wiesbaden: Gabler, 1992.

Simon, H./Bauer, B./Jaegeler, F. (1993): Auf der Suche nach Europas Staerken: Managementkulturen und Erfolgsfaktoren, Landsberg am Lech: Moderne Industrie, 1993.

Simon, H.A. (1959): Administrative Behavior: A Study of Decision-Making Processes in Administrative Organization, 2nd edn., New York, NY: MacMillan, 1959 [1st edn.: 1957].

Simon, H.A. (1988): Management strategischer Wettbewerbsvorteile, in: Zeitschrift fuer Betriebswirtschaft, No. 4, 1988, pp. 461–480.

Simon, H.A. (1991): Bounded Rationality and Organizational Learning, in: Organization Science, Vol. 2, 1991, pp. 176–201.

Sippel, F. (1994): Implementation and Management of Teletraining, Diskussionsbeitrag No. 123, Wissenschaftliches Instituts fuer Kommunikationsdienste, Bad Honnef: WIK, 1994.

Sipser, M. (1997): Introduction to the Theory of Computation, Boston, MA: PWS Publ., 1997.

Sjurts, I. (1998): Kontrolle ist gut, ist Vertrauen besser?, in: Die Betriebswirtschaft, No. 3, 1998, pp. 283–298.

Skiera, B. (1998): Preisdifferenzierung, in: Albers, S./Clement, P./Peters, K. (eds.): Marketing mit interaktiven Medien. Strategien zum Markterfolg, Frankfurt/Main: IMK, 1998, pp. 283–296.

Skiera, B./Spann, M. (2002): Preisdifferenzierung im Internet, in: Schoegel, M./Tomczak, T./Belz, C. (eds.): Roadmap to E-Business – Wie Unternehmen das Internet erfolgreich nutzen, St. Gallen: Texis, 2002, pp. 270–284.

Skinner, W. (1974): The Focused Factory, in: Harvard Business Review, May-June 1974, pp. 114–121.

Smith, A. (1776): An Inquiry into the Nature and Causes of the Wealth of Nations, London: Strahan and Cadell, 1776.

Smith, A. (1999 [1776]): Untersuchung ueber Wesen und Ursachen des Reichtums der Voelker [An Inquiry into the Nature and Causes of the Wealth of Nations], Duesseldorf: Verlag Wirtschaft und Finanzen, 1999.

Smith, K./Carroll, S./Ashford, S. (1995): Intra- and interorganizational cooperation: Toward a research agenda, in: Academy of Management Journal, Vol. 38, 1995, pp. 7–23.

Sorg, S./Zangl, H. (1986): Vorteile integrierter Buerosysteme fuer Fuehrungskraefte – Erfahrungen aus einem Pilotprojekt, in: Jahrbuch der Buerokommunikation, No. 2, 1986, pp. 117–119.

Sowell, T. (1980): Knowledge and Decisions, New York, NY: Basic Books, 1980.

Spremann, K. (1990): Asymmetrische Information, in: Zeitschrift fuer Betriebswirtschaft, No. 5/6, 1990, pp. 561–586.

Staehle, W. H. (1991): Redundanz, Slack und lose Koppelung in Organisationen, in: Staehle, W. H. v./Sydow, J. (eds.): Managementforschung 1, Berlin: de Gruyter, 1991, pp. 313–345.

Staehle, W. H. (1999): Management. Eine verhaltenswissenschaftliche Perspektive, 8th edn., Munich: Vahlen, 1999.

Stalk, G. / Evans, P. H. / Shulman, L. E. (1992): Competing on Capabilities: The New Rules of Corporate Strategy, in: Harvard Business Review, March-April 1992, pp. 57 – 69.

Starke, P. H. (1990): Analyse von Petri-Netz-Modellen, Stuttgart: Teubner, 1990.

Staudt, E. (ed., 1986): Das Management von Innovationen, Frankfurt / Main: FAZ-Institut, 1986.

Steiner, M. (1998): Konstitutive Entscheidungen, in: Bitz, M. / Dellmann, K. / Domsch, M. / Egner, H. (eds.): Vahlens Kompendium der Betriebswirtschaftslehre, Vol. 1, 4th edn., Munich: Vahlen, 1998, pp. 115 – 169.

Steinfield, C.W. / Wigand, R.T. / Markus, M.L. / Minton, G. (2006): Promoting E-Business through Vertical Information Systems Standards: Lessons from the US Home Mortgage Industry. In Shane Greenstein and Victor Stango (eds.), Standards and Public Policy. Cambridge, England: Cambridge University Press, 2006, pp. 160 – 207.

Steinle, C. / Kraege, R. (1998): Kooperationscontrolling: Eine zukunftsorientierte und phasenbezogene Konzeption der Aufgaben und Instrumente des Controlling strategischer Kooperationen, in: Steinle, C. / Eggers, B. / Lawa, D. (eds.): Zukunftsgerichtetes Controlling, 3rd edn., Wiesbaden: Gabler, 1998, pp. 407 – 428.

Sterling, B. (1995): The Hacker Crackdown: Evolution of the US Telephone Network, in: Heap, N. / Thomas, R. / Einon, G. / Mason, R. / Mackay, H. (eds.): Information Technology and Society: A Reader, London et al.: Sage, 1995, pp. 33 – 40.

Stetter, F. (1988): Grundbegriffe der Theoretischen Informatik, Berlin et al.: Springer, 1988.

Steward III, G. B. (1991): The Quest for Value, New York, NY: Harper Business, 1991.

Steyer, R. (1998) : Oekonomische Analyse elektronischer Maerkte, in: Arbeitspapiere WI, No. 1/1998, Lehrstuhl fuer Allg. BWL und Wirtschaftsinformatik (ed.): Johannes Gutenberg-University, Mainz 1998.

Stoffel, K. (1995): Controllership im internationalen Vergleich, Wiesbaden: Gabler, 1995.

Strassmann, P. (1990): The Business Value of Computers, New Canaan, CT: Information Economics Press, 1990.

Strautmann, K.-P. (1993): Ein Ansatz zur strategischen Kooperationsplanung, Munich: VVF, 1993.

Streitz, N.A. / Geissler, J. / Holmer, T. (1998): Roomware for Cooperative Buildings: Integrated Design of Architectural Spaces and Information Spaces, in: Streitz, N. / Konomi, S. / Burkhardt, H. (eds.): Cooperative Buildings – Integrating Information, Organization, and Architecture. Proceedings of CoBuild98, Heidelberg et al.: Springer, 1998, pp. 4 – 21.

Sviokla, J.J. (1998): Virtual Value and the Birth of Virtual Markets; in: Bradley, S. / Nolan, R.L. (eds.): Sense & Respond – Capturing Value in the Network Era, Boston: Harvard Business School Press 1998, pp. 221 – 244.

Sydow, J. (1991): Strategische Netzwerke in Japan, in: Zeitschrift fuer betriebswirtschaftliche Forschung, No. 3, 1991, pp. 238 – 254.

Sydow, J. (1992a): Strategische Netzwerke und Transaktionskosten, in: Staehle, W. H. v. / Conrad, P. (eds.): Managementforschung 2, Berlin / New York: De Gruyter, 1992, pp. 239 – 311.

Sydow, J. (1992b): Strategische Netzwerke: Evolution und Organisation, Wiesbaden: Gabler, 1992.

Sydow, J. (1995): Netzwerkbildung und Kooperation als Fuehrungsaufgabe, in: Kieser, A./Reber, G./Wunderer, R. (eds.): Handwoerterbuch der Fuehrung, 2nd edn., Stuttgart: Schaeffer-Poeschel, 1995, pp. 1622–1635.

Sydow, J. (1996): Erfolg als Vertrauensorganisation?, in: Office Management, issue 7/8, 1996, pp. 10–13.

Szyperski, N./Klein, S. (1993): Informationslogistik und virtuelle Organisationen, in: Die Betriebswirtschaft, No. 2, 1993, pp. 187–208.

Tanenbaum, A.S. (1989): Computer Networks, Englewood Cliffs, NJ: Prentice Hall, 1989.

Tannenbaum, R./Schmidt, W. H. (1958): How to choose a leadership pattern, in: Harvard Business Review, March/April 1958, pp. 95–101.

Taylor, D.A. (1995): Business Engineering with Object Technology, New York: Wiley, 1995.

Taylor, F.W. (1913): Die Grundsaetze wissenschaftlicher Betriebsfuehrung, Munich et al.: Oldenbourg, 1913.

Teece, D.J. (1986): Profiting from Technological Innovation: Implications for Integration, Collaboration, Licensing and Public Policy, in: Research Policy, 1986, pp. 285–305.

Teufel, S. (1996): Computergestuetzte Gruppenarbeit: in: Oesterle, H./Vogler, P. (eds.): Praxis des Workflow-Managements. Grundlagen, Vorgehen, Beispiele, Braunschweig 1996, pp. 35–63.

Thiel, M. (2002): Wissenstransfer in komplexen Organisationen: Effizienz durch Wiederverwendung von Wissen und Best Practices, Wiesbaden: Gabler, 2002.

Thieme, H.-R. (1982): Verhaltensbeeinflussung durch Kontrolle. Wirkung von Kontrollmassnahmen und Folgerungen fuer die Kontrollpraxis, Berlin: Schmidt, 1982.

Thom, N. (1987): Personalentwicklung als Instrument der Unternehmungsfuehrung, Stuttgart: Schaeffer-Poeschel, 1987.

Thome, R. (1998): Informationsverarbeitung als Basis einer neuen zwischenbetrieblichen Firmenkultur, in: Das Wirtschaftsstudium, No. 8/9, 1998, pp. 964–970.

Thome, R. (1999): Unternehmensorganisation durch Software, in: Nagel, K./Erben, R./Piller, F.T. (eds.): Produktionswirtschaft 2000 – Perspektiven fuer die Fabrik der Zukunft, Wiesbaden: Gabler, 1999, pp. 59–73.

Thompson, J.D. (1967): Organizations in Action, New York, NY: McGraw-Hill, 1967.

Thorelli, H.B. (1986): Networks: Between Markets and Hierarchies, in: Strategic Management Journal, No. 7, 1986, pp. 37–51.

Thum, M. (1995): Netzwerkeffekte, Standardisierung und staatlicher Regulierungsbedarf, Tuebingen: Mohr, 1995.

Thurow, L. (1992): Head to Head, New York, NY: Morrow, 1992.

Tietzel, M. (1981): Die Oekonomie der Property-Rights: Ein Ueberblick, in: Zeitschrift fuer Wirtschaftspolitik, No. 3, 1981, pp. 207–243.

Timmers, P. (1998): Business Models for Electronic Markets; in: EM – Electronic Markets, Vol. 8, No. 2, 1998, pp. 3–8.

Tirole, J. (1995): Industrieoekonomik, Munich: Oldenbourg, 1995.

Trist, E.A. / Higgin, G.W. / Murray, H. / Pollock, A.B. (1963): Organizational Choice, London: Tavistock Publications, 1963.

Trivers, R.L. (1971): The evolution of reciprocal altruism, in: Quarterly Review of Biology, Vol. 46, 1971, pp. 35 – 57.

Troendle, D. (1987): Kooperationsmanagement. Steuerung interaktioneller Prozesse bei Unternehmenskooperationen, Bergisch-Gladbach: Eul, 1987.

Ulich, E. (1991): Gruppenarbeit: arbeitspsychologische Konzepte und Beispiele, in: Friedrich, J. / Roediger K.-H. (eds.): Computergestuetzte Gruppenarbeit (CSCW), Berichte des German Chapter of the ACM 34, Stuttgart: Teubner, 1991, pp. 57 – 77.

Ulich, E. (2001): Arbeitspsychologie, 5th edn., Stuttgart: Schaeffer-Poeschel, 2001.

Ulich, E. / Groskurth, P. / Bruggemann A. (1973): Neue Formen der Arbeitsgestaltung, Frankfurt / Main: Europaeische Verlagsanstalt, 1973.

Ullmann-Margalit, E. (1977): The Emergence of Norms, Oxford: Oxford University, 1977.

Ulrich, H. / Probst G. J. (1995): Anleitung zum ganzheitlichen Handeln: Ein Brevier fuer Fuehrungskraefte, 4th edn., Bern et al.: Haupt, 1995.

Ulrich, P. (1993): Transformation der oekonomischen Vernunft. Fortschrittsperspektiven der modernen Industriegesellschaft, 3rd edn., Bern et al: Haupt, 1993.

Underwood, L. (1993): Intelligent Manufacturing, Wokingham et al.: Addison-Wesley, 1993.

van Heck, E. / Ribbers, P.M. (1998): Introducing electronic auction in the dutch flower industry – a comparison of two initiatives; in: Wirtschaftsinformatik Vol. 40., No. 3, 1998, pp. 223 – 231.

Vanberg, V. (1982): Markt und Organisation, Tuebingen: Mohr, 1982.

Vertretung der Europaeischen Kommission in Deutschland (1995): Die Informationsgesellschaft, EU-Informationen, No. 2, Bonn, Februar 1995.

Vester, F. (1980): Neuland des Denkens, Stuttgart: Deutsche Verlags-Anstalt, 1980.

Vickrey, W. (1961): Counterspeculation, Auctions, and Competitive Sealed Tender; in: Journal of Finance 16, 1961, pp. 8 – 37.

Vizjak, A. (1990): Wachstumspotentiale durch Strategische Partnerschaften, Herrsching: B. Kirsch, 1990.

Voskamp, U. / Wittke, V. (1994): Von "Silicon Valley" zur "virtuellen Integration" – Neue Formen der Organisation von Innovationsprozessen am Beispiel der Halbleiterindustrie, in: Sydow, J. v. / Windeler, A. (eds.): Management interorganisationaler Beziehungen: Vertrauen, Kontrolle und Informationstechnik, Opladen: Westdeutscher Verlag, 1994, pp. 212 – 243.

Vroom, V.H. (1964): Work and Motivation, New York, NY: Wiley, 1964.

W3C (1999): Extensible Markup Language (XML), electronically publishes under: http://www.w3.org/XML/, Version of 20.08.1999.

Wagner, D. / Schumann, R. (1991): Die Produktinsel: Leitfaden zur Einfuehrung einer effizienten Produktion in Zulieferbetrieben, Cologn: TUEV Rheinland, 1991.

Wahren, H.K. (1987): Zwischenmenschliche Kommunikation und Interaktion in Unternehmen, Berlin et al.: de Gruyter, 1987.

Whitmore, J. (2002): Coaching For Performance: Growing People, Performance and Purpose, 3rd edn., Nicholas Brealey, 2002.

Wallis, J.J. / North, D.C. (1986): Measuring the Transaction Sector in the American Economy, in: Engerman, S.L. / Gallman, R.E. (eds.): Long-Term Factors in American Economic Growth, Chicago, IL: University of Chicago, 1986, pp. 95 – 161.

Warnecke, H.-J. (1992): Die fraktale Fabrik: Revolution der Unternehmenskultur, Berlin et al.: Springer, 1992.

Watzlawick, P. / Beavin, J.H. / Jackson, D.D. (1990): Menschliche Kommunikation: Formen, Stoerungen, Paradoxien, 8th edn., Bern et al.: Huber, 1990.

Weaver, C.N. (1991): TQM – A Step-by-Step Guide to Implementation, Milwaukee, MI: ASQC Quality Press, 1991.

Weber, A. (1909): Ueber den Standort der Industrien, 1st part: Reine Theorie des Standortes, Tuebingen: Mohr, 1909.

Weber, J. (1995): Modulare Organisationsstrukturen internationaler Unternehmensnetzwerke, Wiesbaden 1995.

Weber, J. (1996): Selektives Rechnungswesen – Schlankes Controlling durch selektive Fuehrungsinformationen, in: krp – Kostenrechnungspraxis, No. 4, 1996, pp. 197 – 201.

Weber, J. (2002): Einfuehrung in das Controlling, 9th edn., Stuttgart: Schaeffer-Poeschel, 2002.

Weber, J. / Kosmider, A. (1991): Controlling-Entwicklung in der Bundesrepublik Deutschland im Spiegel von Stellenanzeigen, in: Zeitschrift fuer Betriebswirtschaft, supplement 3, 1991, pp. 17 – 35.

Weber, J. / Schaeffer, U. (1998): Balanced Scorecard – Gedanken zur Einordnung des Konzepts in das bisherige Controlling-Instrumentarium, in: Zeitschrift fuer Planung, No. 4, 1998, pp. 341 – 365.

Weber, M. (1922): Wirtschaft und Gesellschaft, Tuebingen: Mohr, 1922.

Weiber, R. / Adler, J. (1995a): Informationsoekonomisch begruendete Typologisierung von Kaufprozessen, in: Zeitschrift fuer betriebswirtschaftliche Forschung, Vol. 47., No. 1, 1995, pp. 43 – 65.

Weiber, R. / Adler, J. (1995b): Der Einsatz von Untersicherheitsreduktionsstrategien im Kaufprozess: eine informationsoekonomische Analyse, in: Kaas, K.-P. (ed.): Kontrakte, Geschaeftsbeziehungen, Netzwerke: Marketing und neue Institutionenoekonomik, ZfbF special edition No. 35, 1995, pp. 61 – 77.

Weick, K.E. (1985): Der Prozess des Organisierens, Frankfurt / Main: Suhrkamp, 1985.

Weiner, B. (1994): Motivationspsychologie, 3rd edn., Weinheim: Psychologie-Verl.-Union, 1994.

Weiss, D. / Krcmar, H. (1996): Workflow-Management, in: Wirtschaftsinformatik, Vol. 38., No. 6, 1996, pp. 503 – 513.

Weissner, R. / Klauke, A. / Guse, M. / May, M. (1997): Modulare Fabrikstrukturen in der Automobilindustrie, in: Zeitschrift fuer wirtschaftliche Fertigung und Automatisierung, Vol. 92., No. 4, 1997, pp. 152 – 155.

Weizsaecker, E.U. v. (1974): Erstmaligkeit und Bestaetigung als Komponenten der Pragmatischen Information, in: Weizsaecker, E. U. v. (ed.): Offene Systeme I Beitraege zur Zeitstruktur, Entropie und Evolution, Stuttgart: Klett-Cotta, 1974.

Welge, M.K. (1987): Unternehmensfuehrung, Vol. 2: Organisation, Stuttgart: Schaeffer-Poeschel, 1987.

White Paper on Growth (1993): Growth, Competitiveness and Employment: The Challenge and Ways forward into the 21st century. Bulletin of the European Communities, Supplement No. 6, Bruessel: European Kommission 1993.

Wigand, R.T. (2004): Business-to-business Electronic Commerce: The Convergence of Relationships, Networked Supply Chains and Value Webs. In Preissl, Brigitte, Bouwman, Harry and Steinfield, Charles (eds.). E-Life after the Dot Com Bust. Heidelberg, Germany: Physica Verlag, 2004, pp. 137–155.

Wigand, R.T. (1988): Five Principles for the Successful Introduction of Information Management. Information Management, 1988, 3(2), 24–30.

Wigand, R.T. (1988): High Technology Development in the Phoenix Area: Taming the Desert. In Raymond W. / Smilor, G.K. / Gibson, D.V. (eds.), Creating the Technopolis: Linking Technology Commercialization and Economic Development. Cambridge, MA: Ballinger Publishing, 1988, pp. 185–202.

Wigand, R.T. (1997): Electronic Commerce: Definition, Theory and Context. The Information Society, 1997, Vol. 13, No. 3, pp. 1–16.

Wigand, R.T. (2003): Electronic Commerce. Encyclopedia of International Media and Communications, Vol. 1, San Diego, CA: Academic Press / Elsevier Science, 2003, pp. 489–503.

Wigand, R.T. (2007): Web 2.0: Disruptive Technology or is Everything Miscellaneous? In Huizing, A. / de Vries, E.J. (eds.), Information Management: Setting the Scene. Oxford, England: Elsevier Scientific Publishers, 2007, pp. 273–289.

Wigand, R.T. / Tomoko, I. (1997): Virtual Organization: Enablers and Boundaries of an Emerging Organizational Form. Proceedings of the Americas Conference on Information Systems, August 15–17, 1997, pp. 423–425.

Wigand, R.T. (1985): Integrated Communications and Work Efficiency: Impacts on Organizational Structure and Power. Information Services and Use, Vol. 5, pp. 241 258.

Wigand, R.T. (1995a): Doing Business on the Information Superhighway: Are We Adding Value? Paper presented to the Society for Information Management, Annual Spring Meeting, Syracuse, NY, May, and The Business Journal, Vol. 9, No. 24, pp. 3–15.

Wigand, R.T. (1995b): Electronic Commerce and Reduced Transaction Costs: Firms' Migration into Highly Interconnected Electronic Markets, in Electronic Markets, No. 16/17, pp. 1–5

Wigand, R.T. (1995c): The Information Superhighway and Electronic Commerce: Effects of Electronic Markets. Paper presented to the Annual Conference of the International Communication Association, Albuquerque, NM, May 25–29.

Wigand, R.T. (1995d): Information Technology and Payoff: The Productivity Paradox Revisited. Paper presented to the Annual Conference of the International Communication Association, Albuquerque, NM, May 25–29.

Wigand, R.T. (2003): Facing the Music: Value-driven Electronic Markets, Networks and Value Webs in Economic Integration of Digital Products. In Becker, E. / Buhse, W. / Guennewig, D. / Rump, N. (eds.). Digital Rights Management: Technological, Economic, Legal and Political Aspects, Berlin: Springer Verlag, pp. 250–270.

Wigand, R.T. (1995): Information Technology and Payoff: The Productivity Paradox Revisited. Arbeitsbericht anlaesslich der jaehrlichen Konferenz der International Communication Association, Albuquerque, NM, May 1995.

Wigand, R.T. (1997): Electronic Commerce: Definition, Theory, and Context, in: The Information Society, No. 13, 1997, pp. 1–16.

Wigand, R.T / Chen, H. / Nilan, M.S. (2000): Exploring Web Users' Flow Experiences, in: Information Technology and People, Vol. 14, No. 2, 2000, pp. 263–281.

Wigand, R.T / Crowston, K. (1999): Real Estate War in Cyberspace: An Emerging Electronic Market?, in: International Journal of Electronic Markets, No. 1–2, 1999, pp. 1–8.

Wildemann, H. (1998): Die modulare Fabrik: Kundennahe Produktion durch Fertigungssegmentierung, 5th edn., Munich: TCW, 1998.

Wildemann, H. (1997): Koordination von Unternehmensnetzwerken, in: Zeitschrift fuer Betriebswirtschaft, No. 4, 1997, pp. 417–438.

Wilensky, H.L. (1967): Organizational Intelligence, Knowledge and Policy in Government and Industry, New York, NY: Basic Books, 1967.

Wilkens, A. / Ouchi, W. (1983): Efficient Cultures: Exploring the Relationship between Culture and Organizational Performance, in: Administrative Science Quarterly, No. 28, 1983, pp. 468–481.

Williamson, O.E. (1975): Markets and Hierarchies: Analysis and Antitrust Implications. A Study in the Economics of Internal Organization, New York, NY: The Free Press, 1975.

Williamson, O.E. (1990): Die oekonomischen Institutionen des Kapitalismus: Unternehmen, Maerkte, Kooperation [The Economic Institutions of Capitalism, 1985], Tuebingen: Mohr, 1990.

Williamson, O.E. (1991): Comparative Economic Organization: The Analysis of Discrete Structural Alternatives, in: Administrative Science Quarterly, Vol. 36, No. 2, 1991, pp. 269–296.

Williamson, O.E. (1975): Markets and Hierarchies: Analysis and Antitrust Implications. A Study in the Economics of Internal Organization, New York: The Free Press, 1975.

Williamson, O.E. (1985): The Economic Institutions of Capitalism. Firms, Markets, Relational Contracting, 11th edn., New York: The Free Press, 1985.

Winograd, T. (1986): A Language Perspective on the Design of Cooperative Work, in: Proceedings of the ACM Conference on Computer-Supported Cooperative Work, December 3–5, Austin, New York, NY: ACM, 1986, pp. 203–220.

Winograd, T. / Flores, F. (1986): Understanding Computers and Cognition. A New Foundation for Design, Norwood, NJ: Ablex Publ., 1986.

Winograd, T. / Flores, F. (1992): Erkenntnis, Maschinen, Verstehen – Zur Neugestaltung von Computersystemen, 2nd edn., Berlin: Rotbuch, 1992.

Winter, S. (1998): Zur Eignung von Aktienoptionsplaenen als Motivationsinstrument fuer Manager, in: Zeitschrift fuer betriebswirtschaftliche Forschung, No. 12, 1998, col. 1120–1142.

Wirtz, B. (2001): Electronic Business, 2nd edn., Wiesbaden: Gabler, 2001.

Witte, E. (1984): Buerokommunikation. Ein Beitrag zur Produktivitaetssteigerung, Berlin et al.: Springer, 1984.

Witte, E. (1996): Telearbeit. Protokoll zum Fachgespraech des Bundesministeriums fuer Bildung, Wissenschaft, Forschung und Technologie am 16. Juli 1996 im Wissenschaftszentrum Bonn-Bad Godesberg, Munich: LMU, 1996.

Wittlage, H. (1996): Fraktale Organisation: Eine neue Organisationskonzeption?, in: Das Wirtschaftsstudium, Vol. 25., No. 3, 1996, pp. 223–228.

Wittmann, W. (1959): Unternehmung und unvollkommene Information: Unternehmerische Voraussicht – Ungewissheit und Planung, Cologne et al.: Westdeutscher Verlag, 1959.

Wohlenberg, H. (1994): Gruppenunterstuetzende Systeme in Forschung und Entwicklung: Anwenderpotentiale aus industrieller Sicht, Wiesbaden: Gabler, 1994.

Wolff, B. (1995): Organisation durch Vertraege: Koordination und Motivation in Unternehmen, Wiesbaden: Gabler, 1994.

Wolff, B. / Neuburger, R. (1995): Zur theoretischen Begruendung von Netzwerken aus der Sicht der Neuen Institutionenoekonomik, in: Jansen, D. / Schubert, K (eds.): Netzwerke und Politikproduktion, Marburg: Schueren, 1995, pp. 74–94.

Wolff, M.-R. (1993): Multimediale Informationssysteme, in: Handbuch der modernen Datenverarbeitung, No. 169, 1993, pp 9–26.

Wollnik, M. (1988): Ein Referenzmodell fuer das Informations-Management, in: Information Management, No. 3, 1988, pp. 34–43.

Wollnik, M. (1992): Organisationstheorie, interpretative, in: Frese, E. (eds.): Handwoerterbuch der Organisation, 3rd edn., Stuttgart: Schaeffer-Poeschel, 1992, pp. 1778–1797.

Womack, J. P. / Jones, D. T. / Roos, D. (1990): The Machine that Changed the World, New York, NY et al.: Rawson Ass., 1990.

Worch, A. (1994): Rechtliche Rahmenbedingungen, in: Godehardt, B. (ed.): Telearbeit: Rahmenbedingungen und Potentiale, Opladen: Westdeutscher Verlag, 1994, pp. 205–280.

Wunderer, R. / Grunwald, W. (1980): Fuehrungslehre, Vol. 2, Berlin et al.: de Gruyter, 1980.

Wurche, S. (1994): Vertrauen und oekonomische Rationalitaet in kooperativen Interorganisationsbeziehungen, in: Sydow, J. / Windeler, A. (eds.): Management Interorganisationaler Beziehungen: Vertrauen, Kontrolle und Informationstechnik, Opladen: Westdeutscher Verlag, 1994, pp. 142–159.

Yoffie, D.B. (1997): Introduction: CHESS and Competing in the Age of Digital Convergence, in: Yoffie, D.B. (ed.): Competing in the Age of Digital Convergence, Boston, MA: Harvard Business School, 1997.

Young, D. (1999): Some Reflections on Accounting Adjustments and Economic Value Added, in: The Journal of Financial Statement Analysis, Winter 1999, pp. 7–19.

Zangemeister, C. (1993): Erweiterte Wirtschaftlichkeitsanalyse (EWA). Grundlagen und Leitfaden fuer ein 3-Stufen-Verfahren zur Arbeitssystembewertung, Dortmund: Schriftenreihe der Bundesanstalt fuer Arbeitsschutz, 1993.

Zaepfel, G. (1989): Taktisches Produktions-Management, Berlin et al.: de Gruyter, 1989.

Zenger, T.R. / Hesterly, W.S. (1997): The Dissaggregation of Corporations: Selective Intervention, High-Powered Incentives, and Molecular Units, in: Organization Science, Vol. 8, No. 3, 1997, pp. 209–222.

Zerdick, A./Picot, A./Schrape, K./Artopé, A./Goldhammer, K./Lange, U.T./López-Escobar, E./Silverstone, R. (2001): Die Internet-OEkonomie: Strategien fuer die digitale Wirtschaft, 3rd edn., Berlin et al.: Springer, 2001.

Zink, K.J./Ritter, A. (1992): Mit Qualitaetszirkeln zu mehr Arbeitssicherheit, Wiesbaden: Universum Verlagsanstalt, 1992.

Zuboff, S. (1988): In the Age of the Smart Machine, New York, NY: Basic Books, 1988.

Zucker, L.G. (1986): The production of trust: Institutional sources of economic structure, 1840–1920, in: Research in Organizational Behavior, No. 8, 1986, pp. 55–111.

Zuendorf, L. (1987): Macht, Einfluss und Vertrauen, Lueneburg: Arbeitsbericht des Fachbereiches Wirtschafts- und Sozialwissenschaften/Hochschule, 1987.

# Index